S0-ASK-881

GUIDE TO
MEDIEVAL AND RENAISSANCE MANUSCRIPTS
IN THE HUNTINGTON LIBRARY

GUIDE TO MEDIEVAL AND RENAISSANCE MANUSCRIPTS IN THE HUNTINGTON LIBRARY

By C. W. Dutschke

With the assistance of R. H. Rouse
and
Sara S. Hodson, Virginia Rust, Herbert C. Schulz, Ephrem Compte

VOLUME II

HUNTINGTON LIBRARY

1989

Library of Congress Card Number 88–18999
ISBN 0–87328–082–2
Printed in the United States of America by Kingsport Press
Designed by Ward Ritchie

The preparation and publication of this work was made possible in part through a grant from the Research Collections Program of the National Endowment for the Humanities.

HM 1083
BIBLE

Italy, s. XIII[1]

Bible in the usual order with 66 prologues (of which approx. 2/3 correspond to those listed in Ker, *MMBL* 1:96–97 regarding London, Lambeth Palace MS 1364); of the frequent apocryphal additions to Bibles, only the prayer of Solomon is present, but marked "va-cat."

1. ff. 1–257: Old Testament:

f. 1, *Incipit epistola sancti Ieronimi ad paulinum presbiterum de omnibus divine historie libris,* Frater ambrosius tua michi munuscula perferens detulit . . . , Desiderii mei desideratas accepi epistolas . . . [Stegmüller 284, 285]; f. 3, Genesis; f. 16v, Exodus; f. 28, Leviticus; f. 36, Numbers; f. 47, Deuteronomy; f. 56v, Ihesus filius nave in typum domini . . . , *Incipit prologus in libro iosue,* Tandem finito penthateuco moysi velut grandi fenore . . . [Stegmüller 307, 311]; f. 63v, Judges; f. 69v, Ruth; f. 70v, *Incipit prologus beati ieronimi in libris regum,* Viginti et duas esse litteras apud hebreos . . . [Stegmüller 323]; f. 102, *Incipit prefatio sancti ieronimi presbiteri in libros paralipomenon,* Si septuaginta interpretum pura et ut ab eis . . . [Stegmüller 328]; f. 119v, *Incipit prologus in libros hesdre,* Utrum difficilius sit facere quod poscitis . . . [Stegmüller 330]; f. 126, *Incipit prologus sancti ieronimi presbiteri in librum tobie,* Chromatio et heliodoro episcopis ieronimus presbiter in domino salutem. Mirari non desino exactionis vestre . . . [Stegmüller 332]; f. 128v, *Incipit prologus sancti ieronimi in librum Iudith,* Apud hebreos liber iudith inter agiographa . . . [Stegmüller 335]; f. 132, *Incipit prologus in librum hester,* Librum hester variis translatoribus constat esse viciatum . . . [Stegmüller 341]; f. 135v, *Incipit prefatio sancti Ieronimi presbiteri in librum Iob,* Cogor per singulos scripture divine libros . . . , *Incipit prologus eiusdem,* Iob quoque exemplar patientie . . . [Stegmüller 344, 350]; f. 143, Psalms; f. 159, *Hieronimus prologus incipit super parabolis,* Iungat epistula quos iungit sacerdotium . . . [Stegmüller 457]; f. 165, Ecclesiastes; f. 167, Song of Songs; f. 168, Liber sapientie apud hebreos nusquam est . . . [Stegmüller 468]; f. 172v, Multorum nobis . . . [biblical introduction to Ecclesiasticus treated as prologue]; f. 184v, [Et inclinavit Salo]mon genua sua in conspectu tocius ecclesie . . . [prayer of Solomon, with the first line erased and the entire section marked "va-cat" in a contemporary hand; de Bruyne, *Sommaires,* 562]; f. 184v, Nemo cum prophetas versibus viderit . . . [Stegmüller 482, prologue to Isaiah]; f. 197v, Ieremias propheta cui hic prologus scribitur . . . [Stegmüller 487]; Jeremiah followed by Lamentations on f. 211v; the historical note, Et factum est . . . , missing, although space was reserved for it; f. 213, Liber iste qui baruch prenotatur . . . [Stegmüller 491]; f. 214v, Ezechiel propheta cum ioachim rege iuda . . . [Stegmüller 492]; f. 227v, Danielem prophetam iuxta septuaginta interpretes . . . [Stegmüller 494]; f. 233, Non idem ordo est duodecim prophetarum . . . [Stegmüller 500, prologue to the Minor Prophets]; f. 234v, Ioel filius fatuhel describit terram . . . , In hoc propheta idcirco nec reges . . . quibus osee prophetaverat et ipse prophetavit [Stegmüller 510, 508]; f. 235v, Amos pastor et rusticus et ruborum mora distringens . . . [Stegmüller 512]; f. 237, Abdias qui interpretatur servus domini . . . [Stegmüller 516]; f. 237, Ionas interpretatur columba pulcherrima naufragio . . . [Stegmüller 522]; f. 237v, Micheas de morasthi coheres christi . . . [Stegmüller 525]; f. 238v, Naum consolator urbis . . . [Stegmüller 527]; f. 239, Abacuc luctator fortissimus et rigidus . . . [Stegmüller 529]; f. 239v, Sophonias speculator et archanorum dei cognitor . . . [Stegmüller 532]; f. 240v, Aggeus festivus et letus qui seminavit in lacrimis . . . [Stegmüller 535]; f. 240v, Zacharias memor domini sui multiplex . . . [Stegmüller 540]; f. 243, Malachias aperte et in fine . . . [Stegmüller 544]; f. 243v, Machabeorum libri duo prenotant prelia . . . [Stegmüller 551].

2. ff. 257–324: New Testament:
f. 257, Matheus ex iudeis sicut in ordine primus ponitur . . . [Stegmüller 590]; f. 265v, Marcus evangelista dei electus et petri in baptismate filius . . . [Stegmüller 607]; f. 271, Lucas antiochensis natione syrus arte medicus . . . , Quoniam quidem multi conati sunt . . . [Stegmüller 620 and Lk. 1, 1–4 treated as prologue]; f. 280v, Hic est iohannes evangelista unus ex discipulis dei . . . [Stegmüller 624]; f. 288, Epistole pauli ad romanos causa hec est . . . , Primum queritur quare post evangelia . . . , Romani sunt qui ex iudeis gentilibusque . . . , Romani sunt in partibus italie, hii preventi sunt . . . [Stegmüller 651, 670, 675, 677, prologues to Romans]; f. 292, Corinthi sunt achaici et hi similiter . . . [Stegmüller 685]; f. 295v, Post actam penitentiam consolatoriam scribit . . . [Stegmüller 699, prologue to 2 Cor.]; f. 297v, Galathe sunt greci. Hi verbum veritatis . . . [Stegmüller 707]; f. 299, Ephesii sunt asiani. Hii accepto verbo . . . [Stegmüller 715]; f. 300, Philippenses sunt macedones. Hii accepto verbo . . . [Stegmüller 728]; f. 301, Colossenses et hii sicut laodicenses . . . [Stegmüller 736]; f. 301v, Thessalonicenses sunt macedones, qui in christo ihesu . . . [Stegmüller 747]; f. 302v, Ad Thessalonicenses secundam scribit epistolam . . . [Stegmüller 752]; f. 303, Timotheum instruit et docet . . . [Stegmüller 765]; f. 303v, Item timotheo scribit de exhortatione martyrii . . . [Stegmüller 772]; f. 304v, Titum commonefacit et instruit . . . [Stegmüller 780]; f. 305, Philemoni familiares litteras facit . . . [Stegmüller 783]; f. 305, In primis dicendum est cur apostolus paulus . . . [Stegmüller 793, prologue to Hebrews]; f. 307v, Lucas natione syrus cuius laus . . . [Stegmüller 640, prologue to Acts]; f. 316v, Non ita ordo est apud grecos . . . , Iacobus petrus iohannes iudas septem epistolas . . . , Iacobus apostolus sanctum instruit clerum . . . [Stegmüller 809, 807, 806, prologues to James]; f. 317v, Discipulos salvatoris invictos toto orbe . . . [Stegmüller 816 without first line, prologue to 1 Peter]; f. 318v, Simon petrus per fidem huic mundo mortuos esse declarat . . . [Stegmüller 819, prologue to 2 Peter]; f. 319, Rationem verbi et quod deus ipse . . . [Stegmüller 822, prologue to 1 John]; f. 320, Isque [*sic*] adeo ad sanctam feminam . . . [Stegmüller 823, prologue to 2 John]; f. 320, Gaium pietatis cause extollit . . . [Stegmüller 824, prologue to 3 John]; f. 320, Iudas apostolus fratres de corruptionibus [*sic*] . . . [Stegmüller 825]; f. 320v, Iohannes apostolus et evangelista . . . , Apocalipsis iohannis tot habet sacramenta . . . [Stegmüller 834, 829, prologues to Apocalpyse].

3. ff. 325–352: *Hic sunt interpretationes hebreorum nominum incipientium per a litteram,* Aaç apprehendens vel apprehensio . . . Zucim consiliantes eos vel consiatores [*sic*] eorum [Stegmüller 7709].

4. ff. 352v–354v: List of readings for the Mass, for the temporale from the first Sunday in Advent through the 26th Sunday after Pentecost, and for the sanctorale, from Andrew through Saturninus.

5. f. 354v: List of the books of the Bible, with the number of chapters in each, added in another hand.

Parchment, ff. i (washed parchment; see below) + 354 + i (washed parchment; see below); 208 × 134 (140 × 97; 160 × 115 for art. 4) mm. $1\text{–}12^{12}$ 13^{14}(through f. 158v, the end of Psalms) $14\text{–}26^{12}$ 27^{10}(through f. 324) 28^{12} 29^{16} 30^{2}. Catchwords variously in inside lower margin or in center of lower margin; catchword for quire 28 (in the *Interpretationes*) decorated with brown ink flourishes. 2 columns of 57 lines; 3 columns of 55–60 lines in the *Interpretationes;* 2 columns of 60 lines in art. 4. Ruled in lead, single horizontal bounding lines, double vertical bounding lines, and triple rules between the columns; art. 4 ruled in ink. Round prick marks visible in the lower margins of a few leaves (e.g. ff. 121–144). Written in a small gothic book hand using brown ink, in places badly flaking.

12- to 15-line parted red and blue initials with red and blue flourishing; 2-line initials outside the written space in red with blue flourishing or in blue with red; 1-line initials alternating red and blue; 2-line unornamented initials in red and 1-line initials touched in red in the *Interpretationes.* Running headlines, chapter numbers placed in the margins, and paragraph marks alternating red and blue. Rubrics frequently omitted. Marginal notes in contemporary and later hands. On the front flyleaf recto, an inscription in red capitals, s. XIX, "Sacra Biblia," and on the verso of the same leaf, "Sacra Biblia ad usum Petrarchae" (see below); a scrap of paper, also s. XIX, inserted between ff. 160–161 reads "Postilla di mano del Petrarca," apparently in reference to the otherwise missing verse supplied in the margin of f. 161 for Prov. 13, 13.

Bound in 1972 in brown leather over bevelled wooden boards, with a single fore edge clasp. Pastedowns and flyleaves of washed parchment from the previous binding: the text is a commentary on the gospel of John, chapters 2 and 3, written in Italy, s. XIV, approx. 265 × 197 (220 × 155) mm., 2 columns of 48 (?) lines, lemmata underlined in red, initials within the text touched in red. Formerly bound in parchment, apparently the same as the flyleaves, over boards, and sewn on 3 thongs; boards and parchment retained in Library files.

Written in Italy in the first half of the thirteenth century. A note, s. XIII, on f. 2v, "Hic eusebius fuit de cremona ut narat Cirillus in epistola ad augustinum" suggests, through its orthography and interest in Cremona, early ownership, if not origin in northern Italy. Wrongly said to have belonged to Petrarch and to have been among the books from his house near Milan, and to have been left by him to the Carthusians of Garegnano. In certain copies of Giacomo Filippo Tomasini, *Petrarcha redivivus* (2nd ed., Padua 1650) 281–86, a list of 114 codices, which, ostensibly having belonged to Petrarch, are said to have been bought in Padua by a "Marchese Linterno"; HM 1083 is n. 3 in that list. Of these presumed 114 codices, 26 later belonged to the Visconti di Modrone; ceded in 1834 by Duke Carlo Visconti di Modrone (d. 1836) to the Milanese engineer Giuseppe Bruschetti (1793–1871), who sold them to the bookdealer Gaetano Schiepatti; his sale catalogue of the Linterno codices issued in 1865. Offered to, but refused by the Italian government, because of their false attribution of ownership to Petrarch. Bought by another Milanese bookdealer, Luigi Arrigoni; HM 1083 is n. 2 in his sale catalogue (1883). At Arrigoni's death (1886), the remaining Linterno codices acquired by J. Rosenthal; placed by him at auction. Sotheby's, 12 April 1899; HM 1083 as lot 538 to Quaritch. Belonged to John Boyd Thacher (1847–1909) of New York; his sale, Anderson, New York, 8 January 1914, pt. II, n. 254 to G. D. Smith. Precise source and date of acquisition by Henry E. Huntington unknown.

Secundo folio: de ea vel manifestius

Bibliography: De Ricci, 90. B. L. Ullman, "Petrarch Manuscripts in the United States," *IMU* 5 (1962) n. 83. For the thorough study of the provenance of the Linterno codices, see G. Billanovich, "Nuovi autografi (autentici) e vecchi autografi (falsi) del Petrarca," *IMU* 22 (1979) 223–38, especially pp. 236–38 for the present location of 14 of the codices, and pp. 237–38 for HM 1083. D. Dutschke, *Census of Petrarch Manuscripts in the United States* (Padua 1986) n. 113.

HM 1084 Italy, s. XIV[1]
BIBLE *fig. 67*

Bible in the usual order as described by Ker, *MMBL* 1:96–97 regarding London, Lambeth Palace, MS 1364, but without the Psalms; the prayer of Manasses follows 2 Paralipomenon after 3 prologues placed here out of sequence; 3 Ezra (= Stegmüller 94, 1) occurs in its normal position; the prayer of Solomon follows Ecclesiasticus; the letter to the Laodiceans follows Colossians; there are 97 prologues; variant readings in the margins introduced by "vel" or "aliter."

1. ff. 2–498: Old Testament:

f. 2, *Incipit epistola sancti Ieronimi presbiteri ad paulinum presbiterum de omnibus divine hystorie libris,* Frater ambrosius michi tua munuscula perferens detulit . . . , *Incipit prologus sancti Ieronimi presbiteri in pentatheucum,* Desiderii mei desideratas accepi epistolas . . . [Stegmüller 284, 285]; f. 6, Genesis; f. 33v, Exodus; f. 55v, Leviticus; f. 71v, Numbers; f. 91v, Deuteronomy; f. 109v, *Incipit prologus sancti Ieronimi presbiteri in librum iosue,* Tandem finito pentateuco moysi velut grandi fenore . . . , *Alius prologus,* Iesus filius nave typum dei . . . [Stegmüller 311, 307]; f. 122v, Judges; f. 135v, Ruth; f. 138r–v, blank; f. 139, *Incipit prologus sancti Ieronimi presbiteri in libros regum,* Viginti et duas esse litteras apud hebreos . . . [Stegmüller 323]; f. 203v, *Incipit prologus in libros paralipomenon,* Eusebius ieronimus domnioni et rogatiano suis in christo ihesu salutem. Quomodo grecorum hystorias magis intelligunt . . . , *Alius prologus,* Si septuaginta interpretum pura et ut ab eis . . . [Stegmüller 327, 328]; f. 237, *Primus prologus sancti Ieronimi presbiteri in libros salomonis,* Tribus nominibus vocatum salomonem . . . , *Item alius prologus,* Tres libros salomonis id est proverbia . . . [Stegmüller 456, 455, prologues to Proverbs; text below on f. 292]; f. 237v, *Iste prologus est prologus libri ecclesiastes,* Memini me ante hoc ferme quinquenium . . . [Stegmüller 462; text below on f. 304v]; f. 238, *Oratio manases,* Domine deus omnipotens patrum nostrorum abraham ysaac et iacob et semini eorum iusto . . . [Stegmüller 93, 2; should normally follow 2 Paralipomenon, ending above on f. 237]; ff. 238v–239v, blank; f. 240, Ezra; f. 244, Nehemiah; f. 251, 2 Ezra [= 3 Ezra; Stegmüller 94, 1]; ff. 258v–259v, blank; f. 260, *Incipit prologus in librum thobie,* Cormatio [*sic*] et elyodoro episcopis ieronimus presbiter in domino salutem. Mirari non desino . . . [Stegmüller 332]; f. 264v, *Incipit prologus in librum iudith,* Apud hebreos librum iudith inter agiographa legitur . . . [Stegmüller 335]; f. 271, *Incipit prologus sancti Ieronimi presbiteri in librum Ester,* Librum hester variis translationibus constat esse viciatum . . . , *Incipit argumentum,* Rursum in libro hester . . . [Stegmüller 341, 343]; f. 277, *Incipit argumentum in librum Iob,* In terra quidem habitasse iob . . . , *Alius prologus,* Cogor per singulos scripture divine libros . . . , *Alius prologus,* Si aut fiscellam iunco texerem . . . [Stegmüller 349, 344, 357]; f. 291v, blank; f. 292, *Incipit prologus Sancti Ieronimi presbiteri super tres libros salomonis,* Cormatio [*sic*] et heliodoro episcopis ieronimus. Iungat epistola quos iungit sacerdotium . . . [Stegmüller 457]; f. 292, Proverbs; f. 304 [rubric added in a different hand] *Sequens prologus sancti Ieronimi presbiteri non cadit hic sed ante proverbia salomonis,* Tribus nominibus vocatum fuisse salomonem . . . [Stegmüller 456; same prologue above on f. 237]; f. 304v, *Prolo-*

gus ieronimi presbiteri super ecclesiasten, Memini et cetera [added in a different hand, referring to the prologue already copied on f. 237v]; f. 304v, Ecclesiastes; f. 308v, Song of Songs; f. 311, *Incipit prologus in librum sapiencie,* Liber sapientie aput hebreos nusquam est . . . [Stegmüller 468]; f. 319, *Incipit prologus super Ecclesiasticum,* Multorum nobis et magnorum per legem . . . [biblical introduction to Ecclesiasticus treated as prologue]; f. 341, *Oratio salomonis,* Et inclinavit salomon genua sua in conspectu . . . [de Bruyne, *Sommaires,* 562]; f. 341v, *Incipit prologus sancti Ieronimi presbiteri super ysaiam prophetam,* Nemo cum prophetas versibus viderit . . . [Stegmüller 482]; f. 369, *Incipit prologus in ieremiam prophetam,* Heremias propheta cui hic prologus scribitur . . . , *Item alius prologus,* Ioachim filius iosie cuius tertiodecimo anno prophetare . . . , *Incipit argumentum,* Hieremias propheta anathotites qui est viculus . . . [Stegmüller 487, 490, 486]; f. 402v, Lamentations; f. 405v, *Incipit prologus sancti Ieronimi presbiteri in baruch,* Liber iste qui baruch nomine prenotatur . . . [Stegmüller 491]; f. 409v, *Incipit prologus in librum Ezechiel propheta,* Ezechiel propheta cum ioachyn rege iuda captivus . . . [Stegmüller 492]; f. 434v, *Incipit prologus in danielem prophetam,* Danielem prophetam iuxta septuaginta interpretes . . . [Stegmüller 494], Dan. 14, 42 underlined in red; f. 446, *Incipit prologus in librum xii prophetarum,* Non idem ordo est duodecim prophetarum . . . , *Item alius prologus,* Regule sunt he sub quibus significationibus . . . [Stegmüller 500, 501]; f. 449v, *Incipit prologus in librum Ioel,* Sanctus ioel apud hebreos post osee ponitur . . . , *Alius prologus,* Iohel filius fatuhel describit terram . . . , *Alius prologus,* Ioel propheta qui interpretatur incipiens . . . [Stegmüller 511, 510 and 508 run on, 5208]; f. 451v, *Incipit prologus in amos,* Ozias rex cum domini religionem sollicite emularetur . . . , *Alius prologus,* Amos pastor et rusticus ruborum mora . . . [Stegmüller 515, 512]; f. 454v, *Incipit prologus in abdiam prophetam,* Iacob patriarcha fratrem habuit esau . . . Hebrei hunc esse dicunt . . . , *Incipit argumentum,* Abdias qui interpretatur servus domini . . . [Stegmüller 519 and 517 run on, 516]; f. 455, *Incipit prologus in Ionam prophetam,* Sanctum ionam ebrei affirmant filium fuisse . . . , *Incipit argumentum,* Ionas interpretatur columba pulcherima . . . [Stegmüller 524, 522]; f. 456v, *Incipit prologus in micheam prophetam,* Temporibus ioathan et achaz et ezechie regum iuda . . . , *Incipit argumentum,* Micheas demorasti [*sic*] coheres christi . . . [Stegmüller 526, 525]; f. 458v, *Incipit prologus in Naum prophetam,* Naum prophetam ante adventum regis assyriorum . . . , *Incipit argumentum,* Naum consolator orbis interpretatur . . . [Stegmüller 528, 527]; f. 460, *Incipit prologus in abachuc prophetam,* Quatuor prophete in xii prophetarum volumine . . . , *Incipit argumentum,* Abacuc luctator fortis et rigidus . . . [Stegmüller 531, 529]; f. 461v, *Incipit prologus in sophoniam prophetam,* Tradunt hebrei cuiuscumque prophete pater aut avus . . . neque elati sunt oculi mei, *Incipit argumentum,* Sophonias speculator et archanorum domini cognitor . . . [Stegmüller 534 lacking last lines, 532]; f. 463, *Incipit prologus in ageum prophetam,* Ieremias propheta ob causam periurii sedechie regis . . . , *Incipit argumentum,* Aggeus festivus et letus qui seminavit in lacrimis . . . [Stegmüller 538, 535]; f. 464v, *Incipit prologus in Çachariam,* Anno secundo darii regis medorum . . . , *Incipit argumentum,* Çachariam memor domini sui multiplex in prophetia . . . [Stegmüller 539, 540]; f. 468v, *Incipit prologus in malachiam prophetam,* Deus per moysen populo israel preceperat . . . , *Incipit argumentum,* Malachias aperte et in fine omnium prophetarum . . . [Stegmüller

543, 544]; f. 470, *Incipit prologus in libros machabeorum,* Machabeorum libri duo prenotant prelia . . . , *Alius prologus,* Machabeorum libri licet non habeantur in canone hebreorum . . . [Stegmüller 551, 552].

2. ff. 498v–633: New Testament:

f. 498v, *Incipit prologus sancti Ieronimi presbiteri super iiii*[or] *evangelia,* Beatissimo pape damaso ieronimus. Novum opus me facere cogis ex vetere . . . , *Item alius prologus,* Plures fuisse qui evangelia scripserunt ut lucas . . . magis hereticis quam ecclesiasticis vivis canendas, *Incipit prologus sancti Ieronimi presbiteri in evangelium secundum matheum,* Matheus ex iudea sicut in ordine primus ponitur . . . [Stegmüller 595, 596 lacking last lines, 590]; f. 518, *Incipit prologus in evangelium secundum marcum,* Marchus evangelista dei electus et petri in baptismate filius . . . [Stegmüller 607]; f. 529v, *Incipit prologus super lucam,* Lucas syrus natione antiocensis arte medicus . . . , *Incipit prephacio beati luce in evangelium suum,* Quoniam quidem multi conati sunt . . . [Stegmüller 620 and Luke 1, 1–4]; f. 549v, *Incipit prologus in evangelium beati Iohannis,* Hic est iohannes evangelista unus ex discipulis domini . . . [Stegmüller 624]; f. 564, *Incipit prologus super epistolas pauli,* Primum intelligere nos oportet . . . , Romani sunt in partes ytalie. Hii preventi sunt . . . , *Incipit argumentum,* Romani qui in urbe romana in ihesum christum crediderant . . . [Stegmüller 669, 677, 675]; f. 571v, *Incipit prologus in epistolam primam ad corinthios,* Epistola prima ad corinthios multas causas . . . , *Item alius prologus,* Corinthii sunt achaici et hii similiter . . . [Stegmüller 690, 685]; f. 578, *Incipit prologus in secundam,* In secunda ad corrinphios [*sic*] epistola quasi in parte superiori . . . , Post actam penitentiam consolatoriam scribit eis . . . , Anathema interpretatur perditio . . . interpretatur dominus noster veniet [Stegmüller 697, 699 and 682 run on, lacking the final line]; f. 583, *Incipit prologus in epistolam ad galathas,* Galathas post susceptionem evangelii . . . , *Incipit argumentum,* Galathe sunt greci. Hi verbum veritatis . . . [Stegmüller 709, 707]; f. 585, *Incipit prologus in epistolam ad ephesios,* Devocionem ephesiorum quam et fide . . . , *Incipit proemium,* [E]phesii sunt asiani. Hi accepto verbo veritatis . . . [Stegmüller 724, 716]; f. 587v, *Incipit prologus in epistolam ad philippenses,* Philippis macedonie civitas est in qua apostolus . . . , *Incipit argumentum,* Philippenses sunt macedones. Hii accepto verbo veritatis . . . [Stegmüller 733, 728]; f. 589, *Incipit prologus in epistolam ad colosenses,* Primum colosensibus epaphre verbo fidei . . . , *Incipit argumentum,* Coloscenses et hi sicut laodicenses . . . [Stegmüller 741, 736]; f. 591, *Incipit ad laodicenses,* Paulus apostolus non ab hominibus neque per hominem . . . [Stegmüller 233]; f. 591, *Incipit proemium in epistolam ad tessalonicenses,* Thesalonicenses sunt macedones. Hii accepto verbo veritatis . . . [Stegmüller 747]; f. 592v, *Incipit proemium in secundam mspqryuyfa* [*sic*], Ad thesalonicenses secundam epistolam scribit apostolus . . . [Stegmüller 752]; f. 593, *Incipit proemium in epistolam ad timotheum primam,* Timotheum instruit et docet . . . [Stegmüller 765]; f. 594v, *Incipit proemium in secundam,* Item timotheo scribit de exortatione martirii . . . [Stegmüller 772]; f. 595v, *Incipit proemium in epistolam ad titum,* Tytum comonefacit et instruit . . . [Stegmüller 780]; f. 596v, *Incipit argumentum in epistolam ad phylemonem,* Philemoni familiares litteras mittit . . . [Stegmüller 783]; f. 596v, *Incipit argumentum in epistolam ad hebreos,* In primis dicendum est cur apostolus paulus . . . [Stegmüller 794]; f. 601v, *Incipit argumentum sancti Ieronimi presbiteri in librum actuum apostolorum,* Lucas antiocensis nacione syrus cuius laus . . . , [rubric erased], Nudam quidem et apertam sonare videtur . . . [Stegmüller 640, 631]; f. 617, *Incipit prologus in epistolas canonicas,* Non ita ordo est apud grecos . . . , *Incipit argumentum,* Iacobus apostolus sanctum instruit [*sic*] clerum . . . [Stegmüller 809, 806]; f. 619, *Incipit argumentum in prima epistola petri,* Simon petrus filius iohannis . . . frater andree apostoli [Stegmüller 816, first lines only]; f. 620v, Per fidem huic mundo . . . clarius manifestat de interitu [Stegmüller 818]; f. 622, *Incipit argumentum in epistolam primam Iohannis,* Rationem verbi quod deus ipse sit . . . [Stegmüller 822]; f. 623v, *Incipit argumentum in secundam,* Ad sanctam feminam usque adeo . . . [Stegmüller 823]; f. 624, *Incipit argumentum in tertiam,* Gaium pietatis causa extollit . . . [Stegmüller 824]; f. 624, *Incipit argumentum in epistola Iude,* Iudas apostolus frater iacobi fratres . . . [Stegmüller 825]; f. 624v, *Incipit prologus in apocalipsis,* Iohannes apostolus et evangelista a domino nostro ihesu christo electus . . . , *Incipit argumentum,* Apocalipsis iohannis tot habet sacramenta . . . [Stegmüller 835, 829]; f. 633v, blank.

3. ff. 634–679: Aad testificans vel testimonium adhar predicatio [*sic*] . . . Çuçim consiliantes eos vel consiliatores eorum. Explete sunt interpretationes. Amen. [Stegmüller 7709, the Interpretations of Hebrew Names, beginning with the second entry]; f. 679v, blank.

Parchment, ff. ii (modern paper) + 679 (+ 77 bis, 182 bis) + ii (modern paper); 267 × 203 (170 × 115; 176 × 160 in the *Interpretationes*) mm. 1^{16}(+ 1) $2–5^{16}$ $6–9^{12}$ 10^{10}(through f. 138) $11–18^{12}$(through f. 233) 19^{6} $20–21^{10}$(through f. 259) $22–23^{12}$ 24^{8}(through f. 291) $25–29^{16}$ $30–39^{12}$ 40^{8} $41–48^{16}$ 49^{6}(through f. 633) $50–53^{10}$ 54^{8}(–7, 8). Catchwords in inside lower margin, most in brown ink frames. Signatures of leaves or of quires and leaves variously in vertical, horizontal or oblique strokes (or combinations of these strokes), usually in red ink, but in blue ink for quires 26–28, brown ink for quire 40, and lead (?) for quires 41–43, located in the inside, middle or outside lower margin or just below the bottom right corner of the text frame; the leaves of quire 1 also signed in brown ink arabic numerals. 2 columns of 43–45 lines; 3 columns of 44 lines in the *Interpretationes.* Ruled in lead, single bounding lines; additional double rule in the 3 outer margins and a single rule close to the fore edge. Slash prick marks visible in the outer and lower margins of some leaves. Written in round Italian gothic scripts by several scribes.

Seventy-five historiated initials, usually 9-line, opening most books of the Bible and a few of the prologues, in Bolognese style, with dark tones of blue, olive green, maroon, red, beige and ochre; stylized acanthus leaf extensions into the margins; frequent, but mostly illegible, notes to the illuminator in the margins. The initials are: f. 5v (prologue to Gen.), 7-line, bust of Jerome; f. 6 (Gen.), the length of the text, 7 roundels of the Creation and in a large compartment at the bottom, the Crucifixion with Mary and John the Evangelist; f. 33v (Ex.), Moses and the burning bush with the face of God; f. 55v (Lev.), 8-line, 2 men, one holding a lamb for the offering; f. 71v (Num.), 16-line, Moses kneeling in prayer, as the hand of God reaches down to him; note in the margin, "moyses in oratione coram deo"; f. 91v (Deut.), 7-line, Moses holding a book and preaching; f. 110 (Jos.), death of Moses; f. 122v (Jud.), death of Joshua; f. 135v (Ruth), 28-line letter I, Elimelech, Naomi and 2 children; f. 140 (1 Reg.), Elcana and wives kneeling in front of an altar with a cross; f. 157v (2 Reg.), 10-line, the Amalekite offering Saul's crown to David; f. 172 (3 Reg.), attendants bringing Abishag to David; f. 187v (4 Reg.), Ahaziah falling from stairs on outside of a tower; note in the margin, "rex cadens de scalis palatii cum capite ⟨?⟩"; f. 204v (1 Par.), 11-line, Adam standing in front of his descendants; f. 219v (2 Par.), Solomon praying before an altar with a cross, his crown on the steps beside him; note in the margin, "Salomon orans ⟨?⟩"; f. 240 (1 Ezra), 15-line letter I, a tonsured, hooded figure; f. 260 (Tob.), 8-line, Tobit in bed and the swallow perching on her nest;

f. 265 (Judith), Judith beheading Holofernes as he sleeps; note in the margin, "Iudith truncat capud oloferni dorm[ientis?] in lecto"; f. 271v (Esther), 25-line letter I, Esther receiving the scepter from Ahasuerus; note in the margin, "⟨?⟩ virga regale"; f. 278 (Job), 10-line, Job covered with sores on the dunghill, with his wife and crowned men standing nearby; note in the margin, "sedens ⟨?⟩ tres reges ⟨?⟩"; f. 292 (Prov.), Solomon flogging Rehoboam; f. 304v (Ecclesiastes), Solomon, holding a round object and lecturing to a group of people from an elevated wooden pulpit; f. 308v (Cant.), Virgin and Child; f. 311 (Sap.), 7-line, Solomon with sword; f. 319v (Ecclesiasticus), Christ blessing; note in the margin, "christus [?] in maiestate"; f. 342 (Is.), 10-line, Isaiah being sawn in two; f. 369v (Jer.), 8-line, Jeremiah and the boiling cauldron; note in the margin, "⟨?⟩ ollam ⟨?⟩ ex alto"; f. 402v (Lam.), 8-line, Jeremiah sits by Jerusalem falling into ruin; note in the margin, "⟨?⟩ destructionem [civi]tatis iherusalem"; f. 405v (Bar.), 6-line, the prophet holding a scroll; note in the margin, "⟨?⟩ in manus"; f. 409v (Ezek.), 7-line, a bust of the prophet; note in the margin, "propheta"; f. 435v (Dan.), Daniel in the lions' den; note in the margin, "daniel iuvenis ⟨?⟩ cum leonibus"; f. 446v (Hos.), 8-line, Hosea and Gomer; note in the margin, "⟨?⟩ meretricem uxorem"; f. 450 (Joel), the prophet seated under a fruited tree; note in the margin, "propheta cum arbore ⟨?⟩ a brucis rugis et locust[is]"; f. 452 (Amos), Amos with his sheep; note in the margin, "pastor propheta ⟨?⟩"; f. 455 (Obad.), the standing prophet looking up at Edom; f. 455v (Jon.), Jonah emerging from the mouth of the whale; f. 456v (Mich.), an older man with horns (?) touching the face of a younger man; f. 459 (Nah.), the prophet before Nineveh; note in the margin, "propheta prophetans de civitate"; f. 460v (Hab.), an angel carrying Habakkuk by his hair to Babylon; f. 462 (Zeph.), the prophet standing looking at Nineveh with a ram in a building, and the cormorant and the bittern above the initial; f. 463v (Hagg.), 17-line letter I, the prophet standing; note in the margin, "unus propheta"; initial for Zechariah not historiated; f. 469 (Mal.), 2 tonsured men before an altar with a cross, holding a bundle of sticks (?); note in the margin, "duo sacerdotes offerentes super ⟨?⟩"; f. 470v (1 Macc.), 2 knights on horseback fighting; note in the margin, "duo milites ⟨?⟩"; f. 486v (2 Macc.), 10-line, delivery of a letter; f. 498v (prologue to the New Testament), Damasus blessing; note in the margin, "unus papa"; f. 500 (prologue to Mt.), 5-line, Matthew's angel holding a scroll; f. 500 (Mt.), 26-line, tree of Jesse with 3 kings and the Virgin at the top; f. 518 (prologue to Mk.), 5-line, Mark's winged lion, dressed, holding a scroll; f. 518v (Mk.), 28-line letter I, John the Baptist standing on a mountain, holding a scroll; note in the margin, "sanctus iohannes batista"; f. 530 (prologue to Lk.), 6-line, Luke's winged ox, dressed, holding a scroll; note in the margin, "luca cum ⟨?⟩ bov⟨?⟩"; f. 530 (Lk.), 10-line, Zechariah, tonsured, censing an altar with a cross on it, as an angel appears to him from above; note in the margin, "sacerdos stans ante ⟨?⟩ cum turibulo et angelus ⟨?⟩ ei"; f. 549v (prologue to John), 6-line, John's eagle, dressed; note in the margin, "iohannis ⟨?⟩ cum ⟨?⟩"; f. 550 (John), 29-line letter I, John the Evangelist at the feet of the blessing Christ; note in the margin "⟨?⟩ apostolus"; f. 564 (prologue to the Pauline epistles), bust of Paul holding a book, by a second, less competent artist; f. 565v (Rom.), bust of Paul, holding a book, by the second artist; 1 and 2 Cor. introduced by painted, not historiated, initials; Gal. through Philem. beginning with 5-line initials historiated with a bust of Paul by the main artist; Hebrews with a painted initial; f. 601v (Acts), 6-line, bust of an apostle; f. 617v (James), 16-line letter I, James standing holding a book, and, outside the initial, his staff with the pilgrim's pouch hanging from it; note in the margin, "sanctus iacobus apostolus"; remaining Catholic epistles, 1 Pet. through Jude, introduced by 7- or 6-line initials historiated with busts of the apostles; f. 625 (Apoc.), 7-line, John, as an old man, sleeping as the angel appears to him. Initials to the prologues, 8- to 3-line (usually 4-line), as stylized vegetation in the same colors; 2-line initials outside the written space, alternating blue with good red flourishing or red with purple; on ff. 234–258, 2-line initials with hurried flourishing in blue on red initials or vice versa; unornamented 1-line initials alternating red and blue in the *Interpretationes;* 1-line initials within the text touched in red. Paragraph marks, chapter numbers and running headlines alternating red and blue, except on ff. 234–258, where they are all in red. Most rubrics supplied by the same later, disorderly hand as in the running headlines on these leaves. Contemporary corrections throughout. On f. 1, added probably in the eighteenth century, a full page painting of an arch from which hangs a red banner inscribed, "Veteris Novique Testamenti Libri [*sic*] Omnes in dono accepi ab Ill.mo ac Rev.mo Viro D. G. Vicecomiti"; below the banner, 2 putti supporting the Visconti arms. Added at the same time, f. 2, a U-shaped border in colors with 3 roundels of Christ in the outer margin and the Visconti arms in the lower.

Bound, s. XVIIIex, in English red morocco; gilt edges.

Written in Italy, perhaps Bologna, in the first half of the fourteenth century. Belonged to a member of the Visconti family of Milan in the eighteenth century; their arms added on ff. 1, 2, when the book was given away. The added ex libris "G. Visconti" also appears in a fourteenth century New Testament, Oxford, Bod. Lib., Canonici Bibl. Lat. 18; see E. Pellegrin, *La Bibliothèque des Visconti et des Sforza Ducs de Milan au XVe siècle* (Paris 1955) p. 385. Possibly in the collection of Gerardo Sagredo of Venice, ca. 1710, and to be identified with n. 31 of his printed catalogue (ca. 1745): "Biblia Sacra eleganter scripta in 4 in membrana." In a French bookseller's catalogue; slip in Library files. Belonged to Robert Hoe: Bierstadt (1895) p. 12; *Cat.* (1909) p. 8; his sale, Anderson, New York, 1911, pt. I, n. 2117 to G. D. Smith. Precise source and date of acquisition by Henry E. Huntington unknown.

Secundo folio: [f. 3] indoctus. Et unde
Bibliography: De Ricci, 90.

HM 1086 — Flanders, s. XVmed
BOOK OF HOURS, Sarum use

1. ff. 1–6v: Calendar in red and black with the usual English saints, including the feasts of David (1 March), Chad (2 March), John of Beverley (7 May), Etheldreda (23 June), Visitation (2 July, in red), Winifred (3 November); the qualifier "pape" has been cancelled, although Thomas of Canterbury is not; Latin month verses across the heading [Walther, *Initia* 14563], and the Cisiojanus syllables, here beginning "Cisiojaned," running vertically down the month, of which a version is printed in Grotefend, 24–25.

2. ff. 7–13v [f. 7, blank, except for an added prayer, Auxiliatrix sit michi trinitas sancta . . .]: *Oratio ad dominum nostrum ihesum,* O Domine ihesu christe eterna dulcedo te amancium . . . [the 15 0's of St. Bridget; *HE,* 76–80].

3. ff. 14–16 [f. 14, blank]: *Memoria de sancta trinitate,* Domine deus omnipotens pater et filius et spiritus sanctus da michi famulo tuo N. victoriam . . . , cues of Pss. 53, 66 and 129, and the prayer, Libera me domine ihesu christe fili dei vivi qui in cruce suspensus fuisti . . . [de la Mare, *Lyell Cat.,* 373, n. 88]; f. 16v, ruled, but blank except for prayers added s. XV² running through f. 17: Crux triumphalis domini nostri iesu christi . . . , *Oremus,* Deus qui Tres magos orientales . . . [*HE,* 75]; *A prayer to thy proper angell,* Angele qui meus es custos pietate superna . . . [Wilmart, 554–58]; *Whan thow Enferst* [*sic*] *in to the chyrche say thus,* Domine in multitudine misericordie tue introibo in domum tuam . . . [beg. as in Ps. 5, 8]; *When thou takest holy water say thus,* Aqua benedicta sit michi salus . . . ; *When thou beginnest to praye thus begynne knelyng,* Discedite a me maligni . . . ; O Bone Iesu tu novisti et potes et vis bonum anime mee . . .

4. ff. 17–34v [f. 17 blank, except for added prayers, see above]: suffrages of John the Baptist, Thomas of Canterbury, George, Christopher, Anne, Mary Magdalene, Catherine of Alexandria, Barbara, Margaret; prayers added on ff. 18v–19: Domine libera animam meam de carnali dilectione . . . ; Domine Iesu christe rex virginum integritatis amator . . .

5. ff. 35–84v [f. 35, blank]: *Incipiunt hore beate marie virginis secundum usum Anglie ecclesie,* with the hours of the Cross worked in; suffrages after lauds of the Holy Spirit, the Trinity, the Cross, Michael, John the Baptist, Peter and Paul, Andrew, Lawrence, Stephen, Thomas of Canterbury, Nicholas, Mary Magdalene, Catherine of Alexandria, Margaret, All Saints, prayer for peace; following compline are Salve Regina, the set of versicles, Virgo mater ecclesie . . . , and the prayer, Omnipotens sempiterne deus qui gloriose virginis et matris marie . . . [*HE,* 62–63]; *Oracio de domina nostra,* Gaude flore virginali que honore speciali . . . [*RH* 6810], with the prayer, Dulcissime domine ihesu christe qui beatissimam genitricem tuam . . . ; *De domina nostra,* Gaude virgo mater christi que per aurem concepisti . . . [*RH* 7013], and the prayer, Deus qui beatissimam virginem mariam conceptu et in partu . . . [*HE,* 64]; suffrage of Anthony abbot; prayers added s. XV^{2} on ff. 76–77 as follow: Pater de celos [*sic*] deos [*sic*] miserere nobis. Domine sancte pater omnipotens eterne deus qui coequalem . . . , Domine ihesu christe fili dei vivi qui es verus . . . , Domine spiritu sanctem [*sic*] deus qui coequalis . . . [to the Trinity; *HE,* 124–25]; Deus propicius esto michi peccatori et es custos mei omnibus diebus vite mee . . . with versicle, response and prayer, Deus qui miro ordine angelorum . . . [*HE,* 125]; Salve sancta facies . . . [*RH* 18189].

6. ff. 85–102v: Prayers as follow: *Has videas laudes que sacra virgine gaudes* . . . , Salve virgo virginum stella matutina . . . [a farcing of the Salve Regina, attributed to Bonaventure, *Opera* (Vatican 1668) 6:466–67], with the prayer, Deus qui de beate marie virginis utero . . . [Bruylants, *Oraisons,* v. 2, n. 230]; *Oracio ad dominam nostram,* O Intemerata . . . orbis terrarum. Inclina mater misericordie . . . [masculine forms; Wilmart, 488–90]; Obsecro te . . . et michi famulo tuo . . . [Leroquais, *LH* 2:346]; *Quicumque hec septem gaudia . . . a papa* [this word erased] *clemente qui hec septem gaudia proprio stilo composuit,* Virgo templum trinitatis . . . [Philippus de Grevia; Wilmart, 329, n.]; *Ad ymaginem domini nostri ihesu christi,* Omnibus consideratis . . . [Johannes Lemovicensis; Wilmart, 584, n. to p. 527], with the prayer, Omnipotens sempiterne deus qui unigenitum filium tuum . . . ; *Incipit oratio venerabilis bede presbiteri* . . . , Domine ihesu christe qui septem verba . . . [Leroquais, *LH* 2:342]; Precor te piissime domine ihesu christe propter illam caritatem . . . [Wilmart, 378, n.]; Ave domine ihesu christe verbum patris filius virginis . . . [Wilmart, 412]; *Oracio,* Ave verum corpus natum de maria virgine . . . [Wilmart, 373–76]; Anima christi sanctifica me . . . [Leroquais, *LH* 2:340]; *Oracio,* Ave principium nostre creacionis . . . [Wilmart, 23, n.]; *Cuilibet dicenti hanc oracionem . . . dominus papa* [this word erased] *bonifacius sextus concessit . . . ad supplicacionem philippi regis francie, Oracio,* Domine ihesu christe qui hanc sacratissimam carnem . . . [Wilmart, 378, n.].

7. ff. 103–120 [f. 103, blank]: Penitential psalms, gradual psalms (cues only for the first 12), and litany, including Edward, Quentin and Lambert among the martyrs; Albinus, "Zwithine" and Birinus among the confessors; Petronilla, Sotheris, Edith and Afra among the virgins; f. 120v, ruled, but blank.

8. ff. 121–142v [f. 121, blank]: Office of the Dead, Sarum use.

9. ff. 143–156 [f. 143, blank]: Commendation of souls (Pss. 118, divided into sections, and 138 with the prayers, Tibi domine commendamus animam famuli tui N. . . . , and Misericordiam tuam domine sancte pater . . .); f. 156v, ruled, but blank.

10. ff. 157–162v [f. 157, blank]: Psalms of the Passion (Pss. 21–30, 6 with cues only for Pss. 22–24, 26, 29).

11. ff. 163–176: Psalter of St. Jerome: *Beatus vero iheronimus in hoc modo disposuit psalterium* . . . , [Prayer:] Suscipere digneris domine deus omnipotens . . . , [f. 165:] *Incipit psalterium sancti iheronimi,* Verba mea auribus percipe . . . [*HE,* 116–22] ending with the prayer, Omnipotens sempiterne deus clemenciam tuam suppliciter deprecor . . . ; ff. 176–177, added, s. XV²: *Medesynes to staunch blode,* Scribe hoc in veronica cum sanguine pacientis in fronte eius et dic hanc oracionem, Deus qui solo tactu fimbris vestimenti tui . . . ; *to staunch blode,* In nomine patris . . . , Stabat Jhesus contra fluvium Jordanis . . . ; *to staunch blode,* Jesus that was in bedelem borne and baptyzed in fluvium iorden thou command the blode of this man N. (here name hym) . . . ; *To staunche blode bynde this versyt about thy neke,* . . . ; *To staunch blode wryte this lettirs on thy fote,* . . . [a series of letters and syllables]; [in a different hand, to determine liturgical feasts] After the fyrst monne of the pyphany commyte 4 days and the nexte sonday . . . ; [in a third hand, s. XV^ex] A remembrans that my hosband gyffrey kyffyn deyparted owt of thys worlde un to my lorde god this xxii day of september on sent mauryce ys day the xix year of the rayne of kynge edward the iiii . . . [i.e. 1479, as indicated below in a later hand]; there follow various ownership notes [see below]; f. 177v, blank.

Parchment, ff. i (modern parchment) + 177 + i (modern parchment); 235 × 162 (125 × 80) mm. 1⁶ 2⁸(+ 1, f. 7 and 8, f. 14) 3⁸(ff. 17–24, all singletons, with full page illuminations alternating with text pages, and joined to a "conjunct" text page) 4⁸(ff. 25–32: same as quire 3) 5⁸(+ 1, f. 33 and 3, f. 35) 6⁸(+ 1, f. 43) 7⁸(+ 6, f. 57) 8⁸(+ 2, f. 62 and 9, f. 69) 9⁸(+ 3, f. 73 and 7, f. 77) 10⁴(through f. 84) 11–12⁸ 13⁸(+ 3, f. 103) 14⁸ 15²(through f. 119) 16⁸(+ 1 and 2, ff. 120 [text] and 121) 17⁸ 18⁶(+ 6, f. 143) 19⁶ 20⁸(+ 1, f. 151 [text] and 7, f. 157) 21⁸(+ 3 and 4, ff. 163 [text] and 164) 22⁶(+ 7, f. 177). An occasional catchword survives, in a cursive script in the inner right corner; two signatures on ff. 64 and 130 as letter of the alphabet and roman numeral. 19 long lines, ruled in pale red ink, with pricking usually visible in the 3 outer margins. Written in a gothic book hand.

Twenty-three full pages miniatures on the versos of inserted singletons (rectos are blank) by a somewhat more competent artist than the person who did the smaller miniatures. The miniatures are surrounded by heavy frames of pink or blue segments with gold quatrefoils at the corners; the outer borders around the miniature and those around the text on the facing page are in the same style and hand of black ink spray, with blue and gold acanthus at the corners and centers, and with flowers, strawberries and gold trilobe leaves; in the margins above the miniatures a series of small holes suggests that a protective covering was once sewn in (one piece of silk remains loose in the manuscript, also with a series of holes across one end). The miniatures are: f. 7v (15 0's of St. Bridget), Salvator Mundi; a coat of arms in lower margins of ff. 7v–8 (see below); f. 14v (Trinity), Gnadenstuhl; f. 17v, John the Baptist holding the Lamb on a book; f. 19v, Thomas of Canterbury being assassinated before the altar; f. 21v, George slaying the dragon; f. 23v, Christopher; f. 25v, Anne holding a diminutive Mary on her lap, who, in turn, holds the baby Jesus; f. 27v, Mary Magdalene; f. 29v, Catherine of Alexandria with wheel, sword and Maxentius; f. 31v, Barbara; f. 33v, Margaret; f. 35v (Hours of the Virgin),

Jesus at Gethsemane, and on f. 36, above 7 lines of text, Annunciation; f. 43v (Lauds), Betrayal of Christ, and on f. 44, Visitation; f. 57v (Prime), Pilate washing his hands, and on f. 58, Nativity; f. 62v (Terce), Scourging at the pillar, and on f. 63, Annunciation to the shepherds; full page illumination presumably once present before f. 66 (Sext) now missing; on f. 66, Adoration of the Magi; f. 69v (None), Crucifixion, and on f. 70, Presentation in the temple; f. 73v (Vespers), Deposition from the Cross, and on f. 74, Massacre of the Innocents; f. 77v (Compline), Entombment, and on f. 78, Flight into Egypt; f. 103v (Penitential psalms), Last Judgment, with Christ sitting on a rainbow, Mary and John on either side, and the dead rising from their graves; f. 121v (Office of the Dead), burial in a churchyard; f. 143v (Commendation of souls), angels lifting 2 souls in a sheet to God the Father; f. 157v (Psalms of the Passion), Man of Sorrows, with the emblems of the Passion; f. 164v (Psalter of St. Jerome), Jerome in his study with the lion at his knees, the wounded paw raised. Historiated initials, 7-line, with black ink spray extensions including blue and gold acanthus, flowers, strawberries and gold trilobe leaves and dots: f. 51 (Holy Spirit), the Dove, its feet on the globe; f. 52, Michael; f. 52v, Peter and Paul; f. 53, Andrew; also on f. 53, Lawrence; f. 53v, Stephen; f. 54, Nicholas; f. 55v, All Saints; f. 82 (7 Joys), the Virgin, kneeling before Christ in Majesty; f. 84, Anthony abbot with 2 pigs; f. 85 (Salve virgo virginum), Mary in glory holding the Child; f. 89 (O Intemerata), Pietà; f. 93 (Virgo templum trinitatis), the child Mary on the steps of the temple; f. 95v (Omnibus consideratis), Jesus being nailed to the cross; f. 96 (Omnibus consideratis, to the cross), the 3 crosses, tau-shaped, and empty; also on f. 96 (Omnibus consideratis, to the head of Jesus), Jesus, with blood dripping on his forehead; f. 96v (idem, to the wound on his right hand), the hand, floating on blue clouds, with the wound; f. 97 (idem, to the wound on his left hand); also on f. 97 (idem, to the wound on his side), four small flesh-colored circles, bleeding, surrounding a flesh-colored bleeding heart; f. 97v (idem, to the wound on his right foot), a foot, with clouds at the leg, and the wound; also on f. 97v (idem, to the wound on his left foot); f. 98 (idem, to John the Evangelist), John holding the poisoned chalice; f. 99 (7 Words from the Cross), Crucifixion with the thieves on either side; f. 102v (Domine ihesu christe qui hanc sacratissimam carnem), a priest and others praying before an altar. Major initials, occuring across from full page illuminations, 7-line, white-patterned blue against pink and gold backgrounds, infilled with lush multicolored acanthus leaves, some trilobe leaves and flowers in a style reminiscent of English work. Secondary initials, 3- and 1-line, in gold on patterned pink and blue grounds; initials within the text washed in yellow; ribbon line fillers in pink, blue and gold. Rubrics in red.

Bound, s. XIX, in red velvet with silver filigree clasp.

Written in the middle of the fifteenth century, possibly in Bruges for export to England. Coat of arms placed in the lower margins of ff. 7v–8, very slightly overlapping the flowers of the border decoration: per pale, 1 argent a chevron or between 3 pheons the two in chief lying fesswise point to point and that in base erect sable; 2 or two lions combatant argent supporting a bezant. The first (although with a chevron gules) is given by J. Papworth, *Ordinary of British Armorials* (London 1874) 462 as Kyffin, co. Salop, agreeing with the note on f. 177 by the widow of "Gyffrey Kyffen" (d. 1479). Later notes on the same leaf show that the manuscript belonged to John Somers, 1st Baron Somers (1650/1–1716), whose library passed to his brother-in-law, Sir Joseph Jekyll (1663–1738); his sale, London, 26 February 1739, probably n. 5000 to James West (1704?–1772); the West sale, London, Langford, 27 February 1773, possibly n. 78. Thomas Windus acquired the book (ca. 1820?) from the booksellers John and Arthur Arch; the name Ansley Windus is neatly penned on f. i above an erasure; Thomas Windus sale, 27 February 1858, n. 197. A partially erased note reads "I bought this book at Leigh and Sotheby at auction for . . ." and seems to be signed "W. L‹?›"; another partially erased note, in blue ink, appears to read "T‹?› Henry ‹?›." Sale of Edwin Henry Lawrence, Sotheby's, 9 May 1892, n. 299 to Quaritch. Belonged to Robert Hoe: Bierstadt (1895) 33; *Cat.* (1909) pp.

21–22; his sale, Anderson, New York, 1911, pt. I, n. 2128 to G. D. Smith; precise date and source of acquisition by Henry E. Huntington unknown.

Bibliography: De Ricci, 90.

HM 1087 — Flanders, s. XV^med^
BOOK OF HOURS, Sarum use — *fig. 98*

1. ff. 3–8v: Calendar with major feasts in red; the main English saints are present, as well as Erkenwald (30 April), Ithamar (10 June, in red), Paulinus (10 October, in red); post-1400 saints, including Anne, are missing.

2. ff. 9–14v: *Incipiunt quindecim oraciones de passione,* O Domine ihesu christe eterna dulcedo . . . [*HE,* 76–80].

3. ff. 15–27: *Ad honorem beate trinitatis Oracio,* Domine Deus omnipotens pater et filius et spiritus sanctus da michi famulo tuo N. victoriam . . . , with cues of Pss. 53, 66, and 129, and the prayer, Libera me domine . . . [de la Mare, *Lyell Cat.*, 373, n. 88]; suffrages of John the Baptist [Gaude iohannes baptista . . . , *RH* 26987], John the Evangelist, George, Christopher, Thomas of Canterbury [Gaude lux londoniarum . . . , *RH* 26999], Anne, Mary Magdalene [Gaude pia magdalena . . . , *RH* 6895], Margaret [Gaude virgo gloriosa . . . , *RH* 7002], Catherine of Alexandria [Gaude virgo katherina . . . , *RH* 6991], Barbara; f. 27v, blank.

4. ff. 28–63v: *Cursum beate marie Secundum sarum;* suffrages after lauds of the Holy Spirit, the Trinity, the Cross, Michael, John the Baptist [Inter natos mulierum . . .], Peter and Paul, Andrew, Lawrence, Stephen, Thomas of Canterbury [Tu per thome sanguinem . . .], Nicholas, Mary Magdalene [Maria Magdalena unxit pedes . . .], Catherine of Alexandria [Virgo sancta katherina . . . , *RH* 34646], Margaret [Erat autem margareta . . .], All Saints, for peace; hours of the Cross worked in; compline followed by Salve Regina and the set of versicles, Virgo mater ecclesie . . . [*HE,* 62].

5. ff. 64–71v: *Ad honorem beate marie virginis Salve,* Salve virgo virginum . . . [a farcing of the Salve Regina, attributed to Bonaventure, *Opera* (Vatican 1668) 6:466–67] with response, versicle and prayer, Deus qui de beate marie virginis utero . . . [Bruylants, *Oraisons,* vol. 2, n. 230]; *Oracio devota ad mariam virginem,* O Intemerata . . . orbis terrarum. Inclina mater . . . [Wilmart, 488–90]; *Item alia oracio de nostra domina,* Obsecro te . . . [masculine forms; Leroquais, *LH* 2:346].

6. ff. 72–75v: *Incipiunt septem gaudia beate marie,* Virgo templum trinitatis . . . [Philippus de Grevia; Wilmart, 329, n.].

7. ff. 76–79v: *Ad salutandum ymaginem christi,* Omnibus consideratis . . . [Johannes Lemovicensis; Wilmart, 584, n. to 527] with the prayer, Omnipotens sempiterne deus qui unigenitum filium tuum dominum nostrum ihesum christum crucem coronam spineam . . . ; *Incipit oracio de septem verbis christi,* Domine ihesu christe qui septem verba . . . [Leroquais, *LH* 2:342]; Precor te

piissime domine ihesu christe propter eximiam caritatem . . . [Wilmart, 378, n.].

8. ff. 80–81v: *Salutaciones ad sacrosanctum sacramentum,* Ave domine ihesu christe verbum patris filius virginis . . . [Wilmart, 412]; Ave principium nostre creationis . . . [Wilmart, 23, n.]; *Item alia,* Ave verum corpus natum de maria virgine . . . [Wilmart, 373–76]; *Item alia de eodem,* Ave caro christi cara immolata crucis . . . [Wilmart, 379, n.]; *Alia de eodem,* Anima christi sanctifica me . . . [a version printed in Leroquais, *LH* 2:340]; *Post elevacionem sacramenti,* Domine ihesu christe qui hanc sacratissimam carnem . . . [Wilmart, 378, n.].

9. ff. 82–97: Penitential psalms, gradual psalms (cues only for the first 12), and litany, including Quentin and Denis among the martyrs; Chad, Albinus, Swithun and Birinus (the last 2 corrected in a dark ink to the proper form of the name) among the confessors; Ursula, Petronilla, Bridget, Rosa, Afra, Praxedis, Sotheris, Prisca, Thecla and Edith among the virgins; f. 97v, ruled, but blank.

10. ff. 98–117: Office of the Dead, Sarum use; before the first nocturn are collects *pro corpore presenti, pro tringitalibus* [*sic*], *pro episcopis, pro fratribus et sororibus* and *pro defunctis.*

11. ff. 117v–128v: Commendation of souls (Pss. 118, divided into sections, and 138 with the prayers, Tibi domine commendamus . . . , and Misericordiam taum domine . . .).

12. ff. 129–133: Psalms of the Passion (Pss. 21–30, 6; cues only for Pss. 22–24, 26, 29).

13. ff. 133v–145v: Psalter of St. Jerome: *Beatus vero iheronimus in hoc modo* . . . , Suscipere digneris domine . . . [with the feminine "a" suprascript above the masculine forms of the text; f. 134v, blank], Verba mea auribus percipe . . . [*HE,* 116–22] with the prayer, Omnipotens sempiterne deus clemenciam tuam supplices deprecor . . . [feminine forms suprascript]; ff. 146–147v, blank.

Parchment, ff. ii (modern parchment) + 147 + ii (modern parchment); 205 × 145 (115 × 70) mm. 1^{2}(contemporary flyleaves) 2^{6} $3–4^{8}$ 5^{2}(+1, f. 25) $6–11^{8}$ 12^{6}(through f. 81) $13–14^{8}$(through f. 97) $15–18^{8}$ 19^{4}(+5, f. 134) 20^{8} 21 (? ff. 143–145) 22^{2}(contemporary flyleaves). Indication of cropped leaf signatures on ff. 77, 78 (?). 20 long lines, ruled in pale red ink, the top line full across. Written in a gothic book hand.

Twenty-nine large miniatures above 7 or 8 lines of text in arched compartments with serrated tops, with borders of black vine spray, thin multicolored acanthus leaves, flowers and gold motifs; another manuscript by the same artist and with the same style borders is Brussels, Bibl. Royale, MS IV 1085 (for which see *Vijf Jaar Aanwinsten 1974–78/ Cinq Années d'Acquisition 1974–1978,* n. 41).[1] The miniatures in HM 1087 are: f. 9 (the 15 O's of St. Bridget), Salvator Mundi against a diapered ground; f. 15 (Domine . . . da michi famulo tuo N. victoriam), Gnadenstuhl; f. 17, John the Baptist holding the Agnus Dei on a book; f. 18, John the Evangelist holding the snaky chalice; f. 19, George; f. 20, Christopher; f. 21, Thomas of Canterbury, possibly retouched, against gold-scroll background; f. 22v, Anne sitting in a large chair, the Virgin at her feet, in turn holding the infant Jesus, against a gold-scroll background; f. 23v, Mary Magdalene, against a diapered ground; f. 24v, Margaret, with gold-scroll background; f. 25v, Catherine of Alexandria, standing on the emperor Maxentius; f. 26v, Barbara, her hand resting on a tower of her own height, against a gold-scroll background; f. 28 (Hours of the Virgin), Annunciation, with shelves of books to the right, an enclosed garden behind the Virgin, the angel with multicolored wings; f. 34 (Lauds), Visitation, before a receding landscape of a river, towers and hills; f. 46v (Prime), Nativity, with Joseph holding a candle; f. 50 (Terce), Annunciation to the shepherds, with an angel holding a scroll, and a windmill in the background; f. 52v (Sext), Adoration of the Magi in a shed which occupies exactly the 3 U-shape sides of the picture space; f. 55 (None), Presentation in the temple; f. 57v (Vespers), Massacre of the Innocents before Herod in his throne, against a gold-scroll background; f. 59v (Compline), Flight into Egypt with elaborate towers in the background; f. 64 (farcing of the Salve Regina), Coronation of the Virgin by Jesus, with 4 small angels blowing horns, holding her dress, and worshipping; f. 72 (the 7 Joys), Presentation of the Virgin to the temple; f. 75 (Omnibus consideratis), Adam and Eve on either side of the fruit tree, around which is coiled a female-headed snake with a crucifix in the tree; f. 80 (Ave domine ihesu christe verbum patris), a group of ladies and gentlemen kneeling before a monstrance on an altar; f. 82 (Penitential psalms), Last Judgment, with Christ sitting on a rainbow, Mary on his right, and a pink-robed John on his left, two pink angels above blowing horns and the dead rising from their graves below, against a burnished gold background painted with scroll-work; f. 98 (Office of the Dead), Funeral service in a church with monks and priest in the foreground on one side of the draped coffin, and 4 mourners in black behind it; f. 117v (Commendation of souls), two angels with multicolored wings carry 3 naked souls to heaven in a sheet, while Jesus blesses from a ruffled cloud aperture above; diapered background; f. 129 (Psalms of the Passion), Man of Sorrows and the emblems of the Passion; f. 135 (Psalter of St. Jerome), St. Jerome in his study; close to the painting by Jan van Eyck and Petrus Christus in the Detroit Institute of Arts (see plate, for example, in E. Panofsky, "A Letter to St. Jerome: A Note on the Relationship between Petrus Christus and Jan van Eyck," *Studies in Art and Literature for Belle da Costa Greene,* ed. D. Miner, Princeton University Press 1954, pp. 102–08, fig. 49); here Jerome writes in the book, the window is omitted, and the lion is reversed. Historiated initials, 6-line, with bracket borders and narrow gold and color strip along the length of the text, often with gold-scroll backgrounds, for the suffrages and the Hours of the Cross: f. 40 (Holy Spirit), Pentecost, and (Trinity), Gnadenstuhl, similar to the large one on f. 15; f. 40v (Holy Cross), Helen holding a tau-cross; f. 41, Michael; f. 41v, John the Baptist, generally similar to that on f. 17; also on f. 41v, Peter and Paul; f. 42, Andrew; f. 42v, Lawrence; also on f. 42v, Stephen; f. 43, Thomas of Canterbury; f. 43v, Nicholas; f. 44, Mary Magdalene; also on f. 44, Catherine of Alexandria, generally similar to that on f. 25v; f. 44v, Margaret, similar to that on f. 24v; f. 45, All Saints, in the front row: Anthony abbot, Peter, a bishop, Andrew and one other; f. 45v (for peace), a man kneels before the emperor and the pope while God the Father looks on from a blue ruffled cloud aperture; also on f. 45v (Hours of the Cross), Betrayal, with Judas standing to Christ's right, and Peter and Malchus towards the foreground; f. 49v (Hours of the Cross, prime), Betrayal, with only slight variation from that on f. 45v; f. 52 (Hours of the Cross, terce), Scourging at the pillar; f. 54v (Hours of the Cross, sext), Road to Calvary; f. 57 (Hours of the Cross, none), Crucifixion; f. 59 (Hours of the Cross, vespers), Deposition; f. 62 (Hours of the Cross, compline), Entombment. 6- and 5-line initials in white-patterned blue or pink against a ground of the other color, infilled with colored trilobe leaves against a burnished gold ground; 2-line initials in gold against pink ground and blue infilling; 1-line initials in blue with red penwork, or in gold with black penwork; initials within the text washed in yellow. Blue and gold jigsaw line fillers. Rubrics in pink. The text has been corrected in dark black ink, with a leafy pen flourish as line filler when the correction was shorter than the original text. Rust marks in a long narrow shape along the inner margin of ff. 15v–16. Sixteenth century computistic notes on f. i verso; the phrase "In everi tribulacion thynk on cyr[s]ts dere passion" written on ff. ii and 147; illegible notes in lead and a sketched coat of arms also on f. 147.

Bound by Douglas Cockerell in 1901 for J. B. Thacher, in bevelled wooden boards and stamped calf; 2 plaited fore edge straps to pins on the edge of the top cover; edges in red. Two sets of 2 holes on ff. i and 147, both originally pastedowns suggest long strap and pin closings on an earlier binding.

HM 1087

Written on the Continent (Bruges?) for English use; Ithamar and Paulinus in the calendar may indicate Rochester as the destination. The figure of a man kneeling before pope and emperor (f. 45v) may be intended to represent the owner of the book. The signature "Elizabeth Wyndesor" in an early sixteenth century hand on f. ii may be that of Elizabeth Blount, wife of Andrew Windsor; the same name occurs in a volume of Lydgate's poems, Oxford, Bod. Lib., Hatton 73, ff. 1v, 122 and 123 where an "Elyzabeth Wyndesore" is said to have died in 1531. Another sixteenth century owner was "Anne," to whom the book is dedicated on f. 146v: "Mystres Anne this boke and my hartte ys all yors/ Gode send you good chaunce and meny good New Yersse/ And al halloue that be with yn this boke exprest/ send me yor owne my desyre and harttes Reste/ En dieu essperaunce. A.W." The signature on f. ii of "Sir John Carrill," s. XVII, may be that of Lord John Caryll (1625–1711) whose heir was his nephew, John Caryll (1666?–1736); the latter's grandson held the sale in 1790 referred to on f. ii verso: "Benjamin Rotch, Dunkerque. Bought at a Sale of Lord Carryll's Library 6mo 15th 1790." Belonged to John Boyd Thacher of New York (1847–1909); his sale, Anderson, New York, 8 January 1914, pt. II, n. 253 to G. D. Smith. Source and date of acquisition by Henry E. Huntington unknown.

Bibliography: De Ricci, 91.

---

[1] We thank Prof. James Marrow for this information.

HM 1088 — France, 1513
BOOK OF HOURS, use of Rome — *fig. 30*

1. f. 1, blank; f. 1v: Almanac for 1513–1530.

2. ff. 2–13v: Calendar with standard entries in red and major feasts signified by blue or gold; Latin month verses [Walther, *Initia* 8953 on the recto and 19650 on the verso].

3. ff. 14–19v: Pericopes of the Gospels, that of John followed by the prayer, Protector in te sperantium . . . [Perdrizet, 25].

4. ff. 20–54v: Prayers as follow: *Au matin quant tu te leveras,* Aperi domine os meum ad benedicendum nomen tuum . . . ; *Oratio devotissima dicenda quando aliquis surgit a lecto,* Laudo benedico glorifico et saluto dulcissimum et benignissimum cor ihesu christi . . . ; *Invocatio sanctissime trinitatis valde utilis cum quis vult aliquid incipere,* Nomen dei patris et filii et spiritus sancti sit benedictum . . . , with verses and prayer, Actiones nostras quesumus domine aspirando preveni . . . ; In matutinis domine meditabor in te . . . with verses and prayer, Gratias ago tibi domine omnipotens eterne deus qui me in hac nocte . . . ; Iesus nazarenus rex iudeorum miserere mei, *ter dicitur.* Iesus soit en ma teste et en mon entendement . . . [the first 5 verses in Sonet 991; here continuing for another 4 verses]; pericope from John with versicle, response and prayer as above ff. 14–15v; Sancta regina celi mater domini domina mundi . . . ; *Antienne du sainct esperit,* Veni sancte spiritus . . . , with versicle, response and prayer, Deus qui corda fidelium . . . [Bruylants, *Oraisons,* vol. 2, n. 349]; *En apres il doit dire les oraysons qui s'ensuyvent,* Domine deus omnipotens qui ad principium huius diei nos pervenire fecisti . . . ; *Aultre orayson,* Actiones nostras . . . [as above]; Sub tuum presidium confugimus sancta dei genitrix . . . ; Evigilia super nos eterne salvator . . . ; Salva nos domine vigi-

lantes . . . ; *Quant tu laveras au matin tes mains dy ceste orayson,* Presta quesumus omnipotens et misericordissime deus ut sicut externis abluuntur inquinamenta manum . . . ; *Oratio dicenda quando vis pergere a domo et si quis dixerit devote illa die eterna morte non morietur,* Benedicat me imperialis maiestas . . . [*HE,* 88]; *Ter debet dicere hec sequentes orationes,* Pax domini nostri iesu christi et virtus passionis eius . . . ; *Etiam hec dicat ter,* Largire clarum vespere quo vita numquam decidat . . . ; *Oratio devotissima ad dominum,* Accuso me coram domino meo omnipotenti . . . ; *Alia oratio ad dominum,* Te deum meum vivum et verum creatorem mundi adoro . . . ; *L'orayson qui s'ensuyt est escripte a Rome en l'eglise sainct iehan de latram . . . ,* Gaudium cum pace emendationem vite et spacium vere penitentie . . . ; *Hanc orationem continue dicebat in templo beata virgo maria tempore sue sacre iuventutis,* Domine deus meus qui cuncta de nichillo [*sic*] potenter creasti . . . ; *Oratio brevissima ad impetrandam gratiam apud dominum,* O Bone iesu tu novisti et potes et vis bonum anime mee . . . ; *S'ensuit une devote orayson que fist sainct augustim a nostre seigneur et sainct thomas d'aquin la disoit a son trespassement,* Puro corde credo et ore confiteor te esse verum deum et hominem . . . ; *S'ensuit l'espitre* [*sic*] *de sainct saulveur laquelle pape leon envoya au roy charles . . . De sancta cruce domini antiphona,* O crux gloriosa o crux adoranda . . . with versicle, response and prayer, Adesto nobis quesumus domine et quos sancte crucis letari facis honore . . . ; *Antiphona,* Cruci corone spinee clavis . . . with versicle, response and prayer, Quesumus omnipotens deus ut qui sacratissima nostre redemptionis insignia . . . ; Lancea crux clavi spine mors . . . , *oratio,* Omnipotens sempiterne deus qui in utero beatissime anne . . . ; Crux christi semper sit mecum . . . ; *Quiconques dira devotement a cueur . . . ,* O Domina glorie regina leticie fons . . . ; *Quiconques en grant devotion dira l'orayson qui s'ensuit . . . a la requeste de monseigneur sainct michiel qui l'escrivit en lettre d'or et la bailla es mains d'un hermite . . . ,* Ave domina mea sancta maria mater dei regina celi . . . ; *Quiconques dira devotement l'orayson ensuyante . . . ,* Mater digna dei venie via lux diei . . . [*RH* 11335]; *Oratio ad beatam virginem mariam,* Regina celorum mater misericordie refugium peccatorum . . . ; *Oratio communis de omnibus angelis,* Omnes sancti angeli et archangeli throni et dominationes . . . ; *Oratio pulcherrima et devotissima ad omnes sanctos,* Succurrite michi queso omnes sancti dei . . . ; *Oratio ad proprium angelum,* Obsecro te angele mei custos cui ego ad providendum et custodiendum commissus sum . . . with antiphon, versicle, response and prayer, Deus cuius providentia humano generi . . . ; *L'orayson charlemaigne,* Domine iesu christe pastor bone conserva iustos . . . ; 3 suffrages of Michael; suffrages of John the Baptist, James the Greater, Christopher, Claude, Anne, Catherine of Alexandria, Barbara, Mary Magdalene; *Orayson a tous les saincts,* Ie vous supply tous anges, archanges, patriarches, prophetes . . . [Sonet 932].

5. ff. 55–127: *Incipiunt hore intemerate dei genitricis marie secundum usum romanum,* with suffrages of All Saints, hours of the Cross and of the Holy Spirit worked in; the Salve Regina and the prayer, Omnipotens sempiterne deus qui gloriose virginis marie . . . follow compline; *Orayson apres l'office,* Suscipe clementissime deus precibus et meritis . . . ; f. 127v, ruled, but blank.

6. ff. 128–147: *Orayssons tres devotes a nostre seigneur nostre dame et aux anges,* O Summa deitas inmensa bonitas clementissima et gloriosissima trinitas . . . ; *oratio,* Deus meus pater piissime pater misericordiarum . . . ; *Alia oratio,*

Dulcissime et amantissime domine iesu christe fili dei vivi ad honorem et virtutem . . . ; *Alia oratio,* Domine iesu christe paradisum tuum postulo . . . ; *Dicat istum versum ter,* Disrupisti vincula mea . . . ; *Alia oratio,* Domine iesu christe fili dei vivi propter illam amaritudinem mortis tue . . . ; *Oratio ad beatam virginem mariam,* Regina celorum mater misericordie refugium peccatorum . . . [as above, f. 38v]; *Ad sanctos angelos,* Spiritus celorum angeli beatissimi asistite queso migranti ex hoc seculo . . . ; *Ter debet dicere* [*sic*] *hec sequens Oratio,* Pax domini nostri iesu christi et virtus passionis eius . . . ; *Etiam hec dicat ter,* Largire clarum vespere quo vita numquam decidat . . . [these two as above, f. 27r–v]; *Quicumque dixerit devote istos versos . . . ut dixit sanctus bernardus,* O Bone iesu illumina oculos meos . . . [*RH* 27912] and the prayer, Omnipotens sempiterne deus qui ezechie regi . . . ; *S'ensuivent les huit miserere,* Miserere mei deus et exaudi orationem meam, Miserere mei domine quoniam infirmus sum . . . ; *Orayson a nostre seigneur pour tous les chrestiens,* Omnipotens sempiterne deus in cuius manu sunt . . . ; *S'ensuyvent plussieurs devotes louenges peticions oraysons et requestes . . . Premierement tu diras au soir quant tu t'en yras coucher,* Christe qui lux es et dies noctis tenebras detegis . . . ; *Et puis en toy couchant tu diras,* Illumina oculos meos . . . adversus eum. In nomine patris . . . Angele qui meus es custos . . . [Wilmart, 556], In nomine patris et cetera. Gratias ago tibi omnipotens deus qui me in hac die tua sancta clementia dignatus es custodire . . . ; *Recommendation quant on se couche aux quatre benoys evangelistes,* Huic thalamo presto lucas defensor adesto . . . ; *Devant le lit a genoulz trente huit fois,* Ave maria gratia plena . . . ; *A entrer dans le lit tu doys dire,* Benedicite dominus benedic domine thalamum hunc . . . ; Iesus nazarenus rex iudeorum miserere mei. *Ter dicitur.* Iesus soit en ma teste et en mon entendement . . . [Sonet 991 with the same additional 4 verses as above, ff. 22v–23]; pericope from John with versicle, response and prayer as above, ff. 23–24v; Sancta regina celi mater domini domina mundi . . . [as above, ff. 24v–25]; In manus tuas domine commendo spiritum meum . . . ; *De sainct michiel,* A tres puissant prevost du ciel soyes nous doux . . . ; *Quant tu entreras en ton lit faiz troys foys le signe de la croix et dy,* Mundet et muniat me consignat et salvet titulus triumphalis . . . ; *oratio,* Gloria et iubilatio laus et gratiarum actio, honor et imperium sempiternum sit sancte trinitatis . . . ; *oratio,* Ure igne sancti spiritus renes nostros et cor nostrum domine . . . ; Deus propicius esto michi peccatori miserrimo et custos mei omnibus diebus vite mee . . . [*HE,* 125]; invocations to John the Baptist and All Saints; Angele qui meus es custos . . . [Wilmart, 556]; *Quant on se veult confesser,* Per sanctorum angelorum patriarcharum prophetarum . . . merita orationes et suffragis infunde in corde meo . . . ; *Orayson que l'on doyt dire quant l'on veult recepvoir le corps de nostre seigneur,* Fons sapientie verbum dei in excelsis, domine iesu christe accedo ad sacramentum corporis et sanguinis tui . . . ; *Aultre orayson que l'on doyt dire devant la communion,* Domine sancte pater omnipotens eterne deus da michi indigno famulo tuo N. hoc sacrum corpus tuum . . . ; *Orayson que l'on doyt dire apres la communion,* Laudes et gratias ago domine iesu christe quia me peccatorem saciare dignatus es . . . ; Vera perceptio corporis et sanguinis tui . . . ; Domine iesu christe fili dei vivi qui ex voluntate patris cooperante spiritu sancto . . . ; *Quant il y aura sermon en l'eglise apres que auras dicte l'ave maria dy,* Dominus sit in corde tuo et in ore tuo . . .

7. ff. 147–154v: Weekly variations of the psalms at matins for the hours of the Virgin.

8. ff. 155–163v: Advent office for the hours of the Virgin.

9. ff. 164–168v: *Hec sunt nomina sancta dei que si quis supra se portaverit* . . . , Adonay iesu christe admirabilis deus excercituum deus israel . . . Per hec tua sancta nomina. Trinitas sancta deus, omnipotens homo pater creator eternus . . . ; Obsecro te domine iesu christe per tuam sanctam piissimam passionem tuam [*sic*] et per ista sancta nomina . . . ; *oratio,* Deus messyas deus sother deus emanuel deus sabaoth . . . ; *Icy commencent les noms de nostre seigneur iesucrist que sainct leon pape de rome envoya a charles roy de france lesquelz noms l'ange du ciel luy aporta* . . . , In nomine patris et filii et spiritus sancti amen, messias soter mediator emanuel sabaoth pastor . . . ; *Hec tria qui secum portabit nomina regum solvitur a morbo* . . . *S'ensuyvent les noms de ihesuchrist,* O messyas sother emanuel sabaoth adonay otheos eleyson . . .

10. f. 169: [below a picture of a skeleton pointing to himself with a dead man lying behind him] Comme i'estoye iadis si bien forme/ Mays tout soudain la mort m'a de son dart/ Si fort feru que ainsi m'a deforme/ Pense y donc ung chascun pour sa part; f. 169v: [below a picture of the owner in prayer to Jesus] Sy despourueu es sousprins de la mort/ Et toy vivant n'as fait penitance/ Dampne sera sans te faire nul tort/ Ou feu d'enfer sans avoir allegeance.

11. ff. 170–174v: *Ensuyvent les dix commandemens de la loy* . . . , Ung seul dieu tu adoreras . . . ; *Les cinq commandemens de saincte eglise,* Les dymenches messe orras et festes de commandement . . . ; *Les sept sacremens de saincte eglise,* Baptesme, Confirmation . . . ; *Les sept vertus opposites aux sept pechez mortelz* . . . , Humilite contre orgueil racine de toul [*sic*] mal . . . ; *Les sept dons du sainct esperit,* Pitie, Crainte . . . ; *Les sept vertus divines moralles,* Foy, Esperance . . . ; *Les sept beatitudes,* Povrete d'esperit, Debonnairete . . . ; *Les sept oeuvres de misericorde temporelles,* Donner a menger a ceulx qui ont fain . . . ; *Les sept oeuvres de misericorde spirituelles,* Enseigner les ignorantz, Corriger les defaillans . . . ; *Les troy vertus theologalles,* Foy, Esperance, Charite; *Les vertus cardinalles,* Saigesse, Magnanimite, Continence, Iustice; *Les dix principalles vertus de la glorieuse vierge marie,* Prudence inestimable, Purite incomparable . . .

12. ff. 175–193: *Bonne et briefve doctrine pour retraire l'homme de peche* . . . , Pense es quatre dernieres choses et iamais tu ne pecheras qui sont La mort, Le iugement, Enfer, Et paradis. Premierement en la mort qu'il n'est riens plus horrible . . . ; *Pour soy congnoistre,* Tu as aussi a considerer troys choses et tu n'auras cause de toy orgueillir . . . ; Apres tu noteras que tu doys eviter peche pour troys choses. Premierement pource qu'il desplaist a dieu . . . ; Apres il te fault craindre aymer et honnourer dieu . . . ; Puis il te fault estre acompaigne de troys belles vertus c'est assavoir, Foy . . . ; Si fault aussi que tu soyes arme de sept belles vertus . . . ; Si te fault a complir les dix commandemens . . . ; Ces choses considerees, retourne a ta conscience . . . ; Et si tu te sens en peche ne te couche . . . ; Au matin a ton lever faiz le signe de la croix . . . ; Quant tu seras prest avant que faire aultre chose si elle n'est tropt neccessaire va ouyr messe devotement . . . ; S'il advient qu'il soit feste iceluy iour

commandee de l'eglise soyes a la messe de ta paroysse . . . ; Oultre plus n'actens pas a toy repentir . . . ; *Jeremye xlviii,* Maledictus qui facit opus dei negligenter.

13. ff. 193v–194v: [4 verses per page below death scenes; see physical description] Homme mortel tourne vers moy ta face/ Toy que la mort qui m'a ainsi deffait/ Court apres toy voulant en toute place/ Pource pense ie te prie a ton fait/ Homme insense orguilleux et pervers/ Advise toy considere ces ditz/ Car tu seras embref viande a vers/ Ainsi que sont ceulx qui furent iadiz/ Miserable homme et povre creature/ De terre fait en terre retournant/ Pense a ton cas tant que ta vie dure/ Si evicter veulx d'enfer le feu ardant.

14. ff. 195–205v: *Pour considerer la povrete et misere de ce monde et esmouvoir a devotion,* Tout ce que la terre nourrist/ Certes apres elle pourrist . . . ; *Matth. vi,* Tu autem cum oraveris intra in cubiculum tuum . . . ; *Ysaye lx,* Gens enim et regnum quod non servierit tibi peribit. *La medicine de l'ame pour le dernier trepas d'um chascun bon chrestien,* Se les vraiz amys du malade font grant diligence envers luy . . . [divided in 4 parts, containing respectively 4 exhortations, 6 interrogations, 4 prayers, 10 observations].

15. ff. 206–217: *Fuit quidem papa qui cum ad extrema venisset* . . . , with 3 prayers beginning In honore domini nostri iesu christi . . . , In honore amaritudinis omnium passionum . . . , In honore ineffabilis caritatis iesu christi . . . , followed by a narration of the events after the pope's death and prayers to accompany each of the preceding 3 prayers; *Sainct albert desirant savoir quelle chose plaisoit plus a dieu et luy estoit plus agreable eust de luy cest response,* La premiere chose c'est que en remembrance de moy Tu donnes a ung pouvre . . . ; *Les graces que dieu donne a la personne de ouyr messe devotement. Et premierement,* Maistre iaques de pavye sollempnel maistre en decret . . . Que en oyant la messe bien et devotement sont en especial donnees les vertus et graces qui s'ensuyvent desquelles la premiere est telle. Si tu avoys vendu . . .

16. ff. 217–221v: *Orayson a dieu le pere tres devote,* Mon benoist dieu ie croy de cueur et confesse de bouche . . . [Sonet 1150]; *Oratio ad christum,* Doulx iesu christ filz de dieu redempteur du monde defens moy . . . [Sonet 521]; *Orayson,* Nostre seigneur iesu christ filz de dieu le pere vif par la vertu de ta saincte presence . . . [Sonet 1259].

17. ff. 222–224v: *Pourquoy l'on doit faire abstinence le vendredy,* Pource que a tel iour adam fut forme . . . ; *Ce sont les vendredis blans que les apostres ieunerent en pain et eaue. Et sont appelles les douze vendredis blans, Le premier,* C'est la premiere sepmaine de karesme . . . ; Rendre bien pour bien c'est iustice, Rendre mal pour bien . . . ; Qui timet deum nichil timet preter eum, Et qui deum non timet . . . ; Iusticia sine misericordia crudelitas reputatur, Misericordia sine iusticia . . . ; Deus nunquam aliquod malum permittit nisi . . . ; Il n'est vertu que humilite, Richesse que vraye povrete, Bonte . . . ; Pour venir a la perfection Et paradis avoier ou tous biens sont, Qui en dieu penseroit, En pensant se delecteroit, En delectant . . .

18. ff. 225–226 [f. 225, blank]: [across the opening, below a picture representing Christ carrying the cross, and being helped by the same series of people mentioned] Soustenes bien chascun de vous paciamment portant les faictz comme moy pouvres, malades, ladres et infaitz. Et vous prisonniers sans meffaitz, laboureurs aussi pareillement par moy seres es cieulx parfaictz veufves, orphelins

et mendians; f. 226v, blank; ff. 227–229v, ruled, but blank, except for 6 lines of text at the bottom of f. 228v, in the script of the text: Quant court xvi, vxiii [*sic* for v, xiii], ii, x, xviii, vii, Fertile; Quant court xv, iii [*sic* for iiii?], xii, i, ix, xvii, vi, Sterile; Quant court xiiii, iiii [*sic* for iii?], xi, xix, viii, Tres sterile [apparently the Golden Numbers referring to the succession of years for agriculture?]; f. 229 was the pastedown.

Parchment, ff. iii (modern paper) + i (modern parchment) + 229 + i (modern parchment) + iii (modern paper); 255 × 183 (157 × 105) mm. 1^6(+ 6) 2^6 3^8 4^4 5 (ff. 26–29 of uncertain structure; 28, 29 appear to be singletons) 6^4 7^2 (ff. 34–35, in darker ink) 8^8(+ a leaf in the first half) 9^8(+ a leaf in the second half) 10^6 $11–18^8$ 19^8(+5, f. 128) $20–23^8$ 24^2(through f. 166) $25–31^8$ 32^6(+7, f. 229, the former pastedown). 18 long lines ruled in pale red ink. Written in a gothic book hand of varying sizes according to liturgical function.

Thirty-seven full page illuminations in painted gold architectural frames, with 3 lines of text as if imposed by means of a label, in a style influenced by Bourdichon by possibly more than one artist. The miniatures are: f. 14 (Gospel of John), with 5 lines of text, John on Patmos; f. 20 (Aperi domine os meum), with 5 lines of text, Gnadenstuhl before a choir of angels; f. 28 (Accuso me coram domino meo), the owner kneeling before Christ, the Virgin and the apostles; f. 33v (O crux gloriosa), with no text, the emblems of the passion; f. 36v (O domina glorie regina leticie fons pietatis), Assumption of the Virgin; f. 39 (Omnes sancti angeli et archangeli), rows of the orders of angels, each wearing a different color and labeled; f. 40 (Succurrite michi queso omnes sancti dei), All Saints; f. 42 (Obsecro te angele mei custos), the owner being presented by his guardian angel to God in a landscape; f. 55v (Hours of the Virgin), Annunciation; f. 66 (Lauds), the Tiburtine Sibyl showing Caesar the vision of the Virgin and Child; f. 77v (Matins of the hours of the Cross), Crucifixion with the thieves behind Christ, while Mary and John are on his right, the soldiers on his left; f. 79v (Matins of the hours of the Holy Spirit), Pentecost; f. 81 (Prime), Nativity; f. 88 (Terce), Annunciation to the shepherds; f. 95 (Sext), Adoration of the Magi; f. 102 (None), Presentation in the temple; f. 108v (Vespers), Flight into Egypt, with 2 angels following the Holy Family (by a different artist?); f. 118v (Compline), Coronation of the Virgin; f. 128 (*Orayssons tres devotes a nostre seigneur, nostre dame et aux anges*), with 5 lines of text, enclosed by a simple painted gold rectangular frame, the miniature, on a smaller scale, is restricted to the width of the written space, and may be by a third artist; it represents the owner in prayer before the enthroned Virgin and Child; f. 128v (O Summa deitas), the 3 persons of the Trinity as identical young men, except that the Holy Spirit, in the center, is dressed in white and has large white wings; f. 134v (Christe qui lux es), God the Father, wearing a papal tiara, creating the sun and the moon; f. 169 (Comme i estoy iadis), above 8 lines of text, a skeleton pointing to himself, while behind him lies a corpse; f. 169v (Sy despourueu), above 8 lines of text, the owner kneeling before Christ; f. 170 (*Ensuyvent les dix commandemens de la loy*), above 5 lines of text, Moses and the Burning Bush; f. 170v (Ung seul dieu tu adoreras), Moses, horned, receiving the tables of the Law; f. 175v (Premierement en la mort), Death brandishing an arrow and carrying an empty coffin rides a black bull over the bodies of men, including a pope, a bishop and a king; f. 179 (Secondement pense au iugement final), Last Judgment with Christ on a rainbow showing his wounds, the Virgin and John the Baptist on either side and the resurrecting dead below; f. 180v (Tiercement tu doys penser en enfer), a vision of Hell with devils pushing people into a burning cauldron; f. 182v (Quartement il te fault mediter et penser es ioyes de paradis), the elect in heaven before God the Father who sits on a rainbow with the Virgin and Christ on either side; f. 193v (Homme mortel tourne vers moy ta face), above 8 lines of text, Death with wings and brandishing a large arrow galloping his black horse over a prostrate man; f. 194 (Homme insense orguilleux et pervers), above 8 lines of text, dessicated corpses amid bones and open coffins near a wayside cross; f. 194v (Miserable homme et povre creature), above 8 lines of text, devils carrying the condemned, including a baby, towards a flaming hell-mouth; f. 195v (Tu autem cum oraveris), above 4 lines of text, the owner kneeling before Christ and an angel with a book; f. 196 (Gens enim et regum), above 6 lines of text, Christ appealing to God the Father; f. 196v (Se les vrais amis du malade), a clergyman and relatives around the bed of a sick man; f. 206 (Fuit quidem papa), a dying pope in bed surrounded by a priest, a bishop and 4 cardinals; ff. 225v–226 (Soustenes bien chascun de vous), in a simple gold frame above 4 lines of text, Christ carrying the cross with the help of a cripple, a sick man, a leper, a prisoner, a worker, a nun, a child, mendicant friars (for a similar miniature, see Sotheby's, 9 December 1974, lot 63, with pl. of ff. 205v–206). Smaller miniatures, occupying the width of the page but of varying height, serve as fillers for the space at the end of texts and often pertain iconographically to the following larger miniature; they are enclosed by simple painted gold frames. These smaller miniatures are: f. 15v, 2-line, John the Evangelist (?) in a landscape; f. 17, 6-line, a money changer with scales and coins; f. 18v, 2-line, a turbaned saint (?); f. 27v, 9-line, God the Father with tiara and orb in glory; f. 33, 8-line, an empty sepulchre and a jar of ointment in a landscape; f. 35v, 5-line, Pietà; f. 38v, 4-line, an angel in a landscape; f. 39v, 5-line, Peter (?) and Paul (?) in a landscape; f. 41v, 3-line, an angel in a landscape; f. 47v, 4-line, the hermit with his lantern showing the way to Christopher; f. 55, 7-line, a group of men kneeling before Christ; f. 65v, 9-line, in a bone-strewn landscape, Death with his arrow standing over a corpse while the soul flies to heaven; f. 79, 8-line, God the Father on a cloud while the Dove descends to Earth; f. 80v, 3-line, a landscape; f. 87v, 5-line, a shepherd in a field with sheep; f. 94v, 12-line, the attendants and horses of the Magi waiting at the side of the stable; f. 101v, 13-line, Mary holding the Child, Joseph and friends walking to the temple; f. 118, 3-line, an angel in a landscape; f. 134, 2-line, two men in a landscape, and, 5-line, God the Father wearing a papal tiara blessing the land; f. 168v, 9-line, Christ holding an orb in a landscape; f. 174, 6-line, the Seven Virtues represented allegorically as women with attributes; f. 175, 6-line, Death with a spear rushing upon a man; f. 178v, 3-line, three resurrecting figures; f. 182, 4-line, two angels; f. 193, 8-line, the owner kneeling before a saint (Peter ?); f. 205v, 8-line, a pope followed by 2 cardinals; f. 217, 5-line, the owner in prayer at a prie-dieu; f. 220v, 6-line, again, the owner in prayer at a prie-dieu. Other miniatures, 9-line, in rectangular gold frames: f. 16, Luke; f. 17v, Matthew; f. 19, Mark; f. 32, Christ in a field; f. 44, Michael; f. 46, John the Baptist; f. 47, James the Greater; f. 48, Christopher; f. 49, Claude; f. 50v, Anne; f. 51, Catherine of Alexandria; f. 52, Barbara; f. 53, Mary Magdalene; f. 54, All Saints; f. 143v, Saints and an angel; f. 164v, Ecce Homo; f. 174v, Virgin enthroned and Child; f. 217v, God the Father on a throne with an orb, blessing; f. 221, Christ with an orb and blessing, in a mandorla surrounded by angels. The decoration of the calendar consists of gold architectural frames around miniatures of the monthly occupation, the zodiac symbol and two saints on the recto, and around miniatures of four saints on the verso. The initials of the full page miniatures, 3-line, either as white leaves or in blue with white shading, both types infilled in gold with naturalistic flowers or strawberries, the whole against a gold-decorated rust-colored ground; 2- and 1-line initials in painted gold on alternating rust or blue grounds; initials within the text washed in yellow. Ribbon line fillers either in rust or blue with gold decoration, or as gold logs. Rubrics in blue or, less frequently, in pink; the first word of prayers or of subsections of the text often in burnished gold.

Bound, s. XIX, by Purgold in red morocco with gold tooling; gilt edges.

Written in France just before 1513, according to the almanac for 1513–1530 on f. 1v, which ends "Dixhuit ans entiers et prochains venans"; the first owner's portrait appears repeatedly throughout the volume, and on f. 193 before a saint, possibly Peter. Belonged to the Vicomte de Morel-Vindé (Charles Gilbert Morel de Vindé, 1759–1842?); his sale, Paris, 1823, n. 94; in the sales of the Comte H. de La Bedoyère, Paris, 1837, n. 17 and 1862, n. 24; later in the Leboeuf de Montgermont sale, Paris, 1876, n. 58 to Léon Techener; his sale, Paris, 1887, pt. II, n. 17 to Fontaine. Belonged to Robert Hoe: Grolier Club (1892) n. 54; Bierstadt (1895) p. 28; *Cat.* (1909) pp. 110–13; his sale, Anderson, New

York, 1912, pt. III, n. 2079 with plate of f. 175v to G. D. Smith. Precise source and date of acquisition by Henry E. Huntington unknown.

Bibliography: De Ricci, 91.

HM 1089 ANTIPHONAL

Germany (?), s. XVIII²

Vol. I

pp. 1–324: Temporale, from the first Sunday in Advent to Holy Saturday; antiphons (noted), versicles and responses only; pp. 325–360, blank.

Vol. II

pp. 1–210: Temporale, from Easter to the 24th Sunday after Pentecost; antiphons (noted), versicles and responses only; pp. 211–228, blank.

Vol. III

missing

Vol. IV

pp. 1–281: Sanctorale, from Monica (9 April) to Catherine of Alexandria (25 November); included are the feasts of the Patronage of Joseph (19 or 20 April), Conversion of Augustine (5 May), Our Lady of Mt. Carmel (16 July), Cajetanus (7 August), "Sancti patris nostri Augustini" (28 August), Joseph of Cupertino (18 September), Translation of Augustine (11 October); antiphons (noted), versicles and responses only; pp. 282–300, blank.

Paper (watermark "Pro Patria" similar to Heawood 3696, but with countermark "NB"), 380 × 197 (250 × 145) mm. Contemporary pagination: vol. I, pp. 360; vol. II, pp. 228; vol. IV, pp. 300. Gatherings of 4 leaves. 8 lines of text and music (on red, 4-line staves) or in 25 lines of text, or in variations thereupon. Text ruled in lead with double lines to delineate space for minims; pricking along left and right bounding lines. Written according to a roman font in 2 sizes; major headings in red and black ink; minor headings in an italic script using black ink. 2- and 1-line plain red initials. In vol. IV, running headlines of the names of the months in red.

Bound, s. XVIII, in calf over wooden boards; 2 fore edge clasps; edges in blue or red.

Written perhaps in Germany between 1767 (canonization of Joseph of Cupertino) and 1788 (vol. I, p. 1, in a noting hand in the lower margin: "1788 27 Aprilis F.(?) N.P.L. Haen <cropped>"); Heawood's watermarks "Pro Patria," 3696–3718, are of the eighteenth century. Copied for an Augustinian house, possibly one dedicated to Joseph: in vol. IV, p. 13, invitatory at matins, "Laudemus deum nostrum In veneratione beati josephi protectoris nostri." Belonged to E. Kroencke. Date and source of acquisition by Henry E. Huntington unknown; there is no indication that the missing vol. III was ever held by the Huntington Library.

Bibliography: De Ricci, 91.

HM 1092

HM 1092, "Wilton Codex" Italy, ca. 1480
PTOLEMY, GEOGRAPHIA

Atlas of the world from Western Europe and Africa to Indochina, containing 27 maps and 26 tables:

1. ff. 1v–2: Engraved world map from F. Berlinghieri, *Geografia* (Florence: Nicolaus Laurentii, ca. 1480; Hain 2825), hand colored with gold leaf border, nomenclature overtraced in color or gold (water damaged)
2. ff. 3v–4: British Isles (with part of Thule at top right)
3. ff. 5v–6: Spain and Portugal
4. ff. 7v–8: France
5. ff. 9v–10: Germany
6. ff. 11v–12: Northern Adriatic region, Italy and Yugoslavia
7. ff. 13v–14: Italy, Corsica
8. ff. 15v–16: Sardinia, Sicily
9. ff. 17v–18: Baltic Sea to Black Sea
10. ff. 19v–20: Adriatic Sea to Black Sea
11. ff. 21v–22: Greece
12. ff. 23v–24: Northwest Africa
13. ff. 25v–26: North central Africa
14. ff. 27v–28: Northeast Africa
15. ff. 29v–30: Northern half of Africa
16. ff. 31v–32: Turkey
17. ff. 33v–34: Russia (Sarmatia)
18. ff. 35v–36: Black Sea to Caspian Sea
19. ff. 37v–38: Mediterranean Sea to Persian Gulf
20. ff. 39v–40: Caspian Sea to Persian Gulf
21. ff. 41v–42: Red Sea to Persian Gulf
22. ff. 43v–44: Central Asia, east of Caspian Sea
23. ff. 45v–46: Parts of Russia and Iran (Scythia, etc.)
24. ff. 47v–48: Indus River
25. ff. 49v–50: India
26. ff. 51v–52: Ganges River and Burma
27. ff. 53v–54: Ceylon (i.e., Taprobana, spelled "Tarrogane" on map and "Trapobanem" on accompanying table)

28. ff. 3–53: *Europe Tabula Prima.* Prima europe tabula insulas brittanicas . . . finis Asiae tabularum duodecim; [f. 54v, 2 lines of text:] tunc velut natum permistica santificatum fulgura de sursum depellit omni malignum.

Twenty-six tables alternating with maps; the tables are similar in text and format to the Ebner Manuscript in the Lenox Library at the New York Public Library, published in facsimile by E. L. Stevenson, *Geography of Claudius Ptolemy* (New York 1932) following p. 168. Published in many versions, the first with maps printed in Rome, 1478. See N. A. E. Nordenskiöld, *Facsimile Atlas to the Early History of Cartography* (Stockholm 1889) 9–29.

Parchment, ff. i (early modern paper) + 54 (27 bifolia with maps on center openings and accompanying tables on preceding reverse sides) + i (early modern paper); 457 × 295 mm. (map size, 375 × 440 mm. on double page openings, with many variations). Bifolia attached sequentially with tabs. Tables in a humanistic hand with modern form arabic numerals. Text framed in narrow bands of patterned color (or laurel leaves) outlined with narrow strips of silver or gold, each table beginning with scroll lettered in alternating red and blue square capitals; opening initials 3- or 2-line gold on white-patterned blue ground with parted green and pink infilling. Alternating red and blue 1-line initials placed outside written space; rubrics in red or blue.

Maps are mainly trapezoidal in shape, all maps have rectilinear meridians (except for the engraved world map, which is curvilinear), outside borders are bands of gold leaf. Contemporary arabic numbering of the maps at the top center of the page preceding each map, omitting the engraved world map and counting the British Isles map as number 1, which may indicate that the engraved map was added somewhat later. Heawood (see below, p. 240) suggests it may have been an early proof impression on parchment of Berlinghieri's printed volume. Possibly grouped for binding according to the numbers 1 to 16 written, s. XV/XVI on ff. 1, 7, 11, 15, 19, 21, 23, 27, 31, 35, 39, 41, 43, 47, 49, 51 (thus including the engraved world map). Modern penciled foliation in top right corners.

Nomenclature of maps in black or red ink, with area names in gold, blue or red, and scholia in black or purple ink; cursive noting hand and some use of square capitals; no compass directions or rhumb lines; borders of maps formed by the numbered latitude and longitude scales; no distance scales; sea areas covered with purple wash, cities indicated by small gold circles and mountain ranges with wide ocher bands; no decoration except scrollwork at tops of maps and wind-heads on the engraved world map.

Bound, s. XVIII^{in}, in Pembroke binding of English red morocco, gilt; rebacked. Volume is now disbound and kept in modern case; binding preserved separately.

Made in Italy (judging from the humanistic hand, the abbreviations used and the ornamental borders of the tables), probably ca. 1480; it seems to be an early work with the maps showing a large number of place names still in Greek, lacking the various symbols later used for cities, and omitting the maps that were included in later recensions; Joseph Fisher (see below, 1:370–71) suggests a close similarity to the early work of Pietro del Massaio. Purchased ca. 1700 by Thomas Herbert, 8th Earl of Pembroke (1656–1733) for his library at Wilton House, Salisbury. Pembroke sale, Sotheby's, 26 June 1914, lot 166 to Karl Wilhelm Hiersemann (1854–1938) whose press mark "Kh.9" appears on front flyleaf. Quaritch Handlist, 1923, n. 35. Sold by Hiersemann to Otto Heinrich Friederich Vollbehr (b. 1869). Sale by Sotheby's, 28 July 1924, n. 135 with reproduction of engraved world map, to Maggs for Henry E. Huntington.

Bibliography: De Ricci, 91. J. Fischer, *Claudii Ptolemaei Geographiae* (Turin 1932) 1:218, 365–74 with reproduction of 2 maps (36v–37 and 53v–54) in vol. 2, item L-30. E. Heawood, "The Wilton Codex of Ptolemy Maps," *Geographical Journal* 64 (1924) 237–40.

HM 1097 Italy, s. XV and XVIII
MASS AND OFFICE OF LAWRENCE AND OF THE DEAD

1. pp. 1–5: [recto of the first leaf unnumbered; its verso, with a full page miniature of Lawrence, paginated as "1." Proper of the Mass for the feast of Lawrence; p. 2, Introit:] Confessio et pulcritudo in conspectu eius . . .

2. pp. 6–16: Kyrie eleyson . . . ; Gloria in excelsis deo . . . ; Sanctus, Sanctus, Sanctus . . . ; Agnus Dei . . . ; Credo in unum deum . . .

3. pp. 16–41: [Office of Lawrence at vespers of the vigil and at matins:] *In vigilia sancti Laurentii ad vesperas antiphana* [*sic*], Laurentius ingressus est martir et confessus est . . .

4. pp. 41–68: Office of the Dead, use of Rome.

5. p. 69: [The first verse of the responsorial psalm of matins, Ps. 94:] Venite exultemus domino . . . [pp. 70–72, ruled but blank]

6. p. 73: [K]irie eleison. [C]hriste eleison. [K]irie eleison.

7. pp. 74–85: [Mass for the Dead; Introit:] Requiem eternam dona eis domine . . .

Parchment and paper (watermark scarcely visible in the gutter), pp. ii (modern parchment) + 25 (parchment) + 26–73 (paper) + 74–85 (parchment) + ii (modern parchment); 329 × 240 (265 × 165) mm. 1^4(–1) 2^4(–3, 4; no loss of text) 3^6(through p. 25) 4–9^4 10^6(pp. 74–85). 6 lines of text and music, ruled in lead on the parchment leaves and in dry point on the paper leaves. Written by 3 scribes: i, pp. 2–19 and 74–85 in a round gothic script; ii, pp. 20–25, in a round gothic script; iii, pp. 26–73 in a late humanistic script. Musical notation on red 4-line staves.

Full page miniature on p. 1 (the verso of the first leaf, an added singleton) of Lawrence, with face badly rubbed, holding a book and his gridiron, on a gold and red background with a mosaic border. Opening initial, 55 × 60 mm., in patterned blue and yellow on a gold ground with infilling and C-shaped border of acanthus leaves in blue, pink, green, orange and gold. On p. 74, historiated initial, 58 × 58 mm., in pink and yellow, depicting an insect-covered skeleton with a snake crawling through it; C-shaped border as above. On f. 16, similar initial, 34 × 38 mm. Secondary initials on pp. 2–19, 74–85 alternating in blue with careful red beading and harping or in red with blue; 1-line initials within the text washed in yellow. Secondary initials on pp. 20–69 in plain red. Eighteenth century pagination in red ink beginning on the verso of the first leaf and ending at 60; the following 5 leaves foliated in the same hand; the remaining leaves neither paginated or foliated. Pagination extended throughout the volume for consistency in this description.

Bound, 1972, in quarter calf over wooden boards with a fore edge clasp; formerly bound in eighteenth century parchment.

Written in Italy in the fifteenth century; the portion on paper, pp. 26–73, added in the eighteenth century. A catalogue description in French is affixed to the front pastedown; De Ricci states the manuscript to have been described in a German catalogue, ca. 1900. Date and source of acquisition by Henry E. Huntington unknown.

Secundo folio: [p. 4] Levita laurentius
Bibliography: De Ricci, 91.

HM 1099 France, s. XV^{med}
BOOK OF HOURS, use of Paris *fig. 102*

1. ff. 1–12v: Calendar in French in red with major feasts in blue; included are the feasts of Ansbert (9 February), Austreberta (10 February), Translation of Audoenus (5 May), Translation of Evodius (8 July), Commemoration of Wandregisil (23 July), Transfiguration (6 August, in blue), Victricius (7 August), Commemoration of Audoenus (25 August, in blue), Octave of Audoenus (31 August), "La dedicasse de l'eglise de rouen" (1 October), Evodius (8 October), Nicasius (11 October), Mellonius (22 October), Romanus (23 October, in blue), Octave of Romanus (30 October), "Translation des reliques de rouen" (3 December), "la conception nostre dame" (8 December, in blue).

2. ff. 13–19v: Pericopes of the Gospels, with prayers: John, followed by Protector in te sperantium . . . and Ecclesiam tuam quesumus domine . . . ; Luke, followed by Deus qui de beate marie virginis utero . . . ; Matthew, followed by Deus qui hodierna die unigenitum tuum . . . ; Mark, followed by Concede quesumus omnipotens deus ut qui unigenitum tuum . . . ; f. 20r–v, ruled, but blank.

3. ff. 21–76: Hours of the Virgin, use of Paris; from lauds to compline, prayers to the Holy Spirit, for forgiveness, for the Church; f. 76v, ruled, but blank.

4. ff. 77–83v: *Quant on lieve le corps nostre seigneur,* Ave rex noster fili david redemptor mundi . . . ; *Saultation* [*sic*], Ave verum corpus natum de maria virgine . . . [Wilmart, 373–76]; *Quant on lieve le calice dites,* Ave vere sanguis domini nostri ihesu christi qui de latere eius . . . [Wilmart, 378, n.]; Ave salus mundi verbum miserere mei deus; Ave vere sanguis domini nostri ihesu cristi qui pro salute mundi . . . [Wilmart, 378, n.]; Anima christi sanctifica me . . . [Leroquais, *LH* 2:340]; Ave domine ihesu christe verbum patris filius virginis . . . [Wilmart, 412]; *Oratio,* Domine ihesu christe qui hanc sacratissimam carnem . . . [Wilmart, 378, n.]; *Oratio,* Corpus et sanguis domini nostri ihesu christi et comunicatio sancti spiritus . . . ; *les sept vers saint bernart,* Illumina oculos meos . . . [*RH* 27912] and the prayer, Omnipotens sempiterne deus qui ezechie regi . . . ; Madame sainte margerite/ Digne vierge de dieu eslite . . . [Sonet 1083] followed by a suffrage of Margaret; f. 84r–v, ruled, but blank.

5. ff. 85–102: Penitential psalms and litany, including Hilary, Ivo and Germanus among the confessors; f. 102v, ruled, but blank.

6. ff. 103–110v: Short hours of the Cross.

7. ff. 111–117v: Short hours of the Holy Spirit.

8. ff. 118–125v: Obsecro te . . . [masculine forms; Leroquais, *LH* 2:346]; *Oratio devotissima de beata maria,* O intemerata . . . orbis terrarum. De te enim . . . [Wilmart, 494–95]; f. 126r–v, ruled, but blank.

9. ff. 127–170v: Office of the Dead, undetermined use; the responses to the lessons are: Qui lazarum; Credo quod; Domine quando; Heu michi; Ne recorderis; Domine secundum; Peccantem me; Requiem eternam; Libera me domine; ff. 171–175v, ruled, but blank.

Parchment, ff. ii (contemporary parchment; ruled, but blank) + 175; 210 × 153 (107 × 68) mm. $1\text{–}2^{6}$ 3^{8}(through f. 20) $4\text{–}10^{8}$(through f. 84) $12\text{–}15^{8}$ 16^{10}(through f. 126) $17\text{–}21^{8}$

22^6 23^4(–4). Catchwords usually present in the lower right margin, in the script of the text; quire and leaf signatures, as letters of the alphabet and arabic numerals in the inner left corner of the recto, in a cursive script; a diagonal slash across the gutter indicates the middle of the quire. 15 long lines, ruled in pale red ink; pricking usually visible in the lower margin. Written in a gothic book hand in 2 sizes, according to liturgical function.

Twelve large miniatures by 2 artists above 3 or 4 lines of text, in arched compartments; the more competent work by the Master of Sir John Fastolf.[1] Borders usually consist of a wide gold bar with blue and vermillion leaf patterns in a U-shape around text and miniature, the bars themselves terminating at the 4 corners in multicolored acanthus leaves. The outer border usually contains black ink sprays with colored flowers and gold trilobe leaves, the latter arranged as a row along the outermost edges. The miniatures are: f. 21 (Hours of the Virgin), by the Master, Annunciation, outside the frame of the miniature God, as a Jesus-figure, sends the Dove to Mary; the border, entirely of multicolored acanthus leaves, includes 2 small medallions of an angel with a pitcher and a basket, and of Mary weaving; in the historiated initial, Joseph making a table; f. 32v (Lauds), by the Master, Visitation, with Joseph standing behind Mary; f. 44 (Prime), by the Master, Nativity, against a deep blue starry sky; f. 50v (Terce), by the second, less capable artist, Annunciation to the shepherds; the top of the arched compartment is serrated; f. 55 (Sext), by the second artist, Adoration of the Magi, in a serrated compartment; f. 59v (None), by the Master, Presentation in the temple; f. 64 (Vespers), by the Master, Flight into Egypt and, in the background, the Massacre of the Innocents, against a tessellated ground; f. 71 (Compline), by the Master, Coronation of the Virgin by Jesus, against a tessellated ground; f. 85 (Penitential psalms), by the Master, David praying to God, shown above in a deep blue starry sky; in the background, David as the young shepherd who has just slain Goliath, while in the historiated initial David is shown writing; the entire border of multicolored acanthus leaves; f. 103 (Hours of the Cross), by the second artist, Crucifixion with Mary and John on either side, in a serrated compartment; f. 111 (Hours of the Holy Spirit), by the second artist, Pentecost, in a serrated compartment; f. 127 (Office of the Dead), by the Master, burial scene in a churchyard. Black ink spray band borders with flowers and gold trilobe leaves, traced through, the length of the text in all outer margins and in the inner margins of rectos at the presence of a 2-line initial. On ff. 13 and 77 this type of border surrounds the text on all four sides; on f. 172v, an offset of what was apparently a bracket border of this style, with a 4-line initial [D?]. Major initials, 4- or 3-line, in white-patterned pink or blue on a cusped gold ground infilled with colored trilobe leaves; 2- and 1-line initials in gold against white-patterned pink or blue grounds with infilling of the other color; initials in the text slashed in yellow. Ribbon line fillers of white-patterned red and blue segments. Rubrics in red.

Bound, s. XVIII, in Belgian brown morocco with gilt tooling; gauffered gilt edges; Dutch gilt endpapers.

Written during the middle of the fifteenth century in France, probably for use in Rouen, given the saints in the calendar; the owners may have been in the parish of the Rouen Cathedral, as suggested by Delaissé, Marrow and de Wit, *Waddesdon Manor,* pp. 541, n., and 554. On ff. 1 (erased but legible) and 13, is the note in a rounded gothic hand: "Monasterii et Cellae Abbatis Septimi," which may refer to the Premonstratensians of Septfontaines near Reims. Owned by Brayton Ives (1840–1914); his sale, American Art Association, New York, 5 March 1891, n. 627. Belonged to Robert Hoe: Grolier Club (1892) n. 25; *Cat.* (1909) pp. 45–46; his sale, Anderson, New York, 1911, pt. I, n. 2131 to G. D. Smith. Precise source and date of acquisition by Henry E. Huntington unknown.

Bibliography: De Ricci, 92. M. Meiss, *French Painting in the Time of Jean de Berry: The Boucicaut Master* (London 1968) 140.

[1] We thank Mme Nicole Reynaud for confirming this attribution.

HM 1100 France, s. XV^{med}
BOOK OF HOURS, use of Paris *fig. 100*

1. ff. 1–12v: Full calendar in French of the type printed by Perdrizet; major feasts in gold, the others alternating red and blue.

2. ff. 13–26v: Pericopes of the Gospels, that of John followed by the prayer, Protector in te sperancium . . . [Perdrizet, 25]; the sequence from Mark precedes that from Matthew; *Oroison de nostre dame,* Obsecro te . . . [1 leaf missing after f. 21 with loss of text: . . . clamantem audisti et morien// . . . //danciam omnium bonorum; Leroquais, *LH* 2:346]; *Autre oroison de nostre dame,* O Intemerata . . . orbis terrarum. De te enim . . . michi miserrimo peccatori . . . [Wilmart, 494–95]; f. 27r–v, ruled, but blank.

3. ff. 28–96: Hours of the Virgin, use of Paris; 3 sets of 3 psalms and lessons at matins with rubrics for the nocturns; each hour from lauds to compline ends with the prayer, Ecclesiam tuam quesumus domine benignus . . . ; ff. 96v–97v, ruled, but blank.

4. ff. 98–118v: Penitential psalms and litany including Maurice, Denis and Quentin among the martyrs; Ivo, Germanus, Sulpice and Remigius among the confessors; Syria, Valeria, Radegundis, Opportuna, Genevieve, Ursina (?) and Avia among the virgins.

5. ff. 119–126v: Short hours of the Cross.

6. ff. 127–133v: Short hours of the Holy Spirit.

7. ff. 134–181v: Office of the Dead, use of Paris.

8. ff. 182–191: Prayers as follow: *Cy commencent les quinze ioies de nostre dame,* Doulce dame de misericorde . . . [Leroquais, *LH* 2:310–11]; *Cy s'ensuivent les cinq plaies,* Doulz dieux pere sainte trinite et un dieu . . . [Leroquais, *LH* 2:309–10]; Saincte vray croix aouree . . . [Sonet 1876]; f. 191v, ruled, but blank.

9. ff. 192–211v: Suffrages of the Trinity, All Saints, the Assumption of the Virgin, the Cross, Michael, John the Baptist, Peter and Paul, Andrew, John the Evangelist, James the Greater, Thomas the Apostle, Bartholomew, Matthew the Evangelist, Simon and Jude, Matthias, Luke, Mark, Stephen, Lawrence, Vincent, Denis, Christopher, George, Martin, Nicholas, Maurus, Anthony abbot, Fiacre, Catherine of Alexandria, Margaret, Genevieve, Mary Magdalene, Anne; ff. 212–214v, blank.

Parchment, ff. ii (parchment, with blue silk and gold tooled morocco glued to the recto of the first) + 214 + ii (parchment, with blue silk and gold tooled morocco glued to the verso of the second); 235 × 170 (107 × 65) mm. 1^{12} 2^{8} 3^{8}(–2, after f. 21) 4–11^{8} 12^{6}(through f. 97) 13–23^{8} 24^{6}(through f. 191) 25–26^{8} 27^{8}(–8). Catchwords in a small careful gothic script in the center of the lower margin. 15 long lines, ruled in a rather vivid pink; pricking occasionally present in the upper and lower margins. Written in 2 sizes of gothic script, according to liturgical function.

Nineteen large miniatures usually in arched compartments above 4 lines of text; most borders consist of a decorated wide gold band in a U-shape around both text and miniature, with an outer border of ivy vine and regularly arranged, brightly colored acanthus leaves and flowers. The miniatures, by several artists of the workshop of the Master of the Duke of Bedford, are: f. 13 (Gospel of John), in a square compartment above 5 lines of text, John on Patmos with his eagle holding one end of the scroll, and the devil stealing his inkwell; the acanthus leaves of the outer border in lush, dense foliage form the U-shape frame, and are surrounded by an ivy design of thin, swirling pink or blue branches; f. 15 (Luke), in the same configuration and border as f. 13, the evangelist is shown painting a picture of the Virgin; f. 17 (Mark), configuration and border as on f. 13, Mark sits at his desk writing, with the lion on the floor in front of him; f. 18v (Matthew), configuration and border as on f. 13, Matthew writes while the angel kneels before him; f. 28 (Hours of the Virgin), Annunciation, seen through 3 pale pink arches enclosing respectively the angel, the lilies (within another "frame" of gold curtains), and Mary; the U-shape border consists solely of lush, dense acanthus leaves of bright orange, olive green, rose, red, golden brown and blue, which form spaces for 6 medallions of angels playing musical instruments against burnished gold grounds; the normal ivy leaf decoration has mainly been crowded out, and is reduced to a few gold motifs; f. 52 (Lauds), Visitation, including a young girl accompanying Mary; in the background against a high horizon are 3 islands or peninsulas, and a galleon floating on the river; border as on f. 28; f. 63v (Prime), Nativity, with the Baby lying in the manger on a corner of the Virgin's cloak; behind Mary is an orange and white bed; in the medallions of a border as on f. 28 are angels, men, dogs and sheep, all growing from flowers (reproduced in Meiss, fig. 53); f. 69v (Terce), Annunciation to the shepherds and a shepherdess with a distaff; f. 74v (Sext), Adoration of the Magi; f. 79 (None), Presentation in the temple seen through pale pink architecture; f. 83v (Vespers), Flight into Egypt, with an angel accompanying the Holy Family and a broad river in the background; f. 91 (Compline), Coronation of the Virgin by an angel flying above her together with other angels, as she kneels in prayer before God the Father; f. 98 (Penitential psalms), David on a parapet of his castle above a river praying to God who appears in a circle of gold rays among monochrome blue angels; the background is reminiscent of that in Jan van Eyck's portrait of Chancellor Rolin before the Madonna, reproduced, for example, by M. Meiss, *French Painting in the Time of Jean de Berry: The Boucicaut Master* (New York 1968) fig. 493; f. 119 (Hours of the Cross), with Mary, John and Mary Magdalene on Christ's right along with the 2 Longinus': the soldier who pierces Christ's side and the Longinus who cures his blindness by placing a drop of Christ's blood in his eye; on Christ's left are the soldiers and the converted centurion who holds a scroll bearing the legend "Vere filius dei erat iste"; the border has the same thin swirling pink and blue branches as the borders of the Evangelist portraits; f. 127 (Hours of the Holy Spirit), Pentecost, with Mary centered between 2 columns and exactly below the dome and the Dove; diapered background; f. 134 (Office of the Dead), Burial scene in a churchyard, with 2 men lowering the shrouded corpse into the grave while the small naked soul, aided by the archangel Michael, escapes from the claws of a black devil and is pulled up through an aperture in the sky into heaven where God the Father awaits him; f. 182 (Doulce dame de misericorde), the Virgin standing, holding the Child who has his right arm around her neck and clutches a string of coral beads with the other; 2 angels support a cloth of honor behind them; the pose is directly related to Jan van Eyck's Madonna at the Fountain (dated 1439) in the Musée Royale in Antwerp; in the manuscript, however, there is a canopy above the Virgin, and the fountain has been omitted; see, for example, E. Panofsky, *Early Netherlandish Painting* (Harvard University Press 1953) fig. 255; f. 188 (the 5 Wounds), Man of Sorrows with Mary and John sitting respectively in front and in back of the tomb, while two angels stand behind holding the instruments of the Passion, and a host of orange angels frames the arch; this same scene in Keble College MS 39, f. 164, reproduced in Parkes, *Keble College,* fig. 91; f. 192 (suffrage to the Trinity), God the Father in a brocade and jewelled robe supports the dying Christ, while the Dove perches on Christ's shoulder, with angels at the 4 corners holding the instruments of the Passion; a ruffled gold-starred blue cloud frames the miniature. Small miniatures in the margins, unframed and based on green grass, approximately 40 × 20 mm.: f. 193 (All Saints), placed tightly against the bar frame of the text, a group of male saints among which are identifiable Stephen, James the Greater, Andrew and Lawrence; f. 193v (Assumption of Mary), the Virgin wearing a gold dress, and being supported by 2 angels within a blue cloud; f. 194 (Cross), 2 angels supporting the cross with the INRI legend at the top; f. 195, Michael in full armour, vanquishing the devil; f. 195v, John the Baptist pointing to the nimbed Lamb he holds in his arms; f. 196, Peter with the keys and Paul holding an open book and leaning on the sword; f. 196v, Andrew with open book and his cross; f. 197, John the Evangelist blessing the snake-filled chalice he holds in his left hand together with a palm leaf; f. 197v, James the Greater with staff and open book; f. 198, Thomas the Apostle with lance and open book; f. 198v, Bartholomew with flaying knife and open book; f. 199, Matthew with open book; f. 199v, Jude with the bludgeon and Simon holding an open book; f. 200v, Matthias holding a quill and an open book, evidently through confusion with Matthew the Evangelist; f. 201, Luke with quill and open book; f. 201v, Mark with quill and open book; f. 202v, Stephen with a rock on his head; f. 203, Lawrence with his grate; f. 203v, Vincent dressed in a dalmatic; f. 204, Denis holding his head; f. 205, Christopher, the Christ Child on his shoulders; f. 205v, George on his horse, killing the dragon; f. 206, Martin cutting his cloak; f. 206v, Nicholas blessing the three children, one of whom is stepping out of the barrel; f. 207, Maurus in Benedictine robes with an abbot's crozier; f. 207v, Anthony abbot with the pig and flames; f. 208, Fiacre holding a shovel; f. 208v, Catherine of Alexandria with broken wheel and sword; f. 209, Margaret emerging from the dragon's back; f. 209v, Genevieve with the angel lighting her candle as the devil, using bellows, tries to blow it out; f. 210, Mary Magdalene holding the jar of ointment; f. 211, Anne standing next to the child Mary with one arm protectively around her shoulder, and holding an open book with the other hand. 4-line initials for the first 3 Gospel extracts, and 3-, 2-, and 1-line initials in white-patterned blue on burnished gold grounds with trilobe leaf infilling; the 3-line initials on ff. 52, 98, 119 and 182 against rose-colored grounds; ribbon line fillers in the same colors and in many designs; initials within the text touched in yellow. Blue rubrics for the Gospel sequences and the 2 prayers to the Virgin, thereafter in red. Full borders on every page, consisting of a gold and color U-shaped frame around the text, often terminating in an orange and blue grotesque; outer border of black ivy vine and gold motifs. Similar borders in the calendar, which also include in the lower margin of the recto a miniature of the monthly occupation, and in the middle of the outer margin of the recto a roundel with the zodiac sign. Erased inscription on f. 211v below the text.

Bound, s. XIX, by Charles Smith in worn red velvet with 2 silver-gilt fore edge clasps and four corner-pieces; light blue watered silk doublures and endpapers, dentelle elaborately tooled; gilt edges. This binding, apparently defective, was taken apart in 1945 (?); the book now kept in loose quires in a case.

Written in the middle of the fifteenth century in France, probably Paris, and decorated in the style of the Master of the Duke of Bedford. Given by John Webb to Augustus Frederick, Duke of Sussex (1773–1843); in the *Bibliotheca Sussexiana, A Descriptive Catalogue . . . of the Manuscripts and Printed Books contained in the Library of His Royal Highness, the Duke of Sussex,* by Thomas J. Pettigrew (London 1827) vol. I, pt. 1, n. 129 with a plate of f. 134; his sale, Evans, London, 31 July 1844, pt. II, n. 187 to James Baker; his sale, London, 24 May 1855, n. 473 to Edwin Henry Lawrence (d. 1891); his sale, Sotheby's, 9 May 1892, n. 303 to Quaritch. Acquired by Robert Hoe: Bierstadt (1895) 25–27 with a plate of f. 63v; *Cat.* (1909) pp. 61–62; his sale, Anderson, New York, 1911, pt. I, n. 2130 to G. D. Smith; Smith Cat. [n. 2, 1912?] n. 119 to Henry E. Huntington in April 1912.

Bibliography: De Ricci, 92. M. Meiss, *The De Lévis Hours and the Bedford Workshop* (Yale University Press 1972) fig. 53 of f. 63v.

HM 1101

HM 1101 — France, s. XVI^{in} and XV^{med}
BOOK OF HOURS, use of Rome

1. ff. 5–7v [ff. 1–4 are pastedown and flyleaves]: Full calendar, usually alternating red and blue with major feasts in gold, in 2 columns each of one month; among the saints are: Salvius (10 January), Aventinus (4 February), Austregisil (15 February), Aphrodosius (22 March), Medard (8 June), Philibert (20 August), Basolus (15 October), Magloire (23 October as "episcopi" and 24 October as "confessoris"), Livin (12 November).

2. ff. 8–18v [f. 8, blank]: Pericopes of the Gospels; Passion according to John, followed by the prayer, Deus qui manus tuas . . . ; *Oratio devota ad beatam virginem mariam,* Obsecro te . . . [masculine forms; Leroquais, *LH* 2:346]; *Alia oratio ad beatam virginem et ad sanctum Iohannem,* O Intemerata . . . orbis terrarum. Inclina mater . . . [Wilmart, 488–90]; Salve Regina . . . [*RH* 18147].

3. ff. 19–51v [f. 19, blank]: Hours of the Virgin, use of Rome; suffrages of All Saints from lauds to compline; weekly variations of the psalms at matins begin on f. 43v; Advent office begins on f. 47; *Beatus gregorius papa instituit sequentes orationes et concessit* . . . , O Domine iesu christe adoro te in cruce pendentem . . . [Leroquais, *LH* 2:346, with his n. 3 at the end]; *Quedam devotissima contemplatio beate marie* . . . , Stabat mater dolorosa . . . [*RH* 19416] with versicle, response and prayer, Interveniat pro nobis quesumus domine ihesu christe nunc et in hora mortis . . . ; *Alia oratio,* Inviolata integra et casta es maria . . . [*RH* 9094] with versicle, response and prayer, Deus qui salutis eterne beate marie virginitate fecunda . . .

4. ff. 52–60v [f. 52, blank]: Penitential psalms and litany, including Victor, Denis, Hippolytus, Quentin and Quiriacus among the martyrs; Remigius, Eligius, Magloire and Cloud among the confessors; Genevieve, Anastasia and Chlothildis among the virgins.

5. ff. 61–63v [f. 61, blank]: Short hours of the Cross.

6. ff. 64–66 [f. 64, blank]: Short hours of the Holy Spirit.

7. ff. 66v–85: Office of the Dead, use of Rome.

8. ff. 85v–93v: Suffrage of the Trinity; Pater de celis deus miserere nobis. Domine sancte pater omnipotens eterne deus qui coequalem et consubstancialem . . . , Domine iesu christe fili dei vivi qui es verus . . . , Domine spiritus sancte deus qui coequalis . . . [to the Trinity; *HE* 124–25]; suffrages of the Holy Face, Michael, John the Baptist, John the Evangelist, Peter and Paul, James the Greater, All Apostles, Stephen, Lawrence, Christopher [. . . et michi famulo tuo N . . .], Sebastian, Many Martyrs, Nicholas, Anthony abbot, Anne, Mary Magdalene, Catherine of Alexandria, Margaret, Barbara, Apollonia.

Parchment, ff. 98 (of which 1 is the front pastedown, 2–4 are front flyleaves, 94–97 are back flyleaves, 98 is the back pastedown); 245 × 158 (160 × 83) mm. 1^{4}(ff. 4–7) 2^{8}(+1, f. 8) 3^{12}(+3, f. 19) 4^{4} 5^{12} 6^{4} 7^{12}(+3, f. 52, and 12, f. 61) 8^{4}(+1, f. 64, and 3, f. 66) 9^{12} 10^{4} 11^{10}(−2 leaves in the second half?; ff. 86–93, with stitching between ff. 90–91). One catchword survives, f. 79v, in a small formal cursive script. 30 long lines, ruled in pale red ink; pricking occasionally visible in the outer margin. Written in a rounded script with humanistic influence.

Nine full page miniatures by the Master of Philippe of Guelders[1]; see Plummer, *Last Flowering*, n. 91 and 92; of the 9, 6 are on the versos of inserted singletons, usually blank on the recto: ff. 8v, 19v, 52v, 61v, 64v and 66v; they are enclosed by painted gold architectural frames decorated with Renaissance ornaments and set against a dark background. The miniatures are: f. 8v (Gospel of John), Eve rising from the sleeping Adam's rib, while God, depicted as Jesus, blesses them and water flows from a fountain in the background; f. 19v (Hours of the Virgin), the Cardinal Virtues: Justice (holding a sword), Temperance (holding tablets), Prudence (holding a mirror) and Fortitude (holding an anvil), with an angel standing behind them and the Trinity above; f. 20 (Hours of the Virgin), with 4 lines of text set on a scroll over the architectural frame, the Annunciation; f. 52v (Penitential psalms), David sending Uriah into battle; f. 53 (Penitential psalms), with 4 lines of text set on a scroll, David watching Bathsheba as she bathes in a fountain decorated with 2 gold cupids; f. 61v (Hours of the Cross), Road to Calvary; f. 64v (Hours of the Holy Spirit), the Apostles preaching and the Separation of the Apostles; f. 66v (Office of the Dead), the Rich Man at dinner, with a boy setting dogs on the begging Lazarus; f. 67 (Office of the Dead), the Raising of Lazarus. Smaller miniatures, with ruling visible under the painting, usually 11-line: f. 9, John writing with the eagle holding his inkwell; f. 9v, Luke; f. 10, Matthew; f. 10v, Mark, 10-line; f. 11v (Passion according to John), 20 line, Betrayal with Jesus holding Malchus' bloody ear in his hand; f. 16 (Obsecro te), 18-line, the Virgin holding the baby Jesus on her lap, with an angel at either side; f. 17v (O Intemerata), Pietà; f. 25 (Lauds), 18-line, Visitation; f. 30 (Prime), 18-line, Nativity; f. 32 (Terce), 18-line, Annunciation to the shepherds; f. 34 (Sext), 18-line, Adoration of the Magi; f. 36 (None), 18-line, Presentation in the temple; f. 38 (Vespers), 18-line, Flight into Egypt with the miracles of the corn field and the falling idol in the background; f. 41v (Compline), 18-line, Coronation of the Virgin by an angel as Jesus blesses her, with swirling blue clouds at the lower edge of the picture; f. 60 (Hours of the Cross), 18-line, Crucifixion with Mary, John and others on Christ's right, and the soldiers on his left; f. 65 (Hours of the Holy Spirit), 18-line, Pentecost; f. 85v (Trinity), the Father, as a bearded young man, and the Son with stigmata sit together holding a book while the Dove hovers between them, and (idem, to the Father), God the Father as a young man, sitting, with the orb and gesture of benediction; f. 86 (idem, to the Son), same figure as above, but standing; f. 86v (idem, to the Holy Spirit), Pentecost without the Virgin; f. 86v (prayer to the Holy Face), Veronica holding the cloth with a black image of Christ's face; f. 87v, Michael fighting the devil; f. 87v, John the Baptist pointing to the Agnus Dei which sits on a book; f. 88, John the Evangelist pointing to the poisoned chalice; f. 88, Peter and Paul; f. 88v, James the Greater, with staff and book; f. 89, Stephen; f. 89v, Lawrence; f. 89v, Christopher; f. 90, Sebastian; f. 91, Nicholas; f. 91, Anthony abbot; f. 91v, Anne teaching Mary to read; f. 91v, Mary Magdalene; f. 92, Catherine of Alexandria; f. 92v, Margaret; f. 92v, Barbara; f. 93, Apollonia. In the calendar a narrow strip at the top of the folio, 15 × 90 mm., encloses the 2 signs of the zodiac, while the monthly occupations are below, 35 × 90 mm. On every page, except where there are full page illuminations, traced geometric borders with acanthus leaves, naturalistic flowers, and occasional birds or insects against painted gold, brick-red or blue grounds. 4-, 3- and 2-line initials in painted gold on white-decorated blue grounds; 1-line initials in gold alternate blue or brick-red grounds; line fillers in these 2 colors with gold decoration, or as gold logs. Rubrics in pink.

On both pastedowns and on the front and back flyleaves (foliated as ff. 1–4 and 94–98) are miniatures cut from a French book of hours, s. XV^{med}, in arched compartments above 4 lines of text, 100 × 75 mm. The miniatures, attributed by E. König, *Französische Buchmalerei um 1450: der Jouvenal-Maler, der Maler des Genfer Boccaccio und die Anfänge Jean Fouquets* (Berlin 1982) 254 to the artist of Paris, B.N. fr. 135–136 (by typographical error, this manuscript given as HM 1141), are: f. 1v (the front pastedown; Hours of the Virgin), Annunciation with text and miniature surrounded by a wide U-shaped frame of dark blue decorated with alternating white and orange roses; the outer border consists of white daisy-like flowers and smaller blue ones, growing from yellow-green leafy stems against a gold ground; f. 2v (Lauds), Visitation, in front of lavender city walls; the border is of blue or gold flowers, gold trumpets and yellow-green leaves; f. 3v (Prime), Nativity in the stable, with the Virgin lying on a red-draped pallet, the baby Jesus in a wattle manger; the border is of rather sparse black ink spray vines, gold trilobe leaves and, at regular intervals, a gold log, a rooster, a yellow-green log, a clump of violets, a gold pot of orange carnations; f. 4v (Terce), Annunciation to the shepherds among spiky hills; the U-shaped frame around text and miniature with continuously alternating blue carnations and pink flowers; the ivy spray outer border contains a peacock. On the back flyleaves, f. 94 (Sext), Adoration of the Magi, with the baby Jesus reaching for the gift; red cloth of honor and green wattle in the background; in the ivy spray border a bird and strawberries; f. 95 (None), Presentation in the temple, the interior of which is pale green with orange and blue vaulting; a band of gold and colors forms a U-shape around text and miniature; ivy spray outer border; f. 96 (Vespers), Flight into Egypt, with a similar gold and color U-shaped frame; a gold pot of flowers in the outer border; f. 97 (Hours of the Cross), Crucifixion with Mary and John against a tessellated background; gold U-shaped frame with red and green ivy leaves; in the outer border ivy spray and a clump of growing pink and blue flowers with yellow-green leaves; f. 98 (the back pastedown; Hours of the Holy Spirit), Pentecost, in a lavender building, with some of the apostles' cloaks in bright yellow-green or orange; U-shaped gold frame with blue vine twisted about a red bar; outer border of black ivy spray.

Bound, s. XVIII^{in}, in English gold tooled red morocco; gilt edges; front cover detached; brown morocco slip case by Riviere.

Written in France, the main text in the early sixteenth century, the added miniatures in the middle of the fifteenth. Belonged to Sidney Herbert, 14th Earl of Pembroke (1853–1913); his sale, Sotheby's, 25 June 1914, n. 109 with plates of ff. 19v–20 and one of the added miniatures, f. 2v, to G. D. Smith. Source and date of acquisition by Henry E. Huntington unknown.

Bibliography: De Ricci, 92. A. Shickman, "Shakespeare's 'Figure of an Angel': an iconographic study," *Colby Library Quarterly* 17 (1981) 6–25 with a reproduction of f. 19v.

---

[1] We thank M. François Avril for this identification.

HM 1102 — Rome, 1549
BOOK OF HOURS, use of Rome — *fig. 34*

1. ff. 1–2: f. 1, Title page, in lapidary style in gold letters across the frieze of a temple: "D. Claud Durfe. Reg. Legat. Dicatum"; between the columns in gold square capitals: "Heures de Nostre Dame a l'usaige de Rome escriptes au dict lieu l'an MDXLIX par M. Franc. Wydon et dediees a Messire Claude D'urfe Chevalier de l'ordre du Roy Tres Chrestien et son Ambassadeur au saint siege apostolique"; ff. 1v–2: coat of arms (see below) and an altar; below, 16 lines of verse, "Inventa Alcidae est, catulo duce, purpura fulgens . . ."

2. ff. 2v–21: Full calendar in French; the rubrics for the months begin with etymological information; entries in the calendar also include ancient Greek and Roman festivities. Three contemporary events (in the hand of the scribe):

A tel iour et l'an mil CCCCC vous naquistes monseigneur Messire Claude D'urfe, a semblable iour aussi l'an 1524 fut prins a Pavie Francoys de Valoys, premier de ce nom Roy de France (24 February); Et a tel iour 1529 fut prise et saccaigee la ville de Rome, par le Duc de Bourbon (6 May); Ce iour cy l'an 1549 vous Monseigneur Messire C. D'urfe fustez apelle au sainct college de Mons. S. Michel par le Roy nostre Sire Henry II et faict et cree Chevalier de son ordre (29 September). The full page illustrations for the months of February, April, May, June and November have been cut out, with consequent loss of text; the remaining illustrations have 4-line inscriptions in Latin, referring to the pagan scene depicted.

3. ff. 21v–28v: Pericopes of the Gospels and the Passion according to John; f. 29, with border, but blank.

4. ff. 29v–56: Office of the Virgin, use of Rome, with suffrages of All Saints from lauds to compline; Salve Regina follows compline.

5. ff. 56v–68: Penitential psalms and litany.

6. ff. 68v–79v: Office of the Dead; three lessons at matins.

7. ff. 80–82: Short hours of the Cross.

8. ff. 82v–84: Short hours of the Holy Spirit.

9. ff. 84–85v: Suffrages of the Trinity, Michael, Gabriel, Raphael, Claude; *Ad Deum optimum maximum,* Clementissime mi deus, a te rerum omnium principio incepit oratio mea . . . ; ends, on a decorativcly framed ground: *Regi seculorum immortali, invisibili, soli Deo honor et gloria in secula seculorum Amen.*

Parchment, ff. i (paper) + i (parchment) + 85 + i (parchment) + i (paper); 280 × 195 (232 × 155) mm. 1^8(–4, 8) 2^8(–2, 4) 3^8(–6) $4–11^8$ 12^2. 23 long lines, also in the calendar; no ruling visible. Written by Franc. Wydon, who signed the dedication on f. 1; he has used a variety of scripts; square capitals on f. 1, italic on the cartouches with Latin verses on ff. 1v–2 and on those in the calendar; the main body of the text is in an upright humanistic script. For another manuscript made for Claude d'Urfé, and, although not signed by Wydon, in the same italic script as used in HM 1102, and with the same decoration, see London, Victoria and Albert Museum, L. 1964–1957[1], a *Traicté à la louenge de Dieu* by Victor Brodeau with the inscriptions (f. 2v) "Escript à Rome l'an Iubilé du 1550" and (f. 30) "Escript pour Monseigneur Claude d'Urfé, chevalier de l'ordre et gouverneur de Monseigneur le Daulphin, Conseillier du roy et son Ambassadeur au saint Siege apostolique"; for plates, see J. I. Whalley, *The Pen's Excellencie: the calligraphy of western Europe and America* (Tunbridge Wells 1980). A third manuscript, unsigned, but written in a humanistic script attributable to Wydon is Paris, B.N. n.a. lat. 1506[2], a pontifical made for Claude d'Urfé's successor in Rome, Georges d'Armagnac; the manuscript is dated 1557 in the borders of ff. 34v–35 (although Georges d'Armagnac is not known to have been in residence in Rome at that date); see V. Leroquais, *Les Pontificaux Manuscrits* (Paris 1937) 2:240–41 and pl. 138 (illumination only). Wydon's signature does appear in a book of meditations copied for Georges d'Armagnac in Rome, 1543, now Chantilly, Musée Condé, MS 102 (1398); see L. Dorez, *Le psautier de Paul III* (Paris [1909]) pl. 30–32: pl. 30 shows an architectural opening folio similar to that in HM 1102, and the same humanistic script as the main body of text in HM 1102; pl. 31–32 show the italic script. In the Chantilly manuscript, Wydon identifies himself as "britannus," which Dorez interprets as "breton" (p. 24, n. 2).

Decorated with 24 almost full page illustrations in bistre: f. 1v, coat of arms (see below);

f. 2, an altar for sacrifice; f. 2v, Janus; f. 5v, Mars; f. 10v, Europa and the bull; f. 12v, Pluto and Persephone; f. 14v, Vulcan; f. 16v, Bacchus; f. 19v, the Temple of Vesta; f. 29v (Matins), Annunciation; f. 35 (Lauds), Visitation; f. 41 (Prime), Nativity; f. 43v (Terce), Annunciation to the shepherds; f. 45v (Sext), Adoration of the Magi; f. 47v (None), Circumcision; f. 49v (Vespers), Flight into Egypt; f. 53v (Compline), Coronation of the Virgin; f. 56v (Penitential psalms), Nathan exhorting David to penitence; f. 62v (Litany), Castel Sant'Angelo, with the angel sheathing his sword, and a pope, presumably Gregory the Great, although he may be wearing the Medici arms, kneeling before the propitious vision, while the procession crosses the bridge; f. 68v (Office of the Dead, Vespers), Raising of Lazarus; f. 72v (Office of the Dead, Matins), Pietà; f. 77 (Office of the Dead, Lauds), Last Judgment; f. 80 (Hours of the Cross), Crucifixion; f. 82v (Hours of the Holy Spirit), Pentecost. The four Evangelist portraits and the miniature of Jesus in Gethsemane for the Passion gospel, ff. 21v, 22, 22v, 23v, 24, are 6-line water color. Initials, 6- to 2-line, in painted gold on gold-flourished grounds of blue, purple, green, brown, yellow, rose; 1-line initials in painted gold. Full borders on every page, consisting of narrow purple bands with silver leafy tendrils; in ovals set within the top and bottom band are landscapes or ruins; in the ovals in the bands on the two sides are blue tendrils on a gold ground; square insets of color at the four corners. See Dorez, *op. cit.*, pl. 30–32, for similar borders, which he tentatively attributes to Wydon himself. Rubrics throughout in red.

Bound, s. XVIII^{ex}, in French red morocco; marbled endpapers; gilt edges.

Written in Rome, 1549, by F. Wydon for Claude d'Urfé (1501–58), ambassador of the King of France to the Holy See; his arms appear on f. 1v, ensigned with the collar of the order of St. Michael; see Rietstap, vol. 6, pl. 69. For a history of the d'Urfé library and a list of the surviving books (including HM 1102), see A. Vernet, "Les Manuscrits de Claude d'Urfé (1501–1558) au Château de la Bastie," *Académie des Inscriptions et Belles-Lettres: Comptes-Rendus* (1976) 81–97. The d'Urfé library was bought in 1777 by the Duc de La Vallière; his sale, Paris, 1784, vol. 1, n. 317 (catalogue, dated 1783, compiled by Guillaume De Bure; entry for this manuscript carefully copied out on f. i verso) to De Bure; Duquesroy, Paris, 7 March 1803, n. 28. Belonged to Edward Thurlow, 1st Baron Thurlow (1731–1806); his sale, Christie's, 1804, n. 298 to Hume (apparently a *nom de guerre* to disguise that of J. White of Fleet Street, the bookseller from whom Lord Thurlow had acquired his books originally); see Dibdin, *Bibliomania* (1842) 448–50, for an account of the sale; John White Catalogue 20 (January 1806) n. 466; acquired by Jeremiah Harman, and sold by Evans, 20 May 1844, n. 1154. The manuscript was in the collection of Prof. Manuel John Johnson (1805–59) of the Oxford Observatory, when it was seen and described by G. F. Waagen, *Treasures of Art in Great Britain* (London 1854) 3:116–18; Johnson sale, Sotheby's, 27 May 1862, lot 37 to the dealer Toovey. It appears as property of Stephen Ram in the catalogue of the London bookseller Phillips, 17 December 1862, n. 92; P. Deschamps; Baron S. de la Roche Lacarelle, whose red morocco ex libris is on the front pastedown; his sale, Paris, 1888, n. 21 to Morgand. Belonged to the Count R. de Lignerolles; his sale, Paris, Porquet, 1894, vol. 1, n. 14 to the Marquis d'Albon; the entry from this catalogue is printed by Dorez, *op. cit.*, 49–50; Dorez makes reference to the "Album" of plates for the Lignerolles sale, including one of this manuscript (not available to us). Belonged to Robert Hoe: Bierstadt (1895) p. 34, with a plate of f. 35; *Cat.* (1909) pp. 118–20; his sale, Anderson, New York, 1912, pt. III, n. 2078, with a plate of f. 56v, to G. D. Smith. Source and date of acquisition by Henry E. Huntington unknown.

Bibliography: De Ricci, 92.

---

[1] We thank J. I. Whalley for her kind help.

[2] We are indebted to M. François Avril for examining this manuscript and for providing the information on its date.

HM 1104 France, s. XV^{in} and XV^{ex}
BOOK OF HOURS, use of Rome *fig. 86*

1. ff. 1–12v: Rather empty calendar, alternating red and blue, with major feasts in gold; f. 13r–v, ruled, but blank.

2. ff. 14–19: Pericopes from the Gospels; ff. 19v–20v, ruled, but blank.

3. ff. 21–96v: Hours of the Virgin, use of Rome; suffrages of All Saints from lauds to compline; Salve Regina follows compline; weekly variations of psalms at matins given without rubrics on ff. 78v–87; Advent office begins on f. 87.

4. ff. 97–116v: Penitential psalms and litany, including Martialis as the last of the apostles.

5. ff. 117–160v: Office of the Dead, use of Rome.

Hours for each day of the week, arts. 6–12, as follow:

6. ff. 161–164v: Short hours of the Trinity.

7. ff. 165–168v: Short hours of the Dead.

8. ff. 169–174v: Short hours of the Holy Spirit; rubric for sext miswritten "ad primam."

9. ff. 175–178v: Short hours of All Saints.

10. ff. 179–182v: Short hours of the Eucharist.

11. ff. 183–190v: Short hours of the Cross.

12. ff. 191–194v: Short hours of the Virgin.

13. ff. 195–198v: Short hours of St. Catherine.

14. ff. 199–202: *Septem gaudia beate marie virginis,* Virgo templum trinitatis . . . [Wilmart, 329, n.]; f. 202v, ruled, but blank.

15. ff. 203–236: Prayers in Latin as follow: *Oratio trina Dicenda ad trinitatem,* Aperi domine os meum ad laudandum et benedicendum sanctissimum et ineffabile nomen tuum . . . ; *Ad patrem oratio,* Adoro te domine deus pater ingenite . . . ; *Oratio,* Respice domine quesumus super cunctam familiam tuam . . . [*HE,* 115, first paragraph only]; *Fides catholica,* Credo in deum patrem omnipotentem . . . ; *Oratio ad filium,* Adoro te Domine Iesu christe unicum dei filium verum deum et verum hominem . . . ; *Oratio,* Omnipotens sempiterne deus dirige actus nostros . . . ; *Symbolum angelorum,* Gloria in excelsis deo et in terra pax hominibus bone voluntatis . . . ; *Oratio ad spiritum sanctum,* Adoro te spiritus paraclite verum deum precedentem ab utroque . . . ; *Ultima ad patrem oratio,* Mentes nostras quesumus domine paraclitus spiritus sanctus illuminet . . . ; *Ut gratias referas altissimo oratio,* Gratias ago tibi domine deus eterne de vita mea, salute et sanitate mea . . . ; *Sancti thome de aquino Oratio,* Concede michi misericors deus que tibi placita sunt . . . [Doyle, "Thomas Aquinas"]; *Pro viatgio* [*sic*] *devotissima oratio,* In viam pacis salutis et prosperitatis dirigat dominus gressus nostros . . . [with canticle, verses and responses, ending:] *Vers.* Ora pro nobis beate Iuliane. *Resp.* Ut digni efficiamur. Oremus. *Oratio,* Adesto domine supplicationibus nostris . . . ; *Beate marie virginis devota oratio,*

Benedicat me deus pater qui cuncta de nichilo creavit . . . ; *Sequitur quedam oratio Defunctorum devota,* Avete omnes anime fideles quarum corpora hic et ubique requiescunt in pulvere . . . *Vers.* . . . *Resp.* . . . *Oratio,* Domine ihesu christe salus et liberatio . . . [the set printed in Leroquais, *LH* 2:341]; *Sanctus Gregorius dum fuit summus pontifex* . . . , O domine ihesu christe adoro te in cruce pendentem . . . [Leroquais, *LH* 2:346, but his sections here ordered 1, 2, 4, 7, 3]; *Alia oratio,* Ave vulnus lateris nostri redemptoris . . . [*RH* 24031; on f. 214, a diagram of the wound and of the height of Christ]; *Oratio ad staturam Domini nostri ihesu christi,* Adoro te Domine Ihesu Christe salvator et sacratissimam staturam corporis tui . . . [with an indulgence conceded by Pope Innocent: *Qui orationem precedentem ad vulnus Domini Nostri Ihesu Christi devote dixerit . . . Et hec linea vigesies multiplicata christi longitudinem representat . . . Non patietur Epylentiam, non capietur nec Morte subitanea peribit* . . .]; *Sequitur alia oratio,* Domine deus omnipotens pater filius et spiritus sanctus. Da michi famulo tuo G. victoriam contra Inimicos meos . . . [de la Mare, *Lyell Cat.,* 373, n. 88]; *Oratio phebus,* Domine deus creator et salvator et redemptor omnium Tue bonitati et clementie Regratior humiliter . . . [not identified in G. Tilander, P. Tucoo-Chala, eds., *Gaston Fébus, Livre des Oraisons,* Pau 1974]; Domine ihesu christe redemptor mundi defende me de manu inimicorum meorum . . . ; *Bonifatius papa quartus et innocentius Quintus concesserunt* . . . , Obsecro te . . . Et michi famulo tuo G. . . . [Leroquais, *LH* 2:346]; *Hec de sepulcro sancte et dei genitricis oratio* . . . , Domine ihesu christe fili dei patris omnipotentis, Tu qui es deus angelorum et filius beatissime virginis Marie . . . ; *Alia beatissime virginis Marie oratio,* O intemerata . . . orbis terrarum. Inclina aures . . . [Wilmart, 488–90]; *Oratio septem verborum Domini in cruce,* Domine ihesu christe qui in cruce septem verba . . . [Leroquais, *LH* 2:342]; *De Beata maria Magdalena,* Gaude pia magdalena Spes salutis vite vera . . . [*RH* 6895; suffrage with versicle, response and 2 prayers]; *Oratio sancti augustini ad proprium custodem angelum,* Obsecro te o mi angelice spiritus cui ego ad providendum datus sum . . . [Wilmart, 542].

16. ff. 236–244v: Penitential material in Provençal as follows: *La confession,* Quascun fizel christia segon l'ordenansa De sancta mayre gleisa . . . ; *Las circumstantias En los peccatz* . . . ; *De los sinc sentimens Corporals* . . . ; *De los set peccatz mortals* . . . ; *Rams de superbia* . . . ; *Rams D'avaricia* . . . ; *De luxuria* . . . ; *De Ira* . . . ; *De Gola* . . . ; *De Enuegia* . . . ; *De pigressa* . . . ; *De las vertutz contra los peccatz* . . . ; *Dels set Dos del sant espirit* . . . ; *Dels X mandamens* . . . ; *De los peccatz qe cridan davant dieu* . . . ; *Las iiii*[e] *vertutz cardinals* . . . ; *De las iii vertutz theologals* . . . ; *Dels sagramens de la gleisa* . . . ; *Dels articles de la fee* . . . ; *Dels vii peccatz contra lo sant espirit* . . . ; *Dels peccatz de oration* . . . ; *Las obras de misericorde* . . . ; *De las obras de misericordia Spiritualas* . . . ; *De Los viii*[t] *peccatz D'autruy* . . . ; *Dels peccatz abominatz* . . . ; *De las vii*[t] *Beatitutz Evangelicals* . . . ; *De la vertuz Contra los peccatz venials* . . . ; *De los dotze fruitz del sant espirit* . . . ; *Dels cazes que ammentan La confession* . . . ; ff. 245–248v, ruled, but blank.

C. Brunel, *Bibliographie des manuscrits littéraires en ancien provençal* (Paris 1935) n. 53. E. Roditi, "Huntington Library Manuscript HM 1104: A Religious Orthodox Text in Provençal," *Annali dell'Istituto Universitario Orientale* 22, 1 (Naples 1980) 189–200.

HM 1104

In two parts: 1, ff. 1–202, written in the early fifteenth century; 2, ff. 203–248, added at the end of the century. Parchment, ff. ii (paper, with silk glued to the recto of the first) + 248 + ii (paper, with silk glued to the verso of the second); 263 × 178 (133 × 75) mm. 1^{6} 2^{6}(+1 leaf in the second half; the last leaf is blank) 3^{8}(−1 leaf in the second half; through f. 20, blank) $4–6^{8}$ 7^{6}(through f. 50) 8^{10}(through f. 60) 9^{8} 10^{4}(through f. 72) $11–15^{8}$ 16^{4}(through f. 116) $17–21^{8}$ $22–24^{4}$ 25^{6}(through f. 174) $26–27^{4}$ 28^{8}(through f. 190) 29^{4}(through f. 194) $30–31^{4}$(through f. 202) $32–36^{8}$ 37^{6}. Note that the divisions of the text, arts. 1–14, correspond to breaks between the quires; this is particularly evident for the series of short hours, arts. 6–13, and the Seven Joys, art. 14: each is copied on a separate quire. Catchwords in part 2 only, written vertically along the inner bounding line; quire and leaf signatures in this part as letters, a–[f], and roman numerals, with an X on the first leaf of the second half of the gathering. 15 long lines; part 1 ruled in pale red ink; part 2 in light brown ink. Written by 3 scribes: i, ff. 1–160v, 169–174v (quire 25, Hours of the Holy Spirit) and 183–190v (quire 28, Hours of the Cross) in a gothic book hand; ii, ff. 161–168v, 175–182v and 191–202 in a less precise gothic book hand; iii, Part 2, ff. 203–244v in a careful cursive rounded hand, with some traces of gothic.

Twenty-two large miniatures,[1] the majority executed, s. XV^{in}, in the style of the Master of Luçon[2]; a second artist, contemporary to the first, worked on the supplemental materials; his work coincides with that of the second scribe. At the end of the fifteenth century, part 2 was added to the book with its 3 miniatures by an artist working in the style of Jean Colombe; this artist also retouched the illustration of Part 1 in varying degrees. The miniatures of part 1 occur on the first recto of the quires, except for those on ff. 32, 56 and 65, which are positioned on one of the two rectos of the center bifolium. On f. 14 (Pericopes of the Gospels), John on Patmos with an eagle and a devil, completely done in the ca. 1490 period with continuous painting around the original text and initial, which now appears as if on a scroll; the original spray border is faintly visible below the later painting. On f. 21 (Matins), Annunciation; the faces, angel's wings and the Virgin's hair are retouched ca. 1490; U-shape border around the miniature of acanthus leaves spiraled around a rod; outer border of black ink sprays with gold leaves, flowers, birds and grotesques. The border has been repainted, ca. 1490, in the lower and outer sides, with a narrative sequence: Joachim ejected from the temple by the priests; he prays in the fields; he meets Anne at the Golden Gate; they bring the Virgin to the temple; the Virgin weaving. On f. 32 (Lauds), Visitation; the trees, landscape, hair and faces have been repainted; U-shape inner border of grotesque masks strung along a gold bar; outer border of black ink sprays with gold leaves and putti. On f. 45 (Prime), Nativity; the faces, Joseph's mantle and probably the blue cherubim appear over-painted; U-shape inner border formed by a gold bar and flowers; in the black ink spray outer border, the animal grotesques seem to be retouched in silver. On f. 51 (Terce), Annunciation to the shepherds; comparatively little retouching, only on the angel's face, the trees and grass; U-shape inner border of a gold bar with leaves; grotesques in the usual black ink spray outer border. On f. 56 (Sext), Adoration of the Magi; the faces, trees and the dark blue garments have been retouched, as have the wild men in the border, wherever dark blue or silver occur; U-shape inner border consists of a string of blue flowers. On f. 61 (None), Presentation in the Temple; faces and the areas in dark blue or silver are retouched; U-shape inner border in the form of a gold band with geometric designs; birds in the outer border, some of which were overpainted in silver. On f. 65 (Vespers), Flight into Egypt; faces, trees and Joseph's deep blue mantle are retouched; U-shape inner border of a string of gold crowns; battling cupids in the outer black ink spray border may be unfinished. On f. 73 (Compline), Coronation of the Virgin; the faces, hair and probably the dark blue are added (although some of the dark blue may be the original undercoat, lacking the final modelling); U-shape inner border as a gold bar decorated with leaves; figures of the prophets in the outer border. On f. 97 (Penitential psalms), Last Judgment; Christ showing his wounds sits on the curved rainbow with Mary and John on each side; Christ's hair and beard have been repainted to represent God the Father; the faces are also retouched; U-shape inner border consists of a gold bar of trumpet and leaf patterns; the outer border of oak leaves and acorns (repainted in silver) and hybrids battling, also retouched. On f. 117 (Office of the Dead), a funeral scene; the faces are retouched; U-shaped gold bar with leaves and berries around the miniature; in the outer border are 4 hooded figures, reading, whose faces appear unfinished with only the green-tinged underpainting applied; the dark blue garments also seem to lack the final modelling. On f. 161 (Hours of the Trinity), Gnadenstuhl, without the Dove; corresponding to the change of script at this point is a change of artist; also changed are the borders: the inner bar border is reduced to a simple 2-segmented strip to the right of the illustration; the black ink sprays are more sparse, and may have been traced over in a heavier black. On f. 165 (Hours of the Dead), Raising of Lazarus; done by the same painter as the Trinity; same simpler and more sparse border, with its black ink sprays probably reinforced later. On f. 169 (Hours of the Holy Spirit), Pentecost, by the first artist and scribe; the faces and hair are apparently retouched; U-shape inner border formed of a gold bar with a stream of blue trumpet blossoms; birds in the outer border. On f. 175 (Hours of All Saints), Coronation of the Virgin, as she holds the Child, by the second artist and scribe; a frame surrounds the miniature; sparse black ink spray in the border, perhaps retraced; a green parrot in the lower margin. On f. 179 (Hours of the Eucharist), completely repainted, ca. 1490, over what was probably the second artist's work, as the sparse spray remains visible under the paint, and the script is that common to sections illustrated by him. The miniature depicts a bishop and a deacon kneeling before an altar with a monstrance which shows the image of the Crucifixion on the Host; across the lower margin, a woman receives the consecrated Host from a priest, and then exchanges it with a turbaned Jew for a tunic; in the last scene the Jew kneels before the bleeding Host which has been stabbed by a dagger; see M. A. Lavin, "The Altar of Corpus Domini in Urbino," *Art Bulletin* 49 (1967) 3–10. As on f. 14, the text has been incorporated into a later scroll, held by 2 angels. On f. 183 (Hours of the Cross), Crucifixion, done by the first artist, and the text by the first scribe; the faces, body of Christ and hair were retouched ca. 1490; U-shape inner border as a gold bar decorated with colored leaves; the outer border includes soldiers, somewhat retouched in silver. On f. 191 (Hours of the Virgin), Creation of Adam and Eve, completely in the overpainted style of ca. 1490; it originally would have had the decoration of the second artist, with whom are associated the sparse black ink sprays, visible under the repainting, and the script of the second copyist; the text space has been transformed into a scroll held by 2 angels. The scene shows Adam and Eve kneeling before God while the Devil looks on from behind rocky hills; in the vignettes below, the snake with a female head. On f. 195 (Hours of St. Catherine), completely in the ca. 1490 style, presumably with the work of the second artist underneath; the text is set onto a scroll held by 2 angels; the continuous series of scenes show Catherine praying as angels break the wheel into pieces, a large crowd of people, and a number of slain youths in the lower margin. On f. 203 (prayer to the Trinity); this introduces Part 2, copied ca. 1490, and illustrated by the painter who retouched or repainted the preceding Part 1. In the Trinity depicted here, God the Father sits on a throne, a dove flies from his mouth to the Host set on a chalice and bearing the same shadow image of the Crucifixion as on f. 179; the border is of acanthus leaves, strawberries, grotesques and 2 angels supporting a coat of arms (see below). On f. 213 (prayer), Man of Sorrows with the emblems of the Passion and Mary and John on either side; in the continuous border, the scenes of Noli me tangere, the Crucifixion, Christ before Pilate, and the Road to Calvary; all are by the ca. 1490 painter. On f. 222 (Obsecro te), Virgin nursing the Child; an acanthus border, which includes a pelican; done ca. 1490 by the painter of Part 2.

Major initials, 4- and 2-line, in white-patterned blue or pink against a colored ground (for the 4-line initials) or against a gold ground (for the 2-line initials), both infilled in gold with trilobe leaves; secondary initials, 1-line, gold with purple or black penwork, or blue with red. In Part 2, 2-line initials, painted gold against maroon or grey grounds. Band borders the length of the text, occurring at the presence of a 2-line initial, and consisting of acanthus leaves, flowers, rayed gold dots, in 2 styles: the first appears unfinished (lacking the shading in the leaves), is placed in the outer margins and stops after f. 50; the second style is usually placed to the right of the text and occurs sporadically before f. 50, and exclusively thereafter; the second style may include grotesques or strawberries. There are no band borders in Part 2. Rubrics in red for Part 1, in brownish red for Part 2. Ribbon line fillers in blue and gold in Part 1.

Bound, s. XIX, in tooled red velvet with light blue watered silk endpapers; gauffered gilt edges.

The first portion of the manuscript, ff. 1–202v, was copied at the beginning of the fifteenth century in two stages (probably concurrent). A first scribe copied the more usual texts of a book of hours, including the short hours of the Holy Spirit and of the Cross; he collaborated with the first artist who worked in the style of the Master of Luçon. A second scribe and illuminator were responsible for the less common material (the short hours of the Trinity, the Dead, All Saints, the Eucharist, the Virgin and St. Catherine) which was then meshed with the standard texts to convert the material to a full week of specific devotions. At the end of the century, ca. 1490, a later owner in the south of France added ff. 203–244 and had the illuminations of the first part retouched, sometimes extensively, by an artist whose style derived from that of Jean Colombe. This later owner's coat of arms, f. 203: or a tree proper fructed or on a chief azure a rose gules between 2 leaves (?) in pale or. His name may have been "Julian," as that saint is invoked in the suffrage on f. 210, and the initial "G" appears in the prayers, ff. 216, 220, 224; the prayer on f. 218v reads ". . . Sana me domine et libera me de isto languore B. et a presenti tribulatione G. ab omni infamia . . ." Acquired ca. 1830 by Sir John Hayford Thorold of Syston Park; his book plate and monogrammed label on the front pastedown; his sale, Sotheby's, 12 December 1884, lot 965 to Quaritch; in the Quaritch *General Catalogue* 6 (1887) n. 35711, and in that firm's *Hand-list* (1890) n. 11. The manuscript belonged to E. Dwight Church (1835–1908); his ex libris on the pastedown with "400 Eng" penned on the lower margin; in his *Catalogue . . . of English Literature* (1909) vol. 1, n. 400 with a plate of f. 21. A pencilled note on f. ii calls the manuscript "Heures de la Rose," using the name first applied in the 1887 Quaritch catalogue and taken up in the Church catalogue. Henry E. Huntington bought the Church collection in 1911.

Bibliography: De Ricci, 93. S. C. Chew, *The Pilgrimage of Life* (Yale University Press 1962) fig. 1 of f. 191.

---

[1] This description owes much to extensive notes left by Dorothy Miner.

[2] We thank Prof. James Marrow for this and the following identification.

HM 1121 — Bologna, s. XVI
HYMNAL for vespers

1. ff. 1v–25: [f. 1, blank] Hymns for 31 feasts of the temporale, sanctorale and common of saints at vespers, text only.

2. ff. 25v–27: Suffrages "della Croce, De gli Apostoli, De Sancto Augustino, di San Petronio, della pace."

3. ff. 27v–29v: Office of Petronius.

Parchment, ff. i (contemporary paper) + 29 + i (contemporary paper); 467 × 318 (348 × 244) mm. 1^6(−6, with no loss of text) 2–7^4. 17 long lines, but up to 21 on ff. 5–6, due to rewritten text; cf. erasures in the same area. Ruled in lead; slash pricking along the left and right bounding lines; additional pricking the upper and lower outside corners of the leaves (to mark the size of the leaf?). Written in a round gothic liturgical script.

On f. 1v, 6-line pink initial with yellow and green acanthus leaves wrapped around it, and with floral infilling and border spray. On ff. 2v–3, full border across the opening in panels of Renaissance foliage on a painted gold ground, with roundels of a parrot, a rabbit and the monograms IHS and CPS; 6-line historiated initial on f. 2v of the Nativity, possibly repainted. On ff. 10v (Corpus Christi) and 13 (John the Baptist), 4-line colored initials decorated with acanthus leaves on painted gold grounds. On f. 21, 4-line historiated initial of Stephen (but at hymn for the common of a martyr) in similar style with small floral spray in the upper margin. 4- to 2-line poorly done initials in blue with red flourishing or in red with blue or brown flourishing; 1-line initials alternating red and blue. Rubrics throughout.

Bound, s. XVI, in dark brown leather over bevelled wooden boards; 1 fore edge clasp, closing front to back.

Written in the sixteenth century for use in Bologna, as evidenced by the devotions to Petronius. On the front pastedown, a small square paper label with a red "6" stamped on it; in pencil "64. Orazioni." Date and source of acquisition by Henry E. Huntington unknown.

Bibliography: De Ricci, 93.

HM 1123 — France, s. XV^{med}
BOOK OF HOURS, use of Rome — *fig. 103*

1. ff. 1–12v: Full calendar in French, including the feasts of Genevieve (3 January, in red), Denis (22 April), Marcel (26 July), Denis (9 October, in red), Marcel (3 November, in red), Genevieve (26 November, in red).

2. ff. 13–24: Pericopes of the Gospels; *Oratio beate marie virginis,* Obsecro te . . . [masculine forms; Leroquais, *LH* 2:346]; *Oratio beate marie virginis,* O intemerata . . . orbis terrarum. De te enim . . . [Wilmart, 494–95]; f. 24v, ruled, but blank.

3. ff. 25–95v: Office of the Virgin, use of Rome; variations of the psalms at matins set in the text before the lessons; suffrages of All Saints from lauds to compline; Salve Regina follows compline; Advent office begins on f. 86.

4. ff. 96–116v: Penitential psalms and litany.

5. ff. 117–120: Short hours of the Cross.

6. ff. 120v–123v: Short hours of the Holy Spirit.

7. ff. 124–167v: Office of the Dead; the first and second response at matins are reversed with respect to the use of Rome; for other manuscripts with the same variation, see New York Public Library MS 43 (Paris, ca. 1450) and the manuscript described in the Christie sale catalogue, 18 December 1968, n. 56 (northwestern France, ca. 1470), present location unknown.[1]

8. ff. 167v–172: Prayers as follow: *Quant on se reveille la nuyt on doit dire,* In matutinis meditabor in te . . . ; Gracias ago tibi domine omnipotens eterne

deus qui me in hac nocte . . . ; *Quant on se lieve au matin,* Surrexit dominus de sepulcro . . . oremus. Deus auctor lucis largire michi domine . . . ; *Aultre oroyson,* Gracias agimus tibi domine sancte pater omnipotens eterne deus qui nos de transacto noctis huius spacio . . . ; *Bonne recommendacion,* Benedicat me imperialis maiestas . . . ; *Quant on ot les cloches,* Dulce nomen domini nostri ihesu christi . . . ; *Quant on yst de la mayson,* Vias tuas domine demonstra michi . . . ; *Quant on entre au cimitiere,* Deus fidelium lumen animarum adesto invocacionibus nostris . . . ; *Quant on entre en l'eglise,* Introibo in domum tuam . . . ; *Quant on prent l'eaue benoyte,* Asperges me domine ysopo et mundabor . . . ; Affero me ipsum sacrificium domino . . . ; *Quant le prestre dit orate pro me,* Memor sit dominus omnis sacrificii et holocaustum tuum pinguefiat . . . ; *Quant on se treuve en quelque danger que ce soit soit de tempeste ou aultre,* Ihesus autem transiens per medium illorum . . . ; *Quant on lieve le corps nostre seigneur,* Ave domine ihesu christe verbum patris filius virginis . . . [Wilmart, 412–13]; Anima christi sanctifica me . . . [Leroquais, *LH* 2:340]; Gracias tibi agimus domine sancte pater omnipotens eterne deus qui nos transacto huius diei spacio . . . *Cest oroyson cy devant est bone a dire quant on se couche.*

9. ff. 172v–173: [added by a later cursive hand] *Oratio ad dominam virginem,* Stabat mater dolorosa . . . [*RH* 19416]; ff. 173v–178v, blank.

Parchment, ff. ii (paper, with silk glued to the recto of the first flyleaf) + 178 + ii (paper, with silk glued to the verso of the second flyleaf); 170 × 122 (90 × 56) mm. 1^{12} 2^{8} 3^{4} 4–6^{8} 7^{6}(to f. 54) 8–12^{8} 13^{8}(+ 2, f. 96) 14^{8} 15^{6}(–1, cancelled by the scribe) 16–22^{8} 23^{6}. 16 long lines ruled in pale red ink. Written in a liturgical gothic book hand.

Twelve large miniatures by or certainly related in style to the Master of the *Horloge de Sapience,* in arched compartments, with a bar frame of gold and colors enclosing miniature and text on three sides in a U-shape; outer border of blue and gold acanthus leaves, flowers, strawberries and drolleries: f. 25 (Matins), Annunciation with the angel on the right; f. 43 (Lauds), Visitation, some color has flaked off; f. 55 (Prime), Nativity with a large pink-covered bed in the stall; f. 60 (Terce), Annunciation to the shepherds; f. 64v (Sext), Adoration of the Magi; f. 69 (None), Presentation in the temple; f. 73v (Vespers), Flight into Egypt; f. 81 (Compline), Coronation of the Virgin; f. 96 (Penitential psalms), David in prayer, in an architectural setting, against a brocade cloth drape; f. 117 (Hours of the Cross), the Crucifixion, with Mary and John on Christ's right, the soldiers on his left; f. 120v (Hours of the Holy Spirit), Pentecost; f. 124 (Office of the Dead), burial in a cemetery. 3-line initials on these folios in white-patterned blue on a cusped gold ground, with trilobe leaf infilling; similar 4-line initials for the Obsecro te and the O Intemerata, on a square ground; 2- and 1-line initials in gold on dusky rose ground infilled with blue, and the whole patterned in white, or with the colors reversed; ribbon line fillers in the same style. Band borders in the outer margins at the presence of a 2-line initial, consisting of black ink sprays, gold trilobe leaves and dots, a few colored flowers, strawberries, or leaves. Rubrics in red. A note, f. 68v, s. XVI: "Souveigne vous san sece de vostre bonne messtrese c'est M"; erased notes, possibly of the same date, but illegible under ultra-violet light, on f. 178v; on f. 173v, s. XVI, a sketch of a female saint (Margaret?) standing on what appears under ultra-violet light to be a large animal.

Bound, s. XVIII, in worn blue velvet with heavy gold and silver embroidery, spelling out "Missale Romanum" along the spine; red silk endpapers; gauffered gilt edges; at the time of the Robert Hoe sale (see below), in a silk bag.

Written in France towards the middle of the fifteenth century, for use in Paris, to judge by the saints in the calendar. The Hours of the Virgin are in the use of Rome; the Office of the Dead is unidentified. Two modern erased inscriptions, possibly of ownership, on f. ii verso and f. 1, the latter beginning "Edw . . . C . . ." Belonged to Robert Hoe: *Cat.* (1909) pp. 53–54; his sale, Anderson, New York, 1912, pt. III, n. 2068 to G. D. Smith. Source and date of acquisition by Henry E. Huntington unknown.

Bibliography: De Ricci, 93.

[1] We are indebted to Prof. James Marrow for this information.

HM 1124 — France, s. XVIin
BOOK OF HOURS, use of Rome — *fig. 150*

1. ff. 1–12v: Full calendar, alternating red and blue with major feasts in gold; effort has also been made to fill the space horizontally by adding qualifiers; for example, Oblatio virginis devote, Bibiane virginis gloriose, Lazari resuscitati a christo, Servuli confessoris domini. Most saints registered are the martyrs and confessors of the early Church; the calendar includes Marie de nivibus (5 August, in gold), and four feasts of Mark: Translatio sancti marci (30 January), Marci evangeliste domini (25 April, in gold), Apparitio sancti marci (25 June), Sacra sancti marci evangeliste (8 October).

2. ff. 13–20: Mass of the Virgin, with liturgical variations for the year; [f. 15v] *Oratio devotissima ad beatam virginem mariam,* Obsecro te . . . [masculine forms; Leroquais, *LH* 2:346]; [f. 18] *Alia oratio ad eandem,* O intemerata . . . orbis terrarum. Inclina mater misericordie aures tue . . . mihi miserrimo peccatori . . . [Wilmart, 488–90]; suffrage of Roch; f. 20v, ruled, but blank.

3. ff. 21–36: Pericopes of the Gospels, that of John followed by its usual prayer, Protector in te sperantium . . . ; [f. 25v:] Passion according to John, 18, 1–19, 41, and related prayers: *Ad iesum christum oratio,* Deus qui manus tuas et pedes tuos . . . ; *Alia oratio ad christum,* O Benignissime domine iesu christe respicere digneris super me miserum peccatorem . . . ; *Devota contemplatio beate marie virginis iuxta crucem filii sui lachrymantis et ad compassionem salvatoris singulos invitantis,* Stabat mater dolorosa . . . [*RH* 19416].

4. ff. 36–99v: *Hore intemerate virginis marie secundum usum Romane curie,* with suffrages of All Saints from lauds to compline; Salve Regina follows compline; Advent office begins on f. 91.

5. ff. 99v–105: Hours of the Conception; f. 105v, ruled, but blank.

6. ff. 106–109v: Short hours of the Cross.

7. ff. 109v–118: *Sequitur oratio quam fecit venerabilis beda presbyter de septem verbis* . . . , Domine iesu christe qui septem verba . . . [Leroquais, *LH* 2:342]; *Oratio sancti Augustini devotissima dicenda trigintatribus diebus genibus flexis ad obtinendam omnem gratiam,* O Dulcissime domine iesu christe verus deus . . . ; *Devota contemplatio ad veronicam sanctam,* Salve sancta facies nostri redemptoris . . . [*RH* 18189]; *Simbolum Anathasii* [*sic*], Quicumque vult . . .

8. ff. 118–122v: Short hours of the Holy Spirit.

9. ff. 122v–139v: Penitential psalms and litany, including "bernarde cum sociis tuis" (possibly in error for Berard, who does have companions), and Bonaventure; neither Berard nor Bonaventure are in the calendar.

10. ff. 139v–171: Office of the Dead, use of Rome.

11. ff. 171–188v: *Sequuntur septem versus Sanctissimi patris Bernardi,* Illumina oculos meos . . . [*RH* 27912]; *Sequuntur septem orationes Sanctissimi Pape Gregorii,* O Domine iesu christe adoro te in cruce pendentem . . . [Leroquais, *LH* 2:346]; suffrages of Michael, of one's guardian angel, all angels, Paul, John, Andrew, James, Lawrence, Vincent, Sebastian, Stephen, George, Christopher (in the prayer of this suffrage, f. 179, feminine forms have been added above the masculine, possibly in the hand of the scribe), Ambrose, Gregory, Jerome, Augustine, Francis, Anthony of Padua, Dominic, Benedict, many martyrs, Catherine, Lucia, Barbara, Agatha, Apollonia, Mary Magdalene, Ursula and the 11,000 virgins, Genevieve, Anne; *ends: Horas presentes fecit facere litteratissimus vir magister franciscus de mello pro sorore sua domina maria Manuel;* f. 189r–v, ruled, but blank.

Parchment, ff. ii (parchment, with paper flyleaf glued to the recto of f. i) + 189 + i (parchment, with paper flyleaf glued to the verso); 200 × 133 (123 × 70) mm. 1^8 2^4 3^8(through f. 20) 4–6^8 7^8(+ 7, f. 51) 8–11^8 12^6(through f. 91) 13–14^4 15^6(through f. 105) 16^8 17^8(+ 9, f. 122) 18–25^8 + 3 leaves; catchwords occasionally present in inner right corner; 20 long lines ruled in pale red ink. Written in a humanistic script varying in size according to liturgical function.

Lavishly decorated with 25 full page miniatures, set within painted gold architectural frames by the illuminator referred to as the Master of Morgan 85 by Plummer, *Last Flowering,* nn. 108b, 109b, 118; miniature(s?) apparently derived from woodcuts of Albrecht Dürer, cf. his "Small Woodcut Passion," datable ca. 1509–11, as the source of the miniature on f. 65v.[1] Ten of these, depicting sorrowful scenes, are in grisaille (grey, white, gold, flesh tones, and red for the blood), and tend to be on a somewhat larger scale than the full color illustrations. Most of the grisaille pages are on the verso and face a full color illumination on the recto for the Hours of the Virgin: ff. 36v–37 (Matins), Christ before Pilate and the Annunciation; ff. 51v–52 (Lauds), Scourging at the pillar and Visitation; ff. 61v–62 (Prime), the Mocking of Christ and Nativity; ff. 65v–66 (Terce), Pilate washing his hands as Christ is led away, and Annunciation to the shepherds; ff. 69v–70 (Sext), the Road to Calvary and Adoration of the Magi; ff. 73v–74 (None), Crucifixion and Presentation in the temple; ff. 77v–78 (Vespers), Deposition and Flight into Egypt; ff. 84v–85 (Compline), Entombment and Assumption of the Virgin. The two remaining illustrations in grisaille are on f. 26 (Passion according to John), Betrayal of Jesus, while Peter cuts off Malchus' ear, and on f. 140 (Office of the Dead), Raising of Lazarus. The remaining full color illustrations are: f. 13 (Mass of the Virgin), the Virgin teaching the Christ Child to read; f. 91v (Advent office), the Virgin surrounded by her attributes, each labelled on a scroll (as often found in early printed books of hours); f. 100 (Hours of the Conception), the meeting of Joachim and Anne before the Golden Gate; f. 106 (Hours of the Cross), the Risen Christ and emblems of the passion; f. 110 (prayers), two angels supporting a chalice with the wound of Christ; f. 118v (Hours of the Holy Spirit), Pentecost; f. 123 (Penitential psalms), David penitent. Evangelist portraits for the pericopes, ff. 21, 22v, 23v and 25, 10-line, within gold bar frames, outlined in red; similar frames enclose the 9- to 6-line miniatures for each of the suffrages. Calendar decoration consists of illustrations of the monthly occupations on the recto and of the signs of the zodiac on the verso, placed in rectangles across the top of the folio (55 × 77 mm). A less skillful painter has done the illustration of the calendar, the suffrages, and probably the Attributes of the Virgin, f. 91. Initials, 3- or 2-line, in white acanthus on a gold ground, or in colors on a colored ground with infilling of flowers or berries on gold; 1-line initials, gold, on a ground alternating red, blue or light brown; ribbon line fillers in colors with many variations or as gold logs. The rubrics alternate line by line gold, red, and blue. Every page, except for those with full page miniatures, with full borders, some of which are traced, but with variation in colors and details and in many styles: as multicolored acanthus leaves against a ground of painted gold with black flecks; as illusionistic flowers, or pearl-like berries, or grapes, and insects, also against a painted gold ground; as rope designs; as trellis patterns; as fantastic vases or cornucopiae; most frequent is the compartmentalized border with flowers and grotesques, in considerable variety: background colors may include unusual dark tones of black, grey, brown or olive green; divisions may be in the shape of hearts, fleur-de-lis, scrolls (some with legends: Ave Maria Gratia Plena, or, Domine Iesu Christe fili dei vivi). Many borders bear the initials of Franciscus de Mello (ff. 14, 35, 60v, 65, 138v, 161v, 166v, 182v), of his sister, Maria Manuel (ff. 25v, 32v, 35v, 39v, 42v, 138, 166, 178v), or "A.S." (ff. 60, 77, 90v, 134).

Bound, s. XVIII, in Dutch or Flemish red morocco, with elaborate gilt tooling of a center rosette, fans at the angles, and scattered cupid's heads, roosters, birds, bees, flowers; green silk book marks and sheets protecting the full page illustrations; gilt edges; original green slip case, tooled with the same fan pattern at the angles.

Written in France at the beginning of the sixteenth century at the order of Franciscus de Mello for his sister, Maria Manuel, as stated in the colophon on f. 188v, where there is also a coat of arms: per pale: 1, gules two bars or and six roundels argent, 2, 2 and 2; 2, gules a lion rampant or; the dexter side is similar to the impaled shield for Mello e Castro in Rietstap, vol. 4, pl. 183, which is gules a double traverse cross and six roundels argent, 2, 2, and 2. Belonged to William Horatio Crawford of Lakelands, Cork.; his sale, Sotheby's, 12 March 1891, lot 1609 to Quaritch; acquired at that time by Robert Hoe: Grolier Club (1892) n. 99 (proof sheet for that catalogue entry remaining with the manuscript); *Cat.* (1909) pp. 90–92; his sale, Anderson, New York, 1912, pt. IV, n. 2344 with plate of f. 65v, to G. D. Smith. Source and date of acquisition by Henry E. Huntington unknown.

Bibliography: De Ricci, 93.

[1] We are grateful to Prof. James Marrow for the identification of the artist and his source.

HM 1125 — Flanders or northern France, s. XV^{med}
BOOK OF HOURS, Sarum use — *fig. 99*

1. ff. 1–6v: Calendar in red and black with a number of Franco-Flemish and English saints; Latin month verses [Walther, *Initia* 14563].

2. ff. 7–9v: Short hours of the Holy Spirit; f. 10r–v, ruled but blank.

3. ff. 11–12v: *De sancta trinitate,* Domine deus omnipotens Pater et filius et spiritus sanctus da michi famulo tuo N. victoriam . . . , with Pss. 53 and 66 by cue only, and the prayer, Libera me domine ihesu christe fili dei vivi qui in cruce suspensus fuisti . . . , and Ps. 129 [de la Mare, *Lyell Cat.,* 373, n. 88].

4. ff. 13–23v: Suffrages of John the Baptist, Thomas of Canterbury, George, Christopher, Catherine of Alexandria, Mary Magdalene, Margaret, Barbara.

5. ff. 24–30: *Oracio devota ad christum,* O Ihesu christe eterna dulcedo te amancium iubilus excedens omne gaudium . . . [the 15 O's of St. Bridget; *HE,* 76–80]; f. 30v, coat of arms [see below].

6. ff. 31–68v: Hours of the Virgin, Sarum use; suffrages after lauds of the Holy Spirit, the Trinity, the Cross, Michael, John the Baptist, Peter and Paul, Andrew, Stephen, Lawrence, Thomas of Canterbury, Nicholas, Mary Magdalene, Catherine of Alexandria, Margaret, All Saints, for peace; short hours of the Cross worked in from lauds to compline; Salve Regina after compline, with the versicles, Virgo mater ecclesie . . . , and the prayer, Omnipotens sempiterne deus qui gloriose virginis et matris marie . . . [*HE,* 62–63].

7. ff. 68v–80v: *Has videas laudes qui sacra virgine gaudes . . . Salve regina fulcita,* Salve virgo virginum stella matutina . . . [a farcing of the Salve Regina, attributed to Bonaventure, *Opera* (Vatican 1668) 6:466–67] and the prayer, Deus qui de beate marie virginis utero . . . ; *Oratio de domina nostra,* O Intemerata . . . orbis terrarum. Inclina mater . . . [masculine forms; Wilmart, 488–90]; *oratio de domina nostra,* Obsecro te . . . [masculine forms; Leroquais, *LH* 2:346]; Ave mundi spes maria . . . [Walther, *Initia* 1945]; Adiuvet nos quesumus domine deus beate marie semper virginis intercessio veneranda . . . ; *Quicumque hec septem gaudia in honore beate marie virginis . . . obtinebit a papa clemente qui hec septem gaudia proprio stilo composuit,* Virgo templum trinitatis . . . [Philippus de Grevia; Wilmart, 329, n.].

8. ff. 81–88v: *Ad ymaginem domini ihesu christi,* Omnibus consideratis paradisus voluptatis . . . O maria plasma nati . . . O Johannes evangelista . . . [Johannes Lemovicensis, here in 10 sections; Wilmart, 527 and 584] followed by Kyrie eleison, versicles, and the prayer, Omnipotens sempiterne deus qui unigenitum filium tuum dominum nostrum ihesum christum crucem coronam spineam et quinque vulnera subire voluisti . . . ; *Incipit oratio venerabilis bede* . . . , Domine ihesu christe Qui septem verba . . . [Leroquais, *LH* 2:342] and the prayer, Precor te piissime domine ihesu christe propter illam caritatem . . . [Wilmart, 378, n.]; Deus qui voluisti pro redempcione mundi a iudeis reprobari . . . ; Ave domine ihesu christe verbum patris filius virginis . . . [Wilmart, 497]; *Cuilibet dicenti hanc orationem . . . dominus papa Bonefacius concessit . . . ad supplicationem philippi Regis francie, oratio,* Domine ihesu christe qui hanc sacratissimam carnem . . . [Wilmart, 378, n.].

9. ff. 89–105v: Penitential psalms, gradual psalms (the first 12 by cue only), and a long litany, including "Eswarde," Oswald, Alan, Quentin, Lambert, "Wallepaxde" among the martyrs; Remigius, Vedast, Bavo, Audoenus, Dunstan, Philibert, Leonard, Botulph, Amand among the confessors; Bridget, Christina, Genevieve, Sexburga, Milburga, Osyth, Radegundis, Anastasia among the virgins (the litany appears to coincide with those of Cambridge, Fitzwilliam Museum MSS 52 and 53).

10. ff. 106–127v: Office of the Dead, Sarum use.

11. ff. 128–140v: Commendation of souls (Pss. 118, divided into sections, and 138) with the prayers, Tibi domine commendamus . . . , and Misericordiam tuam domine sancte pater . . . .

12. ff. 141–145v: Psalms of the Passion (Pss. 21–30, 6 with cues only for 22–24, 26, 29)..

13. ff. 145v–158v: *Beatus vero ieronimus in hoc modo psalterium istud disposuit . . . , oratio,* Suscipere digneris domine deus omnipotens . . . , *Incipit psalte-*

rium sancti ieronimi, Verba mea percipe . . . , and the ending prayer, Omnipotens sempiterne deus clemenciam tuam suppliciter deprecor ut me famulum tuum N. . . . ; ff. 159–160v, ruled, but blank.

14. ff. 161–168: *Les xv Joyes nostre dame,* Douce dame de misericorde, mere de pite Et fontaine de tous biens . . . [Sonet 458]; pericopes of the Gospels; f. 168v, ruled, but blank.

Parchment, ff. i (modern parchment) + iii (contemporary parchment) + 168 + iii (contemporary parchment) + i (modern parchment); 212 × 145 (110 × 74) mm. 1^6 2^4 $3–4^8$ 5^4(through f. 30) $6–12^8$ 13^2(through f. 88) $14–22^8$(through f. 160) 23^8. One catchword survives in a cursive script in the lower margin of f. 96v; quires and leaves signed in letters and roman numerals with a cross marking the first folio in the second half of the quire. 19 long lines ruled in pale red ink; pricking visible in the 3 outer margins. Written in a gothic book hand.

Twenty-seven large miniatures in the style of the Master of the Gold Scrolls, above 5 lines of text, with miniature and text enclosed by a U-shaped border of pink, blue and gold segments; outer borders of multicolored acanthus leaves, black ink sprays, gold dots and trilobe leaves, and figures. The miniatures are: f. 7 (Hours of the Holy Spirit), Pentecost, against a gold rinceaux background; f. 11 (prayer to the Trinity), Gnadenstuhl with two worshipping angels in the border; f. 13, John the Baptist holding the Lamb on the book, with a half-figure of a king in the border; f. 14v, martyrdom of Thomas of Canterbury, with a man sitting calmly in the border; f. 16, George, with a small white dog in the border; f. 17, Christopher; f. 18v, Catherine, with wheel and sword, standing on the emperor Maxentius, against a background of rinceaux; f. 20, Mary Magdalene, against gold rinceaux, in the margin a green grotesque; f. 21v, Margaret emerging from the dragon as God the Father sends down a dove from a ruffled blue sky, with a man emerging from a flower in the border; f. 22v, Barbara holding her tower, against a rinceaux background, with an angel in the border; f. 24 (prayer to Christ, O Ihesu christe eterna dulcedo), Salvator Mundi, holding an open book which reads "Ego sum via veritas et vita," with a seated figure in the margin; f. 31 (Hours of the Virgin), Annunciation in a room defined by a low wall, with gold rinceaux above the wall, and God the Father in a ruffled blue cloud, the angel Gabriel holds a scroll, "Ave . . . tecum," while an angel plays a harp in a garden in the margin; f. 37v (Lauds), Betrayal of Christ, Peter with his upraised sword; f. 49 (Prime), Jesus with his hands crossed and hidden by his sleeves, before Pilate, whose wife stands behind his throne; f. 53 (Terce), Flagellation; f. 56 (Sext), Road to Calvary with Jesus looking backwards at a man who kicks him; f. 59 (None), Crucifixion, with Mary and John, she holding a book, and John turning away reading his; in the margin an angel holding the pillar; f. 62 (Vespers), Deposition from the Cross, at the moment of pulling out the nails with tongs; f. 64v (Compline), Entombment; f. 69 (farcing of the Salve Regina), Coronation of the Virgin by two small blue angels, as she sits in a garden holding the Child on her lap, against a background of gold rinceaux; f. 81 (Omnibus consideratis), Adam and Eve each holding an apple before the tree at the top of which is Christ crucified; a small devil with a woman's head holds an apple in the left side of the picture; in the margin a half-figure man rising from a flower; f. 88 (Domine ihesu christe qui hanc sacratissimam carnem), Crucifixion, with Jesus and the two thieves, and the sun and the moon above on either side of the face of God the Father; a man with a cane in the margin; f. 89 (Penitential psalms), Last Judgment, with Christ sitting on the rainbow, Mary and John below, and the dead peering out of their graves; in the margin a devil attacks a woman; f. 106 (Office of the Dead), Funeral in a church with 3 monks singing and 4 other figures in black following the service; a hooded person in the border covers his mouth with his hand; f. 128 (Commendation of souls), 2 angels support 3 souls in a sheet carrying them from their empty graves to God the Father, blessing from above in a blue ruffled sky; in the margin a small man riding a camel; f. 141 (Psalms of the Passion), Man of Sorrows, rising half-length above the tomb and floating on a blue cloud, with the emblems of the Passion around him, while an angel plays a harp in the border; f. 147 (Psalter of St. Jerome), Jerome seated in his study with the lion crouched on the floor; a figure with a scroll in the lower border; this miniature reproduced in H. Friedman, *A Bestiary for St. Jerome, A Study of Animal Symbolism in European Religious Art* (Smithsonian Institute 1980) fig. 163. Major initials, 4-line, in white-patterned blue or pink with trilobe leaf infilling against a cusped gold ground, or ground of the other color with the infilling only in gold; 2-line initials in gold against parted pink and blue grounds with sprays of a few gold leaves and a flower at either end; 1-line initials in blue with red flourishing or in gold with black; initials within the text washed in yellow. Jigsaw line fillers in red and blue with some gold decoration. Rubrics in red. On f. ii verso, a rectangle of cleaner parchment with holes around it, as though something (a pilgrim's badge?) had once been attached, 72 × 55 mm.

Bound, s. XIX, by Chambolle-Duru, in brown morocco with gilt tooling in a Grolieresque design; morocco doublures; gilt edges; brown morocco slipcase.

Written in the middle of the fifteenth century in Flanders or northern France for export to England. A coat of arms, s. XVI (?), has been added on f. 30v; per pale 1 azure a chevron or between three dogs' heads sable langued and collared gules; 2 quarterly, 1 and 4 azure three fish in a bend proper, 2 and 3 argent three escallops gules; above the arms, a stoat proper; below them, a fish or; the whole encircled by a chapelet of carnations. Belonged to Robert Hoe, *Cat.* (1909) pp. 34–36; his sale, Anderson, New York, 1912, pt. IV, n. 2352 with plate of f. 69 to G. D. Smith. Precise date and source of acquisition by Henry E. Huntington unknown.

Bibliography: F. Winkler, *Die Flämische Buchmalerei* (Leipzig 1925) 26.[1] De Ricci, 94.

[1] We are indebted to Prof. James Marrow for this information.

HM 1126 — France, s. XV²
BOOK OF HOURS, use of Amiens — *fig. 119*

1. ff. 1–12v: Full calendar in French, with major feasts in red.

2. ff. 13–27 [f. 13r–v, blank]: Pericopes of the gospels; *oratio de beata maria,* Obsecro te . . . et michi famulo tuo . . . [Leroquais, *LH* 2:346]; *oratio de beata maria,* O Intemerata . . . orbis terrarum. De te enim . . . [Wilmart, 494–95]; f. 27v, ruled, but blank.

3. ff. 28–83v: Hours of the Virgin, use of Amiens; 9 lessons at matins.

4. ff. 84–99v: Penitential psalms and litany, including Quentin, Firmin, Maurice and Fuscianus among the martyrs; Firmin, Honoratus, Romanus and Salvius among the confessors; Ulphia among the virgins.

5. ff. 100–104v [f. 100r–v, blank]: Short hours of the Cross.

6. ff. 105–109 [f. 105r–v, blank]: Short hours of the Holy Spirit.

7. ff. 110–154v [f. 110r–v, blank]: Office of the Dead, use of Amiens.

8. ff. 155–162: Douche dame de misericorde . . . [Leroquais, *LH* 2:310–11]; Quiconque veult estre bien conseillies . . . [Sonet 1760; prologue to the prayer:] Dous dieux dous peres sainte trinite 1 dieu biaux sire dieux . . . [Leroquais, *LH* 2:309–10].

HM 1126

Parchment, ff. i (parchment) + 162 + i (parchment); 196 × 146 (95 × 66) mm. 1^{12} 2^{8}(+ 1, f. 13) 3^{6}(through f. 27) 4–11^{8} 12^{8}(+ 9, f. 100) 13^{8}(+ 5, f. 105, and 10, f. 110) 14–19^{8} 20^{6}(−5, 6). Catchwords in center lower margin in script of text. 16 long lines, ruled in pale red ink. Written in 2 sizes of liturgical gothic book hand.

Eighteen large miniatures above 4 lines of text in arched compartments with serrated tops; the U-shape frame around text and miniature sprouts from the initial, and consists of a narrow gold and color strip on the inner margin and wider bands of gold decorated with colored trilobe leaves or other flowers on the other 2 sides; at the 4 corners are bursts of acanthus leaves, mainly blue and gold; the outer borders are of black ivy spray, flowers, berries and gold motifs. The miniatures, all but one related to the style of Maître François,[1] are: f. 14, John on Patmos, depicted clearly as an island; f. 15v, Luke; f. 17v, Matthew; f. 19v, Mark; f. 28 (Hours of the Virgin), Annunciation; f. 49 (Lauds), Visitation, with Elizabeth kneeling in prayer before the Virgin; f. 58 (Prime), Nativity, with the infant lying on the hem of Mary's cloak, while Joseph holds a candle; the confines of the shed correspond to the shape of the picture; f. 63 (Terce), Annunciation to the shepherds, one of whom holds bagpipes, and a shepherdess; f. 66v (Sext), Adoration of the Magi with Joseph holding his hat; f. 70 (None), Presentation in the temple; f. 73v (Vespers), Flight into Egypt, with an idol falling off its column in the background; f. 79v (Compline), Coronation of the Virgin by an angel, who leans over a low gothic-styled wall, while God the Father, wearing a papal tiara, blesses; blue swirling clouds at the bottom of the picture; f. 84 (Penitential psalms), David in prayer, and an angel with upright sword above; f. 101 (Hours of the Cross), Crucifixion in the center of the picture, with Mary and John to Christ's right, the soldiers on his left, one of whom has a man-faced shield; f. 106 (Hours of the Holy Spirit), Pentecost, with Mary at a prie-dieu, centered between 2 pale blue columns and 2 groups of apostles; f. 111 (Office of the Dead), Funeral service in a church; f. 155 (the 7 Joys of the Virgin), by a different artist, the Virgin, enthroned, holds the Child on her lap, while the owners, man and wife, kneel in prayer, and 2 angels read praises of the Virgin from a scroll; f. 160 (the 7 Requests), by the first artist, the Father and Son, dressed identically, sit on a throne, holding an open book on which the Dove is perched; blue clouds swirl at the lower corners of the picture. 4-line initials in white-decorated blue or pink on a gold ground infilled with colored trilobe leaves. 2- and 1-line initials in gold on white-patterned dark pink or blue grounds with infilling of the other color; ribbon line fillers of the same colors. Rubrics in an orange-tinged red. Traced borders on every page the length of the text. Quire 19 (ff. 151–58) with different border and miniature.

Bound, s. XVI,^{ex} in French brown morocco tooled in silver with leaf sprays and interlaced fillets, originally 2 fore edge straps to pins on lower cover, only 1 remains; gilt edges.

Written during the second half of the fifteenth century for use in Amiens, presumably for a man and wife, as suggested by the miniature on f. 155. On the front pastedown is the bookplate of John Ragsdale, s. XVIII. Belonged to Robert Hoe: *Cat.* (1909) p. 53; his sale, Anderson, New York, 1911, pt. I, n. 2132 to G. D. Smith. Precise source and date of acquisition by Henry E. Huntington unknown.

Bibliography: De Ricci, 94.

---

[1] We thank Prof. James Marrow for this information.

HM 1127 — Netherlands, s. XV^2
BOOK OF HOURS, in Dutch — *fig. 129*

1. ff. 1–10v: Full calendar in Dutch with major feasts in red, including Pancratius (12 May, in red), Servatius (13 May, in red), Odulph (12 June, in red),

Lebuin (25 June, in red), Willibrord (7 November, in red); the months are run on directly after one another; the positions of the 3rd and 4th bifolia were inverted in the binding, so the calendar is to be read ff. 1–3, 5, 4, 7, 6, 8–10; f. 10r–v, computistic notes: Drie besloten tiden sijn int iaer, die eerste opten dach als die advent beghint . . .

2. ff. 11–40: Hours of the Virgin, in the Middle Dutch compilation of Geert Grote; see van Wijk.

3. ff. 40v–42v: Prayers to the Virgin: Heilighe ende onbevlecte maghet moeder gods ende des menschen, welke dat choer der enghelen . . . ; Ic gruet u Maria opgewassen lely der reinicheit. Ic gruet u een welrukende fiole . . .

4. ff. 43–59v: Hours of the Eternal Wisdom, by Henry Suso, in the Middle Dutch version of Geert Grote, with Grote's preface.

5. ff. 59v–60v: Prayers to God and Christ, with indulgences; loss of one leaf between ff. 60–61, with resulting loss of text.

6. ff. 61–78: Long hours of the Cross, in the Middle Dutch translation of Geert Grote, beginning imperfectly due to the loss of the leaf between ff. 60–61.

7. ff. 78–91v: Prayers on the Passion of Christ.

8. ff. 92–106v: Penitential psalms and litany in Middle Dutch.

9. ff. 106v–107v: Prayers to Christ.

10. ff. 108–176v: Prayers for the sanctorale.

11. ff. 177–184v: Prayers for Communion.

12. ff. 184v–188v: Prayers to Christ and to God the Father.

13. ff. 189–216v: Office of the Dead, use of Utrecht, in Middle Dutch.

14. ff. 216v–220v: Prayers with indulgences.

Parchment, ff. ii (parchment) + 220 + ii (parchment); 176 × 125 (110 × 76) mm. 1^{10} $2–5^{8}$(through f. 42) 6^{8} 7^{10}(through f. 60) 8^{8}(−1, before f. 61) $9–11^{8}$(through f. 91) $12–13^{8}$(through f. 107) $14–22^{8}$ 23^{8}(+ 9, f. 188) $24–27^{8}$. Catchwords in a small cursive hand in the inner right corner; ff. 198–199 signed "2" and "3," being their positions in quire 25. 21 long lines, ruled in light brown ink; slash form pricking visible in upper and lower margins. Written in a Dutch book hand.

Elaborate penwork decoration of the type produced at St. Agnes in Delft[1]; see P. J. H. Vermeeren, "Delftse verluchte handschriften ter Koninklijke Bibliotheek," *Oud Delft* 2 (1960) 39–72 esp. the plate on p. 45; J. G. C. Venner and C. A. Chavannes-Mazel, "Delftse handschriften en boekverluchting," in *De Stad Delft: Cultuur en Maatschappij tot 1572* (Stedelijk Museum Het Prinsenhof, Delft 1979) 134–38, esp. fig. 247. Five major initials, 9- or 8-line, in parted red and blue with void white design on a blue penwork ground and infilled by red penwork which surrounds 6–8 roundels of gold or colored flowers; full borders of the same precise red and blue penwork along both sides of a narrow pink strip which sprouts restrained stylized blue, green and gold acanthus at the corners and centers. At the center of the outer border are paintings of animals with blue-lettered scrolls in Latin and in the vernacular: f. 11, a peacock, with a scroll reading "Ave regina celorum, Ave domina angelorum"; f. 43, a deer, with the scroll "Inicium sapiencie timor domini"; f. 92, a wyvern, with the scroll "Die god ontsiet sel niet ontbreken"; f. 108, a unicorn, with the scroll "Een kint is ons geboren ende een soen is ons gege[uen]"; f. 189, a stork standing on its nest with five chicks and a scroll reading "O here verlost se wter pijn die mit dinen bloede behouden sijn." 4- and 3-line initials in blue with void white design on grounds of careful red penwork, infilled by a blue flower with a gold center on a red ground, with bracket borders of red, blue and pink penwork, including flowers and gold balls. 2-line initials alternating red and blue with small bracket borders of both colors. 1-line initials alternating red and blue; line fillers in the litany in the same lacy red and blue penwork. Red rubrics; some initials in the text touched in red.

Bound by Mercier for Robert Hoe in brown morocco with gold tooling and parchment doublures, with the monogram "RH"; gauffered and gilt edges.

Written in the second half of the fifteenth century; the decoration in this manuscript associates it with those produced in the convent of St. Agnes in Delft. Belonged to Robert Hoe: *Cat.* (1909) p. 28; his sale, Anderson, New York, 1912, pt. III, nn. 2066 and 2067 (described as if two manuscripts) to G. D. Smith. Precise source and date of acquisition by Henry E. Huntington unknown.

Bibliography: De Ricci, 94.

[1] We are indebted to Prof. James Marrow for this identification and the relevant bibliography.

HM 1128 — France, s. XV^2
BOOK OF HOURS, use of Paris — *fig. 120*

1. ff. 1–12v: Full calendar in French in alternating red and blue with major feasts in gold.

2. ff. 13–28v: Pericopes of the Gospels; *Oratio ad mariam virginem,* Obsecro te . . . [masculine forms; Leroquais, *LH* 2:346]; *Oratio,* O intemerata . . . orbis terrarum. De te enim . . . [Wilmart, 494–95].

3. ff. 29–98v: Hours of the Virgin, use of Paris; after compline the Salve Regina [*RH* 18147] with versicle, response and prayer, Concede nos famulos tuos quesumus domine deus perpetua mentis . . .

4. ff. 99–119: Penitential psalms and litany.

5. ff. 119v–123v: Short hours of the Cross.

6. ff. 124–128: Short hours of the Holy Spirit.

7. ff. 128v–186: Office of the Dead, use of Paris.

8. ff. 186v–198: [rubric on f. 186] *Les quinze ioyes nostre dame,* Doulce dame de misericorde . . . [Leroquais, *LH* 2:310–11]; *Les VII requests nostre seigneur,* Doulx dieu doulx pere sainte trinite et ung dieu . . . [Leroquais, *LH* 2:309–10]; Sainte vray croix aouree . . . [Sonet 1876]; ff. 198v–200v, ruled, but blank.

Parchment, ff. i (modern paper, with silk glued to the recto) + ii (contemporary parchment, ruled, but blank) + 200 + i (modern paper, with silk glued to the verso); 185 × 130

(82 × 58) mm. 1^{12} $2–3^{8}$(through f. 28) 4^{8} 5^{8}(+ 4, f. 40, text) 6^{8} 7^{8}(+ 4, f. 57) 8^{6}(ff. 63–72; + 2, 3, ff. 64–65, a bifolium; + 8, 9, ff. 70–71, two singletons) $9–11^{8}$ 12^{2}(ff. 97–98) $13–24^{8}$ 25^{4} 26^{2}. Occasional catchwords, in the script of the text on ff. 36v, 45v and 106v, and in a bâtarde script on ff. 62v, 72v and 138v. 13 long lines, ruled in pale red ink; pricking usually visible in the lower margins. Written in a gothic book hand in 2 sizes, according to liturgical function.

Fifteen large illuminations usually above 3 lines of text, with full borders of blue and gold acanthus leaves, flowers and various other figures. The miniatures, attributed to an associate of Maître François, are: f. 13 (Gospel of John), John on Patmos, and a peacock and another bird in the border; f. 29 (Hours of the Virgin), Annunciation, in a room with a pendant traceried arch at the top; in the border a bird and a butterfly; f. 43 (Lauds), Visitation, in front of a large church; in the border, a bird and a gold pot with flowers; f. 57 (Prime), Nativity, before a thatched shed leaning against grey masonry; in the border a peacock and another bird; f. 65 (Terce), Annunciation to the shepherds, including a shepherdess making a garland; in the border a pelican and another bird; f. 71 (Sext), Adoration of the Magi, and, in the border, a stork and another bird; f. 76v (None), Presentation in the temple; both Mary and Simeon have cloths over their hands; seen through a gold arch, in the border a beetle and a butterfly; f. 82 (Vespers), Flight into Egypt, with falling idol, his arms outstretched, in the background; in the border are a peacock and a butterfly; f. 91 (Compline), Coronation of the Virgin before God the Father, who sits in a gothic throne, while one angel, leaning over a low wall, crowns the Virgin and another angel presents her; a duck and another bird in the border; f. 99 (Penitential psalms), David in prayer; f. 119v (Hours of the Cross), above 4 lines of text, Crucifixion, with Mary and John on Christ's right, the soldiers on his left, one with a man-faced shield; in the border, a rooster and another bird; f. 124 (Hours of the Holy Spirit), above 4 lines of text, Pentecost with a shower of bright orange-red fire; in the border a hawk and another bird; f. 128v (Office of the Dead), above 4 lines of text, burial service in a churchyard, with the shrouded body in an open coffin, while a man digs the grave and the priests sprinkle the holy water; behind them is a charnel attic above an arcaded cloister; U-shaped frame around the text and miniature formed of logs; in the outer border, a monkey sitting on a stump holding up his foot in front of him; f. 186v (Doulce dame de misericorde), the Virgin, sitting on the floor, nurses the Child who stands on her knee; at the left Joseph approaches pushing the child's wheeled walker, with a pinwheel toy in his left hand; behind Joseph is a large fireplace, where a fire is burning; a central column in the foreground supports a traceried arch; in the border a peacock and another bird; f. 194 (Doulx dieu doulx pere), Christ, holding a tau-cross, and God the Father, holding an orb, both wearing one cloak, hold up a book, while the Dove hovers between them, and blue clouds swirl at the bottom of the picture; a bird and a gold pot with flowers in the border. Two historiated initials, with bracket borders of blue and gold acanthus leaves: f. 19v (Obsecro te), 7-line, Virgin and Child enthroned between two angels, one with a horn; f. 24 (O intemerata), 4-line, Pietà. In the calendar, roundels at the foot of the recto depict the monthly occupations; roundels at mid-margin on the verso show the zodiac symbols. Band borders running the length of the text in the outer margin, usually between two pink lines, but occasionally with a gold strip on the text side, triggered by the presence of a 2-line initial; when the border is called for on both recto and verso of a leaf, it is traced. 3- and 2-line initials, usually in white-patterned blue against burnished gold grounds with infilling of colored trilobe leaves, or rarely, with an infilling of naturalistic flowers. Occasionally the initial itself may be blue with gold or white shading as if a ribbon or a leaf, set against a brick red ground with infilling of naturalistic flowers or of painted gold acanthus leaves. 1-line initials in burnished gold with infilling of pink or blue against a ground of the other color; ribbon line fillers in the same colors; initials within the text touched in yellow. Rubrics in red. Holes in the upper margins above some of the full page miniatures from protective cloths once sewn in.

HM 1128

Bound by Simier in gold tooled black morocco, purple silk endpapers with 2 silver fore edge clasps; gilt edges.

Written in France during the second half of the fifteenth century. Priced 6,500 fr. as n. 2555 in a French bookseller's catalogue (Belin?). Belonged to E. Dwight Church (1835–1908); in his *Catalogue . . . of English Literature* (1909), vol. 1, n. 404, with plate of f. 128v. The Church collection was acquired by Henry E. Huntington in 1911.

Bibliography: De Ricci, 94.

HM 1129 — Southern France, s. XV^med^
BOOK OF HOURS, use of Paris, in French

1. ff. 2–13v: Full calendar in French with major feasts in red, similar to that printed by Perdrizet, but with frequent inversion of order.

2. ff. 14–19: Pericopes of the Gospels in French; f. 19v, ruled, but blank.

3. ff. 20–77v: Hours of the Virgin, use of Paris, in French verse, rubrics in Latin; portions of the text given by cue only; missing the opening leaves of matins, lauds, prime and terce between ff. 19–20, 32–33, 46–47 and 52–53 respectively.

4. ff. 78–80v: Short hours of the Holy Spirit in French.

5. ff. 81–83v: Short hours of the Cross in French.

6. ff. 84–101: Penitential psalms and litany in French; f. 101v, ruled, but blank.

7. ff. 101–137v: Office of the Dead, use of Paris, in French; ff. 136–137v, *Les sept vers saint bernard,* Sire enlumine mes yeulx . . . , and the prayer, Tout puissant et pardurable dieu qui a ezechie roy . . . [Illumina oculos meos, and Omnipotens sempiterne deus qui ezechie regi, in French, different from Sonet 1980 and 2114].

8. ff. 138–159v: Doulce dame vierge marie tres humblent [*sic*] ie te prye . . . [Obsecro te in French; Sonet 462?]; *La passion selon saint iehan,* En celluy temps pylate prist ihesucriste . . . [catena mainly from John 19, in French; see de la Mare, *Lyell Cat.*, pp. 65–66]; *Oroison,* Sire dieu qui as mis tes mains tes pies et tout ton corps . . . ; *oroison,* Ie te adore corps precieux et sang de nostre seigneur ihesucrist . . . ; *oroison,* Ie te salue tres saintisme et tres precieulx corps de ihesucrist qui fut pose en l'arbre de la crois . . . ; *oroison,* Sire dieu ihesucrist roy tout puyssant qui fis le ciel et la terre . . . ; *oroison,* De celle saincte bouche/ Dont ihesucrist parla/ Et de sa saincte mere/ Que neuf moys le porta . . . [Sonet 351]; *Pape Innocent La fit et conferma, Quant il l'eut confermee Apres il envoya Au bon roy charlemaine* . . . , Saincte cher precieuse/ Je vous aore et pry/ La vierge glorieuse/ Que vous porta et norrit . . . [Sonet 1855]; *oroison,* Ihesu doulx dieu filz de marie Qui par ta mort de mort a vie . . . [Sonet 966]; *oroison,* A Toy royne de hault parage, Dame du ciel et de la terre . . . [attributed to Guillaume Alexis, Sonet 24]; Royne qui fustes mise/ Et Assise/ Lassus ou throne divin . . . [attributed to Guillaume Alexis, Sonet 1804]; f. 160r–v, ruled, but blank.

Parchment (with hair follicles sometimes showing, e.g. ff. 118v–119, as occurs on parchment prepared in southern Europe), ff. ii (modern parchment) + 160 (+ 142 bis) + iii (modern parchment); 180 × 125 (103 × 62) mm. Collation beginning at f. 2: 1^{12} 2^{6}(through f. 19) 3^{8}(–1) 4^{8}(–7) 5^{8} 6^{8}(–6) 7^{8}(–5) $8–10^{8}$ 11^{4}(through f. 83) $12–17^{8}$ 18^{6}(through f. 137) 19^{6} 20^{8} 21^{10}. Catchwords in the script of the text in the center lower margin; leaf signatures visible on quire 12, a–g. 16 long lines, ruled in pale red ink; ruled in purple ink on the first two quires and last two quires. Written in a gothic book hand.

Four large illuminations missing after ff. 19, 32, 46 and 52 (offsets of border designs visible on the versos). Nine large illuminations remain, in slightly rounded compartments; U-shaped bar borders of pink, blue and gold segments enclose the miniature and 4–5 lines of text; outer borders of black ink spray with multicolored acanthus leaves, flowers, strawberries and gold dots. The illuminations, by 3 artists, the first of which has been identified as Enguerrand Quarton,[1] are: f. 57 (Sext), by Quarton, Circumcision; f. 62 (None), by Quarton, Adoration of the Magi, one young, one middle-aged, one old; f. 67 (Vespers), by the second artist, Presentation in the temple; f. 72 (Compline), by Quarton, Flight into Egypt; f. 78 (Hours of the Holy Spirit), by Quarton with some repainting (?), Pentecost; f. 81 (Hours of the Cross), by Quarton, Crucifixion with Mary and John on either side; the INRI legend on a strip of wood attached to the top of the Cross by a thin rod; f. 84 (Penitential psalms), by the third artist, David in prayer facing shining rays that stream downwards; diapered background; nude woman with spindle and distaff in the margin, based on the lost original by the Master of the Playing Cards, see Lehrs, 1:169–70 n. 25; f. 102 (Office of the Dead), by the second artist, Funeral service in a churchyard; f. 138 (Doulce dame vierge marie), by Quarton, the Virgin holding the Child in her lap, in an enclosed garden, with the owner in a pink dress and orange headdress kneeling to the Virgin's right. Major initials, 4- and 3-line, in white-patterned pink or blue with trilobe leaf infilling against a cusped gold ground; the initial on f. 138 contains a large pink flower. 3-, 2- and 1-line initials in gold with infilling of pink or blue on a ground of the other color; initials within the text washed in yellow; ribbon line fillers in segments of pink and blue. Rubrics in an orange-tinged red.

Bound, s. XIX, in purple velvet; gilt edges.

Written in southern France in the middle of the fifteenth century, evidently for a woman: on f. 137, the feminine form "ta servante," and on f. 138, the kneeling figure of a woman. Belonged to Henry William Poor (1844–1915), whose ex libris is on the front pastedown; his sale, Anderson, New York, 7 December 1908, pt. II, n. 769 to G. D. Smith. Precise source and date of acquisition by Henry E. Huntington unknown.

Bibliography: De Ricci, 94. N. Reynaud, "Un nouveau manuscrit attribué à Enguerrand Quarton," *Revue de l'Art* 57 (1982) 61–66 with plates of ff. 57, 62, 72, 78, 81, 138.

[1] We are indebted to Mme Nicole Reynaud and M. François Avril for this identification.

HM 1130
BOOK OF HOURS, use of Paris

France, s. XV^{med}

1. ff. 1–12v: Full calendar in French of the type printed by Perdrizet; major feasts in red.

2. ff. 13–27v: Pericopes of the Gospels, that of John followed by the prayer, Protector in te sperantium . . . [Perdrizet, 25]; *Oratio beate marie virginis,* Obsecro te . . . et michi famulo tuo . . . [Leroquais, *LH* 2:346]; *Alia oratio beate marie virginis,* O Intemerata . . . orbis terrarum. De te enim . . . [Wilmart, 494–95].

3. ff. 28–89: Hours of the Virgin, use of Paris; the prayer, Ecclesiam tuam quesumus domine . . . , concludes the hours from lauds through compline; f. 89v, ruled, but blank.

4. ff. 90–108v: Penitential psalms and litany, including Quentin and Firmin among the martyrs; Amand, Valeric, Nicasius, Leonard and Maurus among the confessors; Genevieve, Austreberta, Juliana and Gertrude among the virgins.

5. ff. 109–112v: Short hours of the Cross.

6. ff. 113–116v: Short hours of the Holy Spirit.

7. ff. 117–170v: Office of the Dead, use of Paris, except for the repetition of the response and versicle of Lesson 5 at Lesson 7 (possibly in error).

8. ff. 170v–188: Prayers as follow: *Les quinze ioyes nostre dame,* Doulce dame de misericorde . . . [Leroquais, *LH* 2:310–11]; *les cincq plaies nostre seigneur,* Doulx dieu doulx pere sainte trinite . . . [Leroquais, *LH* 2:309–10]; Sainte vray croys aouree . . . [Sonet 1876]; Illumina oculos meos . . . [*RH* 27912] with the prayer, Omnipotens sempiterne deus qui ezechie regi . . . ; Ave domine ihesu christe verbum patris . . . [Wilmart, 412]; Ave verum corpus natum . . . [Wilmart, 373–76]; Anima christi sanctifica me . . . [Leroquais, *LH* 2:340]; Domine ihesu christe qui hanc sacratissimam carnem . . . [Wilmart, 378, n.]; Gaude virgo mater christi que per aurem concepisti . . . with the prayer, Deus qui beatissimam et gloriosam virginem mariam in conceptu et partu . . . [both in *HE,* 63–64]; Stabat mater dolorosa . . . [*RH* 19416]; Pietatem tuam clementissime ihesu qui mortem subiciens . . . ; ff. 188v–189v, ruled, but blank.

Parchment, ff. i (modern paper) + ii (parchment) + 189 + ii (parchment) + i (modern paper); 165 × 115 (86 × 56) mm. 1^{12} 2^{8} 3^{6}(+ a leaf in the second half) $4–10^{8}$ 11^{6}(through f. 89) $12–22^{8}$ 23^{4} 24^{8}. Catchwords, usually cropped, but sometimes appearing in the inner lower corner of the last verso, usually written in a bâtarde hand, and once in a noting cursive hand (f. 97v). 15 long lines, ruled in pale red ink; pricking visible in the lower margin. Written in a gothic book hand in 2 sizes.

Twelve large illuminations in arched compartments with serrated tops, above 4 lines of script; the outer borders contain black ivy sprays with gold foliage, thin blue and gold acanthus leaves placed at the corners, various flowers and strawberries. The miniatures, of simple execution, are: f. 28 (Hours of the Virgin), Annunciation, seen below a gothic pendant tracery arch and between 2 white and gold columns, with the half-figure of God the Father appearing in the window; the miniature and text are bounded by a U-frame made of 3 gold logs; f. 40v (Lauds), Visitation; f. 53 (Prime), Nativity, with the Infant lying on a white cloth and Joseph holding the candle; f. 60 (Terce), Annunciation to the shepherds; f. 65 (Sext), Adoration of the Magi, with the Child reaching into the oldest king's coffer; f. 70 (None), Presentation in the temple, seen through 2 white columns and an arch which duplicate the shape of the miniature; f. 75 (Vespers), Flight into Egypt; f. 83 (Compline), Coronation of the Virgin, kneeling on a pillow of clouds and being crowned by an angel, while God the Father blesses and a host of red angels looks on from behind a low wall; f. 90 (Penitential psalms), David praying in an interior framed by white columns and a pendant tracery arch, with God the Father blessing him from the window; f. 109 (Hours of the Cross), Crucifixion, with Mary and John on Christ's right and the soldiers on his left; f. 113 (Hours of the Holy Spirit), Pentecost, viewed through the white columns and arch; f. 117 (Office of the Dead), burial scene in a churchyard with one gravedigger lowering the corpse into the grave, while 2 priests conduct the service and several mourners look on. Initials in 4 styles: 4- and 3-line initials (ff. 40v and 65) in gold- or white-brushed blue set on dark pink grounds, decorated with lighter pink acanthus leaves picked out in gold; 4- and 3-line initials in white-patterned blue on burnished gold grounds with colored trilobe leaves in the infilling; 3-line initials in white-patterned blue against gold-patterned brick red grounds with naturalistic flowers set on the painted gold infillings; 2- and 1-line initials in burnished gold alternate dark pink grounds with blue infilling, or the reverse; ribbon line fillers in the same colors; initials within the text touched in yellow. Rubrics in a bright orange-red. Bracket borders in the same style of ivy sprays, gold motifs, acanthus and flowers, enclosing the text from the outer margin, occur on f. 13 (Gospel of John), f. 19 (Obsecro te), f. 23 (O Intemerata), f. 170v (the 15 Joys), and f. 177 (the 7 Requests). Band borders running the length of the text in the calendar and at the presence of 2-line initials; when applicable, they are traced from the recto to the verso.

Bound by Capé in dark green morocco with red morocco doublures; gilt edges.

Written in France in the middle of the fifteenth century. An engraved book plate on f. i verso with the monogram "RN" (?). Belonged to Robert Hoe: Grolier Club (1892) n. 29; *Cat.* (1909) pp. 70–71; his sale, Anderson, New York, 1912, pt. III, n. 2070 to G. D. Smith. Precise source and date of acquisition by Henry E. Huntington unknown.

Bibliography: De Ricci, 94.

HM 1131 — Flanders, s. XV/XVI

BOOK OF HOURS, use of the congregation of Windesheim — *fig. 144*

1. f. 1v: coat of arms (see below).

2. ff. 2–11v: Calendar, with the months run on; major feasts in red, with those next in importance indicated by red underlining; included are the feasts of Pontianus (14 January, in red), Servatius (13 May, underlined in red), Odulph (12 June, underlined in red), Mary Magdalene (22 July, in another hand), Transfiguration (7 August [*sic*], in red), Remacle (3 September), Remigius and Bavo (1 October, underlined in red), Willibrord (7 November); f. 12r–v, blank.

3. ff. 13–19v: Short hours of the Cross, missing 1 leaf after f. 14, with loss of much of terce; each hour ends with a 4-line stanza to the Virgin, *De domina nostra,* Matutino tempore marie nunciatur quod a iudeis perfidis christus captivatur . . . [*RH* 29562]; *Oracio devota de passione domini,* Precor te piissime domine ihesu christe propter illam eximiam caritatem . . . [Wilmart, 378, n.]; *Item Alia oratio,* Domine ihesu christe qui pro redemptione mundi voluisti a iudeis reprobari . . .

4. ff. 20–52v: Hours of the Virgin, use of the congregation of Windesheim; from lauds through compline, each hour ends with a prayer and responses to the Holy Spirit; ends, *De domina Antiphona,* Salve regina misericordie . . . [*RH* 18147]; *Collecta,* Interveniat pro nobis quesumus domine ihesu criste nunc et in hora mortis nostre . . . ; *In summis festis de domina,* Alma redemptoris mater, que pervia celi porta manes . . . [*RH* 861], with the preceding collect; *Collecta Tempore paschali,* Regina celi letare . . . [*RH* 17170] with versicle, response and prayer, Prosit nobis semper quesumus omnipotens pater et precipue inter hec paschalia filii tui solempnia . . .

5. ff. 53–65v: Penitential psalms and litany, including Crisogonus, Lambert, Denis, Crispin and Crispinian, Pontianus, Pancratius and Theodard among the

martyrs; Hubert, Eligius, Remigius, Bavo, Amand, Willibrord, Servatius, Alexius, Gallus, Aegidius and Odulph among the confessors; Petronilla, Walburga, Gertrude, Oda, Bridget, Ursula and Kunera (Ciwa?) among the virgins.

6. ff. 66–84v [f. 66, blank]: Office of the Dead; 3 lessons at matins; ends with a series of prayers, the last being, *Quando itur in cimiterio oratio pro defunctis dicenda,* Avete omnes fideles anime . . . [Leroquais, *LH* 2:341].

7. ff. 85–107: Prayers as follow: O domine ihesu christe adoro te in cruce pendentem . . . [Leroquais, *LH* 2:346, with his n. 3 at the end]; Obsecro te domine ihesu christe ut passio tua sit virtus mea . . . ; *Quicumque dixerit sequentem coram facie salvatoris promeretur a iohanne papa xx^m^ dies indulgentie,* Salve sancta facies . . . [*RH* 18189]; *Alia oratio de eodom,* Ave facies preclara, pro nobis in crucis ara . . . [*RH* 1787] with versicles and prayer, Deus qui nobis signatis lumine vultus tui . . . [*HE,* 175]; *Alia oratio,* Omnipotens sempiterne deus de cuius munere preeminet hec facies tua expressa . . . ; *De nomine ihesu,* O bone ihesu, O piissime ihesu, O dulcissime ihesu . . . [Wilmart, 'Jubilus,' 267–68]; *Oratio venerabilis bede presbiteri de septem verbis domini in cruce pendentis,* Domine ihesu criste qui septem verba . . . [Leroquais, *LH* 2:342]; *De septem doloribus virginis marie,* O piissima dei genitrix sancta maria cuius cor dolore sanciatum fuit . . . ; *Sequentem orationem edidit dominus sixtus papa quartus et concessit omnibus eam devote dicentibus coram ymaginem beate marie in sole xi^m^ annorum indulgencie,* Ave sanctissima maria mater dei regina celi porta paradisi . . . ; *Officium misse de beata virgine maria,* . . . , Salve sancta parens . . . [with collects, readings, secret, preface and communion]; *Sequuntur devote orationes dicende ad beatam virginem mariam cum multis indulgenciis,* Obsecro te . . . Et michi famulo tuo impetres . . . [Leroquais, *LH* 2:346]; *Oracio pulcherrima de domina nostra,* O Intemerata . . . orbis terrarum. De te enim . . . [Wilmart, 494–95]; *Devota salutacio ad beatam virginem mariam dicenda,* Salve mater salvatoris vas electum vas honoris . . . [*RH* 18051]; *Oratio de gaudiis beate marie virginis,* Gaude dei genitrix virgo immaculata gaude que ab angelo gaudium concepisti . . . ; *Devota oratio de doloribus marie virginis,* Stabat mater dolorosa . . . [*RH* 19416]; *Dulcis oratio beati bernardi ad beatam virginem mariam,* O Piissima dei genitrix virgo maria, Ecce coram dilecto filio tuo . . . ; *Ad mariam virginem salutatio,* Gaude dei genitrix virgo immaculata, Gaude domina angelorum, tu advocata peccatorum . . .

8. ff. 107v–114v: Suffrages of one's guardian angel, Andrew, Stephen, Christopher [masculine forms], Martin, Anne, Mary Magdalene, Catherine of Alexandria, Barbara, Margaret, All Saints.

9. ff. 115–120v: Prayers as follow: *Oratio mane dicenda quando surgis,* In nomine domini nostri ihesu christi surgo . . . ; *Oratio de vesperi dicenda,* Omnipotens sempiterne deus, quidquid ego miser peccator hoc die cogitatione, locutione, opere . . . ; *Oratio quando elevatur corpus domini,* Ave verum corpus natum ex maria virgine . . . [Wilmart, 373–76]; *Ad elevationem calicis,* Ave vere sanguis domini nostri ihesu christi qui de latere eius . . . [Wilmart, 378, n.]; *Oratio dicenda post elevationem quam qui devote dixerit consequitur ab Innocentio papa sexto xx^m^ dierum indulgentie,* Domine ihesu christe qui hanc sacratissimam carnem . . . [Wilmart, 378, n.]; *Commendatio ad deum et sanctos*

eius, Omnipotens deus conditor celi et terre, in hac die commendo tibi animam et corpus meum . . . Nunc deprecor te et omnes sanctos tuos ut me famulam tuam . . . ; *Oracio ante communionem dicenda,* O dulcissime atque amantissime domine ihesu criste quem nunc devote desidero suscipere . . . ; *Oratio sub communione dicenda,* Domine non sum dignus . . . ; *Oratio dicenda post communionem,* Gratias ago tibi omnipotens et misericors deus, gratias ago tremende tue maiestati . . . ; *Item post communionem oratio,* Hec sunt convivia que tibi placent o patris sapientia natus de virgine . . . ; *Oratio post communionem dicenda,* Laudo benedico et gracias ago tibi dulcissime ihesu quia me indignum . . . ; *Antiphona de sacramento,* O quam suavis est domine spiritus tuus qui ut dulcedinem tuam in filios demonstrares . . . with versicle and prayer, Quesumus domine per hec munera nos a peccatorum nostrorum maculis emunda . . .

Parchment (rather stiff), ff. ii (paper) + i (parchment) + 120 + i (parchment) + ii (paper); 153 × 114 (103 × 70) mm. 1^4(+ 1) 2^6(+ 7, f. 12) 3^8(–3, after f. 14) $4–8^8$ 9^6(through f. 65) 10^8(+ 1, f. 66) 11^6 12^4(through f. 84) $13–14^8$ 15^6 16^8 17^8(–7, 8). 20 long lines, ruled in light purple ink; some pricking visible in the lower margin. Written in a gothic book hand.

Two full page illuminations, both on the versos of added singletons: f. 1v, a coat of arms (see below), suspended by a green belt from gold gothic tracery and enclosed by a simple gold picture frame; in the border flowers made from jewels hang from thin gold acanthus branches, against a deep orange-red ground; f. 66v (Office of the Dead), in paler tones than the other miniatures, Last Judgment, with Christ sitting on a rainbow, his feet on a crystal globe and the sword and olive branch on either side of his head, with the blessed gathered behind him, and the dead rising from their graves below. Six large miniatures above 6 lines of text in the style of the artists of the Grimani Breviary, enclosed by simple arched frames, with naturalistic flowers, insects or objects in the outer border; the miniatures are: f. 13 (Hours of the Cross), Betrayal with Judas in a bright yellow robe kissing Jesus, as Peter holds his still unsheathed sword, and Malchus crouches in the foreground, grimacing in pain; f. 20 (Hours of the Virgin), Annunciation, with the Virgin kneeling in front of a long bench in a spacious room; in the foreground are the vase of lilies and a pair of slippers; f. 53 (Penitential psalms), the prophet Nathan, with his hand on David's shoulder, encourages him to repent; David with red eyes and his hands folded in prayer, looks up to a golden opening in the sky, against a landscape of rocky hills, a castle and other towns in a far blue distance; f. 67 (Office of the Dead), Raising of Lazarus, helped by Peter who unties the ropes around his wrists, while his sisters kneel in prayer, and a man with a shovel and another covering his nose, look on; f. 85 (O domine ihesu criste adoro te in cruce pendentem), Mass of St. Gregory; in the outer border grey and pink flowers, some in a blue and white vase with the IHS monogram; f. 93 (Ave sanctissima maria mater dei regina celi), the Virgin and Child, possibly by a different artist, in a style resembling Gerard David; for a similar pose, see the Grimani Breviary, Venice, Biblioteca Nazionale Marciana, MS Lat. I, 99 (2138) f. 830v; in the outer border of this miniature: a red panel lettered in gold "Maria Mater Dei [?]," and niches in gothic architecture containing statues, one of which may be intended to represent Pope Sixtus IV. Sixteen smaller miniatures, 45–55 × 43–50 mm., on leaves with full borders in the same styles: f. 14 (Hours of the Cross, Prime), Christ before Pilate; the opening leaf for terce is missing; f. 15 (Sext), Road to Calvary, with one of Christ's tormentors kicking him; f. 16 (None), Crucifixion with Mary and John, both red-eyed from weeping; f. 17 (Vespers), Deposition from the Cross; f. 18 (Compline), Pietà with John on one side and Mary Magdalene on the other; f. 26 (Hours of the Virgin, Lauds), Visitation, with Elizabeth half-kneeling before Mary (see the Grimani Breviary, f. 610v); f. 33 (Prime), Nativity, with 2 angels with brightly colored wings adoring the Child, as Joseph looks through a hole in the masonry; f. 36 (Terce), Annunciation to the shepherds, one of whom covers his eyes; f. 38v (Sext), Adoration of the Magi, one of whom is black; f. 41 (None), Presentation in the temple; f. 43v (Vespers), Massacre of the Innocents, in pale tones; f. 48 (Compline), Flight into Egypt with a falling idol and the miracle of the corn field in tiny detail in the far upper right corner of the miniature, a city and a person walking are on the left; f. 86v (Salve sancta facies), half-length figure of Jesus in a red tunic, blessing and holding a crystal cross-and-orb; f. 88v (*De nomine ihesu*), the Christ Child nude, seated on a red pillow, holding a tau-cross and blessing, in glory; in the outer margin the sacred monogram formed with pearls and gold branches; f. 91 (the Seven Sorrows of Mary), the Virgin, sitting, with 7 swords piercing her heart, each of which bears on the handle a large roundel with the scenes of Sorrow; in the outer border, gold bells hang from a pearl-encrusted trellis; f. 117 (*Oracio ante communionem dicenda*), 2 angels with brightly colored wings support a monstrance containing the Eucharist, before a red brocade background. Miniatures for the suffrages, ca. 40–30 × 30–25 mm.: f. 107 (Guardian angel), the angel holding a small naked child representing the soul; f. 108, Andrew; f. 108v, Stephen; in the border, pearls and other pendants, including one of the Crucifixion, hanging by gold chains from a deep red cloth; f. 109, Christopher; border as on f. 108v, but here including a gold oval pendant of the Virgin; f. 110, Martin, 48 × 40 mm.; f. 110v, Anne sitting on a throne with a red cloth behind her, reading; the Virgin, holding the baby Jesus, sits at her feet; in the border, the legend "De Sancta Anna"; f. 111, Mary Magdalene, seated reading on a low brick wall covered with grass and flowers; a tall rocky hill rises exactly behind her, with cities in the distance; in the border, the legend "De Sancta Mag."; f. 111v, Catherine of Alexandria, seated on the ground beside the same low brick wall with green grass and scattered flowers on top; f. 112v, Barbara, seated on the floor indoors, with a view from her window of the tower under construction; in the border, the legend "Ora pro nobis beata Barbara ut (followed by cryptic, decorative writing)"; f. 113v, Margaret, emerging from the dragon's back. 3-, 2- and 1-line initials, in grey highlighted and decorated in white against gold-decorated maroon grounds; ribbon line fillers in the same colors. Rubrics in red. Erased inscription on f. 87.

Bound, s. XVII, in Belgian red morocco with gold tooling; blue silk endpapers; gilt edges.

Written perhaps in the Ghent-Bruges area as suggested by the style of the miniatures, but liturgically intended for someone connected with a house of the Windesheim congregation. A reference in an indulgence on f. 93 to Pope Sixtus IV indicates a date certainly after 1471. Although most prayers present masculine forms, one, on f. 116v, refers to "me famulam tuam." The coat of arms on f. 1v bears the elaborate achievement of Margaretha van Bergen, consort of Floris van Egmond. The representation presumably dates from before 1500 when Floris van Egmond's father died, since the Egmond arms are here differenced with a label of six points argent; the representation is also considered to be before 1505 when Floris van Egmond was elected to the order of the Golden Fleece: the collar of that order is not present. Nor could these be the arms of Margaretha's and Floris' son, Maximilian, since she was not an heiress. The arms are: per pale: I, quarterly, 1 and 4, gules three chevrons or (Egmond; Rietstap, vol. 2, pl. 257); 2 and 3, gules one fesse counter-embattled argent (Arkel; Rietstap, vol. 1, pl. 66); over all, or a saltire checky argent and gules (Isselstein; Rietstap, vol. 3, pl. 258); II, per fesse, 1, per pale, sable a lion rampant or (Brabant; Rietstap, vol. 1, pl. 300); and paley gules and or (Berthout; Rietstap, vol. 1, pl. 196); 2, vert three mascles argent (Bautersem; Rietstap, vol. 1, pl. 146). This impaling, for Bergen-op-Zoom, in Rietstap, vol. 1, pl. 185. Belonged to Ambroise Firmin Didot (1790–1876); his sale, Paris, 12 June 1882 n. 18 to Baron de Beurnonville; later owned by William K. Bixby (1857–1931) of St. Louis; acquired by Henry E. Huntington through G. D. Smith in August 1918.

Bibliography: De Ricci, 95.

HM 1132
BOOK OF HOURS, use of Rome

Italy, s. XV^{ex}

1. ff. 2–13v: General calendar in red and black, including "Festum nivis" (5 August).

2. ff. 14–102 [f. 14, blank]: Office of the Virgin, use of Rome; suffrages of All Saints follow each hour from lauds to compline; Salve regina at the end of compline; weekly and seasonal variations begin f. 83; ff. 102v–104v, ruled, but blank.

3. ff. 105–166v [f. 105, blank]: Office of the Dead, use of Rome; ff. 148v–166v, liturgical variations for All Souls and for a funeral; f. 167, ruled, but blank.

4. f. 167v: [Short Hours of the Cross] *Incipit offitium sancte crucis conpilatum a papa iohanne xx Et dedit de indulgentiam* [*sic*] *cuilibet devote dicenti vel audienti pro qualibet hora de septem centum dies im perpetum;* the remainder of this office has been misbound and is on ff. 232–236v [see art. 7].

5. ff. 168–198 [f. 168, blank]: [Long Hours of the Passion] *Incipit officium beatissime pasionis* [*sic*] *domini nostri ihesu christi nazareni crucifixi editum per beatum thomam de aquino;* f. 198v, ruled, but blank.

6. ff. 199–229 [f. 199, blank]: Penitential psalms and litany; ends; *Bernardus doctor in quodam sermone,* Nunquam vidi Nec in scripturis inveni quod devotus virginis dampnaretur. *Facto fine pia Laudetur virgo Maria;* ff. 229v–231v, ruled, but blank.

7. ff. 232–236v [f. 232, blank]: Short hours of the Cross, misbound; should follow rubric on f. 167v [see art. 4]; ff. 237–238v, ruled, but blank.

Parchment, ff. i (contemporary) + 238 (of which f. 1 is a flyleaf) + i (contemporary); 143 × 97 (85 × 45) mm. Collation beginning at f. 2: 1^{12} 2^{10}(+ 1) 3–9^{10} 10^{10}(through f. 104) 11^{10}(+ 1, f. 105) 12–16^{10} 17(2 leaves, ff. 166–167, presumably the beginning of a quire whose remaining leaves are now bound at the end as ff. 230–238) 18^{10}(+ 1, f. 168) 19^{10} 20^{10}(through f. 198) 21^{10}(+ 1, f. 199) 22^{10} 23^{10}(through f. 229, which shows signs of wear on the verso) plus the leaves which would have completed quire 17: 2 blank leaves (ff. 230–231) conjecturally once the conjuncts of ff. 166–167, a leaf blank on the recto and illuminated on the verso (f. 232), which would be a singleton, as are the other illuminated leaves in this codex, and a gathering of 3 bifolia (ff. 233–238); this would give the normal quire of 10 leaves and an added singleton. The quire was evidently misordered while the book was still in Italian ownership: each illuminated leaf and facing recto have been numbered 1–10 in the same color ink as a note on the back pastedown: "dieci Quadretti"; ff. 232–233 bear the numbers 9 and 10, rather than 5 and 6 as they would have if in their correct position. Catchwords centered in the lower verso, decorated with 4 small flourishes; small marks, occasionally visible in the outer right corner of the recto, were possibly leaf signatures. 12 long lines, ruled in pale brown ink. Written in a round Italian gothic book hand.

Five full page miniatures on the versos of inserted leaves, blank on the recto, in a style similar to that of Francesco d'Antonio del Cherico; rectos facing the miniatures with matching full borders and 7-line historiated initials: ff. 14v–15 (Hours of the Virgin), Annunciation, and Virgin and Child in the initial; borders of dense, richly colored acanthus leaves and black-rayed gold dots, with flowers, birds or other animals, urns, medallions of saints or prophets; on f. 14v, a space reserved for a coat of arms; f. 15 with the coat of arms painted in (see below). On ff. 105v–106 (Office of the Dead), Macarius showing a skeleton standing beside an open vault to 3 kings and a young man with a falcon; the initial encloses a crowned winged skeleton holding a scythe; similar border. On ff. 168v–169 (Office of the Passion), Crucifixion with Mary and John; in the initial the dead Christ on the cross, half-length; similar border. On ff. 199v–200 (Penitential psalms), David slaying Goliath; in the initial David penitent, holding a zither, half-length; similar border. On ff. 232v–233 (Office of the Cross), Kiss of Judas; in the initial, Jesus tied to the pillar; similar border. Secondary initials, 3-line, in white-patterned colors on a gold and colored ground with acanthus leaf marginal extensions and black-rayed gold dots; alternating 2-line red or blue initials with very careful and elaborate penwork in both colors extending the full length of the folio; 1-line initials, red with purple harping or blue with red. Red rubrics throughout.

Bound, 1972, in red reverse calf over wooden boards, replacing a previous binding in red velvet; gauffered gilt edges.

Written at the end of the fifteenth century, possibly in Florence as suggested by the style of the decoration. The coat of arms on f. 15, apparently original, is that of the Morelli family of Turin; see J. Gelli, *3500 Ex Libris Italiani* (Milan 1908) fig. 425: gules two lion's jambs or in saltire paws to the chief and in chief a chess-rook or. Other arms added later on f. 1v, and covering an earlier escutcheon: azure five mullets of eight points in a cross or (possibly a variant of the arms of the Lancillotti family of Rome). A note, s. XV, on f. i verso reads: Eugenio quarto, 1431, Condulmeria famiglia, Venetus (referring to the election of Gabriele Condulmer of Venice to the papacy in 1431 as Eugenius IV). Source and date of acquisition by Henry E. Huntington unknown.

Bibliography: De Ricci, 95. S. C. Chew, *The Pilgrimage of Life* (Yale University Press 1962) fig. 140 of f. 105v.

HM 1133 — France, s. XVI^in
BOOK OF HOURS, use of Paris

1. ff. 1–12v: Full calendar in French alternating red and blue with major feasts in gold; included are the feasts of Genevieve (3 January, in gold), Denis (9 October, in gold) and Genevieve (26 November).

2. ff. 13–25v [f. 13, blank]: Pericopes of the Gospels; *Oratio de beate marie virginis* [*sic*], Obsecro te . . . [masculine forms; Leroquais, *LH* 2:346]; *Oratio,* O Intemerata . . . orbis terrarum. Inclina mater . . . [Wilmart, 488–90].

3. Hours of the Virgin, use of Paris; misbound, and should be read as follows: ff. 26–46v [f. 26, blank] and 78r–v, matins, with the weekly variations of the psalms set into the text before the lessons; ff. 79–101, lauds through sext; ff. 101v, 105, 104, 102, none; ff. 103, 108, 109, 107, 106, 47, vespers; ff. 48–52 [f. 52v, ruled, but blank], compline.

4. ff. 53–70v [f. 53, blank]: Penitential psalms and litany, including Denis, Eustachius, Eutropius and Quentin among the martyrs; Remigius, Eligius, Aegidius, Maurice, Lubin and Sulpice among the confessors, and Genevieve among the virgins.

5. ff. 71–74: Short hours of the Cross.

6. ff. 74v–77: Short hours of the Holy Spirit.

7. Office of the Dead; the responses to the lessons are: Qui lazarum; Credo quod; Domine quando; Memento mei; Heu michi; Ne recorderis; Peccantem me; Domine secundum; Libera me domine de morte eterna; misbound, and should be read as follows: ff. 77v, 112, 111, 110, 113, 114, 117, 116, 115, 118–150.

8. ff. 150v–157: Suffrages of the Trinity, Michael, John the Baptist, John the Evangelist, Peter and Paul, Sebastian, Nicholas, Anne, Catherine of Alexandria, Margaret, Genevieve; f. 157v, ruled, but blank.

9. ff. 158–165v: Doulce dame de misericorde . . . [Leroquais, *LH* 2:310–11]; Doulx dieu pere saincte trinite . . . [Leroquais, *LH* 2:309–10].

Parchment, ff. i (parchment) + 165 + i (parchment); 138 × 100 (86 × 52) mm. $1\text{–}2^6$ 3^8(+ 1, f. 13) 4^8(+ 5, f. 26) $5\text{–}6^8$ 7^6(ff. 47–52) 8^8(+ 1, f. 53) $9\text{–}10^8$(through f. 77) $11\text{–}13^8$ 14^8(ff. 102–109) 15^8(ff. 110–117) $16\text{–}20^8$(through f. 157) 21^8. 17 long lines, ruled in pale brown ink. Written in a gothic book hand, apparently by a second scribe on ff. 158–165v.

Three full page illuminations, of mediocre execution, on the versos of inserted singletons, blank on the recto, and enclosed within architectural frames: f. 13v (Gospel of John), John in the pot of boiling oil, and, in the small scenes around the margins, a man tying sheaves of wheat and another man carrying them (?); f. 26v (Hours of the Virgin), Adam and Eve standing on either side of the tree around which is coiled the woman-headed snake; f. 53v (Penitential psalms), David dispatching Uriah into battle, in the surrounding small scenes, two knights jousting and Uriah before the troops. Large miniatures above 4 lines of text, enclosed by architectural frames and with adjacent smaller scenes: f. 14 (Gospel of John), John on Patmos, and in the small scenes, John before an enthroned turbaned man (possibly Aristodemus?), John before 2 young people (miracle of the stones turned into jewels?), and the raising of Drusiana; f. 27 (Hours of the Virgin), Annunciation, and in the 3 small scenes, the meeting of Joachim and Anne before the Golden Gate, the birth of the Virgin, and the betrothal of Joseph and Mary; f. 48 (Compline), Coronation of the Virgin before God the Father; in the small scene in the border, the Virgin in glory; f. 54 (Penitential psalms), David watching Bathsheba as she bathes; in the small scenes, the anointing of David, the slaying of Goliath, and David bringing Goliath's head back to the city in triumph; f. 71 (Hours of the Cross), Crucifixion with Mary and John on either side, and, in the borders, a large inscribed scroll and a scene of the Road to Calvary; f. 74v (Hours of the Holy Spirit), Pentecost; in the borders are a scroll as above and 2 other apostles looking upwards towards the Dove; f. 77v (Office of the Dead), Job on the dunghill; in the margins are the large scroll, and 2 wild men fighting; f. 79 (Lauds), Visitation; f. 89 (Prime), Nativity; f. 94 (Terce), Annunciation to the shepherds, with a landscape in the lower margin; f. 98 (Sext), Adoration of the Magi, with a grotesque in the landscape below; f. 101v (None), Presentation in the temple; in the lower margin, the Holy Family and followers walking to the temple; f. 103 (Vespers), Flight into Egypt, and a landscape in the lower margin; f. 158 (Doulce dame de misericorde), the Virgin holding the Child on her lap. 9- and 8-line illuminations are: f. 15v, Luke; f. 17, Matthew; f. 18v, Mark; f. 19v (Obsecro te), the Virgin with hands joined in prayer; f. 23 (O Intemerata), the Virgin and Child; f. 150v (Trinity), the Father and Son holding a book with the Dove between them; f. 151, Michael; f. 151v, John baptizing Christ; f. 152 (suffrage of John the Evangelist!), John the Baptist in a ragged tunic pointing to the Agnus Dei sitting on a book; f. 152v, Peter and Paul; f. 153v, Sebastian; f. 154, Nicholas; f. 154v, Anne teaching Mary to read; f. 155, Catherine of Alexandria; f. 156, Margaret; f. 156v, Genevieve; f. 163 (Doulx dieu doulx pere), Christ in glory. In the calendar, miniatures in the form of long bands the length of the text depict the monthly occupation on the recto, and the zodiac sign on the verso. Traced geometric band borders the length of the text on every page, with blue and gold acanthus leaves, flowers, strawberries, and small miniatures of grotesques in landscapes on ff. 56v and 59. 3- and 2-line initials, white-patterned blue with colored trilobe leaves or balls as infilling against a burnished gold ground; 1-line initials in gold with either pink or blue infilling against ground of the other color; ribbon line fillers and balls (for the same purpose) in the same colors. Rubrics in blue.

Bound, s. XVII, in French deep red morocco with some gold tooling; gilt edges.

Written in France in the early sixteenth century. On the front pastedown is the modern armorial bookplate of Matthew Ellison, Hadfield; with the manuscript is an American book dealer's slip, numbered 90, identifying the binder as Deseuil.

Bibliography: De Ricci, 95.

HM 1134 — Flanders, s. XV^med
BOOK OF HOURS, use of Rome

1. ff. 1–12v: Calendar in French in red and black, including the feasts of Vedast (6 February, in red, and its octave, 13 February), Vindicianus (11 March), "le relacion de saint vaast" (15 July, in red), Transfiguration (6 August), and, added in a later hand, Veneranda (14 November).

2. ff. 13–41v: Long hours of the Holy Spirit; hymn, Veni creator spiritus . . . [*RH* 21204]; f. 42r–v, ruled, but blank.

3. ff. 43–51: Pericope from John [1, 1–14], and the prayer, Protector in te sperantium . . . [Perdrizet, 25]; *Oraison tres devote a la benoiste vierge marie,* Obsecro te . . . [masculine forms; Leroquais, *LH* 2:346]; *Les sept oraison sainct gregoire,* O Domine ihesu christe adoro te in cruce pendentem . . . [Leroquais, *LH* 2:346].

4. ff. 51–58v: *Offisse de la conception nostre dame;* hymn at matins, Fletus longevi rex regum . . . [*RH* 6367]; in short hours form.

5. ff. 59–115v: Hours of the Virgin, use of Rome; suffrage of All Saints and prayer for peace from lauds to compline.

6. ff. 116–120: Short hours of the Cross; ff. 120v–121v, ruled, but blank.

7. ff. 122–141v: Penitential psalms and litany including Gertrude, Juliana, Genevieve.

8. ff. 142–187v: Office of the Dead, use of Rome.

9. ff. 188–198: Suffrages of Barbara and of Christopher [. . . famulo tuo N. . . .]; *Dominus iohannes papa concessit* . . . , Salve virgo virginum mater salvatoris . . . ; Sa[l]ve splendi[di]ssima virgo maris stella . . . ; *Oracio post celebracionem misse,* Deprecor te domina sanctissima virgo maria . . . ; *Dominus papa gregorius dedit hanc oracionem* . . . , Stabat mater dolorosa . . . [*RH* 19416]; Interveniat pro nobis quesumus domine nunc et in hora mortis . . . ; *Alia oracio,* Domine deus pater omnipotens qui cum eterni filii tui mortem morti superas . . . ; Angeli archangeli, throni et dominaciones . . . ; *Oracio,* Omnipotens sempiterne deus qui nos omnium sanctorum merita . . . ; Salve sancta facies . . . [*RH* 18189] and the prayer, Deus qui nobis signati lumine vultus tui . . . ; f. 198v, ruled, but blank.

10. ff. 199–206: *Passio domini nostri ihesu christi secundum iohannem,* In illo tempore apprehendit ihesum pylatus . . . [catena mainly from John 19; see de la Mare, *Lyell Cat.,* 65–66] and the prayer, Deus qui manus tuas et pedes tuos . . . ; Ave dextra manus christi perforata plaga tristi . . . [*RH* 1771] and the subsequent parts, Ave plaga ihesu leva . . . , Ave vulnus dextri pedis . . . [*RH* 35868], Ave plaga leve plante . . . , Ave latus lanceatum . . . [*RH* 1859]; *Oracio post elevacionem corpus christi,* Deprecor te piissime domine ihesu christe per illam nimiam caritatem . . . ; *Dominus iohannis papa quartus composuit hanc oracionem . . . ,* Anima christi sanctifica me . . . [Leroquais, *LH* 2:340]; *Dominus iohannes papa dedit omnibus dicentibus . . . ,* Salve sancta caro dei . . . [Leroquais, *LH* 2:348]; *Ad peticionem philippi regis francie papa bonefacius sextus concessit . . . ,* Deus qui hanc sacratissimam carnem . . . ; *Quicumque infra scriptam oracionem perlegerit . . . a domino papa bonefacio concessarum,* Ave verbum incarnatum in altari consecratum . . . [Wilmart, 379, n.]; f. 206v, ruled, but blank.

11. ff. 207–224v: *Oraison a dieu le pere,* Pater de celis deus miserere nobis, *oratio,* Domine sancte pater omnipotens eterne deus qui coequalem consubstantialem . . . ; *Au filz,* Fili redemptor mundi deus Miserere nobis, *Oremus,* Domine iesu christe fili dei vivi qui es verus . . . ; *Du sainct esprit,* Spiritus sancte deus Miserere nobis, *Oremus,* Domine spiritus sancte deus qui coequalis . . . [*HE,* 124–25]; suffrages of Michael, John the Baptist, John the Evangelist, Nicholas, Claude, Anthony abbot, Roch, Anne, Catherine of Alexandria, Margaret, Barbara, Mary Magdalene, Genevieve; *Salutation a la benoiste vierge marie mere de dieu,* Ave cuius conceptio solenni plena gaudio celestia . . . [*RH* 1744] with versicle, response and prayer; *Devote oroison,* Ave maria alta stirps lilii castitatis . . . ; *Le pape boniface a donne . . . ,* Avete omnes anime fideles . . . [Leroquais, *LH* 2:341] with its prayer, Domine ihesu christe salus et liberatio . . .

Parchment, ff. i (modern parchment)+ iii (contemporary parchment) + 224 + ii (contemporary parchment) + i (modern parchment); 122 × 90 (72 × 44) mm. 1–2^{6} 3–5^{8} 6^{6}(through f. 42) 7–9^{8} 10^{6} 11^{10} 12^{8} 13–16^{6} 17^{6}(+ a leaf in the second half) 18^{8} 19^{10} 20^{12} 21^{6}(through f. 157) 22–24^{8} 25^{6}(through f. 187) 26^{10} 27^{4} 28^{4}(+ 5, f. 206) 29–30^{8} 31.^{2} Catchwords only on those quires where the second scribe was at work (7–8, 22–23, 29–31) written vertically along the inner bounding line. 15 long lines ruled in pale red ink, or, in the areas written by the second scribe, in a clear red ink. Written by 2 scribes: i, ff. 1–41v [f. 42r–v, ruled but blank], 59–157v and 174–206 [f. 206v, blank] in a liturgical gothic book hand; ii, ff. 43–58v, 158–174 and 207–224v in a more widely spaced gothic book hand. The 2 scribes divide at quire breaks except on the middle of f. 174, the first leaf of the 24th quire.

Twenty large miniatures, simply done in camaïeu gris above 4 lines of text; full border, except where the arch of the miniature reaches to the top of the leaf, of black ink spray with grey, gold and white acanthus leaves, flowers, grotesques and gold dots. The miniatures are: f. 13 (Hours of the Holy Spirit), Pentecost; f. 22 (Lauds of the Holy Spirit), Ascension, with Christ's feet and the hem of his dress disappearing through the clouds; f. 26 (Prime of the Holy Spirit), Gnadenstuhl; f. 28v (Terce of the Holy Spirit), Christ teaching the Creed to the Apostles; f. 31 (Sext of the Holy Spirit), beheading of Paul; f. 33 (None of the Holy Spirit), Peter being tied to a cross made of logs; f. 35v (Vespers of the Holy Spirit), stoning of Stephen; f. 39 (Compline of the Holy Spirit), flaying of Bartholomew; f. 59 (Hours of the Virgin), Judas kissing Christ as he heals Malchus' ear; f. 70v (Lauds), Christ held before Pilate by 2 men wearing animal-like hats; f. 82 (Prime), Scourging at the pillar; f. 87v (Terce), Mocking of Christ by bestial-looking men; f. 92v (Sext),

Road to Calvary; f. 97v (None), Crucifixion; f. 102 (Vespers), Deposition from the Cross; f. 113v (Compline), Entombment; f. 116 (Hours of the Cross), Crucifixion with Mary and John on either side; f. 122 (Penitential psalms), David in prayer; f. 142 (Office of the Dead), Last Judgment with Christ sitting on a rainbow, his feet on the globe, the sword and olive branch on either side of his head and the dead rising from their graves; f. 188, Barbara, seated, reading in front of the tower. Major initials, 5- or 4-line, in pink or blue, on gold grounds with trilobe leaf infilling; 2-line initials in the same style call for band border of varying size (small L around the corner of the text; the length of the text; bracketing the text) of ink spray with gold dots, colored acanthus leaves and flowers; 1-line initials in blue with pink, or in gold with black flourishing; some 1-line cadelled initials on the top line with flourishing into the upper margins, sometimes washed in yellow or forming grotesque faces; initials within the text washed in yellow. Ribbon line fillers in pink, blue and gold segments; rubrics in bright orange-red. In the sections written by the second scribe: 3-line initials in red or blue with void white design, and possibly with simple penwork infilling of the other color; plain 2- and 1-line initials alternating red and blue; initials in the text washed in yellow; some decorative flourishes on the ascenders of the top line, occasionally touched with color; line fillers in either red or blue penwork; rubrics in red.

Bound by Lortic in red morocco with black inlay and gold tooling, including a satyr-face; marble under the gilt edges; dark brown morocco slipcase.

Written in the middle of the fifteenth century in northern France or Flanders, to judge by the prominence given to Vedast in the calendar; note the spellings mikiel, berthelemieu, franche, franchois. Belonged to Brayton Ives (1840–1914); his sale, American Art Association, New York, 5 March 1891, n. 632. Belonged to Robert Hoe: *Cat.* (1909) pp. 37–38; his sale, Anderson, New York, 1911, pt. I, n. 2133 to G. D. Smith; G. D. Smith Cat. 1 [1911] n. 105 and Cat. [2? 1912?] p. 2 to Henry E. Huntington in April 1912.

Bibliography: De Ricci, 95.

HM 1135 — Italy, s. XVI^{in}
BOOK OF HOURS, use of Rome

1. ff. 1–17v: Calendar in red and black, including the feasts of Torpes (17 May), Juvenal (21 May), Zenobius (24 May), "Festum nivis" (5 August), Cassianus (13 August), Miniatus (25 October), Ansanus (1 December).

2. ff. 17v–18v: *Questi sono e versi di sancto Bernardo quid aperie O bone iesu,* Illumina oculos meos . . . [*RH* 27912].

3. ff. 19–103 [f. 19, blank]: Hours of the Virgin, use of Rome; suffrages of All Saints follow each hour from lauds to compline; Salve Regina after compline; weekly and seasonal variations begin on f. 81; ends f. 103, *Finit officium beate marie virginis secundum consuetudinem Romane curie. Deo Gratias. Amen.*

4. ff. 103v–106v: Mass of the Virgin.

5. ff. 107–108v: *Oratio Sancti Anselmi,* Domine deus meus si feci ut essem reus tuus . . . ; suffrage of Roch.

6. ff. 109–137 [f. 109, blank]: Penitential psalms and litany.

7. ff. 137v–139v: [Indulgences] *Papa sixto quarto concesse a ciascuna persona che divotamente diceva la infrascripta oratione undeci milia anni di vera indulgentia per ogni volta,* Ave sanctissima maria mater dei regina celi . . . ; *Oratio piissima sancti Gregori qui concessit omnibus penitentibus et confessis dicentibus eam* . . . , O Domine iesu christe adoro te in cruce pendentem . . . [Leroquais, *LH* 2:346].

8. ff. 140–198v [f. 140, blank]: Office of the Dead, use of Rome.

9. ff. 198v–200v: *Oratio Sancti Sebastiani,* Deus qui beatum Sebastianum gloriosum martyrem tuum in tua fide et dilectione . . . ; *Questi sono e versi di sancto bernardo, O bone iesu,* Illumina oculos meos . . . [repeated as in art. 2]

10. ff. 201–207 [f. 201, blank]: Short hours of the Cross.

11. ff. 207–211v: Short hours of the Holy Spirit.

Parchment, prepared in the southern manner, ff. iii (modern) + 211 (+ f. 27 bis) + iii (modern); 77 × 55 (43 × 30) mm. 1^{10} 2^{8} 3^{10}(+ 1, f. 19) 4–11^{10} 12^{10}(+ 1, f. 109) 13–14^{10} 15^{10}(+ 1, f. 140) 16–20^{10} 21^{10}(+ 1, f. 201). Catchwords written vertically along inner bounding line. 12 long lines ruled in dry point. Written in a humanistic script, using brown ink which has flaked badly on the flesh side.

Major decorated openings consist of an inserted singleton, blank on the recto with a full page miniature of mediocre quality on the verso, and a historiated initial on the facing recto: ff. 19v–20 (Hours of the Virgin), Annunciation and facing historiated initial of the Virgin and Child; borders composed of symmetrical floral patterns, and polylobed medallions against a painted gold ground; IHS monogram in the upper margin of f. 20, and coats of arms (see below) in both lower margins. Folios 109v–110 (Penitential psalms), David penitent, and in the initial David as King; similar border. Folios 140v–141 (Office of the Dead), a winged figure (Death?) rising above a man and a woman, lying on the ground; in the initial, a skeleton in monk's garb holding a cross; similar border, with death's heads in the medallions. Folios 201v–202 (Hours of the Cross), Jesus holding the cross; in the initial, Mary (?) holding the cross; similar border. Two other openings with similar borders and historiated initials, but without the full page inserted miniature: ff. 103v–104 (Mass of the Virgin), with initial of the Virgin; ff. 206v–207 (Hours of the Holy Spirit) with initial showing Pentecost. Individual hours in the Office of the Virgin after matins decorated with a C-shaped border of colored flowers against a diagonally striped gold background; in the lower margin a medallion with the appropriate scene (ff. 33v, 49, 54v, 59, 62v, 66v, 75v). Secondary initials, 3-line, in burnished gold against blue backgrounds with maroon infilling, both patterned in gold; 2-line initials in painted gold on square gold-patterned colored ground; 1-line initials within the text in painted gold on plain colored grounds. Rubrics in reddish-brown ink.

Bound, s. XIX, in tan vellum over pasteboard, with gilt tooling of leafy sprays and onlay deep red morocco flowers; gilt edges.

Written in the early sixteenth century, certainly after 1471, when Sixtus IV was elected to the papacy (see f. 137v), and probably in Tuscany to judge by the saints in the calendar. The coats of arms of the first owners are, f. 19v, azure, on a bend or three mullets azure (possibly the Ginori family of Florence) and, f. 20, gules, four crescents argent 1, 2, 1. Placed by G. D. Smith in a sale by Anderson, New York, 12 December 1917, n. 243 to G. D. Smith. Smith Catalogue [n. 14, 1916?] n. 140 to Henry E. Huntington.

Bibliography: De Ricci, 96.

HM 1136 — Flanders, s. XV^2
BOOK OF HOURS, use of Rome — *fig. 123*

1. ff. 1–12v: Calendar in red and black, including, in red, the feasts of Basilius (14 June), Remigius and Bavo (1 October) and Donatianus (14 October).

2. ff. 13–21v [f. 13, blank]: Short hours of the Cross.

3. ff. 22–29 [f. 22, blank]: Short hours of the Holy Spirit; f. 29v, ruled, but blank.

4. ff. 30–37v [f. 30, blank]: Mass of the Virgin.

5. ff. 38–44: Pericopes of the Gospels; f. 44v, ruled, but blank.

6. ff. 45–106v [f. 45, blank]: *Incipiunt hore beate marie virginis secundum usum romanum;* suffrages of All Saints and prayers for peace from lauds to compline; Salve Regina follows compline.

7. ff. 107–126v [f. 107, blank]: Penitential psalms and litany including Gengulph among the confessors and Godeleva among the virgins.

8. ff. 127–162 [f. 127, blank]: Office of the Dead, with 3 lessons.

9. ff. 162–180: *De sancta maria oratio,* Obsecro te . . . et michi famulo tuo N. impetres . . . [Leroquais, *LH* 2:346]; *Alia oratio de sancta maria,* O intemerata . . . orbis terrarum. Inclina mater . . . [Wilmart, 488–90]; suffrages of Michael, Peter and Paul, John the Baptist, Sebastian, Nicholas, Anthony abbot, Mary Magdalene, Catherine of Alexandria, Barbara, Agnes, Genevieve; f. 180v, ruled, but blank.

Parchment, ff. i (modern parchment) + i (contemporary parchment) + 180 + i (modern parchment); 200 × 140 (105 × 70) mm. 1–2^{6} 3^{6}(+ the miniature, f. 13, and 1 other leaf in the first half) 4^{8}(+ 2, f. 22) 5^{10}(+ 1, f. 30) 6^{6}(+ 5, f. 45) 7^{10} 8^{6} 9^{10} 10^{6} 11^{10} 12^{6} 13^{12}(+ 12, f. 107) 14^{6} 15^{10} 16^{6}(+ 3, f. 127) 17^{10} 18^{6} 19^{10} 20^{6} 21^{10} 22^{6}(+ 1 leaf in the second half). 14 long lines ruled in purple or pale red ink; pricking in the 3 outer margins. Written in a liturgical gothic book hand.

Six full page illustrations in slightly arched compartments, on the verso of inserted singletons which are blank on the recto; the facing page with the same border as the miniature page, in blue and gold acanthus leaves placed at the corners, and remaining space filled with green leaf sprays, flowers, strawberries and grotesques; the opening initials, 5-line, in white-patterned pink or blue on a gold ground, infilled with trilobe leaves. The miniatures, by a follower of Willem Vrelant, are: f. 13v (Hours of the Cross), Crucifixion; f. 22v (Hours of the Holy Spirit), Pentecost; f. 30v (Mass of the Virgin), Virgin enthroned holding the Child to whom she offers a piece of fruit, while four angels playing instruments surround them; f. 45v (Hours of the Virgin), Annunciation; f. 107v (Penitential psalms), David in prayer; f. 127v (Office of the Dead), Raising of Lazarus. Historiated initials, 7- or 6-line, in colors with black ink sprays and a few small blue or red flowers and gold leaves, with the historiation mainly in shades of blue, grey and gold: f. 59 (Lauds), Visitation; f. 72 (Prime), Nativity; f. 77v (Terce), Annunciation to the shepherds; f. 82v (Sext), Adoration of the Magi; f. 87 (None), Presentation in the temple; f. 92 (Vespers), Massacre of the Innocents; f. 100v (Compline), Flight into Egypt; f. 170, Michael; f. 171, Peter and Paul; f. 172, John the Baptist; f. 172v, Sebastian; f. 173v, Nicholas; f. 174, Anthony; f. 175v, Mary Magdalene; f. 176v, Catherine; f. 177v, Barbara; f. 178v, Agnes; f.

179v, Genevieve. A 5-line historiated initial on a gold ground on f. 162 (Obsecro te) represents the Pietà. Secondary initials, 2-line on cusped grounds, 1-line on square grounds, both in gold on pink or blue grounds with infilling of the other color; initials within the text touched in yellow; rubrics in red. Marks from pilgrim badges on f. 1. Contemporary note to the end of the prayer on f. 21v.

Bound, s. XV, in black calf over wooden boards, rebacked; repeated 4 times, both front and back, is a Flemish animal panel (Weale, Netherlands 314, from Bruges, but without the panel of St. Margaret); 2 contemporary worked brass clasps, closing from top to bottom, with inset, glass covered, small miniatures of saints: in the upper clasp, a female saint; in the lower, a male saint with a staff and a string of shells (?) about his neck (James?); A. W. Byvanck, *Les Principaux Manuscrits à Peintures de la Bibliothèque Royale des Pays-Bas* . . . (Paris 1924) p. 80 notes that such clasps with miniatures seem to occur on books from a Vrelant workshop. On the inside of the clasps are the 2 initials "P" and "I" (or "J" for James?) united with a lovers' knot; gauffered and gilt edges; binding restored, 1974. For a similar binding, see D. Miner, *The History of Bookbinding 525–1950 A.D.: an exhibition held at the Baltimore Museum of Art, November 12, 1957 to January 12, 1958,* n. 127 with plate.

Written in the second half of the fifteenth century for use in the diocese of Bruges, to judge from the saints in the calendar. Belonged to William Bateman (1787–1835) and to his son, Thomas Bateman (1821–61); their collection, sold by order of the Court of Chancery, Sotheby's, 25 May 1893, lot 1040 to Quaritch. Belonged to Robert Hoe: *Cat.* (1909) pp. 23–24; his sale, Anderson, New York, 1912, pt. III, n. 2064 to G. D. Smith. Precise source and date of acquisition by Henry E. Huntington unknown.

Bibliography: De Ricci, 96.

HM 1137 — France, s. XV¹
BOOK OF HOURS, use of Besançon (?) — *fig. 96*

1. f. 1, blank; f. 1v: coat of arms (see below).

2. ff. 2–13v: Full calendar in French alternating red, blue and gold entries.

3. ff. 14–20v: Pericopes of the Gospels, that of John followed by the prayer, Protector in te sperancium . . . [Perdrizet, 25]; in the space at the end of Luke, in the hand of the scribe, a suffrage of Catherine of Alexandria; following straight on after Matthew, the prayer, Anime omnium fidelium defunctorum . . .

4. ff. 21–24v: Short hours of the Cross.

5. ff. 25–27v: Short hours of the Holy Spirit.

6. ff. 28–70v: Hours of the Virgin, of undetermined use; the antiphons and capitula at prime and at none are: Ecce tu pulchra . . . ; Ab inicio et ante secula . . . ; Fons ortorum putens . . . ; Quasi cedrus exaltata sum . . . ; each hour ends with a prayer to John the Evangelist; Salve Regina . . . [*RH* 18147] follows compline.

7. ff. 71–85v: Penitential psalms and litany, including Haimo among the apostles and evangelists; Ferreolus, Ferrutius, Antidius, Irenaeus and Maimbod among the martyrs; Columban, Walbert, Deicolus, Ermenfrid and "Lathene" (for Laichtein or Laidhgenn?) among the confessors; Radegundis, Bridget and Sabina among the virgins.

8. ff. 86–109v: Office of the Dead, use of Besançon.

9. ff. 110–114v: Obsecro te . . . et michi famule tue . . . [Leroquais, *LH* 2:346]; O Intemerata . . . orbis terrarum de te enim . . . [Wilmart, 494–95].

10. f. 115: coat of arms (see below); f. 115v, ruled, but blank.

Parchment, ff. iii (modern paper) + i (contemporary parchment; once the pastedown) + 115 (of which f. 1 is a flyleaf) + ii (contemporary parchment; f. ii once the pastedown); 216 × 165 (115 × 81) mm. 1^{6}(from f. 2) 2^{6} $3\text{–}14^{8}$(through f. 109) 15^{8}(–6, 8). 16 long lines ruled in pale red ink. Written in a gothic book hand of varying size according to liturgical function.

Sixteen large illuminations above 3 lines of text within arched compartments by more than one artist; some of the miniatures are based upon compositions of the Boucicaut Master. Borders in 2 styles, the division occurring after quire 3 between ff. 29–30: the first style includes figures in a rather dense ivy leaf outer border, and a narrow U-shaped gold frame around text and miniature; in the second style, a thin gold strip completely encloses the page; the outer border is somewhat more sparse and frequently includes a 180° sun-burst design of thin colored lines emanating from a gold dot set against the edge of the border; a rather wide frame surrounds the text and extends across the top until it meets the arch of the miniature. The miniatures are: f. 14 (Gospel of John), John on Patmos, writing, as a trumpet issues from a golden cloud in the sky; in the border, a bird and a monkey playing a guitar; f. 16 (Luke), the evangelist in an elaborate gothic chair against a tessellated background; in the border, a squirrel and a bird; f. 18 (Matthew), the evangelist below a vaulted gothic ceiling, against a tessellated background, and, in the border, an owl and 2-headed grotesque, the man-half playing a pipe and beating a drum; f. 20 (Mark), the seated evangelist under a gothic vaulted ceiling and against a tessellated background; in the border an owl and a grotesque similar to the one above, but with the monkey-half holding bagpipes; f. 21 (Hours of the Cross), Crucifixion with Mary and John on either side against a tessellated background; in the border are a stork, another bird and a woman spinning; f. 25 (Hours of the Holy Spirit), Pentecost against a tessellated background, and, in the border, a butterfly and two birds; f. 28 (Hours of the Virgin), Annunciation, against a tessellated background, with a peacock and another bird in the border; f. 37 (Lauds), Visitation; f. 46 (Prime), Nativity, with another woman kneeling in prayer; f. 50 (Terce), Annunciation to the shepherds; f. 53 (Sext), Adoration of the Magi; f. 57 (None), Presentation in the temple, with the Baby reaching back to his Mother, seen through a solid grey archway; f. 61 (Vespers), Flight into Egypt; f. 67 (Compline), Coronation of the Virgin, in which the crowned Virgin kneels before Christ who blesses her, against a tessellated background; f. 71 (Penitential psalms), David kneeling, gazing upwards at God the Father who appears in the sky surrounded by orange cherubim; f. 86 (Office of the Dead), burial service in a courtyard with 3 priests, black-dressed mourners and 2 men lowering the body into the grave; the border seems to be of the first type. Band borders the length of the text in the outer margins traced through, with the same division in style as noted above; the calendar with borders of the second type. 3-line initials in white-patterned blue or pink with colored trilobe leaf infilling against a cusped gold ground; 2- and 1-line initials in gold with alternating pink or blue infilling and ground of the other color; ribbon line fillers in the same colors; initials within the text touched in yellow. Rubrics in red, except on f. 23r–v (conjunct with f. 28, with the Annunciation scene) where they are in blue and by a different hand.

Bound, s. XVII, in French red morocco; gilt edges, marbled endpapers and 2 later silver fore edge clasps, closing front to back, one lacking. A diamond-shaped pattern of black-stained holes on the first and last flyleaves and 2 sets of 2 marks each on the outer margins of these flyleaves suggest fore edge clasps and a center boss on an earlier binding.

Written during the first half of the fifteenth century perhaps for use in Besançon, to judge from the Office of the Dead, and the saints in the litany. The arms of early owners on ff. 1v and 115 were identified by A. Van de Put, as those of Jacques d'Archiac, lord of Aveilles (on f. 1v) and of his wife, Louise d'Aumont (on f. 115): his arms, encircled by a laurel wreath, gules two pales vair a chief or; her arms, also encircled by a laurel wreath, per pale, I, gules one [for two] pales vair a chief or (Archiac; similar to Rietstap, vol. 1, pl. 62); II, quarterly of five (2 and 3): 1, argent a chevron gules between, in chief four and in base three, martlets gules (Aumont; see Rietstap, vol. 1, pl. 87); 2, ermine eight horseshoes in orle and a bordure gules (Ferrières; see Rietstap, vol. 2, pl. 317); 3, or three bars azure and a bordure gules; 4, azure two fishes or and seven crosses argent (3 and 4); 5, or a lion rampant azure armed and langued gules. Belonged to Robert Hoe: Grolier Club (1892) n. 18; *Cat.* (1909) pp. 22–23; his sale, Anderson, New York, 1912, pt. IV, n. 2345 with plate of f. 53 to G. D. Smith. Precise source and date of acquisition by Henry E. Huntington unknown.

Bibliography: De Ricci, 96. M. Meiss, *French Painting in the Time of Jean de Berry: The Boucicaut Master* (London—New York 1968) 140.

HM 1138 — Northern France, s. XV[1]
BOOK OF HOURS, use of Paris (?)

1. ff. 1–12v: Full calendar in French with major feasts in red, similar to that printed by Perdrizet.

2. ff. 13–20v: Pericopes of the Gospels, that of John followed by the prayer, Protector in te sperantium . . . [Perdrizet, 25]; Concede quesumus omnipotens deus ut qui unigenitum tuum redemptorem nostrum . . .

3. ff. 21–62v: Hours of the Virgin, possibly of the use of Paris: antiphon and capitulum at none are Sicut lilium and Per te dei. Portions of the text missing due to lost leaves, and other sections misbound; text now arranged as follows: ff. 21–25v, part of matins beginning defectively; ff. 26–27v, end of sext; ff. 28–29v, part of none; ff. 30–40v, end of matins and beginning of lauds; ff. 41–44v, end of lauds (text missing between ff. 40v–41); ff. 45–48v, the last 8 of the 15 Joys of the Virgin (see below ff. 93–94v); ff. 49–51v, part of terce; ff. 52–54v, part of sext (see above ff. 26–27v for the end); ff. 55–59v, part of vespers (text missing between ff. 58v–59); ff. 60–62v, end of compline.

4. ff. 63–74v: Obsecro te . . . [masculine forms; Leroquais, *LH* 2:346]; *Sequitur oratio devota,* O Intemerata . . . orbis terrarum. De te enim . . . [Wilmart, 494–95]; *Oratio devota de nostra domina,* Saluto te beatissima dei genitrix virgo maria angelorum regina . . .

5. ff. 75–90v: Penitential psalms, beginning defectively in the fourth psalm, Ps. 50, 14; litany, including Eustachius and Denis among the martyrs; Magloire, Ivo, Maturinus, Bernard and Lubin as the last confessors; Genevieve among the virgins.

6. ff. 91–92v: Short hours of the Holy Spirit, defective at the beginning and at the end.

7. ff. 93–97v: Three prayers in French as follow: ff. 93–94v, part of the heading and the first 2 of the 15 Joys, of which the last 8 are now bound as ff. 45–48v [Leroquais, *LH* 2:310–11]; ff. 95–97, part of the 5th, then the 4th, the 6th and

the 7th of the 7 Requests [Leroquais, *LH* 2:309–10]; f. 97r–v, *Oroison de la croix,* Saincte vraye croix aouree . . . [Sonet 1876].

8. ff. 98–145: Office of the Dead: ff. 98–100v, matins up to the psalm Verba mea auribus percipe; ff. 100v–145, the remaining parts of the office, with 3 lessons at matins.

9. ff. 145v–150v: Prayers as follow: *S'ensuit tres devote oroison a nostre dame,* O Tres certaine et souveraine esperance deffenderesse et dame . . . [Sonet 1538]; *Oracio de nostra domina,* Sancta maria mater domini nostri ihesu christi in manus tuas . . . ; [added in a bâtarde script:] suffrage of Martin.

Parchment, ff. ix (modern paper) + 150 + lxv (modern paper, all completely blank); 185 × 137 (92 × 60) mm. Because of the amount of missing material, collation represents the quires as they now stand (except in quires 4 and 6 where the missing conjugate of a bifolium is postulated): 1^{6} 2^{6} 3^{8}(through f. 20) 4^{6}(–1; ff. 21–25) 5^{4}(ff. 26–29) 6^{4}(–1; ff. 30–32) 7^{8}(ff. 30–40) 8^{4}(ff. 41–44) 9^{4}(ff. 45–48) 10^{6}(ff. 49–54) 11^{4}(ff. 55–58) 12^{2}(ff. 59–60) 13^{8}(ff. 61–68) 14^{6}(ff. 69–74) 15^{8}(ff. 75–82) 16^{8}(ff. 83–90) 17^{4}(ff. 91–94) $18–24.^{8}$ Catchwords in center of the lower margin in the script of text. 13 long lines ruled in pale red ink. Written in 2 sizes of a gothic book hand.

Only one illumination survives, that of the Office of the Dead, f. 98: in an arched compartment above 4 lines of text, burial service in an enclosed grassy courtyard, with 3 mourners, 2 priests reading from a shared book, while 2 other men lower the white-shrouded body, marked with a long red cross, into the ground; U-shaped frame around text and miniature as a wide gold band, decorated with colored leaf patterns; outer border of black ink ivy spray with gold trilobe leaves. Bracket borders of this ivy spray with small flowers on ff. 63 and 100v; similar band borders, triggered by 2-line initials, placed to the left of the text. Three 4-line initials (ff. 63, 98 and 100v) and 2-line initials alternate white-decorated pink or blue set against a ground of the other color, both infilled with colored trilobe leaves on gold; 1-line initials in gold infilled in blue or pink against grounds of the other color; ribbon line fillers in the same colors; initials in the text washed in yellow. Rubrics in red.

Bound, s. XIX, in French green half-roan; marbled endpapers and edges, including the 65 back paper flyleaves.

Written during the first half of the fifteenth century in France; obtained from Sessler by Henry E. Huntington at an unknown date.

Bibliography: De Ricci, 96.

HM 1139 — France, s. XVI^in^

BOOK OF HOURS, use of Rome

1. ff. 1–12v: Calendar, with major feasts in blue or gold.

2. f. 13: Iudica me deus et discerne causam meam de gente . . . [Ps. 42].

3. ff. 13v–91v: Hours of the Virgin, use of Rome; suffrages of All Saints from lauds to compline; short hours of the Cross and the Holy Spirit worked in; Salve Regina follows compline; f. 81v, suffrage to Anthony abbot [leaf missing between ff. 81–82 with break in text]; f. 82, *Incipiunt mutationes horarum beate marie virginis secundum usum Romanum.*

4. ff. 92–110: Penitential psalms and litany, including Maurice and companions, and Julianus among the martyrs; Gatianus, Maurilius and Renatus among the confessors; Genevieve and Opportuna among the virgins.

5. ff. 110–149: Office of the Dead, use of Rome.

6. ff. 149v–151: Pericope from the Gospel of John [1, 1–14] with antiphon, versicle, response and its usual prayer, Protector in te sperantium . . . [Perdrizet, 25].

7. ff. 151v–159: Prayers in Latin and French as follow: *Oratio ad beatam virginem mariam,* Obsecro te . . . et michi famulo tuo N. impetres . . . [Leroquais, *LH* 2:346]; Royne des cieux glorieuse, Mere et fille de dieu precieuse . . . [Sonet 1793]; *Les dix commandemens de la loy,* . . . ; *Les cinq commandemens de saincte eglise,* . . . [leaf missing between ff. 155–156 with loss of text]; *O vos omnes qui transitis per viam,* Toy qui passes par devant moy, Entens icy et soyes recors . . . [Sonet 2107]; *Pater dimitte illis,* Tres doulx pere a tous pardonne . . . [a continuation of the preceding, with Jesus speaking here also]; suffrage and mass of Genulph; f. 159v, ruled but blank.

Parchment, ff. ii (paper) + i (parchment) + 159 + ii (paper); 233 × 150 (150 × 90) mm. $1–2^6$ $3–4^8$ $5^6(+2, 3)$ $6–10^8$ $11^8(-6$, between ff. 81–82) $12–20^8$ + 4 leaves of uncertain structure with a missing leaf between ff. 155–156. One catchword in the script of the text survives (f. 139v); one quire-leaf signature as letter of the alphabet and an arabic numeral. 20 long lines ruled in pale red ink. Written in a late gothic book hand.

Fifteen full page illustrations, in blue, black, green, gold and flesh tones, enclosed within architectural frames of painted gold: f. 13v (Matins), Annunciation; f. 30v (Lauds), Visitation; f. 41v (Matins of the Cross), Crucifixion with Mary and John; f. 43 (Matins of the Holy Spirit), Pentecost; f. 44v (Prime), Nativity; f. 50 (Terce), Annunciation to the shepherds; f. 55v (Sext) Adoration of the Magi; f. 61 (None), Presentation in the temple; f. 66v (Vespers), Flight into Egypt; f. 75 (Compline), Coronation of the Virgin; f. 92 (Penitential psalms), David, his harp on the ground, in an almost kneeling position in front of figures of War, Death and Pestilence, while an angel from above points to this vision; f. 110v (Office of the Dead), Job on the dunghill; f. 149v (Gospel), John on Patmos, with the eagle offering him his writing tools; f. 151v (Obsecro te), Virgin and Child in glory; f. 156 (Prayer of Jesus on the Cross), Crucifixion with Jesus alone. Initials, 4- to 1-line, in black ink against square painted gold grounds, with black tracery; ribbon line fillers of many patterns, but in the same black and gold colors; initials within the text washed in yellow. Rubrics in blue.

Bound, s. XIX^{in}, in English red morocco, blind and gilt stamped; gilt edges.

Written in France at the beginning of the sixteenth century. The nineteenth century provenance of this manuscript is laid out on the verso of a small slip of paper, now tipped in before the first flyleaf: "This missal was bought by Mr. W. Bateman at the sale of the library of Mr. W. Gates [?] of Manchester ⟨blank space⟩ 1829. It then passed by exchange into the possession of Mr. Duncalf at whose death in 18—⟨left blank⟩ it was purchased along with other books by Mr. James Lowe of Macclesfield from whom I bought it on the 27th of February 1851. [signed] Thomas Bateman [1821–61]." The recto of this slip of paper is inscribed by William Bateman (1787–1835), father of the above Thomas Bateman: "This Missal is the property of the Rev. John Duncalf, Incumbent of Peak Forest, and has been this day placed in my keeping on account of the dampness of his residence, Wetstone Hall, near Tideswell. [signed] Mr. Wm. Bateman, Middleton, 4 December 1834." Bateman sale, sold by order of the Court of Chancery, Sotheby's, 25 May 1893, lot 1367 to Quaritch. Belonged to Robert Hoe: *Cat.* (1909) pp. 148–49;

his sale, Anderson, New York, 1912, pt. IV, n. 2367 to G. D. Smith. Precise source and date of acquisition by Henry E. Huntington unknown.

Bibliography: De Ricci, 96.

HM 1140 — Northwestern Netherlands, s. XV^{ex}
DEVOTIONS, in Dutch — *fig. 140*

1. ff. 1v–13: Full calendar, one month across each opening, in red and black, including the following feasts in red: Pontianus (14 January), Servatius (13 May), Boniface (5 June), Odulph (12 June), Lebuin (25 June), Gereon (17 August), Lambert (17 September), Remigius and Bavo (1 October), Victor and Gereon (10 October), Willibrord (7 November); each month with concluding note on the number and length of days in that month; f. 13v, ruled, but blank.

2. ff. 14–25v [f. 14, blank]: Short hours of the Holy Cross in the Dutch version of Geert Grote; see van Wijk, 87–91.

3. ff. 26–55 [f. 26, blank]: Devotions on the Passion for the canonical hours: *Hier beghinnen deuote oefeningen vander passien ons liefs heren ihesu cristi ende is seer vorderlic die te setten is voor alle ander oefeninghen ende ghebeden behaluen een verbindinghe der ghetiden daermen toe verbonden is vanden rechte der heiliger kerken,* Die grote biscop albertus seit, een simpel ghedacht vander passien ons liefs heren ihesu cristi is oorbaerliker daghelix gheoefent dan of een lase alle daghe een helen souter een iaer lanc . . . [f. 27v:] *Te metten-tijt, O clementissime,* O alre goedertierenste ende soetste heer ihesu criste doe du dijn leuen vloeyndet hadste naden lichhaem in die wtterste ende ellendichste armoede ende pijnlicheit . . . Daer so moet hi ons leiden die voor ons ghestoruen is. Amen.

4. ff. 55–62v: Prayers to the Cross, of the Seven Last Words, of the Seven Sorrows of the Virgin: *Hier begint een goede segheninghe,* Cruus cristi si mit mi + Cruus cristi wese mijn toeuerlaet + Cruus cristi is een gewaer heyl + . . . ; [f. 55v:] *Dit sijn die seuen woerden die onse lieue heer ihesus cristus sprac hanghende inden cruce, ende het is redelic ende seer oerbaerlic datse een yghelick mensche gedenct eens daghes, oracio,* Heer ihesu criste leuende gods soon die inder lester tijt uwes leuens hanghende anden cruce spraecste seuen woorden . . . *Dat eerste woert,* Heer ihesu criste want ghi spraect, vader vergheuet den genen die mi naghelen anden cruce . . . ; [f. 58:] *Hier beghinnen seuen ghetiden vanden medeliden onser lieuer vrouwen mit ihesum haren lieuen soon in sinen heylighen liden. Te metten tijt. O maria,* O maria alre salichste maghet ic bidde di door dat minnentlike liden dijns moederliken herten dat ghi leet te metten tijt doe du vernaems dat dijn ghebenedide enighe soon geuanghen ende ghebonden was . . . haer dan veruroechden mach inder ewicheit mitti ende mit dinen lieuen kinde. Amen.

5. ff. 63–81v [f. 63, blank]: Mass of St. Gregory, prayers for the rosary: *Sinte gregorius ende ander paeusen hebben ghegheuen alle den ghenen die mit berou haerre sonden lesen seuen pater noster ende vii Aue maria mit desen ghebeden voer die wapen ons heren mit gheboghen knien xlvi^{m} ende xii iaer, ende xxiiii*

daghen oflaets, pater noster Aue maria gracia, O heer ihesu christe ic aenbede di hanghende inden cruce ende een doornen croon draghende op dijn hooft . . . ; [f. 65:] *Dit is een exempel van die doornen croon,* Het was een ioncfrou die leefde nader werlt, ende si hadde alte deuoten dienstmaghet die haer dicwijl plach wat goets te seggen . . . ; [f. 67:] *Hier beghint die doornen croon ons heren,* Die die doornen croon onses liefs heren lesen wil, die sel alle souen daghe lesen lxxvii pater noster ende aue maria, ende men selse lesen op die knien sonder spreken . . . O heer ihesu criste verlosser der werlt ghi die v veroetmoedicht hebt ende daelde wtten scoot uwes hemelschen vaders . . . ; [f. 72:] *Hier beghint onser vrouwen cranskijn ende men selse eerst groeten mit groter waerdicheit sprekende dit ghebet,* Ghewaerdighe heilige maghet dat ic di ghebenedie ende die vruchte dijns lichaems louen mach . . . ende bouen allen choeren der enghelen ewelick verheuen. Amen. [f. 80r–v, ruled, but blank]

6. ff. 81–110v: Meditations for the rosary, with a miniature before each Ave Maria and each Pater Noster]: *Hier beghint onser lieuer wrouwen crencskijn dat ghemaect heuet die gloriose doerluchtige doctoor ende honichuloeyende barnaerdus abt van clarendael,* God gruet v maria vol gracien die heer is mitti . . . Wien du alre suuerste maghet ouermits die bootscap des enghels vanden heilighen gheest wonderliken onttincste. Alleluya Ave Maria . . . dat honderdusent werf ghedubbeleert mit een bondeken van roden rosen offer ic v op tot uwen loue Amen.

7. ff. 111–121v: Suffrages of Jerome, one's guardian angel, Michael Archangel, John the Baptist, John the Evangelist, Peter and Paul, Cornelius, Martin, Anne, Catherine of Alexandria, Barbara, Agnes, All Saints; ff. 120–121v, ruled, but blank.

8. ff. 122–138v: [f. 122, blank] Penitential psalms and litany in the version of Geert Grote; see van Wijk, 139–54; included in the litany are Pontianus, Lambert, Boniface and Gereon among the martyrs; Willibrord, Giles, Lebuin, Radbodus, Servatius and Odulph among the confessors; Walburga, Gertrude and Ursula among the virgins.

9. ff. 139–144v: [f. 139, blank] Suffrages of Erasmus (with indulgence) and Christopher; f. 143v, prayer to Anne: *Dit sijn drie pater nosteren van sinte anna der waerder moeder, dimen leest voor een sonderlinghe saec ende sonderlinghe des dinxdages Pater noster. Ave maria gracia,* O ghebenedide ende waerde vrouwe ende moeder sinte anna dit eerste pater noster offer ic di op in die eer der groter vruechden . . . van v gheoffert wort inden tempel god tot enen waerdighe offerhande. Amen.

10. ff. 144v–147v: Four prayers with indulgences: *Dit sijn xv Ave marien daermen mede vercrijcht oflaet van allen sonden, ende men macht oec winnen voor sielen inden vageuier,* Lof eer ende waerdige dancbaerheit si v O waerdighe heilighe drieuoudicheit ende der menscheit cristi dijns soons . . . ; [f. 146v:] *Sixtus die paeus gaf inder vreu sijns doots alle den ghenen die dort ghebedekijn lesen mit beron van sinen sonden xl^{m} iaer oflaet,* O lieve heer ihesu criste als u strenghe oerdel . . . [f. 147:] *Dit nauolghende ghebet staet tot romen tot sinte ians te latranen gheregistert ende daer staet toe lxxx^{m} iaer oflaet,* O heer ihesu criste leuende godes soon ic bidde di dat du door dier minnen dier blijsscap die dijn gheminde moeder hadde als ghi haer openbaerde in die alre salichste

nacht van paesschen . . . ; [f. 147v:] *Sixtus die paeus heeft ghegheuen alle den ghenen die dese oratie deuotelic segghen xi^{m} iaer oflaets van allen sonden elke reyse, Ave maria,* Weest ghegruet alre heilichste maria moeder gods, coninghinne des hemels, poorte des paradijs . . . ende bidde voor mijn sonden. Amen.

11. ff. 147v–154v: Prayers for Mass: *Dit selstu lesen also dicwijl alstu wiwater neemste dat die sonden ofdwaet,* Alhier ontfae ic dat heilighe wi water voor alle mijn sondelike saken . . . ; *Alstu inder kercken coomste* . . . , Ic dancke di lieue heer ihesu christe dattu mi so edelen creatuer ghescepen hebste . . . ; *Alsmen confiteor leest,* Beliet den heer want hi goet is, want in ewicheit is sijn ontfermherticheit . . . ; [f. 150v:] *Alsmen die misse beg.,* Inder teghenwoerdicheit dijns heilighen lichaems ende bloets ghenadige ende ontfermhertighe god huden ende tot allen tiden beuel ic v mijn siel . . . ; [f. 153:] *Alsmen sanctus singet,* Ic bidde di minnentlike heer ihesu criste omder hogher minnen wil daerstu dat menschelike gheslachte mede mindeste doestu hemelsche coninc hingheste anden cruce . . . ; [f. 154:] *Dit selstu lesen nader eleuatien* . . . , God gruet v alre scoonste, alre reynste, alre edelste, alre salichste moeder minnentlike maghet maria . . . ; [f. 154v:] *Hier selstu staen op dine knien ende mit gheuouden handen int eynde vander missen seggende aldus,* Sich in mi onsalich mensche o onghemeten goedertierenheit, o openbaer ontfermherticheit . . . ouermits die menichuodicheit dijnre grondeloser ontfermherticheit Amen.

12. ff. 155–164: Prayers for the week: *Hier beghint een goede oefeninge of ghedenckenisse daer hem een mensche daghelix mede becommeren mach,* Dauid die propheet seit inden souter, Die heer sel spreken vrede den ghenen die hem totter herten keren . . . dat een mensche alte veel meer verdient dan of hi altoes die graci der tranen ende der deuocien hadde tot sinen wille. [ff. 164v–166v, ruled, but blank]

Parchment, ff. ii (modern parchment) + iii (contemporary parchment) + 166 + i (contemporary parchment) + ii (modern parchment); 168 × 113 (90 × 59) mm. Collation beginning with the first contemporary flyleaf: 1–2^{8} 3^{8}(+ 1, f. 14) 4^{8}(+ 4, f. 26; + 6, f. 28; + 10, f. 32) 5^{8}(+ 2, f. 35; + 5, f. 38; + 10, f. 43) 6^{8}(+ 4, f. 48; + 6, f. 50) 7^{8} 8^{8}(+ 1, f. 63) 9^{8}(+ a leaf in the second half) 10–11^{8} 12^{8}(+6, f. 102) 13^{6}(2 central "bifolia" composed of singletons) 14^{10} 15^{8}(+1, f. 122; −9, cancelled by scribe) 16^{8} 17^{8}(+2, f. 139; +5, f. 142; +11, f. 148) 18^{8} 19^{6} 20^{4}. Evidence of quire signatures as letters of the alphabet in red ink in the lower margin of the first leaf recto, beginning with "a" on f. i (thus including the calendar); quire and leaf signatures in brown ink as letters and roman numerals, apparently through each entire gathering, i–viii, but excluding the added illuminated leaves. In quire 14, leaf signatures as arabic numerals. 19 long lines, ruled in ink with single bounding lines. Written in gothic book hands by 3 scribes: i, ff. 1–79v, 123–164; ii, ff. 81–111v (quires 10–13, except for occasional leaves in a more formal script: ff. 81r–v, 102r–v, 109r–v); iii, ff. 112–119v (quire 14).

Eighty-two miniatures by several artists corresponding generally to the divisions in scribal hands. With scribe i, 14 full page miniatures on inserted singletons, blank on the recto and often interrupting the text. With scribe ii, the rosary, 55 (+ 1 miniature for the Jerome suffrage to fill out the quire) integral miniatures by a second main artist, above 3 to 5 lines of text. With scribe iii, 12 10-line miniatures by a third main artist for the suffrages in quire 14.

The full page miniatures associated with scribe i, on inserted singletons and not part of the original plan of decoration, have 2 possible border styles: the first with a narrow gold band around both miniature and border, and with a wide border of strewn flowers, insects and birds set against a dense gold ground; in the second style, the narrow gold band surrounds only the miniature, the border itself is narrower and the ground of the border is a thin gold wash; the illuminations are: f. 14v, with the first style of border, although here on natural parchment ground, Crucifixion with Mary and John; f. 26v, with the first style of border including a Pelican in her Piety, Agony in the Garden; f. 28v, with the second style of border, Betrayal with Peter about to cut off Malchus' ear; f. 32v, with the second style of border, Christ before Pilate; f. 35v, with the first style of border, Scourging at the pillar (by a different artist?); f. 38v, with the second style of border, Mocking of Christ, with the Crown of Thorns; f. 43v, with the second style of border, Crucifixion with Mary and John on Christ's right, Mary Magdalene at the foot of the Cross, and the soldiers on Christ's left; f. 48v, with the first style of border, Deposition from the Cross; f. 50v, with the second style of border, Entombment; f. 63v, with the double gold bands of the first style of border but as grey walls with niches from which various people watch the main scene, St. Gregory's Mass; f. 122v, with the second style of border, David in prayer; f. 139v, with the second style of border, the martyrdom of Erasmus; f. 142v, with the second style of border, Christopher crossing the river with the Christ Child on his shoulders; f. 148, the Virgin, ¾ length, holding the Child, on a crescent. Major initials in this section, 8- or 6-line gold initials on patterned blue or maroon grounds with infilling of the other color (ff. 15, 29, 64, 143) or as branchy gold acanthus stems on a shaded pink ground (f. 123). Secondary initials, 6- to 3-line, usually blue (but red on ff. 55, 59, 60, 132, 155v, 158, 160) with void design on the letter itself and with good quality penwork flourishing of the other color, touched in green; 2- and 1-line initials alternating plain red and blue; some initials within the text touched in red; rubrics throughout.

In the rosary (art. 6), copied by scribe ii, is a similar, but not identical, combination of rosary text and iconographic sequence as in the Latin *Rosarium Beatae Mariae Virginis,* printed by Gerard Leeu (?) in Antwerp, 1489 (Hain 13968) as noticed by S. Hindman and J. D. Farquhar, *Pen to Press: Illustrated Manuscripts and Printed Books in the First Century of Printing* (University of Maryland Art Department Gallery, 15 September–23 October 1977) pp. 120–21 and figs. 45, 46 of the *Rosarium* and fig. 47 of HM 1140, ff. 103v–104. Another related text and analogous miniature style (but not border style) is found in London, Brit. Lib., Add. 15525,[1] reproduced in A. W. Byvanck, *La Miniature Hollandaise* (The Hague 1925) pp. 57–58 n. 130 and pl. 196, figs. 94, 95; here, borders of strewn flowers, birds and insects against an orange-tinged yellow ground, with both miniature and border outlined in red; on the 3 leaves in this section copied by a different scribe (ff. 81r–v, 102r–v, 109r–v), slightly wider borders with a gold wash ground and a narrow gold frame around miniatures executed by a different artist; interventions by this scribe and artist seem to coincide with differences in the iconographic series between HM 1140 and the printed *Rosarium.* The illustrations are: f. 81, rosary with the 4 Wounds of the hands and feet around the perimeter and the Sacred Heart in the center; f. 81v, rosary with the Five Wounds, positioned differently (this and the preceding miniature by a different artist); f. 82, Annunciation; f. 82v, Visitation; f. 83, Annunciation to the shepherds; f. 83v, Adoration of the shepherds; f. 84, Circumcision; f. 84v, Adoration of the Magi; f. 85, Presentation in the temple; f. 85v, Simeon holding the baby Jesus; f. 86, rosary with the Five Wounds, positioned differently; f. 87, Flight into Egypt, with idols falling off columns; f. 87v, Jesus disputing with the Elders in the temple; f. 88, Mary weaving with the child Jesus helping; f. 88v, Baptism of Christ in the river Jordan; f. 89, Temptation of Christ in the desert; f. 89v, Marriage at Cana; f. 90, Jesus liberating a man from a demon and making a cripple walk, while another man walks away, carrying his bed; f. 90v, Raising of Lazarus; f. 91, Mary Magdalene anointing Christ's feet; f. 91v, Last Supper; f. 92, rosary with the Five Wounds, positioned differently; f. 93, Agony in the Garden; f. 93v, Betrayal of Christ; f. 94, Christ before Annas; f. 94v, Slapping of Christ; f. 95, Christ before Pilate; f. 95v, Christ before Herod (this miniature traced through from the recto of the leaf); f. 96, Scourging at the pillar; f. 96v, Mocking of Christ; f.

97, Ecce Homo; f. 97v, Road to Calvary, with spike blocks hanging from Christ's waist; f. 98, rosary with the Five Wounds, positioned differently; f. 99, Nailing to the Cross; f. 99v, Christ on the Cross, asking his Father to forgive his tormentors; f. 100, Christ on the Cross between the two thieves; f. 100v, Mary and John the Evangelist beside the Cross (text with prayer to Mary); f. 101, Mary and John the Evangelist beside the Cross (text with prayer referring to John); f. 101v, Christ on the Cross in despair; f. 102, Christ being offered the bitter sponge by a soldier (Longinus!); f. 102v, Christ being offered the bitter sponge by Stephaton (this and the preceding miniature by a different artist); f. 103, Crucifixion with soldiers throwing dice for the unseamed robe; f. 103v, Wounding of Christ's side; f. 104, rosary with the Five Wounds, positioned differently; f. 105, Deposition from the Cross; f. 105v, Entombment; f. 106, Descent into Hell; f. 106v, Resurrection; f. 107, Christ appearing to the Apostles; f. 107v, Ascension; f. 108, Pentecost; f. 108v, Assumption of the Virgin; f. 109, Last Judgment; f. 109v, Gnadenstuhl (this and the preceding miniature by a different artist); f. 110, rosary with the Five Wounds, positioned differently; f. 111, Jerome standing with the lion (suffrage). In this section, plain 2- and 1-line red or blue initials; some initials within the the text slashed in red; red rubrics.

In quire 14, miniatures by a third artist who has painted over the lines ruled for the text; borders of strewn flowers on a pale yellow wash; the miniatures are: f. 112, owner portrait of a woman kneeling in prayer with her guardian angel beside her; f. 113, Michael; f. 113v, John the Baptist; f. 114, John the Evangelist with the snaky chalice; f. 114v, Peter and Paul; f. 115v, Cornelius holding horn and staff; f. 116, Martin; f. 116v, Anne seated beside Mary, who holds the baby Jesus out to her; f. 117, Catherine of Alexandria; f. 118, Barbara holding her tower; f. 118v, Agnes; f. 119, All Saints. In this section, plain 2-line alternating red and blue initials; some initials within the text slashed in red; rubrics throughout. On f. 28, upside down, an incomplete but finely done sketch of the Annunciation.

Bound by Mercier for Robert Hoe (his monogram on front doublure) in brown mosaic morocco, elaborately tooled and inlaid with an overall pattern of flowers within quatrefoils in the style of Le Monnier; white parchment doublures, gilt tooled with cherub heads and stars; gauffered and gilt edges.

Written at the end of the fifteenth century in the northwestern Netherlands, possibly for use in the diocese of Utrecht, as suggested by the saints in the calendar and litany; the owner portrait on f. 112 is of a woman. Birth and death notices of the Van Nuissenborch family of Dordrecht, from 1598 to 1609, on the front and back flyleaves; on f. ii recto-verso, 18 coats of arms, identified, and with tinctures labelled, of which the first is that of Nuyssenburg of Dordrecht (Rietstap, vol. 4, pl. 299). Belonged to Robert Hoe: reproduced in *One hundred and seventy-six historic and artistic Book-bindings . . . from the Library of Robert Hoe* (New York 1895) vol. 2, pl. 166; *Cat.* (1909) pp. 68–70; his sale, Anderson, New York, 1911, pt. I, n. 2150 to G. D. Smith. Smith Cat. 1 (1911) s. n. (described on the back cover) to Henry E. Huntington in April 1912.

Bibliography: De Ricci, 97.

[1] We thank Prof. James Marrow for this information.

HM 1141 — France, s. XV^med
BOOK OF HOURS, use of Besançon — *fig. 101*

1. ff. 1–12v: Full calendar in French, alternating red and blue with major feasts in gold; f. 13r–v, ruled, but blank.

2. ff. 14–21v: Pericopes of the Gospels, the set of them ending with the prayer, Protector in te sperancium . . . [Perdrizet, 25].

3. ff. 22–93v: Hours of the Virgin, use of Besançon; 9 lessons at matins, each set of 3 preceded by the psalms for the weekdays [Pss. 8, 18, 23; 41, 45, 86; 95, 96, 97]; from lauds to compline, the prayers of John the Evangelist, Ecclesiam tuam quesumus domine . . . and the antiphon, Gaude virgo mater christi que per aurem concepisti . . . , with versicle, response and prayer, Omnipotens sempiterne deus qui beatissimam et gloriosissimam virginem mariam in conceptu . . . [*HE*, 63–64].

4. ff. 94–99: Short hours of the Cross.

5. ff. 99v–103v: Short hours of the Holy Spirit.

6. ff. 104–122: Penitential psalms and litany, including Quentin, Denis, Maurice among the martyrs; Brictius, Remigius, Germanus, and Columban among the confessors; Genevieve and Bridget among the virgins.

7. ff. 122v–171: Office of the Dead, use of Besançon.

8. ff. 171–177v: *Oratio valde devota,* Obsecro te . . . et michi miserrima famula tua N. . . . [Leroquais, *LH* 2:346]; *oratio,* O Intemerata . . . orbis terrarum. Inclina mater . . . [Wilmart, 488–90].

9. ff. 178–188: Doulce dame de misericorde . . . [Leroquais, *LH* 2:310–11]; Doulz dieux pere saincte trinitey et ung dieu . . . [Leroquais, *LH* 2:309–10]; O tres certaine esperance dame et deffenderesse . . . [Sonet 1538]; ff. 188v–189v, ruled, but blank.

Parchment, ff. iii (modern paper, with tooled parchment doublure glued to the recto of f. i) + ii (modern parchment) + 189 + ii (modern parchment) + iii (modern paper, with tooled parchment doublure glued to the verso of the last leaf); 230 × 165 (100 × 70) mm. 1^6 2^6(+ 7, f. 13) 3^8(?, ff. 14–21) 4–13^8 14^2(ff. 102–103) 15–24^8 25^6. Catchwords in center lower margin in scripts of varying degree of formality. 15 long lines, ruled in pale red ink; pricking usually visible. Written in a gothic book hand, in 2 sizes according to liturgical function; ff. 178–188, possibly by a different hand.

Eighteen large miniatures, by an artist who has worked on other Besançon books of hours, e.g. Cambridge, Fitzwilliam Museum MSS 69 and 70, and New York, Public Library MS 41[1]; for this last manuscript, see Plummer, *Last Flowering,* n. 76 with a plate of f. 20; vivid dark colors with a silvery sky and scurrying gold clouds, in arched compartments above 3 lines of text, with both text and miniature enclosed by a decorated wide U-shape frame; the outer border is of dense blue and gold acanthus leaves, flowers, berries, and many grotesques. The miniatures are: f. 14 (Gospel of John), John on Patmos, shown clearly as an island; f. 16, Luke holding his pen up as if to check the point; f. 18, Matthew sharpening his pen; f. 20, Mark; f. 22 (Hours of the Virgin), Annunciation; f. 47 (Lauds), Visitation, in a hilly countryside with large white stones scattered in the foreground; f. 60 (Prime), Nativity, with Mary, another woman and Joseph holding a candle, all kneeling around a rather large baby Jesus, while 3 small angels sing from scrolls in the sky above the stall; f. 65v (Terce), Annunciation to the shepherds; large white stones on the path; f. 71 (Sext), Adoration of the Magi, with the Virgin and Child on a red-draped bed and 2 small angels holding scrolls above the stall; the owners' coat of arms in the lower margin (see below); f. 75v (None), frame around the miniature is unfinished; Presentation in the temple; f. 81 (Vespers), Flight into Egypt, the road with scattered large stones; f. 88v (Compline), Coronation of the Virgin by God the Father, as Jesus blesses and the Dove hovers between them; f. 94 (Hours of the Cross), Crucifixion with the INRI legend on a rather large piece of wood at the top of the cross, and on either side, Mary, and John holding an open book; f. 99v (Hours of the Holy Spirit), Pentecost with the Virgin, on a larger scale than the apostles, seated on a raised dias in the middle of the group with an open book on her knees; f. 104 (Penitential psalms), David kneeling in prayer with his hands open wide, before a half-length figure of God in the sky; f. 122v (Office of the Dead), Raising of Lazarus, with large white rocks in the foreground; f. 178 (Doulce dame de misericorde), owner portrait of a woman, in a blue dress and white veil, kneeling before the Virgin and Child; in the foreground, a cradle and a dog on a cushion; f. 184 (Doulz dieux pere saincte trinitey), Last Judgment, with Christ sitting on a rainbow, his feet resting on a tripart globe (earth, air and water), while 4 blue angels blow their trumpets and the dead rise from their graves. On f. 171 (Obsecro te) a bracket border of the same type as above; traced band borders in the outer margin of every page, each with a grotesque, running the length of the text, and separated from it by a decorated gold strip; these borders also on ff. 188v–189v on ruled, but otherwise blank, leaves. The band borders of the calendar include the monthly occupation on the recto and the zodiac symbol on the verso; on f. 5v, the two Gemini support a coat of arms (see below). 3-line initials in white-patterned blue on a maroon ground decorated with painted gold, or in white-decorated pink with green leaf infilling against a blue ground; occasionally the infilling is of an older style with colored trilobe leaves. 2-line initials, in alternating pink or blue against a gold ground with trilobe leaf infilling; 1-line initials in gold with the two colors as ground and infilling; ribbon line fillers in the same colors; initials within the text washed in yellow. Rubrics throughout.

Bound, s. XIX, in dark blue morocco by Simier and elaborately gilt by Debèse, with tooled parchment doublures; gauffered gilt edges; remains of 2 silver-gilt fore edge clasps.

Written in the middle of the fifteenth century for use in Besançon to judge by the Hours of the Virgin and the Office of the Dead. Arms on f. 5v, gules a bend argent, of the Neufchâtel family. Arms on f. 71 of Guy de La Baume, count of Montrevel (d. 1516; Montrevel is in the department of the Ain) and his wife Jeanne de Longwy: per pale, 1, or a bend indented azure (de la Baume; see Rietstap, vol. 1, pl. 145); 2, azure a bend or (Longwy; see Rietstap, vol. 4, pl. 86). Notes relating to the Rye and Longwy families for the years 1557–67 are on the first leaves of the calendar (the three sons of Simon de Rye and Jeanne de La Baume married the three daughters of Christophe de Longwy and Jeanne de Neufchâtel); a transcription of these notes and information regarding the family members mentioned in them have been carefully copied out in red and black ink on ff. ii–iii verso; the transcription is signed and dated, although by a different hand, "19 Avril 1862. E. M. Bancel"; his sale, Paris, 8 May 1882, n. 12 to Ellis. The manuscript belonged to E. Dwight Church (1835–1908); see his *Catalogue of . . . English Literature* (1909) vol. 1, n. 403 with a plate of f. 65v. The Church collection was acquired by Henry E. Huntington in 1911.

Bibliography: De Ricci, 97.

[1] We are indebted to Prof. James Marrow for this information.

HM 1142 — France, s. XV^{in}
BOOK OF HOURS, use of Paris — *fig. 85*

1. ff. 1–12v: Full calendar in French of the type printed by Perdrizet; major feasts in gold, the others alternating red and blue.

2. ff. 13–22v: Pericopes of the Gospels; Obsecro te . . . Et michi famulo tuo N. impetres. . . [Leroquais, *LH* 2:346]; *oratio,* O Intemerata . . . orbis terrarum, de te enim . . . [Wilmart, 494–95]; f. 23r–v, ruled, but blank.

3. ff. 24–77v: Hours of the Virgin, use of Paris; 9 psalms and lessons at matins with rubrics giving divisions for the nocturns; the prayer, Ecclesiam tuam quesumus domine benignus . . . from lauds to compline at the end of each hour.

4. ff. 78–92v: Penitential psalms and litany, including Ivo, Evurtius, Amand ("amane") and Aegidius among the confessors; Genevieve and Lucia among the virgins; f. 78 was originally the opening leaf of the Hours of the Cross: the first text has been erased and the beginning of the Penitential psalms written in, in an imitative gothic script (s. XVII?).

5. ff. 93–94v, 96–97v, 98r–v, 95r–v: //ciux flans et l'alaitastes . . . Doulce dame priez luy pour moy et pour toutes pe// [the 15 Joys, beginning and ending defectively; Leroquais, *LH* 2:310–11]; //que vous prinstes de vostre propre sapience . . . le larron en la crois quant il vous dist sire remembres// [the 7 Requests, beginning and ending defectively; Leroquais, *LH* 2:309–10].

6. ff. 99–100: Short hours of the Cross, with the offices for none, vespers and compline only.

7. ff. 100v–137v: Office of the Dead, use of Paris; f. 100v was originally the opening leaf for the Hours of the Holy Spirit, as indicated by the rubric, *de sancto spiritu,* on f. 100; the first text was erased and the beginning of the Office of the Dead written in, in an imitative gothic script (s. XVII?).

8. ff. 138–139: Suffrage of Christopher, added in a different hand [. . . michi famulo tuo . . .]; ff. 139v–142v, ruled, but blank.

Parchment, ff. i (paper) + 142 + i (paper); 186 × 128 (99 × 65) mm. 1^{12} 2^{8} 3^{4}(–4, excised) 4–9^{8} 10^{6}(through f. 77) 11^{8}(–1, which has been replaced by a leaf, now f. 78, once at the end of another quire, bearing the catchword "et mortem") 12^{8}(–8, after f. 92) ff. 93–102 (now all singletons with f. 95 bound out of order and with leaves missing before ff. 93 and 98) 13–17^{8}. Catchwords in a cursive script in the center lower margin. 16 long lines, ruled in pale red ink. Written in 2 sizes of a gothic book hand; another gothic script, s. XV, on ff. 138–139; imitative gothic scripts on ff. 78r–v and 100v.

Ten miniatures, usually in square compartments above 5 lines of text, attributed to the Boethius Illuminator by M. Meiss, *French Painting in the time of Jean de Berry: The Limbourgs and their Contemporaries* (New York 1974) 372; see also his *French Painting in the Time of Jean de Berry: The Late Fourteenth Century and the Patronage of the Duke* (London 1967) 354. Both text and miniature enclosed by wide bands of a U-frame deriving from initials and usually composed of pink, blue and gold segments, which sprout narrow pink and blue branches at the four corners; the outer border contains colored and gold trilobe leaves, dots and flowers. The miniatures are: f. 24 (Hours of the Virgin), Annunciation, against a diapered background with God the Father appearing in the arch at the top of the miniature in a gold-ruffled blue aperture, with a lute-playing angel on either side; the U-frame is a gold band decorated with green, orange, and blue leaves; several grotesques in the outer border; f. 43v (Lauds), Visitation, against a diapered background; a man playing a vielle in the border; f. 52v (Prime), Nativity, with a coarsely shaded sky as background; Mary, sitting on a bed, holds the Child, while Joseph sits at a table, his head propped up on his elbow; in the border, a half-human grotesque; f. 57v (Terce), Adoration of the Magi; Joseph not present; in the border, a man sitting with a shield (?) in his hand; f. 61v (Sext), Annunciation to the shepherds, against a dark blue scroll background, with a figure of a man in the border; f. 65 (None), Presentation in the temple, against a diapered background; several grotesques and flowers in the border; f. 68v (Vespers), Flight into Egypt, against a diapered background; in the border, an old man seated tailor-style, reading; f. 74 (Compline), Coronation of the Virgin, with Jesus blessing her; diapered background; in the border, an angel playing a vielle and a grotesque; f. 78 (intended for the Hours of the Cross; now used for the Penitential psalms), Crucifixion, against a diapered ground; f. 100v (intended for the Hours of the Holy Spirit, but now used for the Office of the Dead), Pentecost, with the Dove descending from a white-ruffled blue aperture in the diapered background; a bearded man sits in the border. 3-line initials in white-decorated pink or blue against a burnished gold ground with colored trilobe leaf infilling; 3-, 2- and 1-line initials in burnished gold on pink grounds with blue infilling, or vice versa; ribbon line fillers in the same colors. Borders on every page, including those of the calendar, of a narrow gold and color strip running the length of the text in the outer margin and flourished on 3 sides in bracket form with black ink vines of gold trilobe leaves and blue and pink star-flowers; some leaves contain traced grotesque dragons emerging from either end of the gold and color strip: ff. 25r–v, 29r–v, 56r–v, 63r–v. Figures in the outer borders of ff. 32 (a man with a lute), 40 (a grotesque), 48 (a man reading, holding a sword), 56 (a man with a man-faced shield), 64 (a grotesque), 111 (a half-human grotesque). Where 3- or 2-line initials occur on a recto, a leafy spray grows from the left of the initial into the margin (on the versos, the margin to the left of the initial already contains the bracket border). A bright green leafy spray in the space between text and ivy vine of certain conjugate leaves: 25r–v and 30r–v, 40r–v and 47r–v, 49r–v and 54r–v, 58r–v and 61r–v. Rubrics in an orange-tinged red.

Bound, s. XVII^{ex}, in French brown morocco with later labels on the spine: "Missale Romanum. MSS. In Membrana"; gilt edges.

Written in France in the early fifteenth century; at a later date, perhaps in the seventeenth century when the book was bound in its present form, an effort was made to complete the by-then missing sections at the beginning of the Penitential psalms and of the Office of the dead, by partially erasing (some of the original initials were left untouched) and re-writing respectively the opening leaves of the Hours of the Cross and of the Holy Spirit. Belonged to E. Dwight Church (1835–1908) and is described in his *Catalogue . . . of English Literature* (1909) vol. 1, n. 407 with a plate of f. 43v. The Church collection was acquired by Henry E. Huntington in 1911.

Bibliography: De Ricci, 97.

HM 1143 — France, s. XV^2
BOOK OF HOURS, use of Rome — *fig. 121*

1. ff. 1–12v: Full calendar in French alternating red and blue with major feasts in gold; included are the feasts of Martin (4 July, in gold), Gatianus (23 October), Martin (11 November, in gold), Brictius (13 November) Gatianus (18 December), Perpetuus (30 December).

2. ff. 13–25v: Pericopes of the Gospels; Passion according to John.

3. ff. 26–34v: *Oratio beate marie virginis,* Obsecro te . . . [masculine forms; Leroquais, *LH* 2:346]; *Alia oratio beate marie,* O intemerata . . . orbis terrarum. De te enim . . . [Wilmart, 494–95]; *Sequitur alia oratio beate marie,* Sancta maria virgo virginum mater christi regina celorum noli me miserum propter peccata mea despicere . . . ; *Sanctus bernardus,* Exultet celum terra ridet mundus gaudet . . . , Virginis eximie dum veneris ante figuram . . . ; *Oratio,* Ave maria gratia plena . . . ; *Oratio beate marie,* Stabat mater dolorosa . . . [*RH* 19416]; *Oratio,* Omnipotens sempiterne deus qui gloriose virginis marie corpus . . .

4. ff. 35–79: Hours of the Virgin, use of Rome; weekly variations of the psalms at matins set into the text before the lessons; prayers to All Saints and for peace from lauds to compline; opening leaf of compline missing between ff. 76–77; f. 79v, ruled, but blank, except for rubric to the Hours of the Cross.

5. ff. 80–83v: Short hours of the Cross.

6. ff. 84–87: Short hours of the Holy Spirit; f. 87v, ruled, but blank.

7. ff. 88–103v: Penitential psalms and litany, including Denis and Maurice among the martyrs; Eligius, Ivo and Claude among the confessors; Radegundis, Genevieve, Gertrude and Avia among the virgins; *Sequuntur nomina beate virginis marie magne efficatie,* Digna virgo flos nubes regina theototos [*sic*] theotota Imperatrix . . .

8. ff. 104–135: Office of the Dead, use of Rome.

9. ff. 135v–144: Suffrages of Michael, John the Baptist, John the Evangelist, Peter and Paul, Christopher, George, Adrian, Sebastian, James the Greater, Bernard, Catherine of Alexandria, Mary Magdalene, Martha, Apollonia, Barbara.

10. ff. 144v–155: Domine ihesu christe pastor bone conserva iustos parce peccatoribus . . . ; *Oratio,* Benignissime ac misericordissime domine deus meus si feci ut essem inimicus tuus . . . ; *Oratio,* Domine deus mortem domini nostri ihesu christi obitio inter me et iudicium tuum . . . ; *Oratio,* Domine ihesu christe deprecor te per illas sanctas lacrimas quas pio amore effudisti . . . ; *Oratio,* Creator et rector machine mundi tuum enim catholicum servientem velis taliter inmerere . . . , with versicle, response and prayer, Congregati sunt inimici nostri et se glorificant . . . , with versicle, response and prayer, Benignissime et misericordissime salvator piissime ihesu per merita tue sacratissime incarnationis . . . ; *Oratio,* Firmiter credens ihesum nazarenum esse filium dei . . . ; *oratio,* Domine ihesu christe qui tres magos orientales . . . [different from the version in *HE,* 75]; Firmiter et puro corde credo et ore confiteor ad plenum sanctam fidem catholicam . . . ; *Oratio,* Tu sancte iohannes qui ostendisti mundi tollentem peccata . . . ; *Oratio,* Sana me domine tu cuius es sanare . . . ; Deus propicius esto michi peccatori . . . [Römer, i, 374–75]; *Oratio,* Ne reminiscaris domine delicta nostra . . . ; *Oratio,* Domine ihesu christe qui hanc sacratissimam carnem . . . [Wilmart, 378, n.]; *Oratio,* Ave gloriosum et preciosum corpus domini nostri ihesu christi in manibus sacerdotis . . . ; *Clemens papa V^tus^ dedit remissionem* . . . , Sancte et individue trinitatis ihesu christe crucifixe . . . ; *Oroison tres devote,* Ie te commans N. a dieu le Roy puissant par celle mesmes benediction . . . [Sonet 837]; *Oratio,* Beatus es rex abagar qui non me vidisti . . . ; *Oratio,* Ego rex abagar diligo te ut salus sis . . . ; *Oratio,* Deus qui tres magos orientales . . . [different from the version in *HE,* 75, and from that on f. 148].

11. ff. 155v–186v: *Incipiunt flores psalmorum editi a beato gregorio papa,* Miserere mei deus miserere mei et exaudi oracionem meam. Miserere mei domine quoniam infirmus sum sana me domine quoniam conturbata sunt ossa mea. Miserere mei domine quoniam tribulor . . .

12. ff. 187–194v: *Incipit psalterium sancti augustini episcopi,* [Prayer:] Domine sancte pater omnipotens eterne deus per meritum unigeniti filii tui infunde michi gratiam spiritus sancti ut in horum psalmorum cotidiana frequentia . . . , [f. 187v, Text:] Domine deus omnipotens rex eterne glorie, qui eum sanctis [*sic*] esse beatum qui viam peccatorum spernens . . . [*PL* 40:1135–1138].

13. ff. 195–207v: *Incipit psalterium sancti ieronimi,* Suscipere et exaudire digneris domine deus pater omnipotens hos versiculos tibi consecratos quos ego

indignus peccator decantare cupio . . . , Verba mea auribus percipe . . . , *Oratio,* Suscipere et exaudire digneris deus pater omnipotens hos versiculos quos ego indignus peccator cantavi . . . [*HE,* 116–22]; ff. 208–209v, ruled, but blank.

Parchment, ff. ii (modern parchment) + ii (contemporary parchment, ruled, but blank) + 209 + ii (modern parchment); 195 × 136 (100 × 67) mm. $1–2^6$ $3–4^8$ 5^6(through f. 34) $6–10^8$ 11^6(+ 4, f. 79) 12^6(through f. 87) $13–14^8$(through f. 103) $15–27^8$ 28^2. Quires and leaves signed beginning with quire 19, f. 130, with letters of the alphabet (a–i) and arabic numerals in the upper left hand corner of the band border. 18 long lines, ruled in pale red ink. Written in a bâtarde script, in 2 sizes according to liturgical function.

Thirty-one large miniatures of varying quality by an artist known as the Master of the Vienna Mamerot[1] after his illustrations in Sébastien Mamerot's *Histoire et faits des neuf Preux et des neuf Preuses* in Vienna (Öst. Nationalbibl., Cod. 2577–78); see Plummer, *Last Flowering,* n. 67 citing HM 1143. The miniatures are above 3 lines of text in arched compartments, enclosed by borders of blue and gold acanthus leaves, flowers and strawberries. The miniatures are: f. 13, John on Patmos with a cityscape in the background; f. 14v, Luke writing, with his ox and a painting of the Virgin in front of him; f. 16, Matthew seated frontally at a saw-horse desk; f. 17v, Mark in a room supported by pink twined columns; f. 18v (Passion according to John), Betrayal in a night-time garden scene, with a high fence, Peter sheathing his sword and the soldiers crowding around Jesus and Judas; f. 26 (Obsecro te), by a different artist, Pietà, with only the feet of the 2 thieves visible on the crosses, the rest being beyond the top of the miniature; large single stones scattered prominently in the foreground; f. 32 (Sancta maria virgo virginum), the owner, a man, kneeling before the enthroned Virgin who is nursing the Child, with a cityscape behind; f. 35 (Hours of the Virgin), Annunciation, as if in a gothic church with gold twined columns; the angel's wings are of peacock feathers; the owner's arms in the border (see below); f. 49 (Lauds), Visitation, in which Elizabeth appears quite old; f. 57v (Prime), Nativity, with the shepherds kneeling to the right outside the shed, and peering in, in a composition closely dependent upon that of Fouquet in the Hours of Etienne Chevalier in Chantilly, reproduced, for example, in P. Wescher, *Jean Fouquet and his Time* (trans., New York 1947) pl. 3; f. 61 (Terce), Annunciation to the shepherds, one of whom wears a diagonally striped purple and gold tunic; f. 64v (Sext), Adoration of the Magi, before a red draped city house; a *pentimento* the first king's hat (?) is on the ground before the Virgin; f. 67v (None), Presentation in the temple, with Simeon, in plain blue dress, supporting the Child as it turns back to its Mother; f. 71 (Vespers), Flight into Egypt; illumination for compline missing, as indicated by the offset of a full border on f. 76v; f. 80 (Hours of the Cross), Crucifixion with Jesus and the thieves, while below Mary, on her knees, is being supported by John, and the soldiers, some on horseback, crowd about; f. 84 (Hours of the Holy Spirit), Pentecost, with Mary sitting somewhat apart, to the right, in a large gothic room, the vaulting held up by pink twined columns; f. 88 (Penitential psalms), the young David cutting off Goliath's head, while sheep in the middleground graze or look back at the fighting soldiers; f. 104 (Office of the Dead), the "Trois Vifs et Trois Morts" at a wayside cross; f. 135v, Michael in mid-air above large prominent rocks, stabbing a female devil and looking at another with its tongue out; f. 136v, John the Evangelist and John the Baptist, above 4 lines of text, in one illumination, holding respectively the snake-filled chalice and the Lamb, under a vaulted ceiling supported by a lavender twined column in the center back, and by jewel-studded gold columns at the sides; f. 137v, Peter and Paul, above 4 lines of text; f. 138v, George and Christopher, above 4 lines of text with George, the dragon and the princess in the foreground, and Christopher, the Christ Child and the hermit in the middle and background; f. 139v, Adrian and Sebastian, above 4 lines of text; f. 140v, Bernard and James, above 4 lines of text, each with a book; f. 141v, Catherine of Alexandria, above 4 lines of text, with the angel about to destroy the wheel; f. 142v, Mary Magdalene and Martha, above 4 lines of text, the one with her jar of ointment, and the other holding the container of holy water and the dragon by a leash; the dragon appears to be swallowing someone (conflation with Margaret?); f. 143v, Apollonia and Barbara, above 4 lines of text, in a green-draped room with pink twined columns at either side; f. 144v (Domine ihesu christe pastor), above 4 lines of text, Christ in glory with the symbols of the 4 Evangelists in camaïeu d'or against a blue ground in the 4 corners; f. 155v (*flores psalmorum . . . a gregorio papa*), above 4 lines of text, a scholar, presumably Gregory, dressed in a large green over-tunic and blue headdress, standing reading from a book with other books on the shelves behind him; 2 gold columns frame the scene; f. 187 (*psalterium sancti augustini*), a scholar, presumably Augustine, in a blue tunic with the hood up, a book under his arm and others behind him on shelves, standing in a gold columned room; f. 195 (Psalter of St. Jerome), above 4 lines of text, by the same artist as the Pietà on f. 26, Christ rising from the tomb in a landscape scattered with large rocks. Traced band borders in the outer margin of every page, running the length of the text, composed of blue and gold acanthus leaves, flowers and strawberries. One 5-line initial (f. 29, O intemerata), and the 3- and 2-line initials in white-patterned blue on a burnished gold ground, with colored trilobe leaf infilling; 1-line initials in burnished gold with pink or blue infilling against ground of the other color; in the same colors are ribbon line fillers, dots and 3-leaf flowers (for the same purpose). Rubrics in red.

Bound by F. Bedford in brown morocco; gilt edges.

Written in France during the second half of the fifteenth century, perhaps for use in the diocese of Tours as suggested by the saints in the calendar. The first owner appears kneeling before the Virgin on f. 32; his arms are in the borders of f. 35: barry of six or and sable. Belonged to William Bragge (1823–84); his sale, Sotheby's, 7 June 1876, lot 476 to B. F. Stevens. Belonged to Robert Hoe: Grolier Club (1892) n. 19; Bierstadt (1895) p. 24 with a plate of f. 32; *Cat.* (1909) pp. 56–57; his sale, Anderson, New York, 1912, pt. IV, n. 2338 to G. D. Smith. Precise source and date of acquisition by Henry E. Huntington unknown.

Bibliography: De Ricci, 97.

---

[1] We thank Mme Nicole Reynaud for assistance with this identification.

HM 1144 — Flanders, s. XV^{med}
BOOK OF HOURS, Sarum use

1. ff. 1–12v: Calendar with major feasts in red; includes David (1 March), Visitation (2 July, in red), Anne (26 July, in red); Thomas of Canterbury and the popes have been erased; Latin month verses [Walther, *Initia* 14563] and Cisiojanus syllables, here beginning "Cisioianed" of which a version is printed in Grotefend, 24–25.

2. ff. 13–21 [f. 13, blank]: *Secuntur quindecim orationes composite secundum passionem domini nostri ihesu christi,* O domine ihesu christe eterna dulcedo . . . [*HE,* 76–80]; f. 21v, ruled, but blank.

3. ff. 22–40v [f. 22, blank]: *De sancta trinitate oratio devota,* Domine deus omnipotens pater et filius et spiritus sanctus da michi famulo tuo victoriam . . . with cues of Pss. 53 and 66, the prayer, Libera me domine ihesu christe fili dei vivi . . . , and, at the end, the cue for Ps. 129 [de la Mare, *Lyell Cat.,* 373, n. 88]; suffrages of John the Baptist [Gaude iohannes baptista . . . , *RH* 26988], George, Christopher, Anne, Mary Magdalene [Gaude pia magdalena

. . . , *RH* 6895], Catherine of Alexandria [Gaude virgo catherina . . . , *RH* 6991], Margaret [Gaude virgo margareta . . . , *RH* 7011], Barbara.

4. ff. 41–89v [f. 41, blank]: *Incipiunt hore beate marie virginis secundum consuetudinem anglie;* after lauds suffrages of the Holy Spirit, the Trinity, the Cross, Michael, John the Baptist [Inter natos mulierum . . .], Peter and Paul, Andrew, Lawrence, Stephen; ff. 61v–62, erasure of 11 lines, with the remaining initial "T" for the antiphon ("Tu per thome sanguinem . . ."?) and the "D" for the prayer ("Deus pro cuius ecclesia gloriosus pontifex et martir thomas . . ."?), presumably for Thomas of Canterbury; Nicholas, Mary Magdalene [Maria ergo unxit pedes . . .], Catherine of Alexandria [Virgo sancta catherina . . . , *RH* 34646], Margaret [Erat autem marguareta (*sic*) . . .], All Saints, for peace; hours of the Cross worked in; after compline, Salve Regina and the set of versicles, Virgo mater ecclesie . . . , and the prayer, Omnipotens sempiterne deus qui gloriose virginis et matris marie corpus et animam . . . [*HE,* 62–63].

5. ff. 89v–103: *Quinque gaudia beate marie virginis,* Gaude virgo mater christi que per aurem concepisti . . . , with the prayer, Deus qui beatissimam virginem mariam in conceptu . . . [*HE,* 63–64]; *Has videas laudes* . . . , Salve virgo virginum . . . [a farcing of the Salve Regina, attributed to Bonaventure, *Opera* (Vatican 1668) 6:466–67], and the prayer, Deus qui de beate marie virginis utero . . . [Bruylants, *Oraisons* vol. 2, n. 230]; *ad virginem mariam oratio,* O Intemerata . . . orbis terrarum. Inclina mater . . . [Wilmart, 488–90]; *Alia oratio,* Obsecro te . . . et michi famulo tuo impetres . . . [Leroquais, *LH* 2:346]; *Quicunque hec septem gaudia . . . a domino papa* [this word erased] *clemente qui hec septem gaudia proprio stilo composuit,* Virgo templum trinitatis . . . [Philippus de Grevia; Wilmart, 329, n.]; f. 103v, ruled, but blank.

6. ff. 104–113: *Ad ymaginem christi crucifixi,* Omnibus consideratis . . . [Johannes Lemovicensis; Wilmart, 584, n. to p. 527], with the prayer, Omnipotens sempiterne deus qui unigenitum filium tuum dominum nostrum ihesum christum crucem coronam spineam . . . ; *Oratio venerabilis bede presbiteri* . . . , Domine ihesu christe qui septem verba . . . [Leroquais, *LH* 2:342]; *oratio,* Precor te piissime domine ihesu christe propter illam caritatem . . . [Wilmart, 378, n.]; *oratio,* Ave domine ihesu christe verbum patris . . . [Wilmart, 412]; *oratio,* Ave caro christi cara immolata crucis . . . [Wilmart, 379, n.]; *oratio,* Anima christi sanctifica me . . . [a version in Leroquais, *LH* 2:340]; *Omnibus confessis . . . papa bonificius* [*sic*] *concessit duo milia annorum indulgentiam ad supplicationem philippi regis francie, Oratio,* Domine ihesu christe qui hanc sacratissimam carnem . . . [Wilmart, 378, n.]; f. 113v, ruled, but blank.

7. ff. 114–130v [f. 109, blank on recto, with illumination of the Last Judgment on the verso, has been misbound and should be placed here]: Penitential psalms, gradual psalms (cues only of the first 12), and litany, including Denis among the martyrs; Gildard, Medard, Albinus, "Swichine," "Vrine" [*sic* for Swithun and Birinus], and Germanus among the confessors; Petronilla, Sotheris, Prisca, Thecla, Edith and Afra as the last virgins.

8. ff. 131–155 [f. 131, blank]: Office of the Dead, Sarum use; f. 155v, ruled but blank.

9. ff. 156–170 [f. 156, blank]: Commendation of souls (Pss. 118, divided into sections, and 138 with the prayers, Tibi domine commendamus . . . , and Misericordiam tuam domine . . .); f. 170v, ruled, but blank.

10. ff. 171–177 [f. 171, blank]: Psalms of the Passion (Pss. 21–30, 6, with cues only for 22–24, 26, 29).

11. ff. 177–192v: Psalter of St. Jerome: *Beatus ieronimus in hoc modo . . . ,* Suscipere digneris . . . ; f. 178v, ruled, but blank; f. 179, blank; Verba mea auribus percipe . . . [*HE,* 116–22]; Omnipotens sempiterne deus clementiam tuam suppliciter deprecor . . . ; f. 193r–v, ruled, but blank, except for prayers added, s. XVII: Ave maria gratia plena . . . ; lorde have mercy amen; Deus qui manus tuas et pedes tuos . . . ; O mercifull lorde god hevenly father I render most high Laudes; O lord god have.

Parchment, ff. ii (modern paper) + ii (modern parchment) + 193 + ii (modern parchment) + ii (modern paper); 192 × 135 (102 × 64) mm. Bound too tightly to collate; all the full page miniatures appear to be on separate leaves. 18 long lines, ruled in purple ink on ff. 1–100v, 114–181v, and in pale red ink on ff. 101–113v, 182–193v; pricking usually visible in the lower margin. Written in a gothic book hand; ink varies from black to brown in color.

Twenty-three full page miniatures, on the versos of what are apparently inserted singletons, blank on the recto; the frame around the miniatures is composed of narrow gold and pink strips; the outer border, matched by that on the facing text page, is enclosed by a narrow gold strip and consists of flowers, berries, gold motifs, and thin multicolored acanthus, ribbed with white dots, and whose stems often cross to form patterns. The miniatures are: f. 13v (the 15 O's of St. Bridget), Salvator Mundi with two angels supporting a cloth of honor; the background is of large flat acanthus leaves, monochrome, picked out in gold against a ground of the same color, but in a darker shade; f. 22v (Domine . . . da michi famulo tuo victoriam), Gnadenstuhl, with the Father holding the body of Christ across his knees, and the Dove, barely visible, flying from the Father to the Son; acanthus leaf background as above; f. 25v, John the Baptist pointing to the Agnus Dei who sits on a book; f. 27v, George; f. 29v, Christopher; f. 31v, Anne standing and holding a child-like Mary in her arms, who, in turn, holds a tiny baby Jesus; diapered background; f. 33v, Mary Magdalene; f. 35v, Catherine of Alexandria standing on Maxentius; f. 37v, Margaret emerging from the dragon's back, while God looks on from a cloud aperture above; the prison is indicated by two grey columns adjacent to the sides of the picture, a grey crenellated roof and a grey wall with a locked door across the lower quarter of the picture; f. 39v, Barbara, her hand resting on a tower of her own size; diapered background; f. 41v (Hours of the Virgin), Agony in the Garden; f. 50v (Lauds), Betrayal, with Peter on his knees, sword upraised; f. 66v (Prime), Christ before Pilate, long sleeves covering his hands; diapered background; f. 71v (Terce), Scourging at the pillar, with people watching from a window and a doorway; f. 75v (Sext), Road to Calvary; f. 78v (None), Crucifixion, against a monochrome acanthus background, as on f. 13v; f. 81v (Vespers), Deposition from the Cross, against a monochrome acanthus background, as above; f. 84v (Compline), Entombment, with 3 tau-crosses in the background; f. 109v (misbound here; should precede the Penitential psalms, f. 114), Last Judgment with Christ on a rainbow, his feet resting on a globe, 2 angels blowing horns above, Mary and John below him at either side, and the dead rising from their graves; background of monochrome acanthus leaves, as on f. 13v; f. 131v (Office of the Dead), Raising of Lazarus; f. 156v (Commendation of souls), 2 small naked souls carried in a sheet by 2 angels to God the Father, who appears in glory in a blue cloud aperture above; monochrome acanthus background, as on f. 13v; f. 171v (Psalms of the Passion), Man of Sorrows, in the tomb, rising from a ruffle of blue clouds, the emblems of the Passion surrounding him; f. 179v (Psalter of St. Jerome), Jerome in his study, removing the thorn from the lion's paw; behind him are shelves with books and 2 green vases. Historiated initials, 7- or 6-line, with spray of flowers, gold motifs and blue dots in the margin: f. 58 (Holy Spirit), Pentecost; f. 59, Michael; f. 60, Peter and Paul; f. 60v, Andrew; f. 61, Lawrence; also on f. 61, 3-line, Stephen; f. 62, Nicholas; f. 63v, All Saints; f. 90v (Salve virgo virginum), the Virgin, holding the Child, standing on a crescent; f. 95 (O Intemerata), Pietà; f. 100 (Virgo templum trinitatis), 5-line, the Virgin ascending the steps to the temple; f. 104 (Omnibus consideratis), Christ being nailed to the cross, and (idem, to the Cross), 3 tau-crosses, the center one with the INRI legend; f. 104v (idem, to his head), Veronica; f. 105 (idem, to the wound in his right hand); a right hand, wounded, emerging from a blue cloud ruffle, and (idem, to the wound on his left hand), a left hand; f. 105v (idem, to the wound in his side), a wounded heart, surrounded by 4 circles of flesh, wounded; f. 106 (idem, to the wound in his right foot), a right foot and (idem, to the wound in his left foot), a left foot; f. 106v (idem, to John the Evangelist), John holding the chalice; f. 108 (7 words from the Cross), Crucifixion with the thieves on either side. Illustration in the calendar: 2 square miniatures at the top of the recto, showing the monthly occupation and the zodiac symbol. Major initials, 6- or 5-line, in white-patterned blue against pink and gold grounds, or against a plain gold ground, with infilling of lush acanthus leaves, "English" in style; 2-line initials in gold on pink ground with blue infilling, or vice versa; 1-line initials, blue with red penwork, or gold with black. Line fillers in the litany in alternating rows of blue or gold squiggles. Rubrics in red.

Bound by Lortic for Robert Hoe in brown mosaic morocco in 1884, from a previous binding of "old velvet," according to a note on f. iii signed by Hoe; red morocco doublures; gilt edges.

Written in the middle of the fifteenth century in Flanders, probably Bruges, for export to England; on f. 1, s. XVI, is the note "Jesus have marci a pon us/ Johannes busshells boke tayller," and below this, the name "Arthur," erased. The book was n. 606 in an English book dealer's catalogue, and later, apparently, belonged to Dawson Turner (1775–1858), who signed a slip of paper quoting Sir Francis Palgrave, Sir Frederic Madden, and Mr. Shaw on the date and origin of the manuscript; these opinions are dated 1832 and 1835; Dawson Turner sale, London, 7 March 1853, n. 1880 to Pickering. Robert Hoe signed and dated the same slip mentioned above with his date of purchase (?), 1872. See Robert Hoe, *A Lecture on Bookbinding as a Fine Art, delivered before the Grolier Club February 26, 1885* (Grolier Club 1886) pl. 58; Grolier Club (1892) n. 17; Bierstadt (1895) p. 25; *Cat.* (1909) pp. 50–52; his sale, Anderson, New York, 1911, pt. I, n. 2129 to G. D. Smith. Source and date of acquisition by Henry E. Huntington unknown.

Bibliography: De Ricci, 97.

HM 1145 — France, s. XV²
BOOK OF HOURS, use of Rouen

1. ff. 1–12v: Calendar in French, alternating red and blue entries, with the major feasts in gold, including the feasts of Ansbert (9 February), Austreberta (10 February), Translation of Audoenus (5 May), Ursinus (12 June), Martialis (3 July, in gold), Vivianus (28 August), Nicasius (11 October), Mellonius (22 October), Romanus (23 October, in gold), Octave of Romanus (30 October), Ursinus (30 December).

2. ff. 13–20 [f. 13, blank]: Pericopes of the Gospels, that of John followed by the prayers, Protector in te sperantium . . . [Perdrizet, 25] and Ecclesiam tuam quesumus domine . . . ; f. 20v, blank.

3. ff. 21–86v: Hours of the Virgin, use of Rouen; after lauds, suffrages of the Holy Spirit, Michael, John the Baptist, James the Greater, Lawrence, Eustachius, Denis, Romanus, Nicholas, Catherine of Alexandria, Margaret, All Saints, for

peace; also after lauds, following the suffrages, *Les v ioyes de nostre dame mere de dieu,* Gaude virgo mater christi . . . [*HE,* 63–64], and Salve regina . . . [*HE,* 62–63] and the prayer, Deus qui beatissimam virginem mariam in conceptu . . . ; one leaf missing after f. 66 with the end of sext and the beginning of none; following compline, *Oratio devotissima de beatissima maria virgine,* Inviolata integra et casta es maria. . . . [*RH* 9094], with versicle, response and prayer, Deus qui salutis eterne beate marie virginitate fecunda . . .

4. ff. 87–104v: Penitential psalms and litany, including Nicasius and Eustachius among the martyrs; Romanus, Audoenus, Mellonius, Ansbert and Vivianus among the confessors; Austreberta and Veronica among the virgins; one leaf missing before f. 103 with a portion of the litany.

5. ff. 105–112v: Short hours of the Cross.

6. ff. 113–119v: Short hours of the Holy Spirit.

7. ff. 120–169v: Office of the Dead; responses to the lessons as in Sarum use.

8. ff. 170–194: Prayers as follow: *Oroison tres devote de la benoite vierge marie,* Obsecro te . . . et michi famulo tuo . . . [Leroquais, *LH* 2:346]; *Aultre oroison moult devote de la vierge marie et cetera,* O Intemerata . . . orbis terrarum. De te enim . . . [Wilmart, 494–95]; Quiconque vult salvus esse . . . ; Anima christi sanctifica me . . . [Leroquais, *LH* 2:340]; *les xv ioyes,* Doulce dame de misericorde. . . [Leroquais, *LH* 2:310–11]; Doulz dieu doulz pere saincte trinite . . . [Leroquais, *LH* 2:309–10]; Saincte vray croix aouree . . . [Sonet 1876]; f. 194v, blank.

Parchment, ff. ii (paper) + i (parchment) + 194 + i (parchment) + ii (paper); 178 × 135 (89 × 57) mm. 1^{12} 2^{8}(through f. 20) $3–6^{8}$ 7^{12}(with 1, now a singleton, bound below as f. 70) 8 (ff. 64–71, of which ff. 64–66 apparently constitute the first half of the quire; a leaf missing after f. 66; f. 67 should be bound after f. 102; f. 68 in its correct position; f. 69 should be bound after f. 111; f. 70 should be bound above, before f. 53; f. 71 in its correct position) $9–11^{8}$ 12^{6} 13 (ff. 102, 67, a leaf missing, 103–111, 69, with stitching between ff. 106–107) $14–19^{8}$ 20^{6} 21^{4}(through f. 169) 22^{8} 23^{4}(through f. 181) 24^{8}(+ 1, f. 182) 25^{4}. 14 long lines, very faintly ruled in pale red ink. Written in 2 sizes of gothic book hand according to liturgical function; ink often flaking.

Thirteen large miniatures usually above 3 lines of text in arched compartments with serrated tops; U-shaped frame around text and miniature, consisting of a narrow gold and color strip on the inside, and wide pink and blue segments on the other 2 sides; outer border of black ivy spray with blue and gold acanthus leaves, flowers, strawberries and gold motifs. The miniatures are: f. 13v (the Gospel pericopes), full page, blank on the recto but apparently part of the quire structure; the outer border, while of the same style as the others, is darker in color and finer in execution; the miniature is divided into 4 compartments, one for each evangelist and his symbol; f. 21 (Hours of the Virgin), Annunciation, in a room defined by grey columns, pendant arches and brocaded cloths in the background; f. 33 (Lauds), Visitation, with Mary holding a book, and greeting a rather aged Elizabeth; f. 53 (Prime), Nativity, with Joseph holding a candle and in the background, a kneeling woman; f. 59 (Terce), Annunciation to the shepherds; f. 63v (Sext), Adoration of the Magi; opening leaf of none missing before f. 68; f. 73v (Vespers), Flight into Egypt; f. 80v (Compline), Coronation of the Virgin by an angel, while God the Father, wearing a papal tiara, blesses; f. 87 (Penitential psalms), David in prayer, his harp lying on a table and the angel appearing with upraised sword between David and God the Father; f. 105 (Hours of the Cross), Crucifixion, with Mary and John on either side; f. 113 (Hours of the Holy Spirit), Pentecost; f. 120 (Office of the Dead), burial service in a churchyard, with the white-shrouded corpse being lowered into the grave by a worker, while 2 priests say the service and 3 mourners in black stand in the background; f. 182v, apparently intended to accompany the 15 Joys, which begin on the last 3 lines of f. 183, as if the original plan had been to place the miniature above the text; instead, the miniature was painted on the verso of an inserted singleton, left blank on its recto; the resulting blank space on f. 183 was then filled in by the prayer "Anima christi" in a slightly different hand; the border decoration on this added singleton is the same as that on f. 13v; the artist appears to be more capable; the scene depicts a woman in a red dress and black headdress kneeling before the Virgin and Child. 4- and 3-line initials in white-patterned blue or dark pink against a ground of the other color or against a gold ground, with colored trilobe leaf infilling against a gold ground; except in the presence of full borders, these initials produce marginal extensions of black ivy spray, flowers and gold motifs. 2- and 1-line initials in gold on alternating blue or dark pink grounds with infilling of the other color; ribbon line fillers of the same colors, or as small flowers; initials within the text touched in yellow. Rubrics in an orange-tinged red. Sixteenth century pen trials, now erased: ff. 4 (Jaques), 9v (Jaques du Losc?), 10, 12 (Jaques?), 187v (Jaques?), 188 (a flower), 192 (a bird?), 194, 194v ("venerable," twice).

Bound, s. XVII^ex, in French gilt calf, rebacked, original spine laid down, with small fleurs-de-lis on spine and covers; holes remain from 2 fore edge ties; gilt edges.

Written in France, and probably first owned by a woman to judge by the miniature on f. 182v, although the prayers are copied in the masculine forms; the area was Rouen, as indicated by the liturgical use and the saints in the calendar, suffrages and litany. Modern pencil note on front pastedown, "Lovejoy Library." In the R. H. Charlton collection; sale by Anderson, New York, 12 November 1914, n. 263 to G. D. Smith. Precise source and date of acquisition by Henry E. Huntington unknown.

Bibliography: De Ricci, 98.

HM 1146 — France, s. XV^ex
BOOK OF HOURS, use of Troyes

1. ff. 1–12v: Calendar in French with major feasts in red; included are entries for Frodobert (8 January), Sabinianus martyr (24 January, in red), Sabina (29 January), Helen (4 May, in red), Mastidia (7 May, in red), "Saint loup de troyes" (29 July, in red), Tancha (10 October), Sabinianus and Potentianus bishops and martyrs (19 October).

2. ff. 13–20v: Pericopes of the Gospels, that of John followed by the prayer, Protector in te sperantium . . . [Perdrizet, 25]; Salve regina . . . [*HE*, 62]; *antiphona,* Inviolata integra et casta es maria . . . [*RH* 9094]; *Ad beatam mariam virginem,* Regina celi letare . . . [*RH* 17170].

3. ff. 21–24v: Short hours of the Cross.

4. ff. 25–28v: Short hours of the Holy Spirit.

5. ff. 29–93v: Hours of the Virgin, use of Troyes; Obsecro te . . . [masculine forms; Leroquais, *LH* 2:346]; O Intemerata . . . orbis terrarum. De te enim . . . [Wilmart, 494–95]; f. 94r–v, ruled, but blank.

6. ff. 95–115v: Penitential psalms and litany, including Desiderius, Sabinianus martyr, Leodegar, George, Julianus, Sabinianus bishop and martyr, Potentianus,

Quentin, Christopher, Crispin and Crispinian among the martyrs; Lupus, Julianus, Frodobert, Fidolus and Paul among the confessors; Helen, Mastidia, Julia, Bridget, Sabina, Maura, Potentiana, Petronilla, Juliana, Susanna and Columba among the virgins.

7. ff. 116–164v: Office of the Dead, use of Troyes.

Parchment, ff. iii (paper) + 164 + iii (paper); 184 × 128 (103 × 62) mm. $1–2^6$ 3^8(through f. 20) 4^8(through f. 28) $5–12^8$ 13^2(through f. 94) $14–21^8$ 22^4 23^2. Evidence of a catchword, now almost entirely cropped, on f. 134v, written in a cursive script in the center lower margin. 15 long lines, ruled in brownish ink. Written in a gothic book hand in 2 sizes according to liturgical function.

Thirteen large miniatures above 4 lines of text, in arched compartments with tops decorated in a variety of manners; the outer borders usually geometric, enclosing spaces of dark background. The miniatures are: f. 13 (Gospel of John), John on Patmos; f. 21 (Hours of the Cross), Crucifixion; f. 25 (Hours of the Holy Spirit), Pentecost; f. 29 (Hours of the Virgin), Annunciation, as if in the cloister of a church; border with a diagonal gold trellis against a natural parchment ground, with flowers and grotesques; f. 41v (Lauds), Visitation, with castles and fantastic rock formations in the background; f. 53v (Prime), Nativity; f. 60 (Terce), Annunciation to the shepherds; in the outer border a square gold trellis, with a gold picket fence across the bottom; f. 64v (Sext), Adoration of the Magi, one of whom is black; f. 68v (None), Presentation in the temple; f. 73 (Vespers), Flight into Egypt, in the background the miracle of the cornfield and a falling idol; f. 80 (Compline), Coronation of the Virgin by an angel while Jesus, holding globe and cross, blesses; f. 95 (Penitential psalms), David in prayer, looking up at a bright orange angel who holds an unsheathed sword; God the Father appears in an opening of the clouds directly above David; f. 116 (Office of the Dead), Job on the dunghill with his friends, with a building fallen into ruins behind him; in the outer border a diagonal gold trellis formed by criss-crossed branches. 4-line initials in white-patterned blue against a burnished gold ground with colored trilobe leaf infilling, or as painted gold shaded branches against a maroon ground with naturalistic flowers in the infilling; 2-line initials in white-patterned blue against a gold ground with trilobe leaf infilling; 1-line initials, ribbon and dot line fillers in burnished gold and white-patterned blue and dark pink; initials in the text touched in yellow; rubrics in red. Traced borders on every page running the length of the text, comprised of black ivy spray, blue and gold acanthus, flowers and an occasional bird, insect or grotesque.

Bound, s. XVII–XVIII, in French black morocco, lettered on the spine "Heures Antique [*sic*] P.C." (see below); marbled endpapers; gilt edges.

Written at the end of the fifteenth century in France, for use in the area of Troyes, according to the use of the hours of the Virgin and the office of the dead, and according to the saints in the calendar and litany. Given on 19 May 1700 by the Reverend Father F. Rose, O.S.B., to P. Chalopin (the "P.C." lettered on the spine), according to notes on ff. 1 and 164v. Later belonged to Bronod, Avocat au Conseil, whose bookplate (ca. 1750) is on the front pastedown. Further notes on the lower margins of ff. 1–4 state that Bronod bequeathed the volume to his son who in turn left it to his relative, Charpentier de Boisgibault, Conseiller du Roy. M. Charpentier de Boisgibault left it to his son-in-law, Masson de St. Amand, Conseiller du Roy and later Prefet du Département de l'Eure and member of the Legion of Honor, who was knighted in 1808. On f. 4 are two seals in red wax, being those of Pierre Gilles Masson, Trésorier General de la Marine in 1680 and of Masson de St. Amand, his grandson, in 1808. Sold by Sotheby's, 21 March 1910 lot 427 to Hornstein. Belonged to Beverly Chew (1850–1924); his morocco book label on the front pastedown. Acquired by Henry E. Huntington in 1912.

Bibliography: De Ricci, 98.

HM 1147 — France, s. XVI^{in}

BOOK OF HOURS, use of Paris

1. ff. 1–6v: Full calendar in French with major feasts in gold and the others alternating red and blue.

2. ff. 7–12v: Pericopes of the Gospels, that of John followed by the prayer, Protector in te sperantium . . . [Perdrizet, 25].

3. ff. 13–18v: f. 13, illumination; ff. 13v–14, ruled, but blank; ff. 14v–18v, prayers as follow: *Devote oraison a nostre dame,* Ave cuius conceptio . . . [*RH* 1744] with the prayer, Deus qui nos conceptionis nativitatis . . . ; *Devote oroison a nostre dame,* Salve regina . . . [*RH* 18147] with the prayer, Concede nos famulos tuos quesumus domine deus perpetua mentis et corporis sanitate gaudere . . . ; Inviolata integra et casta . . . [*RH* 9094]; *oratio,* Salve mater pietatis . . . [*RH* 18039]; Ave regina celorum . . . [*RH* 2070]; *S'ensuivent les sept vers saint bernard,* Illumina oculos meos . . . [*RH* 27912, here written as 8 verses] with the prayer, Omnipotens sempiterne deus qui ezechie regi . . . ; *Antienne a nostre dame,* Ave domina sancta maria mater dei; Regina celi letare . . . [*RH* 17170] with versicles, response and prayer, Concede nos famulos tuos quesumus domine perpetua mentis et corporis sanitate gaudere . . .

4. ff. 19–63v: Hours of the Virgin, use of Paris; 9 psalms and lessons at matins without intermediary rubrics; the prayer, Ecclesiam tuam quesumus domine benignus . . . finishes all hours, lauds through compline; the opening leaf of compline missing between ff. 59–60; f. 63v, ruled, but blank.

5. ff. 64–66: Short hours of the Cross.

6. ff. 66v–68v: Short hours of the Holy Spirit.

7. ff. 69–81: Penitential psalms and litany including Denis, Quentin and Quiriacus among the martyrs; Remigius among the confessors; Genevieve among the virgins.

8. ff. 81v–108v: Office of the Dead, use of Paris.

9. ff. 109–127v: Prayers as follow: Obsecro te . . . [masculine forms; Leroquais, *LH* 2:346]; *Devote oroison a nostre dame,* O Intemerata . . . orbis terrarum. De te enim . . . [Wilmart, 494–95]; E Tres doulce dame pour icelle grant Ioye . . . [Sonet 458, the 15 Joys, without the prologue]; Biau sire dieu regardes moy . . . [Sonet 504, the 7 Requests, without the prologue]; Saincte vraye croys aouree . . . [Sonet 1876]; suffrages of Michael, John the Baptist, John the Evangelist, Peter and Paul, James the Greater, Stephen, Lawrence, Mary Magdalene, Catherine of Alexandria, Margaret, Barbara, Apollonia.

Parchment, ff. i (paper) + vi (modern parchment) + 127 + vi (modern parchment) + ii (paper); 170 × 124 (110 × 62) mm. $1\text{–}3^6$ $4\text{–}8^8$ 9^4(+ 5, f. 63) $10\text{–}14^8$ $15\text{–}17^6$(through f. 121) 18^6. Catchwords in the script of the text in the center lower margin. Usually in 22 long lines, but with 17 on ff. 7–12v (quire 2), and with 21 on ff. 13v–26v (quires 3 and 4) and on ff. 109–121v (last leaf of quire 15, quires 16 and 17); the center bifolium of quire 15, ff. 106–107v, written on 23 long lines. Ruled in pale red ink. Written in at least 3 variations of the same stylized round gothic script: i, ff. 1–6v, 19–108v, 122–127v;

ii, ff. 7–12; iii, ff. 14v–18v, 109–121v. Differing sizes of the script used to indicate liturgical function.

Thirteen large miniatures above 4 lines of text, enclosed by painted gold architectural frames; both text and miniature surrounded by full borders of painted gold with multicolored acanthus leaf foliage and grotesques. The miniatures are: f. 7 (Gospel of John), John on Patmos; the frame of gold columns with inset blue panels; f. 19 (Hours of the Virgin), Annunciation, seen through jewelled columns; the outer border consists of a series of small vignettes showing the meeting of Joachim and Anne at the Golden Gate, the birth of the Virgin, Mary ascending the steps to the temple, Mary weaving while an angel holds her book open, the betrothal of Mary and Joseph; this leaf by a less capable artist than the rest of the book; f. 34v (Lauds), Visitation, done by a more competent artist; f. 42v (Prime), Nativity with Joseph warming the infant's swadling clothes by the fire; f. 46v (Terce), Annunciation to the shepherds, with 2 angels in the sky holding a scroll inscribed "Gloria"; f. 49v (Sext), Adoration of the Magi; f. 52v (None), Presentation in the temple; f. 55v (Vespers), Massacre of the Innocents by 2 soldiers while Herod, enthroned, watches; through an open window the Holy Family is seen fleeing to Egypt; opening leaf for compline missing; f. 64 (Hours of the Cross), Crucifixion with Mary, John and others to Christ's right, and the soldiers to his left; f. 66v (Hours of the Holy Spirit), Pentecost; f. 69 (Penitential psalms), David watching Bathsheba at her bath; in place of the usual floral border, the architectural columns occupy the entire space, and bear statues of cupids at the top, and, in a freize at the bottom, images of David handing the letter to Uriah and of Uriah being killed in battle; the 4 lines of text on this leaf decorated to appear as if inscribed on a scroll; f. 81v (Office of the Dead), Death, as a corpse astride a bull, attacking a lady with his lance; others lie already dead on the ground; f. 109 (Obsecro te), Pietà. Smaller miniatures are: f. 9, 8-line, half of the width of the text, in a simple gold frame, Luke; f. 10v, 8-line, Matthew; f. 12, 8-line, Mark; f. 13 (followed by a blank opening, ff. 13v–14), a full page miniature divided into 4 compartments by the painted gold architecture showing the Crucifixion, Deposition, Pietà and Entombment; f. 14v (Ave cuius conceptio), 8-line plus the height of the arch, Anne in prayer with the rayed image of the yet unborn Virgin shining through her womb; f. 17 (Illumina oculos meos), 8-line plus the height of the arch, Bernard writing while the Devil steals his ink-well; f. 112 (O Intemerata), 10-line, the Virgin and Child on a crescent; f. 122, 10-line, Michael, seen in half-length, holding the scales; f. 122v, 9-line, John the Baptist pointing to the Agnus Dei which he holds in his hand; f. 123, 9-line, John the Evangelist holding the snaky chalice; f. 123v, 11-line, Peter and Paul with their attributes; f. 124, 9-line, James the Greater holding his staff and books; f. 124v, 11-line, Stephen; f. 125, 11-line, Mary Magdalene; f. 125v, 12-line, Catherine of Alexandria; f. 126, 11-line, Margaret; f. 126v, 9-line, Barbara; f. 127v, 9-line, Apollonia. Miniatures in the calendar represent the occupations of the month at the top of the page, enclosed by gold columns and a half-oval arch; the zodiac signs are in rectangular frames at the foot of the page; the border completed on all four sides by the same style floral pattern as in the rest of the book. 3-line initials as shaded white ribbons against square painted gold grounds decorated with black ink dots and commas, and with naturalistic flowers or strawberries in the infilling; 3-line initial, f. 7v, in faceted gold against a blue ground decorated with white sprays; some 3-, and all 2- and 1-line initials in painted gold on gold decorated blue, brick red or ochre grounds; ribbon line fillers in these colors. Rubrics in blue. Traced band borders on every page, running the length of the text, outlined in black, in the same style as the full borders, each with a large grotesque.

Bound by Bernard David and finished by Marius Michel for the person who carefully wrote out notes in French regarding the manuscript on the front and back flyleaves; the notes are dated January 1866 and are signed "E.S." (?). Brown morocco binding inlaid with various colors to an entrelac design, green morocco doublures elaborately tooled in the style of Eve; gilt edges gauffered with acanthus and grotesque patterns based on the borders of the manuscript; brown morocco slipcase.

HM 1147

Written in the early sixteenth century in France, where it remained at least through the middle of the nineteenth century. De Ricci suggests that it was bound for William Martin, although it does not appear in Martin's 1869 sale; on f. i verso, the morocco book label of Henri Bordes; not traced in his sales. Belonged to Robert Hoe: Grolier Club (1892) n. 38 with a plate of f. 19; *Cat.* (1909) pp. 79–80; his sale, Anderson, New York, 1912, pt. IV, n. 2349 to G. D. Smith. Precise source and date of acquisition by Henry E. Huntington unknown.

Bibliography: De Ricci, 98.

HM 1148 — Flanders, s. XV^{ex}
BOOK OF HOURS, use of Rome — *fig. 142*

1. ff. 1–11v: Calendar, missing the month of January; including the feast of Macarius (9 May), Rumold (1 July), Amalberga (10 July), Monulph (16 July), Arnulph (16 August), Lambert (17 September), Remigius and Bavo (1 October), Amalberga (27 October), Hubert (3 November).

2. ff. 12–19v: Stabat mater dolorosa . . . [*RH* 19416]; *Devota oratio ad beatam mariam virginem,* Obsecro te . . . [masculine forms; Leroquais, *LH* 2:346]; *Oratio ad beatam virginem mariam,* O Intemerata . . . orbis terrarum. Inclina mater . . . [Wilmart, 488–90].

3. ff. 20–35: Suffrages of the Trinity, John the Baptist, All Angels, Michael, Nicholas, Francis, Anthony of Padua, John the Evangelist, Sebastian, Jerome, Anne, Catherine of Alexandria, Agnes, Apollonia, Elizabeth, Barbara, Mary Magdalene, Margaret, Leonard; f. 35v, ruled, but blank.

4. ff. 36–42v: Short hours of the Cross.

5. ff. 43–48v: Short hours of the Holy Spirit.

6. ff. 49–55v: Pericopes of the Gospels, each beginning at the top of a recto.

7. ff. 56–120v: *Incipiunt hore beate marie virginis secundum cursum romane ecclesie;* with weekly variations of the psalms at matins set into the text before the lessons; suffrages of All Saints and for peace from lauds to compline; f. 112r–v, Salve Regina in a different hand; Advent office begins on f. 113.

8. ff. 121–136: Penitential psalms and litany; f. 136v, ruled, but blank except for a prayer added, s. XVI, in a cursive script: Marie mere de concorde, fontaine de misericorde . . .

9. ff. 137–177v: Office of the Dead, use of Rome.

Parchment, ff. 177 + iii (early modern paper); 168 × 115 (90 × 60) mm. The collation registers the location of what were presumably added singletons, now missing: 1^6(–1) 2^8(–7, 8) $3–5^8$ 6^8(–2 added singletons, before the first and eighth leaf, ff. 36 and 43) 7^8 8^4(to f. 55) 9^8(–an added singleton, before the first leaf, f. 56) 10^8 11^8(–an added singleton, before the second leaf, f. 73) 12^8(–an added singleton, before the fifth leaf, f. 84) 13^8(–2 added singletons, before the second and sixth leaf, ff. 89 and 93) 14^8(–2 added singletons, before the second and sixth leaf, ff. 97 and 101) 15^8(–an added singleton, before the fifth leaf, f. 108) 16^2(–1, to f. 112) 17^8 18^8(–an added singleton, before the first leaf, f. 121) 19^8 20^8(–an added singleton, before the first leaf, f. 137) 21–23^8 24^8(+ 1 added singleton at the end, f. 177). A cropped quire-leaf signature on f. 66, apparently "h3." 16 long lines, ruled in pale red ink, with some pricking visible in the upper and lower margins. Written in a formal bâtarde script.

Twelve full page miniatures, which were all on inserted singletons and presumably blank on the recto, have been cut from the manuscript. The remaining illuminations are those of prayers, suffrages and Gospel pericopes, usually 6-line, in grisaille technique of shaded whites, highlighted in gold, often set against gold-patterned maroon drapes. A number of the miniatures, although simpler in execution, have followed the same model as certain miniatures attributed to the Master of Mary of Burgundy; the references to plates in the following description indicate those in G. I. Lieftinck, *Boekverluchters uit de Omgeving van Maria van Bourgondie, c. 1475–1485* (Brussels 1969). Full borders on the leaves with extant miniatures and on the leaves facing the removed miniatures, with ground of gold paint dabbed over a colored surface or of a color (pink, blue-grey, red, yellow-green), and decorated with realistic flowers, insects, and branchy acanthus leaves (Lieftinck, pl. 39). Depth added to the borders by raised gold dots and ovals, some of which have flaked off down to the base coat; there is no indication here of a previous ivy spray border, in which gold dots were painted over, as noted by J. J. G. Alexander regarding Oxford, Bod. Lib. Douce 219–220 in his introduction to *The Master of Mary of Burgundy* (New York 1970) p. 14. The miniatures are: f. 12 (Stabat mater), Pietà; f. 13v (Obsecro te), the Virgin, standing, holding the Child, 4-line; f. 17v (O Intemerata), the Virgin sitting holding the Child, 4-line; f. 20 (Trinity), the Trinity as three glowing gold circles emanating gold rays through a white field which shades into rose; f. 21, John the Baptist holding the Lamb and pointing to his neck; f. 22 (All Angels), Christ's face in gold highlights surrounded by worshipping angels, also picked out in gold against a deep rose ground; f. 23, Michael with upraised sword vanquishing 2 devils at his feet (Lieftinck, pl. 137); f. 23v, Nicholas seated before the 3 children in a tub (Lieftinck, pl. 196); f. 24, Francis showing the stigmata; f. 25, Anthony of Padua standing before a maroon drape holding a crucifix and a book; f. 25v, John the Evangelist holding a chalice; f. 26, Sebastian; f. 27, Jerome holding a rock with which he has been beating his chest, and gazing at a crucifix, against a background of green foliage; f. 28, Anne standing beside the Virgin, herself a child who holds the infant Jesus (Lieftinck, pl. 34); f. 29, Catherine standing before a maroon drape patterned with gold wheels, and holding a sword and a book; f. 29v, Agnes holding a lamb on a book; f. 30v, Apollonia holding the pincers with a tooth (Lieftinck, pl. 260); f. 31, Elizabeth, crowned, and holding a crown and a coin before a maroon ground; f. 32, Barbara holding a palm frond and touching the tower with her left hand; f. 33, Mary Magdalene holding the pot; f. 34, Margaret with the head only of the dragon visible, stretching up towards her hand and the cross in it; f. 34v, Leonard holding fetters and a book; f. 49, John on Patmos (Lieftinck, pl. 246); f. 51, Luke with the ox (Lieftinck, pls. 117 and 249); f. 53, Matthew with the angel (Lieftinck, pls. 123 and 247); f. 55, Mark with the lion (Lieftinck, pl. 122). Set into the space of the illuminations are 1-line initials, shaped from a white acanthus leaf, against a squared gold-sprinkled light brown ground (Lieftinck, pl. 123). Facing the presumably excised full page illuminations are 6- or 5-line initials, as white or brown branches and leaves, highlighted in gold against a square brick-red or brownish-green ground, lightly stippled in gold, infilled on f. 56 with a bird pecking at a daisy, or with a flower alone (Lieftinck, pl. 149). Minor initials, 2- or 1-line, of white branches against square brown grounds, stippled in gold, with the same colors used for the ribbon line fillers in the litany. Rubrics in red.

Bound, s. XVII^{ex}, in French parchment over pasteboard.

Written in Flanders, probably Ghent and probably decorated by followers of the Master of Mary of Burgundy, ca. 1480. N. 632 in a sale (not Brayton Ives, 1891, according to

De Ricci). Belonged to Robert Hoe: Grolier Club (1892) n. 49 with a plate of f. 23; *Cat.* (1909) pp. 92–93; his sale, Anderson, New York, 1912, pt. IV, n. 2342 to G. D. Smith. Precise source and date of acquisition by Henry E. Huntington unknown.

Bibliography: De Ricci, 98.

HM 1149 — Flanders, s. XVI^in
BOOK OF HOURS, use of Rome

1. ff. 1–12v: Calendar in French in red and black with the feasts of the Elevation of Eleutherius (9 July), "Nostre damme de le nive" (5 August), Transfiguration (6 August), Remigius and Piatus (1 October, in red), Piatus (29 October); erasures of red feasts at 20 February, 9 May and 25 August seem to have been those of Eleutherius, the dedication of the Church of St. Mary in Tournai (?), and the translation of Eleutherius; other erasures of red feasts, now illegible, at 28 July, 10 and 15 August; f. 13r–v, ruled as for a calendar, but blank.

2. ff. 14–22 [f. 14, blank]: Short hours of the Cross; f. 22v, ruled, but blank.

3. ff. 23–29v [f. 23, blank]: Short hours of the Holy Spirit; f. 30r–v, ruled, but blank.

4. ff. 31–102 [f. 31, blank]: Hours of the Virgin, use of Rome; suffrages of All Saints from lauds to compline; ff. 93v–94v, Salve Regina; ff. 95–102, weekly variations of psalms at matins; f. 102v, ruled, but blank.

5. ff. 103–121 [f. 103, blank]: Penitential psalms and litany, including Quentin, Remigius, Eleutherius, Brictius, Amand, Sabina; f. 121v, ruled, but blank.

6. ff. 122–166: Office of the Dead, use of Rome; f. 166v, ruled, but blank.

7. ff. 167–190: Prayers as follow: *Oroison a nostre dame,* Obsecro te . . . et michi famule tue impetres . . . [Leroquais, *LH* 2:346]; O intemerata . . . orbis terrarum. De te enim . . . michi miserrime peccatrici . . . [Wilmart, 494–95]; *Ung religieux et chanoine regulier qui eubt nom arnoul* . . . Missus est gabriel angelus . . . [Leroquais, *LH* 1:95]; *Devote oroison a la vierge marie,* Stabat mater dolorosa . . . [*RH* 19416] with versicle and prayer, Interveniat pro nobis quesumus domine ihesu christe . . . ; O Domine ihesu christe adoro te in cruce pendentem . . . [the 7 prayers of Gregory, with indulgence; Leroquais, *LH* 2:346].

8. ff. 190v–200: Suffrages of the Trinity, Peter and Paul, Sebastian, Anthony abbot, Adrianus, Piatus, Mary Magdalene, Julianus, Catherine of Alexandria, Barbara, Holy Spirit, Roch.

9. ff. 200–204v: *Orison a l'elevation du corps de ihesu crist,* Anima christi sanctifica me . . . [Leroquais, *LH* 2:340]; *Quand on lieve le calice dy,* Ave vere sanguis domini nostri ihesu christi . . . ; *Quant on veult recepvoir le corps de nostre seigneur ihesu crist,* Domine non sum digna ut intres sub tectum meum set tu domine qui dixisti . . . ; *Quand on l'a receu,* Vera perceptio corporis et sanguinis tui . . . ; *Sensieult devote orison que on doit dire pour les trepasses la quelle fu trouvee a romme derriere l'autel en la capelle saint pierre et ordonna et ottroya le pape Jehan XII* . . . , Avete omnes anime fideles . . . , with versicle,

response and prayer, Domine ihesu christe salus et liberatio . . . [Leroquais, *LH* 2:341]; f. 205r–v, ruled, but blank.

Parchment, ff. ii (modern parchment) + ii (contemporary parchment) + 205 + ii (modern parchment); 167 × 117 (94 × 66) mm. 1 (of uncertain structure up to f. 5) 2^8 3^8(+ 1, f. 14) 4^8(+ 1, f. 23 and 9, f. 31) 5^8 6^8(+ 3, f. 43) 7^8(+ 7, f. 56) 8^8 9^8(+ 6, f. 72) 10^8(+ 3, f. 78) 11^8(+ 3, f. 87 and 9, f. 93; with catchword "Domine ne" which refers to quire 13, the beginning of the Penitential psalms) 12^8(ff. 95–102, the weekly variations of psalms at matins) 13^8(+ 1, f. 103) $14–22^8$ 23^6(+ 4, f. 187) 24^8 25^8(–8). Catchwords usually cropped, written in the inner right corner; quire and leaf signatures, often cropped, as letters of the alphabet and roman numerals. 15 long lines, ruled in purple ink; pricking in all 3 outer margins. Written in a gothic book hand.

Full page miniatures, executed on the versos of inserted singletons, blank on the rectos; 11 are extant; presumably another 3 were once in the manuscript for terce, sext and the Office of the Dead. The miniatures are enclosed by brightly painted borders of strewn flowers, branchy acanthus, strawberries, insects and birds, of rather poor quality; the facing rectos have similar borders and 4-line initials of branchy acanthus against square colored grounds with a flower in the infilling. The miniatures are: f. 14v (Hours of the Cross), Crucifixion with Mary and John; f. 23v (Hours of the Holy Spirit), Pentecost; f. 31v (Hours of the Virgin), Annunciation; f. 43v (Lauds), Visitation, outside the gates of a town; f. 56v (Prime), Nativity; f. 72v (None), Presentation in the temple; f. 78v (Vespers), Flight into Egypt with falling idol in the background; f. 87v (Compline), Coronation of the Virgin before the Father and the Son as separate figures with the Dove above them; f. 93v (Salve Regina), the Virgin, standing, holding the Child, before an open book; f. 103v (Penitential psalms), David in prayer, facing God the Father, who is depicted in the historiated initial on the facing page; f. 122 (Office of the Dead), text begins with a historiated initial of a skull, the lower border contains the nude body of a dead woman; f. 187v (the 7 O's of Gregory), John the Baptist, sitting, holding a book and pointing to the Lamb, while in the background he is shown beheaded, as the executioner places his severed head on Salome's plate. An 11-line miniature, f. 177 (Missus est gabriel) depicts the 4th vision of Mary when she saw her Son risen. Fourteen small miniatures, 7-line: f. 167 (Obsecro te), John supports the body of Christ while Mary and another woman worship him; f. 171 (O Intemerata), Christ showing his wound, and Mary her breast, with God the Father in the background; f. 184v (Stabat mater), Crucifixion; f. 190v (Trinity), God supporting the body of Christ, with the Dove above them; f. 191, Peter and Paul; f. 192, Sebastian, in armor, holding arrows; f. 193, Anthony abbot; f. 194, Adrianus in armor with sword and lion; f. 194v, Piatus in priestly garb, holding the sliced-off top of his head; f. 195, Mary Magdalene; f. 195v, Julian and his wife ferrying the leper across the river; f. 196, Catherine; f. 197, Barbara reading in front of the tower; f. 198 (Holy Spirit), Pentecost; f. 199, Roch showing the sore on his leg to an angel. 2-line initials in branchy white acanthus leaves on olive-green square grounds with gold flecked lines for depth; 1-line initials of painted gold on blue or maroon square grounds. Rubrics in red.

Bound by F. Bedford in brown morocco, gilt and blind stamped; gilt edges.

Written in the early sixteenth century in Flanders, possibly for use in the diocese of Tournai, given the presence of Piatus twice in the calendar and in the suffrage, and the possibly 3 entries for Eleutherius in the calendar. Northern spellings: bietremieu, mahieu, franchois (in the calendar), tierche, lichon. Feminine forms used in the prayers. On f. i, two sixteenth century possession notes, the first identifying the owner of the book as the "vefve Franchois houselot"; in the second, the owner "yhalian [?] hogheselot" of Lille declares to have received this book from her grandmother in 1571. Belonged to William Bragge, F.S.A., of Shirle Hall, Sheffield (1823–84); his sale, Sotheby's, 7 June 1876, lot 480 to the dealer B. F. Stevens. Belonged to Robert Hoe: Grolier Club (1892) n. 23; *Cat.* (1909) pp. 55–56; his sale, Anderson, New York, 1912, pt. IV, n. 2341 to G. D. Smith. Precise source and date of acquisition by Henry E. Huntington unknown.

HM 1149

Bibliography: De Ricci, 98. E. Panofsky, *Early Netherlandish Painting* (Cambridge, Mass. 1953) vol. 1, pp. 263, 463 note 4, erroneously identifying the subject of the miniature on f. 177 as the appearance of Christ to a private gentleman. J. D. Breckenridge, "Et prima vidit: The Iconography of the Appearance of Christ to His Mother," *Art Bulletin* 39, 1 (1957) 9–32, especially p. 27 and fig. 13, reproducing f. 177.

HM 1150 — France, s. XV^ex
BOOK OF HOURS, use of Chartres — *fig. 137*

1. ff. 1–6v: Calendar in French with major feasts in red; included are the feasts of Launomar (19 January), Lubin (14 March), Emanus (16 May), Ivo (21 May), Caraunus (28 May), Anianus (10 June), Carileffus (1 July), Evurtius (7 September), Lubin (15 September), Solemnius (24 September), Anianus (7 December).

2. ff. 7–8v: Prayers as follow: O Maria piissima stella maris clarissima mater misericordie . . . [*RH* 13213]; Memento obsecro dulcis maria et domina illius venerande stacionis . . . [masculine forms]; Deus dator gaudii largitor solacii . . . ; Inviolata integra et casta . . . [*RH* 9094].

3. ff. 9–11v: Pericopes of the Gospels (but missing the pericope from John); *Antiphona de virgine maria,* Salve regina . . . [*RH* 18147] and the prayer, Concede nos famulos tuos quesumus domine deus perpetua mentis et corporis sanitate gaudere . . . ; *antiphona Tempore paschale,* Regina celi letare . . . [*RH* 17170].

4. ff. 12–49: Hours of the Virgin, use of Chartres; psalms at matins are Pss. 8, 18, 23, 44, 45, 86, 95, 96, 97, with no intermediary rubrics for the days of the week or for the nocturns.

5. ff. 49v–51: Short hours of the Cross.

6. ff. 51v–53: Short hours of the Holy Spirit.

7. ff. 53v–65: Penitential psalms and litany, including Caraunus and Piatus among the martyrs; Renatus, Sentinus (?), Gilderic, Maturinus and Avertinus (*sic,* for Aventius?) among the confessors; Rosa, Genevieve and Radegundis among the virgins.

8. ff. 65v–95v: Office of the Dead, use of Chartres; *Quiconques dira ceste oroison en ung cymetere . . . ,* Avete omnes anime fideles . . . with versicle, response and prayer, Domine ihesu christe salus et liberatio . . . [Leroquais, *LH* 2:341].

9. ff. 96–112v: Suffrage of one's guardian angel; *Antiphona de sancto michaele archangelo,* Sancte michael archangele domini nostri ihesu christi qui venisti in adiutorio populo dei . . . ; *Oracio devotissima de vulneribus christi,* Omnibus consideratis Paradisus voluptatis . . . [Johannes Lemovicensis; Wilmart, 584, n. to p. 527] with the prayer, Omnipotens sempiterne deus qui unigenitum filium tuum dominum nostrum ihesum christum crucem coronam spineam . . . ; *Oracio ante corpus cristi,* Adoro te domine ihesu christe quem confiteor esse deum verum . . . ; Domine ihesu christe propter illam amarissimam passionem . . . ; Ave domine ihesu christe verbum patris . . . [Wilmart, 412]; Domine

ihesu christe qui hanc sacratissimam carnem . . . [Wilmart, 378, n.]; *Sequitur oracio ad patrem,* Adoro te deus pater ingenite . . . , *Postea dicat,* Credo in deum patrem et cetera, Respice quesumus domine super hanc familiam tuam . . . , *Oratio ad filium,* Adoro te domine ihesu christe unicum dei filium . . . , *Oracio,* Omnipotens sempiterne deus dirige actus nostros in beneplacito tuo . . . , *Postea dicatur,* Credo in spiritum sanctum et cetera, *Oracio ad spiritum sanctum,* Adoro te spiritus paraclite deum verum procedentem ab utroque . . . , *Oracio,* Mentes nostras quesumus domine paraclitus spiritus sanctus . . . , Veni creator spiritus mentes tuorum visita . . . [*RH* 21204]; Deus qui corda fidelium sancti spiritus . . . ; *Sequitur oracio devotissima de vita et passione domini nostri ihesu christi,* Tu domine ihesu christe qui pro nobis miseris peccatoribus dignatus es homo fieri . . . ; *Secuntur quindecim oraciones preclarissime sancte brigide* . . . , O domine ihesu christe eterna dulcedo te amancium iubilus . . . [*HE,* 76–80], followed by a related rubric, *Responsio crucifixi talis est,* Quicumque per circulum unius anni predictas quindecim orationes . . .

10. ff. 113–124: *De sancto michaele archangelo oratio,* Deus propicius esto michi peccatori . . . [*HE,* 125] with versicles, responses and prayer, Beati archangeli tui michaelis intercessione sussulti . . . ; *oratio quando dicitur Sanctus,* Auxiliatrix esto michi sancta trinitas . . . ; *Salutacio coram sacratissimo corpore domini nostri Ihesu cristi,* Ave verum corpus natum de maria virgine . . . [Wilmart, 373–76]; *Salutacio ad elevacionem sanguinis cristi,* Ave sanguis preciosi corporis . . . with versicle, response and prayer, Deus qui nobis sub sacramento mirabili . . . ; *antiphona,* Anima christi sanctifica me . . . [Leroquais, *LH* 2:340]; *Alia oratio,* Ave preciosissimum et sanctissimum corpus domini nostri ihesu christi in ara crucis . . . ; Ave domine ihesu christe verbum patris . . . [as on f. 101r–v; Wilmart, 412]; *oracio valde devota,* Domine ihesu christe qui hanc sacratissimam carnem . . . [as on ff. 101v–102; Wilmart, 378, n.]; *Oracio de eodem,* Domine ihesu christe fili dei vivi qui pro peccatoribus corpus tuum . . . ; Conditor et redemptor corporis et anime esto michi medicus et custos . . . ; *supplicatio ad Requirendum misericordiam deo,* Miserere mei domine et exaudi oracionem meam . . . [the 9 Miserere's] and the verse, Ave domine ihesu doce me facere voluntatem tuam quia deus meus es tu; *oratio,* Obsecro te . . . et michi famule tue . . . [Leroquais, *LH* 2:346]; *Oratio de Beata maria virgine,* Ave cuius conceptio . . . [*RH* 1744] with versicle, response and prayer, Deus cuius conceptionis nativitatis . . . ; *De Sancta maria,* Stabat mater dolorosa . . . [*RH* 19416] and the prayer, Saluto te sancta domina virgo maria celorum regina ea salutacione . . . ; *Oracio edita a beato gregorio,* Domine Ihesu christe redemptor mundi deffende me de manu inimicorum . . . da michi famule tue . . .

11. ff. 124–136: *Oracio de omnibus sanctis,* Omnes sancti cherubim et seraphim throni quoque et dominaciones . . . ; *de omnibus apostolis,* Sancti apostoli dilecti dei vos elegit deus in salutem populi sui . . . ; *de sanctis martiribus,* Gloriosissimi milites sancti martires christi qui pro eius nomine . . . ; *Antiphona de sanctissimis confessoribus,* O Inextinguibiles lucerne mundi confessores cristi . . . ; *Antiphona de omnibus sanctis virginibus,* Inestimabilis et immense glorie sancte virgines christi duplici sorte beate . . . pro me peccatrice . . . ; suffrages of John the Baptist, John the Evangelist [Sancte iohannes evangelista qui cuncta que habere poteras . . .], Eutropius, Stephen, Denis, Sebastian, George, Benedict, Francis, Anthony abbot, Nicholas, Martin, Joachim, Anne, Avia, Catherine

of Alexandria, Mary Magdalene, Barbara, Apollonia, Opportuna, Fiacre, Maturinus, James the Greater [O adiutor omnium seculorum o decus apostolorum . . .]

12. ff. 136–141v: Passion according to John.

13. ff. 141v–146: Suffrages of Peter, Paul, Andrew, John the Evangelist [Iste est iohannes qui supra pectus domini. . .], James the Greater [O adiutor omnium seculorum o decus apostolorum . . . as on ff. 135v–136], Bartholomew, Matthew the Evangelist, Thomas the Apostle, Philip and James the Less, Simon and Jude, Matthias the Apostle, Barnabas, Mark, Luke, the Innocents.

14. ff. 146v–162v: *Oratio devotissima ad deum directa,* Domine deus omnipotens qui trinus es et unus, qui es semper in omnibus . . . [Wilmart, 573–77]; *Alia oratio ad conditorem cunctorum,* Conditor celi et terre Rex regum et dominus dominancium . . . respices me famulam tuam . . . ; suffrages of Leonard, Lupus, the Tears of Christ, Renatus, Cosmas and Damian, Margaret; *Secuntur versus Sancti Bernardi,* Illumina oculos meos . . . [*RH* 27912] followed by the prayer, Omnipotens sempiterne deus qui ezechieli [*sic*] regi . . . ; Deus pater qui creasti Mundum et Illuminasti, Suscipe me penitentem, Et illumina meam mentem . . . [*RH* 4477]; *Consideratio continua nostre vite presentis,* Quis capiti det Rivos aquarum Et oculis fontem lacrimarum . . . ; suffrage of Christopher [. . . michi famule tue N. . . .]; suffrage of Lawrence; O domine ihesu christe adoro te in cruce pendentem . . . [Leroquais, *LH* 2:346]; Gracias et laudes tibi ago domine deus meus misericordia mea qui me dignatus es creare . . .

Parchment, ff. ii (paper) + iv (parchment, of which the first was the pastedown) + 162 + ii (paper); 173 × 115 (100 × 54) mm. 1^8 2^8(–1, the Gospel of John) $3–20^8$ 21^4(–4). One catchword, f. 15v, in the script of the text, written horizontally, to the right of the inner bounding line. 20 long lines through f. 127v (quire 16), thereafter 21 long lines; ruled in a very faint brownish ink. Written in a bâtarde script in 2 sizes according to liturgical function.

Twelve large miniatures above 3 lines of text in squared frames, in an unusual style, the figures being painted with large heads and in dark tones, possibly by more than one artist. The miniatures are: f. 12 (Hours of the Virgin), Annunciation; f. 30 (Prime), Nativity; f. 33v (Terce), Annunciation to the shepherds; f. 36v (Sext), Adoration of the Magi; f. 39 (None), Presentation in the temple; f. 42 (Vespers), Flight into Egypt; f. 46 (Compline), Coronation of the Virgin by 2 angels before God the Father; f. 49v (Hours of the Cross), Crucifixion, with the 2 thieves painted in what would have been the upper portion of the outer border; f. 51v (Hours of the Holy Spirit), Pentecost; in the outer border 2 small strips from an earlier manuscript of geometric blue and gold acanthus design were glued over blank parchment before the illumination was painted; f. 53v (Penitential psalms), David enthroned, his counselors and harp behind him, watching a gentleman handing the letter to Uriah; outer border with glued-in strips as on f. 51v; f. 65v (Office of the Dead), Job on the dunghill; f. 161 (the 7 O's of Gregory), Vision of St. Gregory at Mass; outer border composed of rectangles containing flowers and the initials R, E, GI contracted (?) and N against a painted gold ground. Four historiated full borders: the border for John missing; f. 9, Luke, in the initial M, with the ox in a compartment of the border, which also includes a grotesque playing bagpipes and two half-snail, half-putto figures gathering strawberries; f. 9v, Matthew and his angel, whose wings extend into the initial's space, the initial, therefore, compressed into a small 1-line space of that area; with ox and snail-putti traced through from the recto; f. 10v, Mark in the border, his lion crouching on a bookstand in the space reserved for the initial; in the outer border 2 putti sitting in cherry trees, picking the fruit; f. 23v (Lauds), Visitation, with a grotesque playing an instrument in the border. Small miniatures, ca. 50 × 30 mm., placed in the band border which runs the length of the text, in the outer margin; where applicable, the flowered portions of the border are traced through from recto to verso; the miniatures are: f. 11 (Salve regina), Virgin and Child; f. 102 (Adoro te deus pater), Jesus holding a globe and blessing; f. 102v (Adoro te domine ihesu christe), Man of Sorrows; f. 103 (Adoro te spiritus paraclite), Pentecost; f. 113 (Deus propicius esto michi peccatori), Michael holding a scale with 2 small naked souls, and vanquishing the devil; f. 118 (Obsecro te), the Virgin holding the infant Jesus already covered with his wounds; f. 120v (Ave cuius conceptio), the Virgin as Queen of Heaven, nursing the Child, in a crescent; f. 121 (Stabat mater dolorosa), Pietà; f. 126, John the Baptist pointing to the haloed Lamb whose front hooves are hooked over the edge of the miniature; f. 127, John the Evangelist holding the snaky chalice; f. 127v, Eutropius in bishop's garb, being beheaded; f. 128, Stephen with stones and book; f. 128v, Denis holding his severed head; f. 129, Sebastian; f. 129v, 2 miniatures: George and Benedict; f. 130, 2 miniatures: Francis receiving the stigmata from the winged crucifix, and Anthony abbot; f. 130v, Nicholas; f. 131, Martin; f. 131v, 2 miniatures: Joachim holding a staff, the other hand hooked on his belt, and Anne teaching the Virgin to read; f. 132, Avia in prison receiving the Eucharist from the Virgin; f. 132v, Catherine of Alexandria; f. 133, Mary Magdalene; f. 133v, Barbara; f. 134, Apollonia; f. 134v, Opportuna in her habit as abbess; f. 135, 2 miniatures: Fiacre dressed as a hermit and holding his spade and a book, and Maturinus with his shepherd's crook and the sheep in the background; f. 135v, James the Greater with a pilgrim's staff; f. 136 (Passion according to John), full border, in dark tones, possibly by a different artist, with successive vignettes of the Agony in the Garden, Christ washing the Apostles' feet, and the Last Supper; f. 136v (idem), Judas kissing Jesus who is about to heal Malchus' ear; f. 137 (idem), Christ, blindfolded, being slapped by a group of men; f. 137v (idem), Christ before Caiaphas; f. 138 (idem), Christ before Pilate; f. 138v (idem), Scourging at the pillar; f. 139 (idem), Mockery of Christ; f. 139v (idem), Pilate washing his hands; f. 140 (idem), Road to Calvary, and Christ being stripped of the seamless tunic; f. 140v (idem), Crucifixion with Mary, John and Mary Magdalene, and Stephaton offering the vinegar-soaked sponge; f. 141 (idem), Deposition from the Cross; f. 141v (idem), Entombment and in another miniature, Peter; f. 142, 2 miniatures: Paul and Andrew; f. 142v, John the Evangelist holding a shepherd's crook; f. 143, Bartholomew holding a knife; f. 143v, 2 miniatures: Matthew the Evangelist holding a book and a halberd, and Thomas the Apostle holding a book and a lance; f. 144, Philip holding a tau-cross, and James the Less (or Philip again?) holding a Greek cross on a staff; f. 144v, 2 miniatures: Simon holding a falchion, and Matthias holding an ax; f. 145, Barnabas in prison, holding a book, presumably the gospel of Matthew; f. 145v, Mark; f. 146, Luke; f. 146v (Domine deus omnipotens qui es trinus et unus), Gnadenstuhl; f. 149v (Conditor celi), Christ on a rainbow showing his wounds; f. 151v, 2 miniatures: Leonard with his fetters, and Lupus in bishop's garb; f. 152v, Renatus, the full length of the band border, in bishop's garb; f. 153, 2 miniatures: Cosmas and Damianus, and Margaret; f. 160, Christopher; f. 160v, Lawrence. Simple band border on f. 96 (Rogo te sancte angele). 6-line initial on f. 11 (Salve Regina) formed by a 2-headed snake biting branches with both mouths. 4- and 3-line initials in white-shaded blue, red or grey infilled with naturalistic flowers, set against a painted gold ground; 3-line initials in gold-decorated red on square blue grounds; 2- and 1-line initials in painted gold on blue or brick red grounds; ribbon line fillers in the same colors; initials within the text touched in yellow. Rubrics in a very pale pink.

Bound, s. XIX, in purple morocco by Koehler; silver fore edge clasp closing from back to front; gilt edges.

Written at the end of the fifteenth century in France with the use of Chartres in the hours of the Virgin and in the office of the dead; the saints of the calendar also suggest Chartres. The first owner may have been a woman as the prayers occasionally contain feminine forms (ff. 119v, 123v, 125v, 150, 160). A note on f. ii reads "Je suis a Demoiselle Jeanne de Malherbe, 1567." Belonged to A. Firmin Didot (1790–1876); his sale, Paris,

HM 1150

16 June 1883, n. 12 to Labitte. Belonged to Robert Hoe: Grolier Club (1892) n. 58; *Cat.* (1909) pp. 57–59; his sale, Anderson, New York, 1912, pt. III, n. 2071 to G. D. Smith. Precise source and date of acquisition by Henry E. Huntington unknown.

Bibliography: De Ricci, 99.

HM 1151 — France, s. XV^{in}
BOOK OF HOURS, use of Paris

1. ff. 1–11v: Full calendar in French of the type printed by Perdrizet, including Denis (9 October, in gold); the leaf with the month of January missing; major feasts in gold, the others alternate 2 red with 2 blue entries; particularly on the first few leaves the gold is often entirely rubbed away, so that it appears never to have been applied.

2. ff. 12–17v: Pericopes of the Gospels, that of Matthew with the rubric "Secundum lucam."

3. ff. 18–85: Hours of the Virgin, use of Paris; 9 psalms and lessons at matins in the 3 groups, but without intermediary rubrics; opening leaf of lauds missing between ff. 41–42 with the missing portion of the first psalm for that hour, Ps. 92, 1–3, added in a sixteenth century continental hand in the upper margin of f. 42; the prayer, Ecclesiam tuam quesumus domine benignus . . . completes all hours, lauds to compline.

4. ff. 85v–102v: Penitential psalms and litany, including Denis and Eustachius among the martyrs; Eligius and Aegidius among the confessors and Genevieve among the virgins; breaks defectively in the prayer, Fidelium deus omnium conditor . . .

5. ff. 103r-v, 110–111v, 104–106v: Short hours of the Cross, beginning defectively and misbound as indicated.

6. ff. 107–109v, 112–113v: Short hours of the Holy Spirit.

7. ff. 114–160: Office of the Dead, use of Paris.

8. ff. 160v–183v: Prayers as follow: *Les xv ioies nostre dame,* Doulce dame de misericorde . . . [Leroquais, *LH* 2:310–11]; *Quicunques veult estre bien conseillie de la chose dont il a grant mestier si die par chascun iour les oroisons qui sont cy apres escriptes* . . . , Doulz dieu doulz pere sainte trinite un dieu . . . [Leroquais, *LH* 2:309–10]; Sainte vraie croix aouree . . . [Sonet 1876]; *Oracio beate marie virginis,* Obsecro te . . . [masculine forms; Leroquais, *LH* 2:346]; O Intemerata . . . orbis terrarum, de te enim . . . [Wilmart, 494–95]; suffrages of the Trinity, John the Baptist, Michael, Peter and Paul, Matthew, Simon and Jude, Andrew, Stephen, Lawrence, Denis, and the Innocents (breaking defectively before the prayer).

Parchment, ff. i (paper) + 183 + i (paper); 168 × 121 (98 × 65) mm. 1^6(–1) $2–3^6$ $4–6^8$ 7^8 (–1, before f. 42) $8–13^8$ 14^8(–7, before f. 103) 15^6(ff. 104–109) 16^4(ff. 110–113); these 2 quires originally formed a single gathering with the 2 bifolia of quire 16 as the outer leaves) 17–24⁸ 25 (6 leaves of uncertain structure). Catchwords in the script of the text in the center lower margin. 14 long lines, ruled in pale red ink. Written in a gothic book hand.

Twelve miniatures within square compartments above 4 lines of text; both text and miniature enclosed by U-shaped frames which derive from the initial; the miniatures, set against diapered backgrounds and with green grass as the base, are: f. 18 (Hours of the Virgin), Annunciation, with God the Father appearing in an aperture at the top of the miniature; the outer border contains regular swirls of narrow pink or blue vines with trilobe leaves in these colors and in gold, although both the gold and the miniature itself are badly rubbed; opening leaf for lauds missing; f. 52v (Prime), Nativity with the Virgin lying on an orange-draped bed and reaching to the Infant in a manger, while Joseph, propped against the foot of the bed, dozes; outer border of black ink vines with spiky gold trilobe leaves; f. 59 (Terce), Annunciation to the shepherds; outer border as on f. 52v; f. 64 (Sext), Adoration of the Magi; in the outer border both the pink and blue swirled branches and the black vine spray; f. 68v (None), Presentation in the temple; border as on f. 64; f. 73 (Vespers), Flight into Egypt; outer border formed of black ivy spray completed in the lower margin with spiky gold trilobe leaves, and on the outer and upper margins with orange, blue and gold rayed tear-drop leaves and an occasional star-flower; f. 80 (Compline), Coronation of the Virgin, who sits with hands folded in prayer beside God the Father on a pink bench decorated with acanthus leaves; the outer border contains gold and colored rayed tear-drop leaves and a few fleshy acanthus leaves in orange and blue; f. 85v (Penitential psalms), David, kneeling in a fantastic landscape of twisted green hills and two trees, looks up at God the Father who appears in a dark blue aperture in the diapered background; outer border as on f. 64; opening leaf of the Hours of the Cross missing; f. 107 (Hours of the Holy Spirit), Pentecost, with a dense outer border of bright orange, blue and gold rayed tear-drop leaves and star-flowers and 3 grotesques (plus a fourth in the initial); f. 114 (Office of the Dead), 3 singing monks and a group of mourners clustered about a blue-draped coffin; the outer border of a rather sparse black vine with spiky trilobe leaves in oxidized silver, and, in the lower margin, a few colored or gold tear-drop leaves and star-flowers, larger than those on f. 107; f. 160v (Doulce dame de misericorde), the Virgin sitting on the same pink bench as on f. 80, and putting her arms around the Child who stands next to her on the bench; outer border with oxidized silver trilobe leaves and tear-drop leaves, and, especially in the lower margin, blue and pink circle and star-flowers; f. 167 (Doulz dieu doulz pere), Last Judgment, with Christ on a rainbow showing his wounds; the outer border contains small, dense, rayed gold tear-drop leaves and several clusters of fleshy blue, orange and olive green acanthus leaves, with daisy buds, prickly pear fruit and a trumpet flower; along the inner margin are 4 scrolls, the last out of alignment with the others which are now painted over in white, apparently to cover writing underneath (?); a small dragon-like grotesque in pale ink among the flowers of the lower margin, as if unfinished or due to a change in program. 3-line initials in white-decorated blue or pink on gold grounds with colored trilobe leaf infilling, that on f. 107 also containing a grotesque; 3-, 2- and 1-line initials in burnished gold on pink grounds with blue infilling or vice versa. The flourished extensions of the 2-line initials consist of sprays of black-ink stems and squiggles and some colored buds, in 3 styles: i, up to f. 25v; ii, on the versos and conjuncts of illuminated leaves; iii, the most frequent form, with green also being used for the buds. Ribbon line fillers and single flowers for the same purpose in pink, blue and gold. Rubrics in an orange-tinged red, except for those of the calendar which are in a washed-out pink. The illuminated leaves have an irregular series of holes across the top, possibly where protective coverings for the miniatures were sewn. On f. 128, an additional line ruled at the bottom of the recto and at the top of the verso to add a portion of the text omitted by the scribe; it may be a contemporary correction. The margins of ff. 125 and 180 have been almost entirely replaced with parchment; numerous other small repairs occur throughout the volume; the stub which now holds f. 98 in place (the conjunct to the missing leaf before f. 103) bears writing in a sixteenth century French hand.

HM 1151

Bound, s. XVIII, in blind tooled calf, red sprinkled edges.

Written in the early fifteenth century for use in the area of Paris. The name "Caesar Sacrè" in a sixteenth century (?) hand on f. 112v. Obtained by Henry E. Huntington from the book dealer Charles Sessler of Philadelphia.

Bibliography: De Ricci, 99.

HM 1153 — France, s. XV^2
BOOK OF HOURS, use of Sens (?)

1. ff. 1–12v: Full calendar in French in red and black; included are the feasts of Sabinianus martyr (24 January), Maturinus (10 May), Columba (28 July) and Sabinianus bishop and martyr (19 October, in red).

2. ff. 13–15 [f. 13, blank]: Pericope from John [1, 1–14], and the prayer, Protector in te sperantium . . . [Perdrizet, 25].

3. ff. 15v–63: Hours of the Virgin, possibly in the use of Sens, but with the antiphon to the psalms at vespers "Beatam me dicent omnes generationes . . ."

4. ff. 63v–66: Short hours of the Cross.

5. ff. 66v–69: Short hours of the Holy Spirit.

6. ff. 69v–84: Penitential psalms and litany, including Sabinianus, Potentianus and Maturinus.

7. ff. 84v–106: Office of the Dead, 3 lessons.

8. ff. 106v–115v: Obsecro te . . . [masculine forms; Leroquais, *LH* 2:346]; suffrages of Michael, James, Andrew, George, Adrian, Martin, Nicholas, Eligius, Maturinus, Anne, Mary Magdalene, Catherine of Alexandria.

Parchment, ff. ii (modern parchment, with silk glued to the recto of the first) + 115 + ii (modern parchment with silk glued to the verso of the second); 155 × 108 (90 × 60) mm. 1^8 2^4 3^8(+ 1, f. 13) 4^8(+ 4, f. 25) 5^8 6^6(+ 1, f. 39 and 6, f. 44) 7^8(+ 1, f. 47 and 6, f. 52) 8^8(+ 3, f. 59) 9^4 $10–13^8$ 14^8(+ 6, f. 107) 15^6(–6). 17 long lines, ruled in pale red ink. Written in a bâtarde script.

Fourteen full page miniatures, of which 6 are original (with some retouching), and the others are later additions by Caleb W. Wing (corrected form of the name kindly communicated to us by Janet Backhouse); see J. Backhouse, "A Victorian Connoisseur and his manuscripts: The Tale of Mr. Jarman and Mr. Wing," *British Museum Quarterly* 32 (1967–68) 76–92. The original miniatures are part of the quire structure with text on the reverse side and they introduce major divisions (except for that on f. 34v, for prime); the additions are singletons, blank on the reverse; they are placed at minor divisions (Gospel of John; internal hours of the Virgin, except for prime; Obsecro te) and they interrupt the flow of the text. A number of the bracket borders which surround the facing text at these divisions were also added at the later time. The miniatures and the borders on opposing text pages are: ff. 13v–14 (Gospel of John), John on Patmos, both the miniature and the facing border are added; ff. 15v–16 (Hours of the Virgin), Annunciation, the miniature original with possible retouching on the faces, the facing border added; ff. 24v–25 (Lauds), Visitation, the facing border is original, the miniature added; ff. 34v–35 (Prime), Nativity, the miniature original with possible retouching of the faces, the facing border added; ff. 39v–40 (Terce), Annunciation to the shepherds, both the miniature and the facing border are added; ff. 43v–44 (Sext), Adoration of the Magi, the facing border is original, the miniature added; ff. 47v–48 (None), Presentation in the temple, both the miniature and the facing border are added; ff. 51v–52 (Vespers), Flight into Egypt, the facing border is original, the miniature added; ff. 58v–59 (Compline), Massacre of the Innocents, the facing border is original, the miniature added; ff. 63v–64 (Hours of the Cross), Crucifixion, the miniature is original, the facing border added; ff. 66v–67 (Hours of the Holy Spirit), Pentecost, the miniature is original, the facing border added; ff. 69v–70 (Penitential psalms), Last Judgment, the miniature is original, the facing border added; ff. 84v–85 (Office of the Dead), Funeral in a church, the miniature is original, the facing border added; ff. 106v–107 (Obsecro te), Coronation of the Virgin, the facing border is original, the miniature added. Major initials, 5- or 4-line, in shaded pink or blue, with flowers on a gold infilling, the whole against a shaded ground of the other color; or, more commonly, as a shaded white ribbon with white flowers or leaves on the gold infilling, the whole set against a square of gold-patterned red. 2- and 1-line initials, in painted gold against alternating brown, blue or red square grounds; line fillers in these colors or as gold logs. Rubrics in red.

Bound, s. XIX, in deep purple velvet with 2 silver-gilt fore edge clasps, closing from bottom to top; grey silk linings; gauffered gilt edges; HM 1161 and HM 1175 with similar binding.

Written in the second half of the fifteenth century in France, possibly for use in the diocese of Sens, given the liturgical usage (?), and the saints of the calendar and litany. Possibly lot 25 in the sale of John Boykett Jarman (d. 1864), Sotheby's, 13 June 1864 to de Bure, where it is said to be Flemish; Sir Frederic Madden's annotated copy, however, corrects the origin of lot 25 to French.[1] French sale catalogue slip, n. 200 (pasted to f. i verso and dated by De Ricci "c.1885") describes the book as containing 14 miniatures, some slightly retouched, and with its present binding, which is characteristic of Jarman-owned books. Belonged to Robert Hoe; Grolier Club (1892) n. 67; *Cat.* (1909) pp. 73–74; his sale, Anderson, New York, 1912, pt. III, n. 2065 with plate of f. 63v, to G. D. Smith. Precise source and date of acquisition by Henry E. Huntington unknown.

Bibliography: De Ricci, 99.

[1] We thank Janet Backhouse for this information; the annotated catalogue is in the reference library of the Department of Manuscripts, British Library.

HM 1154 — France, s. XV[2]
BOOK OF HOURS, use of Paris

1. ff. 1–12v: Full calendar in French with major feasts in red, generally similar to that printed by Perdrizet; includes Charlemagne (28 January).

2. ff. 13–22: Pericopes of the Gospels, that of John followed by the prayer, Protector in te sperantium . . . [Perdrizet, 25]; *Oratio de beata maria,* Obsecro te . . . [masculine forms; Leroquais, *LH* 2:346]; f. 22v, ruled, but blank.

3. ff. 23–66v: Hours of the Virgin, use of Paris; the prayer, Ecclesiam tuam quesumus domine benignus . . . , follows by cue all hours after and excepting lauds, where it is written in full; ff. 67–68v, ruled, but blank.

4. ff. 69–86: Penitential psalms and litany, including Denis, Maurice, Eustachius, Eutropius and Quentin among the martyrs; Charles, Remigius, Marcellus, Eli-

gius, Aegidius, Julianus, Maurus and Lubin among the confessors; Genevieve among the virgins.

5. ff. 86v–89v: Short hours of the Cross.

6. ff. 90–92v: Short hours of the Holy Spirit.

7. ff. 93–121: Office of the Dead, use of Paris.

8. ff. 121–135: Prayers as follow: Doulce dame de misericorde . . . [Leroquais, *LH* 2:310–11]; Doulx dieulx doulx pere saincte trinite . . . [Leroquais, *LH* 2:309–10]; Saincte vraye croix aoree . . . [Sonet 1876]; suffrages of Michael, John the Baptist, James the Greater, Christopher, Sebastian, Nicholas, Anthony abbot, Catherine of Alexandria, Margaret, Barbara; ff. 135v–136v, ruled, but blank.

Parchment, ff. i (parchment) + 136 + i (parchment); 148 × 103 (90 × 57) mm. $1\text{–}2^6$ $3\text{–}9^8$(through f. 68) $10\text{–}12^8$(through f. 92) $13\text{–}17^8$ 18^6(–5, 6). Catchwords have occasionally survived cropping and appear in the script of the text in the center lower margin. 16 long lines, ruled in pale red ink. Written in a gothic book hand.

Five large miniatures, simply done, above 4 lines of text, enclosed by a narrow gold frame on 2 sides and with a small amount of gold tracery at the top; the outer borders with compartmentalized divisions of natural parchment or painted gold grounds, both with blue and gold acanthus leaves and colored flowers. The miniatures are: f. 23 (Hours of the Virgin), Annunciation; f. 69 (Penitential psalms), David, supporting his harp with one hand, and kneeling in prayer, while God the Father appears in a blue-rimmed yellow aperture in the sky; f. 86v (Hours of the Cross), Crucifixion with Mary and John on either side; f. 90 (Hours of the Holy Spirit), Pentecost; f. 93 (Office of the Dead), burial scene in a churchyard, with the corpse being lowered into the grave by a young man, while mourners and priests look on. Seven smaller miniatures, 50 × 38 mm., possibly by a different artist, enclosed in frames of simple gold arches, with bracket borders set to the left of the text consisting of a gold and color strip along the text, and acanthus leaves and flowers. The miniatures are: f. 33 (Lauds), Visitation; f. 43 (Prime), Nativity, with the Baby lying on an extension of the Virgin's robe; f. 47v (Terce), 33 × 33 mm., Annunciation to the shepherds; f. 51 (Sext), Adoration of the Magi; f. 54 (None), Presentation in the temple; f. 57 (Vespers), Flight into Egypt; f. 62v (Compline), Coronation of the Virgin, who kneels before Christ, with blue swirling clouds at the lower right corner. 3-line initials in white-patterned blue on gold grounds with colored trilobe leaf infilling; 2- and 1-line initials in gold on dark pink grounds with blue infilling or vice versa; ribbon line fillers in the same colors; initials within the text touched in yellow. Rubrics in dark pink.

Bound, s. XVI, in French calf with gold tooling and the name "Marie" (front cover) "De Rebergues" (back cover); 2 sets of holes on the edges of the front and back covers from fore edge clasps; other holes on both covers from central bosses; gilt edges.

Written for use in Paris in the second half of the fifteenth century. Names of early owners on the back pastedown: Manon dargilliere, francoise dargilliere. A sixteenth century owner was apparently Marie de Rebergues, whose name is stamped on the cover. A cancelled note on f. i identifies a seventeenth century owner as Anne Sa<?> Gaultier of Clermont, who obtained the book from her great-grandmother. Belonged to James Dix of Bristol; his sale, Sotheby's, 11 February 1870, lot 257 to Stevens. In the collection of E. Dwight Church (1835–1908); see his *Catalogue . . . of English Literature* (1909) vol. 1, n. 406 with a plate of f. 93. The Church collection was acquired by Henry E. Huntington in 1911.

Bibliography: De Ricci, 99.

HM 1155 Netherlands, s. XV^med^
BOOK OF HOURS, in Dutch

1. f. 1r–v: [Computistic texts] Soe wanner du paesschen wilste weten so merke op wat ghetale die mane prijmt int iaer . . .

2. ff. 2–13v: Full calendar with major feasts in red; included are the feasts of Pontianus (14 January, in red), Agnes (21 January, in red), Gertrude (17 March, in red), Pancratius, Nereus and Achilleus (12 May, in red), Servatius (13 May, in red), Boniface (5 June, in red), Odulph (12 June, in red), Lebuin (25 June, in red), Remigius and Bavo (1 October, in red), Gereon (10 October, in red), Willibrord (7 November, in red), Lebuin (12 November, in red); added by a later hand are the feasts of the Translation of Bernardinus (15 February), Bernardinus (20 May), the Translation of Francis (25 May), Anthony of Padua (13 June), the Portiuncula Indulgence (2 August), Clare (12 August), Louis (19 August), the Wounds of Francis (17 September), the Translation of Clare (2 October), "Dedicatio salvatoris" (8 November), "Dedicatio petri et pauli" (18 November); f. 14r–v, blank, except for notes.

3. ff. 15–45: Hours of the Virgin in the compilation of Geert Grote, ending with the Salve Regina [van Wijk, 36–70]; Coninginne des hemels verblijt di alleluya . . . [Lievens, 35; 93].

4. ff. 45v–65v: Long hours of the Cross in the compilation of Geert Grote [van Wijk, 113–38].

5. ff. 65v–83: Hours of the Eternal Wisdom in the compilation of Geert Grote [van Wijk, 92–112].

6. ff. 83–97v: Penitential psalms and litany, including Boniface, Victor, Gereon and Pontianus among the martyrs; Willibrord, Remigius, Lebuin, Odulph and Ludger among the confessors; Agnes, Adelgundis, Ursula, Walburga and Gertrude among the virgins [van Wijk, 139–54].

7. ff. 97v–106v: *Hier beghinnen die v groeten van onser lieuer vrouwen, Aue maria,* God gruet v goedertieren maria een blenckende dagheraet een leydsterre des meers . . . ; *Van dinen heilighen engel antiphona,* Behoede nu mijn alre heilichste behoeder uan aenuechtinghe der quader gheesten . . . ; *Van sunte michiel antiphona,* Michael bewaerre des paradijs dien eren alle engelen. *vers.,* Ic gheue di lof in die teghenwoerdicheit der engelen . . . ; *Van sunte andries,* Sunte Andries heilige apostel ons heren ihesum christum ijn dijn ontfermicheit beuele ic mijn ziel ende mijn lichaem . . . ; *van sunte lourens martelaer antiphona,* Die heilige martelaer lourens badt seggende here ihesu christe ontferme di mijnre dijns knechts . . . ; *van sunte iheronimus antiphona,* O heilige iheronimus een lampe der heiligher kerken, een sonderlinge claerheit een leerre der wijsheit . . . ; *van sunte agniet ioncfrou,* O Ionghe suuer maghet sunte agniet mit rechte du besittes dijns brudegoms onsterflicheit . . . ; *van sunte dorothea,* God die dijn alre heilichste maghet dorothea bestort mit rosenden bloede der martelaerscap . . . ; *van sunte katherijn antiphona,* O alre salichste maghet katherijn een leuendige offerhande christi dine passie moet mi sijn een uerlatenis der zunden . . . ; *van sunte barbara,* God groet v heilighe maghet barbara een blenckende licht der claerheit, een spieghel der reinicheit . . . ;

van sunte maria magdaleen antiphona, O heilighe maria magdalena die verdiendes te scouwen alre eerst ihesum verresen vander doot . . . ; *van sunte cecilia antiphona,* O heilighe maghet sunte cecilia du biste een offerhande gods een bruut christi een tempel des heilighen gheests . . . ; *Van sunte margriet antiphona,* O heilighe gloriose maghet ende martelaerster christi sunte margriet coemt mi arme onweerdighe sunder te helpe . . . ; *Vanden elfdusen* [*sic*] *maechden Antiffen,* O bloemen der rosen ende lelye der dalen, O preciose martelaren ende onuerwinlike ridders cristi . . . ; *Van sunte aechte ioncfrou,* Wie soude uolprisen konnen of bewisen mit reden den groten brant der minnen die wi hier verrisen sien . . . ; *Van sunte gheertruut Antiphona,* O heilighe sunte gheertruut onsprekelijc van goedertierenheit tot die vlie ic die aenroep ic dine bedinghe totten here begheer ic . . . ; *Van sunte lucie Antiphona,* O god onse salichgheuer hoer ons ghelijc dat wi uerbliden inder hochtijt der saligher maghet lucien . . . ; *Van sunte scolastica,* O almachtighe god wi bidden di oetmoedelijc dat die ghenadich biste weerdighen wilste aen te sien die uerdiente dijnre heiligher maghet sunte scolastica . . .

8. f. 107r–v: [Christmas Hymn] *Dese ymmen houtmen in kermis daghe totter compleet,* O salighe stat iherusalem gheheten een scouwinge des vreden inden hemel uan leuendighen ghemaect is ende ghecroent mit engelen als een bruut teghen haren brudegom . . . wien is lof ende moghentheit in die ewighe weicheit. *Amen.* [Lievens, 38].

9. ff. 108–110v: [Communion Prayer, with a series of concluding *wel mi* . . . addresses and admonitions to the Lord to be mindful of the suppliant] *Alstu ten heiligen sacrament gaen selte, les dit,* O here huden begheer ic te ontfangen uwen ghebenediden lichame also waerlic ende uolcomelic als en u lieue moeder maria ontfinc . . . ende tot loue so werke in mi dijns uader lof aen den alre hoochsten.

10. f. 110v: [*Dicta*] Augustinus seit, niet en vijntmen dat den mensche meer uan zunden trecket, dan dicke te ouerdencken wat een doot lichaem is. Ysidorus seit, hoe uele wonden dat wi liden, in versmaetheit tot allen tiden also dicke wort ons ghegheuen, een zuuer crone int ewige leuen.

11. ff. 111–142v: Office of the Dead in the compilation of Geert Grote [van Wijk, 156–95].

Parchment, ff. i (modern parchment) + 142 + i (modern parchment); 130 × 93 (93 × 66) mm. 1^{6}(+ 1) 2^{6} 3^{8}(+ 1) $4–10^{8}$ 11^{8}(–4, excised, after f. 82) 12^{8} 13^{8}(–7, 8, after f. 99) 14^{8} 15^{4} (–1; ff. 108–110) $16–19^{8}$. 20 long lines ruled in light brown ink, the top and bottom 2 lines full across. Written in a gothic script in a brownish ink; computistic notes, f. 1r–v, and calendar possibly by another person, using darker ink. Six major initials: ff. 15 and 45v, 8-line, in parted red and blue, infilled with a void leaf design produced by purple cross-hatching; red and blue cascades, and penwork in red, light blue and purple forming bracket border; ff. 66 (7-line), 83 (6-line), 97v (3-line), 111 (6-line), parted red and blue with red leaf infilling, and penwork borders; 4-line initials in plain blue; 2- and 1-line initials alternating red and blue; slashed initials within the text, underlined words and rubrics in red.

Bound, s. XX, in pigskin; yellow stained edges; central fore edge clasp closing from back to front; previous binding in "old paper boards."

Written in the middle of the fifteenth century in the Netherlands, probably for use in the diocese of Utrecht. Later additions to the calendar show Franciscan interest. Belonged to Henry William Poor (1844–1915); his sale, Anderson, New York, 12 January 1909, pt. III, n. 765 to G. D. Smith. Precise source and date of acquisition by Henry E. Huntington unknown.

Bibliography: De Ricci, 99.

HM 1156 — France, s. XV^{in}
BOOK OF HOURS, use of Paris (?) — *fig. 84*

1. ff. 1–11v: Full calendar in French alternating deep red and blue entries, with the major feasts in gold; the leaf with the month of March is missing.

2. ff. 12–22v: Pericopes of the Gospels, that of John followed by the prayer, Protector in te sperantium . . . [Perdrizet, 25]; the rubrics for Matthew and Mark are reversed; *oracio,* Obsecro te . . . [masculine forms; Leroquais, *LH* 2:346]; *oracio,* O intemerata . . . orbis terrarum. Inclina aures . . . [Wilmart, 488–90]; *oracio,* O bone et dulcissime ihesu per tuam misericordiam esto michi ihesus . . . appelo que super exultat omne//

3. ff. 23–69: Hours of the Virgin; the antiphons and capitula at prime and at none are: Benedicta tu . . . ; Felix namque . . . ; Sicut lilium . . . ; Paradisi porta . . . (possibly reversed by the scribe with the capitulum at terce, which here begins "Per te dei"; aside from this reversal, all remaining antiphons and capitula correspond to those of Paris use); matins was presumably set up with the 3 sets of 3 psalms and lessons, but no intermediary rubrics are supplied, and the text begins defectively at Ps. 44, Erutavit [*sic*] cor meum . . . ; the opening leaves of each hour are missing; f. 69v, ruled, but blank.

4. ff. 70–75: Short hours of the Cross, missing the opening leaf.

5. ff. 75v–80v: Short hours of the Holy Spirit.

6. ff. 80v–84v: *Secundum Iohannem,* In illo tempore apprehendit pilatus ihesum et flagellavit eum . . . [catena mainly from John 19, 1–34 *sparsim;* see de la Mare, *Lyell Cat.,* 65–66] with the prayer, Deus qui manus tuas et pedes tuos . . . ; *oratio,* O bone et dulcissime ihesu per tuam misericordiam esto michi ihesus . . . [as on f. 22r–v, ending there defectively]; Stabat mater dolorosa . . . [*RH* 19416].

7. ff. 85–98: Penitential psalms, beginning defectively, and litany, including Blasius, Eutropius and Denis among the martyrs; Silvester, Ambrose, Francis and Marcellus as the confessors; Genevieve among the virgins; f. 98v, ruled, but blank.

8. ff. 99–138v: Office of the Dead, use of Paris, beginning and ending defectively.

9. ff. 139–141: //me sentire vim doloris fac ut tecum lugeam . . . [prayer to the Virgin]; suffrage of Christopher [. . . michi famulo tuo N . . .]; f. 141v, ruled, but blank.

Parchment, ff. iii (paper) + ii (parchment) + 141 + ii (parchment) + iii (paper); 178 × 126 (95 × 58) mm. Collation impracticable, but appears to be in gatherings of 8. 17

long lines, ruled in pale red ink. Written in a bâtarde script in 2 sizes according to liturgical function.

Only one miniature survives; the remaining 12 (?) were apparently cut out, as indicated by the loss of text at the beginning of each section, by the presence of some stubs at those points and by the offset of color onto the presumed facing pages. The surviving miniature, f. 75v, in a square compartment above 5 lines of text with both text and miniature surrounded on 4 sides by a narrow gold and color bar frame out of which sprout narrow dark pink or blue branches with gold, blue and orange trilobe leaves, and a dragon-grotesque, a bird, and a half-man half-cat grotesque with a golden aspergillum and situla; in the space between the bottom of the text and the frame are a dog and a hare on a green grass base. The miniature, for the Hours of the Holy Spirit, shows Jesus being baptized in the river Jordan by John the Baptist who pours water over Jesus' head with his right hand and holds the Agnus Dei in his left; an angel stands on the left bank holding Jesus' tunic, while God the Father from a golden aperture in the gold-patterned blue sky sends down the Dove. The miniature was apparently over-painted in the late fifteenth century as indicated by the deep modelling of the figures, the shadow of Jesus' body seen through the water and the soft trees and grass. 3- and 2-line initials in white-patterned blue on burnished gold grounds with colored trilobe leaf infilling; 1-line initials in burnished gold alternating pink and blue for the infilling and the background; ribbon line fillers in the same colors. Rubrics in deep red. Narrow gold and color bar frames sprouting colored ivy branches on every page, placed on either side of the text; they occasionally terminate in grotesques. On the opening leaves of each month of the calendar and on occasional other leaves (13v, 71), the frame is U-shaped. On ff. 27–34v and 119–126v, which constitute quires, and on the single leaves ff. 139–140v, the border is of somewhat coarser execution. Erased inscription in blue ink, s. XVI (?), on f. 141, in 5 lines, of which the first may read "finis."

Bound, s. XIX, in worn red velvet lettered "Missal" on the spine; 2 engraved silver fore edge clasps; gilt edges.

Written in the early fifteenth century in France. Source and date of acquisition by Henry E. Huntington unknown.

Bibliography: De Ricci, 99.

HM 1157 — Flanders, s. XV[ex]
BOOK OF HOURS, use of Rome — *fig. 141*

1. ff. 1–12v: Calendar in red and black, including, in red, the feasts of Basilius (14 June), Remigius and Bavo (1 October), Donatianus (14 October).

2. ff. 13–14v: *Ad salutandum faciem christi,* Salve sancta facies . . . [*RH* 18189] and the prayer, Deus qui nobis signatis lumen vultus tui . . .

3. ff. 15–22v [f. 15, blank]: Short hours of the Cross.

4. ff. 23–29v [f. 23, blank]: Short hours of the Holy Spirit.

5. ff. 30–37 [f. 30, blank]: Mass of the Virgin.

6. ff. 37–42v: Pericopes of the Gospels.

7. ff. 43–120v [f. 43, blank]: *Incipiunt hore beate marie virginis secundum usum Romanum;* weekly variations of the psalms at matins set into the text before the lessons; suffrages of All Saints and prayers for peace from lauds to compline;

Salve Regina follows compline; Advent office begins on f. 112; [added by a contemporary hand, f. 87r–v, before sext with its miniature of the Magi] Si ambulavero in medio tribulacionis vivicabis me . . . Oremus. Deus qui tres magos orientales . . . ut michi famulo tuo N. . . .

8. ff. 121–144v: Prayers as follow: *Oracio beate marie virginis,* Obsecro te . . . Et michi famulo tuo N. impetres . . . [Leroquais, *LH* 2:346]; *Alia oracio de beata maria,* O intemerata . . . orbis terrarum. De te enim . . . [Wilmart, 494–95]; *Oracio devota ad ihesum christum,* O bone ihesu o piissime ihesu . . . [Allen, *Writings,* 314–17]; *Oracio beati gregorii pape,* Domine ihesu christe exaudi oracionem meam quia iam cognosco quod tempus meum prope est . . . ; suffrages of John the Baptist, Peter and Paul, James, Adrianus, Sebastian, Michael, Francis, Anthony abbot, Nicholas, Anne, Mary Magdalene, Catherine of Alexandria, Barbara, Margaret.

9. ff. 145–167v [f. 145, blank]: Penitential psalms and litany.

10. ff. 168–213 [f. 168, blank]: Office of the Dead, use of Rome.

11. ff. 213v–217v: *Symbolum athanasii episcopi,* Quicumque vult salvus esse . . . ; [added by a second contemporary hand] *versus sancti bernardi,* Illumina oculos meos . . . [*RH* 27912]; f. 217v, 2-line erasure, illegible.

Parchment, ff. i (parchment) + 217 and 2 leaves skipped in the foliation, now numbered ff. 87a, 88a + i (parchment); 124 × 90 (70 × 50) mm. 1^{12} 2^{8}(+ 3, f. 15) 3^{8}(+ 2, f. 23 and 8, f. 30) 4^{8} 5^{8}(+ 4, f. 43) 6^{8} 7^{8}(+ 7, f. 63) 8^{8} 9^{8}(+ 3, f. 76 and 8, f. 82) 10^{8}(+ 5, f. 88) 11^{8}(+ 1, f. 91 and 5, f. 96) 12^{8}(+ 5, f. 105) 13^{10}(+ 2, f. 111; through f. 120) $14–16^{8}$ 17^{8}(+ 1, f. 145) 18^{8} 19^{8}(+ 7, f. 168) $20–24^{8}$ 25^{6}(+ 7). 15 long lines, ruled in pale red ink. Written in a regular bâtarde script, with prayers added by two different hands on ff. 87r–v and 217r–v.

Fifteen full page miniatures on the versos of inserted singletons, blank on the rectos; in slightly arched compartments surrounded by full borders, usually consisting of realistically painted flowers, branchy acanthus leaves, insects, and birds strewn on a gold field, textured through stippling or dabbed paint; matching borders on the facing rectos, with 5-line branchy acanthus leaf initials. The miniatures are: 15v–16 (Hours of the Cross), the Crucifixion, with Mary and John on Jesus' right, the soldiers on his left; in the border, the Passion in a series of vignettes: Christ at Gethsemane, praying to God in the heavens, with the apostles below; Judas kissing Christ who holds Malchus' ear; Christ before Pilate and then being lead away; flagellation; the mocking of Christ; the devil handing a rope to Judas as he climbs a tree; the road to Calvary; Judas hanged. On f. 23v (Hours of the Holy Spirit), Pentecost; f. 30v (Mass of the Virgin), the Virgin supporting the Child on a pillow with a canopy above them; ff. 43v–44 (Hours of the Virgin), the Annunciation, and in the border, the tree of Jesse with the generations of Christ, clusters of grapes and grape leaves; f. 63v (Lauds), Visitation in front of a substantial pink house; f. 76v (Prime), Nativity, above a vaulted stone chamber with a pillar; f. 82v (Terce), Annunciation to the shepherds with the angel in a multicolored cloudy sky; f. 88v (Sext), Adoration of the Magi; f. 91v (None), Presentation in the temple; f. 96v (Vespers), Massacre of the Innocents, with one mother hitting a soldier with a wooden ladle; f. 105v (Compline), Flight into Egypt: the Virgin, riding a donkey, nurses her Child while a palm tree bends over them, with the soldiers and the cornfield in the background; f. 111v (Advent office), Coronation of the Virgin, who kneels before the Father and the Son, both wearing the same cloak while the Dove hovers between them; f. 145v (Penitential psalms), David in prayer and the angel sheathing his sword; f. 168v (Office of the Dead), a man lying dead on his bed; with an angel protecting his small naked soul from an attacking devil. Twenty-three 7-line miniatures with bracket borders to the left of the text in the same style as the full borders: f. 37 (Gospel of John), John on Patmos; f. 38v, Luke writing at a desk; f. 40, Matthew writing, with the angel at a smaller desk; f. 41v, Mark with the lion; f. 121 (Obsecro te), John supporting the body of Jesus while Mary worships him; f. 125 (O Intemerata), the Virgin, holding the Child, sits within a wattle-enclosed garden; f. 129 (O bone ihesu), the Child, sitting on a large pink cushion wearing a coral necklace and playing with another; f. 131v (prayer of Gregory), Vision of St. Gregory; f. 136, John the Baptist, seated, points to the Lamb; f. 136v, Peter and Paul holding their attributes in a green landscape; f. 137, James with staff, pouch and knapsack; f. 138, Adrianus, with sword, anvil and lion (presumably conflating the Adrianus martyred at Caesarea and the one put to death in Nicomedia); f. 138v, Sebastian, fully clothed, holding arrows; f. 139v, Michael fighting 2 devils; f. 140, Francis showing the stigmata; f. 140v, Anthony abbot, reading, his book propped on a wattle fence and the pig behind him; f. 141v, Nicholas seated before the 3 children in a tub; f. 142, Anne, seated, reading in an enclosed garden, while Mary, kneeling, supports the infant Jesus against Anne's knees; f. 142v, Mary Magdalene, nude except for a cloth about her waist, praying, the pot and cave behind her, the entire view seen between parted curtains in the foreground; f. 143, Catherine, holding wheel and sword; f. 144, Barbara; f. 144v, Margaret in prison, emerging from the dragon; f. 213 (Athanasian Creed), Athanasius, with bishop's mitre, sitting before a red drape and holding a book. In the calendar, bracket borders to the left of the text begin each month with square inserts in the upper margin for the sign of the zodiac and in the lower margin for the occupation of the month. Secondary initials, 2- and 1-line, in painted gold on square light-brown grounds with gold tracery; ribbon line fillers in the same colors. Rubrics in pink-tinged red.

Bound, s. XIX, in purple velvet, a silver "gothic" fore edge clasp, closing from bottom to top; gilt edges.

Written at the end of the fifteenth century probably in Bruges as indicated by the saints in the calendar. Date and source of acquisition by Henry E. Huntington unknown.

Bibliography: De Ricci, 99.

HM 1158 — Italy, s. XVII^in
OFFICES — *fig. 38*

1. ff. 1–19: Short hours of the Cross; f. 19v, ruled, but blank.

2. ff. 20–34v: Short hours of the Holy Spirit; ff. 35–36v, ruled, but blank.

3. ff. 37–78v: Penitential psalms and litany; the monks are Anthony, Benedict, Bernard, Dominic and Francis; the prayer for the pope reads "Omnipotens sempiterne Deus miserere famulo tuo Pontifici nostro N. . . ."; ends, f. 78v, in gold square capitals, "G.T.R.S.," evidently for "Giacomo Tarrani Romano Scriveva" which is written out in Latin in the lower corner of f. 79 in a small humanistic script, "Iacobus Tarranus Romanus Scribebat"; ff. 79v–80v, ruled, but blank.

Parchment, ff. v (paper) + 80 + v; 110 × 80 (80 × 53) mm. Bound too tightly to collate, but apparently in quires of 8. Sporadic catchwords from one page to the next. 12 long lines, no horizontal ruling visible; the written space enclosed on all sides by a narrow double rule in painted gold. Written by Iacobus Tarranus of Rome (see f. 79) in a humanistic hand. Initials, 3-line, in painted gold and decorated with pale red flourishes, set within double ruled gold square frames; 1-line initials in red or gold. Major divisions signalled by rubrics in gold square capitals; other rubrics in red or painted gold in the script of the text.

Bound, s. XVII, in Venetian style deep red morocco, elaborately tooled front and back in an all-over pattern of gold swirls and white enamel leaves with center rosettes in the same manner; later English marbled endpapers; gilt edges. For a reproduction of this binding, see *One hundred and seventy-six historic and artistic Bookbindings dating from the Fifteenth Century to the Present Time . . . after the originals selected from the Library of Robert Hoe* (New York 1895), vol. I, pl. 42.

Written ca. 1600 (?) by Iacobus Tarranus of Rome, who also copied an Officio della Beata Vergine Maria; see American Art Association, 20 December 1920, lot 567, the sale of a "Notable American Collection" (Oliver R. Barrett) to Sen. David A. Reed, and De Ricci, 495, n. 11. Most of Senator's Reed's collection is now at Princeton University; this manuscript, however, remains untraced.[1] Although HM 1158 may once have been part of a larger manuscript which included an office of the Virgin, it was not part of Sen. Reed's manuscript, given the latter's larger size (7⁹⁄₁₆ × 5⅜ inches, i.e. approx. 190 × 140 mm.). Acquired by Robert Hoe at least by 1895 (see above); *Cat.* (1909) pp. 145–46; the slip from this catalogue pasted on f. ii; his sale, Anderson, New York, 1912, pt. III, n. 2086 to G. D. Smith. Precise source and date of acquisition by Henry E. Huntington unknown.

Bibliography: De Ricci, 100.

---

[1] We thank Miss Jean Preston for her help in attempting to determine its present location.

HM 1159 — England (?), s. XV^{in}
BOOK OF HOURS, fragment

1. ff. 1–9v: Commendation of souls (Pss. 118, divided into sections, and 138) followed by the prayers, Tibi domine commendamus . . . and Misericordiam tuam domine . . .

2. ff. 9v–10v: [a lengthy prologue and a suffrage of Erasmus, added in a late fifteenth-early sixteenth century cursive hand] [G]od allmyghty hathe graunted that What man or woman or child Redith this preyer that ffolouth eny Sonday or yeveth any almes to a poore man or Woman or a candill of Wax brennyng in the Worship of God and saint Erasme. . . , Sic ffiat omnibus bene credentibus, [O] sancte erasme preciose martir et pontifex ihesu christi qui in die dominica deo oblatus fuisti et cum eo leticiam sancte Resurrectionis suscipisti . . . , with versicle, response and prayer, [P]resta quesimus [*sic*] omnipotens deus ut qui beati erasmi martiris atque pontificis . . .

Parchment, ff. iii (paper) + 10 + iii (paper); 170 × 127 (115 × 73) mm. 1^8 + 2 leaves; no catchword or signatures. 22 long lines, ruled in pale red ink. Written in a gothic book hand.

Opening initial, f. 1, 6-line, in patterned dark pink on a cusped gold ground with infilling of colored trilobe leaves; U-shaped frame around text of colored and gold strips; reversed C-shaped bracket border of black ivy spray, with a burst of red and blue acanthus leaves at the upper right corner, and a dark pink and green burst in the lower right corner; multicolored flowers and gold motifs. 2-line initials in gold on blue or dark pink ground with infilling of the other color; 1-line initials in blue with red penwork or in gold with black penwork. Rubrics in red. Some marginalia, f. 10v.

Bound, s. XIX, in half blue morocco; marbled endpapers.

Written possibly in England, although the border foliage on f. 1 resembles the work of northeastern France; apparently the ending quire and leaves of a book of hours. In the library of Henry Huth (1815–78), and in his catalogue, *The Huth Library* (London 1880) vol. 4, p. 1231; sold by his son, Alfred H. Huth, Sotheby's, 8 July 1918, pt. VII, lot 6248 to G. D. Smith. Acquired from Smith by Henry E. Huntington in September 1918.

Bibliography: De Ricci, 100.

HM 1160 — France, s. XV^{in} and XVI^{in}
BOOK OF HOURS, use of Paris

1. ff. 1–6v: Full calendar in French, alternating entries in red and blue, with major feasts in gold.

2. ff. 7–20v: Passion according to John with the prayer, Deus qui manus tuas et pedes tuos . . .

3. ff. 21–39v: Pericopes of the Gospels, that of John followed by the prayer, Protector in te sperancium . . . [Perdrizet, 25]; *Oratio devota ad virginem mariam,* Obsecro te . . . et michi famulo tuo impetres . . . [Leroquais, *LH* 2:346]; *Alia oratio,* O Intemerata . . . orbis terrarum. Inclina mater . . . [Wilmart, 488–90]; *Alia oratio ad virginem mariam,* Stabat mater dolorosa . . . [*RH* 19416].

4. ff. 40–113v: Hours of the Virgin, use of Paris; 3 sets of 3 psalms and lessons at matins; the prayer, Ecclesiam tuam quesumus domine . . . ends the hours from lauds through compline; opening leaf of terce missing before f. 87.

5. ff. 114–118: Short hours of the Cross.

6. ff. 118v–121v: Short hours of the Holy Spirit.

7. ff. 122–141v: Penitential psalms, with 2 leaves missing between ff. 124–125 containing Ps. 31, 8–11 and Ps. 37, 1–12; litany includes Denis, Maurice, Eustachius, Eutropius, Valentinus and Lambert among the martyrs; Mellonius, Julianus, Fiacre, Eligius, Aegidius, Remigius and Maurus among the confessors; Opportuna and Genevieve among the virgins.

8. ff. 142–195v: Office of the Dead, use of Paris; lacks opening leaf; *Quand on recoit le corps de nostre seigneur ihesucrist,* Domine non sum dignus ut intres sub tectum meum sed tu domine qui dixisti . . . ; *Quant on l'a receu oroison,* Vera perceptio corporis et sanguinis tui . . .

Parchment, ff. iii (paper) + 195 + ii (parchment) + iii (paper); 156 × 108 (93 × 60) mm. 1^6 2^8 3^6(through f. 20) 4^8 5^8(+9, f. 37) 6^2(through f. 39) $7–11^8$ 12^8(–8, after f. 86) $13–15^8$

16^2(+1 at the beginning, through f. 113) 17^8(through f. 121) 18^8(–4, 5, after f. 124) 19^8 20^6 21^8(–1, before f. 142) 22–26^8 27^6(+7, f. 195). 14 long lines, ruled in pale red ink. Written in a gothic script.

Twelve large miniatures above 5 or 4 lines of text, with both text and miniature enclosed by painted gold architectural borders; the paintings may have been added in the early sixteenth century in the empty spaces reserved for that purpose, since the style of the illuminations and that of the initials seem at variance. The miniatures are: f. 7 (Passion according to John), above 5 lines of text, Betrayal in the Garden with Judas holding the bag of silver in his hand and kissing Jesus on his right cheek; Malchus with his bloody ear crouches below Peter; f. 21 (Gospel of John), above 5 lines of text, John, full-length, holding the snaky chalice, with 2 poisoned prisoners at his feet; f. 40 (Hours of the Virgin), Annunciation; f. 68 (Lauds), the Tiburtine Sibyl presenting the vision of the Virgin and Child to Augustus; 4 men stand in an arched cloister in the background; f. 81 (Prime), Nativity; opening leaf of terce missing; f. 91 (Sext), flaking, Adoration of the Magi; f. 95v (None), Presentation in the temple; f. 100 (Vespers), Flight into Egypt, with the Holy Family being accompanied by 2 angels; f. 108 (Compline), Dormition of the Virgin; f. 114 (Hours of the Cross), flaking, Crucifixion, with Mary, John and Mary Magdalene on Christ's right and the soldiers on his left; f. 118v (Hours of the Holy Spirit), Pentecost; f. 122 (Penitential psalms), David sending Uriah into battle; opening leaf for the office of the dead missing. Small miniatures, approximately 45 × 38 mm., enclosed by simple gold frames, while the entire page is framed by painted gold or colored architectural columns, are: f. 23v, Luke, seated in front of an easel painting an image of the Virgin from a smaller one propped above it on the easel, as the winged ox approaches from the left; f. 25v, Matthew, seated writing, with his left hand following the words in a book held by the angel; f. 27v, Mark, writing from 2 books set open on a lectern, with the winged lion below; f. 29 (Obsecro te), Pietà, with John the Baptist presenting a woman to Mary and the dead Christ; f. 34 (O Intemerata), the Virgin, seated, holding the Child with angels playing musical instruments on either side; f. 37v (Stabat mater), Crucifixion with Mary and John. 4- and 3-line initials in white-patterned blue on burnished gold grounds with colored trilobe leaf infilling; 2- and 1-line initials in gold on blue grounds with dark pink infilling, or vice versa; ribbon, dot and flower line fillers in the same colors; initials within the text touched in yellow. Rubrics in a bright orange-red. Two 2-line initials on f. 195r–v in painted gold on square faded maroon grounds; in the lower margin of f. 195 green brush strokes, as if to make a plant; in faded green ink on f. 195v: "finis; christum dominum nostrum."

Bound on the Continent, s. XVIII, in red velvet covered by open-work silver repoussé of 2 lions rampant supporting a blank shield surmounted by a coronet; 2 fore edge clasps, and a chain from front to back cover on the top; red silk endpapers; gilt edges. See R. R. Wark, *British Silver in the Huntington Library* (Huntington Library 1978) n. 373, for description and plate of binding. For a similar binding, see Christie's sale catalogue, 4 April 1962, lot 41 with plate.

Written in France in the early fifteenth century with illuminations apparently added in the early sixteenth century. The owner at that point may have been a woman named "Jeanne," as suggested by the illumination on f. 29. Belonged to Robert Hoe, and discussed by him in his *Lecture on Bookbinding as a Fine Art, delivered before the Grolier Club, February 26, 1885* (New York: Grolier Club 1886) pl. 63; Grolier Club (1892) n. 47; *Exhibition of Silver, Embroidered and Curious Bookbindings* (New York: Grolier Club 1903) n. 32; *Cat.* (1909) pp. 44–45; his sale, Anderson, New York, 1912, pt. III, n. 2072 to G. D. Smith. Precise source and date of acquisition by Henry E. Huntington unknown.

Bibliography: De Ricci, 100.

HM 1161

HM 1161

France, s. XVI^{in}

BOOK OF HOURS, use of Rome

1. ff. 1–12v: Calendar in French, with a saint at each day, alternating red and black, with blue for the major feasts.

2. ff. 1–6: Pericopes of the Gospels, that of John with its prayer, Protector in te sperantium . . .

3. ff. 6v–8v: *Oratio beate marie virginis,* Obsecro te . . . Et michi famulo tuo N. impetres . . . [Leroquais, *LH* 2:346].

4. ff. 9–60v: Hours of the Virgin, use of Rome, beginning defectively in the first psalm: //dominus et rex magnus super omnes deos . . . ; weekly variations of the psalms at matins set into the text before the lessons; loss of text between ff. 14–15, from the end of the Tuesday-Friday psalms to the beginning of the Wednesday-Saturday psalms; prayers to All Saints from lauds to compline; following compline without break are the Salve Regina, and the prayers Omnipotens sempiterne deus qui gloriose virginis matris marie . . . , Deus qui illuminas noctem . . . and Protector in te sperantium . . . ; Advent office begins on f. 54.

5. ff. 61–76v: Penitential psalms and litany, with Martialis as the last apostle, and Eustachius, Eutropius, Nicasius, and Lubin; f. 76v, rubric and antiphon for the Office of the Dead.

6. ff. 77–79v: Short hours of the Cross.

7. ff. 80–82v: Short hours of the Holy Spirit.

8. ff. 83–117v: Office of the Dead, use of Rome.

9. ff. 118–133v: Prayers as follow: *De sanctissima trinitate,* Te invocamus te adoramus te laudamus . . . with versicle, response and prayer; *Oratio ad deum patrem,* . . . , Domine sancte pater omnipotens eterne deus qui coequalem . . . ; *Alia oratio,* . . . , Domine iesu christe fili dei vivi qui es verus . . . ; Domine spiritus sancte deus qui coequalis . . . ; Salve sancta facies . . . [*RH* 18189], with versicle, response and prayer, Deus qui nobis famulis tuis lumine vultus tui signatis; suffrages of Michael, John the Baptist, John the Evangelist, Peter and Paul, James, Stephen, Lawrence, Christopher [. . . michi famulo tuo N . . .], Sebastian, Denis, Nicholas, Claude, Anthony abbot, Anne, Mary Magdalene, Catherine of Alexandria, Margaret, Barbara; f. 134r–v, ruled, but blank.

Parchment, ff. iii (parchment, with silk glued to the recto of the first) + 12 (the calendar) + 134, including 45 bis + ii (parchment, with silk glued to the verso of the second); 212 × 115 (120 × 63) mm. $1–2^{6}$ 3^{8} 4^{8}(–1, 8) $5–8^{8}$ 9^{6} 10^{8}(+9 through f. 60) $11–12^{8}$ 13^{6}(the Hours of the Cross and the Holy Spirit) 14^{8} 15^{8}(+9, f. 99) 16^{8} 17^{10}(through f. 117) 18^{6} 19^{10} + 1 leaf, f. 134. 24 long lines, ruled in pale red ink, with pricking occasionally visible in the outer margin. Written in bâtarde script.

Thirteen large miniatures in painted gold architectural frames, enclosing the full page scene on which the 3 lines of text appear as if imposed. The illuminations are: f. 1 (Gospel of John), John on Patmos; f. 21 (Lauds), Visitation; f. 29v (Prime), Nativity; f. 33 (Terce), Annunciation to the shepherds; f. 36v (Sext), Adoration of the Magi; f. 40 (None), Presentation in the temple; f. 43v (Vespers), Flight into Egypt; f. 48v (Compline), Coronation of the Virgin, sitting before Christ, with a chorus of angels behind them; f. 61 (Penitential psalms), David from a window watching Bathsheba bathing in a fountain; f. 77 (Hours of the Cross), Crucifixion with Mary and John on Christ's right, the soldiers on his left; f. 80 (Hours of the Holy Spirit), Pentecost; f. 83 (Office of the Dead), Job on the dunghill; f. 118 (prayer to the Trinity), the Father and the Son wearing one cloak and holding a book, while the Dove hovers above them. Similar miniatures, also in painted gold architectural frames, varying in size from 16-line on f. 2v to 8-line (the most common): f. 2v, Luke; f. 4, Matthew; f. 5, St. Mark's lion, but without wings, placed below the end of Matthew; f. 5v, Mark; f. 6v (Obsecro te), Virgin and Child; f. 119 (*Oratio ad deum patrem*), God the Father, holding an orb and wearing a papal tiara; f. 119v (prayer to Jesus), standing holding an orb; f. 120 (prayer to the Holy Spirit), Pentecost; f. 120v (Salve sancta facies), Veronica; the remaining 18 miniatures for the suffrages show the saints with their attributes. 3- and 2-line white initials on square brick red grounds with gold tracery, infilled with a flower; 1-line initials in gold paint on alternating brick red or blue square grounds; ribbon line fillers in the same colors. Band borders the length of the text on all pages, except those with architectural frames, in painted gold with acanthus leaves, flowers, berries and strawberries.

Bound, s. XIX, in dark green velvet, rebacked, with 2 brass fore edge clasps, closing from bottom to top, the lower of the 2 is broken; grey silk endpapers; gilt edges; HM 1153 and HM 1175 with similar binding.

Written in northern France at the beginning of the sixteenth century. Belonged to John Boykett Jarman (d. 1864); his sale, Sotheby's, 13 June 1864, lot 1. Source and date of acquisition by Henry E. Huntington unknown.

Bibliography: De Ricci, 100.

HM 1162 — Spain and Flanders, s. XVI[1]
BOOK OF HOURS, use of Rome — *fig. 145*

1. f. 1r–v: *Tabla de las devociones que estan en este libro Primeramente,* El kalendario, *A fojas 2,* Las devociones que la reyna catholica acostumbrava a rezar por la mañana, A fojas *11* . . .

2. ff. 2–10: Calendar with the months following one another directly; major feasts in red; included are the feasts of Ildephonsus "archiepiscopi toletani" (23 January, in red), Our Lady of Peace (24 January, in red), Julianus "archiepiscopi toletani" (8 March), Ermengildus "regis castelle" (13 April), "Festum nivis" (5 August), Transfiguration (6 August, in red), "Bellum de benamarim" (30 October 1340), Eugene "archiepiscopi toletani" (15 November, in red), Leocadia (9 December, in red), Servulus (23 December).

3. ff. 10v–17v: Prayers as follow: *Orationes in surrectione lecti, Oratio,* Gratias tibi ago omnipotens deus qui me in hac nocte non meis meritis . . . ; *Oratio,* Gratias tibi ago domine sancte pater omnipotens eterne deus qui me de transacto noctis spacio . . . ; *Hymnus,* Iam lucis orto sidere . . . [*RH* 9272]; *Oratio,* Domine deus omnipotens pater qui nos ad principium huius diei pervenire fecisti . . . with versicles and responses; *Oratio,* Dirigere et sanctificare regere et gubernare dignare domine deus rex celi et terre . . . with versicles, responses, benedictions and absolution; *Oratio,* Deus qui hodierna die per unigenitum tuum eternitatis nobis aditum devicta morte reserasti . . . ; *Oratio,* Deus qui

pro nobis filium tuum crucis patibulum subire voluisti . . . ; *Oratio,* Indue me domine vestimento salutis . . . with versicles and responses; *Oratio,* Actiones nostras quesumus domine aspirando preveni . . . ; *Oratio,* In viam pacis salutis et prosperitatis dirigat me hodie . . . with versicles and responses; *Oratio,* Deus maiestatis inmense quem nec spacia locorum seu temporum . . . ; *Devotissima Oratio,* In manus tuas domine commendo animam meam spiritum meum . . . et ego misera et peccatrix te invoco . . . ; *Oratio,* Altissime atque gloriosissime domine mi iesu christe illumina cordis mei tenebras . . . ; *Oratio,* Quesumus omnipotens deus ut famulus tuus rex noster qui tua miseratione suscepit regnorum gubernacula . . . ; *Oratio,* Omnipotens sempiterne deus qui dirigis viam iustorum dirige famulum tuum regem nostrum recta via . . . ; *Oratio,* Omnipotens sempiterne deus fac nos tibi semper et devotam gerere voluntatem . . . ; *Oratio,* Mentes nostras quesumus domine lumine tue claritatis illustra . . . ; *Oratio,* Largire nobis domine quesumus semper spiritum cogitandi . . . ; *Oratio,* Sancti nominis tui domine timorem pariter . . . ; *Oratio,* Ecclesiam tuam domine miseratio continuata mundet et muniat . . . ; *Inicium sancti evangelii secundum Ioannem,* In principio erat verbum . . . [John 1, 1–14].

4. ff. 18–22v: Short hours of the Cross, introduced on f. 18r–v by devotional material beginning on f. 18, Hierusalem luge et exue te vestibus iocunditatis, induere cinere et cilicio . . . , and on f. 18v, Christus semel pro peccatis nostris mortuus est . . .

5. ff. 23–27v: Short hours of the Holy Spirit, introduced on f. 23r–v by devotional material beginning on f. 23, Hodie completi sunt dies penthecostes alleluya . . . , and on f. 23v, Repleti sunt omnes spiritu sancto ceperunt loqui . . .

6. ff. 28–34: Short hours of the Conception, introduced on f. 28r–v by devotional material beginning on f. 28, Hylarius. O virgo benedicta super omnes feminas . . . , and on f. 28v, Tota pulchra es amica nostra . . .

7. ff. 34v–92v: *Incipit officium beate marie virginis secundum consuetudinem romane curie,* with variations for the liturgical year worked in for all the hours; weekly variations of the psalms at matins set into the text before the lessons; suffrages of All Saints from lauds to compline; the Hours of the Virgin are introduced by devotional material on f. 34v beginning, Gaude maria virgo quia quem totus non capit orbis . . . ; lauds begins on f. 48, In mariam vite viam matrem veram . . . [*RH* 8671], and on f. 48v, Venit superior ad inferiorem portans in utero . . . ; prime begins on f. 58, Hodie nobis celorum rex de virgine nasci dignatus est . . . , and on f. 58v, Beata viscera marie virginis que portaverunt eterni patris filium . . . ; terce begins on f. 63, Propter nimiam charitatem suam qua dilexit nos deus filium suum misit . . . , and on f. 63v, Mirabile mysterium declaratur hodie innovantur nature . . . ; sext begins on f. 68, Symeon iustus et timoratus expectans redemptionem israel et spiritus sanctus . . . , and on f. 68v, Accipiens symeon in ulnas suas iesum . . . ; none begins on f. 73, Et egressus iesus ibat secundum consuetudinem in montem olivarum . . . , and on f. 73v, Tristis est anima mea usque ad mortem . . . ; vespers begin on f. 78, Pilatus autem convocatis principibus sacerdotum et magistratibus et plebe dixit ad illos . . . , and on f. 78v, Ecce vidimus eum non habentem speciem neque decorem . . . ; compline begins on f. 86 below 5 lines of regular text, Milites autem duxerunt eum intro in atrium pretorii et convocant totam cohortem . . . , and on f. 86v, Non est ei species neque decor . . .

8. ff. 93–98: Mass of the Virgin, Salve sancta parens . . . , beginning with devotional material on f. 93, Ornatam monilibus filiam hierusalem dominus concupivit . . . , and on f. 93v, Tota pulchra es amica mea et macula non est in te . . .

9. ff. 98–111: Penitential psalms and litany, including Leocadia among the virgins; the section begins on f. 98 below 11 lines of regular text, Tradiderunt me in manus impiorum et inter iniquos proiecerunt me . . . , and on f. 98v, Sicut ovis ad occissionem ductus est et quasi agnus . . .

10. f. 111v: Illumination and devotional material to introduce a section now missing after f. 111, which was, according to the Table on f. 1, the Office of the Dead; the devotional material on f. 111v begins, Surge propera amica mea columba mea . . .

11. ff. 140–151: Gradual psalms, in full, in 3 groups of 5 each, followed respectively by versicles and 3 prayers: Absolve quesumus domine animas famulorum famularumque tuarum . . . ; Deus cui proprium est misereri semper et parcere . . . ; Pretende domine famulis et famulabus tuis dexteram celestis auxilii . . . ; *Simbolum athanasii,* Quicumque vult salvus esse . . . ; Ps. 55; the gradual psalms are introduced by devotional material on f. 140, Ecce vicit leo de tribu iuda, radix david aperire librum . . . , and on f. 140v, Surrexit christus de sepulchro qui pro nobis pependit in ligno alleluya . . .

12. ff. 151v–157v: *Orationes in introitu lecti,* Gratias tibi ago omnipotens deus qui me in hac die non meis meritis . . . ; *Symbolum Athanasii,* Quicumque vult salvus esse . . . ; *Initium sancti evangelii secundum Iohannem,* In principio erat verbum . . . [John 1, 1–14]; *Ad sanctum michaelem Commemoratio,* Princeps gloriosissime michael archangele esto memor mei . . . with versicles, response and prayer, Deus qui miro ordine angelorum . . . , *Versus,* Angelum pacis michael ad istam celitus mitte rogitemus aulam nobis . . . with versicles, response and prayer, Deus cuius providentia humano generi . . . , *Ad angelum,* Obsecro te angele dei spiritus bonus cui in custodia sum comissa . . . ; *Confessio generalis,* Confiteor deo omnipotenti et beatissime virgini marie . . . , *Absolutio,* Indulgentiam et remissionem omnium peccatorum meorum . . . , *Oratio,* Gratias tibi reffero domine deus omnipotens pro universis bonis que mihi contulisti . . . Protestor etiam me victuram et morituram in sancta atque catholica fide tua . . . ; *Hymnus,* Christe qui lux es et dies . . . ; *Hymnus,* Te lucis ante terminum rerum creator poscimus ut solita clementia . . . [*RH* 20138] with versicles and prayer, Visita quesumus domine habitationem istam . . . ; *Oratio,* Me mundet et muniat consignetur salvet titulus triumphalis . . . ; *Oratio devotissima,* Pax tua dulcissime ac amantissime iesu et virtus sanctissime incarnationis tue . . . ; this section is introduced on f. 151v by devotional material beginning, Ascendens christus in altum captivam duxit captivitatem . . .

13. ff. 158–162: Suffrages of John the Baptist, Christopher [. . . et mihi famulo tuo N . . .], Jerome, Mary Magdalene, Apollonia, Catherine of Alexandria, Agatha, Elizabeth, Roch, Margaret, Francis, Anthony of Padua; f. 162v, blank.

Parchment, ff. iii (paper) + i (parchment) + 136 (but 162 according to the contemporary foliation in roman numerals used in this description, since "15" was skipped in the foliation and ff. 112–139 are missing) + i (parchment) + ii (paper); 167 × 110 (125 × 75) mm. 1^{10} 2 (5 leaves, ff. 11–16, with the number 15 skipped in the foliation; structure unclear)

3^{12}(ff. 17–31; +2, f. 18; +5 and 6, ff. 21–22, a bifolium) $4–5^{8}$ 6^{8}(+1, f. 48) 7^{8}(+2, f. 58 and 7, f. 63) 8^{8}(+2, f. 68 and 7, f. 73) 9^{8}(+2, f. 78) 10^{6}(+1, f. 81; +8, f. 93; +9, f. 94) $11–12^{8}$ + f. 111 (a singleton, presumably once part of the missing section between ff. 111–140) 13 (?, ff. 140–143, now all singletons but with 4 stubs preceding them) 14^{6}(+1, f. 144 and 8, f. 151) 15^{6}(through f. 157) 16^{8}(?). Catchwords written vertically in the space formed by the double bounding lines of the inner margin. 24 long lines, written between, not on the lines; ruled in pale red ink for the text with double lines full across and full length for the frame of the written space. The illuminated leaves contain 17 lines of text on the recto, and 6 on the verso, below the picture. Written in a round gothic book hand, with dark black ink, often flaking; on the recto and the bottom 6 lines of the verso of leaves with miniatures, the devotional material is written in a humanistic hand in gold ink, against deep red or purple grounds (except for f. 48v which continues the round gothic script).

Seventeen miniatures (all but 2, on ff. 10v, 28), 56 × 39 mm., enclosed by simple gold frames with decorative molding diagonally across the 2 upper corners, probably by Simon Bening. The miniatures with their frames were painted on rectangles of parchment which were then glued to the folios (sometimes singletons, sometimes part of the quire structure); a second artist, less capable, then painted over the join to form an illustrated space of 82 × 84 mm., set above 6 lines of text written in gold humanistic script on dark colored grounds; the entire area is framed in gold strips of wood molding, and the same frame surrounds the text on the facing page. Copies or echoes of engravings by Martin Schongauer occur in the miniatures of the Crucifixion (Lehrs 12), Flagellation (Lehrs 22), Mocking of Christ (Lehrs 23), Road to Calvary (Lehrs 9) and Resurrection (Lehrs 30)[1]; for this practice in other manuscripts illuminated by Simon Bening, see M. Kupfer-Tarasulo, "Innovation and Copy in the Stein Quadriptych of Simon Bening," *Zeitschrift für Kunstgeschichte* 42 (1979) 274–98, and "A Rosary Psalter illuminated by Simon Bening" *Quaerendo* 9 (1979) 209–23.

The miniatures are: f. 10v (*Orationes in surrectione lecti*), the second artist has done the entire picture showing Christ as Salvator Mundi in half-length; in the space below the picture, a coat of arms (see below) instead of text; f. 18v (Hours of the Cross), Crucifixion with Mary and John in the small painting, and Renaissance ornament in the border painted over the join; f. 23v (Hours of the Holy Spirit), Pentecost, with Renaissance ornament in the outer area; f. 28 (Hours of the Conception), a single large miniature, by the second artist, showing the meeting of Joachim and Anne at the Golden Gate, with 2 women on the right, a shepherd on the left, and an angel above; f. 34v (Hours of the Virgin), Annunciation; a line through the angel has been badly rubbed due to buckling in the onlaid parchment; in the outer area the second artist has extended the city seen through the open loggia of Mary's house; f. 48v (Lauds), Visitation, at closer range than the other onlaid miniatures; the second artist has painted 2 angels in camaïeu d'or who support the picture of the first artist; this leaf and the facing one are surrounded by a rich border of dark pink with gold Renaissance ornament, light blue cameos, laurel leaves and a laurel wreath containing a coat of arms (see below); the text on the recto of this singleton leaf is in the usual gold humanistic script on a dark ground; however, on the verso, the text is in 7 lines of the same round gothic script as the main text; f. 58v (Prime), Nativity, with Renaissance ornament in the outer border; f. 63v (Terce), Circumcision, with Renaissance ornament in the border; f. 68v (Sext), Presentation in the temple, with Renaissance ornament in the border; f. 73v (None), Agony in the Garden, with Renaissance ornament in the border; f. 78v (Vespers), Flagellation with Renaissance ornament in the border; f. 86v (Compline), Mocking of Christ; the second artist has painted a pastoral landscape as background to the onlaid miniature; f. 93v (Mass of the Virgin), Coronation of the Virgin by God the Father and the Son, as identical Jesus-like figures with the Dove between them; in the outer border, Renaissance ornament; f. 98v (Penitential psalms), Road to Calvary; the second artist has extended the scene with crowds curving up the hill and he appears to have continued the foliage from his border back into the onlay; f. 111v (Office of the Dead), Dormition of the Virgin, set against a pastoral landscape border; f.

140v (Gradual psalms), Resurrection, with a Renaissance ornament border; f. 151v (*Orationes in introitu lecti*), Ascension of Christ, against a landscape border which continues the scene begun in the inner frame. 6-, 5-, and 4-line initials as white or gold branches or ribbons against square speckled grounds of yellow, green, maroon or blue; those on f. 35 (Hours of the Virgin) and f. 99 (Penitential psalms) enclose naturalistic flowers. 3- and 2-line initials as white or gold branches on square maroon, blue or green grounds; 1-line initials in painted gold on maroon or blue square grounds; ribbon line fillers in gold-decorated olive green, maroon or blue; initials within the text touched in gold. Rubrics in pale red ink.

Bound by Derome le Jeune (with his ticket) in green morocco with gold dentelle tooling; pink silk doublures and endpapers; gilt edges; rust marks on the first and last parchment flyleaves from the clasps of a previous binding.

Written in Spain in the area of Toledo, as the entries in the calendar indicate; feminine forms in the prayers on ff. 14, 155 and 156. The coats of arms on ff. 10v and 48v are those of Charles V and Isabel of Portugal, impaled; the book must have been made between 1526 (their marriage) and 1539 (Isabel's death); miniatures done in Flanders. For another book of hours with the same arms and copied by the same scribe, see Doheny sale, Christie's, 2 December 1987, pt. 2, lot 175. Belonged to Count Justin MacCarthy-Reagh (1744–1811) of Toulouse; his sale through the Parisian bookseller De Bure in 1817, n. 396. Belonged to William Beckford (1759–1844) with his number 2 pencilled in on f. ii; he bequeathed his materials to his son-in-law, Alexander Hamilton, 10th Duke of Hamilton (1767–1852), whose library monogram "HB" and number 654 also appear on f. ii. Catalogued for sale, Sotheby's 1882, lot 461; before the sale, the collection was purchased *in toto* by the Prussian government; W. von Seidlitz, "Die illustrierten Handschriften der Hamilton-Sammlung (Schluss)," *Repertorium für Kunstwissenschaft* 8 (1885) 94–110, esp. 104–05. Sotheby's, 23 May 1889, n. 32 with facsimile (no plates in the catalogue seen by us) to Trübner. Jacques Rosenthal Catalogue 27, n. 31. In the library of William K. Bixby (1857–1931) of St. Louis, whose book plate is on the front pastedown; portions of this collection were acquired by Henry E. Huntington in August 1918.

Bibliography: F. Winkler, *Die Flämische Buchmalerei* (Leipzig 1925) 140. De Ricci, 100. A. Biermann, "Die Miniaturenhandschriften Kardinals Albrecht von Brandenburg (1514–1545), *Aachener Kunstblätter* 46 (1975) 266 n. 93. J. H. Marrow, "Simon Bening in 1521: A Group of Dated Miniatures," in *Liber Amicorum Herman Liebaers* (Brussels 1984) 540.

[1] We are grateful to Prof. James Marrow for pointing out this coincidence and for the relevant bibliography.

HM 1163 — France, s. XV²
BOOK OF HOURS, use of Paris — *fig. 122*

1. ff. 1–12v: Full calendar in French of the type printed by Perdrizet, alternating red and blue entries even for the more important feasts.

2. ff. 13–22: [f. 13, blank; f. 13v, illuminated; f. 14, rubric only:] *Passio domini nostri ihesu christi secundum iohannem,* In illo tempore, Apprehendit pylatus ihesum . . . [catena mainly from John 19; see de la Mare, *Lyell Cat.,* 65–66, and the prayer:] Deus qui manus tuas et pedes tuos . . . ; pericopes of the Gospels.

3. ff. 22v–36v: Obsecro te . . . Et michi famulo tuo N. impetres . . . [Leroquais, *LH* 2:346]; *Alia devota oratio de beata maria,* O [I]ntemerata . . . orbis terrarum. De te enim . . . [Wilmart, 494–95]; *Alia oratio de virgine maria,* O [I]ntemerata . . . orbis terrarum. Inclina aures . . . [Wilmart, 488–90]; *Devote contemplation de nostre dame . . . faicte a la requeste de charles roy de france, par le glorieux confesseur monseigneur saint gregoire pape le quel octroya et donna . . . ,* Stabat mater dolorosa . . . [*RH* 19416]; *S'ensuivent v devots verses salutaires de la vierge marie mere de dieu,* Ave cuius conceptio . . . [*RH* 1744, and the prayer:] Deus qui nos concepcionis, nativitatis . . . ; *A pascha usque ad pentecostem antiphona,* Regina celi letare . . . [*RH* 17170, with versicle, response and the prayer:] Graciam tuam quesumus domine mentibus nostris infunde . . .

4. ff. 37–107: Hours of the Virgin, use of Paris; psalms and lessons at matins for the 3 nocturns; hours from lauds through compline end with the prayer, Ecclesiam tuam quesumus domine . . . , by cue only after lauds; short hours of the Cross and the Holy Spirit worked in; ff. 107v–109v, ruled, but blank.

5. ff. 110–129: Penitential psalms and litany, including Maurice, Denis, Eustachius, Fabianus and Julianus among the martyrs; Julianus, Eligius and Brictius among the confessors; Anne and Radegundis (but not Genevieve) among the virgins.

6. ff. 129v–161: Office of the Dead, use of Paris.

7. ff. 161–169v: *S'ensuivent les vii verses saint bernard, Lesquelz quiconques devotemente les dira le iour une foiz, iamais de mort soubdaine ne mourra, O Bone ihesu,* Illumina oculos meos . . . [*RH* 27912, with the prayer:] Omnipotens sempiterne deus qui ezechie regi . . . ; *Pape boniface donna ii mille ans . . . et la fit fer philippe roy de france,* Domine ihesu christe qui hanc sacratissimam carnem . . . [Wilmart, 378, n.]; *S'ensuit cy apres certaines oroysons de nostre seigneur moult devotes, Et primierement,* Ie te salue ihesu crist parolle du pere, filz de la vierge . . . [Sonet 875]; *Saint Benoist pape fit ceste oroyson, L'an mil trois cens et xxxvii, Lequel donna et octroya a toute personne . . . si comme il fut revele a ung sainct homme nomme saint Iehan crisostome docteur de l'eglise Et monseigneur saint gregoire . . . ,* Tres piteux et benigne redempteur ihesus ie te supplie et requier en grand humilite et recordation . . . [Sonet 2235]; *Oroyson a nostre dame,* O tres certaine esperance deffenderesse de tous maulx [*sic*] qui cy actendent glorieuse vierge marie . . . [Sonet 1538].

8. ff. 170–201v: Suffrages of the Trinity (Libera nos salva nos iustifica nos . . .), Michael, John the Baptist, Peter and Paul (Petrus apostolus et paulus doctor gentium . . .), John the Evangelist (Iohannes apostolus et evangelista virgo est electus . . .), Christopher, Martin, Nicholas, Mary Magdalene, Catherine of Alexandria, Margaret, All Saints, the Trinity (Te deum patrem ingenitum, te filium . . .), All Angels (these 2 suffrages with prayer designated "oratio ut supra"), Peter (Angelus domini astitit et lumen . . .), Paul (Sancte paule apostole predicator veritatis et doctor gencium . . .), Andrew, John the Evangelist (antiphon as above), Thomas the Apostle, Many Apostles, Stephen, Lawrence, Gregory, Blasius, Sebastian, Denis, Gervasius and Protasius, Cosmas and Damianus, Many Martyrs, Anthony abbot, Augustine, Benedict, Maurus, Fiacre, Lazarus (preceded by an indulgence granted by John III), Claude, Many Confessors, Cecilia,

Agnes, Apollonia, Avia, Opportuna, Genevieve, Anne; *De nostre dame par toute l'annee antienne,* Salve regina misericordie . . . [*RH* 18147, with versicle, response and prayer:] Omnipotens sempiterne deus qui gloriose virginis marie corpus et animam . . . ; *Le lundi et le ieude Antienne,* Ave regina celorum ave domina angelorum . . . [*RH* 2070]; *Le mardi et le vendredi,* Virgo parens christi paritura deum genuisti . . . [*RH* 21842?]; *Le ieudi et le samedi antienne,* Alma redemptoris mater que pervia celi porta manens [*sic*] . . . [*RH* 861]; of the Cross, for peace, the Eucharist, Martha.

Parchment, ff. ii (modern parchment) + 201 + ii (modern parchment); 162 × 106 (77 × 53) mm. $1–2^{6}$ 3(ff. 13–16, of unclear structure; f. 13 almost certainly a singleton) $4–5^{8}$ 6^{4}(through f. 36) 7^{8} 8^{8}(–8, excised) 9^{8} 10^{8}(–1 and 2, excised) $11–15^{8}$ 16^{4}(through f. 109) $17–22^{8}$ 23^{12}(through f. 169) $24–27^{8}$. Most catchwords are present, written in the script of the text across the center of the lower margin, on f. 51v written vertically along the inner bounding line. 14 long lines, ruled in pale red ink. Written in a bâtarde script in 2 sizes according to liturgical function.

Fifteen large miniatures, usually above 3 lines of text in arched compartments, surrounded by full borders of blue and gold acanthus, flowers, green pears, strawberries, and a particularly large number of grotesques, frequently obscene. The miniatures have been discussed by Claude Schaefer, "Recherches sur l'iconologie et la stylistique de l'art de Jean Fouquet," Thèse présentée devant l'Université de Paris, IV, 24 February 1971, 2:268–70 and 3:pl. 119–122 (all the miniatures reproduced). The miniature on f. 13v closest to the work of Fouquet; the others, in varying degree, represent styles of Fouquet and Jean Colombe and appear to be products of Fouquet's workshop. The miniatures are: f. 13v (added singleton; the original intent was evidently to paint the miniature for the catena from John directly on the quire leaf, as f. 14 contains only the rubric on the last three lines, leaving the normal miniature space blank), full page miniature, God the Father, holding the orb, and seated in glory, in shades of purple and gold, and, in the corners, the symbols of the 4 Evangelists; f. 22v (Obsecro te), Pietà, with a coat of arms in the border (see below); f. 37 (Hours of the Virgin), Annunciation in a church; f. 62 (Lauds), Visitation, with a coat of arms in the border (see below); f. 74v (Hours of the Cross), Betrayal in the garden, at night, in the left background a woman holds up a lantern, while Judas with the bag of silver in his hand kisses Jesus, and Malchus crouches on the ground; f. 76 (Hours of the Holy Spirit), Pentecost; f. 77v (Prime), Nativity; f. 83v (Terce), Annunciation to the shepherds, one of whom is dressed in white; f. 88 (Sext), Adoration of the Magi, 2 of whom already kneel before the Infant, their crowns on the ground, while the third approaches at the head of a large crowd; f. 92v (None), Flight into Egypt; f. 97 (Vespers), Dormition of the Virgin, with Jesus in a yellow aperture above holding her soul, represented as a small child dressed in white; f. 101 (Compline), Assumption of the Virgin, who is dressed in white and supported by pink angels; f. 110 (Penitential psalms), David killing Goliath; historiated initial on this page of David playing his harp; f. 129v (Office of the Dead), Job on the dunghill with his friends standing before him; f. 170 (suffrage to the Trinity), above 2 lines of text, Gnadenstuhl, on the same model as the miniature on f. 13v. 3-line initial on f. 22v as pink acanthus leaves against a golden acanthus leaf ground with a coat of arms as infilling (see below); the initial on f. 97 formed of white acanthus leaves; that on f. 110 contains an image of David. Other 3-line, and the 2- and 1-line initials in maroon or blue decorated with gold leafy swirls against backgrounds of the other color, also decorated with painted gold leaves. Ribbon line fillers in the same colors. Initials in the text touched in yellow. Rubrics in pale red. Band borders in the outer margin running the length of the text at the presence of 2-line initials, and traced when appropriate, consisting of blue and gold acanthus, flowers, green pears and strawberries.

Bound in brown morocco to a Duodo design by Thibaron-Echaubard and Wampflug, with gold stamped monogram "I C C"; parchment doublures; gilt edges.

HM 1163

Written in France ca. 1480 for a member of the family of Malet de Graville, whose coat of arms appears in the margin of f. 62 (Rietstap, vol. 4, pl. 127); added to the initial on f. 22v are the arms of the Balzac family, seigneurs d'Entragues (Rietstap, vol. 1, pl. 116); the original owners may have been Louis Malet and his wife, Jeanne de Balzac; their daughter, Anne, married Pierre de Balzac in 1505. The book may have passed to Pierre's son-in-law, Claude d'Urfé; see A. Vernet, "Les Manuscrits de Claude d'Urfé (1501–1558) au Château de la Bastie," *Académie des Inscriptions et Belles-Lettres: Comptes-Rendus* (1976) 81–97. His library was bought in 1777 by the Duc de La Vallière; this manuscript, however, does not appear in the Duc's 1784 sale. E. M. Bancel sale, Paris, 8 May 1882, n. 13 to Baron de Beurnonville; his sale, Paris, 16 February 1885, pp. 14–18 to the bookseller D. Morgand (Inv. 23092); Dodd and Mead and Co., Catalogue 11 (October 1885), pp. 27–28. Acquired by E. Dwight Church (1835–1908); in his *Catalogue . . . of English Literature* (1909) vol. 1, n. 402 with a plate of f. 101. The Church collection was acquired by Henry E. Huntington in 1911.

Bibliography: De Ricci, 101. N. Reynaud, *Jean Fouquet,* Les Dossiers du Département des Peintures. Editions de la Réunion des Musées Nationaux (Paris 1981) 55 and footnote 163.

HM 1164 — Flanders, s. XVI^{in}
BOOK OF HOURS, use of Rome

1. ff. 1–6v: Calendar in red and black including the feasts of Gilbert (4 February), Joseph (19 March), Separation of the Apostles (15 July), Transfiguration (6 August), Remigius (1 October, in red); f. 7r–v, ruled, but blank.

2. ff. 8–14v [f. 8, blank]: Short hours of the Cross.

3. ff. 15–21v [f. 15, blank]: Short hours of the Holy Spirit; f. 22r–v, ruled, but blank.

4. ff. 23–88v [f. 23, blank]: *Incipiunt hore beate marie virginis secundum usum romanum;* weekly variations of the psalms at matins set into the text before the lessons; suffrages of All Saints and prayers for peace from lauds to compline; Salve Regina follows directly, with the prayer, Omnipotens sempiterne deus qui gloriose virginis marie . . . ; Advent office begins on f. 81.

5. ff. 89–104v [f. 89, blank]: Penitential psalms and litany, including Martialis as the last apostle; among the martyrs are Denis, Eustachius, Maurice (all with companions) and Eutropius; f. 105r–v, frame ruled, but blank.

6. ff. 106–140 [f. 106, blank]: Office of the Dead, use of Rome; f. 140v, ruled, but blank.

7. ff. 141–153: Prayers as follow: *Symbolum athanasii,* Quicumque vult salvus esse . . . ; *Oratio dominicalis devota,* Pater noster . . . ; *Salutatio angelica ad virginem gloriosam mariam,* Ave maria . . . ; *Symbolum fidei apostolorum,* Credo in deum patrem . . . ; suffrage of the Holy Spirit, Veni sancte spiritus reple tuorum corda fidelium . . . [*RH* 21252]; *Hymus* [*sic*] *devotus de eodem sancto spiritu pro impetranda gratia ipsius sancti spiritus,* Veni creator spiritus mentes tuorum visita . . . [*RH* 21204]; *de beata virgine antiphona,* Salve regina

. . . [*RH* 18147] with the prayer, Omnipotens sempiterne deus qui gloriose virginis marie . . . ; *Prosa de beata virgine maria,* Inviolata integra et casta es maria . . . [*RH* 9094]; *Alia devota oratio de eadem virgine maria,* Stabat mater dolorosa . . . [*RH* 19416] with the prayer, Interveniat pro nobis quesumus domine ihesu christe nunc et in hora . . . ; *Septem orationes beati gregorii,* O Domine ihesu christe adoro te in cruce pendentem . . . [Leroquais, *LH* 2:346]; *Incipiunt octo versus beati bernardi doctoris melliflui,* Illumina oculos meos . . . [the "extra" verse is the second part of the third, Et numerum dierum meorum . . . ; *RH* 27912], with its prayer, Omnipotens sempiterne deus qui ezechie regi . . . ; *De sanctissimo sacramento eucharistie antiphona,* O Quam suavis est domine spiritus tuus . . . ; *alia antiphona de eodem sanctissimo sacramento,* O Sacrum convivium . . . ; with versicle, response and prayer, Deus qui nobis sub sacramento mirabili . . . ; *In elevacione corporis christi,* Anima christi sanctifica me . . . [Leroquais, *LH* 2:340]; *In elevatione sanguinis christi,* Ave vere sanguis domini nostri ihesu christi qui de latere eius . . . ; *ante communionem,* Domine non sum dignus ut intres sub tectum meum sed tu domine . . . ; *Post communionem oracio,* Vera receptio corporis et sanguinis tui. . . .

8. ff. 153–169: Suffrages for peace, one's guardian angel, Michael, John the Baptist, John the Evangelist, Peter and Paul, James, Andrew, Stephen, Lawrence, Vincent, Sebastian, Adrianus, Jerome, Nicholas, Anthony abbot, Benedict, Dominic (2 antiphons), Francis, Anne, Mary Magdalene, Agnes, Apollonia, Cecilia, Agatha, Lucia, Catherine of Alexandria, Barbara; ff. 169v–171v, ruled, but blank.

Parchment, ff. i (modern parchment) + ii (modern paper) + 171 + ii (modern paper) + i (modern parchment); 170 × 95 (114 × 50) mm. 1^{6}(+7, f. 7) 2^{6}(+1, f. 8) 3^{8}(+1, f. 15 and 9, f. 23) 4^{8} 5^{8}(+7, f. 39) 6^{8} 7^{8}(+1, f. 50 and 7, f. 56) 8^{8}(+2, f. 61) 9^{6}(+1, f. 69) 10^{8}(+1, f. 76; – one leaf in the second half, no loss of text) $11–12^{8}$ 13^{8}(+7, f. 106) $14–18^{8}$ 19^{8}(–one leaf in the first half, no loss of text) $20–21^{8}$; evidence of one catchword in the inner corner of f. 99v, all others apparently cropped; 22 long lines, ruled in pale red ink; no pricking visible. Written in a bâtarde script.

Eleven full page miniatures of mediocre quality, all, except for that on f. 89v, on the versos of inserted singletons, blank on the rectos; the full borders, matched by those on the facing page usually of Italianate candelabras with putti, grotesques, and acanthus leaves; both the miniatures and the borders enclosed by rectangular gold frames; 5- or 3-line leaf initials on square colored grounds. The miniatures are: f. 8v (Hours of the Cross), Crucifixion against a dark cloudy sky; f. 15v (Hours of the Holy Spirit), Pentecost, with tongues of fire on the apostles and Mary; f. 23v (Hours of the Virgin), Annunciation; f. 39v (Lauds), Visitation; f. 50v (Prime), Nativity with a small chorus of green-winged angels singing from a scroll; f. 56v (Terce), Annunciation to the shepherds with similar group of singing angels; f. 61v (Sext), Adoration of the Magi, with Joseph peering out from behind a red curtain at the Kings, one of whom is black; no miniature at none; f. 69v (Vespers), Flight into Egypt; f. 76v (Compline), Coronation of the Virgin: one member of the Trinity escorts Mary to the throne where the other two sit (all 3 are identical); the borders on this opening in a monochrome grey-blue of worshiping angels; f. 89v (Penitential psalms), David in prayer; f. 106v (Office of the Dead), Raising of Lazarus. 3- and 2-line initials in white acanthus leaf against square gold grounds with gold stippling for depth; 1-line initials in painted gold against square red or blue grounds; line fillers in this manner also. Rubrics in the same pale red as the ruling.

Bound, s. XIX, by Joly who, on the back flyleaf i, signed his name below the lettered words "Joly, R. D. Ma dernière mosaïque Mai 1891"; binding of olive green morocco, with overall polygonal inlay of red morocco, stamped in gold with quadrifoils, tulips, daisies; vellum doublures; gilt edges; black morocco slipcase.

HM 1164

Written in the early sixteenth century in Flanders. On f. 171v, offset reading "156." Belonged to Robert Hoe: Grolier Club (1892) n. 27; *One hundred and seventy-six historic and artistic Bookbindings . . . from the Library of Robert Hoe* (New York 1895) vol. 2, pl. 167; *Cat.* (1909) pp. 31–32; his sale, Anderson, New York, 1912, pt. III, n. 2077 to G. D. Smith. Precise source and date of acquisition by Henry E. Huntington unknown.

Bibliography: De Ricci, 101.

HM 1165
BOOK OF HOURS, use of Rome

France, s. XVI^{in}
fig. 149

1. ff. 1–12v: Full calendar in French alternating red and brown (the ink of the text), with major feasts in blue; 4 lines reserved at the top of each month, possibly for a miniature.

2. ff. 13–22: Pericopes of the Gospels; *Oracio ad virginem mariam,* Obsecro te . . . [masculine forms; Leroquais, *LH* 2:346]; O intemerata . . . orbis terrarum. Inclina mater misericordie . . . [Wilmart, 488–90]; f. 22v, ruled, but blank.

3. ff. 23–24v: *Pulcrerrime* [*sic*] *laudes marie,* O filia dei patris. Mater ihesu christi, Amica spiritus sancti . . . [17 appellations of the Virgin]; *Septem gaudia beate marie,* Gaude virgo mater christi . . . [*RH* 7013] and the prayer, Deus qui beatissimam et gloriosam virginem mariam in conceptu . . .

4. ff. 25–88: Hours of the Virgin, use of Rome, with weekly variations of the psalms at matins set into the text before the lessons; suffrages of All Saints, and hours of the Cross and of the Holy Spirit worked in; Advent office begins on f. 82; 3 leaves missing before ff. 51, 62 and 77, containing the hours of the Cross at lauds, and the beginnings of sext and compline; f. 57 misbound, should follow f. 61; f. 87 should follow f. 82; f. 88v, ruled, but blank.

5. ff. 89–104v: Penitential psalms and litany, including Gatianus, Martin and Lidorius among the confessors, and Radegundis among the virgins.

6. ff. 105–143v: Office of the Dead, use of Rome.

7. ff. 143v–158: Prayers as follow: Ave domine ihesu christe verbum patris filius virginis . . . [Wilmart, 412] with versicles, responses and the prayer, Deus qui culpa offenderis . . . ; *septem versus beati bernardi,* Illumina oculos meos . . . [*RH* 27912] and the prayer, Deus qui ezechie regi . . . ; *de sancta trinitate,* Adoro te deum patrem et filium et spiritum sanctum unam divinitatem . . . ; suffrages of the Trinity, Michael, John the Baptist, Peter and Paul, John the Evangelist, James, Christopher, Sebastian, Lawrence, Maurice, Gatianus, Martin, Lidorius, Fiacre, Anne, Mary Magdalene, Catherine of Alexandria, Barbara, Agnes, Margaret; *Les sept oraisons saint gregoire,* O domine ihesu christe adoro te in cruce pendentem . . . [Leroquais, *LH* 2:346]; *Oraison pour les trespasses,* Avete omnes anime fideles . . . with versicle, response and the prayer, Domine ihesu christe salus et liberatio . . . [Leroquais, *LH* 2:341]; f. 158v, ruled, and, added in a later hand, a series of 4 prayers, each beginning in a similar manner, Je te commande a dieu le pere tout puissant . . . [Sonet 837].

Parchment, ff. ii (modern parchment) + 158 + ii (modern parchment); 155 × 102 (96 × 57) mm. Quire structure difficult to determine as many leaves are singletons joined to "conjunct" leaves by tabs; collation often relies upon modern binder's numbering of the quires. 1–2^6 3^4 4^6(through f. 22) 5–6^4 7–8^6 9^4 10 (ff. 47–53, but lacking 1 leaf before f. 51) 11 (ff. 54–63, but lacking 1 leaf before f. 62, and misbound: f. 57 should follow f. 61) 12 (ff. 64–72) 13 (ff. 73–80, but lacking 1 leaf before f. 77) 14 (ff. 81–89, misbound: f. 87 should follow f. 82) 15^6 16–21^8 22–23^6 24^4(–4). 21 long lines, ruled in pale red ink. Written in a bâtarde script, the main body of the text in one hand. A second scribe appears to have been responsible for most occurrences of the suffrage of All Saints (after each hour in the hours of the Virgin), and for the short hours of the Cross and the Holy Spirit; he often copies only one side of a leaf or picks up half-way down a page; his larger and more decorative hand usually coincides with a change in ink color (brown to grey), in rubric color (pink to red), in flourishing of the 2- and 1-line initials (finer to simpler). Folios copied by this scribe: 52, 56–58, 64–65, 69r–v, 75v line 12–76v, 80 line 20–81v, 102v line 10–104 line 8 (text at the end of the litany with a variation of Ps. 39, 15–18, versicles, responses and prayers for the pope, benefactors, the dead and absent brothers). A third hand (or a variation of the first?) copied ff. 82r–v, 87v, 88, 156–158.

Three large miniatures apparently missing, for the openings of the hours of the Cross, of sext and of compline (before ff. 51, 62 and 77). Nine large miniatures survive, usually surrounding 5 (but occasionally 6 or 4) lines of text, enclosed by painted gold architectural or picture frames, and set against a rust-colored ground. The miniatures, with subjects in large scale in the foreground in the style of Jean Bourdichon, are: f. 25 (Hours of the Virgin), Annunciation, similar to Paris, Bibl. Mazarine, MS 507, f. 38, reproduced in R. Limousin, *Jean Bourdichon* (Lyons 1954) fig. 162; f. 41 (Lauds), Visitation, as in Bibl. Mazarine, MS 507, f. 47v, reproduced by Limousin, fig. 163; f. 51 (Hours of the Holy Spirit), Pentecost; f. 52v (Prime), Nativity, as in Bibl. Mazarine, MS 507, f. 59v, reproduced by Limousin, fig. 164; f. 58v (Terce), Annunciation to the shepherds; f. 65v (None), Presentation in the temple; f. 70 (Vespers), Joseph with a pack on a stick looking on as the Child Jesus leads his Mother; all 3 walking; Joseph's face similar to that in Bibl. Mazarine, MS 507, f. 82, reproduced by Limousin, fig. 165; f. 89 (Penitential psalms), David, three-quarter length, in armour against a solid color background, in portrait style; the painted gold picture frame surrounding this miniature set with jewels; f. 105 (Office of the Dead), the Three Living and the Three Dead: one of the Dead holds up a mirror reflecting the image of one of the Living, as he is now, still healthy and alive. Four initials, 4-line, in a white leaf pattern with a face in gold camaïeu as infilling: on f. 17 (Obsecro te) and f. 20 (O intemerata), images of the Virgin; on f. 51 (Hours of the Holy Spirit), an old man's face; on f. 89 (Penitential psalms), a bust of a bear (?) in clothes. Initial on f. 23v (Septem gaudia), 7-line, gold, on a square brick-red ground. Other initials, 4- or 3-line, as gold or white leaves on gold-decorated squares of ochre, brick-red or blue; 2- and 1-line initials in painted gold on colored grounds; ribbon line fillers in the same manner. Rubrics usually in the same pale red as the ruling, sometimes in an orange-tinged red (associated with the second scribe).

Bound, 1857, by Duru, in a green and red painted Grolieresque design; gilt edges; red morocco slipcase.

Written in the early sixteenth century in France; the litany and the suffrages indicate Tours. Sold in 1854 by Lamarche of Dijon to Ambroise Firmin Didot (1790–1876); his sale, Paris, 12 June 1882, n. 21 to Lortic. Belonged to Robert Hoe: Grolier Club (1892) n. 65; *One hundred and seventy-six historic and artistic . . . Bookbindings from the Library of Robert Hoe* (New York 1895) vol. 2, pl. 158; *Cat.* (1909) p. 84; his sale, Anderson, New York, 1912, pt. III, n. 2069 to G. D. Smith. Precise source and date of acquisition by Henry E. Huntington unknown.

Bibliography: De Ricci, 101. James H. Marrow, "*In desen speigell:* A New Form of *Memento Mori* in Fifteenth-Century Netherlandish Art," in *Essays in Northern Art Presented to Egbert Haverkamp-Begemann,* ed. A. Logan (Doornspijk, Netherlands, 1983) 154–63, and fig. 5 of f. 105.

HM 1166

HM 1166
France, s. XV^{2}

BOOK OF HOURS, use of Rouen

1. ff. 1–12v: Calendar in French, with major feasts in red; included are the feasts of Valeric (1 April), Hugh (9 April), Eutropius (30 April), Martialis (3 July, in red), Firmin (25 September), Nicasius (11 October), Mellonius (22 October), Romanus (23 October, in red), Ursinus (30 December).

2. ff. 13–28v: Pericopes of the Gospels, that of John followed by the prayers, Protector in te sperantium . . . [Perdrizet, 25], and Ecclesiam tuam quesumus domine . . . ; Obsecro te . . . [masculine forms; Leroquais, *LH* 2:346]; O Intemerata. . . orbis terrarum. De te enim . . . [Wilmart, 494–95]; suffrage of Mary Magdalene.

3. ff. 29–72v: Hours of the Virgin, use of Rouen; suffrage after lauds of Catherine of Alexandria; suffrage after compline of Lawrence, added in a contemporary bâtarde script.

4. ff. 73–90v: Penitential psalms and litany, including Denis, Maurice and Eustachius among the martyrs; Mellonius, Romanus and Fiacre among the confessors; Honorina among the virgins.

5. ff. 91–94: Short hours of the Cross.

6. ff. 94v–97v: Short hours of the Holy Spirit.

7. ff. 98–128v: Office of the Dead, with responses to the lessons as in Sarum use.

8. ff. 129–136v: Prayers as follow: Doulce dame de misericorde . . . [Leroquais, *LH* 2:310–11]; Doulx dieu doulx pere sainte trinite . . . [Leroquais, *LH* 2:309–10]; Saincte vraie croix aouree . . . [Sonet 1876].

Parchment, ff. i (parchment) + 136 + iii (parchment); 172 × 122 (88 × 60; on ff. 129–136, 90 × 65) mm. 1^{12} $2–3^{8}$(through f. 28) $4–8^{8}$ 9^{4}(through f. 72) $10–16^{8}$(through f. 128) 17^{8}. No catchwords or signatures visible. 14 long lines up to f. 128v, thereafter 16 long lines; ruled in pale red ink; pricking occasionally visible in the outer margin. Written in a gothic book hand, in 2 sizes according to liturgical function.

Seven miniatures in arched compartments with serrated tops, above 3 lines of text; both text and miniature enclosed by a U-shaped frame of pink, blue and gold segments, narrower along the inner margin; outer border of black ivy spray, blue and gold acanthus, flowers and berries. The miniatures are: f. 28, Mary Magdalene standing on a green tile floor, holding her jar of ointment; behind her is a blue brocade cloth; f. 29 (Hours of the Virgin), Annunciation, with the angel holding a scroll and the Dove descending from a silvered window; f. 51v, Catherine of Alexandria with the stock portrait of the owner, a woman in a pink dress and squared black headdress, kneeling before her; f. 73 (Penitential psalms), David praying to God the Father who blesses from a deep blue starry aperture in the sky; f. 91 (Hours of the Cross), Crucifixion in a carefully centered scene with the sun and the moon above, and, below, to Christ's right, Mary, John and Mary Magdalene, and the soldiers to his left; f. 94v (Hours of the Holy Spirit), Pentecost; f. 98 (Office of the Dead), Funeral service in a church, with 2 mourners in black near the coffin and priests in front of a lectern in the foreground. Bracket borders of the same style as the full borders on the opening pages of the individual hours of the Virgin and on ff. 129,

133. 3-line initials in blue or dark pink on a gold ground, infilled with colored trilobe leaves; 2-line initials in gold on dark pink or blue grounds with infilling of the other color, and marginal sprays of black ink and gold motifs; 1-line initials in the same style, but without marginal sprays; ribbon line fillers and small flowers for the same purpose also in blue, dark pink and gold; initials in the text touched in yellow. Rubrics in red.

Bound, s. XVI^{ex}, in French red morocco with a simple tooled and painted fanfare design; holes from 2 fore edge ties; gilt edges.

Written in the second half of the fifteenth century for use in Rouen, to judge from the liturgical use of the hours of the Virgin, and from the saints in the calendar and the litany. On f. i is the note "ex libris joannis baptistae de mydorge," possibly written by the same person who filled the 3 back flyleaves with birth notices of Monsieur Mydorge, sieur de Fretay, of his wife, Marie le Bossu, the date of their marriage and the birth and baptism (at the "fons de St. Paul de Paris") of their 12 children, with dates from 1511 to 1561. Monsieur Mydorge, in listing his children's godparents includes his mother, Catherine Asselin, presumably of the well-known family originating in Rouen; this may account for the presence of a fifteenth century book of hours of the use of Rouen in Paris by the early to mid 1500s. Other names on these leaves place Monsieur Mydorge in the upper administrative echelons of his time: Olivier, Brette, Bochetel, Abra de Raconis, Bourdin, Rapoël, Bragelongne (a book of hours of the use of Rouen belonging to a "Magdalene de Brageloigne" is Cambridge, Fitzwilliam Museum, MS 77).

The complete list of names is: Monsieur Mydorge sieur de fretay; Damoiselle Marie le bossu; monsieur Morler du Muse au tresor des ligues; demoiselle Marie Mauque; Claude olivier sieur de Barynuillier; Anne le bossu; Edmond Brette greffier des auditeurs du Chatelet de paris; monsieur le bossu sieur de Montyon (father-in-law of the writer); Jeanne olivier; Jehan Mydorge; Jehan le bossu Archidiacre de Jozes (?); Jaques bochetel secretaire du roy et tresorier de la maison; Catherine Asselin; Galois de Mydorge esveques sieur de fretay commissaire ordinaire de l'artillerie; Gaston Mydorge; Monsieur de Nancy; Gaston olivier grand Archidiacre d'angers; Monsieur Ariole de la planche cure de deneze en Anjou; Madame Marie Mauque; Sarra Mydorge; Jacques olivier archidiacre Doutremarne en l'eglise d'Angers prieur de l'appy en picardie; Madame denise Brette; Monsieur savignac receveur des generaux des Monnoies et de l'hotel dieu; Estienne Mydorge; galois de raconis Commissaire ⟨?⟩ de l'artillerie et lieutenant a paris de Monsieur le grand M. de d<?>dle; Estienne de la planche l'un des quatre esauffesmes de France; Damoiselle Bochetel; Monsieur bourdin conseilleur du roy et secretaire de ses finances; Marie Mydorge; Monsieur le bossu sieur de Montyon (brother-in-law of the writer); Madame la receveuse de l'escurye du roy lyomec (?); Madame la tresoriere de Raconis; Audebert Mydorge; Monsieur Audebert Catin sieur de Clermont; Monsieur francois d'abra dit Raconis tresorier ⟨?⟩ de l'armee (?) et des ⟨?⟩ payes de picardie; Anne Mydorge; Monsieur le commissaire de Raconis; Marguerite Mydorge; Monsieur lyomec (?) sieur de Cueilly receveur de l'escurie du roy; Marguerite pichon; Monsieur le seche; Marie Mydorge; Monsieur de Vandargene; Damoiselle Catherine Rappouel; Monsieur Coigne; Phyles le bossu; Monsieur de villebrosse; Abraham Mydorge; Monsieur Johanne conseiller et argentier du roy; Antoine fayer conseiller du roy et tresorier de le ⟨?⟩ de la guerre; Damoiselle Lamie (?) le bossu; Lois Midorge; Monsieur re⟨damaged⟩ sieur de villebrosse; Monsieur de grantrue (?) receveur des tailles de paris; Demoiselle Catherine de bragelongne; Monsieur Rappouel conseiller du Roy au Chatelet de paris; Rachel Mydorge; Monsieur le bossu sieur de Montyon advocat au parlemen; Damoiselle Brigide d'abra; Catherine de Raconis. Later belonged to Collin Armstrong; his sale, Anderson, New York, 26 October 1909, pt. II, n. 1170 with plate (catalogue not available to us) to G. Wells. Date and source of acquisition by Henry E. Huntington unknown.

Bibliography: De Ricci, 101.

HM 1167
BOOK OF HOURS, use of Amiens

France, s. XV/XVI

1. ff. 1–11v: Calendar in French, missing the month of January, with major feasts in red; included are the feasts of Valeric (1 April), Honoratus (16 May, in red), "Invention saint fuscien" (27 June), Silas (13 July), Transfiguration (27 July), Firmin (1 September, in red), Firmin (25 September, in red), Richarius (9 October, in red), "L'entree de mon sieur saint fremin" (10 October), "Le Response saint fremin" (16 October), Salvius (29 October), Fuscianus (11 December, in red); f. 12r–v, ruled, but blank.

2. ff. 13–14: *Les x commandemens de sainte eglise,* Ung seul dieu tu adoreras Et aymeras parfaitement . . . [Sonet 2287]; *Les v commandemens,* Les dimenches messe orras et festes de commandement . . . [Sonet 1060].

3. ff. 14–22v: Passion according to John, followed by the prayer, Deus qui manus tuas et pedes tuos . . . ; f. 23r–v, ruled, but blank.

4. ff. 24–29v: Pericopes of the Gospels, that of John followed by the prayer, Protector in te sperantium . . . [Perdrizet, 25].

5. ff. 29v–32v: Short hours of the Cross.

6. ff. 32v–34v: Short hours of the Holy Spirit, defective at the end.

7. ff. 35–67: Hours of the Virgin, use of Amiens; leaves missing between ff. 52–53 and 57–58 with loss of text for the end of prime and beginning of terce, and for the end of sext and beginning of none.

8. ff. 67v–80: Penitential psalms and litany, including Fuscianus, Victoricus, Gentianus, Firmin "ter," Achius, Acheolus, Sixtus, Maurice, Denis, Lucianus, Hippolytus, Gervasius, Protasius, Marcellinus and Peter among the martyrs; Remigius, Vedast, Firmin, Honoratus, Salvius, Richarius, Berundus (?), Valeric, Jodocus and Winnoc among the confessors; Regina and Ulphia among the virgins.

9. ff. 80v–100: Office of the Dead; 3 lessons at matins.

10. ff. 100v–120: Prayers as follow: *Oratio de beata maria,* Obsecro te . . . et michi famulo tuo N. impetres . . . [Leroquais, *LH* 2:346]; *Alia oratio de beata maria,* O intemerata . . . orbis terrarum. Inclina aures . . . [Wilmart, 488–90]; *Secundum lucam,* Missus est gabriel angelus ad mariam virginem desponsatam ioseph nuntians ei verbum. Ave maria gratia plena dominus tecum. Missus est gabriel . . . [Wilmart, 334], followed by the prayer, Te deprecor ergo mitissimam piissimam misericordissimam . . . mariam . . . ; *Antiphona pro deffunctis* [*sic*], Avete omnes anime fideles . . . and the prayer, Domine ihesu christe salus et liberatio . . . [Leroquais, *LH* 2:341]; O domine ihesu christe adoro te in cruce pendentem . . . [Leroquais, *LH* 2:346, here ordered 1–2, 4–6, 3, 7]; *Antiphona de beata maria,* Salve regina . . . [*HE,* 62–63] with versicle and prayer, Famulorum tuorum quesumus . . . ; *Antiphona de beata maria,* Stabat mater . . . [*RH* 19416] with versicle and prayer, Interveniat pro nobis quesumus domine ihesu christe nunc et in hora mortis . . . ; *Orison tres devote a dieu le pere,* Mon benoit dieu ie croy de coeur et confesse de bouche . . . [Sonet 1150]; *de la face nostre seigneur,* Salve sancta facies . . . with versicle and prayer, Deus

qui nobis famulis tuis lumine vultus tui signatis . . . [*HE*, 174–75]; *Pape boniface a donne a tous ceux qui diront devotement ceste orison* . . . , Domine iesu christe qui hanc sacratissimam carnem . . . [Wilmart, 378, n.]; *Antiphona,* Ave cuius conceptio . . . [*RH* 1744] with versicle, response and prayer, Deus qui nos conceptionis nativitatis . . .; suffrage of John the Baptist; Ave ihesu christe verbum patris . . . [Wilmart, 412]; Ave principium nostre creationis . . . [Wilmart, 23, n.] with versicle and prayer, Suscipe clementissime deus preces nostras . . . ; *Orison devote a le vierge marie,* O Maria piissima stella clarissima . . . expers paris feminarum me peccatricem . . . ; suffrage of Nicholas; f. 120v, ruled, but blank.

Parchment, ff. i (parchment) + 120 + i (parchment); 190 × 132 (115 × 83) mm. 1^{6}(–1) 2^{6} 3^{8} 4^{4}(through f. 23) 5^{8} 6^{8}(–4, before f. 35) 7^{8} 8^{8}(–7, before f. 53) 9^{8}(–5, before f. 58) $10–16^{8}$ 17^{4}. Some evidence of signatures on ff. 12–14 (?). 16 long lines, ruled in brown-black ink; some pricking visible in the outer margin. Written in a bâtarde script.

Sixteen miniatures of mechanical execution remain, usually enclosed by square painted gold strips; outer border around the text and miniature of white and colored acanthus leaves, and various flowers on a thin wash of gold. The miniatures are: f. 14 (Passion according to John), Betrayal in the garden, with Judas kissing Jesus, who holds Malchus' ear in his right hand; the miniature, of 12-line height, is placed between 2 lines of text above and below; f. 24 (Gospel according to John), full page illumination of John on Patmos, viewed through pink and green marble columns, with the border reduced to a narrow strip; f. 25v (Luke), 10-line, placed below the text, the evangelist viewed through the pink and green marble columns, with a geometric outer border; f. 27 (Matthew), 12-line, placed between 2 lines of text top and bottom, showing Mark [*sic*] and his lion between the 2 columns; f. 28v (Mark), 10-line, with 2 lines of text above and 4 lines below, showing Matthew [*sic*] with his angel through the 2 columns; f. 29v (Hours of the Cross), 14-line, below the text, Jesus putting on his tunic after the flagellation; geometric border; f. 32v (Hours of the Holy Spirit), 9-line, below the text, enclosed by a gold strip frame, Pentecost; miniature missing before f. 35 for matins of the hours of the Virgin; f. 42 (Lauds), above 3 lines of text in an arched compartment, Visitation with 2 angels behind Mary; f. 49v (Prime), above 3 lines of text in an arched compartment, Nativity; miniature missing before f. 53 for terce; f. 55v (Sext), above 3 lines of text in an arched compartment, Adoration of the Magi; miniature missing before f. 58 for none; f. 59v (Vespers), above 3 lines of text in an arched compartment, Flight into Egypt with an angel accompanying the Holy Family; f. 64 (Compline), 12-line, between 2 lines of text top and bottom, seen through columns, Coronation of the Virgin by an angel while God the Father blesses; f. 67v (Penitential psalms), full page, seen through the columns, floral border reduced to a narrow strip, David on his knees before Nathan with God the Father in a gold-rayed circle in the sky; f. 80v (Office of the Dead), full page miniature set between columns, with a narrow floral strip border, Job on the dunghill and his friends; f. 110v (O domine ihesu christe adoro te in cruce pendentem), 10-line, between 2 lines of text above and 4 lines below, the Crucifixion with Mary and John on either side; f. 115 (Salve sancta facies), 6-line and half of the width of the written space, Veronica. Full borders, divided into compartments on ff. 13 (Ung seul dieu), 26 (Luke), 30 (Hours of the Cross), 33 (Hours of the Holy Spirit), 35 (Hours of the Virgin; in painted gold), 68 (Penitential psalms) and 81 (Office of the Dead; in painted gold); bracket border on f. 24v (Gospel of John). 4-, 3- and 2-line initials as shaded ribbons or white branches against painted gold grounds infilled with naturalistic flowers; 1-line initials in painted gold on alternating blue or brown-red square grounds; ribbon line fillers in the same colors; initials within the text touched in yellow; rubrics in brownish-red.

Bound, s. XIX[ex], in Spanish stamped calf.

Written at the turn of the fifteenth century in France for use in Amiens. From the collection of Ricardo Heredia y Livermore, Count of Benahavis, whose book label in bright colors with the monogram R. H. is on the front pastedown; according to a note in Spanish on f. i, Heredia believed the book to have come from the library of the Marques of Isasi; Heredia sale, Paris, 22 May 1891, pt. I, n. 85 to Tumin. Source and date of acquisition by Henry E. Huntington unknown.

Bibliography: De Ricci, 101.

HM 1168 — France, s. XVI^1
BOOK OF HOURS, use of Paris

1. ff. 1–6v: Full calendar alternating red and blue entries with major feasts in gold, indicating generally the north of France.

2. ff. 7–28v: Pericopes of the Gospels, that of John followed by the prayer, Protector in te sperantium . . . [Perdrizet, 25]; Passion according to John; Obsecro te . . . [masculine forms; Leroquais, *LH* 2:346]; O Intemerata . . . orbis terrarum. Inclina mater . . . [Wilmart, 488–90].

3. ff. 29–88v: Hours of the Virgin, use of Paris; 3 sets of 3 psalms and lessons at matins without intermediary rubrics; the prayer, Ecclesiam tuam quesumus domine . . . , completes all hours, lauds to compline.

4. ff. 89–96: Short hours of the Cross.

5. ff. 96v–101v: Short hours of the Holy Spirit.

6. ff. 102–118: Penitential psalms and litany including Martialis as the last apostle; Denis, Maurice, Eustachius, Eutropius and Quentin among the martyrs; Remigius, Marcellus, Eligius, Aegidius, Julianus, Maurus and Lubin among the confessors; Genevieve among the virgins.

7. ff. 118v–160v: Office of the Dead, use of Paris.

8. ff. 161–170v: Suffrages of Michael, John the Baptist, John the Evangelist, Peter and Paul, Lawrence, Eustachius, Fiacre, Nicholas, Claude, Anthony abbot, Maurus, Mary Magdalene, Catherine of Alexandria, Margaret, Genevieve.

Parchment, ff. i (contemporary parchment) + 170 + i (parchment); 188 × 129 (104 × 63) mm. 1^6 2–3^8 4^6(through f. 28) 5–6^8 7–8^4 9^2 10^4 11–13^8 14^6(through f. 88) 15–19^8 20^6 21^8(–8, cancelled by the scribe) 22–23^8 24^6 25^8(+9, f. 170). Catchwords in center lower margin in script of text. 18 long lines, ruled in pale red ink. Written in 2 sizes of a rather round gothic script, but with a humanistic sense of spacing.

Thirteen large miniatures above 4 lines of text, usually framed by colored columns and with gold tracery at the top of the arch; a decorated gold U-frame, narrow in the inner margin, encloses both text and miniature; the outer border composed of compartments with blue and gold acanthus on a natural ground, or with flowers on a painted gold ground; many grotesques. The miniatures are: f. 13 (Passion according to John), above 3 lines of text, Betrayal in the garden with Judas kissing Christ in the middle ground, and Peter about to strike Malchus in the foreground; f. 29 (Hours of the Virgin), Annunciation by a more capable artist than that of the other illuminations in this book, with figures in somewhat larger scale; this leaf does not have the columns and traceried arch or the U-shape frame; f. 49 (Lauds), Visitation, with 2 angels behind the Virgin; f. 59 (Prime), Nativity; f. 64v (Terce), Annunciation to 2 shepherds and a shepherdess; f. 69 (Sext), Adoration of the Magi; f. 73 (None), Presentation in the temple, Joseph not present; f. 77 (Vespers), Massacre of the Innocents, with one dead baby on the floor and a mother showing another one to Herod who crosses his arms over his chest; a soldier in the background killing a child; f. 83v (Compline), Coronation of the Virgin by Jesus, who holds an orb and blesses Mary as she is crowned by an angel, while other angels watch from behind a low gothic wall; blue clouds swirl at Jesus' and Mary's feet; f. 89 (Hours of the Cross), Crucifixion with Mary, John and others to Christ's right, and the soldiers to his left; the border entirely of painted gold, with multicolored acanthus leaves and a frog on a green base across the bottom; f. 96v (Hours of the Holy Spirit), Pentecost, with the Dove sending bright orange-red tongues of flame upon the apostles; f. 102 (Penitential psalms), David from a loggia looks down at Bathsheba bathing; f. 118v (Office of the Dead), Job on the dunghill. The smaller miniatures, in narrow rectangles, enclosed by colored columns and gold tracery at the top, with compartmentalized ¾ bracket borders which leave the inner margin empty, are: f. 7 (Gospel of John), 10-line, John on Patmos, with the eagle holding his ink well, full border; f. 8v, 11-line, Luke studying; f. 10, 10-line, Matthew with the angel holding his ink well; f. 12, 9-line, Mark; f. 23 (Obsecro te), 8-line, the Virgin nursing the Child, with orange angels on either side; f. 26v (O Intemerata), 9-line, Pietà; f. 161, 8-line, Michael vanquishing the devil; f. 161v, 10-line, John the Baptist pointing to the Agnus Dei which he holds on his draped hand; f. 162, 9-line, John the Evangelist holding the snaky chalice; f. 162v, 9-line, Peter and Paul; f. 163v, 9-line, Lawrence; f. 164, 9-line, Eustachius standing in the middle of the Nile, while the lion on one bank and the wolf on the other take his children away; f. 164v, 9-line, Fiacre dressed as a monk, holding his shovel and a book; f. 165, 9-line, Nicholas with the pickled infants; f. 165v, 10-line, Claude; f. 167, 10-line, Anthony abbot; f. 167v, 8-line, Maurus in a Benedictine's habit, holding his abbot's crozier; f. 168, 8-line, Mary Magdalene; f. 169, 8-line, Catherine of Alexandria triumphing over the emperor Maxentius; f. 169v, 9-line, Margaret; f. 170, 8-line, Genevieve with the angel lighting her candle as the devil tries to put it out. The calendar, with bracket borders, contains illustrations of the monthly occupation in the outer border and of the sign of the zodiac in the lower. 3- and most 2-line initials in white-patterned blue on burnished gold grounds with colored trilobe infilling; the 3-line initial on f. 29 (Hours of the Virgin) of white-shaded acanthus leaves on a dark blue initial set against a maroon ground decorated with gold-shaded acanthus leaves. The 2-line initials in quires 17 (ff. 105–112v), 19 (ff. 119–126v) and on ff. 141–144v (2 bifolia) and on f. 153v are in white-patterned blue or dark pink with naturalistic flowers set on painted gold infillings; 1-line initials in painted gold on brown, maroon or blue grounds; ribbon line fillers in the same colors or as gold-lighted logs. Rubrics in blue. Traced borders in the outer margin of every page, running the length of the text, usually compartmentalized, but occasionally entirely of painted gold backgrounds; the borders often contain grotesques.

Bound, s. XVI^{ex}, in French gilt calf; evidence of 2 fore edge clasps; gilt edges.

Written in France during the first half of the sixteenth century. An inscription on the front pastedown shows the manuscript to have belonged to J. G. Smyth, clerk, of St. Gregory's, Norwich in 1790, and to have been given by him on 3 August 1830 to Augustus Frederick, Duke of Sussex (1773–1843), in whose library it bore the shelf mark, VI.H.h.8 (not in the *Bibliotheca Sussexiana,* London 1827, because of the late date of acquisition); sale of the Duke of Sussex, Evans, London, 1844, pt. II, n. 188 to Thorpe. Belonged to Robert Hoe: Grolier Club (1892) n. 20; *Cat.* (1909) pp. 42–43; his sale, Anderson, New York, 1912, pt. III, n. 2073 to G. D. Smith. Precise source and date of acquisition by Henry E. Huntington unknown.

Bibliography: De Ricci, 102.

HM 1169 France, s. XV^{ex}
BOOK OF HOURS, use of Langres

1. ff. 1–12v: Calendar in French with major feasts in blue ink, those of lesser importance in red, the others in the ink of the text; included are the feasts of Gregory "lingonensis episcopus" (4 January), Hilary "pictavensis episcopus" (13 January), the Holy Triplets: Speusippus, Eleusippus and Meleusippus (17 January, in red), Translation of Desiderius (19 January), Translation of Benignus (26 April), Desiderius "lingonensis" (23 May, in red), Mamas (17 August, in blue), Dedication of the church of Langres (26 August, in red), Invention of the Holy Triplets (18 September), Translation of Mamas (10 October, in blue), Benignus (3 November).

2. ff. 13–17: *Orationes dicende a sacerdote ante celebrationem misse,* Summe sacerdos et vere pontifex eterne rex glorie domine ihesu christe, qui temetipsum deo patri pro nobis peccatoribus in ara crucis obtulisti . . . , *Oratio,* Deus qui de indignis dignos facis . . . , *Alia,* O lux mentium repelle a me stulticie noctem . . . , *Alia Oratio,* Omnipotens et misericors deus ecce accedo ad sacramentum corporis et sanguinis . . . , *Ad filium Oratio,* Ihesu dulcissime sit michi sacrum corpus tuum et sanguis . . . , *Ad filium,* Domine ihesu christe fili dei vivi te suppliciter queso et devotissime deprecor ut hodie . . . , *Ad spiritum sanctum,* Accende illumina et sanctifica me vas tuum . . . ; *Post misse celebrationem sacerdos exutus gracias sequentes dicat, psalmus,* Benedicite sacerdotes domini et cetera, Laudate dominum in sanctis eius et cetera, Nunc dimittis servum tuum domine . . . , *Antiphona,* Trium puerorum cantemus hymnum quem cantabant in camino . . . , *Oratio,* Deus qui tribus pueris mitigasti flammas ignium . . . , *Alia,* Da nobis quesumus omnipotens deus viciorum nostrorum flammas extinguere . . . ; *Alia oratio,* Actiones nostras quesumus domine visitando preveni . . .

3. ff. 17–19: *Alie orationes dicende post misse celebrationem,* Quicquid ego indignus et miser peccator in hac missarum celebratione deliqui . . . ; *Alia,* Auge in nobis domine quesumus per sancta sacramenta que sumpsimus . . . ; *Alia Oratio,* Gratias tibi ago domine sancte pater omnipotens eterne deus qui me indignissimum peccatorem . . . ; *Ad beatam mariam,* Serenissima atque inclita mater domini nostri ihesu christi, sancta maria virgo perpetua . . . ; *Item alia oratio post missam dicendam,* Omnipotens sempiterne deus conservator animarum mundique redemptor . . . ; f. 19v, ruled, but blank.

4. ff. 20–59: Hours of the Virgin, use of Langres; weekly variations of the psalms at matins set into the text before the lessons; short hours of the Cross and of the Holy Spirit worked in (but missing the illuminated opening leaf of the hours of the Cross, after f. 37); Advent office begins on f. 58v; f. 59v, ruled, but blank.

5. ff. 60–73v: Penitential psalms and litany including Mamas, Benignus, Lazarus, Gengulph, Desiderius, Achatius, Speusippus, Eleusippus, Meleusippus, and John and Paul among the martyrs; Lupus, Hubert and Bernardinus among the confessors; Radegundis, Juliana, Genevieve, Libaria, Rosa and Regina among the virgins.

6. ff. 74–97v: Office of the Dead, use of Langres; *Sequuntur commendationes defunctorum,* Subvenite sancti dei . . . , *Oratio,* Tibi domine commendamus

. . . , *Alia Oratio,* Misericordiam tuam domine sancte pater . . . , antiphon, psalm, In exitu . . . , and prayer, Omnipotens sempiterne deus qui humano corpori animam . . . , antiphon, psalm, Dilexi . . . , and prayer, Diri vulneris novitate percussi . . . , *Oratio,* Deus cui soli competit medicinam preparare . . . , Partem beate resurrectionis obtineant . . .

7. ff. 98–110v: *Secuntur orationes ad devotionem dicende. Primo de beata maria,* Obsecro te . . . [masculine forms; Leroquais, *LH* 2:346]; *Alia Oratio,* O Intemerata . . . orbis terrarum. De te enim . . . [Wilmart, 494–95]; *Alia oratio ad beatissimam virginem,* Stabat mater dolorosa . . . [*RH* 19416]; *Oratio sancti thome de aquino,* Concede michi queso omnipotens deus que tibi placita sunt . . . [Doyle, "Thomas Aquinas,"]; *Contemplatio sancti anselmi ad dominum ihesum crucifixum,* Respice domine sancte pater de sanctuario tuo . . . [*PL* 158:756D–759A, *passim*]; *Secuntur septem orationes sancti gregorii,* O domine ihesu christe adoro te in cruce pendentem . . . [Leroquais, *LH* 2:346 in the order printed]; *Secuntur septem versus sancti bernardi,* Illumina oculos meos . . . [*RH* 27912] and the prayer, Omnipotens sempiterne deus qui ezechie regi . . . ; suffrages of Desiderius and Denis; ff. 111–113v, ruled, but blank.

Parchment, ff. ii (modern parchment) + 113 (with 14 bis and 49 bis) + iii (modern parchment); 196 × 136 (110 × 69) mm. $1–2^6$ 3^8(through f. 19) $4–5^8$ 6^8(–3, after f. 37) $7–8^8$ 9^2(through f. 59) $10–15^8$ 16^6. 20 long lines, ruled in pale red ink; pricking occasionally visible along the outer margin. Written in 2 sizes of a bâtarde script, according to liturgical function.

Eleven large miniatures above 4 lines of text, enclosed by simple painted gold frames; the outer borders usually compartmentalized. The miniatures, seen at close range, are: f. 20 (Hours of the Virgin), Annunciation in a Renaissance loggia; the outer border of multicolored acanthus, flowers, insects and birds against a painted gold ground, decorated with black ink dots and commas; f. 31 (Lauds), Visitation; the opening leaf of the hours of the Cross, presumably with illumination, missing after f. 37; f. 38 (Hours of the Holy Spirit), Pentecost; f. 39 (Prime), Nativity; f. 43 (Terce), Annunciation to the shepherds; f. 46 (Sext), Adoration of the Magi; the outer border consists of a large gold branch in a U-shaped frame on which perch a fly, a frog and birds, against a dark blue ground set about with blue-grey flowers and acanthus leaves; f. 49 (None), Presentation in the temple, with Joseph holding the candle and the offering of doves; f. 51 (Vespers), Flight into Egypt; f. 55 (Compline), Coronation of the Virgin by an angel, while she kneels before the enthroned Christ, and a host of red angels watches from behind a low wall; f. 60 (Penitential psalms), Last Judgment, with Christ on the rainbow and an angel at either side blowing a horn; the dead are depicted at close range in the immediate foreground; f. 74 (Office of the Dead), Raising of Lazarus, who is helped out of his tomb by a turbaned man, while bystanders, their hands folded in prayer, watch; 2 small figures in the windows of a half-timbered house gaze down at the scene; outer border as on f. 20. A full compartmentalized border on f. 98 (Obsecro te). 4-line initials in white-patterned blue or orange-tinged pink on a burnished gold ground with trilobe leaf infilling; the infilling on f. 43 contains a naturalistic flower; 2- and 1-line initials in burnished gold on alternating dark pink or blue grounds with infilling of the other color; ribbon line fillers in the same colors; initials in the text touched in yellow. Rubrics in a rather orange-colored red.

Bound by F. Bedford in brown morocco with gold tooling; gilt edges.

Written at the end of the fifteenth century in France, for use in Langres, as indicated by the liturgical forms of the hours of the Virgin and the office of the Dead, and by the saints of the calendar and the litany. Belonged to Robert Hoe: Grolier Club (1892) n. 22; *Cat.* (1909) pp. 71–72; his sale, Anderson, New York, 1912, pt. IV, n. 2346 to G. D. Smith. Precise source and date of acquisition by Henry E. Huntington unknown.

HM 1169

Bibliography: De Ricci, 102. P. Kallenburg, O. Carm., *Fontes Liturgiae Carmelitanae.* Textus et Studia Historica Carmelitana 5 (Rome 1962) 263, erroneously listing HM 1169 as Carmelite.

HM 1170 — France, s. XV[ex]
BOOK OF HOURS, use of Rome

1. ff. 1–6v: Calendar, written in 2 columns, with an entry for each day, alternating red and blue; major feasts in gold.

2. ff. 7–10v: Pericopes of the Gospels.

3. ff. 10v–14: *Oratio de beata maria,* Obsecro te . . . [masculine forms; Leroquais, *LH* 2:346]; *Oratio de beata maria,* O Intemerata . . . orbis terrarum. Inclina mater . . . [masculine forms; Wilmart, 488–90]; f. 14v, ruled, but blank.

4. ff. 15–53v: Hours of the Virgin, use of Rome, beginning imperfectly: //damus ante deum ploremus coram domino . . . ; suffrages of All Saints from lauds to compline; weekly variations of the psalms at matins follow the hours; Advent office begins on f. 50.

5. ff. 54–65v: Penitential psalms and litany, including a number of northern saints: Denis, Eustachius, Eutropius, Remigius, Eligius, Aegidius, Julianus, Lubin, Sulpice, Maurus, and, among the virgins, Genevieve.

6. ff. 66–67v: Short hours of the Cross.

7. ff. 68–69v: Short hours of the Holy Spirit.

8. ff. 70–92v: Office of the Dead, use of Rome.

9. ff. 93–98v: Suffrages of the Trinity, Michael, John the Baptist, Peter and Paul, Sebastian, Nicholas, Anthony abbot, Anne, Catherine of Alexandria, Barbara, Margaret, Avia; ff. 99–100v, ruled, but blank except for ownership notes (see below) and, on ff. 99v and 100, 2 prayers added, s. XVI: Priere avant Le Repas. L'Eternel qui crea toutes choses de Rien benisse par sa bonte . . . [dated 1561]; Apres Le Repas. Seigneur Dieu Pere nourrissier de toute creature . . .

Parchment, ff. iv (modern paper with silk glued to the recto of the first) + i (contemporary parchment) + 100 + i (contemporary parchment) + iv (modern paper with silk glued to the verso of the last); 210 × 140 (125 × 68) mm. 1^6 2^8 3^8(–1) 4–9^8 10^8(–2, 4, 6, with loss of text in each case; ff. 70–74) 11^8 12^4 13^6(to f. 92) 14^8. 23 long lines, ruled in pale red ink. Written in a gothic liturgical book hand.

Twelve large miniatures, enclosed within gold columns and a gothic arch, above 4 lines of text; the first 6 borders are compartmentalized with blue and gold acanthus leaves, flowers, strawberries and an occasional grotesque; the second 6 borders have the same acanthus leaf, flowers and grotesques, but against an even gold background. The miniatures are: f. 7 (John the Evangelist), in the cauldron of oil in open countryside; f. 20v (Lauds), Visitation; f. 27v (Prime), Nativity; f. 30 (Terce), Annunciation to the shepherds; f. 33 (Sext), Adoration of the Magi; f. 35v (None), Presentation in the temple; f. 38 (Vespers), Flight into Egypt; f. 42v (Compline), Coronation of the Virgin by God the Father with 2 angels in the background; f. 54 (Penitential psalms), Bathsheba bathing as David watches from a window; f. 66 (Hours of the Cross), Crucifixion, with Mary, John and others on Christ's right, the soldiers on his left, and the sun and the moon above; f. 68 (Hours of the Holy Spirit), Pentecost, with small tongues of flame descending from the Dove to the apostles and Mary; f. 70 (Office of the Dead), Job on the dunghill. Seventeen smaller miniatures, 12-line, also framed by golden columns and arches, with compartmentalized bracket borders; the miniatures for the suffrages are placed in the upper left area of the written space: f. 8, Luke; f. 9, Matthew; f. 10, Mark; f. 10v (Obsecro te), Virgin and Child; f. 13 (O Intemerata), Pietà; f. 93 (Trinity), God the Father and the Son as identical Christ-like figures, wearing one cloak, and the Dove above them; the remaining saints shown with their usual attributes; f. 98v (Avia), as a young girl in prison, receiving the Eucharist from the Virgin and an angel. 3- and 2-line initials in painted gold outlined in red against square blue grounds patterned in white; 1-line initials in painted gold on alternating blue or brownish red square grounds; line fillers in the same colors. Rubrics in blue. Traced compartmentalized band borders the length of the text in the outer margin of every page. In the calendar, the monthly occupations and the zodiac symbols placed at the top of the folio and divided from one another by golden arches; geometric borders in the outer and lower margins.

Bound by Vogel in blue morocco in "Cathedral" style; green silk endpapers; gilt edges.

Written in France at the end of the fifteenth century. Various ownership notes in the book: on f. v verso, somewhat erased, "Phylippes Lyset (?)" and a flourish, possibly the same as that following the prayer and date of 1561 on f. 99v; f. 15, illegible; on f. 99, below an erasure, "Damoyselle Francoyse regnier Dame Des Loges" and "Ces presentes appartiennent De ‹?› a Damoyselle Anne de grugellin Dame du grand et petis Valluer (?)"; on f. 100v, birth and marriage notices for a Catherine of the Grugellin family, and of her children, dating from 1550 to 1570. On the front pastedown, the modern German book plate of Adelrich Benziger. Source and date of acquisition by Henry E. Huntington unknown.

Bibliography: De Ricci, 102.

HM 1171 — France, s. XVI^in
BOOK OF HOURS, use of Rome

1. ff. 1–12v: Full calendar in French with major feasts in red; below the text on the recto are Latin month verses (Walther, *Initia* 8953) and 4-line stanzas in French, Les vi premiers ans que vit l'homme au monde/ . . . (Latin and French texts printed from the Simon Vostre Hours, use of Rome, 16 September 1498, by F. Soleil, *Les Heures Gothiques,* Rouen, 1882, pp. 31–37).

2. ff. 13–23v: *Examen de conscience pour soy congnoistre a bien se confesser Compose par mastre iehan quentin penitencier de paris,* Premierement examine ta conscience sur le peche d'orgueil. Se tu t'es glorifie pour aulcun bien estant en toy . . . ; ff. 23v–24v, prayers added, s. XVII: *Pour Implorer la misericorde de Dieu,* Ne me traite pas, Seigneur, Selon la grandeur de mes offensez . . . ; *oraison,* O Dieu qui ne souhaite pas la mort Du pecheur . . . ; *oraison,* O Dieu qui êtes L'auteur des Saints desirs et des bonnes actions . . . ; *Pour demander a Dieu Une bonne Mort,* Prosternez devant le Trône de Vostre adorable majesté, je vienz vous demander, ô mon Dieu, la derniere de toutes les graces . . . ; *Pour demander la Victoire de ses Passions,* Dieu Saint, Pere de misericordes qui ne m'avez créé que pour servir dans la liberté . . .

3. ff. 25–36v: Pericopes of the Gospels, that of John followed by the prayers, Protector in te sperantium . . . [Perdrizet, 25] and Ecclesiam tuam quesumus

domine benignus illustra . . . ; Passion according to John, followed by the prayer, Deus qui manus tuas et pedes tuos . . . ; *Oratio ad mariam virginem,* Salve regina . . . [*RH* 18147] with versicle, response and prayer, Interveniat pro nobis quesumus domine iesu criste nunc et in hora mortis . . . ; f. 36r–v, prayer added, s. XVII: *Elevation ou Priere Tres devote a Jesu Crist agonisant que chacun peut dire Tous les Jours pour obtenir une heureuse Mort,* Adorable Jesus que je me represente comme Si vous pendiez Encore Sur la croix . . .

4. ff. 37–96v [f. 37, ruled, but blank except for rubric]: Hours of the Virgin, use of Rome, with the short hours of the Cross, the Holy Spirit and the Conception [hymn at matins: Benedicta conceptio virginis matris Marie festivetur cum gaudio . . . (*RH* 2427)] worked in; ends with Salve Regina . . . [*RH* 18147] and prayers for the dead; ff. 87–91, weekly variations of the psalms at matins; ff. 91–96, Advent office; f. 96r–v, prayers added, s. XVII: *Oraison,* Dieu tres misericordieux Soutenez ma faiblesse . . . ; *Prose . . . de la Sainte Vierge,* Vous Estes Sans Tache, Tres pure et Tres chaste O Marie . . . [rubric in the outer margin: Inviolata, Integra et Casta]; *Oraison,* Je vous suplie Seigneur de me pardonner les pechés . . .

5. ff. 97–110 [f. 97, ruled and blank, except for rubric and added prayers, s. XVII: *Antienne a la Sainte Vierge,* Sub tuum presidium, Je me mets sous votre protection . . . ; *Oraison,* Accordez moi Seigneur Dieu s'il vous plaist . . .]: Penitential psalms and litany, including Berardus, Peter, Accursius, Adjustus and Otho [as one entry] as martyrs; Bonaventure and Jodocus among the confessors; the monks are Benedict, Francis, Anthony, Bernardinus, Dominic, Bernard and Louis; Clare among the virgins.

6. ff. 110v–136: Office of the Dead, use of Rome; f. 136v, ruled, but blank, except for rubric and antiphon.

7. ff. 137–144v: Suffrage of the Trinity; *Ad patrem oratio sequitur,* Pater de celis deus miserere nobis. Domine sancte pater omnipotens eterne deus qui coequalem consubstancialem . . . , Domine iesu criste fili dei vivi qui es verus . . . , Domine spiritus sancte deus qui quoequalis [*sic*] . . . [*HE,* 124–25]; suffrage of the Holy Face; *Ad mariam virginem oratio,* Obsecro te . . . [masculine forms; Leroquais, *LH* 2:346]; *Alia oratio ad mariam,* O Intemerata . . . orbis terrarum. Inclina mater . . . [Wilmart, 488–90]; *Devota contemplatio beate marie virginis iuxta crucem filii sui lacrimantis . . . ,* Stabat mater dolorosa . . . [*RH* 19416] with versicle, response and prayer, Interveniat pro nobis quesumus domine iesu criste nunc et in hora mortis . . .

8. ff. 144v–154v: Suffrages of Michael, John the Baptist, John the Evangelist, Peter and Paul, James the Greater, All Apostles, Stephen, Lawrence, Christopher [. . . michi famulo tuo N . . .], Sebastian, Many Martyrs, Nicholas, Claude, Anthony abbot, Francis, Roch, Anne, Mary Magdalene, Catherine of Alexandria, Margaret, Barbara, Apollonia, Genevieve.

9. ff. 154v–174v: Prayers and devotions as follow: *S'ensuyvent pluiseurs* [*sic*] *devotes louenges, petitions, oroisons et requestes qui a toute personne ayant entendement sont necessaires a dire a nostre seigneur iesu crist, Premierement tu diras au matin quand tu te leveras de ton lit,* In matutinis domine meditabor in te quia fuisti adiutor meus, Gratias ago tibi domine omnipotens eterne deus qui me in hac nocte non meis meritis . . . ; *Quand tu seras hors de ta maison,*

Vias tuas domine demonstra michi . . . [for this and a similar set of prayers through Anima Christi see de la Mare, *Lyell Cat.*, p. 73]; *Quand tu prenderas de l'eaue benoite,* Asperges me domine ysopo et mundabor . . . ; *Quand tu seras devant le crucifix antienne,* Salva nos criste salvator per virtutem sancte crucis . . . with versicle, response and prayer, Crucem tuam adoramus et veneramur domine iesu criste . . . ; *Quand le prestre se retourne dy,* Spiritus sancti gratia illustret et illuminet . . . ; *A l'elevation du corps de nostre seigneur,* Anima cristi sanctifica me . . . [Leroquais, *LH* 2:340]; *Quand on lieve le calice,* Ave vere sanguis domini nostri iesu cristi qui de latere eius cum aqua fluxisti . . . [Wilmart, 378, n.]; *Quand on prend le paix,* Da pacem domine in diebus nostris . . . ; *Quand on voeult recepvoir le corps nostre seigneur iesu crist,* Domine non sum dignus ut intres sub tectum meum sed tu domine qui dixisti . . . ; *Quand on l'a receu,* Vera perceptio corporis et sanguinis tui . . . ; *Contre la tempeste,* A domo tua domine spiritales nequitie repellantur . . . ; *Pour le roy,* Deus regnorum et cristiani maxime protector imperii, da servo tuo regi nostro de hoste triumphum . . . ; *Pour impetrer graces des pechies,* Exaudi quesumus domine supplicium preces et confitentium tibi parce peccatis . . . ; *Contre la tentation de la char,* Ure igne sancti spiritus renes nostros . . . ; *Contre les malvaises pensees,* Omnipotens sempiterne deus respice propitius ad preces nostras . . . ; *Pour quelque tribulation,* Ineffabilem misericordiam tuam domine nobis clementer ostende . . . ; *Pour l'amy vivant en tribulation,* Deus qui iustificas impium et non vis mortem peccatorum . . . ; *Pour ceulx qui sont en voiage,* Adesto domine supplicationibus nostris et viam famulorum tuorum . . . ; *Pour nos biensfaicteurs,* Pretende domine famulis et famulabus tuis dexteram celestis auxilii . . . ; *Pour les amis qui sont en necessite,* Omnipotens sempiterne deus salus eterna credentium . . . ; *Pour le tien amy qui est mort,* Suscipe piissime deus in sinu patriarche tui abrahe animam famuli tui N . . . ; *Pour pere et mere,* Deus qui nos patrem et matrem honorare precepisti . . . ; *Les vii vers sainct gregoire,* Domine iesu criste adoro te in cruce pendentem . . . [Leroquais, *LH* 2:346]; *Orison tres devote a dieu le pere,* Mon benoict dieu ie croy de cueur et confesse de bouche . . . [Sonet 1150]; *Oratio dicenda die sabbati ad honorem intemerate dei genitricis virginis marie,* Missus est gabriel angelus ad mariam virginem desponsatam ioseph, nuncians ei verbum, Ave maria gratia plena dominus tecum . . . [Leroquais, *LH* 1:95], *oratio,* Te deprecor ergo mitissimam piissimam misericordissimam speciosissimam dei genitricem mariam semper virginem geminam ut in illo tremendo ac terribili iudicio . . . ; *Antiphona, De sororibus beate marie virginis,* O nobile ternarium sanctarum sororum trium cuius nomen est maria . . . with versicle, response and prayer, Deus qui beatas mariam iacobi et mariam salome genitricis tue marie sorores . . . ; *Specialis salutatio ad beatam virginem mariam,* Ave ancilla trinitatis ave filia sempiterni patris . . . [*RH* 1692] with versicle, response and prayer, Deus qui nos conceptionis nativitatis annuntiationis . . . ; *Oratio devotissima pro fidelibus defunctis in cimiterio inhumatis, Oratio defunctorum,* Avete omnes anime fideles quarum corpora hic et ubique requiescunt . . . with versicle, response and prayer, Domine iesu criste salus et liberatio fidelium animarum . . . [the set in Leroquais, *LH* 2:341]; *S'ensuyvent chincq belles oroysons que monseigneur sainct iehan l'evangeliste fist en l'onneur de la vierge marie dont nostre seigneur donne aulcuns benefices* . . . , Mediatrix . . . , Auxiliatrix . . . , Reparatrix . . . , Illuminatrix . . . , Alleuiatrix . . . ; *S'ensuit le chapelet de iesus et de la vierge marie avec les grans tresors de grace inestimable . . . c'est assavoir que en l'an mil deux cens octante l'ange de dieu s'apparut a ung saint homme nomme iehan de fontaines natif de savoye* . . . , Ave maria gratia plena . . . , Quem tu virgo castissima angelo nunciante de spiritu sancto concepisti . . . [ff. 175–177v, ruled, but blank; f. 177, former pastedown].

Parchment, ff. ii (contemporary parchment, ruled, but blank; f. i, former pastedown) + 177 (f. 177, former pastedown); 195 × 140 (125 × 82) mm. 1–4^{6}(through f. 24) 5^{4}(through f. 28) 6^{8}(through f. 36) 7^{8} 8^{6} 9–13^{8} 14^{6}(through f. 96) 15–19^{8}(through f. 136) 20–23^{8} 24^{8}(–7) 25^{2}. Catchwords written vertically along inner bounding line, usually in the hand of the text, but that on f. 128v in a noting hand; those on ff. 66v and 82v partially erased; quire and leaf signatures occasionally visible as letter of the alphabet and arabic numeral. 23 long lines, ruled in pale brownish ink; pricking usually visible. Written in a bâtarde script.

Sixteen full page miniatures, enclosed by various styles of borders: f. 25 (Gospel of John), John on Patmos gazing upwards at the 7-headed beast, enclosed by a painted gold architectural frame; f. 29 (Passion according to John), Betrayal in a crowded garden, with Malchus on his knees and Peter sheathing his sword; the frame around the miniature is painted yellow to resemble the more normal burnished gold strip, with serrated top arch; outer border of multicolored acanthus leaves and flowers on a painted gold ground; in the lower margin, a coat of arms (see below); f. 37v (Hours of the Virgin), Annunciation, with the owner kneeling at a prie-dieu, his armor decorated with his heraldic devices, and wearing the collar of the order of St. Michael (see below); the miniature is enclosed in a painted gold architectural frame; f. 44v (Lauds), Visitation, with 2 angels in the background; yellow frame around miniature as on f. 29; geometric border with blue and gold acanthus leaves and colored flowers; f. 52 (Hours of the Cross), Crucifixion, with the Sun and the Moon, the 2 Thieves and a large crowd of soldiers; yellow frame around miniature as on f. 29; colored flowers and acanthus leaves against a painted gold ground form the border; f. 53v (Hours of the Holy Spirit), Pentecost, within a painted gold architectural frame; f. 55 (Hours of the Conception), Mary, her hands together in prayer, surrounded by her attributes; yellow frame around miniature as on f. 29; outer border of flowers and acanthus on painted gold ground; f. 56v (Prime), Nativity, with the Baby lying on the hem of Mary's cloak; enclosed by a painted gold architectural frame; f. 61 (Terce), Annunciation to the shepherds; yellow frame around miniature as on f. 29; border of colored flowers and acanthus leaves on a painted gold ground; in the lower margin, the owner's coat of arms (see below); f. 65v (Sext), Adoration of the Magi; yellow frame around the miniature as on f. 29; geometric border of acanthus leaves and flowers; f. 70 (None), Presentation in the temple, enclosed by a painted gold architectural frame; f. 74v (Vespers), Flight into Egypt with the miracle of the cornfield in the background; enclosed by a painted gold architectural frame; f. 80v (Compline), Dormition of the Virgin, with John holding the palm leaf, Peter an aspergillum, the other apostles crowded about the bed, while Jesus approaches unseen; yellow frame around miniature as on f. 29; colored flowers and acanthus against painted gold ground; f. 97v (Penitential psalms), David watching Bathsheba as she bathes, while 4 women attend her with mirror, comb, ointment (?), and a bowl of fruit; her shoes and stockings lie on the ground; frame is painted gold architectural design; f. 110v (Office of the Dead), the Rich Man at dinner, with Lazarus approaching as the dogs lick his sores; on a larger scale than the other miniatures; enclosed by a painted gold architectural frame; f. 137 (De sancta trinitate), the Trinity as 2 identical figures for the Father and the Son, except that the Son is showing his wounds and the Father holds a globe; they support an open book, with the Dove above them; enclosed by a painted gold architectural frame. Smaller miniatures, 7-line, usually of a saint on a green tile floor, against a brocade cloth of honor, either brick red or blue: f. 26v, Luke; f. 27v, Matthew; f. 28, Mark; f. 31 (Passion according to John), Ecce Homo; f. 34 (Passion according to John), Crucifixion with Mary and John; f. 137v (prayer to the Trinity), the Father seated, holding the globe; f. 138 (prayer to the Trinity), the Son, standing and showing his wounds; f. 138v (prayer to the Trinity), Pentecost; f.

139v (Obsecro te), Pietà; f. 143 (Stabat mater), Crucifixion, in a slightly different pose from that on f. 34; f. 145, 2 miniatures: Michael and John the Baptist, the latter of 6-line height; f. 145v, 2 miniatures: John the Evangelist, and Peter and Paul; f. 146, James the Greater; f. 146v, Stephen; f. 147, Lawrence; f. 147v, Christopher; f. 148v, Sebastian; f. 149, Nicholas; f. 149v, Claude; f. 150v, 2 miniatures: Anthony abbot and Francis receiving the stigmata from the winged crucifix; f. 151, Roch showing sore to the angel; f. 151v, Anne teaching Mary to read; f. 152, Mary Magdalene; f. 152v, 2 miniatures: Catherine of Alexandria and Margaret; f. 153, Barbara; f. 153v, Apollonia; f. 154, Genevieve, with an angel lighting the Saint's candle as a devil tries to put it out; f. 159v (Mon benoict dieu ie croy de cueur), Christ holding the Eucharist; f. 160v (Missus est angelus gabriel), the Mother and Child. The decoration of the calendar consists of 2 rectangular miniatures, one of the monthly occupation and one of the zodiac symbol, set into band borders along the outer and lower margins of the recto. 4-line initials in shaded pink, blue or brick red on a painted gold ground decorated with black ink dots and commas, the infilling of naturalistic flowers or berries. 2- and 1-line initials in painted gold on alternating blue or brick red grounds; ribbon and log line fillers in these same colors; initials in the text touched in yellow. Rubrics in red. Marginalia, s. XVII, up to f. 46v, with the "argument" of the psalms.

Bound, s. XVII^{med}, in French red morocco with simple gold ruling; strips of manuscript music, s. XIII^{2}, used as binding reinforcement; gilt edges.

Written in France in the early sixteenth century. The first owner of the manuscript appears kneeling before the Virgin, wearing his coat of arms, on f. 37v; the same coat of arms, ensigned with the collar of the Order of St. Michael, in the lower margins of ff. 29 and 61: argent 3 lions rampant sable, on an escutcheon azure a fesse or between 6 billets or. An English (?) book dealer's slip offset onto f. i verso.

Bibliography: De Ricci, 102.

HM 1172 — France, s. XV^{2}
BOOK OF HOURS, use of St. Quentin

1. ff. 1–6v: Calendar in French, alternating red and blue entries with major feasts in gold; included are the feasts of Quentin (3 January), Regulus (30 March), Quentin (2 May), Bernardinus (13 May), Medard (8 June, in gold), Separation of the Apostles (15 July), Transfiguration (27 July), "aragonne" (for Radegundis? 13 August), "genebault" (4 September), "gaoud" (19 October), Quentin (31 October, in gold).

2. ff. 7–32v: Hours of the Virgin; antiphon and capitulum at prime and at none are: O admirabile; Hec est virgo; Germinavit radix; Per te dei; the antiphon to the Nunc dimittis at compline is Ecce completa sunt omnia, while the other antiphon at compline is Cum iocunditate (cf. breviary of the use of St. Quentin, as identified by a rubric, pr. ca. 1520; copy in Brussels, Roy. Lib., Van Hulthem 658).

3. ff. 33–35: Short hours of the Cross.

4. ff. 35v–38v: Short hours of the Holy Spirit; suffrages of Anthony abbot and Sebastian.

5. ff. 39–48v: Penitential psalms and litany, including Quentin, Denis, Nicasius, Maurice, Eustachius, Lucianus, Lambert, Firmin, Hippolytus and Eutropius

among the martyrs; Remigius, Fursey, Vedast, Amand, Bertin, Germanus, Aegidius, Eligius, Medard and Gildard among the confessors; Cilinia, Ursula, Genevieve, Godeberta, Clare, Radegundis and Bathildis among the virgins.

6. ff. 49–63v: Office of the Dead; 3 lessons at matins.

7. ff. 64–69: Prayers as follow: Ave cuius conceptio . . . [*RH* 1744] with versicle, response and prayer, Deus qui nos conceptionis nativitatis . . . ; *S'ensieut les vii ioyes de la vierge marie,* Gaude flore virginali Que honore speciali . . . , with the prayer, Dulcissime domine ihesu christe qui beatissimam genitricem tuam . . . [*HE,* 64–65]; Stabat mater dolorosa . . . [*RH* 19416], and the prayer, Domine ihesu christe per illam amaritudinem quam pro me sustinuisti in cruce . . . ; suffrages of Anne, Michael, Quentin (Ave martir egregie patrone viromandie . . .) and Adrian.

8. ff. 69–70v, and by tie mark to f. 74r–v: [a long prayer of confession and repentance added in a different hand] [O] Dieu Creteur [*sic*] du ciel et de la terre Roy des Roys seigneur des seigneurs qui m'avez daigne faire et creer a vostre samblance et ymage . . .

9. f. 71r–v: [added by a third hand] [O] Vierge Marie tres saincte Royne du ciel et de la terre comme Dieu le pere selon la divine puissance de sa magnificence vous a en son tres glorieulx trosne . . . ; [O] Glorieuse vierge mere de nostre seigneur Ihesucrist plene de tous biens . . .

10. ff. 72–76: [added by a fourth hand] Obsecro te . . . et michi famulo tuo impetres . . . [Leroquais, *LH* 2:346]; f. 74r–v, continuation of the prayer of confession which began on f. 69; O intemerata . . . orbis terrarum. Inclina mater . . . [Wilmart, 488–90]; f. 76v, ruled but blank.

11. f. 77r–v: [added by a fifth hand] [O] Tres digne princesse dame de pitie fontaine de misericorde comme le benoist sainct esprit vous a acousee et versee en toute vostre tres noble et tres piteuse ame . . . ; f. 78r–v, ruled but blank.

Parchment, ff. ii (paper) + i (parchment) + 78 + ii (paper); 190 × 137 (110 × 75) mm. 1^6 $2–9^8$(through f. 70) 10 (ff. 71–78, of uncertain structure: stitching between ff. 74–75; ff. 75–76 constitute a bifolium; f. 77v bears the offset of a full border of black ivy spray which evidently included some blue acanthus). No catchwords or signatures visible. 22 long lines, ruled in pale red ink, except for ff. 75–76v, ruled in purple ink; pricking visible in all 3 outer margins. Written in a bâtarde script in 2 sizes, according to liturgical function.

Thirteen large miniatures above 8 lines of text, all with a pinkish hue to the coloring; in some, the faces have been outlined in black ink at a later date; compartmentalized borders infilled with blue and gold acanthus, flowers and grotesques, or of flat painted gold with multicolored acanthus, flowers, berries and grotesques. The miniatures are: f. 7 (Hours of the Virgin), by a different artist from the other illuminations in the book, Annunciation, with God the Father sending the Dove to Mary; the room is defined by gold pillars at the sides and gold tracery pendant arches at the top; f. 12v (Lauds), 6-line, in a jeweled frame, Visitation, with 2 angels behind Mary; f. 18 (Prime), in a jeweled frame, Nativity, in which the Infant wears a string of coral beads; f. 21 (Terce), Annunciation to 2 shepherds and a shepherdess; f. 23 (Sext), Adoration of the Magi, with the baby holding a gold flower in a scene set directly outside city walls, while rays from a spoked circle of gold pour down; f. 25 (None), in a brown jeweled frame, Presentation in the temple, with the baby holding a rosary; f. 27 (Vespers), in a brown jeweled frame, Flight into Egypt, with the miracle of the cornfield in the background, while an angel offers fruit to Mary; the Baby wears a coral necklace and holds a flower; f. 30v (Compline), Coronation of the Virgin by 2 angels who fly above her, while God the Father, wearing a papal tiara, blesses; f. 33 (Hours of the Cross), above 5 lines of text, the Crucifixion, with Mary Magdalene at the foot of the cross, Mary and John to Christ's right, the soldiers to his left, and the 2 thieves on crosses behind him; f. 35v (Hours of the Holy Spirit), above 6 lines of text, Pentecost: Mary kneels at a prie-dieu, her book open before her, and her hand raised, while the apostles kneel before her; f. 39 (Penitential psalms), above 6 lines of text, David in prayer inside a room with columns at the sides and an arch forming the top; f. 49 (Office of the Dead), above 7 lines of text, Raising of Lazarus, with columns at the sides. Seven smaller miniatures: f. 37v, 11-line, Anthony abbot sitting with a book open on his knees, staring into the fire, with the pig behind him; f. 38, 11-line, Sebastian; f. 64v (the 7 Joys), 10-line, Mary and Child with angels at either side; f. 68, 10-line, Quentin with iron spikes in his shoulders; f. 68v, 12-line, Adrian wearing armor, standing on a lion, holding the anvil and sword; f. 72 (Obsecro te), 7-line, Pietà, by a different artist; f. 75 (O Intemerata), 7-line, the Virgin and Child, by the same artist as on f. 72. Major initials, 6- and 5-line, as white shaded ribbons, enclosing naturalistic flowers on a gold ground, the outer ground of brick red decorated in gold. On the miniature pages, where the major initials occur, 2- and 1-line initials and line fillers often in painted gold on brick red or blue grounds; this style also for the 3-line initials on ff. 72 and 75. 4-, 2- and 1-line initials in burnished gold on alternating blue or dark pink grounds with infilling of the other color; initials within the text touched in yellow. Full traced borders of blue and gold acanthus, flowers, berries, and gold motifs on all pages, including the calendar; each page with a number of grotesques: unicorns, half-humans, hunters, mermaids, etc.; the text space and the border space outlined in pale red. Rubrics occasionally in blue or gold through f. 14; thereafter only in pale red.

Bound in modern dark red velvet with an earlier silver-gilt fore edge clasp; red silk endpapers; gilt edges.

Written in France, probably for use in St. Quentin, in the second half of the fifteenth century. Belonged to E. Dwight Church (1835–1908); in his *Catalogue . . . of English Literature* (1909) vol. 1, n. 405, with plate of f. 35v. Acquired by Henry E. Huntington with the Church collection in 1911.

Bibliography: De Ricci, 102.

HM 1173 — France, s. XV²
BOOK OF HOURS, undetermined use — *fig. 124*

1. ff. 1–12v: Calendar in French with major feasts in red; included are the feasts of Honoratus (16 May, in red), "Le feste nostre damme" (5 August), Firmin (25 September, in red); f. 13r–v, 2 coats of arms (see below).

2. ff. 14–19: Pericopes of the Gospels; f. 19v, with decorative border, but no text.

3. ff. 20–23v: *Chy apres s'ensieut la messe de nostre damme,* Salve sancta parens . . .

4. ff. 24–27: Short hours of the Cross; f. 27v, blank.

5. ff. 28–64: Hours of the Virgin; the antiphons and capitula at prime and at none are: Ecce tu pulchra . . . , Ab inicio et ante secula . . . , Fons ortorum . . . , Ego quasi vitis . . . ; the hours from lauds to compline end with the prayer, Ecclesiam tuam quesumus domine . . . ; f. 64v, blank.

6. ff. 65–78v: Penitential psalms and litany, including John and Paul, and Gervasius and Protasius among the martyrs; Nicholas and Louis among the confessors; Clare among the virgins.

7. ff. 79–83v: *S'ensieut une devote orison de nostre damme,* Obsecro te . . . [masculine forms; Leroquais, *LH* 2:346]; *Orison de nostre damme,* O intemerata . . . orbis terrarum. Inclina aures . . . [Wilmart, 488–90].

8. ff. 84–114v: Office of the Dead, use of Rome.

9. ff. 114v–116v: Deus propicius esto michi peccatori . . . [*HE,* 125].

10. ff. 117–124 [added s. XVI]: Prayers as follow: *Oratio ad Christum,* Conditor coeli et terrae, rex regum et dominus dominantium qui me de nihilo fecisti ad imaginem et similitudinem tuam . . . ; *Oratio venerabilis Bedae presbiteri* . . . , Domine Iesu Christe qui septem verba . . . [Leroquais, *LH* 2:342]; *Oratio coram crucifixo dicenda . . . contulit Gregorio papa III ad petitionem reginę Angliae,* Precor te amantissime Domine Iesu Christe propter illam eximiam charitatem . . . [Wilmart, 378, n.] with the prayer, Omnipotens sempiterne Deus qui ex nimia charitate unicum filium tuum . . . ; Mon benoist dieu ie croy de cueur et confesse de bouche . . . [Sonet 1150]; ff. 124v–125, blank.

11. ff. 125v–126 [added s. XVII]: *Richardus Pauli Stravius Dei et Apostolicae* [rubric terminating here], Richard Pauli Stravius par la grace de Dieu et du Saint Siege Apostolique Evesque de Denis . . . Donne a Rullant le 29me de Jullet 1652, Par ordonance de Monsieur le R., Charle Briffor secretaire.
An indulgence granted to those who say certain prayers before the images contained in this book; we have found no reference to this bishop or bishopric at this date.

Parchment, ff. iii (of which the first once functioned as a pastedown; all 3 are part of the structure of the first quire) + 126; 205 × 145 (100 × 68) mm. 1–15^8(through f. 117) 16^2 17^{10}(–6, 7, 8, presumably blank). One catchword survives on f. 45v in the script of the text, written vertically along the inner bounding line; the occasional tiny mark at the lower edge of other final quire leaves, however, indicates that the normal system in this book may have been to place the catchwords horizontally in the far inner corner of the leaf. Quire signatures, excluding the calendar, run a–[n?], with the leaves indicated by early form arabic numerals; beginning with the eleventh quire ["i"], another parallel set of quire and leaf signatures begins, a–e and 1–4 in early form arabic numerals, placed in the center of the lower margin. Early modern numbering of the quires in red-tinged ink in the gutter of the first recto. In the main body of the text, 18 long lines, ruled in faint red-brown ink, with the script set above the line; on ff. 118–124, 16–18 lines of text, apparently unruled. Written in a bâtarde script; ff. 117–124 in an italic hand.

Seventeen miniatures in arched compartments enclosed by simple bar frames of leaf gold and color; another strip of painted gold parallels the outer edge of the arch and encloses the 4 lines of text. The outer borders, in a rather spiky blue and dark painted gold acanthus, painted gold dots and a few flowers, berries, clusters of grapes, acorns, pomegranates or thistles of restrained colors: grey, dark rose, pale green. The miniatures were numbered in early form arabic numerals in the center lower margin as suggested by the survival of the numbers 11, 13–17 on ff. 50, 56, 61, 65, 79, 84. The miniatures, which have been attributed to Simon Marmion[1] and helpers (particularly in the backgrounds?), are: f. 14, John sitting on a rocky promontory with the eagle perched on a single rock in the foreground; undulating water surrounds the island and in the far distance a many-spired city is visible; f. 15v, in large scale, the Virgin, holding a diminutive baby Jesus, poses at an open window for Luke who is finishing a portrait of them set on a large easel; the ox lies on the floor at Luke's feet; f. 17, in large scale, with the angel behind him holding a scroll bearing his name, Matthew sits at his desk writing in a thick codex; a convex mirror hangs from the shelf above his desk, upon which there is a clear glass vase; f. 18v, in large scale, Mark concentrates on his writing on a scroll in a barrel-vaulted room, while the lion at his feet stares at the viewer; f. 20 (Mass of the Virgin), seated on a gothic tracery throne in the center of the miniature, Mary holds the tiny baby Jesus in her lap while angels play music at either side; f. 24 (Hours of the Cross), a very thin Christ hangs on the cross, with Mary, John and the holy women on his right, and the soldiers on the left; behind him a city is silhouetted against the golden-colored sky; f. 28 (Hours of the Virgin), Annunciation, set in a gothic church, symmetrically arranged with Mary and the archangel Gabriel at the 2 sides and a gold altar in the center, below a green canopy; f. 35 (Lauds), Visitation, with a farmyard and its dovecote in the middle ground, and an ethereal city in the background; f. 44 (Prime), done by helpers (?), Annunciation to the shepherds, one with a flute tucked in his belt, the other with bagpipes who protects his eyes with an upraised arm, listening to the host of angels, as does a shepherdess who has been interrupted in making a garland; f. 47 (Terce), Nativity, with the tiny doll-like baby Jesus lying on the bare ground in the shed, viewed from directly in front; 2 shepherds gaze over a wattle partition on the left, and Joseph arrives, holding a candle, from the right; f. 50 (Sext), Adoration of the Magi; the oldest Magus, his crown in hand and his gift on the orange-draped bed, kneels to kiss the foot of the tiny baby Jesus who is held up by Mary; Joseph stands to one side with hat in hand; f. 53 (None), Presentation in the temple, which is open frontally to the viewer; a group of men and women observe the scene and each other with interest; f. 56 (Vespers), Flight into Egypt; Joseph, leading the donkey and carrying a bundle on a stick on his back, turns to look at Mary who, wearing a hat and holding the baby, has the donkey's reins in her free hand; in the far distance a group of soldiers is seen pursuing them; f. 61 (Compline), Coronation of the Virgin, who sits on a gold gothic throne while Jesus, with tiara and cross and orb, blesses her, and bands of orange or blue angels frame the scene on either side; f. 65 (Penitential psalms), David, his harp leaning up against a rock, prays to God the Father who appears picked out in gold against the dark blue sky; a small angel in white mediates between them; f. 79 (Obsecro te), the Virgin, seated on a gold throne at the end of a narrow room, nurses the Child, while groups of singing and music-playing angels stand at the sides of the throne; f. 84 (Office of the Dead), Jesus raising Lazarus from the dead, while his sisters kneel in prayer, and a group of men watches intently. 4- and 2-line initials in burnished gold with a design painted on the gold; infillings of dark blue acanthus leaves picked out in gold on maroon grounds of the same style, or vice versa. 1-line initials in burnished gold with infillings of dark blue or maroon on grounds of the other color; initials within the text touched in yellow. Rubrics in red. Full traced borders on every page, contained by 2 thin painted gold lines around the written space and around the outer edge of the border. On ff. 117–124: 3- and 2-line initials in gold curled forms against shaded square red or blue grounds; 1-line painted gold initials on alternating blue or maroon square grounds. On f. 117r–v, the last leaf of the quire, the full acanthus border; on successive leaves the text is framed by illusionistic painted gold molding.

The book has apparently been in loose quires since its acquisition and is kept in a black morocco box made by Lloyd, Wallis and Lloyd; the red velvet back cover from the binding retained in Library files.

Written in northeastern France; note, in the calendar, "michiel," "franchois," "berthelemieu." Among the early owners were members of the family of Berlaymont as indicated by a death note on f. ii for "michiel de Berlaymont" dated 1516; notes on f. 10r–v give the death date of 1558 for "ma femme" whose body was brought to Berlaymont for burial, and again the date of 1558 for the dedication of the church of Berlaymont by the suffragan bishop of Cambrai. Two coats of arms added on f. 13r–v, on a leaf perhaps originally ruled and decorated for a calendar page probably represent the arms of Charles de Berlaymont, Baron of Lens and Knight of the Golden Fleece (1510–78) and his wife, Adrienne, daughter of Louis de Ligne, Baron of Barbaçon. The arms are: f. 13, encircled by a Renaissance wreath, per pale, I, arms of Berlaymont of Namur province (Rietstap, vol. 1, pl. 187); II, quarterly 1 and 4, arms of Ligne (Rietstap, vol. 4, pl. 65); 2 and 3, arms of Barbaçon of Hainaut (Rietstap, vol. 1, pl. 121); on f. 13v, the arms of Berlaymont encircled by the collar of the Order of the Golden Fleece, presumably added between 1556, when Charles received the Golden Fleece, and his death in 1578. The manuscript was in the possession of a book dealer of Prague, Alexander Storch, in November 1896; Christie's, 9 April 1900, n. 234 (bought in); Catalogue 96 (March 1901) of Ellis and Elvey, pp. 1–6 with a long description by J. W. Bradley. Acquired by E. Dwight Church (1835–1908); in his *Catalogue . . . of English Literature* (1909) vol. 1, n. 401 with a plate of f. 24. The Church collection was purchased by Henry E. Huntington in 1911.

Bibliography: J. Destrée, "Un livre d'heures peint par Simon Marmion," *Annuaire de la Société des Bibliophiles et Iconophiles de Belgique* (1918) 131–37. S. R[einach], "Une miniature de Simon Marmion," *Revue archéologique* 9 (1919) 240. De Ricci, 102–03. E. W. Hoffman, "Simon Marmion Re-considered," *Scriptorium* 23 (1969) 243–71 and pl. 80–98; see especially p. 245; also, "Simon Marmion or 'The Master of the Altarpiece of Saint-Bertin': A Problem in Attribution," *Scriptorium* 27 (1973) 263–90 and pl. 17–20; see especially pp. 273 and 275. S. Hindman, "The Case of Simon Marmion: Attributions and Documents," *Zeitschrift für Kunstgeschichte* 40 (1977) 185–204, and especially pp. 203, n. 45 and 204, Appendix. J. Thorpe, introduction to *Book of Hours: Illuminations by Simon Marmion* (Huntington Library pamphlet, no date) with color reproductions of all illuminations, in larger scale than in the manuscript. T. Kren, ed., *Renaissance Painting in Manuscripts: Treasures from the British Library* (J. Paul Getty Museum 1983) n. 11 with reproductions of ff. 44, 47.

---

[1] We thank Mme Nicole Reynaud for confirming this attribution.

HM 1174 — Flanders, s. XV^{ex}
BOOK OF HOURS, use of Rome — *fig. 143*

1. ff. 1–13 [f. 1, blank]: Calendar in red and black including, in red, the feasts of Basilius (14 June), Remigius and Bavo (1 October) and Donatianus (14 October); f. 13v, blank.

2. ff. 14–21 [f. 14, blank]: Short hours of the Cross; f. 21v, ruled, but blank.

3. ff. 22–28 [f. 22, blank]: Short hours of the Holy Spirit; f. 28v, ruled, but blank.

4. ff. 29–35v [f. 29, blank]: Mass of the Virgin.

5. ff. 36–41v: Pericopes of the Gospels.

6. ff. 42–121v [f. 42, blank]: *Incipiunt hore beate marie virginis secundum usum Romanum;* weekly variations of the psalms at matins set into the text before the lessons; suffrages of All Saints and prayers for peace from lauds to compline; Advent office begins on f. 114; f. 122r–v, ruled, but blank.

7. ff. 123–143 [f. 123, blank]: Penitential psalms and litany including Victor, Quentin, Eustachius, Maurice and Denis, all with companions, among the martyrs; among the confessors Bavo, Remigius, Eligius, Aegidius, Audomar, Livin

and Amand; among the virgins Bridget, Genevieve and Apollonia; f. 143v, ruled, but blank.

8. ff. 144–188v [f. 144, blank]: Office of the Dead, use of Rome.

9. ff. 189–206v: *Incipit canticum athanasii,* Quicumque vult salvus esse . . . ; *Oracio ad beatam virginem mariam,* Obsecro te . . . et michi famulo tuo impetres . . . [Leroquais, *LH* 2:346]; *Alia oracio de virgine maria,* O Intemerata . . . orbis terrarum. Inclina mater . . . [masculine forms; Wilmart, 488–90]; *de virgine maria,* Stabat mater dolorosa . . . [*RH* 19416] with the prayer, Interveniat quesumus domine ihesu christe . . . ; suffrages of Sebastian, James, Anthony of Padua, Michael, Francis, Jerome, Peter and Paul.

Parchment, ff. i (contemporary parchment, ruled r–v for a calendar, and conjunct with f. 3) + 206 + iv (contemporary parchment, the last 2 ruled for text); 165 × 117 (100 × 64) mm. 1^8(–1, 2) 2^8 3^8(+1, f. 14 and 9, f. 22) 4^8(+6, f. 29) 5^8 6^8(+2, f. 42) 7^8 8^8(+5, f. 62) 9^8 10^8(+1, f. 75 and 7, f. 81) 11^8(+3, f. 87 and 9, f. 95) 12^8(+5, f. 99) 13^8(+5, f. 108) 14^8 15^2(ff. 121–122) 16^8(+1, f. 123) 17^8 18^8(+5, f. 144) 19–22^8 23^8(to f. 188) 24–25^8 26^2. 16 long lines, ruled in pale red ink. Written in a rounded gothic book hand.

Thirteen full page miniatures on the versos of inserted singletons, blank on the recto, usually with full borders of painted gold strewn with realistic flowers (some in bright orange), berries, insects and birds; matching borders on the facing page with 5-line acanthus leaf initials against square colored grounds and a flower in the infilling. The miniatures are: f. 14v (Hours of the Cross), Crucifixion, with Mary and John on either side, and horsemen as spectators, partially hidden by a hill in the immediate foreground; the miniature is superimposed on a columned fountain with a swan swimming in its waters and landscape visible beyond, presumably in reference to the Fountain of Paradise; the facing page, f. 15, with the normal border as described above. On f. 22v (Hours of the Holy Spirit), Pentecost; the facing border, f. 23, divided into compartments by gold columns and arches, each space occupied by a flower, the lower one by the Holy Spirit as a Dove holding a scroll. On f. 29v (Mass of the Virgin), from an archetype of Roger van der Weyden, the Virgin nursing the Child, with beads and flowers in the border; the facing border holds holy objects in shelves, and a peacock on a table in the lower border; f. 42v (Hours of the Virgin), Annunciation: the Virgin interrupted at her prayers in a small side chapel by the Archangel and 4 smaller angels who salute her from the nave of the church as the dove descends from above; the same composition occurs, for example, in a prayerbook in the Kassel Landesbibliothek, Mss. math. et art. 50; see A. W. Biermann, "Die Miniaturenhandschriften des Kardinals Albrecht von Brandenburg (1514–1545)," *Aachener Kunstblätter* 46 (1975) 15–310, fig. 153; f. 62v (Lauds), Visitation in the courtyard of a manor house; f. 75v (Prime), Nativity in a barn looking out on to an orderly city street; f. 81v (Terce), Annunciation to the shepherds; f. 87v (Sext), Adoration of the Magi, of which one is black, with a black servant; f. 93v (None), Presentation in the temple; f. 99v (Vespers), Massacre of the Innocents; f. 108v (Compline), Flight into Egypt; f. 123v (Penitential psalms), Last Judgment, with Christ on a rainbow, the olive branch and the sword to the right and left of his head, and the elect beside him, while below the dead are rising from the cemeteries; a bird, possibly a pelican, in the lower borders of the opening; another example of this composition is in Vienna, Nationalbib. 1858, f. 105v reproduced in the *Bulletin de la Société française de reproductions de manuscrits à peintures* 2 (1912) pl. 22; f. 144v (Office of the Dead), Raising of Lazarus, with a skull in each of the 2 lower borders of the opening. Smaller miniatures, 7-line, with bracket borders to the left of the text, of painted gold ground strewn with flowers, branchy acanthus leaves, strawberries and insects. The miniatures are: f. 36, John with the eagle holding his inkwell; f. 37v, Luke painting; f. 39, Matthew; f. 40v, Mark; f. 193 (Obsecro te), the Virgin and Child; f. 197 (O Intemerata), Mary and John; f. 199v (Stabat mater), Pietà, with John rubbing his red, swollen eyes; f. 201v, Sebastian, clothed, holding the bow and arrows; f. 202v, James with a staff and open book; f. 203, Anthony of Padua holding a book on which a diminutive Christ Child sits; f. 204, Michael; f. 204v, Francis receiving the stigmata; f. 205, Jerome; f. 206, Peter and Paul. Band borders of the same style, the length of the text, in the outer margin, at the occurrence of a 2-line initial. 2- and 1-line initials alternate grey-and-white leaf designs against brown-and-gold square grounds, or vice versa; ribbon line fillers in the same colors. Rubrics in red. Each month of the calendar written across an opening, both sides with bracket borders in the outer margins so as to almost enclose the opening; in the lower margins, framed by gold columns and arches are, on the verso a monthly occupation, and on the facing recto, a smaller occupation scene continuing the activity of the first and divided by a column from the adjacent zodiac symbol.

Bound, s. XVII, possibly in the Low Countries, with elaborate gold tooling in a lacy pattern around a central panel enclosing an oval with a flower vase; orange Dutch gilt paper pastedowns; gauffered gilt edges; in a slip case intended for a larger book.

Written in Flanders, possibly in Bruges to judge by the saints in the calendar. Belonged to Robert Hoe: Grolier Club (1892) n. 35; *Cat.* (1909) pp. 67–68 (at that time kept in a cloth case with brass clasps, lined with blue satin); his sale, Anderson, New York, 1912, pt. III, n. 2076, with a plate of f. 29v, to G. D. Smith. Precise source and date of acquisition by Henry E. Huntington unknown.

Bibliography: De Ricci, 103.

HM 1175 — s. XIX, from s. XVI originals
BOOK OF HOURS, modern fragments

Nine single leaves, tipped in, with illuminations copied from the Stuart de Rothesay Hours (London, Brit. Lib. Add. 20927), here bound incorrectly, as follows:

Add. 20927		HM 1175
13v	Annunciation	8v
14	rubric for the Hours of the Virgin	7
91v	David penitent	9
92	rubric for the Penitential psalms	1
119v	Jesus before Mary and Martha	2v
120	rubric for the Office of the Dead	5
165v	Crucifixion	6v
166	rubric for the Hours of the Cross	4
172	the Archangel Raphael guiding a very young Tobias to Media	3

Parchment, ff. iii (paper, with the watermark: "Crane and Co. Dalton Mass. 1893 Bond n°25") + 9 folios (misbound, as above, and interleaved with paper bearing the same watermark) + xxiv (paper with the same watermark); 155 × 120 (illuminated space: 127 × 95) mm.

Bound, s. XIX, in burgundy velvet with beige silk endpapers; 2 silver-gilt fore edge clasps; gilt edges; similar binding on HM 1153 and HM 1161.

The original illuminations were executed by Giulio Clovio (ca. 1540) in a book of hours for Cardinal Marino Grimani, whose coat of arms appears on the opening leaf of the Hours of the Virgin (Rietstap, vol. 3, pl. 96, but in HM 1175 lacking the cross). These copies were done by Caleb W. Wing[1] for John Boykett Jarman (d. 1864) as identified by J. Backhouse, "A Victorian Connoisseur and his manuscripts. The Tale of Mr. Jarman and Mr. Wing," *British Museum Quarterly* 32 (1967–68) 76–92 with a reproduction of HM 1175, f. 9 on pl. XXVI. John Boykett Jarman sale, Sotheby's, 13 June 1864, lot 77, where the coat of arms is said to be on pl. 2 (it is now on f. 7). Belonged to Robert Hoe, who may have had it (? re-)bound in its present order, given the date and the American manufacture of the interleaved and filler pages; *Cat.* (1909) p. 193; his sale, Anderson, New York, 1912, pt. IV, n. 2365 to G. D. Smith. Precise source and date of acquisition by Henry E. Huntington unknown.

Bibliography: De Ricci, 103.

---

[1] The corrected form of the name was kindly communicated to us by Janet Backhouse.

HM 1176 PRAYERBOOK — Germany, s. XVI^{in}

1. ff. 1–7: *Sequuntur orationes devote ante sacram Conmunionem ad celestem curiam. Ad patrem,* Domine deus pater omnipotens ego indigna peccatrix accedo ad sacramentum . . . , *Ad filium,* Domine ihesu christe summe sacerdos et rex eterne glorie . . . ; *Ad Spiritum Sanctum,* Spiritus sancte deus qui virtute tua mirabiliter . . . ; *Ad Sanctam trinitatem,* O Super benedicta et beatissima trinitas Da michi creature tue licet peccatrici . . . ; *Ad beatam virginem,* Sanctissima et incontaminata dei genitrix virgo semper Maria que creatorem . . . ; *Ad omnes angelos,* O Vas puritatis angelice spiritus preclara luminaria . . . ; *Ad patriarchas et prophetas,* O Nobilissime radices patriarche et prophete quorum iusticie desideria celos transcendendo . . . ; *Ad appostolos omnes,* O Gloriosi appostoli et ewangeliste discipulique domini quos ipse dei filius . . . ; *Ad omnes martires,* O Invictissimi martires christi qui corpora vestra innumerabilia tradidistis supplicia . . . ; *Ad Confessores,* O pyssimi confessores qui sanctitate operum . . . ; *Ad virgines,* O Inclite et dilecte virgines christi sponsum vestrum virginis filium . . . ; *Ad omnes sanctos,* Omnes sancti et electi dei qui gratia bonitatis ipsius iam in conspectu eius exultatis . . . [f. 7v, blank]

2. ff. 8–13: *Ordinacio Conmunionis,* O here ihesu christe Ich arme ellende sunderin beger dich hilf zur empfanchent In den hochwirdigen Sacrament . . . [13 sections beginning in the same fashion; f. 13v, blank]

3. ff. 14–45: *Hie nach follgent etlich andächtige mainungen von dem hailgen Sacrament uff alle fest, Uff das nuw iar,* O here ihesu christe ich beger dich hutt zů empfanchent zů lob er und danckberkait . . . ; *Uff der hailgen iii tag,* O here ihesu christ ich beger dich hutt zů empfanchent in dem hochwirdigen Sacrament zů lob und er der andächtigen haimsůchung . . . ; *Uff die liecht mess,* O here ihesu christe ich beger dich . . . und er der tieffen dämütikait in der du dich hast . . . ; *Uff den wissen suntag,* O here ihesu christe ich beger dich . . . und Er der tieffen dämütikait In der du das Sacrament des toss [*sic*] hast . . . ; *Uff mit fasten lentarr,* O here ihesu christe ich beger dich

. . . und Er dinen herten strengen tugentrichen leben . . . ; *Uff annunciacionis Marie,* O here ihesu christe ich beger dich . . . und Er diner werden rainen mů̊tter . . . ; *Uff den grienen dornstag,* O here ihesu christe ich beger dich . . . Er und danckberkait der grossen unussprachenlichen angst . . . ; *Uff den oster tag,* O here ihesu christe ich beger dich . . . Er und danckberkait diner günlichen loblichen . . . ; *Uff den may tag,* O here ihesu christe ich beger dich . . . Er und diner ewigen unergrüntlichen wisshait . . . ; O hertz liebster here Ich beger dich och zu empfanchent zů lob und Er dinen hailgen us erwöllten zwöllfbotten Sant philipp und iacob . . . ; *Uff den uffer tag,* O here ihesu christe ich beger dich . . . Er und danckberkait diner wunnicklichen günlichen uffart . . . ; *Uff pfingsten,* O here ihesu christe ich beger dich . . . Er und danckberkait der gnadrichen sendung . . . ; *Uff trinitatis,* O here ihesu christe ich beger dich . . . und Er dem hochsten obresten aller besten gůtt . . . ; *Uff unsers fronlichnams tag,* O here ihesu christe Ich beger dich . . . und Er der grossen unussprechenlichen liebe . . . ; *Uff Visitacionis Marie,* O here ihesu christe ich beger dich . . . und Er diner werden mutter der hochgelobten iunckfrawen Marie . . . ; *Uff Marie Magdalene,* O here ihesu christe ich beger dich . . . und Er diner tieffen unergruntlichen barmhertzikait . . . ; *Uff assumpcionis Marie,* O here ihesu christe ich beger dich . . . und Er diner zarten mutter der hochverdienten iunckfrawen marie . . . ; *Uff nativitatis Marie,* O here ihesu christe ich beger dich . . . und Er diner werden mutter der hochgelobten himel küngin marie . . . ; *Uff Michaelis,* O here ihesu christe ich beger dich . . . und Er minem hailgen und usserwöllten engel den du mir zů geben hast . . . ; *Uff omnium sanctorum,* O here ihesu christe ich beger dich . . . und Er der hochgelobten iunckfrawen Marie allen engeln und allen dinen usserwöllten . . . ; *Uff aspiciens,* O here ihesu christe ich beger dich . . . und Er diner millten guttikait mit der du von ewikait . . . ; *Uff concepcionis Marie,* O here ihesu christe ich beger dich . . . und Er diner Werden mů̊tter irer hailgen und unbefleckten empfengnus . . . ; *Uff wichen nachten,* O here ihesu christe ich beger dich . . . und Er der grossen unusspreckenlichen minn und liebe . . . ; *Ain mainung Uff den tod,* O here ihesu christe ich beger dich . . . Sacrament in der mainung In der ich dich beger zu empfanchent an minen letsten end . . . [f. 45v, blank]

4. ff. 46–47v: //consolatus proficere valeam in cunctis operibus eius prolectissime caritatis . . . [end of prayer *Ad apostolos* as on f. 4r–v]; *Ad omnes martires,* O invictissimi martires christi qui corpora vestra . . . [as on ff. 4v–5]; *Ad confessores,* O pyssimi confessores qui sanctitate operum . . . [as on f. 5v]; *Ad virgines,* Inclite et dilecte virgines christi . . . [as on f. 6]; *Ad omnes Sanctos,* Omnes sancti et electi dei qui gratia bonitatis ipsius . . . [as on ff. 6v–7].

5. ff. 48–59: //*mit dem her nach geschriben mag sich der mensch selbs vor got erklagnen siner sund ee er zu dem sacrament gant,* Ich armer schuldiger mensch vergiech dir aller güttigoster herr das ich so unerstorben bin . . . ; *So du bichten wilt so spricht disse drew pater noster, das pater noster,* Herr ich ermanen dich himelschlicher vater diner vätterlicher geschopft das du mich under allen creaturen . . . ; *das ander pater noster,* Ich ermanen dich herr ihesu christe unser brüder der brüderliche trew erlösung . . . ; *das dritt pater noster,* Ich ermanen dich hailger gaist diner furmen [*sic*] gutti und gewaltige übung . . . ; O lieber herr ihesu christe Ich ermanen dich der grossen angst und not die du hettest am ölberg . . . ; O lieber herr Ich ermanen dich der

erkantnus die du hettest am ölberg . . . ; *und dar nach sprich also,* O herr got byβ mir sünderin genedig O du aller senftmütigost lam . . . ; *So du sorgost das du in sünden syest so sprich also,* O brosts gůt ich bekenn das ich wider dinen willen han gethan . . . ; *das ander,* O brosts güt wann du mir das liebst soltost sin ob allen dingen . . . ; *Das dritt,* O brosts güt ich han ain beraiten willen das ich geren diner wirdikait . . . ; *Nach der bicht,* O min liebster herr ihesu christi ain furst und unmässiger wirdikait des lebendigen gottes son . . . ; *Vor der bicht,* O herr ihesu christe du ewiger hailmacher . . . ; *Nach der bicht,* O vater der ewigkait dem alle hertzen offennbar sind . . . ; O herr ihesu christe ich senck die grössy [*sic*] miner sünd In die bitterkait dins lidens . . .

6. ff. 59–69v: *Bett iii pater noster dinen engel und bett dar nach xv pater noster,* Das erst pater noster sy dir herr zu lob und ere gesprochen diner grossen armůt die du ye gehept hast . . . [15 prayers]; O herr ich han mich nit geübt in fasten wachen betten und in anndern güthaiten als ich solt und dick wol vermugt hett . . .

7. ff. 70–89: //des hailgen gaists O herr ich beger dich ze entpfachent in dem hochwirdigen sacrament das min gemiet zů himelschlichen dingen erhebt werde . . . ; *Sprich xii pater noster vor der enpfachung des sacramens,* O miniclicher herr min hertz lieber got und schöpfer erlöser und behalter Ich ermanen dich der grossen liebin und begierd in der du din viertzig tägig vasten volbracht hast . . . [12 prayers]

8. ff. 89v–98: *So dir wilt das hohwirdig sacrament empfachen sprich diβ gebett vor hin ain tag oder dry mit rew und andacht und gůten fürsatz,* O barmhertziger vater ich arme sünderin rüf dich an uβ grund mins hertzen . . . ; *pater noster,* O du küng der engel ich elende unwirdige sünderin vermiβ mich das ich dich wil enpfachen der du bist ain richter der lebendigen . . . ; O du aller lieblichoster und barmhertziger herr ich ermanen dich das du dich selbs für uns enpfiengost und ufopfrotost got dinen himelschlichen vater . . . ; O himelschlicher vater ich will dir bessren mit allen den wercken die din aingeborner son unnser herr ihesus christus . . . ; *kyrieleonson* [*sic*], herr erbarm dich über uns *christeleyson* Erbarm dich uber uns Vater von himel erbarm dich über uns der du grosser liebi dinen aingebornen son gesent hast in diβ welt . . .

9. ff. 98v–101v: O du hailger gaist ain warer tröster aller betrübten herzen der gnad all menschen ist beschirmen . . . ; *Veni sancte,* O du hailige drivaltikait got vater got sun got hailger gaist dry persona ain wars ewiges wesen du bist gerecht und barmhertzig . . . ; Sancta maria du gebererin gottes dem himel und erd nit hat mügen begryffen . . . ; O Ir all himelschlich gaist und engel Ich bit uch das ir mich behüttend . . . ; O Ir hailgen patriarchen und prophetten mit was groβer begierd hand ir begerot . . . ; O Ir hailgen zwelfpotten und ewangelisten und all Iünger ihesu christi Cristus hat üch uf erd selbs gespist . . . ; O Ir hailgen martrar ewer hailig blůt hond Ir mit fröden vergossen von des willen . . . ; O Ir hailgen bichter und vatter aller orden nach ewerm strengen leben . . . ; O Ir hailgen rainen Iunckfrowen mit künschen [*sic*] armen sind ir umb fachen ewern gesponsen . . . ; O Ir hailgen witwen die nach dem Eelichen stat nit mer gangen sind . . . ; O Ir all gottes hailgen gemainlich den ewer got unser herr von ewigkait hat berait . . . ; O herr nun versprich mich und verantwürt mich hüt . . . [each prayer of this article followed by an Ave Maria]

10. ff. 101v–105: *Item wenn du das hailig wirdig sacrament des zarten fronlichnams unsers herren ihesu christi empfachen wilt oder meß hören . . .*, Allmächtiger ewiger got als ich dir schuldig bin lob und danck zesagen . . . ; O serenissima et inclita virgo maria mater domini nostri ihesu christi regina celi et terre . . . ; O Beata maria pia dei genitrix virgo inmaculata que dominum ihesum eterni patris filium es enixa . . . ; *Ain anders gebett,* O aller liebster herr min trost und hoffnung berait mich hütt durch die gnad des hailgen gaists . . .

11. ff. 105–113v: *Diß nach geschriben sint gebet die gand uf die dry tugend gelob hoffnung liebi die sol der mensch begeren das im verlyhen werd,* O herr min got und schöpfer ich kom hüt zu dir in ainem waren cristenlichen globen . . . ; *Das ist die annder,* O herr ich kom zu dir In ainer waren vesten hoffnung die ich han zu dir . . . ; *Das ist die drit,* O herr ihesu christe Ich kom zů dir in ainer waren liebin die ich han zu dir . . . ; *Ain gůt gebett zespreche vor der enpfanchung des sacraments,* O almächtiger got ich getar mine ougen mit uf heben in den himel . . . ; O herr ihesu christi du hast gesprochen zů augustin Credo et manducasti in dem selben . . . ; O du unussprechenliches gut herr ihesu christi kom zu dem kunglichen tisch . . .

12. ff. 113v–116v: *Sant thomas spricht der mensch der zů den sacrament wil gen . . . Das ist der gegenwürtig andacht die beger und sprich also,* O güttiger und milter herr ihesu christi der du begriffen bist in dem hailgen sacrament . . . ; *Die erst mainung ist hoffnung zů got vergebung der sünd,* Almächtiger ewiger vater Ich wil dir hüt uf opfren unsern herren ihesum christum . . . ; *Die ander bekantnus aigner blödikait,* Güttiger barmhertziger got ich opfren dir hüt uf unsern herren in dem sacrament . . . ; *Die drit ist so der mensch sol in kumer und lyden ist so enpfach das sacrament,* Almächtiger got ich opfren dir uf din aller liebsten sun . . . ; *Die vierd begierd ist von got ze erwerbend ain sonder genad,* O barmhertziger herr ich wil dir hut uf opfren ihesum christum und bit dich durch die grundloße barmhertzikait . . . ; *Die funft ist das der mensch got well loben und danck sagen,* O milter uf geber aller gab und genad Ich bekenn demütiklich . . . ; *Die vi fur dinen nechsten oder dinen gůten fründ der in lyden ist,* O himelscher vater du hast mir gebotten das ich min nechsten lieb hab . . . ; *Zů dem vii fur die den du ain ursach zů den sünden gewesen bist,* O herr ain erkenner aller hertzen Ich bit dich über alle menschen den ich ain ursach bin gewesen . . . ; *Wenn du das sacrament fur ainen todsünder ouch fur din sünd,* O Ewiger got der du uß natur güttig bist Ich bitt dich . . . ; *Wenn du das sacrament fur ain sel wilt empfachen so sprich also,* O herr ain tröster der gefangnen selen in dem fegfür den allen ze trost . . .

13. ff. 117–120: *Incipiunt orationes bone et devote ante communionem dicende Et primo ad patrem et deinde ad omnem celestem curiam per ordinem. Ad patrem,* Domine sancte pater qui unigenitum tuum misisti in mundum ut carne sua nos cibaret . . . ; *ad filium,* Domine ihesu christe qui pro salute nostra animam tuam dilectam in mortem tradidisti . . . ; *ad spiritum sanctum,* Sancte spiritus ubi vis spirat et tua infusio letificat cor hominis . . . ; *Ad sanctam trinitatem,* Sancta trinitas unus deus magnus et terribilis et multum miserians . . . ; *ad beatam virginem mariam,* Sancta maria que unigenitum dei filium quem celi capere non poterant . . . ; *Item alia ad virginem mariam,* Sancta dei genitrix

que maternis oculis amabilissimum et desiderantissimum aspiciens ipsum . . . ; *alia,* Sancta virgo virginum que te matrem dei incorruptam agnoscens verbum dei patris . . . ; *Ad angelos,* Omnes sancti beatorum spiritum ordinis quos deus a lapsu cadencium reservavit . . . ; *Ad patriarchas et prophetas,* Omne sancti patriarche et prophete qui domini dominum desiderasti ipsum . . . ; *ad appostolos et ewangelistas,* Omnes sancti appostoli et ewangeliste quesumus ad huc nobiscum inter nos conversans . . . ; *Ad martires,* Omnes sancti martires qui ob amorem domini nostri ihesu christi sanguinem vestrum fudistis . . . ; *ad confessores,* Omnes sancti confessores quod ad confessionem sui nominis in celeste dominus transtulit convivium . . . ; *Ad virgines sanctas,* Omnes sancte virgines que in castis cristi amplexibus requiescitis . . . ; *Ad omnes sanctos,* Omnes sancti quibus ab eterno sanctitatis sanctus sanctorum eternas eppulas preparavit . . .

14. ff. 120v–124v: O herr zu diner gnad nach ich mich in din erbermd enpfilch ich mich . . . ; O sapiencia que ex ore altissimi prodisti veni et dare me . . . ; *Sprich dar nach,* Fiat domine per virtutem tuam pax in cordibus nostris . . . ; *Die collect dar nach,* Deus qui dilectionem nos mutuam doces . . . ; *Das sprich in der stillen meß och so du zů den sacrament gan wilt,* Oriens splendor lucis eterne et sol iusticie veni et illumina me . . . ; *Gries das wirdig sacrament sprich diß verß mit ernst,* Ave corpus sanctissimum in ara crucis torrdium [*sic*] . . . ; *So man glich wil gan so sprich,* Ave domine ihesu christe verbum patris filius virginis . . . ; *Wenn du an hin gast so sprich dise verß,* Introibo ad altare dei et desidero accipere ihesum christum amatorem anime mee . . . ; O herr in dem globen der aller hailgosten můter der cristenhait So kom ich . . .

15. ff. 125–132v: *Diß sprich nach dem so du das wirdig sacrament empfangen hast,* Herr ich sag dir lob err und danck das ich enpfangen han das lieb . . . ; O zarter minneklicher got O min lieber herr ihesu was hast du durch mich erlitten . . . ; O Ewiger himelschlicher vater wer bin ich das du mir dinen wirdigen son zů ainer spys geben hast . . . ; *Achtag nach dem enpfachen sprich altag zů danckberkait,* O aller miltoster vater min schopfer und behalter Ich unwirdige sünderin sag dir lob und danck . . . ; *von sant maria,* O du aller rainoste und hailgoste můter und Iunckfrow maria ain kungin des himels und der erd den du under dinen rainen hertzen getragen und geboren hast . . . ; *So man die vene niempt,* O herr ihesu christi mach mich hüt empfengklich diner gnad . . . ; *So man an hin gat, . . . ; Die gebett sol man nach der empfachung des wirdigen sacramentz mit ernst sprechen,* Eya bys wilkomen zů hundert tusent malen du min aller liebster//

16. ff. 133–140: //und besonder als du dich selbs hast uf geopfrot am hailgen ölberg in als din lyden und als du dich dinen himelschlichen vater hast uf geopfrot . . . ; Himelschlicher vater in der ewigkait Ich opfren dir hüt uf din aingebornen son ihesum christum . . . ; *Denck mer,* O du min aller liebster herr wa ich dise und annder din gaben und gnad . . . ; O himelschlicher vater ich opfren dir hut uf din aingebornen sun im hohwirdigen sacrament . . .

17. ff. 140–147v: *her nach volgent fast kostliche gebett nach dem und du das wirdig sacrament hast empfangen,* Lob und danck sag ich dir barmhertziger ewiger milter got das du mich arme sünderin So gnädiklich gespyst hast . . . ; Lob und danck sag ich dir lieber herr ihesu christi der du uns uß nichten geschaffen hast nach diner bildung . . . ; Aller liebster herr Ich dancken dir so vast

ich kan und mag . . . ; O herr ich bit dich durch die kraft dins zarten fronlichnams das ich in diser kurtzen seit müg . . .

18. ff. 148–155: *Am tag so ain mensch empfangen hat das wirdig sacrament mag er die ůter gotz bitten das si im erwerb syben gaben. Die erst,* O maria erwirb mir das ich dinen lieben son wirdigclich hab enpfangen . . . ; *die ander,* O maria erwirb mir ob ich ye in kainer todsund das wirdig sacrament . . . ; *die drytt,* O maria erwirb das ich furbaß das wirdig sacrament . . . ; *die vierd,* O maria erwirb mir durch die empfanchung des sacraments . . . ; *die fünft,* O maria erwirb mir an minem end ain ware rẅ laid bicht . . . ; *die sechst gab,* O maria erwirb mir von dinem lieben son an minem end ain frölich angesicht . . . ; *die sybend gab,* O du můter aller barmhertzikait Ich bit dich beruf alles himelschlich her zu dir . . . ; O du minnereiche kungin aller gnaden Ich klagnen dir das ich dem hohwirdigen kostlichen schatz das hailig wirdig sacrament . . . ; O muter aller gnaden Erwirb mir das min hertz und sel berait werd mit seiner gnad . . . ; Es sprechent die hailgen lerer das under aller übungen das hertz nütz als treffenklich enzünd . . . ; *Pulchra oratio post communionem sanctam,* O anima mea rex angelorum venit ad nos et hospitatus est nobiscum letemur ergo . . . ; Te christum te ihesum benedicimus te regem regum et dominum dominancium confitemur . . . ; *Oratio sancti augustini de sancta trinitate,* Summe omnipotentissime misericordissime iustissime sanctissime potentissime pulcherrime fortissime stabilis incomprehensibilis . . .

19. ff. 155v–172: *Hie nach stond geschriben nün gebetlin die sol ains sprechen e das sacrament genossen hat. Das erst,* O almächtiger ewiger got Ich unwirdige ellende sünderin fal für din götliche gnad . . . ; *das ander,* O ewiger barmhertziger got Ich sag dir gnad lob und danck der unussprechenlichen liebin . . . ; *das dritt,* O aller getrewoster lieb haber miner armen sel Zarter herr ich sag lob . . . ; *Das vier,* O barmhertziger got Ich sag dir lob eer und danck durch die kraft des hohwirdigen sacramentz . . . ; *das fünft,* O aller süssoster herr ihesu christe Ich sag dir lob err und danck durch die kraft dins hailgen hochwirdigen sacramentz . . . ; *das sechst,* O ewigs gůt getriwer herr Ich sag dir gnad lob err und danck . . . ; *Das sybend,* O aller getrewoster lieb haber miner armen sel herr ihesu christe . . . ; *Das achtend,* O himelsclicher vater Ich fal für din gotlich almächtikait und opfren dir uf in kraft diser spyß des hailgen wirdigen sacraments . . . ; *das nund,* O geliepter herr ihesu christe du milter erlöser gedenck min so du stast in der angesicht gotz . . . ; *das zehend,* O milter erlöser herr ihesu christe ich beger mit gantzer begierd mins hertzes . . . ; *Ain gebett uber den ersten gegen wurf,* Barmhertziger schöpfer hailger herr almächtiger vater ewiger got der du von ewigkait für genomen und geordnot hast . . . [f. 172v, ruled, but blank]

20. ff. 173–192: *Feria secunda,* In nomine domini omne genuflectatur celestium terrestrium et infernorum quia factus es obediens patri . . . ; Obsecro domine ihesu criste per msera [?] misericordie quibus visitasti nos oriens ex alto . . . ; *feria tercia,* Adoremus dominum nostrum ihesum christum nobis et pro nobis baptisatum in baptisma te tuo beatissimam trinitatem nobis revelantem . . . ; *Oratio,* Peto domine ihesu qui es animarum eternus amator fac . . . ; *feria* 4ta, Adoremus dominum nostrum ihesum christum in oracionibus pernoctantem diebus in predicationibus laborantem . . . ; *Oratio,* Peto domine ihesu per talem perfectam bonitatem cordis tui . . .; *feria quinta,*

Adoramus te dominum nostrum ihesum christum ad redemcionem nostram iherosolimam ingredientem . . . ; *Oratio,* Peto domine ihesu christe per illam noctem quam ultimum in hoc mundo vixisti . . . ; *feria sexta,* Adoramus te dominum nostrum ihesum christum pilato iudici presentatum coram eo false acusatum . . . ; *Oratio,* Peto domine ihesu christe qui pro peccatoribus et inter peccatores ignominosam mortem pati dignatus es . . . ; *Sabato,* Adoramus te dominum ihesum christum speciosum forma pro filys hominum cuius sol et luna mirantur pulchritudinem . . . ; *Oratio,* Peto domine ihesu eternus dies glorie et sol iusticie nesciens occasum qui pro nobis pati dignatus es . . . ; *Dominica,* Adoremus te dominum ihesum christum a morte resurgentem super omnia creatura . . . ; *Oratio,* Peto te domine ihesu christe per divinam glorificationem humane nature tue . . . ; *Oratio,* Ante ymaginem pietatis dicenda de qua concessit beatus gregorius omnium peccatorum remissionem, In mei sind memoria ihesu pie singnacula que passionis tempore pertulisti durissime . . . [with versicle and prayer:] Domine ihesu christe fily dei vivi salvator mundi rex glorie clementissime qui sanctissimum passionis tue misterium . . . da michi queso misera peccatrice . . . ; Domine ihesu christe hic sum ante te tamquam medicus [*sic*] ante divitem . . . [5 prayers beginning in like fashion]; *Oratio,* Rogo te dilectissime deus et mors tua amarissima et passio omnium membrorum tuorum mortificet . . . [f. 192v, frame ruled, but blank]

21. ff. 193–200: [prayers and psalms on the Passion] *De passione domini,* Pater noster Ave maria Credo in deum. *Vers.* Tuam crucem adoramus domine tuam gloriosam recolimus passionem miserere nobis qui passus est pro nobis. Adiutorium nostrum in nomine domini . . .

22. ff. 200v–204v: *Diß nach geschriben bett haist die dry todschrecken unnsers herren ihesu christi Amen,* O herr ihesu christe min got ich ermanen dich und dancken dir des grymen todschreckes . . . ; *der ander schreck,* O lieber herr ihesu christe min got ich ermanen dich und dancken dir des schrecken den din minnekliches hertz enpfieng . . . ; *der dryt schreck,* O herr ihesu christe min got Ich ermanen dich und dancken dir des schrecken und der wiß die all din zart menschait . . . ; Eya abgrund der wyshait die da uber trift aller creaturas vernunft . . . ; Grusisto es ihesu christe blüender spons Ich arme sünderin . . .

23. ff. 205–210v: *Wer diß bett mit andacht sprich: zů lob dem lyden christi der hat got als vil gedienet als ob er tusent pater noster . . . ,* Alle herschaft dienet alle wißhait sorget alle unschuld forcht ir . . . ; *Ain ander bett vom lyden christi,* Herr Ich ermanen dich der ewigen minn in der du dich gebt in gefengknust . . . ; *Ain annders schäns gebett von dem leben und liden christi,* Herr ihesu criste din menschwerdung naig mich zu demütikait und tugenden . . .

24. ff. 211–222: *Wer das bett spricht mit andacht dem volgent dar us vil guter nütze,* Herre ihesu christe Ich bit dich durch das zittron und durch der angst ere die du hettest . . . [18 prayers beginning in like manner]; *Das gnadreich enpfelchen,* Allmachtiger got gedenck an mich in miner letsten zeit Ich enpfilch mich . . . [with Pater noster and Ave Maria]; Herr ihesu christe Ich ermanen dich des wercks das du dinen iungeren tettost . . . [with Pater noster and Ave Maria]; Herr ihesu christe Ich ermanen dich der willigen gehorsann . . . [with Pater noster]; *An dem frytag vor dem palmtag sol man anheben viiii pater*

noster . . . , Herr ihesu christe Ich ermanen dich der trübsälikait die din hailge mensch ait . . . [with Pater noster]; Herr ihesu christe ich ermanen dich der demutikait und der senftmutikait . . . [with Pater noster]; Herr ihesu christe ich ermanen dich der bittren angst . . .

25. ff. 222–229: *Diß sind die zechen inwendigen lyden unsers lieben herren ihesu Cristi* . . . , Das erst lyden oder inwendig sterben ist min got . . . ; Das ander Min süsser herr ihesu criste Ich ermanen dich . . . ; Das drit du gemachel aller rainer hertzen ihesu criste Ich ruffe . . . ; Das vierd Minneklicher herr ihesu Criste Ich ermanen dich dines vierden lydens . . . ; Das fünft Getriwer vater ihesu criste Ich rüff dich . . . ; Das sechst Du edler gemachel miner sel ihesu criste . . . ; Das sybent Du hocher maister lieber herr ihesu criste du bist ermanet von mir . . . ; Das achtett Getrewer herr ihesu christe und brüder gedenck . . . ; Das nünd Du ainiger got und gemachel und ußerwolter lieb . . . ; Das zechend Du alpfa und o das ist du ursprung und end aller ding . . . [each followed by a Pater noster and an Ave Maria]; *Fünf rosen von den fünf wunden unsers lieben herren ihesu Cristi. Der erst roß,* Herre ihesu criste ich ermanen dich des bittren lydens das du hettest an der wunden der glinggen hand . . . ; *Der annder ros,* Ach susses hertz ihesu christe und lieber herr Ich ermanen dich dines strengen bittren lydens . . . ; *Der drit ros,* Du gemachel aller rainer hertzen ihesu criste . . . ; *der vierd ros,* Ach du getrewer und brůder ihesu criste . . . ; *der funft ros,* Du getrewes hertz herr ihesu criste Ich ermanen dich der grossen verschmächt . . . ; *Von disen iii pater noster hat man xviiii tusent jar ablaß und wirt nit von got geschaiden,* O herr ihesu criste das pater noster opfren ich dir dinen sünfzgen . . . ; *das ii pater noster,* O herr ihesu criste ich opfren dir diß pater noster dem sunftzgen den du hettest da du din crütz nider letost . . . ; *das iii pater noster,* O herr ihesu criste diß pater noster opfren ich dir dinen sunftzgen den du tatest da du sachost . . . [ff. 229v–232v, frame ruled, but blank]

26. ff. 233–240v: *Diß viertzehen Innwendigen liden und sterben unsers herren ihesu cristi die er gelitten hat ain crütz,* O himelscher vater Ich din arme sündige unwirdige creatur Ermanen und dancken dir der unußsprechelichen liebi . . . ; O du ewigs wort des vätterlichen hertzen herr ihesu christe . . . ; O du unerschöpflichs gůt der ewigen wishait herr ihesu christe . . . ; O du zarter trost aller andächtigen hertzen . . . ; O du milter vergeber aller schuld herr ihesu christe . . . ; O du ursprung aller sälikait herr ihesu criste . . . ; O du kreftiger wircker alles gůts herr ihesu christe . . . ; O du süsser weg der obrosten warhait herr ihesu criste . . . ; O du küng aller tugent herr ihesu criste . . . ; O du ainige zůversicht aller rainer hertzen herr ihesu christe . . . ; O du userwelts ainigs lieb aller himelschen gemüt herr ihesu criste . . . ; O du wunnekliche fröd aller engel herr ihesu criste . . . ; O du glantz des vätterlichen hertzen herr ihesu christe . . . ; O du obroster byschoff herr ihesu criste . . . ; O du hochs hailigs erwirdigs opfer des almechtigen vaters herr ihesu christe . . .

27. ff. 240v–244v: An der guten mitwochen so betracht das liden Cristi in rüwender wys und bekantnuß . . . ; An dem güten donrstag betracht das liden christi in nachvolgender wys das du all sünd lassest . . . ; An dem hailgen karfrytag betracht das scharpf liden unsers herren ihesu christi mit grossem mitliden . . . ; An dem oster aubent betracht das liden unsers herren nach den früchten in danckberlicher wiß . . . ; An dem hailgen ostertag betracht das liden christi

in ainem waren globen in wunderbärlicher wis . . . ; An dem ostermontag betracht das liden christi in lernender wiß . . . ; An dem afterzinstag betracht das liden cristi in růwender wiß . . . ; An der aftermittwoch betracht das liden cristi in frölicher winschender wiß . . . ; An dem donrstag in dem ostren betracht das liden christi in schlechter wiß . . .

28. ff. 245–250v, 252: *Diß sind dis acht vers unser lieben frowen wer sy der mit andacht ermanet den verlant sy nymer,* Maria ain milte uß geberin aller gnaden Ich ermanen dich der verserung . . . ; Maria du hochgelopte můter gotz Ich ermanen dich des grossen hertzen laids . . . ; Maria ain sichere zůversicht aller sünder . . . ; Maria ain trost aller ellenden wislosen menschen . . . ; Maria ain gewaltige frow himelreichs und ertrichs . . . ; Maria ain bewärter trost aller der die in angsten und notten sind . . . ; Maria an gantzer trost und zůversicht aller betrübten hertzen . . .

29. ff. 251–260 [f. 251, blank]: *Septem psalmi penitentiales beate virginis Antiphona Sancta maria,* Domina ne in furore dei sinas corripi me . . . ; Sancta casta florigera ubera tua que florem viriditatis perpetue eruperunt . . . ; Domina ne in furore arguat me dominus, nobis veniam obtine . . . ; Miserere mei domina que mater misericordie nucuparis . . . ; Domina exaudi orationem meam et clamor meus ad te veniat . . . ; De profundis clamavi ad te domina, domina exaudi vocem meam . . . ; Domina exaudi oracionem meam percipe tuis auribus supplicacionem meam . . . ; Sancta maria sic curre [*sic*] miseris . . . [followed by a litany to the Virgin, ff. 254–256v]; *Psalmus,* Domina in adiutorium meum intende . . . [with versicles and prayer:] Omnipotens sempiterne deus qui pro nobis de castissima virgine maria . . . ; Te matrem dei laudamus te maria virginem confitemur . . .

30. ff. 260v–274: *Diß salve regina zů tütsch oder latin sol sprechen ain Ieglicher mensch all wochen ain mal . . . ,* Also spricht der andächtig lerer maistor iohannes gerson cancelarius parisiensiß in tractatu de temptacionibus, So ain mensch sol sterben Er sey frum oder bös . . . ; *Sprich yetz drew salve regina,* Dar nach so kompt den der bos gaist . . . ; *Von den dryssigoste unser lieben frowen schribt alanus ir andachtiger caplan über das buch cantica canticorum,* Der engel gabriel nach dem und setzt ecclesiastica hystoria bracht maria dor der wirdigen muter gottes . . . , Die erst palm ist die erst und gröst fröd des ersten kors der engel die den allain besitzen uf der barmhertzikait . . . ; Die ander palm ist . . . der engel die säglich und unussprechenlich grösser ist denn die erst . . . ; Die dritt palm ist do maria komen ist in den dritten kor der engel die klarich bewysent . . . ; Die vierd palmen ist die fröd . . . der engel das sind die kreftigen engel . . . ; Die v palm ist die fröd marie des fünften kors und sind die gewaltigen engel . . . ; Die vi palmen ist die vi frod marie . . . der engel und haissend die herschenden engel . . . ; Die vii palmen ist die fröd marie . . . der engel die haissend troni das sind die rubenden engel . . . ; Die viii frod und palm is die fröd marie . . . der engel die haissent cserubin [*sic*] . . . ; Die ix palmen ist die ix fröd . . . der engel die habent die grosten fröd und haissent die brinenden engel . . . [each section followed by a prayer to Mary]; Ascendit christus super celos et preparavit sue castissime matris . . .

31. ff. 274v–281: *Wer mit andacht betrachten wil das mit liden der muter gotz der sol betrachten xv stuckli mit xv ave maria den lant sü nymer,* Das erst do maria die Iunckfrow an dem grienen donrstag schaiden must . . . ; Das

ander ist do maria die Iunckfrow ain karfrytag an dem morgen gieng zu Ierusalem . . . ; Die drit ist do maria die Iunckfrow sach und hort das geschray der Iuden . . . ; Das vierd do maria die hailig Iunckfrow sach christum den herren iren liebsten sun . . . ; Das funft do maria die hochgelopt Iunckfrow sach das antlit ihesu christi verspuwen . . . ; Das sechst do maria die hailige Iunckfrow hort pylatum sprechen . . . ; Das sybend do maria die Iunckfrow sach Iren lieben sun tragen das crütz . . . ; Das achtot do maria die hailige Iunckfrow sach Iren lieben sun sitzen uf dem krütz . . . ; Das nünd do maria die hailge Iunckfrow sach unsern herren ihesum christum irn liben sun an das crütz naglen . . . ; Das zechend do maria die muter gotz hort schryen ihesum am crütz . . . ; Das ailft do maria die hailige Iunckfrow hort ihesum am crutz sprechen . . . ; Das zwelft do maria die hailge Iunckfrow hort sprechen den herren am hailgen crütz . . . ; Das dryzechend do maria die hailige Iunckfrow hört den herren am crütz sprechen vater in din hend . . . ; Das viertzehend do maria die hailige Iunckfrow sach unnsern herren ihesum nemen von dem crütz . . . ; Das fünftzehen und das letst do maria die hailig Iunckfrow sich müst schaiden . . . [each section completed by a prayer to Mary]

32. ff. 281–288: *Diß ist unser frowen psalter uß gezogen uß irem . . . , den verß dignare,* Er wirdig mich dich zů lobent du aller hailgoste maria . . . , *Sprich letz das gebett also,* Allmächtiger ewiger got Ich dir vil lobs und danckberkait schuldig bin zesagent . . . , *Sprich ainen Credo und ainen magnificat und das bett,* O ewiger got von grund mines hertzen sag ich dir lob . . . ; *dar nach fach an und sprich das ave maria* . . . [50 prayers for the rosary] . . . *und beschlüß mit dem gebett,* O herr ihesu criste durch die giettikait . . . ; O herr ihesu christe du wars liecht . . .

33. ff. 288–292: *Das ander krentzlin, Sprich das gebett und dar zů ain Credo und den benedictus zacharie,* Eya barmhertziger got himelschlicher vater us diner ungemessnen miltikait . . . [50 prayers for the rosary] . . . *und beschlüß mit dem gebett,* O herr ihesu christe setz din bitter lyden . . .

34. ff. 292–296: *Es facht das drit krentzlin mit dem frolichen alleluia . . . ,* Lob und danck mit iubel mines hertzen . . . [50 prayers for the rosary] . . . Durch des lyden ouch durch din verdienen . . . ; *Sprich pater noster ave maria salve regina celi und das gebett,* O barmhertziger got wir bittend dich ernstlich verlich hilf . . .

35. ff. 296–300: *Von sant anna,* O maria ain edle hailge tochter sant anna und Ioachim . . . [with hymn, versicle and prayer]; *Das gebet sprich und opfer das psalterlin dar mit uf,* O mater pietatis et misericordie virgo benedicta maria Ecce ego misera peccatrix et indigna ancilla tua . . . ; *Oratio Iohannis pape ccc die indulgencie,* Benedicta sit hora in qua deus homo natus est . . . ; *Dis nach geschriben drew bett sprich mit drew pater noster* . . . ; O herr ihesu christe das pater noster sy zů lob und ere gesprochen diner grossen angst . . . ; *Das ander pater noster,* O herr ihesu christe das pater noster sy dir zů lob und ere gesprochen und ermanen dich das du woltest . . . ; *Das dritt pater noster,* O herr ihesu christe das pater noster sy dir zu lob und ere gesprochen und ermanen dich das du durch den wyssagen gesprochen hast . . . ; *Ain bett von unnser lieben frowen umb ain güts end,* O můter got Ich ermanen dich das got der vater . . . ; O muter gotz ich ermanen dich das dir der hailig gaist . . .

36. ff. 300v–307v: *Iste sunt novem gaudia beate marie. Quicumque ea de voce legerit novem diebus ante festum annunciacionis assumpcionis nativitatis purificationis eiusdem beate virginis faciem eius letus videbit ante finem suum certe in fine vite sue,* Ave maria mater misericordie, Ave et miserere mei nunc et in hora exitus mei . . . [9 prayers each followed by a Magnificat]; *Nomen beate marie Maria de prima litera dic magnificat,* Maria virgo semper letare . . . , Alma redemptoris mater . . . , Recordare virgo mater . . . , In odore ungentorum tuorum . . . Ave stella matutina . . . ; *Collecta,* Letificet nos quesumus ihesu christi nunc et hora mortis nostre . . . ; Omnipotens sempiterne deus misterium consolator laborancium . . . ; *Valde bone orationes pro homine laboranti in extremis,* Ihesu domine deus noster adesto famule tue et lumen sancte fidei illi infunde . . .

37. ff. 307v–311: *Diß sind ix ave maria die sol man betten in advent,* Item das erst dem Iunckfrölichen hertzen marie mit dem danck . . . ; Das ander gries sy und Ir demutikait . . . ; Das dritt grieß Ir andächtige hailikait . . . ; Das vierd grieß Ir liebi . . . ; Das fünft grieß sy und Ir flyssig behaltung . . . ; Das sechst Irem mit lyden das sy allzeit het . . . ; Das sybend Irem gantzen ergeben gelaßnen . . . ; Das achtend Irem gebett das sy altzeit bitt . . . ; Das nünd das sy mit Irem gebett und verdienen . . . ; *In advent Sprich altag die vii antiphone mit den Collecten,* Consciencias nostras et excita . . . ; *Im advent,* Ihesum wenn du fur unser frowen bild gast . . . ; *In der crist nacht,* In der crist nacht wenn nun an schlecht spring von dem bet Surge vigili animo . . . ; *Zu aim guten Iar,* Item gang zů dem kriplin bitt umb v ding, Item das erst bit das kindlin ihesus . . .

38. ff. 311–316: *Contra pestilencia experto dicatur in me et in teritu lecti,* Regina celi letare alleluia quesumus quem meruisti portare . . . ; *Oratio Sixti pape quarti contra pestem,* Signum + a peste et insanie liberi nos . . . Gegrüsset und gebenediet syest du gemintes kind ihesus . . . ; Rogo te domine deus nate et fily ut me et omnes illos velis salvare . . . ; *Item dar nach so sprich vii magnificat dar nach des gebett,* O maria ich ermanen dich der wirdigkait in der dich got der vater . . . ; *Das sind die vii ave maria in der crist nacht,* Maria ich ermanen dich der wirdikait die du dinen kind . . .

39. ff. 316–320: *Wer sant annen brüderschaft tailhäftig sin wil, der sprech Ir ye ain krentzlin oder psalterlin . . . ,* Griest syest du gebererin der můter gotz anna die aller angenemest . . . ; *Ain anders das magst du auch fur das vorgendig sprechen,* Griest bist du maria volle gnad . . . und gesegnet sy din aller hailgoste můter anna . . . ; *Wer sant anna lieb hab der sprech das alweg nach dem ave maria,* Und gesegnot sy din aller hailgoste und wirdigoster muter sant anna . . . ; *Item hie nach folgent die v gebet die sant anna die beriempt und hailig witwe hat geben der andächtigen Iunckfrowen anna zů augspurg uß Irem mund, Sprich das erst,* Erfrow dich O hailige můter anna die du gewirdiget bist . . . ; *das ii,* Erfrow dich o hailige muter anna ain gebererin . . . ; *das iii,* Erfrow dich o selige muter anna die du verdient hast . . . ; *das iiii,* Erfrow dich o selige muter anna des hohen grossen kindes . . . ; *das v,* Erfrow dich o selige muter anna mit fröden . . . ; *Dis nach volgende gebett spricht anna zů augspurg altag zu x, 1,* O herr ihesu cristi ain sun des lebendigen gottes . . . ; *Ihesus maria anna de sancto ioachim Oratio,* Famule dei ioachim sanctissime pater beatissime virginis marie ex tuo semine salus hominum orta

est . . . ; *de sancto ioseph oratio,* Laudem tuam nemo enarrare potest beatissime pater . . .

40. ff. 320–327: *In festo concepcionis beate marie,* Benedicta es maria laus nostra et domina te collaudat . . . ; *Alia antiphona de eandem* [*sic*], Maria plena gratia stirpe concepta . . . ; *de nativitate beate marie,* Precor te pyssima dei genitricis maria per sanctam tuam nativitatem . . . ; *de presentacione sancte marie,* Deus qui sanctam dei genitricem virginis mariam templum spiritus sancti . . . ; *de annunciacione beate marie,* Ave mundi domina regina angelorum ave virgo virginum per te venit redempcio noster [*sic*] . . . ; *Alia oratio de annunciacione sancte marie,* Saluto te sancta maria ea salutacione qua te salutavit angelus gabriel . . . ; *de assumpcione beate marie,* Salve dei genitrix virgo maria rogo te regina celorum per sanctam assumpcionem tuam . . . ; *de purification sancte marie,* Angelorum sanctorum et hominum domina virgo sancta maria in sinu pietatis tue . . . ; *de concepcione sancte marie fily dei in utero,* Gaude dei genitrix sancta maria obsecro te matrem benignitatis . . . ; *de visitacione sancte marie,* Veni precelsa domina maria tu nos visita egras mentes . . . ; *Alia oratio de visitacione beate marie,* O clementissima mater misericordie fons tocius bonitatis et clemencie mater dei . . .

41. ff. 328–333v: *Wie man den sonnentag sol firren und hailgen. Ain mensch sol sich uf den sonnentag vor an ouch all ander panen firtag am morgen frie versamlen . . . ;* Zum ersten sol er in firen und das bestant uf zway stucken . . . ; O du warer babst herr ihesu christi Ich arme sunderi fal hüt für dich . . .//

42. ff. 334–351v: *Oratio bona de nativitate domini,* Sanctam et inmaculatam humanitatem tuam ihesu nostra redempcio devote salutamus . . . ; *Oratio de sancta maria,* Gaudeamus omnes rei maria peperit filium dei sanctum . . . ; *Oratio de circumcisione domini,* O ihesu clementissime qui de virgine natus sub lege circumcidi voluisti . . . ; *de epiphania domini,* Ave domine ihesu christe in cuius virtute tres reges vehementer sunt letati . . . ; *dominica prima in quadragesima,* Ave ihesu christe qui tuo spiritu ductus in desertum elongasti fugiens conforcia hominum . . . ; *Oratio in cena domini,* Flecto tibi genua mea quia tua flexisti cum tuis discipulis . . . ; *Am grienen donrstag nach completorium Sprich xv pater noster und das betlin,* Gracias agimus tibi dilecto patris unigenito qui in tua sancta humanitate . . . ; *Oracio in die parasceve,* Omnipotens sempiterne deus qui ex nimia caritate unicum filium tuum pro nobis . . . ; *Sabato in vigilia pasce oracio,* Gloria tibi domine qui sacratissima nocte descendisti ad inferos . . . ; *In die sancte pasce oracio,* Salve dies sanctitatis leticie et felicitatis que es celsior universis . . . ; *Oracio de ascensione domini,* O unigenite altissimi genitoris deus dei quia sumus filius . . . ; *In die pentecostes oracio,* Veni sancti [*sic*] spiritus visita me miseram peccatricem per tuam gratiam . . . ; *In festo sancte trinitatis,* O beata trinitas in auxilium meum te in voce et tu in adiutorium meum intende . . . ; *In festo corporis christi oratio,* O ihesu benigne salus vera sanctificatio nostra sacietas . . . ; *In festo transfiguracionis domini oratio,* Ave domine ihesu christe cui divina voluntas virtutem prestitit . . . ; *In festo spine corone domini,* Ave ihesu christe rex regum gloriosissimus dominus dominancium . . . ; *In adventu domini oracio,* Ave ihesu criste fructus dulcis vite eterne ortus de nobili virga iesse . . .

43. ff. 352–358: [prayers added in the same hand as ff. 46–47v] *Diß send ain und LXXX stuck von unsers lieben herren Ihesu christi lyden und marter,* Daß uß zerren siner klaider Er<?> siner wunden . . .

44. ff. 358–371v: 21 prayers added in a cursive hand; f. 372r–v, blank.

Paper (Piccard, *Ochsenkopf* XI, 447, Bruch 1509–12 and XVI, 441, Innsbruck 1506–09; a third watermark generally similar to Briquet, *Couronne* 5057, Ulm 1523), ff. i (paper) + 372; 150 × 100 (103 × 68) mm. 1^8(includes f. i) 2^6 3^8 4^6 5^8 6^{10}(through f. 45) $7–8^{10}$ 9^{10}(–5, 6) $10–13^{10}$ 14^{10}(+11, f. 124) 15^{10}(–9) 16^8(text complete) 17^{10}(+ one leaf in the first half of the quire) $18–19^{10}$(through f. 172) $20–21^{10}$(through f. 192) $22–25^{10}$(through f. 232) 26^{10} 27^{10}(+9, f. 251) $28–34^{10}$ 35^{10}(catchword doesn't match) $36–37^{10}$ 38^{12} 39^8(–8, now the pastedown?). Catchwords in the hand of the text in the inner right corner. 19 long lines, frame ruled in pale brown ink or in lead, with divisions at quire breaks. Written by possibly as many as 4 hands: i, ff. 1–45, in a cursive script; ii, ff. 46–47v and 352–358, in a more calligraphic script; iii, ff. 48–351v, in a hybrida script; iv, ff. 358–371v, in a more hurried version of i (?). Plain 2- and 1-line red initials, red rubrics, underlining, slashed initials in the text and some punctuation in red; no decoration on ff. 358–371v.

Bound, s. XVI^1, in wooden boards and German stamped calf, rebacked, with metal ornaments at the 4 corners of each cover (one lacking), with 2 fore edge clasps closing to hooks on the front cover, only one remaining; both center bosses gone; fragments from a manuscript as pastedowns, Germany, s. XII.

Written in Germany in the early sixteenth century; feminine forms used throughout; on ff. 317 and 318, prayers revealed to or regularly recited by the "Iunckfrowen anna zů augspurg." On f. i, in a late nineteenth century hand, "Aus Buxheimer Klosterbibliothek." Belonged to Hugo, Graf von Waldbott-Bassenheim (1820–95), whose stamp appears on f. 1; his manuscripts sold in Munich, 20 September 1883; this manuscript not identified by De Ricci in the catalogue (catalogue not available to us). Source and date of acquisition by Henry E. Huntington not known.

Secundo folio: (virtu-)te tua mirabiliter
Bibliography: De Ricci, 103.

HM 1177 — s. XIX
BOOK OF HOURS, modern fragment

A bifolium with full page facing miniatures, both modern copies.

1. f. 1v: David penitent, with his hands spread, kneeling on a parapet of his castle, his crown lying on the throne behind him, and his harp on a desk with an open book; this portion of the painting from the same source as HM 1100, f. 98. In the background, a wide river with an island and a towered bridge spanning the river, similar to the background in Jan van Eyck's painting of Chancellor Rolin before the Madonna, now in the Louvre[1] (see, for example, M. Meiss, *French Painting in the Time of Jean de Berry. The Boucicaut Master,* New York, 1968, fig. 493). The outer border consists of 2 long branches of pomegranate and many insects, against a painted gold ground, in the late fifteenth century French manner.

2. f. 2: Adoration of the Magi, with the Virgin holding the naked Child upright on her lap; she sits to the right of the picture; the Magi, one of whom is black,

approach with their followers from the left; the oldest Magus, with white hair but a young beardless face, already kneels in adoration, his crown on the ground beside him; the ass and the donkey are in the shed with a sheaf of hay, and a young shepherd peers in at the scene from a window in the left side of the shed. The outer border consists of 6 medallions of the Flight into Egypt set in a Renaissance ornament and foliage border.

Parchment, 1 bifolium, with another added around it as flyleaves; 153 × 103 (painted area: 142 × 100) mm. Bound in an English red morocco folder inscribed on the front cover "An Illuminated Sheet from a 15th Century Manuscript." On f. i verso, in pencil in the upper corner: "8–8–09, pm 1/5."

Date and source of acquisition by Henry E. Huntington unknown.

Bibliography: De Ricci, 103 .

---

[1] We are grateful to Prof. James Marrow for noting this coincidence.

HM 1179 BOOK OF HOURS

France, s. XV^{in}
fig. 87

1. f. 3v: *Sequuntur hore beatissime virginis marie* . . . , Ave maria gratia plena . . . ; at the bottom of the written space an erasure of red ink which appears to read: Sequuntur hore beate virginis marie ad matutinas; the Hours of the Virgin are no longer present.

2. ff. 4–50v: Hours of the Passion; prayers to the Virgin, John the Evangelist, and All Saints follow lauds to compline; opening leaf of none missing between ff. 34–35; f. 51r–v, ruled, but blank except for rubric.

3. ff. 52–74: Hours of the Holy Spirit, with one lesson; hymn at matins, Veni creator spiritus . . . [*RH* 21204]; f. 74v, ruled, but blank except for rubric.

4. ff. 75–114v: Long hours of the Trinity.

5. ff. 115–136v: Suffrages of Michael, All Angels, John the Baptist, Peter and Paul, John the Evangelist, Andrew, James the Greater, All Apostles, Stephen, Denis, Lawrence, Christopher, All Martyrs, Martin, Nicholas, Anthony abbot, Godo, Maurus, All Confessors, Mary Magdalene, Anne, Catherine of Alexandria, Margaret, All Virgins, All Saints, for peace.

6. ff. 137–139: Prayers as follow: Domine ihesu christe qui hanc sacratissimam carnem . . . [Wilmart, 378, n.]; *Item alia oratio,* Anima christi sanctifica me . . . [Leroquais, *LH* 2:340]; *Alia oratio,* Ave domine ihesu christe verbum patris . . . [Wilmart, 412]; *Alia oratio,* Ave verum corpus natum de maria virgine . . . [*RH* 2175]; *Memoria de trinitate antiphona,* Te invocamus te adoramus . . . with versicle, response and prayer, Domine deus pater omnipotens nos famulos tuos tue maiestati . . .

7. ff. 139v–152v: 64 short prayers for the Sundays of the year and major feasts.

8. ff. 153–154v: Prayers as follow: *Ad impetrandam gratiam spiritus sancti,* Deus cui omne cor patet et omnis voluntas loquitur . . . ; *Contra malas cogita-*

tiones, Omnipotens et mitissime deus respice propicius ad preces nostras et libera corda nostra . . . ; *Contra temptationes carnis,* Ure igne sancti spiritus renes nostros . . . ; *Ad postulandam gratiam lacrimarum,* Omnipotens et mitissime deus qui sitienti populo . . . ; *Ad postulandum fidem spem et caritatem,* Omnipotens sempiterne deus respice propicius ad preces ecclesie tue . . . ; *Sequitur oratio pro vivis et deffunctis* [*sic*], Omnipotens sempiterne deus qui vivorum dominaris simul et mortuorum . . .

9. ff. 155–166v: Prayers as follow: Deus pater qui creasti Mundum et illuminasti . . . [*RH* 4477]; *oratio,* O celi terre domina O angelorum agmina . . . ; *oratio,* Domine ihesu tuorum Propter merita sanctorum . . . ; *Oratio De beata virgine et de omnibus sanctis,* Sancte dei genitricis marie semperque virginis gloriose . . . ; Iuste iudex ihesu christe rex regum et domine . . . [*RH* 9910]; *De sancto guillermo antiphona,* O Guillerme pastor bone . . . [*RH* 13077] with versicle, response and prayer, Adesto supplicationibus nostris omnipotens deus . . . ; ff. 167–168v, ruled, but blank.

Parchment, ff. ii (modern parchment) + 168 + ii (modern parchment); 195 × 137 (97 × 60) mm. 1 (ff. 1–8: ff. 1–3, singletons, ruled, but blank, except for the now inappropriate rubric on f. 3v; ff. 4–5, center bifolium; ff. 6–8, singletons, with text following correctly) $2–4^8$ 5^8(–3, before f. 35, the opening leaf of none) 6^8 7^4(through f. 51) $8–14^8$ 15^8(–7, excised; through f. 114) $16–21^8$ 22^6. Catchwords, when present, usually in the script of the text and washed in yellow; occasionally in a small cursive (ff. 51v, 107v). Quires and leaves signed with letters of the alphabet, a–y, and arabic numerals in the gutter. 15 long lines, ruled in a pale brown-red ink, the top line full across; pricking visible in the lower margin. Written in a gothic book hand in 2 sizes according to liturgical function.

Twenty-two large miniatures above 4 lines of text, both text and miniature enclosed by a U-shaped frame of narrow pink, blue and gold segments, growing out of the initial and sprouting ivy vines at the 4 corners; outer border of regularly positioned ivy vine with pink, blue and gold trilobe leaves. The miniatures have been attributed to the Master of Troyes by M. Meiss, *French Painting in the Time of Jean de Berry: The Late Fourteenth Century and the Patronage of the Duke* (London–New York 1967) 359; and *French Painting in the Time of Jean de Berry: The Limbourgs and their contemporaries* (New York 1974) 407; they are: f. 4 (Hours of the Passion), Betrayal, against a diapered ground; f. 20 (Prime), Scourging at the pillar, beneath a diaphragm arch; Christ is completely nude; background blue with gold squares; f. 24 (Terce), Christ before Pilate; blue-grey ground with white squares; f. 29v (Sext), Road to Calvary; red ground with gold squares; miniature for none missing before f. 35; f. 41 (Vespers), Deposition from the Cross, against a diapered ground; f. 46 (Compline), Entombment; blue ground decorated with gold squares; f. 52 (Hours of the Holy Spirit), Baptism of Christ with a tiny swan swimming in the stream; John pours the water from a bowl, while an angel holds Christ's tunic, and a half-figure of God breaks through a star-shaped shatter of clouds; a scroll carries the words, "Hic est filius meus . . ."; f. 57v (Prime), Christ in a white robe with globe and staff followed by Peter, John the Evangelist and James (?), meeting Moses, horned, and Elijah in a bleak, mountainous desert; the Old Testament figures are in smaller scale; f. 60 (Terce), Pentecost, in an outdoor setting of bleak, spiral hills, under a blue sky split by the descending dove, with red rays curving down to the apostles; f. 62v (Sext), Peter, the keys over his arm, preaching to men and women sitting on the ground; red rays from the aperture in the sky above; f. 65 (None), Peter, holding a book, converting a group of men and women to the left, while John the Evangelist, holding the snaky chalice, converts people on the right in a setting of craggy hills, with red rays curving out of a ruffled quatrefoil aperture in the sky; f. 67v (Vespers), John the Evangelist and Peter with a crowd of disciples meeting Simon Magus, who has a large purse hanging from his arm and gold coins in his hand; a scroll against a square-patterned ground reads "Pecunia tua tecum sit in perdicione"; f. 71 (Compline), Peter, John the Evangelist and disciples meeting Ananias, who falls dead, dropping silver coins, while Sapphira, to the right, also offers a handful of silver, in the hilly desert; f. 75 (Hours of the Trinity), the 3 Persons sit side by side on a wide throne: to the left, a Christ-like figure with a brown beard holds a haloed dove on his lap and blesses; in the center the figure for God the Father, with a grey beard, holds an orb and blesses; to the right, a young man, like the first, but with a cross-nimbus holds a cross on which is hung the Crown of Thorns; all are dressed alike; background of blue angels; f. 115, Michael; f. 117v, John the Baptist sitting in the hilly desert in a hair shirt and blue mantle, and holding the forefeet of the Lamb; f. 120, Peter; f. 124, Stephen holding 3 small stones like a trefoil with the same arrangement of stones on his head; f. 127v, Martin, on horseback, with elaborate saddle, shares his cloak with a peg-legged beggar; tooled burnished gold ground; f. 130v, Mary Magdalene, against a square-patterned pink ground, each square being filled with a grotesque face; f. 132, Catherine of Alexandria, against a burnished gold ground patterned with squares; f. 166, William, bishop of Bourges, in miter, cope and dalmatic before the kneeling owner of this manuscript. 4-line initials in white-patterned pink or blue against cusped gold ground, infilled with colored trilobe leaves; 3-, 2-, and 1-line initials in alternating blue with careful red penwork, or gold with black; initials within the text touched in yellow. Jigsaw line fillers in blue and gold. Rubrics in red.

Bound perhaps for Emile Bancel with interlaced initials "BB" by Thibaron in brown morocco with blue inlay, finished by Marius Michel; one of 2 silver fore edge clasps closing to pins on edge of top cover remains; gilt edges; parchment doublures.

Written in the early fifteenth century in France; the suffrages to Godo and Maurus may suggest Verdun as the book's destination; the first owner was apparently named William, and may have been connected with Bourges. Belonged to E. M. Bancel; his sale, Paris, 8 May 1882, n. 9 to Ellis. In the collection of E. Dwight Church (1835–1908), and in his *Catalogue . . . of English Literature* (1909) vol. 1, n. 399 with a plate of f. 41. The Church collection was acquired by Henry E. Huntington in 1911.

Bibliography: De Ricci, 103.

HM 1180 — France, s. XV$^{4/4}$
BOOK OF HOURS — *fig. 138*

1. ff. 3–27 [f. 3, ruled, but blank]: Hours of the Passion; 5 lessons at matins; weekly variations of the psalms set into the text for each hour; from lauds to compline a suffrage for each of the 7 Joys of the Virgin; after lauds, suffrages of Catherine of Alexandria, John the Evangelist, and Peter and Paul; after none, a suffrage "de annunciatione dominica."

2. ff. 27v–30v: Passion according to John.

3. ff. 31–40v [f. 31, ruled, but blank]: Hours of the Compassion of the Virgin.

4. ff. 41–44 [f. 41, ruled, but blank]: Prayers to the Holy Spirit as follow: *Secuuntur orationes de sancto spiritu,* O Sancte Spiritus creator et vivificator omnium qui in principio . . . ; *Alia oratio,* O Sancte spiritus qui es amator sensorum cogitacionum . . . ; O Sancte spiritus qui es fons vivus et purificator omnium . . . ; *de sancto spiritu oratio,* O Sancte spiritus qui lugentibus et merentibus apostolis missus es consolator . . . ; *oratio,* O Sancte spiritus vivificator omnium quia fecundas aquas et vivificas animas . . . ; O Sancte spiritus qui aspirando

das homines esse spirituales . . . ; *Oratio,* Sancti spiritus gracia domine deus omnipotens queso . . . ; *Alia oratio,* O Sancte optime ceterorum magister qui per tuum magisterium . . . ; O Sancte spiritus qui digitus dei dixeris . . . ; O Sancte spiritus qui gracia dei dixeris . . . ; O Sancte spiritus qui ideo in specie columbe venisse ostenderis . . . ; O Sancte spiritus qui ideo ignis appellaris . . . ; O Sancte spiritus qui deus proprie nuncuparis . . . ; *Alia,* Omnipotens sempiterne deus clemenciam tuam devota mente suppliciter exoro . . . ; *oratio,* Omnipotens sempiterne deus qui nimie unigeniti tui misisti . . . ; *Item alia de sancto spiritu,* O gracia ineffabilis caritas inseparabilis . . . ; *Oratio,* Veni sancte spiritus doctor amabilis omnium fidelium . . .

5. ff. 44v–55: Long hours of the Holy Spirit, beginning with the verses, Unctio doctorem det quem devotus adorem . . . , *Isti versiculi dicuntur ante qualibet* [*sic*] *horam.*

6. ff. 55–58v: Prayers to Jesus as follow: *Oratio ad dominum nostrum ihesum christum,* Ihesu dulcis memoria ihesu dulce solacium ihesu tuta fiducia . . . ; Ihesus salutis hostia salutis sacrificium ihesu salutis gracia . . . ; *Alia oratio,* Ihesu largitor venie ihesu solamen tristium ihesu laus penitencie . . . ; *Oratio,* Ihesu lux et rex glorie fili dei et hominis ihesu flos pudicitie . . . ; *Alia oratio,* Ihesu nostra redemptio ihesu redemptor omnium ihesu nostra dilectio . . . ; *Oratio,* Ihesu patris unigenitus virtus et sapiencia . . . ; *Alia,* Ihesu via rectissima ihesu salutis ostium ihesu porta tutissima . . . ; *Item alia oratio,* Transfige domine dulcissime ihesu christe vere deus amoris medullos anime mee . . . ; *Alia,* Domine ihesu christe fili dei vivi in honore tuarum sanctissimarum orationum . . . ; *oratio,* Ihesu nostra redemptio amor et desiderium . . .

7. ff. 59–68 [ff. 59–60, blank]: Hours of the Holy Name of Jesus, with the rubric, f. 58v, *Incipit iubilus cum iubilo beati bernardi de ihesu. Ad omnes horas diei;* in long hours form; see A. Wilmart, *Le 'Jubilus' dit de St. Bernard* (Rome 1944).

8. ff. 68–73v: *Incipiunt orationes devote beati bernardi abbatis ad ihesum christum dominum nostrum,* Ihesu fili dei vivi qui ex voluntate patris cooperante spiritu sancto . . . ; *oratio,* Ihesu dulcis qui de ancilla humili tu humilis humiliter natus . . . ; *Alia ad eiusdem* [*sic*], Ihesu clemens qui de virgine natus circumcidi sub lege voluisti . . . ; *oratio,* Ihesu bone qui de virgine natus te ipsum magis stella duce revelasti . . . ; *Oratio,* Ihesu desiderabilis qui in templo presentatur visto symeoni . . . ; Ihesu mitissime qui de virgine natus in partibus egypti secessisti . . . ; *Alia ad eundem,* Ihesu clementissime qui per manus beati iohannis baptiste baptizari voluisti . . . ; *Oratio,* Ihesu bone qui ductus in deserto a spiritu . . . ; *oratio,* Ihesu clemens qui deprehensam in adulterio clementer ab accusatoribus liberasti . . . ; Ihesu spes penitencium qui ree peccatrici stanti retro secus pedes tuos . . . ; *Alia oratio,* Ihesu benignissime qui marthe et marie fide et precibus quatriduarum lazarum iam fetentem a sepulchro . . . ; *oratio,* Ihesu benignissime qui pro credentibus et crediturus [*sic*] in te ante tempus passionis patrem suppliciter exorasti . . . ; *oratio,* Ihesu clementissime qui nimia ductus caritate et misericordia . . . ; *Oratio,* Ihesus mitis vere paciencie forma et humilitatis exemplum . . . ; *Alia oratio ad eundem,* Ihesu misericors qui pendens in cruce venerabilem matrem et virginem . . . ; *Oratio,* Ihesu bone cruci affixus ab eadem descendere voluisti . . . ; *oratio,* Ihesu vera clemencia qui positus in sepulchro a visu hominum . . . ; *oratio,* Verum has inter hec o anima in ea deponamus piissimas tristicie querelas . . . ; *Alia ad eundem*

dominum, Ihesu nostra redemptio amor et desiderium qui devotis mulieribus te querentibus . . . ; *oratio,* Ihesu corona celsior qui resurgens a mortuis . . . ; *oratio,* Ihesu largitor donorum omnium qui super apostolos tuos . . . ; Tua sunt omnia hec ihesu bone hee sunt misericordie tue antique domine . . . ; Deprecor te domine ihesu christe pro omnibus illis pro quibus decrevi orare . . .

9. ff. 73v–79: *Incipiunt orationes de passione domini quas composuit beatus bernardus abbas,* Dulcissime domine ihesu christe qui pro miseris peccatoribus dignatus es descendere de celo . . . ; *Alia oratio,* Dulcissime ihesu per vocationem et longam ac triplicem orationem post agoniam . . . ; *oratio,* Dulcis ihesu postea ductus fuisti ad caypham . . . ; *Alia oratio,* Dulcis ihesu postea ductus fuisti ad consilium factum mane . . . ; *oratio,* Dulcis ihesu quo ductum condamnatum et ligatum preduxerunt . . . ; Dulcis ihesu tunc herodes remisit te ad pilatum . . . ; *oratio,* Dulcis ihesu per istam postposicionem qua dignatus est . . . ; *Oratio,* Dulcis ihesu postea pilatus ducit te foras ad iudeos dicens . . . ; Dulcis ihesu iterum pilatus te reduceris ad pretorium querit unde es tu . . . ; *Alia oratio Ad eundem,* Dulcis ihesu ex inde querebat te pylatus omnino dimittere . . . ; Dulcis ihesu cum ergo ducerent te extra civitatem ad crucem . . . ; Dulcis ihesu postea eiecerunt te extra civitatem et imposuerunt humeris ferre crucem tuam . . . ; Dulcis ihesu per illam crucis baiulacionem fac me dignum tanto honore . . . ; *Oratio,* Dulcis ihesu ducis ad locum passionis ubi rei pro suis sceleribus torquebantur . . . ; Quis dabit capiti meo aquam et oculis meis fontem lacrimarum ut defleam vulnera anime mee. Conversi sunt dies festi mei in luctum et cantica in lamentacionibus . . . ; *Item Alia Oratio,* Culter que circumcidisti sacrosanctam carnem christi resera nocencia ihesum ioseph ut est scriptum. Tollens fugit in egyptum . . . ; *Oratio Ad christum,* Rogo te domine ihesu christe per illa salutifera vulnera cum quibus passus es . . .

10. ff. 79–86v: Prayers as follow: *Ad deum patrem Oratio,* Ad te domine lacrimabili ingemisco ad te domine de magna necessitate . . . ; *ad deum filium oratio,* Domine ihesu christe fili dei vivi creator et resuscitator generis humani . . . ; *Ad spiritum sanctum Oratio,* Temeritatis quidam est apud me o spiritus alme ut ego infelix et peccator . . . ; *Ad christum oratio,* Verbum secretum habeo ad te rex seculorum misericordia et refugium . . . *Psalterium ad deum patrem,* Letifica domine peccatricem animam meam et concede michi ob amorem tue beatitudinis consiliare . . . with kyrie eleison and prayer, Domine sancte pater omnipotens eterne deus qui coeternum et substancialem tibi ante secula . . . [*HE,* 124]; *Psalterium ad deum filium,* Miserere mei deus secundum magnam misericordiam tuam . . . with kyrie eleison and prayer, Domine ihesu christe fili dei vivi verus et omnipotens deus . . . [*HE,* 124]; *Psalterium ad spiritum sanctum,* Propicius esto omnibus iniquitatibus nostris et sacia in bonis desiderium meum . . . with kyrie eleison and prayer, Domine sancte spiritus omnipotens deus qui cum patre filioque semper existans . . . [*HE,* 124–25].

11. ff. 86v–89v: *Sequitur psalterium beati iheronimi,* Verba mea auribus percipe . . . [*HE,* 116–22]; ff. 90–92v, ruled, but blank.

Parchment with hair follicles apparent, ff. 92 (+f. 43 bis; the pastedowns, the first 2 and the last 3 leaves ruled, but blank); 200 × 140 (132 × 80) mm. Collation beginning at f. 3, including f. 43 bis and ending at f. 89: 1^8 2^8(–4, before f. 14) 3^8(–2, before f. 19; this leaf now Baltimore, Walters Art Gallery, W. 781a[1]) 4^8 5^8(–2, before f. 34; this leaf now Baltimore, Walters Art Gallery, W.781b) $6–7^8$ 8^8(+5 and 6, ff. 59, blank, and 60, blank on the recto) 9^8 10^8(+ 1 at the beginning, f. 73) 11^8. Some catchwords remain, although partially erased, in the inner margin of ff. 32v and 46v. A quire and leaf signature on f. 43 "m iiii" may indicate that the book once contained an additional 5 or 6 quires at the beginning. 31 long lines, ruled in pale red ink; some pricking uncropped. Written in a gothic book hand of 2 sizes according to liturgical function.

Sixteen full page miniatures in arched compartments with serrated tops, enclosed by U-shaped frames, with the decorated outer and lower bars wider than the inner strip; border usually of blue and gold acanthus leaves, multicolored flowers, strawberries, insects, birds and grotesques or figures; miniatures frequently framed by columns and arches duplicating the shape of the arched compartments. Several of the miniatures derive directly from contemporary engravings, as indicated below; many have been retouched to lighten the dark skin tones and to repair flaking: f. 3v (Hours of the Passion), Entry into Jerusalem; f. 7v (Lauds), Last Supper; f. 11v (Prime), Christ washing the disciples' feet; illumination for terce missing before f. 14; f. 16v (Sext), Betrayal in the garden at night, with Peter holding the sword in one hand and grasping Malchus' arm with the other; U-shaped frame around the miniature formed of logs; illumination for none missing before f. 19 and now in the Walters Art Gallery: Christ before Caiaphas; f. 21v (Vespers), Christ before Pilate, based on the print by the Master with the Banderoles, reproduced in A. I. Lockhart, "Four Engravings by the Master with the Banderoles," *Bulletin of the Cleveland Museum of Art* 60 (1973) p. 248 fig. 1; in HM 1180, but not in the print, the initial "S" on the tunic front of one of the soldiers; f. 24v (Compline), Mocking of Christ, with 2 tormentors pressing the crown of thorns down on his head with large sticks; the initial "G" on the tunic front of one of the tormentors; U-shaped frame around the miniature formed of logs; f. 27v (Passion according to John), Flagellation; f. 31v (Hours of the Compassion), Christ on the road to Calvary, with a spike block hung from his waist; frame around the miniature formed of logs; the miniature based on the print by the Master with the Banderoles, reproduced in Lockhart, p. 249 fig. 4; illumination for lauds missing before f. 34 and now in the Walters Art Gallery: the Disrobing of Christ, based on the print by the Master of the Berlin Passion, Lehrs n. 28, pl. 94 fig. 244; f. 35v (Prime), Nailing to the Cross; f. 36v (Terce), Crucifixion, between the 2 thieves, with Mary, John and others on Christ's right and the soldiers on his left; f. 37v (Sext), Deposition from the Cross; f. 38v (None), Entombment, set beneath an open-sided grey masonry vault; frame around the miniature formed of logs; f. 39v (Vespers), the Harrowing of Hell, based on the print by the Master with the Banderoles, Lehrs n. 38 reproduced in F. W. H. Hollstein, *Dutch and Flemish Etchings, Engravings and Woodcuts, ca. 1450–1700* (Amsterdam 1949–81) vol. 12, under the Lehrs number; f. 41v (Compline), Resurrection set beneath the same grey gothic vault as on f. 38v; in the place of the usual U-shaped frame, a border of painted gold ground decorated with colored flowers and leaves and with black ink commas and dots; the miniature based on the print by the Master with the Banderoles, Lehrs n. 39, pl. 114 fig. 336; in HM 1180, but not in the print, the initial "L" on the tunic front of one of the soldiers; f. 44v (Hours of the Holy Spirit), Pentecost; in place of the usual U-shaped frame, a compartmentalized border; the miniature based on the print by the Master E. S., Lehrs n. 35, pl. 83 fig. 217; f. 60v (Hours of the Holy Name of Jesus), 4 angels support the IHS monogram in glory; possibly by a different artist; in a rectangular frame with the IHS monogram throughout the border. Full borders of similar style on the leaves facing the miniatures and on ff. 14, 19, 34 (to face the missing miniatures); the borders on ff. 40, 42, 45 are geometric with many figures; those on ff. 48, 49, 50, 51 (compartmentalized), 52, 53 (painted gold ground), 54 do not face illuminations but are triggered by the presence of 9-line initials; those on ff. 61, 62, 63, 64r–v, 65v, 66, 67, also with 9-line initials, decorated with the IHS monogram. 9-line initials in white-patterned pink or blue on burnished gold ground with colored trilobe leaf infilling; 2- and 1-line initials in gold on blue or pink with infilling of the other color; initials within the text touched in yellow. Rubrics in red.

Bound, s. XVII, in coarse grained black morocco over bevelled wooden boards; evidence of 2 fore edge straps closing to pins on edge of lower cover; gilt edges.

HM 1180

Written in France during the fourth quarter of the fifteenth century. HM 1180 may be only the second half of the book, since it lacks many usual texts of a book of hours: calendar, hours of the Virgin, office of the dead, penitential psalms and litany. Robson Catalogue 94 (London, ca. 1900) n. 11 with a plate of f. 16v. Belonged to Herschel V. Jones (1861–1928) of Minneapolis; his sale, Anderson, New York, 29 January 1919, pt. II, n. 907 to G. D. Smith. Precise source and date of acquisition by Henry E. Huntington unknown.

Bibliography: De Ricci, 104.

---

[1] We are grateful to Prof. James Marrow for this information and for the following identification of compositional sources of some miniatures in contemporary prints; we thank Dr. Lilian Randall for her kind assistance.

HM 1181 — France, s. XV/XVI
BOOK OF HOURS, use of Rome

1. ff. 1–6v: Full calendar with an entry for each day, alternating red and blue with major feasts in gold.

2. ff. 7–11: Pericopes of the Gospels.

3. ff. 11v–16: *Oratio ad beatam virginem mariam,* Obsecro te . . . [masculine forms; Leroquais, *LH* 2:346]; *Alia oratio ad beatam virginem mariam,* O Intemerata . . . orbis terrarum. Inclina aures tue pietatis . . . [masculine forms; Wilmart, 488–90]; f. 16v, ruled, but blank.

4. ff. 17–67v: Hours of the Virgin, use of Rome, with weekly variations of the psalms at matins set into the text before the lessons; opening leaf of prime missing between ff. 39–40; suffrage of All Saints and prayer for peace from lauds to compline; Salve Regina follows compline, with versicle, response and the prayer, Omnipotens sempiterne deus qui gloriose virginis matris marie . . . ; Advent office begins on f. 62.

5. ff. 68–70v: *Oratio valde devota ad ihesum christum,* O bone ihesu o dulcis ihesu o piissime ihesu . . . [Wilmart, 'Jubilus']; *Incipiunt septem versus sancti bernardi, O bone ihesu,* Illumina oculos meos . . . [*RH* 27912; breaks imperfectly after the fifth holy name "Deloy," after f. 69]; prayer beginning imperfectly in its heading: *//et fut aportee au noble empereur charlemaine. Sensuit l'oraison,* Benedictio dei patris cum angelis suis . . . [Leroquais, *LH* 1:170]; Nam et si ambulavero . . . ; O Domine ihesu christe pastor bone per hanc passionem tuam . . . ; *Alia Oratio,* Ave verum corpus . . . [Wilmart, 373–76]; *Alia oratio,* O Passio magna, o profunda vulnera . . .

6. ff. 71–72v: Short hours of the Cross, beginning imperfectly: //sti mundum. *Vers.* Omnes terra adoret . . .

7. ff. 73–75v: Short hours of the Holy Spirit.

8. ff. 76–88v: Penitential psalms and litany.

9. ff. 89–119v: Office of the Dead, use of Rome.

10. ff. 120–135: Suffrages of Michael, John the Evangelist, Peter and Paul, James, Bartholomew, Stephen, Lawrence, Sebastian, Christopher [. . . me famulo tuo

N . . .], Ivo, Nicholas, Claude, Anthony abbot, the 10,000 Martyrs, Leonard, Anne, Mary Magdalene, Catherine of Alexandria, Margaret, Barbara, Apollonia, Avia, Genevieve, the 11,000 Virgins.

11. ff. 135–143v: *Septem orationes beati gregorii,* O domine ihesu christe adoro te in cruce pendentem . . . [Leroquais, *LH* 2:346]; *Les xv Ioyes de nostre dame,* Doulce dame de misericorde . . . [Sonet 458]; *Les sept Requestes a nostre seigneur Ihesucrist,* Doulx dieu doulx pere saincte trinite ung seul dieu . . . [Sonet 504]; Saincte vraye croix aouree . . . [Sonet 1876]; *Pape Boniface a donne a tous ceulx qui diront devotement* . . . , Domine Ihesu christe qui hanc sacratissimam carnem . . . ; *Quant on veult recepvoir le corps de nostre seigneur ihesucrist,* Domine non sum dignus ut intres sub tectum meum, sed tu domine . . . ; *Quant on l'a receu,* Vera perceptio corporis et sanguinis tui . . .

Parchment, ff. i (paper) + i (parchment) + 143 + i (parchment) + i (paper); 175 × 120 (107 × 60) mm. 1^6 2^8 3^2(to f. 16) $4–5^8$ $6^8(-8)$ $7–9^8$ $10^8(-7)$ $11^8(-1)$ $12–19^8$ 20^2. Catchwords written vertically along the inner bounding line. 22 long lines ruled in pale red ink. Written in a bâtarde script.

Thirteen full page miniatures, in painted gold architectural frames, often with colored marble panels or columns: f. 7, John on Patmos, with the devil hiding behind the rocks, attempting to steal the inkwell, and God and angels above; f. 11v (Obsecro te), Virgin and Child, enthroned, with angels playing instruments on either side; f. 17 (Hours of the Virgin), Annunciation, with the Dove resting on Mary's head; f. 31 (Lauds), Visitation; illumination missing at prime, between ff. 39–40; f. 43 (Terce), Annunciation to the shepherds; f. 46v (Sext), Adoration of the Magi, one of whom is black; f. 50 (None), Presentation in the temple; f. 53 (Vespers), Flight into Egypt with Mary nursing the Child and an angel following behind; f. 58v (Compline), Assumption of the Virgin, standing on a crescent and rising into heaven supported by 2 angels; illumination missing for the Hours of the Cross, between ff. 70–71; f. 73 (Hours of the Holy Spirit), Pentecost; f. 76 (Penitential psalms), Bathsheba bathing as David watches from a window; f. 89 (Office of the Dead), Job on the dunghill; f. 124v, Christopher with the Christ Child standing on his shoulders. Thirty-two smaller miniatures, 11- or 10-line: f. 8v, Luke; f. 9v, Matthew; f. 10v, Mark; f. 14v (O Intemerata), Pietà; f. 68 (O bone ihesu), Man of Sorrows; f. 69v (Illumina oculos meos), Bernard holding the devil by a cord around his neck; f. 120, Michael; f. 120v, John the Evangelist with the chalice; f. 121, Peter and Paul; f. 121v, James, with staff, pouch, book and a shell on his hat; f. 122, Bartholomew holding a knife and a book; f. 122v, Stephen; f. 123, Lawrence; f. 123v, Sebastian; f. 126, Ivo holding legal papers; f. 126v, Nicholas; f. 127, Claude as a bishop, blessing; f. 128, Anthony abbot; f. 129, 10,000 Martyrs; f. 129v, Leonard, with book and fetters; f. 130, Anne teaching Mary to read; f. 130v, Mary Magdalene; f. 131, Catherine; f. 131v, Margaret; f. 132, Barbara; f. 133, Apollonia; f. 133v, Avia, in prison with Mary bringing the Eucharist to her; f. 134, Genevieve (unfinished or badly rubbed); f. 134v, 11,000 Virgins, lead by Ursula and a bishop; f. 135 (7 O's), Gregory; f. 136 (15 Joys), Virgin and Child; f. 140 (7 Requests), God the Father. Major initials, 6-line, in white-patterned blue with infilling on gold ground of a realistic flower, the whole set against a red ground; 2- and 1-line painted gold initials against alternating brick-red or blue square grounds; line fillers in the same colors. Compartmentalized band borders the length of the text in outer margins of every page, traced through. Rubrics in a deep rose color. In the calendar, illustrations of the monthly occupations with the zodiac symbols usually in monochrome blue set on the lighter blue of the sky; traced geometric borders as above. On f. ii recto, a small sketch of a man's head in profile.

Bound, s. XVII[1], in French red morocco with the arms and monogram of Philippe de Béthune; see J. Guigard, *Nouvel Armorial du Bibliophile* (Paris 1890) 2:56; marbled endpapers; gilt edges.

HM 1181

Written in France at the turn of the fifteenth century for owners whose monograms BL and BI (?) tied with a lovers' knot, appear 24 times in the borders; one of the B's may indicate Bartholomew, a suffrage of that saint being included in this book. Owned by Philippe, comte de Béthune (d. 1649) whose books passed to his son Hippolyte; he, in turn, bequeathed them to Louis XIV in 1658. Belonged to Robert Hoe: *Cat.* (1909) pp. 95–96; at that time kept in a wrapper of dark red striped silk and satin; his sale, Anderson, New York, 1912, pt. IV, n. 2337 to G. D. Smith. Precise date and source of acquisition by Henry E. Huntington unknown.

Bibliography: De Ricci, 104.

HM 1200 — Flanders, s. XV^med
BOOK OF HOURS, undetermined use

1. ff. 1–12v: Calendar, rather empty, in French with major feasts in red.

2. ff. 13–20: Pericopes of the Gospels; *Oroison A nostre dame,* O Intemerata . . . orbis terrarum. Inclina aures . . . [Wilmart, 488–90]; f. 20v, ruled, but blank.

3. ff. 21–25 [f. 21, blank]: Short hours of the Cross; f. 25v, ruled, but blank.

4. ff. 26–30 [f. 26, blank]: Short hours of the Holy Spirit; f. 30v, ruled, but blank.

5. ff. 31–85 [f. 31, blank]: Hours of the Virgin; the antiphons and capitula at prime and at none are: Assumpta est . . . ; Hec est virgo . . . ; Germinavit radix . . . ; Et radicavi . . . ; f. 85v, ruled, but blank.

6. ff. 86–87: *Oroison de sainte veronne,* Salve sancta facies . . . and the prayer, Deus qui nobis signastis lumen vultus tui . . . [*HE,* 174–75]; f. 87v, ruled, but blank.

7. ff. 88–106v [f. 88, blank]: Penitential psalms and litany, including Blasius, Quentin and Livin among the martyrs; Amand, Vedast, Remigius, Eligius, Aegidius, Audomar, Bertin and Bavo among the confessors; Ursula, Amalberga, Walburga, Dorothea, Anastasia, Agatha, Pisca (for Prisca?), Cita (for Zita?), Gertrude and Adelgundis among the virgins.

8. ff. 107–132 [f. 107, blank]: Office of the Dead; 3 lessons at matins; ff. 132v–134v, ruled, but blank.

9. ff. 135–137v: Mass of the Virgin, Salve sancta parens . . . ; f. 138r–v, ruled, but blank.

10. ff. 139–149v: Prayers as follow: *Oroison a nostre dame,* Obsecro te . . . [masculine forms; Leroquais, *LH* 2:346]; *Oroison A la vierge marie,* Salve regina misericordie . . . [*RH* 18147] with versicle, response and prayer, Concede nos famulos tuos quesumus domine deus perpetua mentis . . . ; *Devote oroison a nostre dame,* Inviolata integra et casta . . . [*RH* 9094]; *Salutacion a nostre dame,* Ave regina celorum Ave domina angelorum . . . [*RH* 2070]; *Deprecation A nostre dame,* Regina celi letare . . . [*RH* 17170]; *S'ensieut moult bonne et devote oroison du saint esperit,* Veni creator spiritus . . . [*RH* 21204] with versicle, response and prayer, Deus qui corda fidelium . . . [Bruylants, *Oraisons,* 2, n. 349]; *S'ensieut le psalme de le foy,* Quicunque vult salvus esse . . .

11. ff. 150–160v: Suffrages of the Trinity, Michael, John the Baptist, John the Evangelist, Peter and Paul, All Apostles, James the Greater, Christopher (masculine forms), Sebastian, Lawrence, Anthony abbot, Nicholas, Adrianus, Francis, Mary Magdalene, Catherine of Alexandria, Barbara, Margaret; ff. 161–162v, ruled, but blank.

Parchment, ff. ii (early parchment; the first formerly the pastedown) + ii (modern parchment) + 162 + i (early parchment, conjunct with the pastedown); 180 × 129 (104 × 71) mm. 1^{12} 2^{8} 3^{8}(+1, f. 21 and 6, f. 26) 4^{10}(+1, f. 31) 5^{10}(+10, f. 51) 6^{10}(+5, f. 57 and 10, f. 62) 7^{10}(+3, f. 67 and 8, f. 72) 8^{10}(+4, f. 80) 9^{10}(+1, f. 88) 10^{8} 11^{10}(+1, f. 107) 12^{10} 13^{8}(–5, excised by the scribe; through f. 134) 14^{10}(–8 and 10, both excised by the scribe) 15–16^{10}. One catchword survives, in a small cursive hand in the inner corner of f. 117v. 18 long lines, ruled in purple ink with the top and bottom 2 lines full across; pricking visible in all 3 outer margins. Written in 2 sizes of a gothic book hand.

Eleven full page miniatures on the versos of inserted singletons, blank on the recto; the miniatures in arched compartments framed by wide, colored bands decorated with lettering, fine arabesques, or painted gold spiky leaves twisted about a blue rod; the outer border consists of thin, long-stemmed multicolored acanthus leaves, symmetrically arranged around flowers, birds, grey grapes, strawberries and occasional figures of men, angels, or grotesques. The miniatures are related in style to those of the Master of Guillebert de Mets and the Master of the Privileges of Ghent,[1] but have been repainted in varying degree, perhaps in the seventeenth century: f. 21v (Hours of the Cross), Crucifixion with Mary and John; f. 26v (Hours of the Holy Spirit), Pentecost; f. 31v (Hours of the Virgin), Annunciation; f. 51v (Prime), Nativity; f. 57v (Terce), Annunciation to the shepherds; f. 62v (Sext), Presentation in the temple; f. 67v (None), Adoration of the Magi; f. 72v (Vespers), Massacre of the Innocents: a turbaned mother kneels before Herod as soldiers enter with bloody heads of children on the tips of their swords; f. 80v (Compline), Flight into Egypt, with Mary nursing the Baby; f. 88v (Penitential psalms), David in prayer; f. 107v (Office of the Dead), Raising of Lazarus. Historiated initials usually 3-line, enclosed by frames of gold and color strips, and with narrow bracket borders of black ink vine, flowers, strawberries and gold motifs; they have not been repainted: f. 13, 4-line, John seated at a chair, indoors, with the eagle perched on his desk; f. 14, 4-line, Luke; f. 15v, 4-line, Matthew; f. 17, 4-line, Mark; f. 41 (Lauds of the hours of the Virgin), 5-line, Visitation against a diapered background; f. 86 (Salve sancta facies), 6-line, Veronica holding the cloth, against a diapered background; f. 150 (Trinity), 4-line, Gnadenstuhl without the Dove; f. 150v, Michael vanquishing a bright orange devil; f. 151, John the Baptist; f. 151v, John the Evangelist; f. 152, 4-line, Peter and Paul; f. 152v, All Apostles; f. 153, James the Greater; f. 153v, Christopher; f. 154v, Sebastian; f. 156, Lawrence; f. 156v, Anthony abbot; f. 157v, Nicholas; f. 158, Adrianus standing on a lion; f. 158v, Francis receiving the stigmata from a bright orange seraph-crucifix; f. 159, Mary Magdalene; f. 159v, Catherine of Alexandria; f. 160, Barbara; f. 160v, Margaret, coming out of the back of a green-spotted, yellow dragon. Major initials on text pages facing the miniatures, 7- or 6-line, white-patterned blue or pink on burnished gold grounds, with infilling of shaded leaves of many colors; a decorated, wide, burnished gold band in U-shape encloses the written space on 3 sides; the full border does not match that of the inserted miniature pages, but is formed of a dense pattern of acanthus leaves in gold and dark blue, with the ribs picked out by a row of white dots; also in the outer border are flowers, some growing out of pots, grapes, pears, birds and grotesques. On f. 135, a 6-line initial in the same style as above, but with bracket border; a 6-line initial (f. 139), a 5-line initial (f. 143), and the 4-, 3-, and 2-line initials in burnished gold on parted pink and blue grounds, and producing a bracket border to the left of the text; 1-line initials in gold on blue grounds with pink infilling, or vice versa; ribbon line fillers of the same colors. Some flourishes touched in pink on the top-line ascenders or on the bottom-line descenders. Bracket borders in the calendar. Rubrics in pale pink. Note on f. 160v, below the text, in a later hand: "act. x Ja. a. mlii."

HM 1200

Bound, s. XVI, in pink velvet, very worn, over wooden boards; 2 gilt fore edge clasps; gilt edges; offset of binding reinforcement, apparently a document in French, s. XV^2, on inside front cover and on the recto of the now lifted pastedown.

Written in the middle of the fifteenth century in Flanders; liturgical use undetermined. The miniatures may not have been originally intended for this book, since the borders don't match; those for sext and none appear reversed, with the Presentation in the Temple preceding the Adoration of the Magi; all the full-page miniatures have been repainted. A possession note on the back flyleaf identifies a late sixteenth century owner as Johannes Hullandt; in another inscription, ca. 1600 (?), Carolus Hullandt "vicecomes Rolariensis villae" (Rousselaere?) gives the book to Catarina van Huerne. On the front flyleaf, f. i verso, are pious phrases and the inscription "Vertu pour guide, Jacqueline van." On f. ii verso, the inscriptions: "This Book belonged to Queen Mary of Scotland And shee used it at her death upon the Scaffold" (legible only under ultra-violet light), and "The above the Hand writing of King James the [?] 2," (s. XIX). A letter from Charles Browne Mostyn to Sir Gregory O. Page-Turner dated 1822 repeats this information, adding that the book eventually passed to the Scots College in Paris, where Mostyn obtained it during the Revolution. The letter, once loose in the manuscript, is now shelved as HM 46702. Sold at the Page-Turner sale, Battlesden House, 19 October 1824, probably n. 2524; Samuel Addington sale, Sotheby's, 24 May 1886, n. 285 to Nattali; belonged to Charles Butler (1821–1910); his sale, Sotheby's, 18 March 1912, pt. III, n. 2377 to Sabin. Purchased from the Minneapolis bookseller and collector, Edmund D. Brooks by William K. Bixby (1857–1931) of St. Louis (*St. Louis Republic,* 18 March 1917, Feature section, p. 1). Acquired from him by Henry E. Huntington through G. D. Smith in August 1918.

Bibliography: De Ricci, 104.

---

[1] We are indebted to Prof. James Marrow for this identification.

HM 1248 — Flanders, 1478
PSALTER and PRAYERS — *fig. 28*

1. ff. 1–4v: Flyleaves with owners' notes (see below).

2. ff. 5–16v: Calendar with major feasts in red; included are the feasts of the Octave of Thomas of Canterbury (5 January), Milburga (23 February), Richard de Wych (3 April), Elphege (18 April), Fremund (11 May), Brendan (16 May), Dunstan (19 May), Augustine "anglorum" (26 May), Boniface (5 June), Translation of Edmund archbishop (9 June), Translation of Edward martyr (20 June), Albanus (21 June), Mildred (13 July), Kenelm (17 July), Oswald (5 August), Milburga (31 August), Thecla (23 September), Leodegar (2 October), Translation of Edward (13 October), Wulfram (15 October), Frideswide (19 October), Willibrord (7 November), Edmund archbishop (16 November), Edmund king (20 November), Thomas of Canterbury (29 December, in red); Latin month verses (Walther, *Initia* 14561).

3. ff. 17–33v [f. 17, blank]: Penitential psalms, gradual psalms with cues only of the first twelve, and litany, including Leodegar, Edmund and Albanus among the martyrs; Cuthbert, Inan (? "inniane"), Duthac and Ternan among the confessors; Lucia, Margaret and Bridget among the virgins; *Devota oratio de sacramento,* Adoro te latens veritas, Tu qui sub formis vere latitas . . . [*RH* 518?];

Alia oratio de sacramento, Ave sanctissimum corpus dominicum in hoc sacramento contentum . . . [Wilmart, 379, n.]

4. ff. 34–55v: Office of the Dead; the responses at matins are: 1. Credo quod . . . ; 2. Qui lazarum . . . ; 3. Domine quando veneris iudicare terram ubi me abscondam a vultu ire tue quia peccavi nimis in vita mea; 4. Heu michi . . . ; 5. Ne recorderis . . . ; 6. Domine quando veneris iudicare terram secundum actum meum noli me iudicare nichil enim dignum in conspectu tuo egi, Ideo deprecor maiestatem tuam tuam [*sic*] ut tu deus deleas iniquitatem meam; 7. Peccantem me . . . ; 8. Requiem eternam . . . ; 9. Libera me . . . de morte.

5. ff. 56–69v [f. 56, blank]: Commendation of souls (Pss. 118, divided into sections, and 138) with the prayers, Tibi domine commendamus . . . and Misericordiam tuam domine . . .

6. ff. 70–77: Psalms of the Passion (Pss. 21–30 v. 6, with cues only for Pss. 23, 26 and 29); f. 77v, blank.

7. ff. 78–94: Prayers as follow: O domine Ihesu christe eterna dulcedo te amancium . . . [*HE,* 76–80]; Gracias tibi ago domine ihesu christe qui voluisti pro redemptione mundi a iudeis reprobari . . . ; *Devota oratio,* O bone ihesu o dulcissime ihesu o piissime ihesu o ihesu fili marie virginis plenus misericordia . . . [Wilmart, *'Jubilus,'* 267–68]; Deus propicius esto michi peccatori et custos mei omnibus diebus vite mee . . . [*HE*, 125]; suffrage of Christopher; *Oratio dicenda quando aliquis accipit sacramentum eukaristie,* Omnipotens et misericors deus ecce ad sacramentum unigeniti filii domini nostri ihesu christi accedo . . . ; suffrage of Barbara; *Utilis oracio et devota,* Domine ihesu christe qui septem verba . . . [Leroquais, *LH* 2:342]; *Oracio multum devota,* Crucem coronam spineam . . . [with versicle, response and prayer; *HE*, 176–77]; *Oracio in honore sancte crucis,* Crux salve preciosa o crux salve gloriosa . . . [with prayer]; *In elevacione corporis christi,* Ecce salutem mundi verbum patris . . . ; ff. 94v–95v, blank.

8. ff. 96–102v: Suffrages of John the Baptist, Thomas of Canterbury, Erasmus, John the Evangelist, the Holy Face; *Oracio dicenda de nocte,* Gracias ago tibi domine sancte pater omnipotens eterne deus qui me dignatus es hac nocte custodire . . . ; *Oracio pro animabus defunctorum,* Avete omnes anime quarum corpora . . . [with versicle, response and prayer:] Domine ihesu christe salus et liberacio . . . [Leroquais, *LH* 2:341].

9. ff. 103–112 [f. 103, blank]: *Oracio ad nostram dominam,* Ave mundi spes maria ave mitis ave pia . . . [*RH* 1974, with versicle, response and prayer]; *Collecta,* Obsecro te . . . [masculine forms; Leroquais, *LH* 2:346]; *De beata maria virgine,* Ave virgo florens rosa semper decens formosa . . . [with versicle, response and prayer]; *De gloriosa virgine maria,* Ave gloriosa virginum regina vitis generosa vite medicina . . . [*RH* 1828]; *Oracio devota,* Stabat mater dolorosa . . . [*RH* 19416]; f. 112v, blank.

10. ff. 113–269 [f. 113, blank]: Psalter with 8-part liturgical division; the psalms which appear elsewhere in the book are given here by cue only; ff. 270–271v, containing Pss. 5, 8 though 7, 17, are misbound and should follow f. 116.

11. ff. 269r–v, 272–284v: Ferial canticles; Te deum laudamus . . . ; Quicumque vult . . . salvus esse non poterit. Anno domini 1478; ff. 285–291v, blank.

HM 1248

Parchment, ff. iii (paper) + ii (modern parchment) + i (contemporary parchment) + 291 + iii (paper); 110 × 74 (75 × 44) mm. Collation for ff. 5–285 (ff. 1–4 and 286–291 are contemporary flyleaves): 1–2^{6} 3^{8}(+1, f. 17) 4^{8} 5–6^{10} 7^{2}(singletons) 8^{10}(+1, f. 56) 9^{2}(singletons) 10^{8}(+8) 11^{10} 12^{8}(through f. 95) 13^{6}(+5) 14^{8}(+1 and 10, ff. 103 and 112) 15^{6}(+1, f. 113; original central bifolium now bound in quire 35 as ff. 270–271) 16^{16}(+17, f. 136) 17^{6}(+1, f. 137) 18^{10} 19^{6}(+1, f. 154) 20^{10} 21^{4}(+1, f. 171) 22^{12} 23^{4}(+1, f. 188) 24^{12} 25^{4} 26^{6}(singletons) 27^{8}(+1, f. 210) 28^{8} 29^{3}(singletons?) 30^{2}(+1, f. 230) 31^{14} 32^{2}(+3) 33^{8}(+1 and 2) 34^{8} 35^{8}(+3 and 4, ff. 270–271) 36^{8}. Catchwords faintly inscribed in the script of the text in the inner corners of ff. 53v, 66v, 87v. 18 long lines; no ruling visible up to f. 112v; thereafter ruled in pale red ink. Written by 2 people, both using a bâtarde script: i, ff. 1–112; ii, ff. 114–284v.

Ten full page illuminations on inserted singletons, blank on the rectos, in semi-grisaïlle in a style derived from Vrelant; the first three in rectangular frames of a gold and color strip with borders of dark grey, painted gold and blue acanthus leaves, flowers and berries, and scattered black dots and small gold balls; the seven remaining illuminations, for the Psalter, are in arched compartments, serrated at the top, and framed by a narrow gold strip; outer border of the same style as above. The miniatures, somewhat worn and flaked off, are: f. 17v (Penitential psalms), Last Judgment with Christ sitting on a rainbow, 2 angels with trumpets in the sky, and Mary and John kneeling below, while the dead rise from their graves; (illumination missing for the Office of the Dead? or now misbound before the Penitential psalms?); f. 56v (Commendation of souls), angels carrying a sheet with 3 small naked souls to God the Father, who blesses from an aperture in the sky; (no illumination before the Psalms of the Passion); f. 103v (Ave mundi spes), the Virgin standing on a crescent and holding the Child, with 4 adoring angels around them; f. 113v (Psalter, Beatus vir), David in prayer, his harp lying on the ground; an armorial shield painted silver in the lower border; f. 137v (Dominus illuminatio mea), David pointing to his eyes; f. 154v (Dixi custodiam vias meas), David kneeling on a path with a road behind him; f. 171v (Dixit insipiens in corde suo), David on his throne with the fool before him; f. 188v (Salvum me fac), David, his hands folded in prayer, waist-deep in water; f. 210v (Exultate deo adiutori nostro), David playing the bells; f. 230v (Cantate domino canticum novum), a group of priests singing before a lectern in a church. Historiated initials in white-patterned grey on cusped gold grounds with full borders, as above: f. 85 (O bone ihesu), 6-line, the baby Jesus sitting naked on a cushion between Catherine and Barbara; f. 88v, 6-line, Christopher fording the river; f. 90, 4-line, Barbara standing beside her tower, which is of her same height; f. 96, 6-line, John the Baptist; f. 97, 6-line, martyrdom of Thomas of Canterbury; f. 98, 5-line, Erasmus with his entrails being wound out of him; f. 99v, 5-line, John the Evangelist with the snaky chalice; f. 100 (Salve sancta facies), 5-line, the Holy Face. Major initials, 6- and 5-line, in white-patterned grey on gold grounds with grey and white trilobe leaf infilling; secondary initials, 2- and 1-line, and line fillers up to f. 112 in burnished gold on blue grounds with pink infilling, or vice versa; after f. 112 (the Psalter), secondary initials in gold on black grounds. Rubrics, only up to f. 112, in orange-tinged red.

Bound by Gruel in red morocco, the doublures inlaid with the covers of an eighteenth century armorial calf binding (see below).

Written in Flanders, dated 1478 on f. 284v, and perhaps meant for export to England, given the English saints in the calendar; the office of the dead may also have been intended to follow the Sarum liturgical use. On f. 1, the signature "Pedro micault" and a prayer; on ff. 1–5, birth and death notices in Flemish of the Micault family, 1581–1600; places mentioned are Brussels, Mechelen (Malines) and Bruges. On the back flyleaves, ff. 286–288, birth and death notices in French of the Micault family, 1510–1606; places mentioned are Brussels, Utrecht, Rome, Valladolid. Added in a space in the calendar, f. 5, s. XVIII, "Ad numeros libris Christiani Geller Parochi in Lebach" (in the Saarland). Arms, s. XVIII^{2}, of "Joannes D[ei] G[ratia] S[acri] R[omani] I[mperii] Princeps Salm Kyrburg Comes Rheni et Sylv." (Rietstap, vol. 5, pl. 233), whose lands were in Westphalia, from the covers of a previous binding, now as pastedowns. Belonged to William K. Bixby (1857–1931) of St. Louis; his bookplate on f. i verso; acquired by Henry E. Huntington through G. D. Smith in August 1918.

Bibliography: De Ricci, 104.

HM 1249 DEVOTIONS

Netherlands, s. XV²

1. ff. 1–28: *Incipiunt centum meditaciones passionis domini nostri ihesu christi,* Eya dei sapiencia domine ihesu christe in qualemcumque vicissitudinem . . . [100 *articuli* divided out through the week, alternating mainly with the prayer "Ave benigne domine ihesu christe gracia plenus misericordia tecum. Benedicta passio wlnera et mors tua et benedictus sanguis wlnerum tuorum. Amen," or sometimes with the Ave Maria].

2. ff. 28–35: *Incipit planctus beati bernardi* [the rubric continues with an indulgence conceded by Urban V], Salve meum salutare, salve salve ihesu care, cruci tue me aptare, vellem vere tu scis quare, da michi tui copiam . . . [in 5-line stanzas; *RH* 18056]; *Ad genua ihesu,* Salve ihesu rex sanctorum, spes votiva peccatorum . . . [*RH* 17989]; *ad latus ihesu,* Salve, salve summe bonus ad percendem vivus provus . . . ; *Ad pectus ihesu,* Salve salus mea deus ihesu dulcis amor meus, salve pectus reverendum cum tremore contingendum . . . [*RH* 18164]; *Ad cor ihesu,* Summi regis cor aveto, te saluto corde leto . . . [*RH* 19737]; *Ad manus,* Salve salve ihesu bone, fatigatus in agone . . . [*RH* 18166]; *Ad faciem ihesu,* Salve ihesu reverende, nunc et semper inquirende . . . [*RH* 17986].

3. ff. 35–43: *Incipiunt quindecim pater noster honore vulnerum christi,* O Ihesu eterne [*sic*] dulcedo te amancium iubilus excedens omne gaudium . . . [the 15 O's of St. Bridget; *HE,* 76–80; at the end, the collect:] Domine ihesu christe fili dei vivi gracias agimus te pro sexaginta quadringentis quinques mille wlneribus . . .

4. ff. 43–52: Papal indulgences as follow: Ave dextera manus christi perforata plaga tristi . . . [Gregory, on the 5 Wounds; *RH* 1771]; O domine ihesu christe adoro te in cruce pendentem . . . [Leroquais, *LH* 2:346]; Deprecor te domine ihesu christe in honorem mortis tue . . . [Callistus]; Salve sancta facies nostri salvatoris, in qua nitet species divini splendoris . . . [John XXII; *RH* 18191]; Ave principium nostre creacionis, Ave primum nostre oracionis . . . [Innocent III at the Elevation; Wilmart, p. 23 and elsewhere]; Anima christi sanctifica me, corpus christi salva me . . . [Benedict XII; *RH* 1090]; Salve tremendum caput cunctis potestatibus nostri salvatoris pro nobis spinis coronatum . . . [Boniface VIII]; Precor te piissime domine ihesu christi per illam eximiam caritatem . . . [Benedict XII; Wilmart, 378, n.]; Mundi creator et redemptor ihesu christi qui ad passionem iturus . . . [John XII].

5. ff. 52–67v: *Oracio beati ambrosii episcopi ante communionem dicendam,* O summe sacerdos et vere pontifex qui teipsum obtulisti pro nobis miseris peccatricibus . . . ; *Ante communionem devota oracio,* Ad mensam dulcissimi convivii

tui domine ihesu christe ego rea et peccatrix immunda . . . ; *Ante communionem,* Ave sanctissimum corpus dominicum in hoc sacramento contentum . . . [Wilmart, 379, n.]; *Oracio beati gregorii pape Ante communionem,* Deus inestimabilis misericordie deus immense pietatis et venie . . . ; *Ante communionem,* Domine non sum dignus ut intres sub tectum meum sed confisus de tanta pietate et clementie . . . ; *Post communionem,* Gracias tibi ago piissime deus quia me ad officium sacerdotale elegisti . . . ; *Oracio de* [*sic*] *beate marie virginis post communionem,* Gracias tibi ago piissima mater misericordie et inclita dei genitrix virgo maria regina mundi . . . ; *Post communionem,* Precor eciam te piissime deus pro omnibus specialibus amicis meis . . . ; *Post communionem,* Pignore salutis eterne corpore sanctum et preciose sanguine tuo domine ihesu christe . . . ; *Post communionem,* O amantissime et piissime domine ihesu christe, Ecce ego assum miser et indignus peccator coram throno . . . ; *Post communionem,* Sanctissimo nomine tuo domine ihesu christe crucifixe creatori et redemptori ac salvatori meo . . . ; *Post communionem,* Agne dei qui tolles peccata mundi miserere michi indigno famulo tuo et parentibus meis . . .

6. ff. 67v–79: *Hanc oracionem beatus augustinus fecit cum angelo et est valde devota oracio,* Domine deus pater omnipotens qui es trinus et unus . . . ; *Beatus augustinus hanc oracionem scripsit* . . . , Deus propicius esto michi peccatori omnibus diebus vite mee . . . [*HE,* 125]; *Oracio valde devota,* Gracias tibi ago domine ihesu christe quia passionem tuam inchoasti potenter . . . [Parkes, *Keble College,* 13, 8, i]; *Oracio de domina nostra,* O gloriosa domina sanctissima virgo maria in sinum tue pietatis . . . ; *Ave maria,* O consolatrix pauperum maria tuis precibus auge . . . ; *Oracio beati augustini ad patrem,* O amantissime pater respice queso tuum dilectissimum filium . . . ; *Oracio beati barnardi ad patrem celestem,* Pater celestis offero tibi unigeniti filii tui domini nostri ihesu christi fratris et redemptoris mei . . .

7. ff. 79v–86: *Incipit rosarium beate marie virginis,* Magnificat anima mea dominum et cetera. Gaude dei genitrix virgo immaculata . . . [*RH* 6757, followed by a collect and a prayer, then the rosary itself: the Ave Marias, each followed by a verse, in sets of 10, then a Pater Noster].

8. ff. 86–102v: *Incipiunt hic quinque dolores beate marie virginis que habuit sub cruce,* O gloriosissima et nobilissima mater dei virgo maria regina celorum et domina mundi, Quantus dolor et compassio fuit tibi . . . ; *Incipiunt hic septem gaudia beate marie que habuit in terris primum,* O gloriosa virgo sancta maria quam ineffabilem graciam apud dominum meruisti . . . ; *oracio thome,* O domina mea sancta maria perpetua virgo virginum mater summe benignitatis . . . [indulgence; Wilmart, 516, n.]; *Hic postula que desideras. Ave.,* Et sicut certa sum quod ille nichil negans te honorat . . . ; *Oracio ad cor beate marie virginis,* Loquar ad cor tuum o maria, loquar ad cor tuum mundum . . . ; *Oracio de domina nostra et de beato iohanne evangelista,* O intemerata et in eternum benedicta . . . Inclina aures tue pietatis . . . et esto michi in omnibus pia auxiliatrix . . . benignissimus paraclitus . . . [Wilmart, 488].

9. ff. 102v–113: *Incipit dictamen egregium beati augustini episcopi de domina nostra de centeno versu,* Salve mater misericordie, mater spei et mater venie . . . [100 verses, *RH* 18032, ending with the collect:] Suscipe domine deus precibus et meritis beatissime semper virginis marie . . .

10. ff. 113–117: *Sequentes tres oraciones revelavit beata virgo maria sancte machtildi ut eas cotidie cum tribus Ave Maria diceret,* Deprecor te gloriosissima virgo maria ut sicut deus pater secundum omnipotencie sue magnificentiam . . . ; *Oracio bona,* Domine omnia tua sunt que in celo et que in terra. Desidero meipsum . . .

11. ff. 117–136: *De sancta trinitate Oratio bona,* O gloriosa trinitas et individua tue tremende maiestati . . . ; *Oracio,* O gloriosa domina sancta maria in sinum me pietatis . . . ; *De proprio angelo,* O preciosissima et nobilissima creatura dei mei angelice species qui ad custodiam fragilis vite mee deputatus es . . . ; *De sancto michaheli,* O sancte michael archangele christi qui potestatem a domino accepisti . . . ; *De sancto iohanne baptista Oracio,* O sancte iohannes lucerna dei ardens qui ab eodem quo dominus angelo nunciatus . . . ; *De sancto petro apostolo,* O sancte petre apostole pastor universe ecclesie . . . ; *De sancto paulo apostolo,* O sancte paule apostole dei vide angustias et tribulaciones meas . . . ; *De sancto andrea apostolo,* O sancte andrea fortissime predicator . . . ; *De sancto iacobo apostolo,* O iacobum minorem virtutibus et signis supplantantem hostem . . . ; *De sancto iohanne apostolo et evangelista,* Gaude iohannes electe fili dei preelecte amoris privilegio . . . , *oracio,* O sancte iohannes dilecte dei apostole rogo te propter familiaritatem quam habuisti . . . ; *De sancto stephane prothomartire,* Ave senior stephane Ave martyr paradoxe . . . ; *De decem milibus martiribus,* O decus sanctorum gloria angelorum eterni regis milites incliti . . . ; *De sancto laurentio martire,* Obsecro te sancte laurenti dux egregie triumphalis exercitus domini . . . , *collecta,* Deus qui beato laurencio levite et martiri tuo per amorem tuum . . . ; *De sancto panthaleone martire,* O candens lilium et dilicatissime flos fulgens adolescens . . . , *collecta,* Adesto quesumus domine supplicationibus nostris . . . ; *De sancto sebastiano martire,* O beate sebastiane magna est fides tua intercede pro nobis . . . , *Collecta,* Omnipotens sempiterne deus qui meritis beati sebastiani martyris tui gloriosissimi generalem pestem epidemie . . . ; *De sancto Augustino,* O doctor eximie dilectissime pater augustine intercede pro me peccatrice que sub specie monastice sanctitatis fallaciter vivo . . . ; *De sancto martino,* Rogo te dilecte sacerdos dei martine ut pro me miserrimo atque scelestissimo . . . ; *De sancto nycolao,* O beate nycolae confessor christi gloriose quem sibi in sacerdotem magnum elige dignatus est . . . ; *De sancto bernardo,* O bernarde sancti spiritus organum atque virtutum speculum posce . . . ; *de sancto rocho,* O lampas ardens in virtute, O speculum pudicitie . . . , *collecta,* Deus qui nos beati rochi confessoris tui meritis et intercessione letificas . . . ; *De sancta katherina,* Gaude virgo katherina quam refulsit lux divina . . . ; *De sancta barbara,* Sancta barbara virgo deo devota que pro fide christi denutata, a ministris fuisti dire flagellata . . . , *Oracio,* Gaude barbara regina summe pollens in doctrina . . . , *collecta,* Intercessio nos quesumus domine barbare virginis ac martiris tue . . . ; *De sancta Agneta virgine,* Sanctissima ac beatissima agnes virgo et martir que terrenum et transitorium repulisti sponsum . . . ; *De sancta ursula,* Salve et gaude O tu vere preciosissima christiane religionis . . . ; *Oracio ad XI mille virginum,* O preclare vos puelle, nunc implete meum velle . . . [*RH* 13425], *vers.,* Orate pro nobis undecim mille virgines . . . , *collecta,* Deus qui affluentissime bonitatis tue prudentia beatissimam ursulam . . . ; *De sancta cecilia,* O Gloriosa virgo et amica filii dei cecilia inclina aures tue pietatis clementer ad me famulum tuum . . . ; *De sancta maria magdalena,* Gaude pia magdalena spes salutis

vite vena lapsorum fiducia . . . ; *De sancta anna,* Gaude felix anna que genuisti prolem . . . , *collecta,* Deus qui beate anne ut mater sancte dei genitricis . . . ; *De sancta elyzabeth,* O beata sponsa christi elyzabeth que meruisti apud regem angelorum . . . ; *De sancto herasmo,* Gaude herasme martyre cristi dilectissime qui die dominico oblatus fuisti . . . , *Collecta,* Deus qui nos beati herasmi martyris tui meritis et intercessione letificas . . . ; *De omnibus sanctis oracio,* Omnes sancti spiritus et anime iustorum et sanctorum dei qui meruistis confortes . . . , *vers.,* Letamini in domino et exultate iusti . . . , *collecta,* Omnipotens sempiterne deus qui nos omnium sanctorum tuorum merita sub una tribuistis commemoratione . . . ; ff. 136v–138v, ruled, and now blank, but visible under ultraviolet light is an added text or words in square capitals, written partially in Latin, partially in French.

Parchment, ff. i (modern parchment) + 138 + i (modern parchment); 117 × 85 (70 × 47) mm. $1–5^8$ 6^8(–6, cancelled by scribe) $7–14^8$ 15^8(–7, cancelled by scribe) $16–17^8$ 19^6(–3, 6). Quires and leaves signed in letters of the alphabet and roman numerals. 17 long lines, ruled in ink with single bounding lines, the first and the last 2 horizontal rules full across. Text set between, not on, the lines. Pricking visible in the outer margin. Written in a cursive, non-looped, Dutch book hand.

Full page borders on ff. 1, 28, 80 of multicolored acanthus leaves, green foliage, colored flowers, black-rayed gold dots, and one bird, with initials on gold cusped grounds respectively as 9-line blue acanthus foliage with elaborate floral infilling, a 5-line dragon, and a 6-line twined stem. Full page borders on ff. 35 and 52 in painted gold with black flecks and scattered flowers; 4-line blue initials on cusped gold grounds with thistle infilling. Similar 6-line initial on f. 94v, with a border of acanthus leaves and rayed gold dots the length of the text. Secondary initials, 4- or 3-line, in gold on a white-patterned blue ground, with floral or white-patterned rose infilling; floral spray in the border with gold dots and tear drops, rayed in black. 2- and 1-line initials alternating red and blue; initials touched with red within the text; rubrics throughout. The text has been carefully corrected; it once had a large number of fore edge tabs, topped by embroidered knots in red, green or blue, of which only 15 survive.

Bound, s. XX, in blue velvet over wooden boards.

Written in the Netherlands in the second half of the fifteenth century. The manuscript may have been copied for a nun, to judge by the use, though not exclusive, of feminine forms; note especially f. 125, the prayer to St. Augustine ". . . intercede pro me peccatrice que sub specie monastice sanctitatis fallaciter vivo . . ." Belonged to the American banker, Beverly Chew (1850–1924), whose library was bought by Henry E. Huntington in 1912.

Secundo folio: (op-)probrium maliciosum
Bibliography: De Ricci, 104.

HM 1250 — France, s. XV^{ex}
BOOK OF HOURS, undetermined use

1. ff. 1–6v: Full calendar alternating red and blue, with gold for major feasts.

2. ff. 7–14: Pericopes of the Gospels, that of John followed by the prayer, Protector in te sperantium . . . [Perdrizet, 25]; *oratio devota,* Obsecro te . . . [masculine forms; Leroquais, *LH* 2:346]; f. 14v, ruled, but blank.

3. ff. 15–66v: Hours of the Virgin of undetermined use [Prime, ant. O admirabile, cap. In omnibus; None, ant. Germinavit, cap. Et radicavi; Vespers, ant. Beata

mater, cap. Beata es virgo]; prayers for health and peace from lauds to compline; hours of the Cross and of the Holy Spirit worked in.

4. ff. 67–79v: Penitential psalms and litany.

5. ff. 80–118: Office of the Dead of undetermined use; the responses to the lessons at matins are: Credo quod; Qui lazarum; Requiem eternam dona; Peccantem me; Ne recorderis; Requiem eternam dona; Subvenite sancti dei; Libera me domine de viis inferni; Libera me domine de morte eterna; ff. 118v–121v, ruled, but blank.

Parchment, ff. iii (ruled, but blank) + 121; 170 × 115 (94 × 53) mm. 1^6 2^8(through f. 14) $3–8^8$ 9^4(through f. 66) $10–15^8$ + unclear structure of ff. 115–121. Evidence of catchwords written in a cursive script in the lower right margin. 21 long lines, ruled in pale red ink. Written in a bâtarde script.

Twelve large miniatures, the width of the page, with the 3 lines of text superimposed as if a label at the bottom of the picture; acanthus leaf border across the width of the lower margin. All but one of the miniatures in half-length close-up, highlighted with fine gold hatching in a style influenced by Bourdichon. The miniatures are: f. 15 (Hours of the Virgin), Annunciation; f. 23 (Lauds), Visitation; f. 32 (Hours of the Cross), Crucifixion with Mary, John and others on Christ's right, the soldiers on his left; f. 33v (Hours of the Holy Spirit), Pentecost, with all the figures concentrated on the right; f. 34v (Prime), Nativity, the Child lying in a wattle basket or manger; f. 41 (Terce), Annunciation to the shepherds; f. 46 (Sext), Adoration of the Magi, with the Child reaching out towards the gift; f. 50v (None), Presentation in the temple; f. 55v (Vespers), a mother showing her dead infant to Herod; f. 61v (Compline), Coronation of the Virgin; the crowned Virgin kneeling in prayer before Jesus who wears a tiara; f. 67 (Penitential psalms), Bathsheba bathing in a fountain decorated with a gold cupid, while David watches from a loggia; f. 80 (Office of the Dead), Job on the dunghill. Small miniatures, 10- to 8-line, by a different artist: f. 7 (Gospel of John), John on Patmos; f. 8, Luke at a desk with the ox and Mary behind him; f. 9v, Matthew holding a book on his knees, while looking at another held up by the angel; f. 10v, Mark; f. 11v (Obsecro te), Virgin and Child, with 4 angels supporting a canopy over them. The double set of miniatures in the calendar represents the signs of the zodiac (45 × 25) and the monthly occupations (35 × 40). Band borders on every page, traced through, with acanthus leaves, flowers, birds or insects or grotesques, all in muted shades of grey, pale blue, pink and gold. Compartmentalized bracket borders on ff. 7, 8, 9v, and 10v with acanthus leaves in the usual blue, gold and colors; the bracket border on f. 11v bears the normal acanthus leaves against a solid gold ground. Major initials, 4- and 3-line, as white leaves with gold infilling on a gold-patterned brick-red ground; 2- and 1-line initials in gold on white-patterned blue grounds, or in blue on gold-patterned red grounds, or as white leaves infilled with a bird or insect against a gold-patterned red ground. Ribbon line fillers in blue and white, or in red and gold, or as gold logs. Rubrics in blue.

Bound in green velvet, rebacked, over wooden boards; gauffered gilt edges.

Written at the end of the fifteenth century in France, but of undetermined liturgical use, with general calendar and litany. On the first front and back flyleaf the same name has been written and crossed out; on the front is also the date "ce 26 Sept. 1811" and several flourishes, all in the same ink as the name. A note in French on the front pastedown discusses text and miniatures. Belonged to Robert Hoe: Grolier Club (1892) n. 24; *Cat.* (1909) pp. 89–90, where it is said to be in a "modern case of brown morocco"; his sale, Anderson, New York, 1912, pt. IV n. 2351 to G. D. Smith. Precise source and date of acquisition by Henry E. Huntington unknown.

Bibliography: De Ricci, 105.

HM 1265 — France, s. XVI^{in}
BOOK OF HOURS, use of Châlons-sur-Marne

1. f. i r–v [added, s. XVI]: [M]issus est angelus gabriel ad mariam virginem desponsatam Joseph nuncians ei verbum Ave maria gratia plena dominus tecum, Missus est gabriel . . . [responsorial prayer; Wilmart, 334 and Leroquais, *LH* 1:95].

2. ff. 1–6v: Calendar in French with importance of feasts indicated by blue or red ink, then that of the text; included are the feasts of Alpinus (2 May, in blue), Memmius (5 August, in red), Alpinus (7 September), Maurilius (13 September), "la dedicasse saint estienne" (26 October, in blue).

3. ff. 7–8v, 10–11: Pericopes of the Gospels; f. 11r–v, continuation of the responsorial prayer from f. i verso.

4. ff. 13–14v: Obsecro te . . . Et michi famulo tuo impetres . . . et pacienciam michi tribuat// [Leroquais, *LH* 2:346, ending defectively].

5. Hours of the Virgin, apparently use of Châlons-sur-Marne (the antiphons at prime and none are Quando natus and Ecce maria genuit; the capitula for both are missing). The book lacks leaves and is misbound, particularly in this section of the text, and should be read as follows: matins: 40, 39, 41–43, 23, 12; lauds: 20–22, 27, 15, one leaf missing, 30; prime: 25–26, 34, one leaf missing; terce: 9, 16, one leaf missing; sext: one leaf missing, 19, one leaf missing; none: 35–36, one leaf missing; vespers: 37–38, one leaf missing; 24; compline: two leaves missing, 29.

6. ff. 44–54v: Penitential psalms and litany, including Memmius, Donatianus, Domicianus, Alpinus, Elaphius and Leodomir among the confessors; Poma among the virgins; one leaf missing between ff. 48–49, containing Ps. 101, 5–24; f. 54r–v, prayer added, s. XVI, in the same hand as on f. i r–v: [M]ediatrix . . . , [A]uxiliatrix . . . , [R]eparatrix . . .

7. ff. 31–32, 17–18, 33, 28, 55–71v: Office of the Dead, use of Châlons-sur-Marne.

8. ff. 72–77v: Prayers as follow: Stabat mater dolorosa . . . [*RH* 19416]; *Oroison devote a la glorieuse vierge marie,* O Tres certaine esperance deffenderesse et dame . . . [Sonet 1538]; *Pape Innocent donna C Jours de pardon* . . . , Ie te prie tres doulce vierge marie, Mere de dieu plainne de pitie . . . a moy qui suis ta familiere . . . [Obsecro te; Sonet 846]; f. 77r–v, completion of prayer from f. 54v: [I]lluminatrix . . . , [A]lleluiatrix . . .

Parchment, ff. i + 77; 168 × 125 (111 × 73) mm. 1^6 2^6(–4) $3–5^4$ 6^6 7^6(–5, after f. 33) 8^6(–4, after f. 37; –6, after f. 38) 9^6(–5, after f. 42) 10^6(–6, after f. 48) $11–14^6$ 15^4(+5, f. 77). Catchwords (ff. 15v and 23v) in bâtarde script written vertically along the inner bounding line. 20 long lines, ruled in brown ink. Written in a gothic script in two sizes.

Eight large miniatures, above 5 lines of text, in arched compartments, with flesh of figures in a greenish tinge; outer border of multicolored acanthus leaves and black ivy spray vines with gold foliage. The miniatures are: f. 40 (Matins of the Hours of the Virgin), Betrayal of Jesus who is being pulled away by a soldier, while Peter sheathes his sword and Malchus kneels beside his lantern; f. 20 (Lauds), Flagellation; f. 25 (Prime), Mocking of Christ by a man to Christ's left who is pulling his mouth into a grimace with his hands; 2 other men, one with his back to Christ's back, press down on the Crown of Thorns; f. 9 (Terce), Christ before Pilate, whose throne is placed outdoors; illumination missing for sext; f. 35 (None), Crucifixion with Mary and John on either side; f. 37 (Vespers), Deposition from the Cross; illumination missing for compline; f. 44 (Penitential psalms), David, in a lavender cut-away church, prays to God the Father who appears in a dark blue opening in the sky; f. 31 (Office of the Dead), Burial scene in a churchyard with an old man standing in the grave and holding the shrouded corpse, while 2 priests and 2 mourners watch. 5-line initials in white-patterned blue or pink on a ground of the other color with infilling of colored trilobe leaves set against a gold ground, and a gold bar forming an outer frame to the initial; 2-line initials in burnished gold with blue infilling and pink ground, or vice versa; 1-line initials alternate plain red and blue; jigsaw line fillers of both colors in the litany. Rubrics in red or, rarely, in blue (f. 19v). Pen trials on ff. 77v and on the facing pastedown (see below).

Bound in very worn blue velvet with 4 holes (for ties?) in the center and edge of both covers.

Written in the early sixteenth century in France, apparently destined for use in the area of Châlons-sur-Marne; the feminine form in the prayer on f. 76 suggests that the first owner was a woman. A note on the back pastedown identifies a sixteenth century owner as Margueritte Morelz. Date and source of acquisition by Henry E. Huntington unknown.

Bibliography: De Ricci, 105.

HM 1313 — Italy, s. XVI[ex]
REPORT ON SWITZERLAND

ff. 1–36v: *Relatione de svizzeri, Bernesi, Grisoni et Vallesani,* Terra de svizzeri è una Regione posta in Germania quasi sul Dorso del mondo . . . senza Capitoli di novita, ma solamente con gl'oblighi et conditioni generali, Laus Domino.

The account is geographical, then historical, canton by canton, and outlines the growth of the confederation. The latest date mentioned is 1552, on f. 36v, discussing a pact between Charles V and the Swiss.

Paper (Briquet, *Arbalète,* 728, Ferrara 1586; another watermark not in Briquet: crossbow within a circle, countermark: 2 C's surmounted by a trefoil, same as in HM 773), ff. 36; 302 × 206 (250 × 130) mm. $1\text{–}2^{10}$ 3^{10}(–8, text is complete) 4^{8}(–8). Catchwords on each verso. 19 long lines with vertical bounding lines produced by folding or dry point. One hand in an italic script, same as HM 773. Contemporary foliation, 1–36, although possibly not by copyist of text. Unbound; but once part of the same volume as HM 773 and 1316; later bound with HM 772, 775 and other materials.

For provenance, see description of HM 772.

Bibliography: De Ricci, 105.

HM 1316 — Italy, s. XVI[ex]
INSTRUCTIONS TO THE AMBASSADOR TO THE COURT OF SPAIN

ff. 1–9v: *Instruttione per negotii nella Corte di Spagna al Signor Ludovico Orsino mandato* [*a*] *Sua Maesta Cattolica dal Signor Duca di Bracciano, la quale puo servire anco per avvertimenti molto utili ad ogni Agente di Principe che habbia da negotiare in quella o in altra Corte,* Perche si conduchino a buon fine tutte le cosse che si trattano in ogni corte . . . Terza, si parlera delli suoi aggi, si per la reputatione, come perche servendo lontano dagli stati proprii, non potra cosi facilmente prevalersi delle sue facolta.

Instructions to Ludovico Orsini, to be sent as Ambassador to Spain by Paolo Giordano Orsini, Duke of Bracciano, who desires the title of "Generale d'Italiani" (f. 9); dating from 1567–79, when Antonio Perez was the Spanish minister in charge of the affairs of Italy (f. 3v). This seems a later fine copy made to win patronage.

Paper (not dissimilar from Briquet, *Arbalète,* 731, but with small mountains as countermark, Laibach 1591, var. ident. Reggio Emilia 1592), ff. 9; 302 × 210 (235 × 130) mm. 1 quire of 8 leaves with an additional leaf at the beginning (possibly the missing last leaf of HM 1313). 20 long lines with vertical bounding lines produced by folding. One hand in italic script, the same as HM 773 and 1313, but more hurried. Contemporary foliation, 1–9, by the same person who foliated HM 1313. Unbound, but once part of the same volume as HM 773 and 1313; later bound with HM 772, 775 and other materials.

For provenance, see description of HM 772.

Bibliography: De Ricci, 105.

HM 1336 — England, s. XV^med
MEDICAL RECIPES, in English — *fig. 109*

1. f. 1: *For ye Emerawdis . . . , For alle maner hote gowtte . . .*

Two medical recipes, possibly the last of a series begun on a previous quire, now missing.

2. ff. 1–2v: *Here begynnyn ye namys of herbis in latyn & also in englis,* Artamessia, Matertera, Mater herbarum [bracketed to:] Moderworte . . .

Latin-English herbal glossary of approximately 130 entries.

3. ff. 2v–18v, 29–34v: *Forto make water of lyne,* Recipe Notmuges glowes galingale ye seed of ye cardmoyn . . . & if you felle it sore ley yerto rotes stampid welle of smalache & do yus tille you be hole.

Approximately 220 recipes in no readily discernible order, giving recipes for the same illness or affliction in various places; included are several non-medical recipes: pigments (f. 3v), an incantation against the "fallynge euylle" (ff. 8v–9), red or green sealing wax (f. 12), a charm against being deceived in the market place (f. 13), rat poison (f. 14), ink and glue for parchment (f. 15), indices to determine if a sick person will die (f. 32).

4. ff. 19–28v: //tak sowþernewode & hony eysel & powne yt togeder . . . *For alle manere brosynge,* nyme persely rote & al & sowrebred//

A quire from another manuscript, beginning and ending defectively, and lacking its center bifolium, now containing approximately 168 recipes, arranged somewhat more systematically than those of art. 3, here proceeding roughly from the head downwards and treating each subject in one place; the latter part of this text lists beneficial herbs and harmful behaviours for different parts of the body; non-medical recipes in this section: indices to determine if a sick person will die (f. 27), rat poison, egg-white ink legible only by candle light, method of preparing eggs so hard that they will not break when thrown against a wall, herbs to make chickens seem dead, means of making a man seem headless, how to make white crows (these 6 on f. 27v).

5. ff. 34v–35: *Of thundrynge in diuerse tymis of ye ȝere,* If it thundire in ye monthe Ianeuere it betoknyth gret wyndis & habundance of fruet & gret batelle . . . If it thundere in ye monthe of decembre it toknith finalle pace & good reste & pese amonge cristen men.

Similar text in M. Förster, "Beiträge zur mittelalterlichen Volkskunde," *Archiv für das Studium der Neueren Sprachen* 128 (1912) 287–88.

6. f. 35: *Howe diuerse ȝeres oftyn fallyn thorw chonging of dais,* If sunday falle on ye kalendes of Ianereuer [*sic*] yat signifieth hot somer . . . If kalendes of Ianeuere falle on saterday copiouse wyndis drie somere dere qwhet diuerse seknesse.

Similar, but shorter text in Förster, p. 295.

7. f. 35: *Good dais to be lat blode,* Hosoeuer blede on ye rith hande ye xvii day of marche . . . also hoso bled on sent lamberte day he xalle not haue ye fallynge euyll god scheld vs yerfro.

8. f. 35r–v: *In ye ȝere arn xxxii perlouse dais,* In qwich if a man falle seke he xalle not liue . . . In ye monthe of Ianeuere i^us^, ii, iiii, v, xv, x, xviii day . . . In ye monthe of Decembre vi, vii, xv day.

Similar text of the *dies nefastae* or *egyptiacae* in W. R. Dawson, ed., *A Leechbook or Collection of Medical Recipes of the Fifteenth Century* (London 1934) 328.

9. ff. 35v–36: *How ye xalle be gouernd euery month in ye ȝere,* In ye monthe of Ianeuere qwhit wyn is good to drynke & blodletynge forebere for ye vii perlouse dais, in ye monthe of feuerere potages of hokkes to etyn is goode . . . and hoso gouerne his yat monthe welle it xalle be gret hele to hym all ye next ȝere folwyng on warentise. *Explicit goode gouernanse quod symon. Nunc scripsi totum pro christo da michi potum. Iste liber constat Roberto Taylour de Boxforde. Omnibus omnia non mea sompnia dicere possum. Quod symon Wysbech scolaris cantabrig. inceptor canonum et legens sive studens in iure canonico. Symon Wysbech studens in iure canonico. Hec predicta scripsit benedicatur deus.* [f. 36v, blank]

Similar text in Dawson, pp. 58–62.

Parchment, ff. i (modern parchment) + i (medieval parchment) + 36 + i (medieval parchment) + i (modern parchment); 216–219 × 145 (167–178 × 110) mm. 1^{10} 2^{8}(through f. 18) 3^{12}(–6, 7) 4^{8}; leaves signed in roman numerals. 30–34 long lines, frame ruled in ink. Written by Symon Wysbech in an anglicana script; 1-line initials beginning art. 2 slashed in red; rubrics, paragraph marks and line fillers in red. Rough sketch of 2 faces, f. 13. In quire 3 (ff. 19–28) of separate origin, no leaf signatures, ruling or red decoration; copied by a different hand.

Bound, s. XIX, in green parchment over pasteboards, gold tooled. Flyleaves, once the wrappers of the book, from a late fourteenth century or early fifteenth century English liturgical book, possibly a missal: "Ite missa est" on the front flyleaf and blessing for meals on the back flyleaf; 208 × 145 (160 × 105) mm., 20 long lines, 2- and 1-line red initials, red decoration along the outer border of the back flyleaf.

HM 1336

Written in England, both the main text and the inserted quire (ff. 19–28), in the middle of the fifteenth century. The main text copied for Robert Taylor of Boxford (Suffolk) by Symon Wysbech, a student of canon law at Cambridge (not identified in Emden, *BRUC*); Wysbech's name and English forms such as "xalle," "qwich" point to East Anglia. On the modern front flyleaf, a description of the manuscript, signed "T" (or "J"?), possibly copied from a bookdealer's catalogue, referring to "Bohn, a former possessor"; this may be Henry George Bohn (1796–1884), the bookdealer, publisher and bibliographer. HM 1336, however, does not appear in his famous "Guinea" catalogue (1841) nor in his sales by Sotheby's, 10 February 1868 or 9 May 1870. Erased inscription, ca. 1900, on the front pastedown, "J.M. Da Costa from B. Coxe." Acquired by Henry E. Huntington from A. S. W. Rosenbach in February 1926.

Secundo folio: lentigo
Bibliography: De Ricci, 105.

HM 1339 England, s. XV[1]
NICHOLAS LOVE, MIRROUR OF THE BLESSED LYF OF JESU CHRIST

ff. 1–105: [Chapter list:] *O*[rubricator's error for *A*]*t þe bigynnynge þe proheme of the Book þat is cleped þe mirour of þe blissed lif ihesu criste. þe firste parte for þe moneday,* A deuoute meditacioun of þe grete counsell in heuene for þe restorynge of man and his sauacioun, capitulum primum . . . [f. 2, first Latin prefatory passage:] Attende lector huius libri, Aput sequitur in anglico scripti quod ubicunque in margine ponitur litera N verba sunt translatoris . . . , [f. 2, second Latin prefatory passage, the approbation of Thomas Arundel:] Memorandum quod circa annum domini Millesimum cccc decimum originalis copia huius libri scilicet speculi vite christi in anglice presentabatur london. per compilatorem eiusdem. Reverendissimo in christo patri et domino Domino Thome Arundel cantuariensi archiepiscopo . . . , [f. 2v, Prologue:] *Quecunque scripta sunt ad nostram doctrinam scripta sunt ut per pacienciam et consolacionem scripturarum spem habeamus ad romanos xv,* Thise be þe wordes of þe gret doctour & holi apostle Poule . . . , [f. 4v, Text:] *A deuoute meditacioun of þe grete consell in heuene for þe Restorynge of man & his sauacioun. Capitulum primum et prima pars libri,* Afftir þe tyme þat man was exiled oute of þe hiȝ cite of heuene . . . with þe to liff euerlastynge Ihesu lorde bi vertue & grace of þi lif blissed withoute endynge. Amen. Amen. Amen. Ihesu lorde þi blissed lif, helpe & conforte oure wrecch[ed lif]. Amen. Explicit speculum v‹leaf damaged› *Drede Shame and Thynkon.* [Some text lost from f. 97 to the end, due to damaged leaves; ff. 105v–107v, blank.]

L. F. Powell, ed., *The Mirrour of the Blessed Lyf of Jesu Christ, a Translation . . . by Nicholas Love.* Roxburghe Club 151 (Oxford 1908); in the introduction Powell thanks Sir Henry Ingilby for the loan of his copy, presumably this manuscript. The edition does not print Arundel's approbation. On f. 2, a biographical note regarding Arundel, s. XVI[1]: "Is primo Eliensis antistes deinde Eboracensis archiepiscopus et anglici regni Cancellarius ad postremum Guilielmo Corteneio qui vix annum pontificatum gesserat in Cantuariensi sede successit. 1415 henrici quinti primo." See E. Salter, *Nicholas Love's "Myrrour of the Blessed Lyf of Jesu Christ."* Analecta Cartusiana 10 (Salzburg 1974) 8 and, for a revised list of the manuscripts, E. Salter, "The Manuscripts of Nicholas Love's *Myrrour of the Blessed Lyf of Jesu Christ* and Related Texts," in A. S. G. Edwards and D. Pearsall, eds., *Middle English Prose: Essays on Bibliographical Problems* (New York 1981) 115–27.

Parchment (varying quality), ff. i (early modern paper) + 107; 280 × 196 (203 × 135) mm. $1\text{–}13^8$ 14^2 (+3, flyleaf). Catchwords in scrolls; quire and leaf signatures as letters and arabic numerals, some worn or trimmed away. 32 long lines, ruled in ink; top and bottom 2 lines full across; pricking visible in outer margins of most leaves. Written in an anglicana formata script; final motto, f. 106, in textura. The same scribe copied Cambridge University Library Mm.5.15 and Oo.7.45, both Nicholas Love manuscripts.[1] 6-line initial, f. 2v, and 4-line initial, f. 4v, each parted red and blue; 4-line blue initial with simple void white design on f. 97; 3- or 2-line initials in blue begin the chapters. Alternating red and blue paragraph marks; running title and marginal notes in the hand of the scribe. Biblical texts underscored in red. Damage due to damp on ff. 97–106.

Bound in limp parchment, adapted from a larger binding, ca. 1600. On front cover: "The Book that is cleped the Mirror of the blissed Life Jesus Criste." On Spine: "No. 13" and "Speculum ⟨?⟩ the life of Jesus Christe."

Written in England in the first half of the fifteenth century. Said by E. M. Thompson, *The Carthusian Order in England* (London 1930) 331 and 339 to have once belonged to Mount Grace because of its later Ingilby ownership; however, the manuscript seems to have entered the Ingilby library at a relatively late date, given the frequence of other sixteenth century ownership notes. Notes and pen trials include: f. 21, s. XV, in plummet, recorded in the 1930s, but no longer visible, "F a mersy quod s"; in the same hand apparently, and only barely visible, f. 36v, "W. Saxy." In late sixteenth century hands are: f. 1v, twice, "Christofer ⟨?⟩"; f. 80, "Thys indenteuer mayd þe xiiii day of fabruary in the xi year of the reayne of oure soferayng lady Elezabeth by the g." (1569); f. 96v, "Wylliam Barkar est verus possessor," "William Barkar ons this booke" 3 times (possibly the Cambridge scholar, William Barker, fl. 1572); f. 97, "Thys Indenture mayd the xxiii day of iuli in the xi day [*sic*] of the reande of our soferyegn lady Quen," and, in a different hand, "Thomas Allyn of ronla ys a good felo ⟨?⟩ honorificatibilitudinitatibus ⟨?⟩" (this same playful word in New Haven, Yale University, Beinecke Library, MS 60, f. 141); f. 106v, "Peter sa <?>"; f. 107, a copy of a receipt in which "Lorances Baynes" is paid for one close for a term of 6 years, to be occupied by "Rychard Stewenson," 18 October 1556. Belonged to Sir William Henry Ingilby (1874–1950); his sale, Sotheby's, 21 October 1920, lot 160; Sotheby's, 30 January 1922, lot 876 to Archer; Sotheby's, 31 July 1922, lot 627 to Maggs; Maggs Catalogue 456 (1924) n. 268. Acquired by Henry E. Huntington from A. S. W. Rosenbach in February 1926.

Secundo folio: [Chapter list] How þat; [f. 3, Text] children haue
Bibliography: HMC, *6th Report, App.* (1877) 355–56. De Ricci, 105.

[1] We thank Mr. Jeremy Griffiths for this information.

HM 1342 — England (?), s. XV^{med}
HISTORICAL MISCELLANY

1. ff. 1v–2v: *Copia littere magni teucri misse domino pape,* Magno sacerdoti romanorum iuxta merita dilectionem. Nuper auribus nostris intonuit quod in partibus italie ad preces et ad postulaciones venetorum in basilicis nostris [*sic*]

facitis publice divulgari quod quicumque sumpserit arma contra nos et nostros suorum in seculo remissionem peccatorum eisque beatam vitam promittitis in futurum . . . intendimus pertransire et septentrionem plagam presertim circa croaciam et dalmaciam visitare. Datum Anno Machameti M° in introitu Mensis Celidon. [f. 3, blank]

The letter protests hostilities of the Venetians against those who descend from the Trojans, progenitors also of the Romans, and against those who accept Christ as a prophet; it threatens war to avenge the loss of Crete.

2. f. 3v: List of the contents of the manuscript, with 3 additions in a later hand: "copia littere magni teucri ad papam in folio precedenti [placed before the original entries]; Item de dedicacione ecclesie Westmonasterii per beatum petrum; Item tractatus de pestilencia orta in Anglia anno millesimo ccc xlviii°" [these 2 entries written at the end of the list, but with a tie mark to their relative position in the manuscript; the treatise on the plague in England was apparently never copied].

3. ff. 4–15v: *Incipit vita Ade,* Post casum luciferi qui superbia inflatus ait, Ponam sedem meam in aquilone . . . [f. 6:] Cum autem Adam et Eva expulsi essent de paradiso voluptatis fecerunt tabernaculum . . . simul cum corpore et anima numquam de cetero morientur sed regnabunt per infinita secula seculorum. Amen. *Explicit vita ade.*

W. Meyer, ed., "Vita Adae et Evae," *Abhandlungen der Münchner Akademie der Wissenschaften,* Philos.-Philol. Klasse, 14.3 (1878) 187–250; S. Harrison Thomson, "A Fifth Recension of the Latin 'Vita Ade et Eve'," *Studi Medievali* ser. 3, vol. 6 (1933) 271–78, printing part of the text from this manuscript. See also M. E. B. Halford, "The Apocryphal *Vita Adae et Evae:* Some comments on the manuscript tradition," *Neuphilologische Mitteilungen* 82 (1981) 417–27, listing 73 manuscripts, including HM 1342.

4. ff. 16–23v: [title added in the margin, *de invencione veronice*] In diebus Tyberii claudii cesaris sub tetracho poncio pilato traditus fuit christus Iudeis . . . ipse regit nos et det nobis adiutorem et perducat nos ad vitam eternam qui es laudabilis et benedictus et gloriosus in secula seculorum. Amen. *Et sic est finis.*

Related by M. R. James, *The Apocryphal New Testament* (Oxford 1924) 159–60 as "Vengence of the Saviour."

5. ff. 24–63v: [title added in the margin, *Gesta Romanorum moralizata*] Pompeyus rex dives et potens valde unicam filiam pulcherrimam habebat . . . et sic eternam coronam finaliter optineamus Quod nobis concedat deus noster iesus christus in secula seculorum. Amen. *Et sic est finis huius.*

H. Oesterley, ed., *Gesta Romanorum* (Berlin 1872); the chapter sequence of this manuscript appears most similar to Oesterley's III, Cod. Götting. Luneb. 46, fol.; see his pp. 16–17. Following the Göttingen chapter numbers, this manuscript is in the following order: 1–6; 8; 7; 9–17; ff. 35v–36v, the moralization alone, relating to the Balance (not the one printed by Oesterley on pp. 331–34); 19–26; 43; 45; 27–29; 33–35; f. 50r–v, unidentified, although beginning in the same manner as 36; 30–32; 36–42; 44; f. 60r–v, unidentified, referring to Alexander; 47–49. See J. T. Welter, *L'Exemplum dans la littérature religieuse et didactique du moyen âge* (Paris 1927) 373 n. to supplement Oesterley's list of manuscripts.

6. ff. 64–65: [added by a different hand] *De dedicacione* [word expunged] *ecclesie Westmonasterii per beatum petrum Apostolum angelis eidem ministrantibus nocte dominica xi kalendis Aprilis Anno domini vi^c^ iiii^to^,* [T]empore quo rex Adelbertus qui regnavit in Cancia predicante beato Augustino fidei sacramenta susceperat . . . mox tam diu artis caruit beneficio donec confessus reatum et ablatum restituerat et promittere correccionem.

Ailred of Rievaulx, *Vita Sancti Edwardi Regis; PL* 195:755–757.

7. ff. 65–67: [added by the same hand as art. 6] *Item de revelacione beati Petri Apostoli ac de Dedicacione ecclesie Westmonasterii et de litteris inclusi cuiusdam ad sanctum et gloriosum regem Edwardum directis,* [E]rat vir quidam dilectus deo et hominibus qui Specu subterraneo multis annis inclusus suorum erat . . . quia non solum ut supra diximus celestis visionis oraculo sed etiam antiquissimi attestacione miraculi istum ei didicit pre omnibus cariorem.

Aelred of Rievaulx, *Vita Sancti Edwardi Regis; PL* 195:752–755.

8. f. 67v: *hii versus scribuntur Rome in porta sancte marie transtiberim,* Roma vetus veteres dum te rexere quirites . . .

Walther, *Initia* 16879.

9. ff. 68–99v: [entitled in the contents list, f. 3v, *Cronica de fundatoribus et mirabilibus Rome*] Sicud dicit orosius in cronica sua quod a mundi creatione usque ad urbem conditam . . . [f. 99v, *De pynea que stabat in Roma,* . . . :] Ita quod a longe quasi aureus mons videbatur cuius pulchritudo ad huc cernitur ad sanctum// [Catchword, "petrum"; f. 100r–v, blank except for the rubric *Indulgentie* at the top of f. 100]

Apparently breaks defectively with the end of this quire. The compilation is mainly of historical nature with at least certain sections derived from the later versions of the *Mirabilia Romae;* it contains: a chronology, a mention of the kingdoms of Babylon, Carthage, Greece and Rome; a history of Rome beginning (f. 70v) with Aeneas; from f. 75 on, a description of Rome discussing: *Muri, Porte, Arcus triumphales, Pontes, Montes, Palatia, Capitolium, Templa* (including the Coloseum as "templum solis"), and *Caballi marmorei;* on f. 82v, a return to the historical material, from the kings of Rome through a relatively long section on the Punic wars; the vision of the Virgin and Child (*Ara Coeli*) shown to Octavianus by the Tiburtine Sibyl; *Cimiteria;* information on the Tiber, including a reference to a flood on 30 November 1422; descriptions of the offices of *Primicerius, Secunderius, Nomenculator, Arcarius, Secellarius* and *Bibliothecarius;* on the Columns of Antoninus and Trajan; on the pine cone said to have covered the opening in the roof of the Pantheon. Orosius is the only source cited by name.

10. ff. 101–113: [list of the churches in Rome with their relics and indulgences] Sanctus Silvester scribit in cronica sua quod Rome fuerunt mille quingente quinque ecclesie . . . in via pelegrinacionis degressu vel ingressu ab omnibus peccatis mortalibus et venialibus veraciter est absolutus. Amen. *Et sic est finis harum indulgenciarum. Deo gracias. Amen.* [f. 113v, blank]

11. ff. 114–132: [entitled in the contents list, f. 3v, *Cronica de translacione Imperii Romani ad almanos*] Multipharie multisque modis dominus universorum in diebus sue carnis dignatus est honorare Romanum imperium . . . [f. 118, lines 9–11] sicud scriptum est oculos habent et non videbunt et cetera.

Sunt quidem temporis huius clerici et layci . . . sic ego nullam puto admiscuisse falsitatem petens veniam cum humilitate de ⟨cancellation⟩ erratis. *Amen deo gracias sic est finis huius voluminis.* [ff. 132v–133v, blank]

H. Grundmann, ed., *Alexander von Roes, De translatione imperii und Jordanus von Osnabrück, De prerogativa romani imperii.* Veroffentlichungen der Forschungsinstitute an der Universität Leipzig (Leipzig 1930). This manuscript lacks the prologue to Jordanus of Osnabrück's treatise and runs straight on into the work of Alexander of Roes, ending incompletely at p. 33 line 25 of the printed text.

12. ff. 134–165v: Section on Catholic hierarchy, broken down as follows: [f. 134: on papal jurisdiction] In urbe Romana sunt Quatuor ecclesie patriarchales sive Cathedrales . . . ; [ff. 134v–137v: list of Christian emperors and kings] Imperatores christiani sunt duo scilicet Imperator Romanorum . . . ; [ff. 137v–139v: list of types of religious orders] Infrascripti sunt ordines Religiosorum per Romanam ecclesiam approbati . . . ; [ff. 139v–165v: Provincial] In civitate Romana sunt quinque ecclesie que patriarchales dicuntur . . . Archiepiscopus Cambaliensis in dominio tartarorum creatus de novo per dominum C. papam quintum. *Et sic est finis huius provinciale.*

The Provincial includes lists of presbiter and deacon cardinals, archbishops with their suffragans, a passage on the dignity of Jerusalem, and a list of bishops of the Holy Land. A slightly variant form of the *Liber Provincialis* appears in Matthew Paris, *Chronica Majora,* RS 57 pt. 6 (1857) 446–63.

13. ff. 166–175v: [Johannes Jacobi, *Regimen contra pestilentiam*] Ad honorem sancte trinitatis ac virginis gloriose et ad utilitatem rei publice ac pro conservacione sanorum et reformacione lapsorum volo aliquid de pestilencia scribere ex dictis medicorum magis autenticorum breviter complilandi [*sic*] . . . Et hec dicta quo ad pestilenciam sufficiant. Ergo si quis ⟨cancellation⟩ se rexerit secundum modum predictum huius morbi contagiosi seu pestilencie periculo evadere poterat Prestante domino nostro ihesu christo sine quo nichil potest fieri qui est benedictus in seculorum secula. Amen. *Et sic est finis.*

Edited, although in a form different from HM 1342, by K. Sudhoff, "Pestschriften aus den ersten 150 Jahren nach der Epidemie des 'schwarzen Todes' 1348. XVIII, Pestschriften aus Frankreich, Spanien und England," *Archiv für Geschichte der Medizin* 17 (1925) 12–139, and especially 23–29. On the authorship of the treatise, see A. Klebs and K. Sudhoff, *Die ersten gedruckten Pestschriften* (Munich 1926) 141–59.

14. ff. 176–187: [Peter of Eboli; title added in the margin, *Nomina balneorum in terra laboris*] *Incipiunt nomina et virtutes Balneorum putheoli et Bayarum sicud in libro decimo Oribasii vetustissimi Medici continentur,* [Prologue:] [I]nter opes operum deus est laudandus in illis . . . [Text:] *De Balneo Sudatorii,* Absque liquore domus bene sudatoria dicta . . . Pauper in augusto nemo poeta fuit/ Ebolei vatis cesar reminiscere vestri [*sic*]/ Ut possit nati scribere facta tui.

For an edition of the text, see J. M. D'Amato, "Prolegomena to a critical edition of the Illustrated Medieval Poem *De Balneis Terre Laboris* by Peter of Eboli (Petrus de Ebulo)," unpublished Ph.D. dissertation, Johns Hopkins University, 1975. For a list of manuscripts, see C. M. Kauffman, *The Baths of Pozzuoli: A Study of the Medieval Illuminations of Peter of Eboli's Poem* (Oxford 1959) 21–22.

15. f. 187v: Diagram of the vices from *Avaricia* to *Dolus.*

Paper with deckle edges (a variety of watermarks, of which the most probably identifiable is Briquet, *Fleur,* 6385, Vicenza 1429; some of the other watermarks may also be Italian); ff. i (modern paper) + 187 (ff. 1–3, contemporary parchment flyleaves) + i (modern paper); 225 × 145 (approx. 140 × 90) mm. Collation beginning at f. 4: 1^{12}(through f. 15) 2^{8}(through f. 23) $3–5^{12}$ 6^{8}(through f. 67) $7–8^{12}$ 9^{8}(through f. 99) 10^{14}(through f. 113) 11^{12} 12^{8}(through f. 133) 13^{10} 14^{12} 15^{10}(through f. 165) 16^{10}(through f. 175) 17^{12}. Catchwords only occasionally present, written horizontally in inner corner. 24–27 long lines, frame ruled in dry point or faintly in lead with single bounding lines; pricking visible in all 4 margins. Possibly as many as 8 cursive hands: i, f. 3v; ii, ff. 4–15v; iii, ff. 16–23 and 134–165v; iv, ff. 24–63; v, ff. 68–99v and 114–132; vi, ff. 101-113; vii, ff. 166–175v; viii, ff. 176–187. Initials, 2- and 1-line, in ink of text, sometimes with cadel decoration; on ff. 24–28, touches of red in the opening initials, initials in the text and lines through the rubrics. The later additions to the text, ff. 1v–2v, 3v, 64–67, 187(note) and other marginalia by at least 2 hands are in an English script; ff. 1v–2v and 64–67 have 32–33 long lines to the page, ruled in lead; the script is a textura quadrata; rubrics in red.

Bound, s. XIX, in English polished brown calf, ruled in blind; same binding on HM 127 and 1343.

Written after 30 November 1422 when a flood of the Tiber, mentioned of f. 99, occurred. The manuscript may have been written in Italy given the watermark and the subject matter, but was in England soon thereafter as shown by the added material in distinctly English hands, some of which pertains to Westminster; it is attributed to Westminster by Ker, *MLGB,* 197, with a question mark. Belonged to Edward Herbert, first Baron Herbert of Cherbury (1583–1648), whose calligraphic monogram, "E" superimposed on an "H," appears on f. 4; his indication of price is on f. 1. He bequeathed his Latin and Greek printed books to Jesus College, Oxford; see C. J. Fordyce and T. M. Knox, "The Library of Jesus College, Oxford," *Proceedings of the Oxford Bibliographical Society* 5.2 (1937) 53–115; the plate following p. 72 shows Herbert's monogram and price notation. Herbert's manuscripts were left to his grandson, Edward, the third Baron; later they belonged to George Charles Herbert, 4th Earl of Powis (1862–1952); his sale, Sotheby's, 20 March 1923, lot 338 to Rosenbach; acquired from him by Henry E. Huntington in February 1926.

Secundo folio: [f. 5, Text] gloria quanto
Bibliography: De Ricci, 106.

HM 1343 France, s. XIV^1
GRAND COUTUMIER, in Latin; DECISIONS OF THE NORMAN EXCHEQUER

1. ff. 1–89v: *Incipit liber de iuribus et consuetudinibus normannorum,* [Second prologue:] Cum ineffrenare cupiditatis malicia humanum genus ardore suo insaciabili teneat irretitum . . . , [f. 1v, Text:] *De iure,* Ius itaque quoddam est naturale . . . [f. 43v:] *Incipit secunda pars huius libri De querelis et legibus,* Post predicta de querelis agendum est et legibus per quas ipse querele habent terminari . . . usque ad quindecimum diem post submonitionem factam. *Explicit textus consuetudinum normannorum.*

The text generally corresponds to that published by E. J. Tardif, *Coutumiers de Normandie,* vol. 2, "La Summa de Legibus Normannie in curia laicali"

(Rouen-Paris 1896, repr. Geneva 1977) 2–341; it contains the end of the chapter "De lege apparenti" and the chapter "De prescriptione" (third family). On ff. 18v–20, the treatise of consanguinity with tables, beginning "Quia tractare intendimus de consanguinitate et eius gradibus de arboribus consanguinitatis exponere ad eius evidenciam pleniorem . . ."; in the margins, by the same scribe as the main text, are decisions of the Exchequers of Falaise, Rouen and Caen, and a few of the Parliament of Paris, dating up to 1299; also in the margins: on f. 68r–v, letter of the prelates of Normandy to Philip Augustus on matters of patronage, for which see A. Teulet, *Layettes du Trésor des Chartes* (Paris 1863–66) 1:310–11, n. 828; on f. 76, ordinance of St. Louis on tithes (here, March 1279) and the relative document of Philip IV (1294), for both, see *Ordonnances des Roys de France de la Troisième Race,* vol. 1, ed. E. J. de Laurière (Paris 1723) 102–03 and 325.

2. ff. 89v–97v: Decisions of the Exchequers of Falaise, Rouen and Caen, 1207–1237.

Similar groups of texts edited by L. A. Warnkoenig, *Französische Staats- und Rechtsgeschichte* (Basel 1848) 2:70–119.

3. ff. 98–100v: Proceedings of the assize of Rouen, 1205.

Cf. Léchaudé d'Anisy, "Grands rôles des Echiquiers de Normandie," *Mémoires de la Société des Antiquaires de Normandie* 15 [1841?] 151–68.

4. ff. 100v–101v: [added by another hand, in French] Exchequer, session of Michaelmas, 1282, and in Rouen, 1291.

5. ff. 101v–102v: [added by the same hand as art. 4; first prologue and chapter list:] Cum nostra sit intentio in presenti opere iura et instituta normannie in quantum poterimus declarare . . . et eius que pertinent ad ipsam reprimendam. *Capitula prime distinctionis prime partis hec sunt,* De iure, De iurisdictione . . . De lege desrasnie, De legibus.

First prologue, printed by Tardif, *op. cit.,* pp. 1–2. The chapter list in this manuscript lacks 2 headings of chapters which are in the text: "de officio senescalli" (in the text, ff. 3v–4v, between "de iusticiario" and "de officio vicecomitis") and "de exercitu" (in the text, ff. 17v–18v, between "de forisfacturis" and the treatise on consanguinity, followed in turn by "de successione").

Parchment, ff. i (modern paper) + 102 + i (modern paper); 220 × 160 (155 × 103) mm. $1–12^8$ 13^6. Catchwords in lower right corner, enclosed in frames, usually retraced in red; quires and leaves signed in red with letters of the alphabet and roman numerals; an arabic "2" marks the beginning of the second half of the quire. 2 columns of 27 lines, ruled in lead with single bounding lines, and all horizontal lines full across. Pricking visible in upper and lower margins, slash form. Text written between, not on, the lines. Written in a gothic book hand.

Space reserved, f. 1, ca. 90 × 120 mm., presumably for a miniature. Opening initial, f. 1, 5-line, parted blue and pale green with red leaf filigree as infilling; secondary initials, 2-line, alternating red with purple penwork or blue with red; alternating 1-line red and blue initials in the chapter list. Red rubrics and paragraph marks throughout. On ff. 19–20, 2 columns of 48 lines; on ff. 19v–20, tables of consanguinity. Guide letters and rubrics in black ink in a noting hand in the margins have not been erased.

Bound, s. XIX, in English polished brown calf, ruled in blind; same binding on HM 127 and 1342.

Written in France in the first half of the fourteenth century. Belonged to Edward Herbert, first Baron Herbert of Cherbury (1583–1648), whose calligraphic monogram, "E" superimposed on an "H," appears on f. 1, along with the indication of price. He bequeathed his Latin and Greek printed books to Jesus College, Oxford; see C. J. Fordyce and T. M. Knox, "The Library of Jesus College, Oxford," *Proceedings of the Oxford Bibliographical Society* 5 pt. 2 (1937) 53–115; the plate following p. 72 shows Herbert's monogram and price notation. His manuscripts were left to his grandson, Edward, the third Baron; later they belonged to George Charles Herbert, 4th Earl of Powis (1862–1952); his sale, Sotheby's, 20 March 1923, n. 199 to A. S. W. Rosenbach; acquired from him by Henry E. Huntington in February 1926.

Secundo folio: quod dicitur
Bibliography: De Ricci, 106. *Legal Manuscripts,* n. 4.

HM 1344 — Flanders, s. XVI^in
BOOK OF HOURS, Sarum use

1. ff. 1–12v: Full calendar, including the feasts of David (1 March), Chad (2 March), Erkenwald (30 April, in red), Crown of Thorns (4 May), John of Beverley (7 May), Etheldreda (23 June), "Festum nivis" (5 August, in red), Transfiguration (6 August), Holy Name (7 August), Etheldreda (17 October), Frideswide (19 October), Winifred (3 November), Translation of Erkenwald (14 November), Osmund (4 December); erasures at 5 January, 29 December (Thomas of Canterbury) and of the qualifier "pape"; Latin month verses at the end of each month [Walther, *Initia* 8953].

2. ff. 13–17 [f. 13, blank]: Pericopes of the Gospels, that of John followed by the prayer, Protector in te sperantium . . . [Perdrizet, 25]; f. 17v, ruled, but blank.

3. ff. 18–33v [f. 18, blank]: Passion according to John; *These prayers folewynge ought for to be sayde or ye departe out of your chamber at your uprysynge. De sancta trinitate,* Auxiliatrix sis michi trinitas sancta deus in nomine tuo . . . me indignum famulum tuum N. . . . ; *Whan thou goost firste oute of thy house blysse the saynge tus,* Crux triumphalis domini nostri ihesu christi ecce vivifice crucis . . . ; Deus qui tres magos orientales . . . [short version of *HE,* 75]; *Ad crucem,* Crucem tuam adoramus et veneramur . . . [de la Mare, *Lyell Cat.,* 372, n. 75]; *Whan the prest tourneth after the lavatorye,* Spiritus sancti gratia illustret et illuminet . . . [de la Mare, *Lyell Cat.,* 398, n. 395]; *At the levacion of oure lorde,* Anima christi sanctifica me . . . [Leroquais, *LH* 2:340; for the succession of this and the 2 preceding prayers, see Lyell MS 30, f. 307v]; *Whanne thou entrest in to the church say thus,* Domine in multitudine misericordie tue introibo . . . [beginning as in Ps. 5, 8]; *Whan thou takest holy water say thus,* Aqua benedicta sit michi salus . . . ; *Wan thou begynnest to pray say thus knelynge,* Discedite a me maligni . . . ; O bone ihesu tu novisti et potes et vis bonum anime mee . . . ; Ascendat ad te domine deus oratio mea . . . ; *Pro carnali dilectione,* Domine libera animam meam a carnali dilectione . . . ; *Pro temptacione carnis,* Domine ihesu christe rex virginum integritatis amator . . . ; *Pro vera penitencia oratio,* Omnipotens sempiterne deus precor te ut non permittas me perire . . . ; *hora prima,* Domine deus qui nos ad principium huius diei pervenire fecisti . . . [through the hours of the day]; *Oratio sancti*

augustini in nocte, Deus pater noster qui ut oremus hortaris . . . ; *Oratio sancti anselmi,* Domine deus meus si feci ut essem reus tuus . . . ; Pater noster qui es in celis . . . ; Ave maria gratia plena . . . ; Credo in deum patrem omnipotentem . . . ; Confitebor tibi domine ihesu christe . . . ; Suscipere dignare domine deus omnipotens has orationes quas ego indigna peccatrix decantare desidero . . . ; *Whan thou resceyvest the pax say thus,* Da pacem domine in diebus nostris . . . ; *Whan thou shalt receyve the sacrament,* Domine non sum dignus ut intres sub tectum meum sed tu domine qui dixisti . . . ; *Whan thou haste receyved,* Vera perceptio corporis et sanguinis tui . . . ; *To gete grace for syn,* Exaudi quesumus domine supplicum preces et confitencium . . . ; *Ayenst evyll thoughtes,* Omnipotens mitissime deus respice propicius ad preces nostras . . . ; *For the kynge,* Deus regnorum christiane maxime protector imperii da servo tuo N. regi nostro de hoste triumphum . . . ; *For thy frendes lyvynge,* Deus qui iustificas impium . . . ; *For wayfaringe men,* Adesto domine supplicationibus nostris et viam famulorum tuorum . . . ; *For frendes in sekenes or in necessite,* Omnipotens sempiterne deus salus eterna credentium exaudi nos pro famulo tuo seu pro famula tua N. . . . ; *For thy fader and moder deed,* Deus qui nos patrem et matrem honorare precepisti . . . ; *For thy frende dat is dede,* Suscipe piissime deus in sinu patriarche tue abrahe animam famuli tui N. . . . ; *For all lyvynge and dede,* Omnipotens sempiterne deus qui vivorum dominaris simul et mortuorum . . .

4. ff. 34–72v [f. 34, blank]: *Incipiunt hore beate marie virginis secundum usum sarum;* suffrages after lauds of the Holy Spirit, the Trinity, the Cross, Michael, John the Baptist, Peter and Paul, Andrew, John the Evangelist, Lawrence, Stephen, Thomas of Canterbury (cancelled), Nicholas, Mary Magdalene, Catherine of Alexandria, Margaret, Many Apostles, All Saints, for peace; hours of the Cross worked in; following compline are the Salve Regina, the set of versicles, Virgo mater ecclesie . . . and the prayer, Omnipotens sempiterne deus qui gloriose virginis et matris marie . . . [*HE,* 62–63].

5. ff. 72v–111v: Prayers as follow: Gaude virgo mater christi que per aurem concepisti . . . [*RH* 7013], and the prayer, Deus qui beatissimam virginem mariam in conceptu . . . [*HE,* 64]; Gaude flore virginali honoreque speciali . . . [*RH* 6810] with the prayer, Dulcissime domine ihesu christe fili dei vivi qui beatissimam gloriosissimam humilem benignam et pulcerrimam virginem mariam matrem tuam . . . [*HE,* 66]; De profundis clamavi . . . with versicles and prayer; O Intemerata . . . orbis terrarum. Inclina mater misericordie . . . et esto michi miserrime peccatrici . . . [Wilmart, 488–90]; *Alia oratio,* Sancta maria dei genitrix semperque virgo benedicta . . . [*HE,* 68]; *Oratio de virgine maria,* Obsecro te . . . et michi famule tue impetres . . . [Leroquais, *LH* 2:346]; Sancta maria regina celi et terre mater domini nostri iesu christi . . . ; Stella celi extirpavit . . . [*RH* 19438] with versicle, response and prayer, Deus misericordie deus pietatis deus indulgentie qui misertus es . . . ; *Ad elevationem corporis christi salutatio,* Ave verum corpus natum de maria virgine . . . [Wilmart, 373–76]; Ave ihesu christe verbum patris filius virginis . . . [Wilmart, 412]; In presentia sacrosancti corporis et sanguinis tui domine iesu christe tibi commendo me miseram famulam tuam N. . . . [*HE,* 71–72]; *oratio,* Domine ihesu christe qui hanc sacratissimam carnem . . . [Wilmart, 378, n.]; Sancta trinitas unus deus . . . [*HE,* 72]; Deus qui superbis resistis et humilibus das gratiam . . . [*HE,* 72]; Deus qui liberasti susannam de falso crimine . . . [*HE,* 73]; Domine ihesu

christe qui me creasti . . . [*HE*, 73]; Domine ihesu christe qui solus es sapiencia tu scis que michi peccatrici expediunt . . . [*HE*, 73]; Rex iaspar, rex melchior, rex baltasar rogo vos per singula nomina . . . , with versicle and prayer, Deus illuminator omnium gentium . . . [*HE*, 74]; Trium regum trinum munus christus homo deus unus . . . , with versicle and prayer, Deus qui tres magos orientales . . . [*HE*, 74–75]; O Domine iesu christe eterna dulcedo te amancium iubilus . . . [the 15 O's of St. Bridget; *HE*, 76–80]; *To all them that before the ymage of pyte devoutly say* . . . , Adoro te domine ihesu christe in cruce pendentem . . . [Leroquais, *LH* 2:346, in the order 1–2, 4–7, 3], with versicle and prayer, Benignissime domine iesu christe respice super me miseram peccatricem . . . ; *Dominus papa sixtus quartus composuit* . . . , Pie crucifixe redemptor omnium populorum . . . propicius esto michi peccatrici et exaudi preces famule tue . . . , followed by 5 prayers referring to the wounds of Christ, each ending "super me N. peccatrice," and with the final prayer, Deus qui voluisti pro redemptione mundi nasci et circumcidi a iudeis reprobari . . . [*HE*, 82–83]; *Sequitur oratio sancti bernardini confessoris ordinis minorum,* O bone iesu, o dulcis iesu, o iesu fili marie virginis . . . propicius esto michi peccatrici . . . [Wilmart, 'Jubilus']; O rex gloriose inter sanctos tuos . . . , with versicle and prayer, Deus qui gloriosissimum nomen iesu cristi . . . [*HE*, 84–85]; Sanctifica me domine iesu christe signaculo tue sancte crucis . . . [de la Mare, *Lyell Cat.*, 62]; *Antiphona,* Angele qui meus es custos . . . [Wilmart, 554–58, with versicle and prayer, Deus qui sanctorum angelorum tuorum . . . , and O sancte angele dei minister celestis imperii . . . [Wilmart, 552 and 581]; suffrages of James the Greater, James the Less, Sebastian, Christopher, George, Martin, Anthony abbot, Francis, Anne, Barbara, the 11,000 Virgins, Apollonia, All Saints; *A devoute prayer in englysshe,* O gloriosus iesu, o mekest iesu, O most swettest iesu, I pray the tha I may have true confession . . . [*HE*, 85]; O the moost sweteste spouse of my soule crist iesu desiring hertely evermore for to be with the . . . [*HE*, 86]; *Iste orationes debent dici in agonia mortis per sacerdotem pro infirmo in mutando verba. Et quilibet potest dicere pro semetipso sicut hic stat. Et dic primo kirieleison,* . . . , *Oratio,* Domine iesu christe per agoniam et orationem tuam sanctissimam . . . , *Tercio dic,* . . . et me famulam tuam . . . ; *oratio,* Domine iesu christe qui redemisti nos precioso sanguine tuo scribe in anima mea . . . ; *Oratio ad patrem,* Pater de celis deus miserere nobis. Domine sancte pater omnipotens eterne deus qui coequalem . . . , Domine iesu christe fili dei vivi qui es verus . . . , Domine spiritus sancte deus qui coequalis . . . [to the Trinity; *HE*, 124–25]; *Oratio bona cotidie dicentibus revelatione divina transmissa uni monaco de bynhym circa annum domini M.cccc.lxxxv* . . . , Deus propicius esto michi peccatrici et esto custos mei omnibus diebus vite mee . . . [*HE*, 125]; *Ad sanctum gabrielem oratio,* Precor te et princeps egregie gabriel fortissime . . . [Wilmart, 580]; *Oracio ad sanctum raphaelem,* Auxiliare michi et tu princeps obsecro eximie raphael . . . [Wilmart, 580–81]; Benedicat me imperialis maiestas . . . [*HE*, 88]; A [*sic*] blyssed trinite fader sonne ond holy goost, thre persones and one god, I byleve with myn herte . . . [*HE*, 86–87]; O lorde god almightye all seynge all thynges knowynge wysdome and sapyence of al, I poore synner . . . [*HE*, 87–88].

6. ff. 112–128v [f. 112, blank]: Penitential psalms, gradual psalms (cues only of the first 12), and litany, including Edmund, Denis, Maurice and Gereon among the martyrs; Edward, Albanus, Swithun, Birinus, Erkenwald, Dunstan and Cuth-

bert among the confessors; Afra, Edith, Osyth, Winifred, Frideswide, Gertrude, Othilia, Bridget, Ursula and Wilgefortis among the virgins; *Sequuntur versiculi sancti bernardi,* Illumina oculos meos . . . [*RH* 27912]; Ihesu fili dei omnium conditor . . . [3 prayers, each with a Pater noster and an Ave Maria]; *Oratio,* Omnipotens sempiterne deus parce metuentibus . . . ; Peto domine ihesu christe largire michi in amore tuo . . . ; Domine iesu christe ego cognosco me graviter peccasse . . . ; *Oratio,* Deus qui culpa offenderis . . .

7. ff. 129–149 [f. 129, blank]: Office of the Dead, Sarum use, with variations for the liturgical year.

8. ff. 149–159: Commendation of souls (Pss. 118, divided into sections, and 138) with the prayer, Tibi domine commendamus animam . . . ; Avete omnes anime fideles . . . [Leroquais, *LH* 2:341]; *Oratio ad sanctam crucem,* Salve salve rex sanctorum . . . [*RH* 18170]; Salve salve iesu bone . . . [*RH* 18166]; f. 159v, ruled, but blank.

9. ff. 160–167v: Psalms of the Passion (Pss. 21–30, 6; here all in full); Respice quesumus domine super hanc familiam tuam . . . ; Interveniat pro nobis domine ihesu christe apud tuam clementiam . . . ; *Oratio,* Beati iohannis apostoli tui et evangeliste quesumus domine deus noster nunc et in hora mortis nostre . . . [these 3 as one prayer, *HE,* 115]; Ave benigne ihesu gratia plenus misericordia tecum . . . [*HE,* 116].

10. ff. 167v–177v: Psalter of St. Jerome: *Beatus ieronimus hoc modo disposuit* . . . , Verba mea auribus percipe . . . , and the prayer, Dona michi queso omnipotens deus ut per hanc sacrosanctam psalterii celestis melodiam . . . [*HE,* 116–23].

11. ff. 177v–183: *Oratio ad sanctum ieronimum antiphona,* Ave amator quam famose . . . , with versicle and prayer, Deus qui gloriosum confessorem tuum ieronimum . . . ; *Oratio sancti gregorii pape,* Dominator domine deus omnipotens qui es trinitas in filio [*sic*] . . . [*PL* 101:589–591]; *Incipit rosarium beate marie virginis,* Ave maria gratia plena . . . ; f. 183v, ruled, but blank.

Parchment, ff. iii (modern parchment) + 183 + iii (modern parchment); 215 × 160 (126 × 90) mm. 1–2^6 3^8(+1, f. 13 and 6, f. 18) 4^8 5^4(–4) 6^8(+1, f. 34 and 7, f. 40) 7^8 8^6(+1, f. 52, and 5, f. 56 and 8, f. 59) 9^6(+2, f. 62 and 5, f. 65 and 8, f. 68) 10–14^8 15^8(+3, f. 112) 16^8 17^8(+3, f. 129) 18–23^8. 20 long lines, ruled in pale red ink. Written in a gothic book hand.

Twelve full page illuminations of mediocre quality on the verso of inserted singletons, blank on the recto, except for 6 lines of text on f. 40. Full borders on the miniature page and the facing text page usually of naturalistic flowers, birds and insects against a thin yellow-gold wash. The miniatures are: f. 13v (Gospel of John), John on Patmos, the eagle holding his pen case, with a vision of the Virgin and Child on a crescent in the sky; in the lower margin, John in the pot of oil; f. 18v (Passion according to John), Man of Sorrows sitting on the inner edge of the tomb with the emblems of the Passion around him; historiated margins on ff. 18v–19 depict Gethsemane, Betrayal, Christ before Pilate, Flagellation, Mocking of Christ, Road to Calvary and Veronica, Nailing to the Cross, and Pietà; f. 34v (Hours of the Virgin), Annunciation; in the margins of ff. 34v–35, the tree of Jesse; f. 40v (Lauds), Visitation; f. 52v (Prime), Nativity; in the margins of ff. 52v–53, gothic architecture with a peasant dance across the lower border of f. 52v; f. 56v (Terce), Annunciation to the shepherds; f. 59v (Sext), Adoration of the Magi, one of whom is black; in the margins of ff. 59v–60, gothic architecture; f. 62v (None), Presentation in the temple; f. 65v (Vespers), Massacre of the Innocents; f. 68v (Compline), Flight into Egypt, with the miracle of the cornfield in the background; f. 112v (Penitential psalms), Last Judgment with Christ sitting on a rainbow, Mary and John on either side and, below them, the resurrection of the dead and a hell-mouth; f. 129v (Office of the Dead), Raising of Lazarus; in the borders on ff. 129v–130, gothic architecture forming compartments containing skulls or hooded monks. Small miniatures, 7-line, with C-shaped strewn borders: f. 15, Luke; f. 15v, Matthew with a compartmentalized border filled with naturalistic flowers; f. 16v, Mark; f. 24v (to the Trinity), Gnadenstuhl; f. 75 (O Intemerata), Mary and John at the foot of the cross; f. 149 (Commendation of souls), an angel protecting the small naked soul of a dead man from the devil; f. 160 (Psalms of the passion), Jesus kneeling in prayer on the cross, his hands tied together, while God the Father watches from above; f. 168 (Psalter of St. Jerome), Jerome beating his chest with a rock before a crucifix, with the lion beside him; f. 178 (Prayer of St. Gregory, Dominator domine), Mass of St. Gregory; f. 180v (Rosary), Mary and Child on a crescent in a mandorla formed of the beads of a rosary. Major initials, 5-line, as brown or dark green branches against variously colored grounds; that on f. 35 (Hours of the Virgin) in white-patterned blue with red and gold infilling against a brown and gold ground. Secondary initials, 2- and 1-line, in shaded white leaf patterns against a gold-decorated terra cotta ground; ribbon line fillers in the same colors. Rubrics in pale red.

Bound, s. XIX, by Riviere in black morocco, decorated with various tools, gold dots and circular inlays of light brown morocco; gilt edges.

Written in the early sixteenth century in Flanders for export to England; a number of feminine forms (ff. 31, 75v, 78v, 82, 84v, 92v, 93, 95v, 106v, 108v) indicate that it was intended for a woman. Obtained by Henry E. Huntington from A. S. W. Rosenbach in 1926.

Bibliography: De Ricci, 107.

HM 1345 THEOLOGICAL MISCELLANY

England, s. XIV^in^

1. ff. 1–17: *Incipit epistola Bede in librum de ymagine mundi,* Septiformi spiritu in trinitatis fide illustrato . . . *De ymagine mundi liber i^us^,* Mundus dicitur quasi undique motus . . . Sed nos temporis volubilitatem postponamus ad evi stabilitatem dei gratia mente tendamus. Amen. Explicit. *Hec sunt capitula precedentis libri,* De ymagine mundi, i; De quinque zonis ii . . . De celo, xiiii.

Honorius of Autun, *De imagine mundi,* Bks. 1 and 2. *PL* 172:119–165.

2. ff. 17–19: Secundus fuit philosophus qui philosophatus est omni tempore silencium tenens . . . quia secundus philosopharetur tacens precepit eius libros sacre bibliotece inseri et intitulari. Explicit vita secundi philosophi de greco in latinum translata a magistro Willelmo medico nascione provinciali quam secum a constantinopoli detulit qui postea factus est monachus in cenobio sancti Dionisii et demum preficiebatur abbas eiusdem loci.

B. E. Perry, ed., *Secundus, the Silent Philosopher.* Philological Monographs 22 (Ithaca 1964) 92–100. On the Life of Secundus and on the Latin translation by William le Mire, see P. O. Kristeller and F. E. Cranz, eds., *Catalogus translationum et commentariorum* . . . (Washington, D.C. 1971) 2:1–3.

3. f. 19r–v: Annus ab origine mundi usque ad incarnacionem domini, v̄ Cxix; Annus ab Incarnacione domini, M° cci; Annus a passione domini, M° cc lxxii;

HM 1345

A prima successione fidei christiane misse in britanniam lucio Regi ab eleutherio papa, M° c xxi . . . ; Anniversaria a bissexto, iii; Annus indictionis, xiii; Ciclus decemnovenalis, xv . . . ; Tres filii Noe regnum inter se diviserunt . . . Aquitannia, Britannia, Hybernia, Austraua [*sic*].

Chronological table of important dates in English history and of computistic information, with many inconsistencies, evidently composed ca. 1310, followed by a brief account of the 3-part division of the world and a list of the provinces in each.

4. ff. 19v–40: *Transcripta testamentorum xii patriarcharum. Et primo testri* [*sic*] *Ruben de hiis que in mente habebat de vii spiritibus,* Transcriptum testamenti Ruben quecumque mandavit filiis suis . . . et habitaverunt in egipto usque ad diem exitus eorum ex terra egypti et cetera. [added, s. XVI[ex], in the same hand as arts. 11, 14] Finis testamentorum 12 patriarcharum.

Stegmüller 87, 7. *PG* 2:1038–1150. S. Harrison Thomson, *The Writings of Robert Grosseteste* (Cambridge 1940) 42–44, listing HM 1345.

5. ff. 40–46v: *Incipiunt Capitula de naturis Rerum,* De quadrifario opere dei, *i;* De mundi formacione, *ii* . . . Divisio terre, *xlix* [f. 40v:] *Incipiunt excepta que Beda ex libris plinii secundi de naturis rerum extraxit; primum capitulum de quadrifario opere dei,* Operacio divina que secla creavit et gubernat quadriformi ratione distinguitur . . . Atque inde affrica a meridie usque ad occidentem extenditur.

Bede, *De natura rerum. PL* 90:187–278. M. L. W. Laistner, *A Hand-List of Bede Manuscripts* (Cornell University Press 1943), recording HM 1345 on p. 143. P. O. Kristeller and F. E. Cranz, eds., *Catalogus translationum et commentariorum* . . . (Washington, D.C. 1980) 4:303 n. 12.

6. f. 46v: Regnum scottorum fuit inter cetera mundi/ Terrarum quondam nobile forte potens . . . hostibus expulsis iudicis usque diem. Explicit.

Song on the Kings of Scotland; see Ward, *Cat. of Romances* 1:327. J. Pinkerton, *An Enquiry into the History of Scotland* (2nd ed., Edinburgh 1814) 1:501–02, here lacking the last 14 lines of the printed text.

7. ff. 47–97: [title added, s. XV:] *Lucidarius. Gloriose magister rogo ut ad inquisita michi ne pigriteris respondere ad utilitatem* [*sic*] *dei et utilitatem ecclesie.* Equidem faciam quantum vires ipse dabunt [*sic*] . . . [f. 63v:] hoc in sompnis ymaginatur et in timore positus per tristiciam modificatur. *Quid est quod parturiente thamar unus ex filiis qui in utero eius erant manum foras misit capite clauso in ventre,* Hoc significabat quod non dum nato christo patriarche et alii boni operati sunt bene . . . [f. 92v:] perfecto nichil obstat qui tota te ipso prophetia dicta fuerit [remainder of column left blank; f. 93:] *Duo.* Magister. In ea etate in qua assumpti sunt qui etiam ab antichristo . . . Si enim aliquid Plus cuperent plenum gaudium non haberent. *Explicit liber iste.*

Honorius of Autun, *Elucidarium,* pr. in Y. Lefèvre, *L'Elucidarium et les Lucidaires.* Bibliothèque des Écoles Françaises d'Athènes et de Rome 180 (Paris 1954) 361–452, 453–472, with a long interpolation on ff. 63vb–92vb containing questions and answers on the liturgy and sections on the liturgical seasons from Rogationtide, through Ascension, Pentecost, Trinity, 24 Sundays after Pentecost, Advent, on the mass, on the Jews. This manuscript is of the family that answers the question on the nature of free will, "libertas eligendi bonum vel malum" (f. 56b).

8. ff. 97–103v: *De captione Ierosolimitani et antiochie a christianis,* Anno millesimo xc^{mo} vi^{to} facta est motio ierosolimitana predicatione urbani pape . . . [f. 101:] Hoc etiam anno descessit osmundus episcopus salebyrie [*sic*]. *Liber i^{us} editus ab henrico archidiacono hundendunense anno gracie M^{o} c^{o} xxxv^{to} directus ad alexandrum Lincolniensem episcopum De situ britannie,* Britannia igitur beatissima est insularum . . . quam unam inter ceteras deus ab exordio linguarum instituit mirandum videtur.

T. Arnold, ed., *Henrici Archidiaconi Huntendunensis Historia Anglorum.* RS 74 (London 1879) 219–32, 5–13 for Bk. 7, chapt. 5–21, Bk. 1, chapt. 1–8.

9. ff. 103v–107v: *Epistola de serie bruduum directa Regi henrici primo,* Eneas igitur Romani generis auctor genuit ascanium . . . Quorum si prolixitatem desideras librum grandem Galfridi arturi quem apud lecium [*sic*] inveni queras ubi predicta diligenter et prolixe tractata videbis.

Apparently Henry of Huntingdon, *Historia Anglorum,* Bk. 8, ep. 2, although here addressed to Henry I, rather than to Warinus; not printed by Arnold, but see pp. xix–xxiv.

10. ff. 107v–111: *Hec est prophecia merlini ambrosii,* Sedente itaque vortegerno rege britonum super ripam exhausti stagni egressi sunt duo dracones . . . Confligent venti diro sufflamine et sonitum inter sydera conficient. *Explicit expliciat ludere scriptor eat.*

A. Griscom, ed., *The Historia Regum Britannie of Geoffrey of Monmouth* (New York 1929) 384–97, for Bk. 7, chapt. 3–4.

11. f. 111v: [note added, s. XVI^{ex}] *In chartula quadam Patris, carmina quaedam a Merlino scripta,* Draco maximus et fidelis in potentissimo brachio . . . et tandem cum Rege, ut Cedar, venerabitur.

12. ff. 112–184: *Incipit breviloquium de virtutibus antiquorum philosophorum,* Quoniam misericordia et veritas custodiunt regem et roboratur clemencia thronus eius. Prov. 20. Immo iiii^{or} virtutes cardinales . . . serenitas sine nube ad quem diem festum nos deducat qui cum patre usque modo operatur et parat amen. *Explicit liber iste.*

John of Wales, *Breviloquium.* Glorieux, 322b. Bloomfield, *Virtues and Vices* 4971.

13. f. 184: [added, s. XIV^{med}] Post consumati sunt dies octo. Si vus dirai un conte petit de une seint home que out a nonn seint benet qui se fu done del tout a deu . . . tentacion le dyable. [f. 184v, ruled, but blank]

French version of Gregory I, *Dialogues,* 2, 2 of the temptation of St. Benedict by the black bird and the beautiful woman; for the Latin, see *PL* 66:132.

14. f. 185: [2 index notes added, s. XVI^{ex}] Mos Saxonum in puniendis luxuriosis, fol. 161; Quae necessaria pro religiosorum castitate servanda, f. 170.

15. f. 185v: [added, s. XIV] Quinque modis a domino flagellantur homines . . . ; *Quatuor sunt mortes et quatuor vite,* Prima mors anime in peccatis . . . resuscitari ad vitam vel a viciis ad virtutes. [added, s. XVI:] Finis breviloquii.

16. ff. 186–198v: *Incipit liber magistri hugonis de sancto victore,* [Prologue:] Quia fratres largiente domino de vana conversacione huius seculi . . . [f. 186v, Text:] *Quibus modis invenitur scientia recte vivendi,* Primum igitur scire debetis quod hanc scientiam . . . bonitatem vero orate ut vobis det deus. Amen.

HM 1345

Hugh of St. Victor, *De institutione novitiorum. PL* 176:925–952. See Goy 2.2.5.1 (pp. 340–67), this manuscript recorded as n. 143.

17. ff. 198v–214: *Incipit liber claustralis magistri Hugonis de sancto victore,* Congruum nobis videtur edificia fratrum . . . solve vincula colli tui. Tolle grabatum et ambula. *Explicit liber claustralis.*

Hugh of Fouilloy, *Liber de claustro animae. PL* 176:1053–1104, here in abbreviated form.

18. ff. 214v–217: Prima ala confessio est non laudis unde Confitemini domino quam bonus et cetera sed criminis . . . celestia appetens et requiescam vera libertate eterna et fruens beatitudine. Amen.

Clement of Llanthony (?) or Alan of Lille (?), *De sex alis cherubim. PL* 210:273–280. Bloomfield, *Virtues and Vices* 4055.

19. ff. 217–224: [Brief exegetical texts] Ieronimus, An nescitis quia corpora nostra templum sunt dei. Si quis templum dei violaverit . . . ; Petrus accepit romam in sua sorte, andreas achaiam . . . ; Locutus est dominus ad moysen dicens descende in egyptum, dic pharaoni dimitte populum meum ut sacrificet michi in deserto. Ex egypto vocavi filium meum. Tria loca esse ex sacre scripture erudicione cognovimus . . . ; Sic autem commedetis agnum, renes vestros accingetis, calciamenta habeatis in pedibus, tenentes baculos in manibus, commedetis festinanter. Verba fit moysi in exodo immo domini per moysen ad papam isrealeticum. De hoc agno hic fratres loquitur de quo ait Iohannes baptista . . . ; Cantemus domino Gloriose enim magnificatus equum et ascensorem proiecit in mare. In hoc versiculo moysi tria continentur, primum est quod deus equum . . . ; Dum complerentur dies pentecostes erant omnes disciputi pariter in eodem loco et cetera. Singulorum que in ecclesia geruntur cognitio fidelibus est facienda pro eorum capacitate . . . ; Fratres christus assistens pontifex futurorum bonorum. De quibus confidens psalmista aiebat Credo videre bona domini in terra vivencium . . . ; Dominicis diebus resurrectionis duo alleluia canimus, unum de percepta leticia . . . ; Post baptismum manet originale peccatum in puero superatum et peremptum nisi illicito consensu . . . Nisi dominus cor illustraverit auditorum doctor in nocte laborat.

20. ff. 224–227: *Ieronimus de membris domini nostri,* Omnipotens deus et pater et filius et spiritus sanctus. Unus atque trinus est, unus fidelis [*sic*] in natura, trinus in personis. Solus invisibilis . . . et ultionem inimicorum se manifestum demonstrare.

Eucher of Lyon, *De formulis spiritualis intelligentiae. PL* 42:1199–1206.

21. ff. 227–231v: [7 texts:] Paulus dicit. Eundum est de fide in fidem. Sunt enim multe partes fidei. Est enim principium et fundamentum christiane fidei ut credamus patrem . . . ; Fratres karissimi cuilibet christiano mittendum [?] est ad hoc ubi in se talem mansionem edificet . . . ; Si quis ad ea profecit quod fidem habet tunc obnixe rogandus est deus ut det caritatem . . . ; Fundamenta iam collato parietibus in altum constructis restat extremus labor disponendi tectum. Contra bestias enim muniti sumus . . . ; Dominus dixit vetustissima veterum comedetis et nova venientibus vetera eicietis. Vetustissima veterum vocat deus scilicet ut cognoscamus unitatem in trinitate . . . ; David futuram spiritu previdens liberavit inquit dominus pauperem a potente cui non erat adiutor. Non omni est scientia. Ignoravit aliquid pauperem istum . . . ; Ante

diem festum pasche sciens ihesus quia venit hora eius ut transseat de hoc mundo ad patrem, cum dilexisset suos qui erant in mundo in finem dilexit eos. Iohannes evangelista ait de christo filio marie appropinquante die transitus sui ut deus qui omnia novit . . . quos in finem dixisti pro quibus misericorditer mori voluisti qui cum domino patre nostro vivit et regnat per omnia secula seculorum amen.

22. ff. 231v–233v: Sicut miles temporalis armis temporalibus munitus est sic miles spiritualis debet munitus esse . . . Valde itaque ut prediximus sunt necessaria spirituali militi sua arma.

Alexander of Canterbury, "Similitudo militis." *PL* 159:702–707 under Eadmer, *Liber de sancti Anselmi similitudinibus.*

23. ff. 233v–234: [3 texts, the first, of 13 lines, run on without break after art. 22:] Ideo septimale in ecclesia pro defunctis celebratur per tres dies ut quod per tres proprietates anime scilicet racionem maledictam . . . ; Est superbia cordis Superbia oris superbia operis . . . ; Opera trinitatis individua sunt. Opponitur soli filio convenit assumpsisse carnem . . . sed soli patri convenit quia solus pater significatus est per ea que fiunt. *Explicit liber iste.*

24. ff. 234–257v: [Prologue:] Primi parentes generis humani per culpam primam . . . [f. 234v, Text:] Nupcie facte sunt in chana galilee et erat ibi ihesus cum maria matre eius. Chana interpretatur zelus . . . quam largitur immutabiliter et summus bonus deus conversatur et non peribit. *Explicit liber iste.*

Richard of St. Victor, *Allegoriae in Evangelia. PL* 175:751–767, 789–828 under Hugh of St. Victor, but here in quite different order, the manuscript ending with chapter 3, col. 810.

25. ff. 257v–260v: *Hic incipit summa de penitencia abreviata per sanctum Augustinum,* Notandum quod vii sunt criminalia peccata scilicet inanis gloria . . . [f. 260v:] *Isti sunt excommunicandi sed non extra ecclesiam ponendi,* Pro istis autem peccatis tenes extra ecclesiam penitentes . . . culpa parentum vii annorum est iii diebus//

Bloomfield, *Virtues and Vices* 3441, here ending defectively.

Parchment, ff. i (medieval parchment) + 260 ("7" skipped in foliation) + i (early modern paper); 222 × 162 (183 × 120) mm. $1–9^{12}$ 10^{14} $11–14^{12}$ 15^{14} $16–17^{12}$ 18^{16} 19^{14} 20^{12} 21^{12}(–10, 11, 12). Catchwords in yellow-tinted frames. 2 columns of 41 lines, ruled in lead, top and bottom 3 lines full across, triple lines between the columns, narrow double rule in the outer and lower margin. Written in a conservative littera textualis (numerous ampersands).

Parted red and blue initials, 4-line, infilled with cross-hatching and void designs of leaves or grotesques, and with flourished extensions in both colors (e.g. ff. 198v, 214v, 234); secondary initials, 3- and 2-line, in alternating red and blue with flourishing of the other color through f. 133, thereafter initials only in blue with red flourishing; initials within the text touched in yellow; red and blue paragraph marks; nota bene marks in the hand of the scribe; rubrics usually in red, but sometimes underlined in yellow. Foliation, s. XV, in arabic numerals. On f. i verso: [list of contents, s. XVI^{in}; altered, s. XVI^{med}] Contenta: Beda de ymagine mundi, folio primo; Vita secundi philosophi, 17°; Transcripta testamentorum xii patriarcharum, fol. 19; Excerpta Bede de libris plinii de naturis rerum, 40°; Lucidarius id est questiones de theologia et missa, et cetera, 47; Liber de situ Britanie editus a magistro henrico Archidiacono huntyngdonensi, 101; Epistola eiusdem de serie britonum missa regi Henrico primo, 103; Ex valerio maximo et aliis compositum; Breviloquium de virtutibus antiquorum philosophorum, 112°. A fragment, France, s. XIII^{in}, of an expanded version of the commentary on Lucan's *Pharsalia,* Bk. 6.321–409, by Arnulf of Orleans, once loose in HM 1345, now shelved separately as HM 47937.

HM 1345

Bound, s. XVII, in English brown calf stamped in gold with Ley arms (Rietstap, vol. 4, pl. 58) on both covers; red sprinkled edges.

Written in England in the early fourteenth century. Belonged to the historian Sir James Ley, first Earl of Marlborough (1550–1629). On f. i, the date, 1811, and the signature of John J. Conybeare (1779–1824), Oxford professor of Anglo-Saxon. Belonged to William Loscombe; sale of Clifton Wintringham Loscombe, Sotheby's, 19 June 1854, n. 1155 to Upham for Bertram Ashburnham, 4th Earl of Ashburnham (1797–1878); in his "Appendix," n. CXI, with that number in arabic numerals on a yellow circular label on the spine. The Ashburnham "Appendix" sold privately to Henry Yates Thompson (1838–1928) in May 1897; the manuscripts he did not wish to keep were sold at Sotheby's, 1 May 1899, this manuscript lot 60 to Quaritch. Quaritch Cat. 193 (1899) n. 29. Acquired by Henry E. Huntington from A. S. W. Rosenbach in February 1926.

Secundo folio: sunt non
Bibliography: De Ricci, 107.

HM 1346 England, s. XIV[1]
BOOK OF HOURS, Sarum use *fig. 68*

1. ff. 1–6v: Calendar, with major feasts in blue, secondary in red, and lesser in ink of text; the entries of the most important feasts have been traced over in gold; note the feasts of Cuthbert (20 March), Augustine of Canterbury (26 May, in red), Boniface (5 June, in red), Albanus (22 June, in red), Etheldreda (23 June, in red), Translation of Thomas of Canterbury (7 July, in red), Translation of Cuthbert (4 September), Translation of Edward confessor (13 October, in red), Frideswide (19 October, in red), Edmund archbishop (16 November, in blue), Edmund king (20 November, in blue); entries added in a later hand are: "Sancti Dunstani archiepiscopi. Obitus domini Johannis de Clifford militis" (19 May), and "Obitus thome de schobholl Anno domini M CCC lxv [?]" (17 July).

2. ff. 7–84v: Hours of the Virgin, Sarum use, missing the opening leaves of matins (before f. 7), lauds (before f. 22), terce (before f. 55), none (before f. 65), vespers (before f. 69) and compline (before f. 77); suffrages after lauds of the Holy Spirit, the Trinity, the Cross, Michael, John the Baptist, Peter and Paul, John the Evangelist, Edmund king and martyr, Lawrence, Stephen, Nicholas, Mary Magdalene, Catherine of Alexandria, Margaret, All Saints, for peace; after compline are the Salve Regina and the prayer, Omnipotens sempiterne deus qui gloriose virginis et matris marie corpus et animam . . . [*HE,* 62–63].

3. ff. 85–118v: Penitential psalms, gradual psalms and litany, including Edmund king, Oswald, Albanus, Denis and Maurice among the martyrs; Dunstan, Hilary, Martialis, Leonard, Maurus and Botulph among the confessors; Etheldreda, Sexburga, Anne, Anastasia, Mildred, Thecla and Frideswide among the virgins.

4. ff. 119–184v: Office of the Dead, Sarum use; one leaf missing before f. 131 with loss of text.

5. ff. 185–186: [added, s. XIV–XV] Un apostolie fu iadis ke out une mere ke mout fu tenu par prode femme de tote gent . . . en la manere cum vous avez fet serrunt sauvez. Dieu seit gracie. *Oratio,* Deus qui es nostra redemptio in terra promissionis . . .

A version of this trental printed from MS Ff.6.15 by P. Meyer, "Les Manuscrits français de Cambridge," *Romania* 15 (1886) 236–357, esp. pp. 282–83; the prayer for deliverance of the soul and the Holy Land printed by R. W. Pfaff, "The English Devotion of St. Gregory's Trental," *Speculum* 49 (1974) 75–90, esp. pp. 82–83.

6. f. 186v: [added, s. XIV–XV, in a different hand from above] *Les advousouns que sonnt en les mayns mon sieur le c. de D.*, iii portionns en l'esglise de Dodsam, l'esglise de Sotton Courtenay . . . [listing 35 churches, chapels and chantries, mainly in Somersetshire and Devonshire, with a few in Berkshire such as Sutton Courtenay; 3 are later additions]; *Les Advousouns des esglises que serraunt en les mayns mon sieur le count,* . . . [lists another 3].

7. f. 187: [added, s. XV^{in}] *Prophecia hermerici ab origine mundi vi m D xxxvi.* Est hermericus in historia almannorum sicut merelinus in historia Britanorum. Lilium in meliori parte annis multisque remanebit et veniet in terram leonis . . . et filius hominis accipiet signum mirabile et transibit ad terram promissionis. *Exposicio eiusdem hermerici:* Lilium Rex Francie, leo Flandria, Filius leonis dux Flandrie . . .

A version of the prophecy of the Lily, the Lion and the Son of Man is printed by J. H. Todd, *The Last Age of the Church by John Wyclyffe* (Dublin 1840) p. lxxxiv; see also Ward, *Cat. of Romances* 1:314, *passim;* and R. Taylor, *Political Prophecy in England* (New York 1911) 61, n. 21.

8. f. 187v: [added, s. XV^{in}, in the same hand as the prophecy] Ces sont les pointz par out le Pape Iohannes [XXIII] feu deposez par la generalle conseille c'est a ssavoir par ses Cardinals legats et cubiculers la veille de corpus christi l'an du grace M CCCC xv . . . Item que le dit Pape enpoisona les deux Antecessers c'est a ssavoir Innocentz et urban.

Parchment, ff. ii (early parchment) + 187 + ii (early parchment); 190 × 115 (113 × 72, measurement of the ruling immediately surrounding the written space) mm. 1^{6} 2^{12}(–1) 3^{12}(–5) 4^{10} 5^{8} 6^{12}(–9, before f. 55) 7^{12}(–8, before f. 65) 8^{12}(–1, before f. 69 and –10, before f. 77) 9^{6}(through f. 84) $10–11^{12}$ 12^{10}(through f. 118) 13^{12} 14^{12}(–1, before f. 131) $15–17^{12}$ 18^{8}(through f. 185) ff. 186–187, contemporary flyleaves. Catchwords in the script of the text (ff. 38v, 165v) or in a small noting hand (17v, 28v, 141v) and usually covered by the decoration. Leaf signatures, when present, in varying systems: ff. 32–33, slashes (roman numerals?) in the far right corner; ff. 58–63, letter of the alphabet and roman numerals; ff. 97–102, roman numerals within a space formed by the ruling; ff. 131–135, roman numerals in the center lower margin. 12 long lines, with complex ruling which includes horizontal rules for the text, bounding lines around the text space, a narrow ruled strip in the 3 outer margins and additional rules at the outer edge of all 3 outer margins; all ruling, both horizontal and vertical, is formed of 2 parallel lines, pink and green. Pricking in the intersections of the marginal strips, but no longer present in the outer margins. Written in a gothic book hand, set between the rules.

Five historiated initials survive (presumably of an original 11), to some extent mutilated by effacing and by slashing with a knife: opening leaves of matins and lauds, before ff. 7 and 22 respectively, missing; f. 47 (Prime), 7-line, Christ before Pilate, but all the faces are completely scraped off; opening leaf of terce, before f. 55, missing; f. 60 (Sext), 6-line, Crucifixion, the face of a kneeling figure at the right is scraped, and the leaf bears a large Y-shaped knife slash; opening leaves for none, vespers and compline, before ff. 65, 69 and 77 respectively, missing; f. 85 (Penitential psalms), 7-line, by a more capable artist, Christ enthroned holding globe and blessing, slashed with a knife; f. 103 (Gradual psalms), 5-line, a figure, kneeling before an altar, prays to God who appears above; the face of the figure is obliterated; f. 119 (Office of the Dead), 7-line, Funeral mass with a woman watching; slashed by a knife; f. 137 (the first lesson of the Office of the Dead), 2-line, a face. 2-line initials in white-decorated blue or pink on grounds of the other color, filled with colored trilobe leaves on a gold ground. 1-line initials in gold against blue or pink grounds and infilling of the other color. Ribbon line fillers in blue, pink, gold and orange-tinged red decorated with geometric designs, trilobe leaves or grotesques. Rubrics in red. Full borders on all pages: up to f. 38v (end of quire 4), they consist of cusped pink and blue segments across the top and the sides, with a large grotesque forming the lower border; from f. 39 on at the occurrence of a 2-line initial, the borders are of pink and blue segments in bracket form, with the fourth side given by a single-strand colored vine; after f. 38v, pages without 2-line initials have full borders solely of the single-strand colored vine. 2 coats of arms and various grotesques or decorative elements across the lower margin of every page. The borders in the calendar consist of wide bands broken by medallions of faces in the outer border, and of the monthly occupation and signs of the zodiac in the lower margin; birds perch along the cusping of the outer border, which terminates in a grotesque in the upper right corner; one coat of arms in each lower border of the calendar.

Bound in old black leather over bevelled wooden boards.

Written in England in the first half of the fourteenth century; it has been suggested that the "count de D." on f. 186v is to be identified with Edward Courtenay, Earl of Devonshire (d. 1419). See J. Backhouse, *The Madresfield Hours* (The Roxburghe Club, 1975), especially Appendix, pp. 30–33, for a list of 24 other books of hours made for English owners between about 1240 and the middle of the fourteenth century (this manuscript not listed). On the front pastedown, a square label bearing, within a blue circle, the pressmark "A. III. 72." Quaritch Gen. Cat. (1880) n. 8557; Howell Wills sale, London, 1894, n. 375 to Quaritch. Quaritch catalogues: 144 (1894) n. 33; 149 (1895) n. 11; 154 (1895) n. 167; 193 (1899) n. 173; 211 (1902) n. 62. Belonged to George Clifford Thomas (1839–1909); his *Catalogue* (Philadelphia 1907) p. 33. Obtained by Henry E. Huntington from A. S. W. Rosenbach in February 1926.

Bibliography: De Ricci, 108.

HM 1548 ANONYMOUS, PORTOLAN CHART

Italy, s. XV[ex]

Nautical chart of the Mediterranean area, including Europe with British Isles and part of Scandinavia.

Parchment, f. 1 (full skin), 675 × 810 (660 × 810 including extension to the right) mm. Borders are triple ruled in black and red on top and bottom only. Black and red ink for nomenclature in a minuscule hand; land masses outlined in black ink (Ireland overtraced in green, Scotland in pale red, traces of ocher on other coasts) with islands painted gold, green, red or blue; no compass roses, instead the symbols for the 4 principal directions are inscribed on two rhumb line intersections, one on the upper and one on the right sides; several rhumb line patterns, some with 32 lines, many only partial; a simple latitude scale numbered from 24° to 54° N (scale appears to have been added later since it is drawn over portions of islands in the Atlantic and seems to be in another hand), no longitude; 2 unnumbered scales of distance (drawn in conjunction with upper and lower borders); simple decoration with a few vignettes of cities, banners, and one large figure, little color.

Unbound: formerly mounted on a roller, now flattened in a modern portfolio.

Probably made in northeastern Italy (Venice?), judging from linguistic characteristics, and possibly before 1492, since map appears to precede Spanish reconquest of Granada. Sold in 1867 by Henry Stevens (1791–1867) to Henry Huth (1815–78), *The Huth Library* (1880), pt. 4, 1171. Sale of Alfred Henry Huth (1850–1910), Sotheby's, 11 July 1917, pt. VI, n. 5913 to G. D. Smith for Henry E. Huntington.

Bibliography: De Ricci, 108. J. E. Kelley, Jr., "The Oldest Portolan Chart in the New World," *Terrae Incognitae* 9 (1977) 38–39.

HM 1549 — Lisbon, ca. 1600
LUÍS TEIXEIRA, PORTOLAN CHART

Nautical chart of Mediterranean area, including Europe with British Isles and portion of Scandinavia.

Parchment, f. 1 (full skin), 595 × 950 (557 × 920 including extension at left) mm. Border is red band outlined in black. Black and red ink for nomenclature in a minuscule hand with area names in display script; Mediterranean Sea, Black Sea coasts and Scotland outlined in red ink, other Atlantic coasts colored green, with islands painted gold, green, red or blue; 15 elaborate compass roses, 7 with the symbols for the 8 wind directions; usual 32 rhumb line network in black, red and green ink for the principal directions; latitude scale numbered from 20° to 63° N, no longitude; 2 distance scales on borders and 2 within body of the map, all unnumbered; highly decorated with colorful vignettes of cities, banners, coats of arms and with a crucifix on the left extension.

Unbound: formerly mounted on roller, now flattened in a modern portfolio.

Inscribed on a scroll "Por Luis Te[ixe]ira em Lix[bo]a." Sold in 1867 by Henry Stevens (1791–1867) to Henry Huth (1815–78), *The Huth Library* (1880), pt. 4, 1171. Sale of Alfred Henry Huth (1850–1910), Sotheby's, 11 July 1917, pt. VI, n. 5914 to G. D. Smith for Henry E. Huntington.

Bibliography: Cortesão, *Cartografia*, 2:271–72. De Ricci, 109. *PMC*, 3:63 with reproduction on pl. 361.

HM 1555 — Germany, s. XV^{med}
ANTIPHONAL

1. ff. 1–99v: Temporale from vespers before the first Sunday of Advent to lauds of Holy Saturday.

2. ff. 100–112: Sanctorale, for the Immaculate Conception, Conversion of Paul, Purification, Chair of Peter and Annunciation.

3. ff. 112v–133v: Common of saints.

4. f. 133v: Responses of the office of the Dead, ending defectively.

Parchment, ff. ii (modern paper) + 133 (and a small tipped-in leaf, foliated 120, as is the following full leaf) + ii (modern paper); 309 × 225 (253 × 175) mm. 1–14^{8} 15^{8}(+8, f. 120) 16^{8} 17^{6}(–6). Catchword in a noting hand in the inner margin of f. 8v. 10 lines of text and music. Double vertical bounding lines in red ink, a single bounding line full across the bottom; the upper line of the top staff forms the top boundary line of the written space. Slash prick marks in the 3 outer margins. Music on red 4-line staves. Written in a gothic liturgical book hand. On f. 1, opening initial for Advent, 45 × 55 mm., in blue with simple void pattern and red flourishing; secondary initials in plain red or as cadels in the ink of the text filled in red. In later hands: foliation in early form arabic numerals, except for 100, designated as "C"; hymns and verses numbered in arabic numerals in the margins; marginalia, including on f. 58v, "Maria mutter königin mutter der bahrmhertzigkeit." Running titles added, s. XVII.

Bound, s. XVI, in German white pigskin over bevelled wooden boards, stamped with panels of full length allegorical representations of the Virtues, and of Renaissance foliage; evidence of 4 bosses, front and back; 2 fore edge clasps of leather and brass, back to front; red leather fore edge tabs; modern marbled endpapers.

Written in Germany in the middle of the fifteenth century. In the lower margin of f. 1, the stamp "G.W.B.D." of Hugo, Graf von Waldbott-Bassenheim (1820–95) who acquired many manuscripts from the Carthusians of Buxheim; his sale, Munich, 20 September 1883, n. 2381 (German sale catalogue slip affixed to the front pastedown). Synder collection. Date and source of acquisition by Henry E. Huntington unknown.

Secundo folio: (benignita-)tem et terra
Bibliography: De Ricci, 109.

HM 1727 — Flanders, s. XVI$^{2/4}$
MEDITATIONS ON THE PSALMS, in Flemish — *fig. 152*

1. f. 1: Portrait; f. lv: Monogram of two facing and overlapping C's crossing an I.

2. ff. 2–173v: [f. 2, Prologue:] *Prologhe* Aengesien die psalter des coninclijken prophetes Dauids, enen onwtsprekelijken ende costelijken schat is inden welcken Christus handelinghe, cracht, werckinge, lof ende heerlijcheyt sijns rijcx . . . , [f. 3v, Psalter] *Om een oprecht Christen leeuen Beatus vir Psalmus i,* O Almoghende Heere der heyscharen, mij een alderghenaedichste godt doer Jesum Christum uwen enighen soone ende een alder goetgunstichste vader . . . [f. 172v, *Een ghemeyn ghebet Laudate domino Psal. cl,* O Lieue Heere ende Godt wij loouen v in v seluen:] . . . O Heere al wat asem heeft moet v loouen ghij die haerder alder leeuen sijt maer der ghelouighen eewighe leeuen door Jhesum Christum onsen Heere met welcken ghij heemelsche Vader tsamen met den heyligen Geest een Godt sijt ghedanct ende gheloost in der ewicheit. Amen.

See C. C. de Bruin, "Bijdrage tot de geschiedenis der Middelnederlandse psalmenvertaling," in *Bundel opstellen van oud-leerlingen, aangeboden aan C. G. N. Vooys* (Groningen 1940) 46–74, and the editions in *Verzameling Middelnederlandse bijbelteksten* (Leiden); psalms have Hebrew numeration.

3. ff. 174–205: [Excerpts from Proverbs and Ecclesiastes on the theme of a good wife] *Proverbiorum i capittel,* Die vreese des Heeren is een beghinsel der wijsheyt. *Proverbiorum 2 capittel,* Ist dat ghij die wijsheyt aenroept ende v hertte neycht nae der voersichticheyt. Eest dat ghij haer soect ghelijck die schatten. Als dan suldij die vreese des heeren verstaen ende Gods kennisse

vinden . . . Maer bouen deese beyde, is te prijsen een eerbaer vrouwe. Mijn kint alle den tijt ws leeuens en schickt v niet te bedelen: want het is beeter te steruen dan te rabbauwen, oft te bedelen.

4. f. 205r–v: [Closing Prayer] *Een schoon ghebedeken,* Dontfermherttighe Heere ghij hebt mij gheheeuen dat ick een Christen ben gheworden sonder alle mijn verdienste . . . soe houdt mij nochtans bij den Euangelio ende v goddelijck woert Amen.

5. f. 205v and back flyleaf i: Prayers added in a contemporary noting hand.

Parchment, ff. iii (contemporary parchment) + 205 + iii (contemporary parchment); 100 × 70 (80 × 50) mm. 1^4(+1, the portrait) 2^2 $3–22^8$ 23^8(–7, 8, after f. 173) $24–27^8$. 15 long lines ruled in pale brownish-red ink. Written in a late hybrida script. On f. 1, a portrait of excellent quality (French?), 62 × 54 mm., of a woman with delicate features, holding a flower, the usual indication of a wedding portrait; in the upper corner, "Etatis 32." Opening initial, f. 2, 5-line, in gold arabesques on a patterned blue ground, enclosed by a simple gold frame; 2-line initials in gold or white on rose, brown, green or blue grounds, patterned in gold; 1-line initials within the text slashed in red; punctuation and rubrics in red; light blue-grey paragraph marks. Numerous attractively colored gesticulating hands in the margins, as many as 3 to an opening, to call attention to underscored sections of the text.

Bound, s. XVIII, in German calf.

Written in Flanders in the second quarter of the sixteenth century; "Anno 1478" is written in a contemporary hand on the front flyleaf i verso and on the back flyleaf iii. The first owner was probably the woman whose portrait is on f. 1; on f. 1v, the initials of her name or of her motto. The book may have been a wedding gift. Purchased by Henry E. Huntington in September 1926 from R. Koehler of Portland, Oregon.

Bibliography: De Ricci, 110.

HM 1729 — France, s. XVI^ex
STUDENT NOTEBOOK

1. [ff. 1–2v, blank except for name "Andreas Gruellius" on f. 1; f. 2r–v, ruled] ff. 3–187: *praefatio in laudem eloquentiae, In cipriani zoaris rhetoricam annota, 1587,* Quod philosophorum illi princeps homerus et quasi quidam dens apolinis . . . [f. 8v, Text:] *de nomine rhetoricae,* Quoniam ut scribis aristoteles . . . firmitatis. *Finis.* [f. 182:] *Tabula in cipriani zoaris rhetoricae annotationes, A,* Artis significatio eiusque aceptio, 13; ars non cadrat in rhetoricam, 13 . . . Virtus quid, 61; Vitiosum in exordio quid, 110. *Finis tabulae.*

Notes, presumably on the *De Arte Rhetorica Libri tres* of Cyprian Soarez, S. J. (1524–1593), first printed 1565 (n.p.).

2. ff. 187v–188: *Totius rhetoricae actiomata,* Quod convenit de fintioni convenit et definitio . . . sublato autem enim ⟨?⟩ tollitur consequuen⟨?⟩. *Finis.* [ff. 188v–189v, ruled, but blank]

3. ff. 190–271v: *De Geographiae Nomine, Caput Primum,* Mobar In Geographiam navigantibus provincias nullus commodum visus est Exordium quam si Geographiam . . . quondam artium gloria revelatur musarum ⟨?⟩ modo turca-

rum ⟨?⟩ gratia Nature ⟨?⟩. *Finis laudabat opus. A. Gruel.* [ff. 272–273v, ruled, but blank]

Paper (watermarks not in Briquet), ff. ii (contemporary parchment scrap) + i (contemporary paper) + 273 + i (contemporary paper) + stubs of the same parchment as the front flyleaf; 172 × 130 (123 × 68) mm. 1^{8}(–8) $2–3^{4}$ 4^{6} 5^{4} 6^{6} $7–8^{2}$ $9–27^{4}$ 28^{2} $29–35^{4}$ 36^{2} $37–47^{4}$ 48^{8}(–7, 8 but apparently no text missing) $49–68^{4}$. Quire signatures for the notes on geography, ff. 190–271v, as letters of the alphabet on first leaf on the quire. 20–29 long lines, frame ruled in ink with a narrow space allotted at the top for titles, and a wide strip in the outer margin for notes; pricking visible in the lower and outer margins. Written in a rapid secretary hand. Some titles written in a display script and underlined in brown ink; some underlining in yellow in the index, ff. 182–187. Contemporary foliation in arabic numerals, beginning the count again at f. 190, with art. 3; marginalia in the hand of the main texts, concentrated on the rhetorical material. Pages frequently left blank, and marked "nihil deest." Original text on f. i–ii, washed and illegible; notes on f. iii in French, s. XVI, making reference to Lyons.

Bound, s. XVI, in French brown calf; gold stamped laurel wreath on front and back cover.

Written in France; owned and possibly written by Andreas Gruellius, whose name appears on f. 1; perhaps from the area of Lyons, given the note on f. iii. Francis Edwards Catalogue 483 (1926) n. 864; acquired by Henry E. Huntington at that time.

Bibliography: De Ricci, 110.

HM 1735 — Italy, s. XII^{1}
BREVIARY, fragment

ff. 1–2v: //Alleluia. Dum presens est imitantur illam et desiderant eam . . . [f. 2v:] *Incipiunt responsoria d*[*e*] *diurnis horis usque* ⟨?⟩ *in quadr*[*agesima*], Adiutor meus esto deus ne derelinquas me . . . *Vers.*, In te confirmatus sum ex uter//

Fragment of a noted breviary with responses for matins and lauds on the Saturday before Septuagesima, and responses for the day hours in Lent.

Parchment, 2 consecutive leaves; 302 × 214 (247 × 180) mm. 14 lines of text, ruled in dry point on the hair side with triple vertical bounding lines; pricking in slash form visible in the outer margin of f. 2. Written in a minuscule script; music in neumes on a 3-line stave, F in red and the other 2 lines ruled in dry point; clefs A, C and F written to the left of the text. On f. 1, opening initial, ca. 75 × 50 mm., in red and green with blue and green infilling, decorated with white vine stem. Secondary initials, ca. 15 × 15 mm., alternating ink of the text and red, set outside the written space; rubrics in red.

Written in the first half of the twelfth century in Italy, perhaps Lucca, given the form of the neumes; the presence of 12 responses shows monastic origin. Formerly as endleaves in RB 89742, a copy of Johannes Annius, *Auctores vetustissimi* (Rome: Eucharius Silber, 1498) *GW* 2015, Mead, n. 2164, acquired by Henry E. Huntington from A. S. W. Rosenbach in September 1924. The leaves were removed from the printed book and catalogued separately in February 1927.

Bibliography: Aspects of Medieval England, n. 37.

HM 1788 DERROTERO

Spain, s. XVI/XVII

ff. 1–168v: *Derotero Del Mundo,* [Prologue:] La lignea equinoçeal divide en dos partes . . . [f. 2, Text:] Pues bolviendo a la obra començada . . . cuya gracia sea en nuestro favor.

Geographical description of the coasts of the world: Europe, Africa, southern and eastern Asia (including Japan and the East Indies), the Americas from the La Plata River to the Carribean, Peru, the east coast of North America to Labrador and Greenland, with descriptions of the inhabitants, customs, products and brief historical notices, especially for Europe and the Holy Lands. Possibly composed after 1582 as Fernando Alvarez de Toledo, Duke of Alba is apparently referred to as no longer living (f. 81); the latest date given in the text is 1570 (f. 46v). Few interlinear or marginal corrections or additions, and those in several different hands.

Paper (arrow of the type of Briquet, *Flèche* 6299, Augsburg 1554 with sim. var. Fabriano 1554 and 1576; also somewhat similar to Heawood, Arrow 40, Rome 1561), ff. iv (paper s. XVII?) + 168 + ii (paper, s. XVII?); 284 × 222 (225 × 143) mm. $1^8(+1)$ 2–20^8 21^8(8 is flyleaf). 25–27 long lines, frame ruled in dry point, possibly following the chain marks. Written in an italic script; a later addition (?), the prologue on f. 1r–v, and later replacements (?), ff. 162–163v and 168r–v (conjunct with 163) by a different hand and on paper of different watermark. First words of each chapter in pale red square capitals often decorated with flourishes, those on f. 83v with an angel's head. Within the text, place names and numbers for distances, degrees and dates in the same pale red; same color for finding notes in the margin.

Bound, s. XVII?, in Spanish limp parchment; remains of 2 fore edge ties; red edges.

Written in Spain after 1570, the earliest possible date of composition of the text. On f. 83, otherwise blank, contemporary pen trials including the names "Gonzalo de Faloxa ⟨?⟩" and "Antonio"; other pen trials on f. 164v. On ff. 1 and 168v, ownership note and rubric (in the Spanish sense) of Don Vicente Antonio de Rendon C° Burgos; the added mention of Burgos to the text on f. 4 is probably attributable to this owner. Also on f. 1, a monogram of superimposed letters "A.R.O.T.E. (or L.)" and a note "Año de 76 [?]." Belonged to the Spanish writer, philologist and politician, Diego Clemencín (1765–1834), whose shelf mark on a slip of paper is pasted to the first flyleaf over an inked out inscription. On the front pastedown, a modern armorial bookplate, imitative of a late medieval woodcut, with the initials "A.G." and the motto "Que Quede Vida En La Muerte Velar Se Deve En La Vida De Tal Suerte." Purchased in February 1927 by the Huntington Library from Karl W. Hiersemann, Cat. 1, new series (1926) n. 53.

Bibliography: De Ricci, 111.

HM 2098 ANONYMOUS, PORTOLAN CHART

England, s. XVII^{in}

Nautical chart of west coast of Europe from southern Scotland to Cape Palmas on the coast of Africa.

HM 2098

Parchment, f. 1, 590 × 400 (570 × 390) mm. Border is yellow band edged in black with simple arabesque and dot design, on three sides only, which suggests it may be a "half-chart" of the North Atlantic. Black and red ink for nomenclature, in a cursive hand with area names in display script; land masses outlined in color, islands painted red and green; 2 compass roses (main one with Tudor rose in center); usual 32 rhumb line network with black, red and green ink for the principal directions; latitude scale numbered from 5° to 56° N, no longitude; numbered distance scale in cartouche decorated with stylized leaf and fruit design; no decoration except for the distance scale and compass roses.

Unbound: possibly originally mounted on boards since there is a sharp vertical crease in the center of this chart, but there are no cut-outs for hinges. A lesser horizontal fold was possibly made to fit a later binding. Chart is now flattened and in modern portfolio.

Probably made in London by a member of the Thames School of Chartmakers at the beginning of the seventeenth century. No owners' markings; according to Anderson sale catalogue, chart was found in chest of documents related to Plymouth district of Devonshire, all dated before 1601. Belonged to E. Williams. Sale by Anderson, New York, Cat. 1430, 13 May 1919, n. 304 to G. D. Smith from whom it was acquired by Henry E. Huntington.

Bibliography: De Ricci, 111. T. R. Smith, "Manuscript and Printed Sea Charts in Seventeenth-century London: The Case of the Thames School," *The Compleat Plattmaker*, ed. by N. J. W. Thrower (Berkeley 1978), 98.

HM 2515 — Marseilles, 1619
SALVATOR OLIVA, PORTOLAN CHARTS

Two nautical charts by Salvator Oliva bound with the chart of the Aegean Sea by Estienne Bremond (HM 31, *q.v.*):

1. Mediterranean

2. Western coast of Europe and northwestern Africa

Parchment, ff. 3 (2 sheets folded in center and pasted back to back), 404 × 286 mm. (map size, 386 × 562 mm., on double page openings). Bifolia attached sequentially with tabs. Border is a red band with a single black rule on each side. Black and red ink for nomenclature, in a humanistic hand with display script in square capitals; land masses outlined in color, islands painted blue, red, green or gold; chart 1 has 10 compass roses, chart 2 has 6; usual 32 rhumb line network in black, green, and red for the principal directions; no latitude or longitude; chart 1 has 3 unnumbered scales of distance and chart 2 has 2; elaborate vignettes of Marseilles on both charts and highly decorated cartouches for scales of distance.

Bound, ca. 1830, with HM 31, in pink marbled paper over cardboard, brown calf spine.

Inscribed "Salvator Oliva fecit in civitate marsiliae, Anno 1619." Sale of the library of Abate Luigi Celotti (ca. 1768–ca. 1846), Sotheby's, 14 March 1825, lot 207. A sale catalogue slip affixed to front pastedown describes a ". . . map of the World on three leaves." Since this volume also contains the Mediterranean chart made by Estienne Bremond

(HM 31) which forms the third leaf and since neither is a "World map," the sale catalogue entry either was carelessly made or the slip actually refers to a different portolan chart and was erroneously placed in this volume. This volume may instead have been lot 210 or lot 283 in the Celotti sale: both numbers are pencilled on the pastedown. Number 391 on back pastedown refers to Cochrane's sale of the library of Frederick North, 5th Earl of Guilford (1766–1827), to Sir Thomas Phillipps, 8 December 1830 as dated by A. N. L. Munby, *The Formation of the Phillipps Library up to the Year 1840,* Phillipps Studies (Cambridge 1951–60) 3:56. Front pastedown bears his number "Phillipps MS 6360." Obtained privately by A. S. W. Rosenbach for Henry E. Huntington in 1924.

Bibliography: De Ricci, 41.

HM 2590 — France, s. XV^2
BOOK OF HOURS, use of Rouen

1. ff. 2–13v: Full calendar in French, alternating blue and red with gold to indicate major feasts; included are the feasts of Austreberta (10 February), Honorina (27 February), Rumpharius (17 April), Hildebert (27 May), Martialis (3 July, in gold), "Nostre dame des neiges" (5 August), Vivianus (28 August), Nicasius (11 October), Austrebert (20 October), Mellonius (22 October), Romanus (23 October, in gold), Ursinus (30 December).

2. ff. 14–48v, 53–73v: [misbound] Hours of the Virgin, use of Rouen; the weekly variations of the psalms at matins set into the text before the lessons; suffrages after lauds of the Holy Spirit, John the Baptist, Peter and Paul, Lawrence, Nicholas (ends on f. 69), Catherine of Alexandria (on f. 69); opening leaves of the little hours missing before ff. 53, 59, 61, 63.

3. ff. 49–52v: Pericopes of the Gospels, beginning defectively in John 1, 8 and ending with the first words of the prayer, Protector in te sperantium; Luke begins defectively at 1, 31; Matthew begins defectively at 2, 5; Mark has only the rubric and "recumbentibus unde//."

4. ff. 74–91v: Penitential psalms and litany including Martialis as the last apostle; Nicasius, Clarus, Hippolytus, Leodegar and Adrianus as the last martyrs; Romanus, Maclovius and Vivianus among the confessors; Honorina as the last virgin.

5. ff. 92–124v: Office of the Dead, use of Rouen.

6. ff. 124v–125v: Suffrages of Peter and of James the Greater; f. 126r–v, ruled, but blank.

Parchment, ff. i (modern paper) + i (contemporary parchment) + 126 + ii (modern paper); 123 × 95 (68 × 50) mm. Collation beginning with f. 2: 1^{12} $2–5^8$ 6^2(+1 at the beginning; ff. 46–48) 7^8(–1, 3, 5, 8; ff. 49–52) 8^8(–1, 8; ff. 53–58; f. 53 misbound, should follow f. 58) 9^{10}(–1, 4, 7; ff. 59–65) 10^6(+4, f. 69 misbound, should follow f. 48; + 8, f. 73) $11–12^8$ 13^2(ff. 90–91) $14–17^8$ 18^2(+3, f. 126). 14 long lines, ruled in pale red ink; pricking occasionally remains in the upper margin. Written in a gothic book hand, in 2 sizes according to liturgical function.

Seven large miniatures, somewhat rubbed, above 3 lines of text in arched compartments with serrated tops; borders of acanthus leaves, flowers and grotesques against a flat painted gold ground. The miniatures are: f. 14 (Hours of the Virgin), Agony in the Garden; f. 35 (Lauds), Betrayal, with Peter and Malchus on the left; f. 52v (Gospel according to Mark), Christ addressing the apostles; f. 66 (Vespers), Deposition from the cross; f. 70 (Compline), Entombment; f. 74 (Penitential psalms), David in prayer, with the young David slaying Goliath in the background; f. 92 (Office of the Dead), funeral service in a church. 3-line initials in 3 styles: in white-patterned blue against burnished gold ground with multicolored trilobe leaves in the infilling; or as shaded white leaves against a painted gold ground and infilling of a naturalistic flower; or in blue on a brick-red ground, decorated with painted gold. 2-line initials in shaded white against a painted gold ground; 1-line initials in painted gold on alternating brick-red or blue grounds; ribbon line fillers in these colors also; initials within the text washed in yellow. Rubrics in red. Traced band borders in the outer margin of every leaf running the length of the text.

Bound, s. XVIII, in English red morocco, with gold tooling; marbled endpapers; gilt edges.

Written in France, probably Rouen, in the second half of the fifteenth century. Belonged to Joseph Granville Stuart Goff of Hale Park; his armorial book plate, s. XIX, on the front pastedown. P. M. Pittar sale, Sotheby's, 4 November 1918, pt. II, n. 340 to Finnigan; again P. M. Pittar sale, Sotheby's, 17 December 1919, n. 124 to G. D. Smith. Pencilled price code of Dawson's Book Shop, Los Angeles on f. i verso. Given to the Huntington Library in May 1939 by Miss Bella Mabury (d. 1964) in memory of her brother, Paul Rodman Mabury.

Bibliography: De Ricci, 22.

HM 3027 — France, s. XIII[ex]
JACOBUS DE VORAGINE, LEGENDA AUREA — *fig. 62*

ff. 1–163v: [Jacobus de Voragine, *Legenda aurea*] *De sancto andrea apostolo,* Andreas et quidam alii discipuli . . . et alienum hunc vultum a te conffugabo et proprium coram omnibus reddam [catchword:] hoc tamen nullo//; [f. 164r–v:] //animal stare poterit. Sed ad solum omnia prosternentur. Nona equabitur . . . sicut oculis suis viderant conscripserunt.

Th. Graesse, ed., *Jacobi a Voragine Legenda Aurea* (Bratislava 1890) p. 7, line 13 to p. 783, line 17; the last folio was misbound in its present position, and should be the first. According to the roman-numbered Lives in the Graesse edition, this manuscript is arranged: 1–18; text missing between ff. 21–22: end of De Sancto Felice, De Sancto Marcello and beginning of De Sancto Antonio; 22–30; text missing between ff. 29–30: De Septuagesima and beginning of De Quinquagesima; 34; text missing between ff. 30–31: end of De Ieiuniis, De Sancto Ignatio and the beginning of De Purificatione BVM; 38; text missing between ff. 33–34: end of De Sancta Agatha, De Sancto Vedasto, De Sancto Amando and the beginning of De Sancto Valentino; 43–45; text missing between ff. 38–39: end of De Sancto Gregorio, De Sancto Longino, De Sancta Sophia and beginning of De Sancto Benedicto; 50–51; De Sancto Timotheo, 52, not copied in this manuscript; 53–54; text missing between ff. 46–47: end of De Sancto

Secundo and beginning of De Sancta Maria Aegyptiaca; 57–58; text missing between ff. 50–51: end of De Sancto Marco Evangelista, De Sancto Marcellino, De Sancto Vitali and beginning of De Sancto Petro Martire; De Sancto Fabiano, 64, not copied in this manuscript; 65; De Sancta Apollonia, 66, not copied in this manuscript; 67–70; De Sancto Bonifacio, 71, not copied in this manuscript; 72–82; text missing between ff. 66–67: end of De Sancto Quirico, De Sancta Maria and beginning of De Sanctis Gervasio et Prothasio; 86–89; text missing between ff. 75–76: end of De Sancto Paulo, De Septem Fratribus, and beginning of De Sancta Theodora; 93–101; text missing between ff. 86–87: end of De Sanctis Nazario et Celso, De Sancto Felice Papa, De Sanctis Simplicio et Faustino, De Sancta Martha, De Sanctis Abdon et Sennen and beginning of De Sancto Germano; 108–131; 134; text missing between ff. 122–123: end of De Sanctis Gorgonio et Dorotheo and beginning of De Sanctis Protho et Jacincto; 137–138; 62 (De Virgine Anthiochena); 132 (De Sanctis Cornelio et Cypriano); 139; 133 (De Sancto Lamberto), 140–170. Kaeppeli, *SOPMA* 2154.

Parchment, ff. i (late medieval parchment) + 164 + ii (late medieval parchment); 350 × 247 (245 × 145) mm. 1^{12}(–1, 2, 3; this last now f. 164) 2^{12} 3^{12}(–1, 10, 11) 4^{12}(–1, 5, 11) 5^{12}(–8) 6^{12}(–1; note that the 2nd, 3rd, 9th and 10th leaves—ff. 52, 53, 58, 59—are singletons, their conjuncts having evidently been cancelled, since the text runs continuously) 7^{12}(–6) 8^{12}(–4) 9^{12}(–4, 5) 10^{12} 11^{12}(–2, no text missing) 12^{12}(–7) $13–15^{12}$ + one leaf (the third leaf of the first quire, misbound). Catchwords in simple yellow-washed frames through quire 5, that of quire 6 noted in a cursive hand, thereafter decorated with elaborate mouse-designs touched in red. Leaf signatures in a variety of methods: letters of the alphabet, a-h; an individual letter repeated, d, dd, ddd, dddd, vd (on quire 6); a series of horizontal slashes; letters of the alphabet surmounted by diacritical marks; a series of tangent circles. 2 columns of 59 lines, ruled in scratchy brown lead; pricking visible in the 3 outer margins. Written by 2 scribes in a gothic book hand: i, ff. 1–50 and 164; ii, ff. 51–163.

Extensively illuminated with 135 miniatures, usually 16 lines in height and width of 1 column (approximately 67 × 67 mm.). Written instructions to the illuminator are present for approximately one third of the miniatures; they tend to be more complex and closer to the text than the resulting miniature. Rudimentary sketches, or evidence of sketches, for the miniatures occur in about one quarter of the cases; a number of miniatures have both the written directions and the preliminary sketch. The illuminations are: f. 1, Andrew being tied to a Latin cross; f. 3, Nicholas before the children in the tub and the repentant butcher; f. 4v, Lucia standing in the fire with boiling oil thrown on her and a sword being run through her stomach; f. 5, Thomas the Apostle commanding the idol to destroy itself as the high priest smites him with a sword; f. 6v, Nativity: the Virgin lies on a bed looking away into the distance while Joseph stands to the right and the Christ Child lies in a manger in the background; f. 8, Anastasia being burned at the stake at a king's orders; f. 8v, Stephen being stoned; f. 10, John the Evangelist in the pot of boiling oil; f. 11v, Massacre of the Innocents; f. 12v, Thomas of Canterbury; f. 13v, Silvester tying a cord around the dragon's neck; f. 16, Circumcision; f. 17v, Adoration of the Magi; f. 19v, Paul the Hermit, his body still kneeling in prayer, while angels carry away his soul; f. 20, Remigius baptizing the king with oil brought by an angel from heaven; f. 20v, Hilary seated among the other bishops; f. 21, Macarius carrying a sack of sand on his shoulders; f. 21v, Felix being stabbed by his students with their styluses; f. 22, Fabianus chosen pope by the white dove; f. 22v, Sebastian; f. 23v, Agnes being burned, and with a sword through her neck; f. 24v, Vincent tied to a St. Andrew's cross, being lacerated with metal combs; f. 25, Basil rising from his deathbed to baptize his Jewish doctor; f. 26v, John the Almoner giving money to the poor; f. 27, Conversion of Paul; f. 27v, Paula and Eustochium in a boat leaving for the Holy Land; f. 28v, Julianus and Julius asking passers-by to help build the church, even though one of them pretends to be dead; f. 30, for Lent, a man confessing; f. 30v, for the Ember days, 2 groups of monks praying or singing from books; f. 32v, Blasius being decapitated at a king's orders; f. 33, Agatha, her breasts being cut off; f. 34, Juliana in prison binding the demon's hands and, later, being beheaded; f. 34v, Peter on his throne in Antioch; f. 35v, Matthias and Joseph Barsabas casting lots to take Judas' place; f. 36v, Gregory giving his silver bowl to a beggar; f. 40v, Patrick accidentally piercing the king's foot with his staff; f. 41v, Annunciation, with both Gabriel and Mary standing; f. 42v, Crucifixion between Mary and John; f. 45, Resurrection; f. 47, Ambrose protecting the church from the emperor; f. 49, George bound to the wheel of swords; f. 50, Mark writing; f. 53v, Philip tied to the cross; f. 54, James the Less felled by a blow of a club; f. 56, Finding of the Holy Cross; f. 57v, John the Evangelist in the pot of oil before the Latin Gate; f. 58, Procession with cross and banners; f. 59, Ascension; f. 61, Pentecost; f. 63, Gordianus being beheaded at a king's orders; f. 63v, Nereus and Achilleus being decapitated; f. 64, Pancratius being decapitated; f. 64, Urbanus with 5 companions being decapitated; f. 64v, Petronilla in bed receiving communion before dying, and Felicula being tortured; f. 64v, Peter the Exorcist and Marcellinus being beheaded in the forest; f. 65, Primus and Felicianus being decapitated at a king's orders; f. 65v, Barnabas held by ropes about his neck and kneeling in the flames; f. 66v, Vitus, tonsured, on a St. Andrew's cross with 2 sleeping (?) people at his feet, presumably Modestus and Crescentia; f. 67, Birth of John the Baptist, while Elizabeth in bed gazes off into the distance; f. 69, John and Paul being decapitated; f. 69v, Leo, his hand being kissed, and, later, cutting off the offending hand; f. 70, Peter crucified upside down; f. 72v, Paul being beheaded at a king's orders; f. 76v, Margaret coming out of the dragon's back; f. 77, Alexius accepted as a beggar in his father's house; f. 78, Praxedis and Pudentiana burying the bodies of martyrs; f. 78v, Mary Magdalene before the Risen Christ in the garden; f. 80v, Apollinaris being beaten by the mobs; f. 81, Christina being shot with arrows; f. 81v, James the Greater about to be decapitated; f. 84, Christopher holding the Christ Child in his arms; f. 85, the Seven Sleepers and the emperor Theodosius; f. 86, Nazarius and Celsius being beheaded; f. 87v, Eusebius being stoned by the heretics; f. 88, Maccabean Martyrs; f. 88v, Peter in chains talking with an angel, while the guards gather outside the prison; f. 90, Stephen the Pope being beheaded after mass; f. 90, Stephen protomartyr's, and Gamaliel's, Nicodemus' and Abibas' open coffins lie before the wondering bishop; f. 91v, Dominic and his brethern kneeling before the pope (?); f. 96, Sixtus and 2 companions being beheaded; f. 96v, Donatus being beheaded; f. 97, Cyriacus and 2 companions being beheaded; f. 97v, Lawrence on the gridiron; f. 100v, Hippolytus drawn between 2 horses; f. 101, Dormition of the Virgin, while Jesus holds her soul, as a small child, in his arms; f. 106, Bernard and Malachy in prayer; f. 108, Timothy and a companion decapitated at a king's orders; f. 108, Symphorianus being decapitated; f. 108, Bartholomew being flayed; f. 110v, Augustine, disputing; f. 114v, Decollation of John the Baptist, while Herod and Herodias watch from their banquet; f. 116v, Felix and Adauctus being decapitated at a king's orders; f. 117, Sabinianus of Troyes being decapitated by soldiers; f. 117v, Lupus receiving Clotaire who is returning the church bell to Sens; f. 118, (for the feast of Mamertinus, although the rubric reads "De sancto martino") Marinus, a monk of Mamertinus' monastery, releasing the bear from the trap; f. 118v, Aegidius wounded by the huntsman's arrow, while protecting the tame deer; f. 119v, Birth of the Virgin, who is being washed by a midwife, while Anne, lying in bed, props her head up on her elbow; f. 122, Adrianus' hands being severed from his body and his wife Nathalia carefully holding one of them; f. 123, Heraclius approaching Jerusalem with the Holy Cross; f. 124v, John Chrysostom, dying, his soul being received by an angel; f. 126v, the Antiochene Virgin, kneeling before a man, with a group of people in the background; f. 127v, Cornelius and 2 other martyrs being decapitated; f. 128, Euphemia being pierced by the executioner's sword as he himself is attacked by a lion; f. 128v, Lambert killed by 2 soldiers as a king watches; f. 129, Matthew being beheaded beside the altar; f. 130, Maurice and his companions being beheaded by soldiers; f. 131, Justina and Cyprian in the pot of pitch, while the flames jump out on to the priest of the idols; f. 132, Cosmas and Damian, attaching the black leg to the sick man; f. 133, Fursey in bed, as his soul is received by 2 angels, while a third protects it from devils shooting arrows; f. 133v, Michael helping a saint in his fight against devils; f. 136, Jerome commands the lion to guard the donkey bearing wood, while another monk watches; f. 137v, Translation of Remigius by angels carrying his coffin to the crypt; f. 138, Leodegarius being decapitated; f. 138v, Francis about to receive the stigmata from the crucified seraph; f. 141, Pelagia repenting before Veronus; f. 141v, Margaret leaving her marriage feast; f. 142, Thais burning her goods; f. 142v, Denis holding his severed head and standing between Rusticus and Eleutherius as they are being decapitated; f. 143v, Callistus being thrown from a window into the well; f. 144, Leonard releasing the man who had been in the pit below the tower; f. 145, Luke writing; f. 147, Chrysanthus and Daria in the pit being crushed by the stones and earth thrown in upon them; f. 147, Ursula and the 11,000 Virgins being decapitated; f. 148, Simon and Jude being decapitated; f. 149, Quentin being decapitated; f. 149, Eustachius kneeling before the stag with the image of Christ between its antlers; f. 150v, All Saints: Christ in majesty holds a sheet containing the souls of the saints in his hands, with the symbols of the Evangelists at the 4 corners of the miniature; f. 153, All Souls; f. 155v, the Four Crowned Martyrs being cast into the sea; f. 155v, Theodore standing in the flames and giving forth his soul to the angel above; f. 156, Martin cutting his cloak to share it with a beggar; f. 156v, Brictius commanding the infant to declare the falsity of the paternity charges brought against him; f. 157, Elizabeth kneeling, reading her prayers before Master Conrad who holds a whip; f. 161, Cecilia being beheaded as she burns in the flames; f. 162v, Clement being cast into the sea with a weight hung from his neck. Major initials, 9- to 7-line, in dull pink or blue, patterned in white against a cusped ground of the other color, infilling in a darker shade of the same color as the initial, with grotesque or leaf forms decorated with burnished gold, and marginal extensions. Initials, 4-line, to introduce the *Etymologia* of similar style; secondary initials, 2-line, alternating red and blue with flourishes of the other color. Running headlines across the opening alternate red and blue letters; rubrics in red throughout; line fillers in the shape of mice, the same as the decoration on the catchwords. Frequent notes to the rubricator. Carefully corrected throughout by the scribe of the text, corrections in yellow boxes. Some marginalia in various hands up to s. XVI.

Bound in original (?) oak boards, quarter backed in modern mottled calf; remains of 2 fore edge straps of pink leather closing to pins on the center back; flyleaves, washed, contained a prose text in French in 2 columns, written in a bâtarde script, s. XV.

Written in France, perhaps in Paris, during the next to the last decade of the thirteenth century, but in England by the third or certainly the last quarter of the fourteenth century, to judge by the script of the note added on f. 11v, correcting the king's name from "Edmundus" to "Edwardus." A modern note on f. i states that the manuscript came from Fountains Abbey, Yorkshire; rejected by Ker, *MLGB,* 89. Belonged to Sir Henry Ingilby, Bart., of Ripley Castle, Yorkshire and later to Lt. Col. Sir William Henry Ingilby, Bart. (1874–1950); his sale, Sotheby's, 21 October 1920, lot 172 to Sabin; at this point the current f. 164 began the volume. Purchased by the Huntington Library from the G. D. Smith Book Company in January 1927.

Bibliography: HMC, *6th Report, Appendix* (1877) 352–95, especially 356; *Proceedings of the Society of Antiquaries of London* (1885–87) 179; De Ricci, 112; *Aspects of Medieval England,* n. 23 open at f. 161, Cecilia. For reproductions of the miniatures, see Sotheby's, 21 October 1920, frontispiece, of ff. 118v, 138v and 117, respectively Aegidius, Francis and Sabinianus with the adjacent preliminary sketch; G. Ryan and H. Ripperger, trans., *The Golden Legend of Jacobus de Voragine* (London 1941) pl. 2 of f. 64, Pancratius and Urbanus; Princeton Index of Christian Art, of the full series of miniatures; *New Catholic Encyclopedia,* "Hagiography" of f. 8, Anastasia; R. Zuccaro, *Gli affreschi nella Grotta di San Michele ad Olevano sul Tusciano.* Studi sulla pittura medioevale campana 2 (Rome

1977) pl. 200 of f. 66v, Vitus; H. Friedman, *A Bestiary for Saint Jerome* (Smithsonian Institution 1980) fig. 156 of f. 136, Jerome.

HM 15241 England, s. XIV$^{1/4}$
YEAR BOOK, fragment

ff. 1–4v: Fragment of a year book containing assizes of novel disseisin, including the following names of speakers as they occur in the text (information from J. H. Baker, *The Order of Serjeants at Law,* London 1983, appendix IV and from G. O. Sayles, *Select Cases in the Court of King's Bench under Edward I,* Selden Society 55, London 1936, pp. cxxix–cxli): Gilbert de Toutheby (*narrator* by 1293, d. by 1328); Robert de Malberthorpe (*narrator* by 1299, judge from 1320, d. by 1332); William Herle (*narrator* by 1300, judge by 1320); Edmund de Passelewe (*narrator* by 1299, Baron of the Exchequer by 1323); Nicholas de Warrewik (*narrator* by 1287, d. by 1311); Geoffrey de Hertilpole (*narrator* by 1291, d. ca. 1324); Gilbert of Roubury (judge of the king's bench 1295–1316, judge of the common bench 1316–1321); "Scrop," either Henry (*narrator* by 1292, judge from 1308, d. 1336) or Geoffrey (serjeant in 1309, judge from 1323, d. 1340); John de Cantebrigge (serjeant from 1309, judge from 1329, d. before June 1335); John de Wescote (*narrator* by 1300, d. after 1316); Henry le Spigurnel (*narrator* by 1291, d. 1328); John de Ingham (serjeant in 1309, d. after 1325); John de Stonore (serjeant from 1311, judge from 1320, d. 1354); "Bradford," perhaps John de Bradenstoke (*narrator* by 1293); Walter de Friskeney (*narrator* by 1293; judge from 1323, probably d. by 1328); John de Haverington (*narrator* by 1292); "Cave"; Roger de Scoter (*narrator* by 1291, Baron of the Exchequer in 1310, d. by 1312); "Cressing[ham]"; William de Kellaw (*narrator* by 1286, known until 1292); William Howard (*narrator* in 1293–94, judge from 1297, d. ca. 1308); William de Bereford (*narrator* by 1285, judge from 1292, d. 1326); Adam de Kyngeshemede (*narrator* by 1276, known until 1312); Ralph de Stalinburgh (*narrator* by 1294, known until 1301); John of Mettingham (judge of the common bench 1290–1301). The following names of parties appear: Mestre Thomas; Roger vs. John; Robert le Orfevre and his wife Joan vs. William Dewere; William de Norton vs. William de Haston; Robert Turry and his wife Beatrice vs. John de Coverelle; Robert de Stureye vs. James, Alice de T. and her son Geoffrey; Henry vs. Robert and Richard; John de Thornton vs. Robert de Holoynd; Renald son of Renald vs. Renald son of John and William de N.; John Benk vs. A. de N.; John son of Giles de Brewes; Thomas Corbridge archbishop of York (1300–04) vs. Davy de Kauode.

Parchment, ff. 4; 227 × 163 (205 × 142) mm. 2 bifolia, possibly not consecutive. 43–50 long lines, ruled in lead; slash prick marks. Written in an anglicana script. Marginalia in the hand of the scribe.

Formerly bound, s. XIX, in Middle Hill blue pasteboards with a fragment of a register of writs, now shelved separately as HM 15242.

Written in England in the first quarter of the fourteenth century. Owned by Sir Thomas Phillipps; his n. 11002 in the lower margin of what is now f. 2. Acquired by the Huntington Library from Sotheby's, 24 June 1935, lot 250.

Bibliography: Aspects of Medieval England, n. 3 open at ff. 2v–3. *Chronica,* 2.

HM 15242
REGISTER OF WRITS, fragment

England, s. XV[2]

ff. 1–8v: Register of writs, beginning with a writ of right dated 26 November, 25 Henry [VI], 1447 brought by John Shirland against William Asthill for a messuage in "N.," and ending defectively with a Recordari addressed to the council of Dover castle.

Parchment, ff. 8; 275 × 195 (195 × 130) mm. 1^8, signed "a iiii" on f. 4 and with a catchword on f. 8. 39 long lines, ruled in ink with an additional set of double rules in the 3 outer margins. Written in a secretary script with anglicana forms. 8-line gold initial on a particolored blue and maroon ground with white patterning; from the initial, a black ink spray with green leaves and gold trefoils; alternating red and blue paragraph marks. Running headline on all leaves, "capitulum primum." Contemporary foliation, i–viii.

Bound, s. XIX, in Middle Hill blue pasteboards.

Written in England in the second half of the fifteenth century. In the lower margin of f. 1, in a textura hand in blue ink with a red initial, the name "Folbery," possibly the Robert Folbery/Fulberry of Newcastle (1420–85) admitted to Lincoln's Inn in 1443–44; see J. C. Wedgwood and A. D. Holt, *History of Parliament, Biographies . . . 1439–1509* (London 1936) 343. Belonged to Sir Thomas Phillipps; his n. 11002. Phillipps sale, Sotheby's, 24 June 1935, lot 250, at that time bound with a fragment of a year book, now shelved separately as HM 15241. Acquired by the Huntington Library in 1935.

Bibliography: Chronica, 2.

HM 19079
MEDICAL TREATISES

England, s. XV[1/4]

1. ff. 1–15v: [Broþir] in crist þat þyng þat ȝe desyreþ of me y wol don hyt wyþ goddes grace her beþ medycynes þat beþ ydrawen out of goode leches bokes. *For þe hed ache* mak lye of verueyne oþer of beteyne . . . & ȝef þe arm be broke let hym bere a bal of herbes in hys hond for crokynge of hys fyngeres deo gracias Amen.

Approximately 150 medical recipes, including 2 on f. 3 for determining if a sick man will live or die.

2. f. 15v: Forto rede & vnderstonde þe wrytynge þat comeþ heraftur & such oþer wrytynge as leches wryteþ in makynge of hur medycynes wheþer it be in englysch oþer in latyn þow schalt vnderstonde þat a pound is þus ywryte li. i & half a pound . . . & þus þey beþ ywryten in latyn bokes.

For a similar text on pharmaceutical weights and how they are written, see W. R. Dawson, *A Leechbook or Collection of Medical Recipes of the Fifteenth Century* (London 1934) 294.

3. ff. 16–237: *Hed Ache,* A mon þat wol helpe men in hure seknesses hym byhofeþ to knowe þe enchesones & þe kyndes of þe seknesses þat is to sugge wheþer þey ben hote oþer colde oþer druye oþer moyst And þys is yknowe by mony dyuerse tokenes as by þe vryn & by þe pous . . . And furst we wolleþ

bygynne at þe seknesses of þe hed & furst of þe hed ache þat may come to a mon þroȝ hete oþer colde oþer druyenesse . . . Anoynte hem wyþ þe oyle of eyren oþer of roses oþer wyþ þe mys of þe lylye rote oþer wyþ fresch botter oþer wyþ lard ymedled wyþ botter oþer wyþ oyle of whete oþer wyþ þe whyt of an ey.

Treatise on sicknesses, arranged from the head down (headache to hemorrhoids) defining for each the humors, diagnostic symptoms and remedies.

4. f. 237v: In al þys bok þer as þou seest vyolet idon in electewaryes . . . it restoreþ colere & consumeþ malencolye & it sleþ þe cancre & þe festre & it druyeþ qwyture & abateþ a monnes fatuesse. Deo gracias. *Amen.*

Notes on the preparation of violet, saffron and iron rust for medicinal use.

5. ff. 238–242: *Seknesses of þe hed,* 16, Ache of hed, Suger roset, Suger vyolet . . .

Table of contents to ff. 16–237 (art. 3), listing part of the body affected and appropriate medicines with reference to folio numbers.

6. ff. 16v, 18v, 50v, 96, 141v, 203, 208v, 209, 241v, 242v, 243, 244: Medical recipes in Latin and in English added by several different hands, s. XV and XVI.

Parchment, ff. 244 (the last is 3 leaves pasted together); 125 × 89 (80–88 × 59–69) mm. $1\text{–}3^{12}$ 4^{10} $5\text{–}19^{12}$ 20^{12}(12 drawn past quire 21 and originally used as pastedown; now pasted to the last 2 leaves of quire 21) 21^{8}(7, 8 and the last leaf of quire 20 now pasted together as f. 244). Catchwords in lower right margin, usually in ink or green frames. 18–25 long lines, frame ruled in lead; slash prick marks in the upper and lower margins. Written in an anglicana script with some secretary forms.

In quires 1–4, 2- and 1-line green initials filled in yellow with simple borders to the right of the text in the same colors; green paragraph marks filled in yellow; running headlines in green frames washed in yellow. From quire 5 to the end, 1-line red initials, red paragraph marks, running headlines enclosed in red frames washed in yellow, and, intermittently, also written in red ink to the right of the upper margin. In the hand of the scribe: "Maria Ihesus Iohannes" in the upper margin of the first leaf of each quire; finding notes in the outer margins, sometimes in red frames; foliation in arabic numerals, 1–237, numbering each leaf recto and verso (not the opening). Nota bene hands washed in yellow on, e.g., ff. 149v, 154v, 214; sketch of a leg (to show vein for blood letting), f. 199v; sketch of an herb, f. 223v. On f. 244, s. XV, "prec. x s."

Bound, s. XV, originally in white doeskin over bevelled wooden boards; recovered in pink leather with turn-ins nailed to the previous cover; fore edge strap fastening to a pin on the back cover; sewn on 3 thongs, with head and tail bands. As front pastedown, a fragment from a Latin saint's life (?), England, s. XIII; a narrow strip of parchment used as sewing guard before the first leaf, s. XII.

Written in England in the first quarter of the fifteenth century. Visible on the strip of the white leather binding which extends beyond the pink leather turn-in on the front cover, s. XVI, "Liber Ric. clere [?] rectoris sancti panc<?> <?> Edward Horden." On f. 1, "Sum Gulielmi Moore 1657" and on f. 244, "William Moore [?]." In modern pencil on the front pastedown "£ 300," underlined. Quaritch Cat. 699 (1952) n. 94; acquired from Quaritch in 1952 by the Huntington Library.

Secundo folio: & hold it in

HM 19913

Bibliography: L. MacKinney, *Medical Illustrations in Medieval Manuscripts* (Berkeley 1965) p. 174 n. 148.2. *Aspects of Medieval England,* n. 45 open at f. 16. *Chronica,* 2.

HM 19913 — England, s. XV^in
BOOK OF HOURS, Sarum use — *fig. 80*

1. ff. 1–6v: Calendar in blue, red and black, including Edward martyr (18 March), Richard of Chichester (3 April), Translation of Edmund archbishop (9 June, in red), Translation of Richard of Chichester (16 June), Translation of Edward martyr (20 June), Etheldreda (23 June), Translation of Thomas of Canterbury (7 July, in red), Anne (26 July, in red), Cuthburga (31 August), Edith (16 September), Translation of Edward confessor (13 October, in red), Edmund archbishop (16 November), Hugh (17 November, in red), Edmund king (20) November), Thomas of Canterbury (29 December, in blue).

2. ff. 7–42: Hours of the Virgin, use of Sarum with the hours of the Cross worked in; suffrages after lauds of the Holy Spirit, the Trinity, the Cross, Michael, John the Baptist, John the Evangelist, Peter and Paul, Andrew, Lawrence, Stephen, Thomas of Canterbury (erased), Nicholas, Catherine of Alexandria, Margaret, All Saints; after compline are the Salve Regina and the prayer, Omnipotens sempiterne deus qui gloriose virginis . . . ; f. 42v, ruled, but blank.

3. ff. 43–62v: Penitential psalms, gradual psalms (the first 10 by cue only), and litany including Swithun, Birinus, Sotheris, Afra and Edith; ff. 63–64, ruled, but blank.

4. ff. 65–103: Office of the Dead, Sarum use, with variations for the liturgical year; f. 103v, ruled, but blank.

5. ff. 104–119: Commendation of souls (Pss. 118, divided into sections, and 138), and the prayer, Tibi domine commendamus animas . . . ; f. 119v, ruled, but blank.

6. ff. 120–137v: Psalter of St. Jerome, with the heading and the opening prayer, Suscipere dignare domine deus omnipotens hos psalmos consecratos . . . ; f. 122, Verba mea auribus percipe . . . ; ending prayer, Liberator animarum mundi redemptor . . .

7. ff. 138–142v: //baris spinis coronaberis arundine . . . O Ihesu vitis vera et fecunda // [the 15 O's of St. Bridget, beginning and ending defectively in the first and last prayer; *HE,* 76–80].

Parchment, ff. iii (modern paper) + iv (parchment) + 142 + iv (parchment) + vii (modern paper); 110 × 82 (63 × 38) mm. 1^6 $2–5^8$ 6^4(through f. 42) $7–8^8$ 9^6(through f. 64) $10–18^8$ 19^{10}(? ff. 137–142, one leaf missing before f. 138, stitching between ff. 140–141, at least one leaf missing after f. 142). Catchwords in lower right margin, sometimes on a scroll. 19 long lines through f. 42, thereafter 18 long lines, ruled in pale red ink with upper and lower 2 lines full across. Written in a gothic book hand, with hierarchy of size denoting different liturgical functions.

Four miniatures, 13- or 12-line, enclosed by painted illusionistic frames in orange, blue or pink decorated with clusters of 3 white dots; the frame on f. 65 consists of alternating orange and green ribbons twined around a blue rod. Outer borders of narrow gold and colored bars, lush multicolored acanthus leaves, and some black ink spray extensions with gold dots and green tendrils. Three of the miniatures are attributed to followers of Herman Scheerre (ff. 43, 65, and 104); the last miniature, f. 122, is attributed to Scheerre himself by C. Kuhn, "Herman Scheerre and English Illumination of the early Fifteenth Century," *Art Bulletin* 22 (1940) 138–56, especially p. 149 and fig. 11 of f. 122. The miniatures are: f. 43 (Penitential psalms), the Last Judgment with Christ sitting on a rainbow showing his wounds, and the heads of 4 dead visible in their graves (similar composition in the Bedford Psalter, London, Brit. Lib., Add. 42131, f. 37); f. 65 (Office of the Dead), a burial service with hooded mourners in black holding candles, and 3 priests (a more elaborate composition in the Hours of Elizabeth the Queen, London, Brit. Lib., Add. 50001, reproduced in *Illustrations from One Hundred Manuscripts in the Library of Henry Yates Thompson,* London 1914, vol. 4, pl. 67 of f. 55b); f. 104 (Commendation of souls), God the Father holds 3 naked souls in a sheet against a background of angels in vermilion camaïeu (see London, Brit. Lib., Add. 16998, f. 44); f. 122 (Psalter of St. Jerome), Jerome in his study. The individual hours of the Virgin are introduced by the same style of acanthus leaf borders as above, and by 7-line shaded initials in colors with infilling of lush acanthus leaf and ground of another color; 3- and 2-line initials in gold on a colored ground, infilled with an acanthus leaf, and with black ink spray extension. 1-line initials, gold with purple flourishing or blue with red; jigsaw line fillers in blue and gold. On ff. 138–142, by a different illuminator, only 2-line initials in gold on white-patterned blue or dusky pink ground, infilled with the other color and with small sprays. Rubrics throughout.

Bound in modern polished blue calf with 4 parchment tabs at the head.

Written in England and dated ca. 1405 by C. Kuhn (see above) on the basis of style. In the lower margin of f. 1 are the initials "I.G." in a late sixteenth or early seventeenth century hand. Acquired by Dr. Eric G. Millar (1887–1966) from James Thorp in London, 1934; his notes, ff. i–ii, and on file; his sale, Sotheby's, 15 June 1959 lot 190 with a plate of all 4 miniatures. Acquired by the Huntington Library at that time.

Bibliography: Burlington Fine Arts Club Exhibition of British Medieval Art, May–July 1939, n. 14; f. 122 exhibited. E. Panofsky, *Early Netherlandish Painting* (Cambridge, Mass. 1953) pp. 116, 403, footnote. Eric G. Millar, "Fresh Materials for the Study of English Illumination," *Studies in Art and Literature for Belle Da Costa Greene,* edited by D. Miner (Princeton 1954) 286–94, especially p. 294, and fig. 252 which reproduces all 4 miniatures. D. H. Turner, "List of the Medieval and Renaissance Manuscripts owned by Eric Millar," *British Museum Quarterly* 33 (1968–69) 9–16, this manuscript n. 50. *Aspects of Medieval England,* n. 36; f. 122 exhibited and as frontispiece of the catalogue. *Chronica,* 2. H. Friedman, *A Bestiary for Saint Jerome* (Smithsonian Institution 1980) p. 39 fig. 13 of f. 122. Scott, *Later Gothic Manuscripts* (forthcoming).

HM 19914 — England, s. XIII^med
PASTORAL COLLECTION — *fig. 161*

Composite volume

I.

1. ff. 1–2v [flyleaves]: f. 1, an incomplete motet; ff. 1v–2, a complete motet, Maria diceris mater amabilis; f. 2v, a 3-part Kyrie. All are polyphonic music, with notation in separate parts on ff. 1–2 (alternating groups of black and red notes on one line of f. 2), and score notation on f. 2v; in 8 red five-line staves

per page for the motets ad 9 for the Kyrie. Written ca. 1350. Listed in *RISM* B.IV² pp. 369–71.

II.

2. ff. 3–114: *Brevis compilacio supe[r psalterium]* [Prologue:] Quisquis ad divine pagine lectionem accedit . . . [f. 3, Text:] Beatus vir qui non abiit, Homo quando cogitacionem suam ad terrena flectit . . . sola enim perseverantia accipit bravium. Finis distinctionum post meldensem collectarum. Amen. *Explicit compendiosa exposicio super psalterium.* [f. 114v, blank]

Michael de Meaux, archbishop of Sens, Stegmüller 5638, but often attributed to Bonaventure and printed in his *Opera omnia* (Lyons 1668) 1:72–293.

III.

3. ff. 115–158: *Incipit speculum sacerdotum secundum magistrum Richardum de leycestria cancellarium Cantebrigensem,* [Prologue:] Qui bene presunt presbiteri . . . Presbiter grece senex latine dicitur . . . [f. 115v, Text:] Ad manifestationem singulorum prenominatorum per ordinem possunt introduci auctoritates sanctarum scripturarum . . . Siquid autem residuum fuerit, filiis aaron relinquo. Faciendi quidem libros, nullus est finis. Hic ergo erit consumatus. Finito libro reddatur gloria christo amen. *versus. Explicit speculum sacerdotum secundum magistrum Richardum de Leycestria quondam cancellarium Cantebrigensem.* [f. 158v, blank]

Richard of Leicester, also known as Richard Wetheringsett (Emden, *BRUC,* 367 and 679); for a list of manuscripts, see Bloomfield, *Virtues and Vices* 4583.

4. ff. 159–184: [top line cropped] //In primis igitur ut ab unitate exordiamur innotescendum est, quod scriptum est. *Unus deus.* Deus unus est. Contra Deut. xix ysay. cxxx. Apostolus ait, sunt multi dii et cetera. Resp. Dicitur deus essencialiter . . . et hic deo gracias agendo huius summe finem facimus cui nomen numerale imponimus, plura quidem hic omissa in aliis opusculis nostris copiosius sunt exarata. *Explicit numerale magistri Willelmi lincolnensis ecclesie cancellarii. Sancta Ositha Deo gracias.* [followed by the chapter on the Four Arms of the Cross marked "vacat"; it had already been copied in its correct position on f. 170.]

H. Mackinnon, "The Life and Works of William de Montibus," unpublished D. Phil. thesis, Oxford, 1959, and, "William de Montibus, a medieval Teacher," in *Essays in Medieval History presented to Bertie Wilkinson,* ed. T. A. Sandquist and M. R. Powicke (Toronto 1969) 32–45. For a list of the rubrics of the *Numerale,* see B. Smalley and G. Lacombe, "The Lombard's Commentary on Isaias and other Fragments," *The New Scholasticism* 5 (1931) 147–51.

5. ff. 184v–188v: Ante dies omnes mundi fuit omnis in uno/ Machina momento facta iubente deo . . . Illic absque metu pax est risus sine fletu/ Absque labore quies et sine nocte dies. Amen.

A verse compendium of the Old and New Testament in 706 lines; it lacks the prose preface with which it sometimes circulates (see London, Brit. Lib., Roy. 6.B.XI, f. 54v); Walther, *Initia* 1291.

6. ff. 189–200: *Incipit tractatus domini pape de contemptu mundi,* Domino patri karissimo petro dei gracia portuensi episcopo lotarius . . . Modicum ocii quod inter multas angustias . . . Quare de vulva . . . terrores et punctiones,

amaritudines, fames et sitis, frigus et sulphur et ignis ardens a quibus omnibus liberet nos deus. Amen. *Explicit tractatus lotharii de contemptu mundi. Sancta Ositha virgo et martir pretiosa miserere supplicibus tuis. Amen. Deo gracias.*

M. Maccarrone, ed., *Lotharii Cardinalis (Innocentii III) De Miseria Humane Conditionis.* Thesaurus Mundi (Lugano 1955). The manuscript shows chapters 9 and 10 of the printed Book I run on; chapters 15 and 16 of the printed Book II in reversed order; chapter 1 of the printed Book III here ends Book II; chapters 2 and 3 were not copied; what is chapter 4 in the printed edition begins Book III in the manuscript. See also R. E. Lewis, ed., *Lotario dei Segni (Pope Innocent III), De Miseria Condicionis Humane.* The Chaucer Library (Athens, Georgia 1978) with list of manuscripts, including HM 19914.

7. ff. 200v–226v: [Alan of Lille, *Summa de arte predicatoria*] *Incipit compilacio notabilium pro predicantibus utilis et devota, capitulum primum quod scala est perfectus catholici,* Vidit iacob scalam a terra usque ad celum attingentem . . . Nube ergo illi de quo dicitur, Potestati eius quis resistit, et alibi, Regni eius non erit finis. Ad quem pervenire valeamus. Amen. *Explicit liber artis predicandi. PL* 210:111–195.

8. ff. 227–228v: *Penitentiarius magistri Willelmi de montibus,* Bernardus super cantico sermone xvi° Confessio eo periculosius noxia quo subtilius vana . . . [Text:] Peniteas cito peccatorum . . . Secundum ea que peccaverit homo oportet pretium reddi. Quod gula peccaverit ieiunium// [f. 229:] *Explicit penitentiarius magistri Willelmi de montibus sed incompletus.* [followed by 2 lines in red ink, erased; f. 229v, blank]

William de Montibus' didactic poem in its glossed form (with small red suprascript letters tying text to gloss) which runs here for 87 lines and breaks incomplete as shown by the rubric on f. 229; the poem is preceded by a short citation from a sermon of St. Bernard. See H. Mackinnon (art. 4 above), thesis, and *loc. cit.,* 40–45.

IV.

9. ff. 230–334: *Incipit proemium Beati gregorii pape in exposicionem Iob. Reverendissimo atque Sanctissimo fratri Leandro coepiscopo Gregorius servus Servorum Dei,* [Epistle:] Dudum te frater beatissime in constantinopolitana urbe cognoscens cum me illic sedis apostolice responsa constringerent . . . *Incipiunt moralia beati gregorii pape per contemplacionem sumpta in librum Iob Libri quinque pars prima,* [f. 231, Prologue:] Inter multos sepe queritur quis libri beati iob scriptor habeatur. Et alii quidem moysen alii unum ex prophetis scriptorem huius operis fuisse suspicantur. Quia enim in libro geneseos . . . [f. 234, Text:] Vir erat in terra hus nomine iob. Idcirco sanctus vir ubi habitaverit dicitur . . . Quia is qui in desiderio carnalis corruptionis exestuat ad fetorem putredinis anhelat. *Explicit. Coram quo de quo quid ubi cui quomodo quando/ Dicas provideas ne male peniteas. Expliciunt quedam notabilia moralium beati gregorii excerpta pro utilitate contemplativorum.* [followed by an erasure of red ink; f. 334v, blank]

This text follows the organization of Gregory's work; it does not appear to correspond to any of the works studied by R. Wasselynck, "Les compilations des *Moralia in Job* du VIIe au XIIe siècle," *RTAM* 29 (1962) 5–32, and successive articles.

HM 19914

Parchment (thick and velvety), forming a composite volume, 180 × 135 mm. (but severely cropped) of ff. 334 in 4 parts.
I. ff. 1–2v, music copied ca. 1350, functioning here as flyleaves (see above).
II. ff. 3–114v; ruled space: 140 × 83 mm. 1–8^8 9^{10}(through f. 76) 10–13^8 14^8(–7, 8). Quires signed in roman numerals on the verso of the last leaf, 1–9 and then 1–4. 28–30 long lines, ruled in brown crayon with double bounding lines. Written in a littera textualis. Major initials, ff. 3, 3v and 77, 3-line, light blue patterned in white or red patterned in light blue, both with leaf infilling in red touched with a light green wash; the initial on f. 3 enclosed in a square red frame with a leaf extension the length of the text; slashed initials within the text, underlining, paragraph marks and rubrics in red; running headlines numbering the chapters, and marginal notes at the beginnings of chapters in brown ink.
III. ff. 115–228v; ruled space: 147 × 110 mm. 1^6(+7) 2^8 3^8(+8, a half leaf, f. 137) 4^8 5^8(+5, a half leaf, f. 151) 6–13^8 14^{10}(–10). In 2 columns of 40–43 lines, ruled in brown crayon with double bounding lines. Written in littera textualis by 2 people: i, ff. 115–226v, except for ff. 137 and 151, additions, each by a different hand, s. XIV; ii, ff. 227–229v. Initials, 4- to 1-line, placed outside the written space, the first in parted red and blue with stylized acanthus extension and flourishing; the others in combinations of pale blue, red or green; slashed initials in the text, paragraph marks, chapter numbers, underlining, rubrics and running headlines, all in red. On ff. 204–205, pouncing or pricking in lower margins.
IV. ff. 229–334v; ruled space: 155 × 120 mm. 1^8(+1, f. 229) 2^8 3^8(+8; the ninth leaf, between ff. 253–254, has been almost entirely cut away) 4–12^8 13^8(+9). In 2 columns of 35–36 lines, ruled in lead, with a center line between the columns and a double line in the far left margin; pricking visible in the inner margin. Written in a littera textualis. Opening initial, 3-line, green with red leaf-pattern infilling, and rubric in alternating lines of red and green; secondary initials set into the written space, 3- and 2-line, in plain red or green; tinted initials in the text, rubrics and running headlines in red.

Bound, s. XVII, in English brown calf over pasteboards; paper label on the front cover, also s. XVII, "Exposition on the Psalms, Lat. Liber artis praedicandi. Gregorii expositio in Job, et cetera"; edges speckled in red.

A composite volume in 4 parts, written in England in the middle of the thirteenth century; all the scribes write above the top line. Although the 1959 Sotheby catalogue (see below) suggests that the manuscript may have belonged to the Augustinians of St. Osyth near Colchester because of the invocations of St. Osyth on ff. 184 and 200 (and possibly in the erasures on ff. 229, 334), there is no formal evidence to this effect. The manuscript was almost certainly in an institutional library in the fifteenth century, since below the rubric on f. 3, a later hand has added "2° folio; causa distinctionis." Marginal notes by early owners: f. 2, s. XV: "Thoma Northall solvit domino Iohanni Wynton v s. viii d.," and on f. 334, s. XVI: "prec. xvi s." followed by an erasure. Belonged to the Welsh antiquary Robert Davies of Llannerch and Gwysaney (ca. 1658–1710). The earliest known catalogue of the Llannerch manuscripts, dated 1740, lists this manuscript as n. 14 (that number in ink on the front pastedown); the manuscript also appears in the 1778 catalogue as n. 69 (the cover of the manuscript has been rebacked, and thus probably lost its label with this designation). Later, when the collection had passed through inheritance to Philip Bryan Davies Cooke, a list of its contents was printed by the HMC, *6th Report,* pt. I (1887–88); this manuscript on p. 419. When owned by Lt.-Col. Philip Ralph Davies-Cooke (b. 1896), the collection was placed on deposit in the National Library of Wales, 1947–59, where this book bore the number "Gwysaney 19" (in pencil on the inner front cover). For the history of the collection, see H. D. Emanuel, "The Gwysaney Manuscripts," *National Library of Wales Journal* 7 (1952) 326–43. Davies-Cooke sale, Sotheby's, 15 June 1959, lot 203 to Maggs for the Huntington Library.

Secundo folio: [f. 4, flyleaves included in foliation] causa distinctionis

HM 19914

Bibliography: Schenkl 4797. *Chronica,* 2. *Aspects of Medieval England,* n. 39, open at f. 2.

HM 19915 — England, s. XII/XIII
AUGUSTINE; POMERIUS — *figs. 47, 48, 155*

1. ff. 1–61: *Incipit prologus sancti augustini episcopi in enchiridion,* Dici non potest dilectissime fili laurenti . . . [f. 2:] *Incipiunt capitula libri sequentis, i,* De proprio catholice fidei fundamento; *ii,* Quid inter sperare et timere . . . [f. 3:] *lxx,* De lege quod impleri non possit; *lxxi,* De baptismo boni hominis vel mali; *lxxii,* De karitate. *Expliciunt capitula. Incipit liber sancti augustini episcopi yponiensis qui dicitur Enchiridion. De proprio fidei catholice fundamento, i,* Certum vero propriumque fidei catholice fundamentum christus est . . . a quo enim quis devictus est huic servus addictus est. [f. 59:] *De baptismo boni hominis vel mali, lxxi,* Non est melior baptismus per manus sancti cuiuslibet hominis . . . et non ipse sacerdos corpus christi consecrat sed ipse christus per ipsum. [f. 59v:] *De caritate, lxxii,* Karissimi fratres qui ad ymaginem dei facti sumus . . . sed cum electis premium vite eterne recipere mereamur quod ipse prestare dignetur qui cum patre et spiritu sancto vivit et regnat deus per omnia secula seculorum. Amen. *Explicit liber sancti augustini yponensis episcopi qui vocatur enchiridion.*

Aurelii Augustini Opera. CC 46 (Turnholt 1969), "Enchiridion" ed. by E. Evans, pp. 21–112 line 20; the last 2 sections, on baptism and charity, not in printed text.

2. ff. 61–63v: [note, s. XVI, in upper margin: Ex libro D. Paschasii Abbatis Corbiensis ordinis sancti Benedicti ad Placidum abbatem de Sacramento altaris qui claruit temporibus Caroli Crassi imperatoris anno domini 880. Cap. 14] *Relatio cuiusdam sapientis de manifesta visione corporis christi,* Nemo qui sanctorum vitas et exempla legerit . . . et sacerdotis desiderium impletur ex miraculo nostraque fides firmaretur ex relatu. *De proprietate corporis christi quod sumimus in altari,* Vere credere et indubitanter scire debemus . . . et spirituali intelligentia degustetur. Et ut mirabilius loquar non alia plane quam que nata est de virgine maria . . . nisi a quo creata est in utero virginis ut verbum caro fieret amen.

B. Paulus, ed., *Pascasii Radberti De Corpore et Sanguine Domini.* CC Cont. Med. 16 (Turnholt 1969) 85–91, 76–77.

3. ff. 63v–66: Unidentified short passages: *Contemplatio abbatis macharii,* Eo tempore quo fratres accedebant ad sacramenta vidit abbas macharius . . . et manum suam in sacramentorum distributione super sacerdotis manum ponere. [f. 63v:] *De superbia,* Omni vitio deterior est superbia propter quod a summis personis summisque viris assumitur . . . quia tam per virtutes quam per vicia humanam mentem exterminat. [f. 64:] *De periurio,* Sicut mentiri non potest qui non loquitur sic periurare non poterit qui iurare non appetit . . . hoc accipit sicut ille cui iuratur intelligit. [f. 64:] *Distancia publice et occulte peccandi,* Maioris culpe est manifeste quam occulte peccare . . . de facto suo erubescit ipse si iam iudex fit. [f. 64v:] *De tribus peccatorum causis et earum remediis,*

Satis nos oportet timere tres causas fratres karissimi per quas totus perit mundus . . . sed hic et in eternum salvus erit deo auxiliante amen. [f. 65v:] *De omnipotencia dei,* Cum quicquid vult dominus facere et mortem peccatoris non vult . . . moritur quidem in peccato deo patiente sed nolente. [f. 65v:] *Item alia s.,* Septem sunt gradus quibus abstrahitur peccator a tenebroso puteo perdicionis . . . et timor dei ne iterum homo iste cadat in puteum. [f. 66:] *De triplici spelunca vulpium,* Vulpes foveas habent. Per vulpes que tres foveas in quibus se occultent habere dicuntur . . . hoc est deitatem suam super eum reclinare velit. [f. 66:] *Augustinus,* Preces valent ad ea impetranda que se precantibus concessurum esse prescivit deus. *Item,* Homo si nolit omnino non peccat. Sed si peccat aut si non peccat hoc totum etiam prenoscit deus. [f. 66v, ruled, but blank]

4. ff. 67–168v: *Incipiunt capitula libri primi,* Quod ea sit vite contemplative [added in pencil in the margin: proprietas] ubi deus mundo corde videbitur; *ii,* De qualitate vite future . . . [f. 68:] *Incipit prologus,* Diu multumque renisus sum voluntati tue mi domine studiosissime pontificum iuliane . . . [f. 70:] *Incipit prosperi liber primus de vita contemplativaque activa. Quod ea sit vite contemplative proprietas ubi deus mundo corde videbitur,* Contemplativa vita est in qua creatura creatorem suum . . . sed pro rebus enunciandis verba sunt instituta. *Explicit prosperi liber tercius de viciis et virtutibus.* [ff. 169–170v, blank]

Julianus Pomerius, *De vita contemplativa,* here attributed to Prosper of Aquitaine. *CPL* 998. *PL* 59:415–520. For a list of manuscripts, HM 19915 not included, see M. L. W. Laistner, "The Influence during the Middle Ages of the Treatise 'De Vita Contemplativa' and its surviving Manuscripts," in *Miscellanea Giovanni Mercati,* Studi e Testi 122 (Vatican City 1946) 2:344–58.

Parchment, ff. i (contemporary parchment) + 170; 231 × 166 (143 × 100) mm. $1–7^8$ 8^{10}(through f. 66) $9–21^8$. Catchwords of scribe i in the gutter, and of scribe ii in a small script in the center lower margin. Quire signatures in roman numerals in the middle of the upper margin, first leaf recto, "vii" on f. 49 and "viii" on f. 57; another signature (?) trimmed away in the middle of the lower margin, last leaf verso, f. 24v. 21 long lines; 2 columns of 21 lines in the chapter list to art. 1, ff. 2v–3; ruled in lead, the 2 top and bottom lines full across and an additional narrow double rule in the 3 outer margins through f. 66; thereafter, usually only the single top and bottom line full across and with ruling in the lower margin omitted; slash prick marks in the 3 outer margins; 2 parallel sets of pricking in the outer margin of quire 8. Written in a minuscule script by 2 scribes, both writing above the top line and using the flex mark in punctuation: i, ff. 1–66; ii, ff. 67–168v.

Opening initial, f. 3v, 6-line, tan and blue, infilled with stylized vines and leaves in blue, tan, green and orange-red, on a tan ground within a green frame; 2-line initials in light blue, green or orange-red with infilling and extensions of stylized leaves through f. 66; thereafter 5- to 2-line unornamented initials in the same colors, except for a poor attempt at leaf infilling on ff. 123v–124; in art. 4, some folios with 1-line initials within the text filled in red (e.g. ff. 86v–88, 89v–90). Notes in the margins in the scribe's (?) hand for art. 1, enclosed in decorated and tinted frames, e.g. f. 5, within a ship; f. 6, on a pedestal; f. 36v, supported by grotesques with a dog's and a rabbit's head and with fish tails; f. 46, encircled by a dragon sprouting leaves from his mouth. In the lower margin of f. 42, a half figure of Christ (?) blessing, in good style. Crude sketches in lead of a man riding a grotesque on f. 41v, and of dogs' heads on ff. 139v, 140; sketches for initials on ff. 30, 114v. Instructions to the rubricator frequently remaining, written vertically in the outer margins. Art. 1 corrected in ink in the margins; corrections not entered into the text; art. 4 corrected in lead in the margins; corrections then entered into the text over erasures or carefully rewritten in ink in the margin. Medieval pagination in early form arabic numerals in lead in the middle of the upper margin, ff. 3v–34, [1]–62; foliation in ink, s. XIII/XIV, in roman numerals in the middle of the outer margin verso, i–clxx. Considerable damage from water from f. 155 on.

Bound in contemporary white calf (?) over boards (back board gone), sewn onto 4 bands; semi-circular tabs at head and foot of spine, lined with pink deerskin and embroidered around the edges in blue and white; the whole covered, s. XV (?), by a heavy parchment or deerskin wrapper with a fore edge flap (now partially cut off) from the front cover to the back; remains of a pink strap closing to a central pin (now missing) on the back cover; 3 (of 4) bosses on front cover in the characteristic fluted, truncated cone shape of St. Mary's at Holme Cultram (also on Oxford, Bod. Lib., Lyell 2; see de la Mare, *Lyell Cat.*, entry and pl. 37); holes from former label at bottom center of back cover; bookmark of white skin, now loose, but once tied to a loop at the foot of the spine. Modern red morocco label on spine.

Written, ca. 1200, in England. Belonged from an early date to the Cistercian abbey of St. Mary at Holme Cultram, Cumberland: on f. i verso, s. XII^{ex}, "Liber Sancte Marie De Homcoltran. Hec Continentur in hoc volumine Enchiridion Augustini, Prosper De vita contemplativa"; on f. 1, in the lower margin, s. XIII, "Liber sancte Marie de holmo" (see de la Mare, *Lyell Cat.*, pl. 1c); on the same leaf, in the upper margin, the pressmark, s. XV, "liber lxxvi^{us}." Ker, *MLGB*, 102. Belonged to the Welsh antiquary Robert Davies of Llannerch and Gwysaney (ca. 1658–1710). The earliest known catalogue of the Llannerch manuscripts, dated 1740, lists this manuscript as n. 17 (that number in ink on f. i); the manuscript also appears in the 1778 catalogue as n. 42 (on a paper label on the spine). Later, when the collection had passed through inheritance to Philip Bryan Davies Cooke, a list of its contents was printed by the HMC, *6th Report,* pt. I (1887–88); this manuscript on p. 418. When owned by Lt. Col. Philip Ralph Davies-Cooke (b. 1896), the collection was placed on deposit in the National Library of Wales, 1947–59, where this book bore the number "Gwysaney 2" (in pencil on the front pastedown). For the history of the collection, see H. D. Emanuel, "The Gwysaney Manuscripts," *National Library of Wales Journal* 7 (1952) 326–43. Davies-Cooke sale, Sotheby's, 15 June 1959, lot 197 with a plate of f. 3v to Maggs for the Huntington Library.

Secundo folio: diligenter sciendo
Bibliography: Schenkl 4796. Römer, i, 340. *Chronica,* 2.

HM 19916 — England, s. XIV$^{1/4}$
GUILLELMUS DURANTIS, SPECULUM IUDICIALE

ff. 1–295v: [Prologue] *In nomine domini et gloriose virginis matris eius incipit speculum iudiciale a magistro Guillelmo duranti compositum. Rubrica,* Reverendo in christo patri ac domino suo octobono dei gratia sancti adriani diacono cardinali magister guillelmus duranti domini pape subdiaconus et capellanus . . . De throno procedunt fulgura, voces, atque tonutrua . . . [f. 2, Text:] Quoniam parum esset nosce iura foreprodita nisi persone quarum causa prodita sunt note essent . . . Pensans insuper non ministri meritum, sed ministerii effectum favorem profecto non querentes humanum sed solum bravium sempiternum. Ad quod nos perducat qui sine fine vivit et regnat. Amen.

Several early editions; Schulte, 2:148–52.

HM 19916

Parchment, ff. i (early parchment) + iv (paper) + 295 + iv (paper); 405 × 270 (330 × 210) mm. 1–24[12] 25[10](–8, 9, 10, excised). Quires signed in modern form arabic numerals on the first leaf recto; contemporary quire and leaf signatures: a-z, the tironian 7 and the "cum" abbreviation indicating the quire, and i–vii indicating the leaf. Catchwords in the inner corner, enclosed in a small ink frame. 2 columns of 75 lines, ruled in brown crayon. Written in a small semi-quadrata textura.

Opening historiated initial, 50 × 58 mm., depicting a doctor with an open book on his lectern, teaching 2 students, against a burnished gold background, from which grows a C-shaped frame of pink and blue segments, cusped corners, a grotesque, daisy buds, and occasional gold motifs. Major initials for the book divisions on ff. 2, 78v, 192v, 204, 9- to 5-line, in parted red and blue with void infilling of leaves produced by red cross-hatching, and with filigree and cascades of both colors; 2-line blue initials with red penwork. Paragraph marks alternating red and blue, in bracket shape when at the left of the text. Rubrics and running headlines in red and ink of the text. Genealogical diagram, f. 284; simple profile-head brackets by annotator, e.g. ff. 197, 200; f. 135a, ruled, but blank with note on f. 134v, "Hic nichil deficit"; copious marginal notes in several hands of the third quarter of the fourteenth century. On f. 295v, Latin and English verses in a mid-fourteenth century hand: "Nulli crostico [?] reor esse fidem neque dico/ hosti pro modico fit amicus hostis amico./ O vos causidici qui linguas venditis issy aliter hic cy [Walther, *Initia* 13058] / vos vocat infernus vous [?] respuit ordo supernus." The English verses are: "Twenty wynter glad and blyth/ Twenty wynter þe and þryf/ Twenty wynter stond in stede/ Twenty wynter byde þy bede" [*IMEV* 3815.3]. Also in the lower margin on f. 295v, a statement regarding the distance between the earth and the sky, pronounced by "quidam Bacalarius in theologia ⟨?⟩ in predicatione sua in ministerio sancti Pauli London."

Bound, s. XVII, in English speckled calf, with gilt-tooled spine; rebacked, original spine laid down; stains suggest that a former binding included 2 fore edge clasps. Two leaves, once used as pastedowns to judge from the stains (although not in this manuscript), and formerly laid in this volume, have been removed and catalogued as HM 46015.

Written in England in the first quarter of the fourteenth century. It appears similar in style of production, script and decoration to portions of a copy of the Apparatus on the Sext (Oxford, Bod. Lib., Lat. misc. b.16, ff. 1–72v, 151–276); for a reproduction from that manuscript, see Pächt and Alexander, 3, pl. 63, n. 610b; see also Sotheby's, 15 June 1959, lot 199. Erased inscriptions on f. 295: "Liber magistri Richardi Langton Rectoris de Lythe," and, in a second hand, "⟨?⟩ mense ⟨?⟩ xvi"; Richard Langton, a bachelor in canon law, flourished 1457–58 (Emden, *BRUO*, 1100); Lythe is in Yorkshire. Belonged to the Welsh antiquary Robert Davies of Llannerch and Gwysaney (ca. 1658–1710). The earliest known catalogue of the Llannerch manuscripts, dated 1740, lists this manuscript as n. 3 (that number in ink on f. i); the manuscript also appears in the 1778 catalogue as n. 2 (on a paper label on the spine). Later when the collection had passed through inheritance to Philip Bryan Davies Cooke, a list of its contents was printed by the HMC, *6th Report*, pt. I (1887–88); this manuscript on p. 419. When owned by Lt.-Col. Philip Ralph Davies-Cooke (b. 1896), the collection was placed on deposit in the National Library of Wales, 1947–59, where this book bore the number "Gwysaney 6" (in pencil on the front pastedown). For the history of the collection, see H. D. Emanuel, "The Gwysaney Manuscripts," *National Library of Wales Journal* 7 (1952) 326–43. Davies-Cooke sale, Sotheby's, 15 June 1959, lot 205 to Maggs for the Huntington Library.

Secundo folio: principiis quibus licet
Bibliography: Chronica, 3.

HM 19918
MISSAL, Sarum use

England, s. XIV^{1} and XV$^{1\text{-}ex}$
fig. 4

Composite volume

I.

1. f. i r–v [added, s. XV^{ex}]: Votive masses: collect, secret and postcommunion for the dead, Concede quesumus omnipotens et misericors deus ut anime quorum quarumque commemoracionem . . . ; collect, secret and postcommunion of Catherine, Margaret and Mary Magdalene; full office of Anne.

2. ff. 1–6v: Graded calendar in red and black including Julianus (27 January), Juliana (16 February), Chad (2 March), Translation of Edmund of Abingdon (9 June), Etheldreda (23 June), "festum Reliquiarum duplex festum" (15 September, in red; see below), Edith (16 September), Remigius, Germanus and Mylor (1 October), Thomas of Hereford and Leger (2 October), Hugh of Lincoln (6 October), Edmund of Abingdon (16 November, in red), Anianus and Hugh of Lincoln (17 November), Edmund king and martyr (20 November); later additions, in several hands: Anthony abbot (17 January), Osburga (23 January), David (1 March), "Bellum" (14 April; possibly referring to the battle of Barnet, 14 April 1471), Anne (26 July), Winifred (3 November); here, as elsewhere in the manuscript, the feasts of Thomas of Canterbury were not damaged; Latin month verses (Walther, *Initia* 14563).

3. ff. 7–90v: Temporale, beginning defectively in the first Sunday of Advent, through Easter Eve; Gloria; Credo; on f. 24, secret for the second Sunday after Epiphany, Ut tibi domine grata sint . . .

4. ff. 91–93v: Prefaces, that for All Apostles and the common preface are noted.

5. ff. 94–96vb: Canon of Mass, beginning defectively: //accepit panem in sanctas ac venerabiles manus suas . . . ; Pater noster, noted; Corporis et sanguinis tui domine ihesu christe sacramentum . . . substitutes in the lower margin for an erased prayer which began with a flourished initial "A."

6. ff. 96vb–145v: Temporale, Easter through the 25th Sunday after Pentecost; Sabbato iiii^{or} temporum; De dedicatione ecclesie.

7. ff. 145v–188: Sanctorale with full offices, Andrew through Linus, including the saints mentioned in the calendar and Laudus, f. 179; added in several later hands in the lower margins are prayers for David (f. 154v), Leger (f. 181), Edward king and confessor (f. 182v), Winifred (f. 185v), Hugh, Anianus and Martin (f. 186v) and Hugh (f. 187).

8. ff. 188–204v: Common of saints, ending defectively in the office for Many Virgins: . . . *Sapientie,* O quam pulcra est casta generatio cum claritate. Immortalis est enim memoria//

II.

9. ff. 205–212v [added quire from another book, s. XV^{1}]: Votive masses, collect, secret and postcommunion only, beginning defectively: //ne cunctorum. Per dominum [unidentified]; *pro quacumque tribulacione* [2 sets]; *contra aereas potestates* [*sic*]; *pro infirmo; pro benefactoribus vel pro salute minorum; pro*

specialibus amicis; pro defunctis [many sets]; *orationes generales pro vivis et defunctis;* Gloria, with 6 inset phrases mainly referring to the Virgin.

III.

10. ff. 213–215v [added quire from another book, s. XV^{ex}]: f. 213 [secretary hand], Mass for St. Gregory's Trental, collect, secret and postcommunion only; ff. 213v–215a [book hand], Masses with full office of Anne and Anthony abbot; f. 215b [secretary hand], Mass *pro mortalitate evitanda,* introit, "Recordare," through part of the lection from Luke.

IV.

11. ff. 216–222v [added quire from another book, s. XV^{med}]: 32 sequences from the first Sunday of Advent, ending defectively in the Purification; one leaf missing after f. 216, with loss of text from the end of the sequence for Stephen through the beginning of the sequence for the Circumcision; *RH* 17777, 17240, 16496, 9816, 11890, 19215, 3413, 11032, 5323, 5497, 6601, 22256, 15601, 3714, 4567, 21505, 10417, 17479, 18557, 17353, 5312, 10840, 10370, 822, 2435, 10222, 10013, 16071, 17733, 3795, 19168, 7494.

Parchment (poorly prepared), ff. i + 220.
I. s. XIV^1, ff. 1–204; 310 × 210 (230 × 140) mm. 1^6 2^{12}(–1) 3–8^{12} 9^{12}(–5, before f. 94) 10–12^{12} 13^{10} 14–17^{12} 18^{12}(–11, 12). 2 columns of 36 lines for the main text, 29 lines for the canon, ff. 91–96vb (first 5 lines). Ruled in brown crayon with double ruling between columns, top 2 lines full across, and occasionally a narrow double rule in the outer margin; pricking visible in the 3 outer margins. Written in a littera textualis, using brown ink; on ff. 92v–95v, notation on 4-line red staves. Opening leaf of the canon, presumably with decoration, now missing. Parted red and blue initials infilled with void leaf design or red whorls on ff. 93 (13-line), 17 (7-line) and 96v, 108v, 113, 120, 145v, 189 (5- or 4-line). 2-line initials alternating red and blue with simple flourishing; 1-line initials within the text in red or blue; blue paragraph marks; rubrics throughout.
II. s. XV^1, ff. 205–212; 292 × 195 (215 × 137) mm. One gathering of 8 leaves. 2 columns of 36 lines ruled in black ink, top and bottom 2 lines full across; pricking visible in the 3 outer margins. Written in a littera textualis with black ink. 3- and 2-line blue initials with red flourishes and simple red infilling; initials within the text filled in yellow; rubrics.
III. s. XV^{ex}, ff. 213–215; 305 × 195 (235 × 125) mm. One gathering originally of 4 leaves, now missing the last. Formal text on ff. 213v–214v only: 2 columns of 39 lines ruled in brown crayon, top and bottom 2 full across; pricking in outer margin and against inner bounding line. Written in a littera textualis in brown ink with added passages on ff. 213, 215r–v in a secretary script. 2- and 1-line plain red initials, space reserved for rubrics.
IV. s. XV^{med}, ff. 216–222; 296 × 197 (225 × 137) mm. A gathering once of 8 leaves, now missing the second. Leaf signatures in roman numerals on ff. 216, 217; catchword, f. 222, with pattes-de-mouche on either side, set towards the right corner. 2 columns of 37 lines ruled in ink; pricking visible in the 3 outer margins. Written in a littera textualis in black ink. One 4-line initial, f. 216, and 2-line initials in blue with rudimentary red flourishing and infilling; 1-line initials in the text alternating red and blue; rubrics.

Bound, s. XV^{ex}, in calf over bevelled wooden boards; 2 replacement straps to pins on back cover; rebacked; restored by Gertrude Weadock of New York, March 1939.

Written in England; pt. **I** was possibly copied in the first quarter of the fourteenth century: the calendar and sanctorale, f. 181, include Thomas of Hereford, canonized in 1320, but the calendar still places the feast of the relics on 15 September rather than at the moveable date of the first Sunday after the Translation of Thomas of Canterbury (between 8–14 July); this change of date was established in 1319. Pts. **II–IV** were written during the fifteenth century. A note added to the calendar at 1 July in the late fifteenth century reads: Obitus iohannis Nuby, katerine uxoris eius et agnetis Nuby et omnium fratrum et sororum istius loci. The volume was n. 398 in a book dealer's catalogue, with the relevant slip now glued to the front pastedown. Acquired with funds of the Friends of the Huntington Library from Scribner in July 1958.

Secundo folio: [f. 7, Text] Deus qui de beate marie
Bibliography: Chronica, 3.

HM 19920 STATUTES

England, s. $XV^{1/4}$
fig. 82

1. ff. 1–3v: Magna Carta, 9 Henry III, followed by a brief clause dated at Westminster, 18 March, 28 Henry III, on observing all articles of the charter; *SR* 1, charters, 22–25.

2. ff. 3v–5: Carta de foresta, ending ". . . quas prius habuerunt. Omnes autem illas consuetudines ut supra in magna carta. Nos autem donaciones et concessiones et cetera. Omnia ut supra," 23 Edward I; *SR* 1, charters, 42–43.

3. ff. 5–6v: Provisions of Merton, 20 Henry III; *SR* 1:1–4.

4. ff. 6v–10: Statute of Marlborough, 52 Henry III; *SR* 1:19–25.

5. ff. 10–17: Statute of Westminster I, 3 Edward I; *SR* 1:26–39.

6. ff. 17–18v: Statute of Gloucester, beginning in the chapter on damages in novel disseisin, 6 Edward I; *SR* 1:47–50.

7. ff. 18v–19: *Iste Articulus sequens in quadam billa scriptus consutus est statuto consignato in banco,* Come contenu soit en nostre estatut que nul homme de nostre court n'empreigne plee en champert . . . et ne purquant soient reintz a la volunte le Roi; *SR* 1:216, first paragraph; see also art. 33 of this description.

8. f. 19: Article of the statute of Gloucester, ending "Memorandum quod iste articulus in forma predicta consignatus fuit sub magno sigillo domini Edwardi Regis . . . non obstante quod articulus ille in omnibus cum dicto statuto Glouc. non concordat," 9 Edward I; *SR* 1:52 and footnote on that page.

9. ff. 19–33v: Statute of Westminster II, 13 Edward I; *SR* 1:71–95.

10. ff. 33v–34v: Prerogativa regis; *SR* 1:226–27.

11. ff. 34v–35: Statute of bigamy, 4 Edward I; *SR* 1:42–43.

12. f. 35r–v: Of persons vouched to warranty who are present, 20 Edward I; *SR* 1:108–09.

13. ff. 35v–36: Statute of defending right, 20 Edward I; *SR* 1:110.

14. ff. 36–37v: Statute of the exchequer, copied as 3 separate instruments, the second and third beginning, "Purce que la communalte du Roialme ad eu graunde damage . . ." and "Purce que les mareschals Conestables et les Chaumberleins que sont de fee al Escheqer . . ."; *SR* 1:196–98.

15. ff. 37v–38: Statute of Ireland concerning coparceners, 20 Henry III (here dated 14 May, 24 Henry III); *SR* 1:5.

16. f. 38r–v: Statute of Westminster IV, 14 Edward II; *SR* 1:180–81.

17. ff. 38v–39v: Provisions made in the exchequer, 12 Edward I (dated in the rubriç 23 May, 10 Edward I): *SR* 1:69–70.

18. ff. 39v–40: Quia emptores, 18 Edward I; *SR* 1:106.

19. ff. 40–42: *Incipit Statutum Suthamptoun,* In Octabis sancti Michaelis anno quinquagesimo secundo coram N. de litt. precipe priori de monte forti quod iuste et cetera reddat I. et A. uxori eius unum molendinum et lv acres terre cum pertinentibus in N. in quas idem prior non habet ingressum . . . et non liberum tenementum est id quod in villenagio tenetur sive ad terminum vite perpetuo sibi et heredibus suis possidendum.

Notes of law and cases, 3 of which are dated 52 Henry III; named persons are "N. de litt.," "A. Malleb'ge" vs. "C. de B. coram S. de littilbure in Banco," "J. de lande" vs. the abbot and convent of Selby, "G. de Sutton" vs. "A. Husse coram M[artin] de l[ittlebury] in Banco," "Walter de Wyburnam" and "W. de Cantilupo" bishop of Worcester (1237–66) "qui postea fuit collega S. de monte forti Com. leyc."

20. f. 42r–v: Statute for religious men, 7 Edward I; *SR* 1:51.

21. ff. 42v–43: *Articuli contra prohibicionem Regis,* Sub qua forma non impetrent laici Regis prohibicionem super decimis oblacionibus obvencionibus . . . si reus velit redimere libere recipiat prelatus pecuniam licet regia prohibicio porrigatur; *SR* 1:171.

22. ff. 43–44v: Articles for the clergy, 9 Edward II; *SR* 1:171–74.

23. ff. 44v–45v: Statute of Carlisle, without concluding writ, 35 Edward I; *SR* 1:150–52.

24. ff. 45v–46: Circumspecte agatis, ending ". . . regia prohibicione non obstante," 13 Edward I; *SR* 1:101.

25. f. 46: Statute of the writ of consultation, 18 Edward I; *SR* 1:108.

26. f. 46: *Incipit Statutum Indicavit,* Quia eciam lites Curia christianitatis hactenus indebitas dilationes multociens paciebantur . . . super hoc cercioretur. In cuius rei et cetera. Teste me ipso et cetera apud Westmonasterium anno xxxiiii°," 34 Edward I; *SR* 1:147.

27. f. 46r–v: Statute of ragman, 4 Edward I; *SR* 1:44.

28. ff. 46v–47: Statute of persons to be put in assizes and juries, ending ". . . prout temporibus retroactis fieri consuevit," 21 Edward I; *SR* 1:113.

29. f. 47: Statute concerning wards and reliefs; *SR* 1:228.

30. f. 47r–v: Statute of breaking prisons, 23 Edward I; *SR* 1:113.

31. f. 47v: Statute for persons appealed, 28 Edward I; *SR* 1:141.

32. f. 47v: Statute against allowing protections, dated at Westminster, 18 November, 34 Edward I; *SR* 1:217.

33. ff. 47v–48: Statute concerning conspirators, dated at Berwick, 12 March, 18 Edward I; *SR* 1:216, first paragraph; see also art. 7 of this description.

34. f. 48: *Incipit Statutum de Conspiratoribus,* Dominus Rex mandavit nunciante Gilberto de Thornetoun . . . apud Westmonasterium quinto die maii Anno regni nostri vicesimo quinto; *SR* 1:216, second paragraph.

35. f. 48: Ordinance concerning conspirators, 33 Edward I; *SR* 1:145.

36. f. 48: *Statutum de iure calumpn. pro Rege,* De requisitionibus coram Iusticiis quibuscumque capiendis et in quibus dominus Rex est pars qualitercumque . . . Ita [*sic*] ordinacio et ordinacio de foresta facte fuerunt in parliamento apud Westmonasterium die dominica proxima post festum sancti michaelis Anno regni Regis Edwardi filii Regis henrici tricesimo quinto.

37. f. 48v: Of the chattels of felons; *SR* 1:230.

38. f. 48v: *Incipit Statutum de utlagaria,* Omnibus ad quos presentes litere pervenerint salutem. Nos legem habemus de tempore . . . Et ideo dicimus quod Aldemarus Wyntoun in regno nostro Anglie introduci non debet quia de morte hominis et roberiis appellatus fuit et non comparavit et ideo propter suam contumaciam utlagatus est.

39. ff. 48v–49: Statute forbidding bearing of armor, 7 Edward II; *SR* 1:170.

40. f. 49: Statute of arms, beginning "A nostre seignour le Roi priont et requiront les Countes . . ."; *SR* 1:230–31.

41. f. 49r–v: Statute for respiting of knighthood; *SR* 1:229.

42. ff. 49v–50v: Statute of fines levied, beginning "Quia fines in Curia nostra levati . . . ," 27 Edward I; *SR* 1:128–30.

43. ff. 50v–51: Statute concerning fines and attorneys, dated at Carlisle, 4 February, 35 Edward I; *SR* 1:215.

44. ff. 51–52: Statute of merchants, 13 Edward I; *SR* 1:98–100.

45. ff. 52–53: Statute of joint tenants, 34 Edward I; *SR* 1:145–47.

46. f. 53: Statute concerning the sheriff and his clerks; *SR* 1:213.

47. f. 53r–v: Statute of sheriffs, without concluding writ, 9 Edward II; *SR* 1:174–75.

48. ff. 53v–54: Oath of the sheriff; *SR* 1:247.

49. f. 54: *Officium vicecomitis,* Ceux sont les articles touchants nostre coroune et nostre pees enfreint pleablez par viscont autre foitz . . . Et ceux de xii ans que ne sount venuz a hundrede toutz les articles que sont contenuz en vewe de frankplegge et cetera.

50. ff. 54–55: Office of the coroner, 4 Edward I; *SR* 1:40–41.

51. f. 55: *Sacramentum Coronatoris,* Ceo oiez sire viconte que R. de B. Coroner nostre seignur le Roy deinz le Wapentake de G. loialment et sanz lower demander . . . et quanque a mon office de Coroner appent sanz rien prendre si dieu m'aide et cetera.

52. ff. 55–57: Statute of Exeter, with the articles, dated 28 December, 14 Edward [I], as a separate instrument; *SR* 1:210–12.

53. f. 57r–v: Abjuration and oath of thieves, beginning "Hoc audis domine Coronator quod ego Robertus Rounde sum latro . . . versus portum de P. . . ." and ending ". . . sicut deus me adiuvet. Et avant q'il foriure le Roialme . . . et une crois de fuiste en sa main et cetera"; *SR* 1:250.

54. ff. 57v–58v: Statute of Winchester, 13 Edward I; *SR* 1:96–98.

55. ff. 58v–59: Articles of inquiry upon the statute of Winchester; *SR* 1:245–46.

56. f. 59r–v: Statute for escheators, 29 Edward I; *SR* 1:142–43.

57. f. 59v: Oath of escheators, ending ". . . ou par quoi droiture soit destourbe"; *SR* 1:249.

58. ff. 59v–61: Articles of the office of escheator, differing from the text in *SR* 1:238–41.

59. ff. 61–62: Statute of Gloucester, up to the chapter on damages in novel disseisin, and ending with a "Precipimus tibi" clause, text here in Latin, 6 Edward I; *SR* 1:45–46.

60. f. 62: Quo warranto II, here in Latin, 18 Edward I; *SR* 1:107.

61. f. 62r–v: Quo warranto I, 18 Edward I; *SR* 1:107.

62. ff. 62v–64: *Incipiunt Notabilia de quo Waranto,* Utrum domino Regi competat accio ad recuperandum dominicum corone sue a corona sua separatum per breve . . . se possent tueri si calumpniati fuerint per quam se tuerentur huiusmodi magnates vel eorum heredes et cetera.

63. f. 64: *Statutum de antiquo dominico corone,* Licet in antiquo dominico corone non currat aliquod breve nisi parvum breve de recto clausum . . . propter quod si ego fuissem assignatus Iusticiarius ego secure procederem in assisa sicut pluries consuevi quid alii faciunt ignoro.

A. J. Horwood, ed., *Year Books of the Reign of King Edward the first, years XX and XXI.* RS 39 pt. 16 (London 1886) xviii–xix, here ending incomplete with respect to the printed text.

64. ff. 64–65: View of frankpledge, here in Latin; *SR* 1:246–47.

65. f. 65r–v: Extenta manerii; *SR* 1:242–43.

66. ff. 65v–66: Statutes concerning money, with articles copied as a separate instrument; *SR* 1:219–219a.

67. f. 66r–v: *Capitula de tonsura Monete,* De tonsura monete tam de Iudeis quam de christianis de hiis qui tradiderunt denaros suos retonsore pro habendo lucro tonsure . . . cum multis de populo ad hoc teneretur licet expresse non consentirent.

68. ff. 66v–67: Statutum de moneta parvum, dated 21 July, 20 Edward [I]; *SR* 1:220.

69. f. 67r–v: Statute for oaths of the king's officers in the eyre, with introductory material here in French, "Primes doit le Iustice faire lire devant lui . . ."; *SR* 1:232.

70. ff. 67v–68v: Articles of the eyre, ending " . . . per quod iusticia et veritas suffocantur"; *SR* 1:233–34.

71. ff. 68v–71: New articles in eyre; *SR* 1:235–38.

72. ff. 71–72: Ordinance of the forest, ending " . . . salvis arentacionibus nostris in forma predicta. In cuius et cetera. Teste et cetera apud Westmonasterium xxvii die [month not given] Anno regni nostri xxxiiii," 34 Edward I; *SR* 1:147–49.

73. f. 72: Statute of trespassers in parks, 21 Edward I; *SR* 1:111–12.

74. ff. 72v–73: Customs and assize of the forest, ending " . . . quia sufficientem habet inde Warantum"; *SR* 1:243–45.

75. f. 73r–v: Ordinance of the forest, ending with the note "Irrotulatur in Banco," 33 Edward I; *SR* 1:144.

76. f. 73v: General days in banc, ending " . . . et sic respondet quilibet terminus alii"; *SR* 1:208.

77. f. 73v: General days in dower, ending " . . . Si in quindena sancti Iohannis Baptiste in crastino animarum et cetera"; *SR* 1:208.

78. ff. 73v–74v: Judgment of the pillory, ending " . . . si in mercato venissent"; *SR* 1:201–02.

79. f. 74v: Assize of bread and ale, here in French and copied as 3 separate instruments, the second and the third headed "lucrum pistoris" and "Assisa cervisie"; *SR* 1:199–200; text ends "Quando quarterium ordei venditur pro ii solidis . . . et diminuetur per vi denarios"; *SR* 1:202.

80. ff. 74v–75: Assize of weights and measures, beginning "Nunc dicendum est de ponderibus plumbi et aliarum rerum. Notandum quod le charre de plumbo constat ex xxx formellis [*sic*] . . ."; *SR* 1:205.

81. ff. 75–76: Statute concerning bakers, copied as 3 separate instruments, of which the first ends ". . . et idem fiat de cocis transgredientibus. Siqui coci decoquant carnes vel pisces in pane vel aqua vel alio modo non sanas corpori humano . . . puniantur primo secundo tercio et quarto ut supradictum est de carnificibus et cetera" and the third ends ". . . et cum necesse fuerit per eandem cedulam cerciorari possunt"; *SR* 1:202–04.

82. f. 76: *Incipit composicio ulnarum et perticarum,* Ordinatum est quod tria grana ordei . . . faciunt acram et cetera; *SR* 1:206, footnote.

83. f. 76r–v: Statute for the measuring of land, ending ". . . Quando xlv tunc iii et di. et cetera"; *SR* 1:206–07.

84. f. 76v: Assize of weights and measures, first paragraph only, "Per discrecionem tocius regni Anglie . . . set carra de peck est multo minus. Denarius sancti petri est elemosina Regis et solvitur in festo sancti petri et pauli"; *SR* 1:204.

85. ff. 76v–77: Manner of doing homage and fealty, here with directions in Latin and copied as 2 separate instruments, with a passage on the nature of homage inserted between the 2 parts, "Homagium est iuris vinculum per quod dominus tenetur et distringitur ad Warantizandum . . . non propter hoc cadit homagium in persona superstitis licet cadat in persona morientis"; *SR* 1:227–28.

86. f. 77: *De villenagio,* Vous vous [*sic*] savoir q'en deux maners sont vileins, les uns sont celes que sount del auncien demesne le Roi . . . il demoura vilein a celui a qi il dist q'il fuist avant sokeman et cetera.

87. f. 77r–v: Statute concerning tallage, 25 Edward I; *SR* 1:125.

88. f. 77v: Statute for view of land and essoin in the king's service; *SR* 1:218.

89. f. 77v: Statute concerning the great assizes and battle; *SR* 1:218.

90. ff. 77v–78: Statute of the justices of assize, 21 Edward I; *SR* 1:112.

91. ff. 78–80v: Articles upon the charters, 28 Edward I; *SR* 1:136–41.

92. ff. 80v–81: Statute concerning the lands of the Templars, ending ". . . si voluerint audire concordatum provisionem et assignacionem predictas in forma predicta," 17 Edward II; *SR* 1:194–96.

93. f. 81r–v: Statute that the rector not cut down trees in the churchyard; *SR* 1:221.

94. ff. 81v–82: *Decretum Walteri Grey Archiepiscopi Eboracensis,* Decretum domini Walteri Grey Eboracensis Archiepiscopi Anglie primatis . . . et memoriam omnium futurorum. Cum plerumque inter Rectores seu vicarios in provincia Eboracensi constitutos . . . secundum hanc ordinacionem sive constitucionem alias in hac parte probatam.

D. Wilkins, ed., *Concilia Magnae Britanniae et Hiberniae* (London 1737) 1:698.

95. f. 82r–v: *Exposicio vocabulorum,* Sek hoc est secta de omnibus in Curia nostra secundum consuetudinem regni . . . Sak . . . Tolhost . . . Ton . . . Infangenthef . . . Ferdwite quietus esse de mora in hostagio; ff. 83–92, ruled, but blank.

96. f. 92v: Table of golden numbers and leap years, 1413–1500.

97. ff. 93–98v: Graded calendar, with rank of feast, number of lessons, number of singers or indication of soloist for the invitatory, responsories; in the lower margin, list of the most prominent feasts of the month, headed "ab omnibus operibus"; usual Latin month verses, "Prima dies mensis et septima truncat ut ensis . . ." (Walther, *Initia* 14563), indication of sun entering the zodiac sign and number of hours in the day and night; among the feasts are Translation of Wilfrid, bishop of York (24 April, in red, identified as "non sarum"), John of Beverley (7 May, in red, identified as "non sarum"), William, archbishop of York (8 June, in red, identified as "non sarum"), Anne (26 July, in red), Translation of John of Beverley (25 October, in red, identified as "non sarum"); the qualifier "pape" and the feasts of Thomas Becket erased.

98. ff. 99–100: Statute I, beginning defectively "//doune fait si trove soit en la court le Roi par conissance du partie . . . ," 1 Edward III; *SR* 1:253–54.

99. ff. 100–101: Statute II, 1 Edward III; *SR* 1:255–57.

100. ff. 101–102v: *Item aliud Statutum editum Anno primo,* Come nadgairs en temps le Roi E. fitz le Roi E. fitz le Roi henri plusours graundz du Roialme D'engleterre surmeissent a hugh le despenser le fitz et hugh le despenser le piere plusours malveistes . . . desobeissances et rebellions soient quitz par ceste acorde assent et estatut a touz iours.

101. ff. 102v–104v: Statute made at Northampton, without concluding writ, 2 Edward III; *SR* 1:257–61.

102. ff. 104v–106v: Statute, without concluding writ, 4 Edward III; *SR* 1:261–65.

103. ff. 106v–108v: Statute, ending ". . . a deliverance come desuis est dit. Auxint est accorde par nostre seignur le Roi . . . ne par autre nul robbeour meffesour n'endite," 5 Edward III; *SR* 1:265–69.

104. ff. 108v–110v: Statute made at York, without concluding writ, 9 Edward III; *SR* 1:269–72.

105. ff. 110v–111: Second statute made at York, ending ". . . qe vous facez publier et ferment tenir ceste chose suisdit dover et cetera," 9 Edward III; *SR* 1:273–74.

106. ff. 111–112: Statute I, 10 Edward III; *SR* 1:275.

107. f. 112r–v: Statute II, ending ". . . auxibien a la suite le Roi come a la suite de partie. Done a Westmonstr et cetera," 10 Edward III; *SR* 1:276–77.

108. ff. 112v–113: Statute, without concluding writ, 11 Edward III; *SR* 1:280–81.

109. ff. 113–118v: Statute I, 14 Edward III; *SR* 1:281–89.

110. ff. 118v–119v: Statute IV, 14 Edward III; *SR* 1:292–94.

111. ff. 119v–120: Statute III, 14 Edward III; *SR* 1:292.

112. ff. 120–121: Statute II, 18 Edward III; *SR* 1:300–01.

113. f. 121: Statute I, 18 Edward III; *SR* 1:299.

114. ff. 121–122: Statute III, 18 Edward III; *SR* 1:302–03.

115. ff. 122–123: Ordinance made for the state of the land of Ireland; *SR* 1:193–94.

116. ff. 123–124: Ordinance for the justices, 20 Edward III; *SR* 1:303–05.

117. ff. 124–125v: Statute, ending ". . . et applicare suo usui quod per ipsum conceditur prosequenti. Explicit et cetera," 23 Edward III; *SR* 1:307–09.

118. ff. 125v–127: Statute II, 25 Edward III; *SR* 1:311–13.

119. ff. 127–130: Statute V, copied as 2 separate instruments, the second beginning "Auxint pur ce que diverses opinions ont este avaunt ces heures . . ." and without concluding writ, 25 Edward III; *SR* 1:319–24.

120. ff. 130–131v: Ordinance for the clergy, 25 Edward III; *SR* 1:324–26.

121. ff. 131v–133: Statute of provisors of benefices, 25 Edward III; *SR* 1:316–18.

122. f. 133r–v: Statute for those who are born in parts beyond sea, 25 Edward III; *SR* 1:310.

123. ff. 133v–135: Statute III, 25 Edward III; *SR* 1:314–16.

124. ff. 135–141v: Ordinance of the staples, 27 Edward III; *SR* 1:332–43.

125. ff. 141v–142: Et puis apres fuist ordene par nostre dit seignur le Roi prelates et autres gentz du conseil nostre dit seignur le Roi q'une autre estaple seroit tenuz a kyngestoun sur hull . . . a Westm. le lundy prochein apres la feste de seint marc l'evangelist l'an du regne nostre dit seignur le Roi d'engleterre vint et oeptisme et de France quinzisme et come assent de tout le parlement horspris certeins articles contenuz en un estatut fait en le parlement avaundit.

126. f. 142: Fait a remembrer q'ia soit ce q'il fuist ordene a conseil tenuz a Westm. le lundy prochein apres le fest de seint matheu l'apostoil darrein passe par les grauntz et autres illeoques este antz que leins et plumbe seroient poisez . . . et illeoques la custume paie les dites leins pealx quirs et plumbe a mesmes les Custumers.

127. f. 142r–v: Ordinance of the fees of the mayors and constables of the staple, 27 Edward III; *SR* 1:343–44.

128. ff. 142v–143v: Come contenu soit en les ordinances de l'estaple fait a graunt conseil tenuz a Westm. le lundy proschein apres le fest de seint matheu l'apostoil darrein passe que chacun marchant qi vende ses leins a l'estaple . . . soient les boundes des ditz estaples parmy toute la ville. *Expliciunt ordinaciones staple; SR* 1:348–49.

129. ff. 143v–145: Statute against annullers of judgments of the king's court, 27 Edward III; *SR* 1:329–31.

130. ff. 145–148: Statute, 28 Edward III; *SR* 1:345–49.

131. ff. 148–149v: Statute I, without concluding writ, 31 Edward III; *SR* 1:349–52.

132. ff. 149v–150v: Ordinance concerning the salt fish of Blakeney, 31 Edward III; *SR* 1:355–56.

133. ff. 150v–151v: Ordinance made concerning the selling of herrings, 31 Edward III; *SR* 1:353–55.

134. ff. 151v–152: Ordinance of herring, 35 Edward III (here dated 34 Edward III); *SR* 1:369–70; see also art. 136 of this description.

135. ff. 152v–155v: Statute, 34 Edward III; *SR* 1:364–69.

136. ff. 155v–156: Ordinance of herring, 35 Edward III; *SR* 1:369–70; see also art. 134 of this description.

137. ff. 156–159: Statute I, 36 Edward III; *SR* 1:371–76.

138. ff. 159–160: Of the pardon made to the commonalty of the realm of England, without concluding writ, 36 Edward III; *SR* 1:376–78.

139. ff. 160–163: Statute concerning diet and apparel, 37 Edward III; *SR* 1:378–83.

140. ff. 163–164: Statute I, 38 Edward III; *SR* 1:383–85.

141. ff. 164–165: Statute II, 38 Edward III; *SR* 1:385–87.

142. f. 165: Accorde est par nostre seignur et son conseil a ce parlement de Northamptoun que touz les oiers et terminers grauntez contre la fourme d'esta-

tut fait en temps le Roi E. Aiel le Roi qor est . . . mes ce est baille en Chauncellerie par bille.

This text also in HM 906, f. 125r–v, HM 930, f. 12 and EL 9 H 10, ff. 55v–56.

143. ff. 165–166: Statute, 42 Edward III; *SR* 1:388–90.

144. ff. 166v–167v: Statute, 43 Edward III; *SR* 1:390–92.

145. ff. 167v–168: Statute, 45 Edward III; *SR* 1:393.

146. f. 168r–v: Statute, 47 Edward III; *SR* 1:395.

147. ff. 168v–169v: Statute, 50 Edward III; *SR* 1:396–98; ff. 170–172v, ruled, but blank.

148. ff. 173–175v: Statute, 1 Richard II; *SR* 2:1–5.

149. ff. 175v–178v: Statute I, 2 Richard II; *SR* 2:6–11.

150. ff. 178v–179: Statute II, 2 Richard II; *SR* 2:12.

151. ff. 179–180v: Statute, 3 Richard II; *SR* 2:13–15.

152. ff. 180v–181: Statute, 4 Richard II; *SR* 2:16.

153. ff. 181–184v: Statute I, 5 Richard II; *SR* 2:17–23.

154. ff. 184v–186: Statute II, ending ". . . et ent requis come desuis est dit," 5 Richard II; *SR* 2:23–26.

155. ff. 186–188v: Statute I, 6 Richard II; *SR* 2:26–30.

156. ff. 188v–189: Statute II, 6 Richard II; *SR* 2:30–31.

157. ff. 189v–191v: Statute, 7 Richard II; *SR* 2:32–36.

158. f. 192r–v: Statute, without concluding writ, 8 Richard II; *SR* 2:36–37.

159. ff. 192v–193v: Statute, 9 Richard II; *SR* 2:38–39.

160. ff. 193v–200v: Statute, 11 Richard II; *SR* 2:43–55.

161. ff. 201–203v: Statute, without concluding writ, 12 Richard II; *SR* 2:55–60.

162. ff. 203v–207v: Statute I, without concluding writ, 13 Richard II; *SR* 2:61–68.

163. ff. 207v–209: Statute II, without concluding writ, 13 Richard II; *SR* 2:68–74.

164. ff. 209v–210: Statute III, 13 Richard II; *SR* 2:74–75.

165. ff. 210–211: Statute, without concluding writ, 14 Richard II; *SR* 2:76–77.

166. ff. 211–213: Statute, without concluding writ, 15 Richard II; *SR* 2:78–82.

167. ff. 213v–216: Statute, without concluding writ, 16 Richard II; *SR* 2:82–87.

168. ff. 216–217v: Statute, ending ". . . et si sovent come bon leur semblera," 17 Richard II; *SR* 2:87–90.

169. ff. 217v–218v: Statute, 20 Richard II; *SR* 2:92–94.

170. ff. 218v–226: Statute, 21 Richard II; *SR* 2:94–110; f. 226v, ruled, but blank.

171. ff. 227–231v: Statute, 1 Henry IV; *SR* 2:111–19.

172. ff. 231v–238v: Statute, 2 Henry IV; *SR* 2:120–31.

173. ff. 238v–244v: Statute, 4 Henry IV; *SR* 2:132–43.

174. ff. 245–247v: Statute, 5 Henry IV; *SR* 2:143–48.

175. ff. 247v–248v: Statute, 6 Henry IV; *SR* 2:148–50.

176. ff. 248v–253: Statute, 7 Henry IV; *SR* 2:150–58.

177. ff. 253–254: Statute, ending ". . . come par lour procuratours notaires et executours avantditz," 9 Henry IV; *SR* 2:159–61; ff. 254v–258v, ruled, but blank.

Parchment, ff. iv (early modern paper) + iv (contemporary parchment) + 258 + iv (early modern paper); 348 × 230 (230 × 142–145) mm. $1–10^8$ 11^8(–4, 5 after f. 83) 12^8(–2, 3 after f. 87) 13^6(calendar) 14^8(–1 after f. 98) $15–22^8$ 23^4(–2 after f. 170) $24–29^8$ 30^6(through f. 226) $31–34^8$. Catchwords in flourished ink frames in the inner lower margin; signatures mostly cropped: red plus sign on the first 4 leaves of quires 15, 17–18, 22, 24–29; red "a" in quire 1; brown ink "m," "n" and "o" in quires 26, 27 and 28. 2 columns of 40 lines, ruled in ink with additional double rules in all 4 margins (omitted in lower margins of quires 8, 9, 12, 23, 31, 32); slash prick marks occasionally remaining in upper and lower margins. Written in a calligraphic anglicana formata hand of chancery type. The hand is not dissimilar from that of Richard Frampton who signed Glasgow, University Library, Hunterian T.4.1 (84) (not 80 as in Somerville, below) and who was paid for copying the Great Cowchers (London, P. R. O. Duchy of Lancaster. Misc. Books, D.L. 42, 1 and 2), for which see R. Somerville, "The Cowcher Books of the Duchy of Lancaster," *English Historical Review* 51 (1936) 598–615 and *History of the Duchy of Lancaster* (London 1953) vol. 1 pl. 2 facing p. 22 and pl. 7 facing p. 140.

Historiated initials, 8- and 7-line, in the style of the Dutch Master of the Carmelite Missal (and related to the historiated initials in the Great Cowchers), containing portraits of Henry III (f. 1), Richard II (f. 173) and Henry IV (f. 227); the leaf beginning the statutes of Edward III has been excised, but the offset of a full border remains on f. 98v. The initials are in white-highlighted blue or pink on gold grounds, with full bar borders decorated with leaves in gold, pink, blue and orange and with coats of arms (see below) possibly added on ff. 1 and 173, but integral on f. 227; the initial on f. 227, more delicately shaded than the previous 2, and with border of a slightly later style, including thimble leaves, kite leaves and green touching on the ink sprays. 3- and 2-line blue initials and blue paragraph marks, both with red flourishing; rubrics in red. In the calendar, 2-line gold initials with purple flourishing and blue initials with red; 1-line initials alternating blue with red flourishing and red with purple. Running headlines on ff. 99–105v only; chapter numbers in the margins; "ex[aminatur] per rotul[um]" in the hand of the scribe at the end of arts. 1, 2, 9, 98, 100–102, 136, 148, 149, 151, 153–160, 162–167; notes in another hand identifying regnal year for some statutes; on f. 92, s. XV or XVI, a small sketch in ink of a young man's head; on f. iv recto and verso, s. XVII, a table giving the moral significance of various tinctures of arms.

Bound, s. XVII, in English brown calf, gold tooled; gilt center lozenge flanked by the initials "H.N." (the "N" stamped backwards) on both covers; rebacked with original spine laid down; remains of 2 green fore edge ties; red speckled edges.

Written in England in the first quarter of the fifteenth century, but after 1407, the date of the last statute (art. 177); the table on f. 92v with dates from 1413 to 1500 may constitute a later addition. Possibly intended for owners in York, given the presence of Yorkshire saints in the calendar and the text of art. 94. The somewhat finer border on f. 227, incorporating (rather than adding) the coats of arms, suggests that the eventual owner may have decided to purchase the book rather late in its production. The coats of arms on f. 1 are: in the upper corner, the arms of England; in the outer margin, barry of 6 or and azure, on a canton argent a chaplet gules (Holme, of Yorkshire or of Lancashire); across the lower margin, the first coat of arms, Holme impaling sable a lion rampant argent (Wastneys), the second Holme, and the third Holme within a bordure engrailed gules; below these 3 coats of arms are faint sketches of the same arms, perhaps as instructions to the illuminator; the arms themselves appear to be later additions over larger, blank shields, now erased. On f. 173, in the upper corner, the arms of England and France quarterly, impaling the arms attributed to Edward the Confessor (azure, a cross flory between 5 martlets or); in the outer margin, within a bordure or, quarterly, 1 and 4 argent 3 chaplets gules (Lascelles? Hilton?), 2 and 3 argent 2 bars azure (unidentified); across the lower margin, the first coat of arms, Holme impaling Wastneys, the second Holme, the third argent a lion rampant sable (also for Wastneys?); the 3 coats of arms in the lower margin appear to be later additions over larger, blank shields, now erased. On f. 227, in the upper corner, the arms of England and France; in the outer margin, azure 3 chevronels interlaced and a chief or (Fitzhugh); across the lower margin, the first coat of arms, Holme impaling Wastneys, the second Holme, the third Holme within a bordure engrailed gules. The arms may be those of John Holme (d. 1438; Foster, *Yorkshire Pedigrees,* 1874, ii), of Paull-Holme, who married Elizabeth, daughter and co-heir of Sir Adam Wastneys; his son, also named John Holme, married Joan, daughter of John Ellerker of Riseby, serjeant at law ca. 1441; the younger John Holme was probably Baron of the Exchequer, 1446–49 (Foss, *Judges of England,* iv, p. 331). On f. v verso, twice, the signature of Sir Thomas Bourchier (1442–1512), nephew to the Cardinal Archbishop of Canterbury of the same name (see J. C. Wedgwood and A. D. Holt, *History of Parliament,* London 1936, 1:95–96); the same inscription occurs in Princeton University, Garrett 150, a *Brut,* and in Oxford, Bod. Lib., Ashmole 39, a copy of Lydgate's *Life of our Lady.* Also on f. v verso, s. XVI, "Constat Roberto plummer." The book belonged to "H.N." who had it rebound with his initials on the covers and who may have written the notes on tinctures on f. iv recto and verso. On f. iii, s. XVII, "Roger Allestry his book 1291 [*sic*]." Armorial bookplate, s. XIX, of Thomas William Evans, in which the first quarter (gironny of 8 argent and vert, a lion rampant gardant or) and the crest (in a charger a boar's head erased argent) correspond to those of W. Evans of Allestree Hall, Derbyshire. Sold by J. and J. Leighton to C. W. Dyson Perrins (1864–1958) in 1905. Dyson Perrins sale, Sotheby's, 1 December 1959, lot 71 with plate of f. 173 to the Huntington Library.

Secundo folio: et hoc modo
Bibliography: G. Warner, *Descriptive Catalogue of Illuminated Mavuscripts in the Library of C. W. Dyson Perrins* (Oxford 1920) vol. 1, pp. 62–63, and vol. 2, pl. 23 of details of ff. 1, 173, 227. E. G. Millar, *English Illuminated Manuscripts of the XIVth and XVth Centuries* (Paris and Brussels 1928) 89, n. 287. *Aspects of Medieval England,* this manuscript mentioned in n. 36, the entry for HM 19913. *Chronica,* 3. Scott, *Later Gothic Manuscripts* (forthcoming).

HM 19960 — England, s. XV^med^
ENGLISH HISTORICAL COLLECTION — *fig. 114*

ff. 1v–175: *De orbis indagacione facta per Iulium Cesarem,* [E]x olim senatus consulto censuit Iulius Cesar . . . in Scotia tunc existens dicti Regis Camisiam postmodum domino papa ut dicitur deferebat. [ff. 175v–179v, ruled, but blank]

A geographical and historical compilation from various sources: Augustine, Bede, the 1399–1437 version of the Latin *Brut,* Gildas, the Chester chronicler (Higden), Geoffrey of Monmouth, William of Malmesbury (often named or quoted by chapter), a 50-line metrical life of William of Wykeham (on ff. 150–151v; see G. H. Moberly, *Life of William of Wykeham, sometime Bishop of Winchester and Lord High Chancellor of England,* Winchester and London 1887, pp. 293–308; only 5 lines correspond), a list of the heresies of Wyclif. About half of the text pertains to material before 1066; material is fuller for the fourteenth century, and extends to 1437. Its authorship is attributed by a fifteenth century owner of the manuscript (see below) to John Tiptoft; the attribution is accepted with some confusion by R. J. Mitchell, *John Tiptoft 1427–1470* (London 1938) as referring to his father, Sir John Tiptoft (ca. 1375–1443) on pp. 9–10, although she lists it both among John Tiptoft's supposed works on p. 242, and as in his library on p. 243. The attribution to John or to Sir John Tiptoft is rejected, and the manuscript's contents are briefly analyzed by Roberto Weiss, *Humanism in England during the Fifteenth Century* 2nd. ed. (Oxford 1957) 118. See also A. Gransden, *Historical Writing in England* (London 1982) 2:480.

Parchment, ff. i (modern parchment) + i (early modern paper) + ii (contemporary parchment) + 179 (but one number skipped in the foliation after f. 14) + i (modern parchment); 200 × 135 (145 × 90) mm. $1\text{–}2^{14}$ 3^{10} $4\text{–}7^{12}$ 8^{14} 9^{20} 10^{12} 11^{10} $12\text{–}14^{12}$. The first quire is bound out of order and should be read: 1, 13, 6, 3, 4, 10, 8, 7, 5, 11, 12, 9, 2, 14. Quires and leaves signed with letters of the alphabet and early form arabic numerals on the first quire, with roman numerals on the successive quires. Catchwords written horizontally in inner right corner. 26–28 long lines frame ruled in brown lead; pricking visible at the 4 corners of the written space. Written in an anglicana script. Space reserved on f. 1v for a miniature (?); space reserved for initials; on f. 13v (which should have been f. 2v), a drawing in red of a T-O world map; on f. 8v (which should have been f. 7v), the lines to project the size of Christ's tomb. Rubrics, slashed initials in the text, and paragraph marks through f. 121. A few marginal notes, including dates in the *Brut* chronicle section.

Bound in 1972 in brown calf; one singleton and a quire of 8 blank leaves removed at the end.

Written in England in the middle of the fifteenth century. On f. iiii, a note in a fifteenth century hand reads: "Cronice Regum Anglie de diversis historiografis per dominum Iohannem Wigornensem Comitem sparsim collecte. Sheldwych. De orbis indagatione, divisione et descriptione per Iulium Cesarem in provincias et regiones factus; inter quas hic liber maxime de Regno Anglorum et Regibus eiusdem similiter A Bruto usque in Annum decimum sextum henrici sexti que magna famosa et rara sunt declarat." On f. iiii verso, "Sheldwych" signs a chronology list: "Anno ante christum M° C° venit Brutus in Angliam . . . Henricus VI[us] etatis XVIII eodem incepit regnare que nunquam vidit patrem suum nec pater suus eum. Sheldwych"; on f. 1, a note in another hand refers to Plutarch; an erased note on f. 179v, barely legible under ultra-violet light, ends with the name "Iohannes." Said to have belonged to the Scottish antiquary and historian, George Chalmers (1742–1825), whose books passed to his nephew and upon the latter's death were sold at auction by Evans, 27 September 1841, and 7 March and 10 November 1842; this manuscript not identified in these sales. Owned by the antiquary John Sidney Hawkins (1758–1842) and sold by Fletcher, 8 May 1843 (manuscripts are lots 2616–2649; this catalogue not available to us); the sale and a description of the book's contents are mentioned in *The Chronicles of the White Rose of York* (London 1843) 192–93. Sold to Sir Thomas Phillipps, whose number 11301 is on f. ii in modern pencil below his name, the Middle Hill stamp, and the date 1843. Phillipps sale, Sotheby's, 11 November 1946, lot 134; acquired by the Huntington Library in 1960 from Bernard Rosenthal, Special Offer Catalogue 17 (n.d.) n. 214.

HM 19960

Secundo folio: [now f. 13] puplice nunciarent
Bibliography: Chronica, 3.

HM 19999 — France, s. XIII^{ex}
GREGORY IX, DECRETALS; etc. — *figs. 64, 65*

1. ff. 1–241v: [Prologue:] Gregorius Episcopus servus servorum dei Dilectis filiis doctoribus et scolaribus universis parisius bononieque commorantibus salutem et apostolicam benedictionem. Rex pacificus pia miseracione disposuit . . . [f. 1v, Text:] Innocencius iii^{us} in concilio generali, *De summa trinitate et fide catholica Rubrica,* Firmiter credimus et simpliciter confitemur . . . Indignum est et a romane ecclesie consuetudine alienum ut pro spiritualibus facere quis homagium compellatur. *Expliciunt decretales deo gracias.*

A. Friedberg, ed., *Corpus iuris canonici* (Leipzig 1879, repr. Graz 1959) 2:6–928.[1]

2. ff. 1–241v: [Prologue to gloss:] In huius libri principio quinque sunt precipue prenotanda videlicet que sit intentio . . . [f. 1v, Gloss to text:] Firmiter, ideo dicit firmiter quia ordo fidei nostre probari non potest . . . et si interveniret nullam obligationem de iure vel de facto inducit supra de pactis pactiones. Bernardus. *Explicit apparatus decretalium.*

Gloss of Bernardus Parmensis de Botone on the Decretals of Gregory IX; Schulte, 2:115. This manuscript contains all the variants of Bernardus' later redactions listed by S. Kuttner and B. Smalley, "The 'Glossa Ordinaria' to the Gregorian Decretals," *English Historical Review* 60 (1945) 97–105, except for the reference to Octavian's consecration. See also S. Kuttner, "Notes on the Glossa ordinaria of Bernard of Parma," *Bulletin of Medieval Canon Law* 11 (1981) 86–93.

3. ff. 241v–251v: [Prologue:] Gregorius episcopus servus servorum dei dilectis filiis universitati magistrorum et scolarium parisius salutem et apostolicam benedictionem. Cum nuper in generali concilio lugdunensi . . . [Text:] *De summa trinitate et fide catholica,* Fide [added: -li] ac devota professione fatemur . . . ab ea non possint nisi per sedem apostolicam absolutionis beneficium obtinere. *Expliciunt constituciones nove gregorii x^{i}.*

J. Alberigo et al., eds., *Conciliorum Oecumenicorum Decreta* (Bologna 1973) 314–31.

4. ff. 241v–255: [Prologue to gloss:] Gregorius iste priusquam papa fieret vocabatur thealdus . . . [Gloss to text:] Fidei primo dicit quod spiritus sanctus eternaliter procedit . . . Apostolica secus esset si hoc dictum non fuisset ut supra c. nuper. *Expliciunt glose guillelmi durandi super constitucionibus gregorii x in generali consilio lugdunensi.*

Gloss of Guillelmus Durantis on the Decretals of Gregory X; Schulte, 2:154. See also M. Bertram, "Zur wissenschaftlichen Bearbeitung der Konstitutionen Gregors X.," *Quellen und Forschungen aus italienischen Archiven und Bibliotheken* 53 (1973) 459–67 at 464–65; L. Boyle, "The Date of the Commentary of William Duranti on the Constitutions of the Second Council of Lyons," *Bulletin of Medieval Canon Law* 4 (1974) 39–47.

5. ff. 255–262: [Prologue to gloss:] In nomine domini amen. Quoniam natura rerum introductum est ut plura sint negocia quam vocabula . . . [f. 255v, Gloss to text:] *De summa trinitate et fide catholica,* Fideli fuerunt quidam et adhuc sunt hodie . . . sunt excommunicati ut in c. tua nos alii incendiarii sunt excommunicandi xxiii q. ultima pessimam. *Expliciunt glose ordinarie novarum constitucionum domini gregorii pape decimi a garsia iuris civilis et canonici professore composite Anno domini M° cc° lxxxii°.*

Gloss of Iohannes Garsias Hispanus on the Decretals of Gregory X; Schulte, 2:161. See also S. Kuttner, "Decretalistica," *Zeitschrift für Rechtsgeschichte* Kan. Abt. 23 (1937) 436–70 at 459 n. 1.

6. ff. 262v–270v: [Prologue:] Nicholaus servus servorum dei dilectis filiis suis universitati magistrorum et scolarium parisius salutem et apostolicam benedictionem. Cum quasdam constituciones super certis articulis duxerimus promulgandas . . . [Text:] *De electione et electi potestate Rubrica,* Cupientes ecclesiarum vacationibus periculosis occurrere . . . vel prefata premissa tua humili confessione aliisque circumstanciis mansuetudine temporandi. Datum rome apud sanctum petrum x° kalendas aprilis Pontificatus nostri anno tercio.

J. F. von Schulte, "Die Dekretalen zwischen den 'Decretales Gregorii IX' und 'Liber VI. Bonifacii VIII' . . . ," *Sitzungsberichte der Akademie der Wissenschaft* (Vienna) 55 (1867) 701–69 at 719–21.

7. ff. 262–268: [Prologue of gloss:] In nomine domini amen. Licet ad occurrendum ecclesiarum vacationibus essent multa . . . [Gloss to text:] Cupientes et cetera. Hec decretalis valde utilis est quia ad expeditionem ecclesiarum dummodo curia servet eam . . . Equitas canonum, hanc equitatem colliges per iura allegata in glosa proxima. *Explicit apparatus domini nicholai.*

Gloss of Iohannes Garsias Hispanus on *Cupientes,* as in, e.g., Philadelphia, University of Pennsylvania, Latin MS 280, ff. 3–16 (but ending differently). See A. García y García, "Canonistas gallegos medievales," *Compostellanum* 16 (1971) 101–24 at 119–20.

8. ff. 270v–273v: *Incipiunt nove constituciones alexandri iiii*[ti] *pape ad perpetuam rei memoriam de Rescriptis,* Cum per illam generalem clausulam quidam alii frequenter apostolicis inseritur litteris . . . Nec premissi per ea se ulterius iuvare valerat ulterium. Nulli genere et cetera, nostre revocationis et cetera, si autem et cetera. Datum anagnie xv kalendas septembris pontificatus nostri anno primo. *Expliciunt constituciones alexandri iiii*[ti].

Schulte, "Die Dekretalen . . . ," 713–14, regarding Erlangen, Universitätsbibliothek, MS 464.

9. f. 273v: *Incipiunt constituciones clementis pape iiii*[ti], Clemens episcopus servus servorum dei ad perpetuam rei memoriam. Sepe accidisse precipimus quod nonnulli clerici in suis partibus vinculo excommunicationis ast⟨?⟩e apostate aut irregulares seu alii suscepti- [catchword:] -one sacr⟨?⟩//

Schulte, "Die Dekretalen . . . ," 714–16.

10. f. 274r–v: Table of contents, added in a later hand, to the *Decretals* and to the *Liber Sextus* (not mentioning VI.4.2); there is no other evidence that the *Liber Sextus* was ever part of this volume.

11. back flyleaf: [added, s. XV[med or ex]] Thre flourys in a nyȝt can spryng/ From euery floure a streme rennyng/ A clerk among the flourys lyyng/ Hem fond but noȝt durst say nor syng/ For drede of the mone.

HM 19999

IMEV 3708.5. Printed by G. Warner in the Dyson Perrins catalogue (see below) and by Hanna, "Addenda," n. 55.

Parchment, ff. ii (modern parchment) + ii (contemporary parchment) + 274 + i (contemporary parchment) + ii (modern parchment); 448–453 × 270 (204–241 × 120–137 for text frame, 337–481 × 218–247 including gloss) mm. $1–4^{10}$ 5^{12} $6–11^{10}$ 12^{12}(–10, 11, 12, through f. 121) 13^{6} $14–15^{10}$ 16^{12} $17–24^{10}$ 25^{12} 26^{10} 27^{12}(+13, f. 274). Catchwords to following text (not to the gloss) in inside corner, enclosed in light brown ink frames washed in yellow. Leaf signatures in letters, variously with a single stroke or an "x" above, below or alongside the letter; through quire 16, the signatures are in red, thereafter in the ink of the text; the leaf following the middle of the quire often marked with an "x." Quire signatures in a late medieval hand in the lower right corner of the first leaf recto, from A to Dd, with f. 274 marked Ee. 2 columns of 20–48 lines for the text; typically 92–104 lines for the gloss; slash prick marks visible in the upper and lower margins. Written in a round Italianate gothic script, with a somewhat smaller size for the gloss, using a brown or light black ink.

Five miniatures by Maître Honoré, approximately 65 × 60 mm. in blue and maroon frames, edged in gold, with gold oak leaves along the outer sides, and with half or ¾ border extensions of colored trilobe leaves. See G. Warner in the Dyson Perrins catalogue (see below), quoting Sir Sydney Cockerell, and Eric G. Millar, *An Illuminated Manuscript of La Somme le Roy attributed to the Parisian Miniaturist Honoré* (Roxburghe Club 1953) 12; also mentioned by C. Nordenfalk, "Maître Honoré and Maître Pucelle," *Apollo* 79 (1964) 357. Other law books associated with this atelier are a Justinian, formerly Chester Beatty MS 67 and later in the Major J. R. Abbey collection (sold, Sotheby's, 4 June 1974, lot 2917) as well as copies of the Decretum of Gratian in Tours, Bibliothèque Municipale, MS 558, one formerly Yates Thompson MS 88, one in Copenhagen, Kongelige Bibliotek, Thott 160.2° and another of which only 2 leaves survive, formerly in the collection of Sir Sydney Cockerell. The miniatures are: f. 1, Gregory IX receiving a book from one of a group of ecclesiastics; f. 64, a judge, seated, between a man and a woman, each with an advocate; f. 122, a priest celebrating mass, while a layman is ejected from that part of the church reserved for clerics; f. 173v, a bishop performing a marriage; f. 191, a seated pope listening to a monk kneeling before him, as others stand behind. On f. 121v, a miniature, 113 × 78 mm., added during the first half of the fourteenth century by an English artist, showing the Virgin and Child under a gothic arch, and to their left, under another arch, Agnes standing, holding book and sword, with her lamb at her feet; below the miniature (instructions to the artist?), "Sanctissima Agnes virgo et martir gloriosa ad cuius dextrum stat ["a dextris" cancelled] agnus nive candidior." On f. 1r–v, 3 historiated initials, 7- to 4-line, of a seated doctor instructing students, of a seated king, and of the Trinity, with Father and Son side by side as the Dove descends between them. Other books of the Decretals begin with 6- or 5-line initials, in white-patterned pink on blue grounds, or vice versa, infilled with colored trilobe leaves; 3-line initials in similar style, some with partial borders, often ending in drolleries or infilled with busts of many kinds: men clean-shaven or bearded, women with or without elaborate headdresses, kings, queens, a figure with a wing-like cap, rabbits, dogs; 4-line initials, placed outside the written space, in blue with red flourishing; 2-line initials in the same colors; 1-line initials within the text in red or washed in yellow; red paragraph marks; running headlines across the opening in red and blue numbering the books of the Decretals only. "Corr. in textu" in the lower margin of the last leaf verso of each quire. Considerable marginalia in contemporary French hands, and in contemporary and later English hands (on f. 92v, a note dated 1470); running headlines giving the subject in the upper right corner of each leaf recto in an English hand. Modern fore edge tabs. First leaf defective along the inner margin, with some loss of text; now hinged.

Bound in 1903 by Douglas Cockerell, in wooden boards with red morocco spine decorated in gilt and blind with the initials of Michael Tomkinson (see below), 2 3-part braided straps to catches on the front cover. Rust marks from chain hasps on top and bottom center of f. iii, once the pastedown.

Written during the last years of the thirteenth century possibly in Avignon or Montpellier, or by a southern scribe working in Paris, and painted in Paris by Maître Honoré. Concerning a similar group of legal manuscripts, see the review by C. Nordenfalk in *Zeitschrift für Kunstgeschichte* 43 (1980) 318–37, especially pp. 336–37, of A. Melnikas, *The Corpus of the Miniatures in the Manuscripts of the Decretum Gratiani* (Rome 1975); another manuscript written by a southern scribe and illuminated by Maître Honoré is Cambridge, Mass., Harvard University, Houghton Library, fMS Typ 228, Augustine, *De civitate dei*. A *terminus post quem* for the copying of HM 19999 is the date of composition of art. 5, 1282, as noticed in the explicit on f. 262. Contemporary notes of an early owner in a French hand, but soon acquired by an Englishman, as shown by the numerous notes in early fourteenth century anglicana, and by the miniature added by an English artist on f. 121v. In the spandrels of the arches in this miniature are what may represent coats of arms: gules, a fess or (in the 2 outer spandrels); azure, a cross saltire or (in the center); this last may be intended for the arms of St. Albans abbey, although a St. Albans provenance seems doubtful and the volume was not listed by Ker, *MLGB;* the choice of Agnes in the miniature suggests particular devotion on the part of an individual or institutional owner. Owned before 1436 by William Meelys, rector of Tarporley, Cheshire: on f. iv verso, "Decretales apparate F. de dono Magistri Willelmi Meelys, rectoris de Tarpurley pro anima sua ex procuracione ⟨?⟩ David Bromfelde anno domini M° cccc xxxvi"; on the contemporary back flyleaf, "Constat Willelmo Meeles [cancelled: "1450"?]." A draft of a letter on f. iv recto includes a mention of Chester and the date 1470. In a fifteenth century hand on the back flyleaf, "Percy [?] de Burscho [?] desiderat emere istum librum cum bello troianorum et libro de passione christi," and, in the upper margin of f. 274, in possibly the same hand, "frater p., precio lx li." Belonged to Richard Bulkeley, archdeacon of Merioneth (1483–ca. 1500) and Anglesey (1504 until his death in 1524); see J. Le Neve, *Fasti Ecclesiae Anglicanae 1300–1541*, pt. XI, *The Welsh Dioceses*, comp. by B. Jones (University of London 1965) 10–11, and Emden, *BRUO*, p. 303: on f. 274v, over an erasure (?), "Constat ricardo bulkeley archidiacono Meryoneth"; on f. iv recto, "Precario conceditur domino Iohanni Gwyn ad tempus per Ricardum bulkeley archidiaconum Anglesey," and "Constat fratri Ricardo Bulkeley Teste reddatur ad Signum ea quod servi." Belonged to John Ruskin (1819–1900) by 1857, when he discussed its decoration in his *Elements of Drawing* (London 1857) 301–02; Ruskin's bookplate on the inside front cover. His estate inherited by Mr. and Mrs. Arthur Severn, who sold this manuscript ca. 1903 to Michael Tomkinson (1841–1922?), of Franche Hall, Kidderminster, Worcestershire, for whom the book was rebound; sold by Tomkinson in 1911 to C. W. Dyson Perrins (1864–1958). Dyson Perrins sale, Sotheby's, 29 November 1960, lot 109 with reproductions of the miniatures on ff. 1, 64, 122, 173v on pl. 15. Acquired at that time by the Huntington Library.

Secundo folio: [Text:] et sanguis; [Gloss:] omnia non
Bibliography: Burlington Fine Arts Club, *An Exhibition of Illuminated Manuscripts* (London 1908) n. 93 open at f. 122. G. F. Warner, *Descriptive Catalogue of Illuminated Manuscripts in the Library of C. W. Dyson Perrins* (Oxford 1920) 1:99–100 and pl. 40 of the miniature and text (not gloss) of f. 64. J. S. Dearden, "John Ruskin, the Collector, with a catalogue of the Illuminated and Other Manuscripts formerly in his Collection," *The Library* ser. 5 vol. 21 (1966) pp. 136–37 n. 22. *Aspects of Medieval England,* n. 21 open at f. 122. *Chronica,* 3.

---

[1] We are grateful to Dr. Thomas M. Izbicki for the bibliography on the texts in this manuscript.

HM 21720 Honduras, 1545
BARTOLOMÉ DE LAS CASAS, PRESENTATION to the Audiencia de los Confines

ff. 1–2: *Muy poderosos señores,* El obispo de chiapa don fray bartolome de las casas por cumplir con mi officio pastoral . . . presentada y leyda a los dichos presidente y oydores en su acuerdo jueves veynte y dos del mes de otubre de 1545. Fray bartolome de las casas, obispo de chiapa.

Colección de documentos inéditos del archivo de Indias (Madrid 1867) 7:172–78 probably from this manuscript, and A. M. Fabié, "Vida y escritos de fray Bartolomé de las Casas," in *Colección de documentos inéditos para la historia de España* (Madrid 1879) 70:535–41.

Paper (*Main,* roughly similar to Briquet 11136–11139), ff. 2; 316 × 220 (226–284 × 190) mm. 1 bifolium. 54 long lines, unruled. Written in the hand of the author.

Unbound; formerly bound, ca. 1890, with HM 21721 by Riviere in red morocco.

Written in the hand of the author, dated 22 October 1545, to be delivered before the Audiencia de los Confines in the town of Gracias a Dios (Honduras). On f. 2v, the note "Papeles tocantes al Padre Casas" in an eighteenth century hand; on f. 1, a small pencilled "c" in upper left corner. Sold in 1874 by Ellis Booksellers to Henry Huth (1815–78); *The Huth Library* (1880) 5:1681–82. Sale of Alfred Henry Huth (1850–1910), Sotheby's, 12 June 1911, lots 32–33, to Frank T. Sabin. Sold through Charles Sessler to Henry E. Huntington in August 1925.

Bibliography: De Ricci, 119. H. R. Wagner and H. R. Parish, *The Life and Writings of Bartolomé de las Casas* (Albuquerque 1967) 145–46, 274 n. 36.

HM 21721 Madrid, 1563
BARTOLOMÉ DE LAS CASAS, LETTER to the Dominicans in Chiapa and Guatemala

ff. 1–8: *Muy Reverendos y charissimos padres mios,* Nuestro señor sea siempre en las animas de Vuestros padres . . . vel apprehenditis ut dicitur. [f. 8v, blank]

A. M. Fabié, "Vida y escritos de fray Bartolomé de las Casas," in *Colección de documentos inéditos para la historia de España* (Madrid 1879) 71:367–82.

Paper (*Main,* similar to Briquet 11213 and 11214, Clemont-Ferrand 1565 and 1570), ff. 8; 305 × 215 (255–270 × 150) mm. 33–36 long lines, unruled. One gathering. Written in an italic script by a copyist, but signed by Bartolomé de las Casas.

Unbound; formerly bound with HM 21720.

Written in 1563 in Madrid, probably at Santa María de Atocha. On f. 8v, "193 . . . 13," written in ink in a seventeenth century Spanish hand; in the upper left corner of f. 1, a small "k" in pencil; traces of a red ink stamp in the left margin of f. 1. For provenance, see description of HM 21720.

Bibliography: De Ricci, 119. Wagner and Parish, 222, 293–94 n. 70.

HM 25771 Germany, s. XV[ex]
DOMINICAN BREVIARY

1. ff. 1–6v: Graded calendar in red and black, including the feasts of the Octave of Stephen (2 January, 3 lessons), Erhard (8 January), Translation of Thomas Aquinas (28 January, in red, totum duplex), "Anniversarium patrum et matrum" (4 February), Cunigundis (3 March, in red, simplex), Thomas Aquinas (7 March, in red, totum duplex), Octave of Thomas Aquinas (14 March), Vincent Ferrer (5 April, in red, totum duplex), Octave of Vincent (12 April), Peter martyr (29 April, in red, totum duplex), Translation of Peter martyr (7 May, in red, totum duplex), Apparition of Michael (8 May, totum duplex), Translation of Dominic (24 May, in red, totum duplex), Ulric (4 July), "Anniversarium in cymiteriis nostris sepultorum" (12 July), Henry emperor and confessor (13 July, in red, simplex), Invention of Stephen (3 August, simplex), Dominic (5 August, in red, totum duplex), Transfiguration (6 August, totum duplex), Octave of Dominic (12 August, simplex), Sebald (19 August, in red, simplex), "Anniversarium familiarum et benefactorum" (5 September), Translation of Cunigundis (9 August, in red, simplex), Michael (29 September, in red, totum duplex), Otto (30 September, in red, duplex), Octave of Michael (6 October), "Anniversarium omnium fratrum et sororum ordinis nostri" (10 October), Stephen (26 December, in red, totum duplex); numerous additions to the calendar of saints canonized in the sixteenth century, many of them Dominican; the later personal entries all by a different hand: Raymond of Pennafort (7 January), Chair of Peter (18 January, duplex), Martina virgin and martyr (30 January, duplex), "Anniversarium gilg. scheckenpach" (16 February), Casmir (4 March, duplex), "Anniversarium pater meus Nacht." (6 March), Gabriel (18 March, totum duplex), Joseph (19 March, totum duplex), Joachim (20 March, totum duplex), Ambrose of Sansedoni (22 March, totum duplex), Francis de Paola (2 April, duplex), Agnes of Montepulciano (20 April, totum duplex), Antoninus Florentinus (2 May), Athanasius (5 May), Gregory Nazianzen (9 May), Stanislas (11 May, duplex), Philip Neri (26 May, duplex), James Salomone (31 May, totum duplex), Petronilla (1 June, 3 lessons), Norbert (6 June, duplex), ⟨?⟩ (22 and 27 June), "Anniversarium mea anfraw" (17 June), "Anniversarium Marx scheckenpach mein anher 1491" (26 August), "Anniversarium pater meus 1494" (31 August), "Anniversarium hanns Repogen 1590 [*sic*]" (3 September), "Anniversarium ⟨Nicholas?⟩ Regenpogin mein anfraw" (10 September), Eustachius (20 September, duplex), Emmeram (23 September, totum duplex), Guardian Angel (30 September, totum duplex), Bruno (6 October, duplex), Bridget (8 October, duplex), Teresa of Avila (15 October, duplex), Louis Beltran (19 October, totum duplex), "Anniversarium mater mea" (27 October), Wolfgang (31 October, totum duplex), Charles Borromeo (4 November, totum duplex), Albertus Magnus (15 November, totum duplex), "dedicacioni basyli" (Peter & Paul; 18 November, duplex), Bibiana (2 December, duplex); verses in German on the Golden Number in the lower margin of January, March, May.

2. ff. 7–11v: Commemorations of the Virgin, Dominic, Catherine of Alexandria, Peter martyr, Thomas Aquinas and the Eucharist.

3. ff. 12–14: Prayers and lessons for the dead.

4. ff. 14–15v: Office for matins.

5. ff. 16–19v: Prayers for various occasions: *zu dem frumal, Nach tisch, Zum abentesse, zu abent, zu mette zeit, umb ein schon weter, An dem ascher mitwochen und hohen donerstag uber dy vii ps., An den creutz tagen fur dy heiligen cristenheyt.*

6. ff. 19v–43: Hours of the Virgin: matins, lauds and vespers, and variations for the liturgical year; on f. 27, an added leaf, a computistic calendar based on the 19-year Golden Number cycle (blank on the verso).

7. ff. 43–67v: Office: prime through none and vespers of Sunday and part of Monday.

8. ff. 67v–78: Hours of the Virgin, Dominican use: prime through none, and compline.

9. ff. 78–117v: Office: vespers of part of Thursday through Saturday, and compline, ending with the Salve Regina and a suffrage of Dominic; ff. 97–100v, antiphons and hymns for various feasts; ff. 100v–117v, changed office for the temporale, from the first Sunday after the octave of Epiphany through the 25th Sunday after Pentecost.

10. ff. 117v–153: Office of the Dead, Dominican use.

11. ff. 153–169v: Penitential psalms and litany, including Peter among the martyrs; Dominic (twice), Thomas, Vincent and Sebald among the confessors; Catherine (twice), Ursula and Cunigundis among the virgins; ff. 168–169v, alternate litany for the dead, beginning with Elizabeth of Thuringia.

12. ff. 170–190v: *Psalmi communes* (Pss. 1–5, 8, 10, 14–15, 18, 20–25, 53, 92, 32–33, 44–46, 60, 63, 74, 86, 95–98, some by cue only).

13. ff. 190v–194: Office of Dominic.

14. ff. 194–213v: Common of saints; worked in under the office of each classification (one martyr, many martyrs, one confessor, etc.) are collects for various saints: a list of saints' names is given in the rubrics, the prayers having only the generic "N."

15. ff. 214–240v: Temporale, day offices only, from Advent through the Octave of Corpus Christi; no major feasts are present; ff. 238–240v, Octave of the dedication of a church.

16. ff. 240v–281: Sanctorale, day offices only, from the octave of Andrew (7 December) through Saturninus (29 November), including Cunigundis, Octave of Vincent Ferrer, Catherine of Siena, Henry, Invention of Stephen, Octave of Dominic, Sebald, Octave of Michael, Otto; no major feasts are present; ff. 277–281, psalms and antiphons *in passione domini nostri ihesu christi* and versicles for the nocturns of the feast of the Annunciation.

17. ff. 281–285v: Additions by later hands: f. 281v, s. XV, prayer to Apollonia; ff. 281v–283, s. XVI, antiphons and capitula for the hours of the office during Lent and Passion Sunday; ff. 283v–284, ruled, but blank; f. 284v, s. XVI, "Quoniam non delectat dulcis organica Cantus/ Rudibus Ac truncis Erit Emmerandus"; f. 285r–v, s. XV, antiphons for the vigil of the Separation of the Apostles.

18. ff. 286–289v: Office of Catherine of Alexandria.

Parchment, ff. i (paper) + 289 + i (paper); 127 × 90 (93–94 × 59–60) mm. 1^6 2^{10} 3^{10}(+ 11, f. 27) 4–26^{10} 27^8 28^{10} 29^{10}(–10, plus one short leaf tipped in at end of quire) 30^4. Catchwords in inner lower margin. 16 long lines, ruled in brown ink, the second rule from the top and from the bottom full across. Written in a gothic book hand with additions in a hybrida script (f. 281v), in 2 cursive scripts (ff. 281v–283 and 284v), in a littera textualis script (f. 285r–v) and in a contemporary gothic book hand (ff. 286–289v).

Opening historiated initial, f. 7, 7-line, in white-highlighted blue, enclosing the Virgin and Child against an embossed gold ground, the whole within a frame of narrow green, orange and red segments, with multicolored acanthus leaf extensions; 4- and 3-line initials in blue with void design on initial, infilled and decorated with penwork flourishing in the ink of the text; 2-line initials alternating red or blue, occasionally with flourishing in ink or other color; plain red or blue 1-line initials; initials within the text slashed in red. Music in square notation on 4-line red staves for the antiphons and responses of the office of the dead; on 3-line red staves for cues of the antiphons, ff. 43v–95. Initials in music in red, blue or calligraphic black, often touched with red. Brown leather tabs along fore edges. Some later marginalia.

Bound, s. XVI (?), in worn blue velvet over wooden boards; 2 fore edge clasps of brass and leather, closing from back to front.

Written at the end of the fifteenth century for use in a Dominican convent for nuns, probably in the diocese of Bamberg, as shown by the presence of Cunigundis, Henry and many Dominican saints in the calendar. Feminine forms, "Sorores sobrie estote . . ." (f. 91v) begin compline, where responses are headed "Das spricht dy priorin" and "Der convent spricht." It was still presumably in Dominican ownership in the seventeenth century, when additions were being made to the calendar, the latest being that of Louis Beltran (here 19 October), beatified in 1608 and canonized in 1671. On the back flyleaf verso, release stamp of the Denkmalschutz. Belonged to Mary W. T. Dickinson, who had acquired it by June 1945, probably from Dawson's Book Shop, Los Angeles (their price code in pencil on the front pastedown). Received by the Huntington Library in April 1953 as a bequest from Mary Dickinson (d. September 1952).

Secundo folio: [f. 8] (do-)minici confessoris
Bibliography: Chronica, 3.

HM 25772 — Italy, s. XV^ex^
LECTIONARY

1. ff. 1–24v: *Incipiunt epistule et evangelia festorum solemnium. Et primo ad primam missam in nativitate domini. Ad titum,* Carissime Apparuit gratia dei salvatoris . . . [f. 24, *In sancti Mauri abbatis et martyris Lectio libri sapientie,* Beatus vir qui inventus est sine macula . . .] Si quis mihi ministraverit honorificabit eum pater meus qui est in celis.

Readings from the Epistles and Gospels for 24 main feasts of the liturgical year, from the first mass of Christmas through All Saints' Day and Maurus (abbot and martyr? the only saint present); between the feasts of the Apparition of Michael in Mt. Gargano (8 May) and Ascension, are readings for the anniversary of a dedication of a church.

2. ff. 24v–26v: [added in a different hand] *In cena domini Lectio epistule beati pauli ad corinthios,* Fratres, Convenientibus vobis in unum . . . [f. 26, *Feria iii post resurrectionem domini. Secundum lucam,* In illo tempore. Stetit yesus

in medio discipulorum suorum . . .] et predicari in nomine eius penitentiam in remissionem peccatorum in omnes gentes.

Readings for these 2 feasts added out of sequence, the second with a tie mark to its proper position on f. 11.

Parchment, ff. i (contemporary paper) + 30 + ii (contemporary paper; watermark, not in Briquet, of a C within a circle, with a trilobe flower above the circle and an N below it); 282 × 213 (192 × 132) mm. $1–2^{10}$ 3^{10}(1, 2 replacements, attached to stubs). Catchwords in the center of the lower margin enclosed by designs of black ink dots. 2 columns of 23 lines, ruled in ink. Written in a round gothic script by two scribes: i, ff. 1–24v; ii, ff. 24v–26v.

Opening initial, 7-line, in dusky rose decorated with green and blue acanthus leaves, and infilling with rose-colored flowers against a blue ground, the whole set on a square gold ground; C-shaped border in Ferrara-style flowers and regular, compact penwork with a medallion of the archangel Michael in the lower border and the Holy Monogram, YHS, in the upper. Also on f. 1, a 2-line gold initial on a rose and green ground; the entire written and decorated space enclosed by a narrow frame of blue and gold strips. Other initials up to f. 24v, 2-line, alternating blue with red harping and beading, or red with purple; 1-line initials washed in yellow. Opening initial of art. 2 on f. 24v in red with poorly done brown penwork; remaining 2-line initials of art. 2 in plain red; 1-line initials stroked through in red. Rubrics throughout.

Bound, s. XIX (?), in green brocade silk over wooden boards, with 5 bosses on the front and on the back covers; red and green speckled edges; a small pendant seal, with a worn legend, "IMPORTAZIONE [?]," attached to a cord along the spine.

Written in Italy at the end of the fifteenth century. Armorial bookplate on the front pastedown stated on bookdealer's slip to be that of Prince Odescalchi, presumably referring to Prince Pietro Odescalchi (1789–1856), whose books were sold at auction by the Libreria Bonifazi, Rome in 1856. The bookplate bears the same charges in chief as Rietstap, vol. 4, pl. 304, but with 5 chalices (?) instead of the vair field; motto: "Per servire s'acquista, Servi quando poi." N. 153 in an American bookseller's catalogue (slip on file); "n. 546" in pencil on f. i. Received by the Huntington Library in April 1953 as a bequest from Mary W. T. Dickinson (d. September 1952).

Secundo folio: deo et in terra
Bibliography: Chronica, 3.

HM 25773 — Flanders, s. XV^{ex}
BOOK OF HOURS, use of Rome

1. ff. 1–12v: Calendar in red and black, including the feasts of Basilius (14 June), Remigius and Bavo (1 October) and Donatianus (14 October).

2. ff. 13–14: *Oracio de sancta veronica,* Salve sancta facies nostri redemptoris . . . [*RH* 18189]; *Oracio,* Deus qui nobis signatis lumen vultus tui . . . [*HE,* 174–75]; f. 14v, blank.

3. ff. 15–23 [f. 15, blank]: Mass of the Virgin; f. 23v, blank.

4. ff. 24–89 [f. 24, blank]: *Incipit officium beate marie secundum usum romanum;* weekly variations of psalms follow matins; suffrages of All Saints and prayer for peace follow hours from lauds to compline; f. 88, Salve Regina; f. 89v, blank.

5. ff. 90–99: Variations on the office for the Virgin for the liturgical year; f. 99v, blank.

6. ff. 100–119v: Penitential psalms and litany including Eleazar among the monks.

7. ff. 120–123v [f. 120, blank]: *Devota oracio de sancta maria,* Obsecro te . . . [masculine forms; Leroquais, *LH* 2:346].

Parchment, ff. i (paper) + ii (parchment) + 123 + i (paper); 60 × 46 (37 × 23) mm. For the collation, the structure of (the 2 flyleaves and?) ff. 1–4 is unclear, 2^8 3^8(+3, f. 15) 4^8(+3, f. 24) 5–12^8 13 (ff. 96–99 of uncertain structure) 14–15^8 16^8(+5, f. 120). Catchwords written vertically along the inner bounding line. 17 long lines ruled in very pale brown ink. Written in a gothic book hand.

Three inserted singletons, blank on the recto, and with a miniature of simple execution on the verso; the leaves facing the miniatures with the same style borders and 5-line white acanthus initials: f. 15v, Virgin and Child, on the crescent; f. 24v, Annunciation; f. 120v, Pietà; the same style border on ff. 13 (with a coat of arms, see below) and 100. Secondary initials, 5-line, white-patterned blue or pink on a gold cusped ground with trilobe leaf infilling; 2-line initials in gold against blue or pink square ground with infilling of the other color; 1-line initials, blue with red penwork or gold with black. Rubrics in pale red.

Bound, s. XVIII, in Italian red morocco; gilt edges; black morocco slip case.

Written in Flanders at the end of the fifteenth century for use in Bruges, according to the saints in the calendar. The coat of arms on f. 13 appears to be original, and is probably that of the Esneval family of Normandy (Rietstap, vol. 2, pl. 280). The book bears the number "26" on the spine and on f. i; also on f. i, the erased press mark "D.8.1," the cipher "$\frac{1673}{2629}$," and what is probably the price code for Dawson's Book Shop, Los Angeles. Received by the Huntington Library in April 1953 as a bequest from Mary W. T. Dickinson (d. September 1952).

Bibliography: Chronica, 3.

HM 25774 — Seville, s. XVI²
REGLA DE LA COFRADIA DE SANTA ANA

1. ff. vi–ix verso: [Chapter list with reference to contemporary foliation] *Tabla de los Capitulos y obligationes que tiene esta rregla,* Capitulo primero de la orden que se a de tener en hazer la fiesta de sancta anna, v. . . . Capitulo lxxvi que habla que el prioste que a la sazon fuere sea obligado a mandar a sentar a los hermanos, lii.

2. ff. 1–4: Pericopes of the Gospels.

3. ff. 4v–48v: [Prayer] En el nombre de dios todopoderoso padre e hijo e spiritu sancto tres personas, una essençia . . . e complir todo quanto en esta Regla se contiene. [f. 5, Text:] *Capitulo primero que habla de nuestra fiesta de la bien aventurada señora sanctana,* Primeramente ordenamos e estableçemos para siempre jamas . . . y al bien e pro deste nuestro ospital e pobres del.

4. ff. 48v–52v: Added regulations, dated 1574 on f. 49; included in the chapter list.

5. ff. 53–54v: Added regulations, in a different hand.

6. ff. 55–60v: Additional modifications of the Rule, in various cursive hands, including these dates: f. 57, 1633; f. 58v, 1574; f. 59, 1562 (?); f. 60v, 1645; ff. 61–62v, ruled, but blank.

Parchment, ff. ix (contemporary parchment) + 62 + i (contemporary parchment); 188 × 142 (140 × 102) mm. 1^2(1 is pastedown) 2^2 3 (two singletons ? ff. iv–v) 4^8(–1 through 4) 5–10^8 11^4(ff. 49–52) 12^6(–2) 13^4(–1) 14^4(–3, 4) 15^2(flyleaf and pastedown). Catchwords written vertically in the inside lower margin of quires 6–8 and horizontally in quire 9. 20 long lines through f. 48v, ruled in lead; in art. 4, 20 long lines (unruled?); in art. 5, 16 long lines; in art. 6, 14–22 long lines. Round prick marks at left and right bounding lines repeated in a slightly different position on each recto and verso of the folios in quire 4 (ff. vi–ix) only. Written by 8 people: i, ff. vi–ix, 48v lines 10–20, 49–52v in a round gothic script; ii, ff. 1–48v line 9, in a round gothic script; iii, ff. 53–54v, in a round gothic script, possibly the same as i; iv, ff. 55–57, in a cursive script; (f. 57v, blank; f. 58, erased); v, f. 58 top, in a cursive script; vi, f. 58 bottom, in a cursive script; vii, f. 59, in a cursive script; (f. 59v, blank); viii, f. 60r–v, in a cursive script with italic features (ff. 61–62, blank).

Full page miniature of the Crucifixion with Mary and John on f. iv verso and, facing it on f. v, a full page miniature of Anne, Mary and the infant Jesus; both of mediocre quality. 6- to 4-line parted red and blue initials with red and lavender penwork on the first 4 leaves of text. 3- and 2-line initials alternating blue with red, and red with purple penwork through f. 48v. On each leaf through f. 48v, double blue line to the left of the text on each recto and a double red line on each verso; the borders on ff. 1, 1v, 2v, 3v, 4v and 5 decorated with red and purple flourishing (predominantly red for the blue borders, and predominantly purple for the red borders). Rubrics and chapter numbers in red through f. 48v. On ff. 49–57v, double bounding lines in red around the written space; on ff. 49–54v, plain red initials, 3- and 2-line. Two sets of contemporary foliation through f. 52: in red roman numerals in the upper right corner, and in brown arabic numerals in the lower right corner.

Bound in old red velvet with modern brass ornaments on both covers; 2 old fore edge clasps of red velvet and brass, back to front.

Written, ca. 1574, for, and probably by, the Cofradia de Santa Ana in the parish of that saint in Triana, in the vicinity of Seville. Circular label with scalloped edges on the front pastedown, "N° 18/1.40.00." Received by the Huntington Library in April 1953 as a bequest from Mary W. T. Dickinson (d. September 1952).

Secundo folio: [f. ii] alcaldes, xvii; [f. 2] ad virginem desponsatam
Bibliography: Chronica, 3.

HM 25775 — Italy, s. XV²
EPHRAEM; PELAGIUS; PAULINUS AQUILEIENSIS — *fig. 156*

1. ff. 1–92v: [Ephraem, *Sermones,* trans. Ambrogio Traversari; Prologue of the translator:] *Prefatio auctoris incipit,* Ambrosius monachus Cosmo suo viro clarissimo plurimam salutem dicit. Peregrinum nuper offendi e syria ut aiebant profectum . . . illum amplectere illique potius aures atque animum applica. Iam enim tecum illum relinquo. Vale. [f. 2v, Text:] *Incipit Sermo sancti Ephren de penitentia et hora novissima et iudicii die et retributione,* Dilectissimi nihil sanctę caritati prȩferamus. Multa enim negligendo peccamus . . . adhuc enim tu veraci-

ter vivis amboque fleverunt pariter et glorificaverunt deum. Et nos igitur pro his omnibus referamus gratiam patri et filio et spiritui sancto nunc et semper in sęcula sęculorum. Amen. *Explicit Sermo de laudibus Ioseph patriarche a beato Ephren Syro ędita feliciter. Amen.*

Ephraem Syrus, *Sermones,* trans. Ambrogio Traversari (Florence: Antonio Miscomini, 1481), *GW* 9331; the manuscript and the printed book present the 20 sermons in the same order and under the same rubrics.

2. ff. 93–103v: [Pelagius, *De vita christiana*] *Aurelii Augustini liber de vita christiana ad sororem suam incipit feliciter. Leti animo lege,* [Prologue:] Ut ego peccator et ultimus insipientior cęteris et imperitior universis te ut sanctitatis et iustitię viam pergas crebrioribus audeam litteris admonere . . . [f. 93v, Text:] Christum unctum interpretari sapientum et fidelium nullus ignorat . . . memento nostri qui diligimus tantum ut quod tibi pręstare presentes non possumus conferamus absentes auxiliante illo qui semper vivit et regnat in secula seculorum. Amen. *Beati Augustini liber explicit.* [f. 104r–v, ruled, but blank]

CPL 730. *PL* 40:1031–1046.

3. ff. 105–128v: [Paulinus Aquileiensis, *Liber exhortationis*] *Incipit liber exhortationis beati Augustini ad Iulianum Comitem carissimum sibi atque singularissimum,* Frater mi si cupias scire quamvis ego nesciam quam perfectissima atque plenissima sit iustitia. Iustitia est deum colere ex toto corde . . . [f. 106, Chapter 2:] Igitur quotienscunque bonis actibus mandata christi facimus . . . et electis tuis ęternaliter regnare concedis quia tibi est cum ęterno patre et spiritu sancto una deitas par gloria eadem virtus imperium et potestas in secula seculorum. Amen. *Liber beati Augustini ad Iulianum feliciter explicit. Amen.*

PL 40:1047–1078, here in 25 chapters.

Paper (watermarks ff. 1–18 and 93–104: *Tête de boeuf,* Briquet 14660, Verona, 1430–40; ff. 19–92 and 105–128: *Monts,* Briquet 11704, Verona, 1443), ff. ii (modern paper) + 128 + ii (modern paper); 207 × 148 (167 × 88) mm. 1^{8} $2–5^{10}$ $6–7^{12}$ $8–9^{10}$ 10^{12}(ff. 93–104) $11–12^{12}$. 38 long lines, horizontal rules in ink, vertical in lead. Written in a humanistic script.

Initials, 11-line on f. 1, thereafter usually 6-line in gold with whitish-brown or colored acanthus foliage against blue, pink, red or light green grounds; that on f. 19 (*Sermo de vita et exercitacione monastica*) in gold with white vinestem on a dotted green, red and blue ground; 2-line initials for beginning of the text of art. 2, f. 93v, and throughout art. 3, alternating red and light blue; initials in the text washed in yellow on ff. 13v–31, 52–55, 57v–62, 90v–96 or washed in red, ff. 50v–52, 86–90. Rubrics usually in pale red, but in blue on f. 41v, in green on f. 40v, in purple on ff. 103v and 128v, and in alternating lines of purple and green on ff. 93 and 105. YHS monogram in blue in the upper margin of f. 105. Manicules of varying forms.

Bound, s. XIX, in English ¾ blue straight grain morocco.

Written in Italy in the middle of the fifteenth century, possibly in the Veneto given the Veronese watermarks and the ownership note on f. 128v, which at one time was concealed by a new section of paper glued over the bottom of the page, but was uncovered by N. C. Starr (see below): "Iste liber est congregationis Sancte Iustine deputatus monachis habitantibus verone 53 [this number cancelled; added in a different hand:] signatusque in inventario numero 4 ex littera E." What was possibly another possession note has been cut away from the lower margin of f. 1, as the top of a letter still shows above the new paper now forming the margin. Notes by several owners or readers, s. XVI, also on f. 128v: "franciscus bodius" (?, cropped), "⟨cropped⟩ expliciunt xii maii 1539," "Amor dei et amor proximi," "Alma redemptoris voluisti templum fieri immaculatum,"

HM 25775

"Guta cavat lapidem non bis [*sic*] sepe cadendo" [Walther, *Proverbia* 10508], "O quam sunt utilliores quam laudaciores isti sermones in hoc libello," "O quam sermones isti in hoc libello sunt utiliores et laudaciores a quibus sepe legentur legerentur." Belonged to the Rev. Henry J. Drury (1778–1841) who wrote the table of contents on f. ii and signed his name; his sale, Evans, 19 February 1827, n. 4220 to F. North (not ascertained if Frederick North, 5th Earl of Guilford, 1766–14 October 1827; his sale catalogues not available to us). On the front pastedown, signature of Thomas Mills; on f. i verso, "Rev. Thos. Hodges from ⟨?⟩." Ellis Cat. 206 (1922) n. 93 to Nathan Comfort Starr (b. 1896), at that time living in Cambridge, Massachusetts, but in Anapolis, Maryland when the book was described by De Ricci. Dawson's Book Shop, Los Angeles, Cat. 189 (Fall 1944) n. 13 to Mrs. Mary W. T. Dickinson (d. September 1952); received by the Huntington Library in April 1953 as her bequest.

Secundo folio: minime implere possumus
Bibliography: De Ricci, 751. *Chronica,* 3.

HM 25776 BIBLE

Italy, s. XIII²

Bible in the order of London, Lambeth Palace, MS 1364 as described by Ker, *MMBL,* 1:96–97, but here including the prayer of Solomon after Ecclesiasticus; Daniel ending at 14, 41; 63 prologues, lacking Stegmüller 327, 343, 521 and 547 but with the additional prologues, Stegmüller 414, 430, 480.

1. ff. 1–409v: Old Testament:
f. 1, *Incipit epistola sancti Ieronimi presbiteri de omnibus divine hystorie libris ad paulinum presbiterum,* Frater ambrosius tua michi munuscula perferens detulit . . . , *Incipit prologus sancti ieronimi in pentateuchum,* Desiderii mei desideratas accepi epistolas . . . [Stegmüller 284, 285]; f. 4, Genesis, with f. 5 containing Genesis 15, 16–18, 8 bound incorrectly in its present position, it should follow f. 9; f. 24v, Exodus; f. 41v, Leviticus; f. 53, Numbers; f. 69, Deuteronomy; f. 84, *Incipit prologus in librum Iosue,* Tandem finito pentatheuco moysi velut grandi fenore . . . [Stegmüller 311]; f. 94v, Judges; f. 105, Ruth; f. 106v, *Incipit prologus in libros regum,* Viginti duas esse litteras aput hebreos . . . [Stegmüller 323]; f. 160v, *Incipit prologus in libros paralipomenon,* Si septuaginta interpretum pura et ut ab eis . . . [Stegmüller 328], 2 Paralipomenon followed on f. 189v by the prayer of Manasses, Domine deus omnipotens patrum nostrorum abraham ysaac et iacob et semini eorum iusto . . . [Stegmüller 93, 2]; f. 189v, *Incipit prologus esdre primus,* Utrum difficilius sit facere quod poscitis . . . [Stegmüller 330], with Ezra, Nehemiah, 2 Ezra [= 3 Ezra; Stegmüller 94, 1]; f. 207, *Incipit prologus in librum tobie,* Chromatio et helyodoro episcopis ieronimus presbiter in domino salutem. Mirari non desino . . . [Stegmüller 332]; f. 211v, *Incipit prologus in librum iudith,* Aput hebreos liber iudith inter [correction over erasure:] apocrifa legitur . . . [Stegmüller 335]; f. 217v, *Incipit prologus in librum hester,* Librum hester variis translatoribus constat esse viciatum . . . [Stegmüller 341]; f. 223, *Incipit prologus in iob,* Cogor per singulos scripture divine libros . . . , *Incipit alius prologus,* Si aut fiscellam iunco texerem . . . [Stegmüller 344, 357]; f. 235, *Incipit prologus in libro psalmorum,* David filius iesse cum esset . . . , *Incipit epistola ad paulum et eustochium,* Psalterium

rome dudum ponitus emendaram . . . [Stegmüller 414, 430], with major initials at the usual 8-part division and at Pss. 114, 121; f. 263, Iungat epistola quos iungit sacerdocium . . . [Stegmüller 457, prologue to Proverbs]; f. 271, *Incipit prologus in libro ecclesiastes,* Memini me hoc ferme quinquennium . . . [Stegmüller 462]; f. 274, Song of Songs; f. 275v, *Incipit prologus in librum sapiencie,* Liber sapiencie apud hebreos nusquam est . . . [Stegmüller 468]; f. 281, *Incipit prologus in ecclesiasticum,* Multorum nobis et magnorum per legem . . . [biblical introduction to Ecclesiasticus treated as prologue]; f. 297, Et inclinavit salomon genua sua . . . [prayer of Solomon, following Ecclesiasticus directly; de Bruyne, *Sommaires,* 562]; f. 297, *Incipit prologus sancti ieronimi presbiteri in ysaya propheta,* Nemo cum prophetas versibus viderit . . . [prologue added in the margin:] *Incipit argumentum,* [Y]sayas in ierusalem nobili genere ortus est . . . [Stegmüller 482, 480]; f. 316v, *Incipit prologus Ieremie,* Ieremias propheta cui hic prologus scribitur . . . [Stegmüller 487], ending with the historical note for Lamentations, . . . suspirans et eiulans ait; f. 339, Lamentations; f. 341, *Incipit prologus in baruch,* Liber iste qui baruch nomine prenotatur . . . [Stegmüller 491]; f. 343v, *Incipit prologus in ezechiele propheta,* Eiezechiel [*sic*] propheta cum iohachim rege iuda . . . [Stegmüller 492]; f. 363, *Incipit prologus in danielem prophetam,* Danielem prophetam iuxta lxx interpretes . . . [Stegmüller 494], Daniel ends at 14, 41; f. 371v, *Incipit prologus in librum duodecim prophetarum,* Non idem ordo est xii prophetarum . . . , *Incipit secundus,* Temporibus ozie et ioathan achaz et ezechie . . . [Stegmüller 500, 507]; f. 374v, *Incipit prologus sancti Ieronimi in Iohelem prophetam,* Sanctus Ioel apud hebreos post osee ponitur . . . , *Incipit secundus,* Ioel Phatuel filius describit terram . . . [Stegmüller 511, 510]; f. 375v, *Incipit prologus primus in amos prophetam,* Ozias rex cum dei religionem . . . , *Incipit secundus,* Amos pastor et rusticus et ruborum mora . . . , *Incipit tercius,* Hic amos propheta non fuit pater ysaye . . . [Stegmüller 515, 512, 513]; f. 378, *Incipit prologus abdie prophete,* Iacob patriarcha fratrem habuit esau . . . , *De eodem capitulo,* Hebrei hunc esse dicunt qui . . . [Stegmüller 519, 517]; f. 378v, *Incipit prologus in ionam prophetam,* Sanctum ionam hebrei affirmant filium fuisse . . . [Stegmüller 524]; f. 379v, *Incipit prologus in micheam prophetam,* Temporibus ioathe et achaçe et ezechie . . . [Stegmüller 526]; f. 381, *Incipit prologus in Naum prophetam,* Naum prophetam ante adventum regis . . . [Stegmüller 528]; f. 382, *Incipit prologus in abacuch propheta,* Quatuor prophete in xii prophetarum volumine sunt . . . [Stegmüller 531]; f. 383, *Incipit prologus in Sophoniam prophetam,* Tradunt hebrei cuiuscumque prophete pater aut avus . . . , *Item alius prologus,* Iosiam regem iuda cuius temporibus . . . [Stegmüller 534 in 2 parts]; f. 384, *Incipit prologus in aggeum prophetam,* Ieremias propheta ob causam periurii sedechie regis . . . [Stegmüller 538]; f. 385, *Incipit prologus in zachariam prophetam,* Anno secundo darii regis medorum . . . [Stegmüller 539]; f. 388v, *Incipit prologus in malachiam prophetam,* Deus per moysen populo israeli preceperat . . . [Stegmüller 543]; f. 389v, *Incipit prologus machabeorum,* Machabeorum libri duo prenotant prelia . . . , *Incipit secundus,* Reverentissimo et omni caritatis officio dignissimo Geraldo . . . Memini me in palatio huagionum civitatis . . . [Stegmüller 551, 553].

2. ff. 409v–509: New Testament:
f. 409v, *Incipit prologus mathei evangeliste primus,* Matheus ex iudea sicut in ordine primus ponitur . . . , *Incipit secundus,* Matheus cum primo predicasset

evangelium in iudea . . . [Stegmüller 590, 589]; f. 422v, *Incipit prologus in evangelium secundum marchum,* Marcus evangelista dei electus et petri in baptismate filius . . . [Stegmüller 607]; f. 431, Lucas syrus natione antiochenus arte medicus . . . , Quoniam quidem multi conati sunt . . . [Stegmüller 620 and Luke 1, 1–4 treated as prologue]; f. 445v, *Incipit prologus in evangelium Iohannis,* Hic est iohannes evangelista unus ex discipulis dei . . . [Stegmüller 624]; f. 456v, *Incipit prologus in epistola ad romanos,* Romani sunt in partibus ytalie . . . [Stegmüller 677]; f. 462, [rubric erased], Corinthi sunt achaici et hii similiter . . . [Stegmüller 685, prologue to 1 Cor.]; f. 467, *Incipit prologus* [erasure], Post actam penitentiam consolatoriam scribit . . . [Stegmüller 699, prologue to 2 Cor.]; f. 470v, *Incipit* [erasure], Galathe sunt greci. Hii verbum veritatis . . . [Stegmüller 707]; f. 472v, *Incipit* [erasure], Ephesi sunt asiani. Hii accepto verbo veritatis . . . [Stegmüller 715]; f. 474, *Incipit* [erasure], Philipenses sunt macedones. Hii accepto verbo veritatis . . . [Stegmüller 728]; f. 475, *Incipit* [erasure], Colossenses et hii sicut laodicenses . . . [Stegmüller 736]; f. 476v, *Incipit* [erasure], Thessalonicensses sunt macedones qui accepto verbo veritatis . . . [Stegmüller 747]; f. 477v, [erasure], Ad tessalonicensses secundam scribit apostolus epistolam . . . [Stegmüller 752]; f. 478, *Incipit* [erasure] *ad thimotheum,* Timotheum instruit et docet . . . [Stegmüller 765]; f. 479, *Incipit* [erasure], Item thimotheo scribit de exortatione martirii . . . [Stegmüller 772]; f. 480, *Incipit* [erasure], Titum comonefacit et instruit . . . [Stegmüller 780]; f. 480v, *Incipit* [erasure] *ad phylomenem* [*sic*], Philemoni familiares litteras facit . . . [Stegmüller 783]; f. 481, *Incipit prologus in epistola ad hebreos,* In primis dicendum est cur apostolus paulus . . . [Stegmüller 793]; f. 484v, *Incipit prologus in actibus apostolorum,* Lucas anthiocensis natione sirus cuius laus . . . [Stegmüller 640]; f. 497v, *Incipit prologus in epistolis canonicis,* Non ita est ordo apud grecos . . . [Stegmüller 809]; f. 497v, James; f. 499, 1 Peter; f. 500, 2 Peter; f. 501, 1 John; f. 502v, 2 John; f. 502v, 3 John; f. 502v, Jude; f. 503, *Incipit prologus in apochalipsi Iohannis,* Omnes qui pie volunt vivere . . . [Stegmüller 839].

3. ff. 509–539v: *Hec sunt interpretationes hebraicorum nominum incipiencium per a litteram,* Aat [*sic*] apprehendens vel apprehenssio . . . Tharacha superfluus eis vel elongatus ab eo sive superfluus eius aut elongatio eius// [Stegmüller 7709, breaking defectively without approx. the last 275 entries].

Parchment, ff. i (modern parchment) + i (early modern paper) + 539 (+ ff. 145 bis, 146 bis, 303 bis; "309" skipped) + i (early modern paper) + i (modern parchment); 161 × 116 (112 × 75) mm. 1^{12}(+ f. 5, an added singleton; should be bound after f. 9) $2–9^{16}$ $10–12^{18}$ $13–15^{16}$ 16^{12} 17^{12}(–4, 5, 6; through f. 262, end of Psalms; last column with only 5 lines of text) $18–24^{20}$ 25^{18} 26^{22} 27^{18} 28^{22} 29^{18} 30^{22} 31^{18}(–18). Catchwords or evidence of catchwords visible only in beginning of book in a noting hand in the inner right margin. 2 columns of 46–44 lines ruled in lead; after f. 263, 2 columns of 47 lines; in the *Interpretationes,* 3 columns of 47 lines; some pricking remains in the upper and lower margins. Written in 2 gothic book hands: i, ff. 1–262v (end of Psalms); ii, ff. 263–539v.

Painted initials with extensions in the margins in white-patterned beige, brown, blue, grey, ochre, dark orange and olive green, usually as stylized, fleshy leaves, but occasionally also including animal heads; historiated with a picture of Jerome seated and gesturing on f. 1, and as a wide decorated band between the columns on f. 4; through f. 262v, 10- to 6-line for the books and 7- or 6-line for the prologues, followed by the first words of the text in a display script, sometimes touched in red. After f. 263, painted initials for the books only, 6- to 4-line, apparently by the same artist. In both sections, alternating red and blue initials with flourishing of the other color: 4- to 2-line and placed outside the written space through f. 262v; 2-line within the written space for all those after f. 262v. Unornamented alternating red and blue 1-line initials in the Psalms and in the *Interpretationes;* 1-line initials within the text touched in red. Running headlines across the opening and chapter numbers in alternating red and blue letters. Rubrics throughout, possibly all by the scribe of ff. 1–262v. Lower margin of f. 334 cut away.

Bound by Riviere in purple morocco over wooden boards with 2 brass fore edge clasps (added from a different binding?), the lower with the initials IFPM; gauffered and gilt edges; purple morocco slip case.

Written in Italy in the second half of the thirteenth century. Acquired by Mrs. Mary W. T. Dickinson from Dawson's Book Shop, Los Angeles. Received by the Huntington Library in April 1953 as a bequest from Mary Dickinson (d. September 1952).

Secundo folio: celi ezechieli qui
Bibliography: Chronica, 4.

HM 25777 — CISTERCIAN BREVIARY

Germany, s. XV^{in}

1. ff. 2–6v: Graded calendar, beginning defectively in March, with numerous astrological entries; major feasts in red or lined through in red; included are the feasts of Cuthbert (20 March), "Resurrectio domini vera" (27 March, 12 lessons), Robert of Molesme (29 April, lined through), Bernard (20 August, in red, 12 lessons), "Defunctorum ordinis nostri" (18 September, in red, commemoration), Wenceslas (28 September), Malachius (5 November, lined through), Edmund Rich (16 November, lined through, 12 lessons), "Commemoratio patrum et matrum" (20 November, in red); added in a later hand are the feasts of Thomas Aquinas (7 March), Hugh of Cluny (29 April), Ivo (19 May), "Anniversarium [?] fratrum et sororum" (20 June), 10,000 Martyrs (22 June), Visitation (2 July), Octave of the Visitation (9 July), "Divisio apostolorum" (15 July), Margaret (erased from 13 July and rewritten for 20 July), Anne (26 July), Simplicius and Faustinus (29 July), Octave of Bernard (27 August), Octave of the Nativity of the Virgin (15 September), Conception (8 December).

2. ff. 7–89v: Temporale, no lessons or psalms, from Advent through the 25th Sunday after Pentecost.

3. ff. 89v–151: Sanctorale, no lessons or psalms, from Stephen through Thomas the Apostle; included are offices or prayers for William of Bourges, Speusippus, (Eleusippus) and Meleusippus, Cuthbert, Robert of Molesme, Hugh of Cluny, Magnus (f. 126v, added in the upper margin), Agapitus (f. 126v, added in the lower margin), Bernard, Wenceslas, Hedwig, Malachius, Edmund Rich.

4. ff. 151–168: Common of saints, no lessons or psalms, with collects under martyrs for (1) Fabian, Sebastian, Denis, John and Paul; (2) Maurice; under confessors for (1) Gregory, Augustine, Silvester, Martin; (2) Ambrose, Peter, Remigius, Nicholas, Julianus, William, Malachius, Edmund, Eligius; (3) Hilary, Remigius, Vedastus, Amandus, Germanus; under virgins for (1) Agnes, Cecilia, Margaret; (2) Catherine, Agatha, Lucia; (3) Scholastica.

5. ff. 168–195: Sixty-three hymns in full for the week, the temporale, the sanctorale, the common of saints and the dedication of a church; a few others by cue only; generally as in the Cistercian breviary printed in Basle, 1484 (*GW* 5198).

6. ff. 195–203: Monastic canticles for Sundays, Christmas, Easter (Mearns, set 1 in each case), for the common of apostles and martyrs (Mearns, sets 9 and 1), of virgins (Mearns, set 2); canticles *de sancta cruce,* cues only: Domine audivi, Pro iniquitate, Egressus es (Mearns, p. 89); canticles *in dedicatione ecclesie,* cues only: Letatus sum, Nisi dominus, Lauda ierusalem (Mearns, p. 89).

7. ff. 203–204: Prayers: *pro amico in tribulacione constituto; pro pluvium* [*sic*]; *pro serenitate; contra tempestatem.*

8. ff. 204–205v: Added material in 4 fifteenth century hands: i, f. 204r–v, antiphons for Paul; ii, f. 204v, antiphons; iii, ff. 204v–205v, rubrics *quando de beata virgine antiphona obmittitur* and prayer to Anne; iv, f. 205v, office of Mary Magdalene.

Parchment, ff. i + 205; 132 × 97 (96–97 × 65–70) mm. 1^{2}(ff. i–1) 2^{6}(–1) $3–21^{10}$ 22^{10}(–10). Catchwords in the middle of the lower margin. 18 long lines, ruled in ink, with top and bottom 2 lines full across; slash pricking in outer margins. Written in a gothic book hand in 2 sizes according to liturgical function. Plain 3- to 1-line initials in red; 1-line initials within the text touched with red. Contemporary foliation, i–xx, in brown ink in roman numerals on the versos of ff. 7–26, written between the double rules of the text frame; a second set of foliation, i–lxii, in red ink in roman numerals on the versos of ff. 89–150 (the sanctorale), written in the outside margin; and a third set, 1–15, in red ink in arabic numerals on the versos of ff. 151–165 (the common of saints), written in the middle of the upper margin. Passages on ff. 7–8 and 20v erased.

Bound in contemporary German brown panelled calf over wooden boards (the front board badly worm eaten) with 10 bosses (3 of 5 remaining on front cover, and all 5 on back cover) and with brass edging along top, bottom and fore edge of both covers; 2 fore edge clasps of leather and brass, back to front; 3 later notes on spine, including a paper label, "[Miss]ale ⟨?⟩ 5," barely decipherable due to considerable disintegration along the spine.

Written in the early fifteenth century in northern Germany for Cistercian use as shown by the saints of the calendar and the sanctorale. Early, if not first owners were the Cistercians of Riddagshausen in the diocese of Halberstadt, Brunswick; on f. i verso, in green ink in a fifteenth century hand: "⟨?⟩r liber perpetue virginis Marie. Sub custodia fratris Iohannis ⟨?⟩ professi ibidem in Riddageshussen." On f. 1v: "Dis buch gehöret dem Kloster Riddageshausen 1689." A slip of paper with the number ⟨?⟩225 is pasted to the inside front cover so that the part with the number is visible above the top of the book. In modern pencil, f. i verso: "1136 1 Nov." With the book is a letter from Dawson's Book Shop, Los Angeles, dated 15 April 1948, offering it for sale to Mrs. Mary W. T. Dickinson; another slip, signed by her, shows that she had bought it by 29 April of the same year. Received by the Huntington Library in April 1953 as a bequest from Mary Dickinson (d. September 1952).

Secundo folio: [f. 8] Domine deus
Bibliography: Chronica, 4.

HM 25778
PERALDUS, DE ERUDITIONE PRINCIPUM

France, s. XIV^{in}

1. ff. 2–92v: *Incipit prologus in librum eruditionis principum,* Cum pars illustris ecclesie sit cetus principum et multum ab eis dependeat vita minorum . . . ; [f. 2v, Chapter list:] *Incipiunt capituli primi libri,* Quod potestas terrena pocius est timenda quam appetenda, i . . . ; [f. 5, Text:] *Incipit liber primus quod potestas terrena pocius est timenda quam appetenda,* Cum inordinatus amor potestatis terrene multum noceat . . . eo quod corpori dominico ad modicum tempus fuit associata. Liber eruditionis principum explicit. Benedictus deus qui incepit et complevit. Amen.

For attribution to Guillelmus Peraldus, see Kaeppeli, *SOPMA* 1626; printed several times among the works of Thomas Aquinas, including *Opera Omnia* (Parma 1865, repr. New York 1950) 16:390–476. Two quires and 15 leaves missing with loss of text as follows: after f. 3, Chapter list, Book 5, 21 to Book 7, 5; after f. 16, Book 1, 7 to 1, 9; after f. 24, Book 1, 15 to 2, 1; after f. 26, Book 2, 3 to 2, 6; after f. 30, Book 2, 10 to 2, 11; after f. 32, Book 2, 13 to 3, 3; after f. 34, Book 3, 4 to 3, 5; after f. 36, Book 3, 7 to 3, (?); after f. 37, Book 3, (?) to 3, 9; after f. 42, Book 4, 5 to 4, 7; after f. 54, Book 5, 10 to 5, 12; after f. 66, Book 5, 25 to 5, 38; after f. 77, Book 5, 50 to 6, 1.

2. f. 93: [former pastedown] List of authorities, mainly the books of the Bible, but also Bernard, Augustine, Seneca, Isidore and Aristotle with appropriate abbreviations; f. 93v, ruled, but blank.

Parchment, ff. i (modern parchment) + 93 (of which the first and last, although part of the quire structure, were formerly used as pastedowns) + i (modern parchment); 269 × 180 (185 × 126) mm. 1^{12}(–4, after f. 3) 2^{12}(–6, 7 after f. 16) 3^{10}(–4, 7 after ff. 24 and 26) 4^{10}(–2, 5, 6, 9 after ff. 30, 32, 34) 5^{12}(–2, 4, 10 after ff. 36, 37, 42) 6^{12}(–11, 12 after f. 54) 7^{12} one quire missing here 8^{12}(–1 after f. 66) one quire missing here 9^{8} 10^{8}. Catchwords in lower right margin; quires signed in lead on last leaf verso in early form arabic numerals. 2 columns of 31 lines, ruled in ink with double bounding lines at left and right of written space, with top and bottom 2 lines full across and with additional sets of double rules in the upper margin (used for the running headlines) and in the lower margin. Written in a well formed book hand. Parted red and blue initials, 6- and 5-line, with filigree infilling, tendrils and cascades in both colors; alternating red and blue initials, 2-line, with similar decoration. Alternating plain red and blue initials, 1-line, in the chapter list at the beginning of the book and in those that remain before the individual Books (for Books 4, 5 and 7). Running headlines across the opening, alternating colors. Rubrics throughout. Scattered marginalia.

Bound, s. XV, in leather over wooden boards, with diagonal rules, horseshoe and dot tooling; 4 corner and 1 center brass bosses (2 missing on the back cover); 2 fore edge straps closing to pins on the front; on the front cover, 2 paper labels: "Liber eruditionis principum" and "B" or possibly "8"; rebacked and repaired in 1972.

Written in France in the first third of the fourteenth century. Belonged to Isham Keller of Redlands, California who may have removed the missing quires and leaves before selling it to Dawson's Book Shop, Los Angeles, in April 1947; acquired from Dawson's by Mrs. Mary W. T. Dickinson. Received by the Huntington Library in April 1953 as a bequest from Mary Dickinson (d. September 1952).

Secundo folio: [f. 3] est vanitas; [f. 6] non adducet
Bibliography: Chronica, 4.

HM 25779
BOOK OF HOURS, use of Rome

Italy, s. XV²

1. ff. 1–12v: Calendar in red and black, including the feasts of Maurelius (7 May, in red), Alo (25 June), "Festum nivis" (5 August), Cerbonus (10 October).

2. ff. 13–85: *Incipit offitium beate et gloriose virginis marie secundum consuetudinem romane curie;* suffrages of All Saints after each hour except matins; weekly and seasonal variations begin on f. 67v; ff. 85v–86v, ruled, but blank.

3. ff. 87–110: Penitential psalms and litany.

4. ff. 110v–115: Short hours of the Cross; ff. 115v–116v, ruled, but blank.

5. ff. 117–166v: Office of the Dead, use of Rome.

Parchment prepared in the southern manner, ff. i + 166 + i; 98 × 70 (55 × 37) mm. 1^{12} $2–8^{10}$ 9^{4}(to f. 86) $10–11^{10}$ 12^{10}(to f. 116) $13–17^{10}$. Catchwords to the right in the lower margin. A few quire and leaf signatures remain uncropped, as letters of the alphabet and arabic numerals. 15 long lines ruled in pale brown ink. Written in a round Italian gothic book hand.

Opening page, f. 13, 10-line, rose-colored historiated initial of the Virgin and Child on a square gold ground with acanthus leaf extensions; IHS monogram in the lower margin; full border, composed of regular black ink sprays, gold dots and flowers in the Ferrara style. On f. 87 (Penitential psalms), 9-line, rose-colored historiated initial of David praying, half-length, against a gold cusped ground with marginal extensions of acanthus leaves and gold dots; f. 110v (Hours of the Cross), similar initial containing a cross on a square ground; f. 117 (Office of the Dead), similar initial containing a skull. The hours of the Virgin after matins designated by a 6-line rose-colored initial against a square gold ground with acanthus leaf extension; infilling is a green and gold petalled flower. Secondary initials, 2-line blue with red harping and beading, or red with purple; 1-line initials within the text alternating red or blue. Rubrics in red.

Bound, s. XVII, in Italian calf over wooden boards with gilt tooling of a pomegranate design; gilt edges.

Written possibly in Florence, given the style of the illuminations. On the front pastedown the engraved heraldic bookplate of C. W. Loscombe; Sotheby's, 16 December 1946, lot 547 to the London booksellers McLeish and Sons; sold by them to Dawson's Book Shop in Los Angeles with correspondence to that effect dated November 1947 now in Huntington files; sold by Dawson's to Mary W. T. Dickinson by that date. Received by the Huntington Library in April 1953 as a bequest from Mary Dickinson (d. September 1952).

Bibliography: Chronica, 4.

HM 25780
PETER COMESTOR, HISTORIA SCHOLASTICA, fragment

England or France, s. XIII^in

ff. 1–10v: //veniet tibi fames in regno tuo, aut tribus mensibus fugies adversarios tuos . . . non essent. Porro in extremitatibus cuiusque// [bifolium missing; f. 3:] //ad mare eneum et abluebat ibi pedes et manus . . . Ecce filii tui israel qui eduxerunt te de terra// [2(?) quires missing; f. 5:] //quibus iratus es. Iste iam . . . respondit, sed paulo post tempore usque ad//

Peter Comestor, *Historia scholastica,* on sections of 2 and 3 Kings, Daniel, Judith and Ester; *PL* 198:1346–1355, 1364–1373, 1473–1499.

Parchment, ff. i (early modern paper) + 10 + i (early modern paper); 332 × 238 (211 × 140) mm. 2 columns of 48 lines, some columns divided into 2 narrower columns (e.g. on ff. 5, 10v), ruled in lead, single bounding lines. Two quires, probably originally sexterni; the first lacks its inner bifolium. Written by one person in a spiky littera textualis. Spaces reserved for 2-line initials. Notes to rubricator in the lower margin. Occasional corrections and index notes in a contemporary hand. Running headlines added.

Bound in blue cloth over pasteboard probably by Bretherton.

Written in England or France in the opening years of the thirteenth century. Probably originates in a French collection, for the 2 quires are wrapped in a paper bifolium inscribed on the back leaf in a late eighteenth or early nineteenth century hand, "Chevaux D'artillerie De Campagne." Folio i bears the number "510" and a contents note, s. XVIII, "fragmentum epistolarum Sancti hyeronimi ad Sanctos Augustinum et Alipium Episcopos. MS XII s.," surmounted by a cross, signed with a two-letter monogram, D[?], and numbered 6. Sold ca. 1824 by Thomas Thorpe to Sir Thomas Phillipps. On f. 1, the Phillipps Middle Hill stamp and his number 2520. Phillipps sale, Sotheby's, 15 June 1908, lot 90, to Parkes. Acquired by Nathan Comfort Starr (b. 1896) of St. John's College, Annapolis, Maryland; his bookplate on front pastedown. N. 313 in a book dealer's catalogue. Acquired by Mary W. T. Dickinson. Received by the Huntington Library in April 1953 as a bequest from Mary Dickinson (d. September 1952).

Bibliography: De Ricci, 751; *Chronica,* 4.

HM 25781 — Netherlands, s. XV^{med}
ADMONITIO AD NONSUINDAM RECLUSAM

ff. 1–14v: [Anon.] Tue non immemor petitionis o karissima mater tibi ut rogasti scribere studui . . . sed illi qui in te hoc operatur et velle et perficere pro bona voluntate cui est honor et potestas et imperium per infinita secula seculorum. Amen. *Explicit epistola Sancti augustini* [name erased] *ad matrem suam.* [Entire attribution marked "Vacat" by the same person who inserted a more general statement:] *Explicit epistola cuiusdam devoti patris ad quandam spiritualem singularis devotionis matrem doctrinaliter conscripta.*

PL 134:915–938.

Paper (watermark, a letter "P," similar to Briquet 8685, Düsseldorf, 1464), ff. i (early modern paper) + 14; 210 × 140 (160 × 105) mm. 1^{12} + 2 single leaves. 35 long lines, ruled in hard point. Written in a hybrida script. Opening initial, 13-line, parted red and blue with lacy red leaf infilling, and red or olive green penwork decoration; initials within the text slashed in red. Carefully corrected throughout.

Bound in an eighteenth century German document on vellum.

Written in the Netherlands. Sotheby (?) sale slip attached to the front pastedown. Dawson's Book Shop of Los Angeles, Catalogue 83, March 1932, n. 6 to Mary W. T. Dickinson. Received by the Huntington Library in April 1953 as a bequest from Mary Dickinson (d. September 1952).

Secundo folio: (dis-)tantibus nos hoc
Bibliography: Chronica, 4.

HM 25782

HM 25782 STATUTES

England, s. XIII[ex]
fig. 3

1. ff. 1–6v: Magna Carta with rubric, *"Incipiunt provisiones de Ronnemede scilicet carta Regis Iohannis,"* 17 John; J. C. Holt, *Magna Carta* (Cambridge 1965) pp. 304–12 for the "Articles of the Barons," and pp. 313–37 for the charter itself with a translation; here with variants suggesting it to be a draft of the charter. See V. H. Galbraith, "A New MS of the Statutes," *HLQ* 22 (1958–59) 148–51, "A Draft of Magna Carta (1215)," *Proceedings of the British Academy* 53 (1967) 345–60, and "Statutes of Edward I: Huntington Library MS HM 25782," in *Essays in Medieval History presented to Bertie Wilkinson,* ed. by T. A. Sandquist and M. R. Powicke (Toronto 1969) 176–91 with a pl. of f. 85v.

2. f. 7r–v: [Note for rubric in the upper margin] *Exposiciones verborum antiquorum anglicorum,* Munthbreche, Trepas vers seignur; Burgbreche, Quite de forfeture de Citee depescer . . . Danegeld, Estre quit de doner ou ayder al tribut ke les Roys de Engleterre soleient doner a Danays e al Roy de Danemarche.

List of 34 Old English legal terms and their French meanings.

3. f. 8r–v: Assize of weights and measures, beginning "Notandum quod la charre plumby constat ex triginta fotmall . . . ," followed by the first paragraph of this assize, "Per discrecionem tocius regni Anglie fuit mensura domini Regis composita . . . Et octo galones frumenti faciunt bussellum london. hoc est octavam partem quarterii"; *SR* 1:204–05.

4. ff. 9–12: Dictum of Kenilworth, 51 and 52 Henry III; *SR* 1:12–17.

5. ff. 12–14: Articles of the eyre; *SR* 1:233–34a.

6. ff. 14–15: Extenta manerii; *SR* 1:242–43.

7. ff. 15v–16: Assize of bread and ale (the latter with its own heading); *SR* 1:199–200.

8. f. 16r–v: View of frankpledge, here in Latin; *SR* 1:246–47.

9. ff. 17–20v: Magna Carta, ending ". . . Hiis testibus Domino S. Cantuariense Archiepiscopo," 9 Henry III; *SR* 1, charters, 22–25.

10. ff. 21–23: Carta de foresta, ending ". . . Hiis testibus Domino S. Cantuariense Archiepiscopo et cetera," 9 Henry III; *SR* 1, charters, 26–27.

11. f. 23r–v: Sentence of curse given by the bishops against the breakers of the charters, 37 Henry III; *SR* 1:6–7.

12. ff. 23v–24v: *Capitula foreste,* Videnda sunt assarta facta in foresta post principium secundi anni prime Coronationis domini Henrici Regis Tercii . . . vel aliquod ingenium aliud ad malefaciendum domino Regi de feris suis.

Chapters of the Regard, in *Patent Rolls of the reign of Henry III . . . 1225–1232* (London 1903) 286–87.

13. f. 24v: General days in banc; *SR* 1:208.

14. ff. 25–26v: Provisions of Merton, 20 Henry III; *SR* 1:1–4.

15. ff. 27–32: Statute of Marlborough, 52 Henry III; *SR* 1:19–25.

16. f. 32v: [added in a later hand] Beginning of a copy of the will of Gylbart Forman of Rodwell, Yorkshire, dated 21 May "M d et cetera."

17. ff. 33–35v: Chapter list of the statutes of Westminster I, Gloucester, Westminster II.

18. f. 36: [added, s. XV] Hec sunt capitula que inqueri debent a capitalis franci plegii in singulis locis Anglie ubi homines sunt in decena scilicet bis per annum in festo sancti Michaelis et Pasche. Et de hoc etiam primo iuratus iurare quod verum dicet de capitalis que ab eo exiguntur ex parte domini Regis et quod pro nullo dimittet quando verum dicet. Si omnes libere tenentes ⟨?⟩ summoniti fuerint . . . Si aliqua via vel legalis Semita sit obstructa vel consternata vel levata contra libertatem domini et quis est ille qui hoc fecit. [f. 36v, ruled, but blank]

19. ff. 37–48: Statute of Westminster I, 3 Edward I; *SR* 1:26–39.

20. ff. 48v–51v: Statute of the exchequer ". . . *les estatuz del Escheker fez a Westmuster a la cluse Paske en l'an le roy Edward fiz le Roy Henry tierz*"; *SR* 1:197–98.

21. ff. 51v–53v: Statute of jewry ". . . *les estatuz de la Ieurie ke nostre seignur le Roy Edward fiz le Roy Henry fist a Wemuster* [*sic*] *a son parlement a la Quinzeyne de seint Michel l'an de son regne tierz,*" followed straight on by the *Districciones scaccarii,* "E purceo ke le commun del Reaume ad eu graunt damage . . . le viscunte avera reconu sey aver receu"; *SR* 1:221–21a and 197b.

22. ff. 53v–56: Statute of Gloucester, beginning with the chapter on damages in novel disseisin, and with the dating clause added in a later hand, 6 Edward I; *SR* 1:47–50.

23. f. 56v: Exposition of the statute of Gloucester, 6 Edward I; *SR* 1:50.

24. f. 57r–v: Statute for religious men, with dating clause added in a later hand, 7 Edward I; *SR* 1:51.

25. ff. 58–59: Statute of merchants, with dating clause added in a later hand, 11 Edward I; *SR* 1:53–54.

26. ff. 59v–61v: Statute of merchants, 13 Edward I; *SR* 1:98–100.

27. f. 62r–v: Statute for respiting of knighthood; *SR* 1:229.

28. ff. 63–82v: Statute of Westminster II, ending ". . . seit puni a la volente le Roy ausi bien cely ki le purchacera come cely ki le fra," 13 Edward I; *SR* 1:71–95.

29. f. 82v: [added in a different hand] Quia emptores, 18 Edward I; *SR* 1:106.

30. ff. 83–85: Statute of Winchester, with dating clause added in a later hand, 13 Edward I; *SR* 1:96–98.

31. ff. 85v–87v: Statute of Exeter ". . . *les estatuz le Roy Edward fiz le Roy Henry fez a Excester a la feste seint Hillarii l'an de son Regne Quatorzim,*" with loss of a leaf after f. 86; *SR* 1:210–12.

Parchment, ff. ii (modern paper) + 87 + ii (modern paper); 217 × 147 (156 × 97) mm. $1–4^{8}$ 5^{4}(ff. 33–36) 6^{8} 7^{10} $8–10^{8}$ 11^{10}(–9). Catchwords in inner lower margin, some in red ink frames; some leaf signatures as vertical slashes in crayon visible in quires 7 and 9. 32 long lines, ruled in lead with double vertical bounding lines to the written space, with additional single rules in the inner and outer margins, and with additional double rules in the upper and lower margins. Written in an anglicana script, with brief texts on ff. 32v, 36 and 82v added in other hands.

5- and 4-line parted red and blue initials with flourishing and infilling in whorl designs in both colors; 4- to 2-line initials alternating red and blue with infilling and flourishing of the other color; paragraph marks alternating red and blue. Running headlines added, s. XV; chapter numbers in the hand of the scribe and by later hands, some correcting the first numbers. Later corrections to the text in the statutes of Westminster I, II and Gloucester. Evidence of fore edge tabs once sewn to upper corners of leaves. Early modern foliation in ink in the lower right corner of the recto, frequently cropped.

Bound, s. XVIII, in English tan calf; rebacked; gilt edges.

Written in England towards the end of the thirteenth century; the text contains the statute of Exeter (1286) in the main hand and *Quia emptores* (1290) added by a second hand. An allusion to the manor of Nasby in Northamptonshire in the text of the statute of Westminster II (f. 66v) seems to refer to the legal struggles of Isabella de Fortibus (1237–93) regarding those lands. On f. 32v, the will of Gylbart Forman of Rodwell, Yorkshire dated 21 May 1500. On f. 1, s. XVIII (?), "No. 84 JP." Bookplate on front pastedown of Lowther, possibly of the earls of Lonsdale. Acquired by the Huntington Library from H. P. Kraus in 1957.

Secundo folio: (ha-)beat maritagium
Bibliography: Aspects of Medieval England, n. 1 open to f. 6v. *Chronica,* 4.

HM 25862 — France, s. XIV²
GRAND COUTUMIER; CHARTE AUX NORMANDS

1. ff. 1–271v: *Cy commencent quoy que nul die/ les droiz qui sont en normendie/ et les establissemens aussy,* [First prologue:] Pource que nostre entencion est a esclarier en ceste oeuvre au mieux que nous pourrons les drois et les establissemens de normendie . . . [f. 2, Chapter list:] De droit *i,* De iurisdicion *ii* . . . [f. 6, Second prologue:] Pource que la malice de convoitise avoit si ardanment enlacie l'umain lignage . . . [f. 7, Text:] *De droit i,* Droit est parti en ii parties . . . [f. 123v:] *Cy ensuit la ii*[e] *partie de cest livre de querelles 1,* Or nous convient traitier des querelles dez loys pour quoy les querelles doivent estre fineez . . . que quant l'en fait une exoine tous ceulz qui firent celles devant y doivent estre presens.

W. Laurence De Gruchy, *L'Ancienne Coutume de Normandie* (Jersey 1881); text ends in the chapter "De lois apparissant," corresponding to Family 2 of the Latin texts as discussed by E. J. Tardif, *Coutumiers de Normandie* (Rouen-Paris 1896, repr. Geneva 1977); quires 22 and 23 (ff. 165–180) reversed in binding.

2. ff. 271v–283: *La chartre aux normans,* Louys par la grace de dieu roy de france et de navarre A tous nos feaulx et nos iusticiers salut et paix. Nous avons receue la grief complainte des barons des chevaliers et de tous aultrez noblez . . . Et commandons qu'elles soient gardeez perpetuellement sans enfraindre de tous nos iusticiers. Donne a vincennes soubz nostre seel du quel nous usions

nostre seigneur de pere vivant le xixe iour du moys de mars l'an mil ccc xiiii. [f. 284r–v, ruled, but blank]

Ordonnances des Roys de France de la Troisième Race, vol. 1, ed. E. J. de Laurière (Paris 1723) 587–94.

Parchment, ff. i + 284; 92 × 70 (55 × 38) mm.; 1^{8} 2^{10}(–9, cancelled by the scribe) $3–8^{8}$ 9^{8}(–7, cancelled by the scribe) $10–13^{8}$ 14^{8}(–3, cancelled by the scribe) $15–19^{8}$ 20^{6}(–1, cancelled by the scribe) 21^{8}(with a catchword also on f. 162v, the 6th leaf) $22–36^{8}$. Catchwords in lower right corner in flourished red frames. 16–17 long lines ruled in ink with single bounding lines; the top line ruled full across. Pricking visible in outer margin. Written in a gothic book hand.

Opening page, f. 1, 6-line, parted red and blue initial with blue filigree infilling, and a C-shaped border of red and blue cascade motifs. Secondary initials, 2-line, alternating red and blue with tendrils of the other color; alternating red and blue paragraph marks; initials within the text slashed in red; red rubrics; chapter list alternates 1-line red and blue initials.

Bound, s. XVII, in French brown calf over pasteboards; rebacked, original spine laid down; repaired; marbled endpapers in the front; edges speckled in red; green silk bookmark loose in volume.

Written in France in the second half of the fourteenth century. An early owner, s. XVI (?), has signed f. 283v "Le [M?]oulins." Purchased by the Huntington Library from Dawsons of Pall Mall, Cat. 102 (1960) item 4, with a plate of f. 1.

Secundo folio: [f. 2, Prologue] droit en la; [f. 7, Text] les princes
Bibliography: Chronica, 4.

HM 26012 — England, s. XV¹
PROCESSIONAL, Sarum use — *fig. 90*

1. ff. 1–3v: Blessing of salt and water.
W. G. Henderson, ed., *Processionale ad usum insignis et preclarae Ecclesiae Sarum* (Leeds 1881) 1–6. For a study on the processional and brief descriptions of the 23 known manuscripts, excluding HM 26012, see T. Bailey, *The Processions of Sarum and the Western Church* (Toronto 1971).

2. ff. 3v–107v: Temporale from the first Sunday of Advent to the Sundays after Trinity, and the Dedication of a church; on ff. 11v–12v, ceremony of the Boy Bishop at vespers of the feast of the Holy Innocents; 2 litanies after the blessing of the Easter candle in the usual form.
Processionale, 6–135.

3. ff. 107v–133: Sanctorale from Andrew (30 November) to Catherine of Alexandria (25 November); included are processions for the feasts of the relics according to Sarum use, Anne and the Discovery of Stephen (2 August); no provision was made for processions for Brictius or for the later feasts of the Visitation, Transfiguration and Holy Name; Osmund is not present (as usual for Sarum processionals even after his canonization; see Bailey, 74); feast of Edward king and confessor with prayer only.
Processionale, 135–62.

4. ff. 133–136: Common of saints.
Processionale, 162–64.

5. ff. 136–138v: Processions *pro serenitate aeris, ad pluviam postulandam, contra mortalitatem hominum et in tempore belli, pro pace petenda.*
Processionale, 164–66.

6. ff. 138v–144v: Votive masses *pro fratribus et sororibus, pro serenitate aeris, ad pluviam petendam, in tempore belli, pro quacumque tribulacione, pro pace;* litany to be said after mass.
Processionale, 166–67 (*pro fratribus et sororibus* only).

7. ff. 144v–145v: Processions for the reception of prelates and royalty.
Processionale, 169–70.

8. ff. 145v–147: Procession for a burial.
Processionale, 167–68.

9. ff. 147–149v: Litany, including Gildard, Medard, Swithun and Birinus among confessors; Afra and Edith among virgins; final prayers of the Office of the Dead.

10. f. 150: Procession for the translation of Edward king and confessor, of which only the prayer was copied above (f. 129) in the correct order.
Processionale, 158.

Parchment, ff. ii (modern parchment) + 150 + ii (modern parchment); 266 × 187 (180 × 112) mm. $1\text{–}18^{8}$ 19^{6}; the leaves in quire 1 now separated and mounted on tabs. Catchword survives on f. 8v written in the middle of the lower margin and enclosed in a circle. Quire and leaf signatures in letters (a–s) and roman numerals through quire 19, variously written in the inside, outside or middle of the lower margin. 27 long lines of text or 9 staves of text and music, or variations thereupon. Ruled in brown ink, with the bottom 2 lines full across; slash prick marks in the 3 outer margins. Written in a liturgical gothic book hand. Music on red, 4-line staves. On f. 1, 3-line parted blue and ochre initial, with a full border of a narrow blue strip, flourished in red and decorated with a series of regular curled tendrils in alternating ochre and blue. 3- and 2-line initials in blue with red flourishing; 1-line initials alternating in red and blue; 1-line initials within text filled in yellow. Paragraph marks alternating in blue and red. Liturgical directions in red throughout. Initials in sung portions in blue with red flourishing or as cadels, in black ink infilled in blue, pink or yellow and flourished in a light greenish black ink, sometimes worked in to human or animal faces (e.g. ff. 43v, 74, 75v, 79v). Marginal annotations in sixteenth century hands.

Bound, s. XIX, in brown morocco by F. Bedford.

Written in England for Sarum use, probably in the first half of the fifteenth century as the feasts of the Visitation, Transfiguration and Holy Name are absent. Sixteenth century owners erased and cancelled the procession for Thomas of Canterbury on ff. 13–14, erased the procession for his translation on f. 122 and substituted "epescope" for "pape" after the name of Clement on f. 132. The name "Scheppys Wyllem," s. XVI, occurs on f. 24. Acquired by the Huntington Library in April 1958 from Quaritch.

Secundo folio: (sacramen-)ta in aquarum
Bibliography: Chronica, 4.

HM 26052 England, s. XII²
AUGUSTINE, ENARRATIONES IN PSALMOS 101–150 *fig. 45*

ff. 1–287: [A]*urelii Augustini Egregii Oratoris Tractatus prior de psalmo centesimo primo incipit D*[omine exaudi orationem meam et clamor meus] *ad te veniat,* Unus pauper orat et non orat in silentio . . . Et quia sapere secundum carnem mors est, omnis spiritus laudet dominum. *Aurelii Augustini Episcopi Tractatus de Psalmo Centesimo Quinquagesimo Explicit. Amen.* [f. 287v, blank]

E. Dekkers and J. Fraipont, eds., Augustine, *Enarrationes in Psalmos,* CC 38–40 (Turnholt 1956).

Parchment, ff. ii (contemporary parchment) + 287; 350 × 250 (250 × 164) mm. $1–8^{12}$ $9–10^{10}$ $11–12^{8}$ 13^{8}(–5, no loss of text) $14–31^{8}$ 32^{8}(–5 through 8). Catchwords in the center of the lower margin through quire 8, thereafter in inner right corner. 2 columns of 40 lines through quire 6, of 38 lines in quires 7–10, of 36 lines in the rest of the book. Ruled in lead and brown crayon, double bounding lines, triple rules between the columns, top and bottom first and third lines full across through quire 10, thereafter top and bottom 3 lines full across. Pricking remains in the 3 outer margins and in 2 parallel lines in the inner margin of quires 7–10. Written, above the top line, by 2 people in well-formed book hands: i, ff. 1–115va (quire ends with f. 116); ii, ff. 115va–287.

On f. 1, fine large initial, approx. 95 × 83 mm., of pen-drawn ornaments, vines, palmette forms and biting dragons, reserved, against a blue and green ground, with some red in the dragons; on f. 5v, a smaller initial in the same style, but without colors; initials, 6- to 3-line, up to f. 99 in plain red, yellow, green or blue, occasionally with simple foliage tendrils in the same or another color; from f. 99v on, more elaborate initials, often using several colors and a few animal forms, but of varying quality (among the better, ff. 162, 177, 189v, 224v, 235); from f. 116 (with change of scribal hand), 3- and 2-line initials in colors with simple foliage of another color; also from f. 116, 1-line single color initials; initials within the text filled in red and biblical passages underlined in red on ff. 1–46, 197v–199, 201–287; biblical texts noted by the first scribe with single S strokes in the margin in the ink of the text. Display script for beginning line of f. 1 not filled in; opening lines of each psalm in a bastard uncial script; one heading in green ink on f. 82v; other rubrics in red. Numbers of psalms added, s. XIII/XIV, in running headlines in arabic numerals. Some marginalia in red. Later sketches, imitative of the dragons in the initial on that leaf, in the lower margin of f. 120v. Bad stains on ff. 173v–174; lower ⅔ of f. 287 cut away.

Bound, s. XII²/XIII, in leather over wooden boards with square edges flush to the book block; sewn on 3 wide bands; spine flat. Lunette-shaped tabs at the head and foot (partially cut away) of the spine, lined with a fabric woven in pink and green and embroidered around the edge. This binding covered in thin parchment, possibly in the eighteenth century. Remains of a paper label on the spine.

Written in eastern England in the second half of the twelfth century. In the upper margin of f. 1, the pressmark "B.B." Listed by Ker, *MLGB,* 170 as possibly from the Augustinian abbey of St. Osyth in Essex. Belonged to the Tollemache family of Helmingham Hall, Suffolk, who began collecting at the turn of the seventeenth century. For a brief history of this collection, see Sotheby catalogue, 14 June 1965, iii–viii. N. 63 in the old Helmingham catalogue; small paper label on inside front cover "L.J.V.9" corrected to "L.J.III." with pressmark of Sir Lionel Tollemache. Tollemache sale, Sotheby's, 6 June 1961 with plate of f. 1, to the Huntington Library.

Secundo folio: dicit. A finibus
Bibliography: Schenkl 4695. Römer, i, 339. *Chronica,* 4.

HM 26053 England, s. XV^2
HERBAL and MEDICAL TRACTS

1. ff. 1–17v: [A]brotanum istius herbe due sunt species scilicet Domesticus et agrestis et alio nomine dicitur sichuum Armenicum sed quando simpliciter potius pro domestica intellectus que alio nomine vocatur camphorata que et anglice dicitur Southernwodde et gallice Averoique. Calidus est in secundo gradu et siccus in primo. Archemesia [*sic*] . . . Absinthium . . . Apium . . . Ameos . . . Affodillus . . . [Z]uccoraria . . . zedoar anglice cetwalle, zirumbet idem, zufe id est ysopus, zinzar id est viride or⟨?⟩, zarnet id est [blank], zeg id est attramentum. Explicit.

2. ff. 17v–26: [A]gnus castus, Andra, Salix marinus, Sigillum salamonis, Diptana silvestris folia habens ut atriplex, Rubeum florem . . . Apium . . . Anetum . . . Zodoarum zedewale, zinziber zinziber [*sic*] anglice Gyngeuer. Explicit.

3. ff. 26v–31: [A]garigus fungus arboris est scilicet abietis. Acacia succus prunellarum immaturarum. Attramentum quedam terra gallica et sunt 2^e species et secundum quosdam vitriolum dicitur. Antimonium . . . Pionia maior et minor debent colligi in yeme. Pigamum anglice wilde Rewe. [ff. 31v–34, blank]

4. ff. 34v–36 [added by a different hand]: *De qualitatibus similibus remittentibus,* Calidum in 4to, Calidum in 3° . . . , *De qualitatibus contrariis,* Calidum in 4to, Frigidum in 4to, *De qualitatibus obtundentibus,* Humidum in 4to, Calidum in 4to . . . *De qualitatibus Augentibus,* Siccum in 4to, Calidum in 4to . . . ; [f. 35v:] Qualitates augentes promovent remissiones secundum merita et retinent proprium gradum. Gradus est excessus alicuius qualitatis notabilis super temperamentum secundum distanciam . . . ut que est dupla per comparacionem ad primum gradum erit quadrupla per comparacionem ad temperamentum et ita de aliis. [f. 36v, blank]

5. ff. 37–39: [L]argus amans hillaris ridens ruberque coloris/ Cantans carnosus satis audax atque benignus/. Nota quod sanguineus est humidus et calidus. Multum enim appetit quia calidus et multum potest quia humidus. Iste concordat veri et tunc peius se habet propter nimiam humiditatem cum caliditate. Melius enim habet se in autumpno . . .

The four complexions, each with a verse couplet and a prose text; verses in Thorndike and Kibre, 811.

6. ff. 39–41: *De Fleobothomia,* Nota quod Fleobothomia tot effectus habet. Mentem sincerat, memoriam probet, vesicam purgat . . .

7. ff. 41–42: *Qualiter homo debet se servare per singulos menses,* In mense Ianuarii vinum album ieiunus bibe nullum sanguinem penitus minue a pocionibus que ventrem laxant abstine . . .

Thorndike and Kibre, 691.

8. f. 42r–v: *De 4^{or} temporibus Anni,* Estuat Urbanus. Autumpnat Bartholomeus . . . Estas incipit a festo sancti urbani et durat usque ad festum sancti Bartholomei . . .

9. f. 43r–v: *De vocabulo morborum,* Nota quod *frenesis* impedimentum mentis quia inde leditur mens quia greci mentem frenas vocant vel quia dentibus infredunt . . .

10. ff. 43v–44v: *Nota consideraciones in colleccione urinarum,* Sciendum est quod in collectione urinarum vii^{tem} a phisicis considerantur scilicet tempus collegendi, quanto sit colligenda . . .

11. ff. 44v–45: *De colore urinarum,* Calor intendit urinam quia per eum fit resolucio terrestrium et aquosarum parcium in aereas et igneas colores . . .

12. ff. 45–46v: *De 4^{or} complexionibus hominis,* Quia homo est compositus ex appositis elementis et ex 4^{or} contrariis humoribus . . .

13. ff. 46v–47v: *Incipiunt quedam consideraciones ad medicinam pertinentes,* Nota quod in primis attendendum est utrum corpus indigeat purgari an non, habundante ergo humore pregandus est nisi impediatur ab hiis, scilicet Etate, Virtute, Complexione . . .

14. ff. 47v–55: *Nota de diversitate purgacionum,* Sciendum est quod purgacio Alia fit per vomitum, Alia per urinam, alia per emoroidas, Alia per menstrua, Alia per pessaria, Alia per sudorem . . . *Expliciunt consideraciones ad medicinam pertinentes.*

15. ff. 55–67: [I]n medendis corporibus et maxime purgandis sepe molestamur in contramedendis non quia medicina que datur sit incongrua sed quia ab imperitis medicis est oblata. Est ergo opus hoc medendi inventum . . . Tribus modis medemur scilicet Dissoluendo, Constringendo, Restaurando . . . *Expliciunt consideraciones circa medicinas.*
Thorndike and Kibre, 691.

16. ff. 67–76v: *Incipit Liber viaticus,* [P]erfecte dicuntur temperatina [*sic?*] que illius qualitatis habent excessum in quibus sunt caliditatis, Frigiditatis, Siccitatis, Humiditatis non invenitur dominium ut aurum . . . *Explicit Liber Viaticus.*
Thorndike and Kibre, 1034.

17. ff. 76v–80v: *Hic incipit tractatus medicinarum et laxativorum simplicium. Primo de comprimentibus,* Incipiendum est a medicinis que purgant comprimendo. Tamarindi sunt fructus cuiusdam arboris qui conquassatur . . . *Expliciunt medicine laxative simplices.*

18. ff. 80v–87: [G]audet epar spodio cor mace cerebrum quoque musto/ Pulmo liquoricia splen capare stoma galanga . . .
Walther, *Initia* 7108.

19. ff. 87–90: *De apio,* Apium idem est quod merg sive Smallage. Apium est calidum et siccum. Iram mitigat . . .

20. ff. 90–92v: *Sequitur de nocivis corpori humano in diversis partibus eius, Ista valent cerebro,* Cerebro valent fedid⟨?⟩ in quam oppressione ut in epilencia Serenus aer, Sonus delectabilis, Omne aromaticum . . .

21. ff. 92v–97: *Hec est dieta bona pro colericis,* In primis valet eis aer humidus panis frumentatus et digestibilis, potus sit vinum etate quidem medium . . .

22. ff. 97–102: *Nota diversitates passionum in aure,* Diverse sunt passiones in aure scilicet dolor cum apostemate, dolor sine apostemate, Vulnus, vermes, casus lapilli, Surditas . . .

23. ff. 102–103: *Ista valent Stomacho,* Marrubium scilicet Horehofe, Plantago Plantayne, Ruta Rewe . . .

HM 26053

24. f. 103: *Nota de aceto,* Acetum frigidum est in primo gradu et siccum in 2° gradu, habet digerendi et dividendi virtutem Penetrativam ex subtilitate substancie . . .

25. f. 103v: Four tables of Aqua, Aer, Ignis, Terra with the colors and grades, added by a different hand; f. 104, blank; f. 104v, added in a cursive hand: "A booke of fesyke begynnyng with namys of herbys xx s"; below, another price blacked out "viii s. vi d."

Paper (similar to Briquet *Lettre Y* 9183, Brittany 1475; *Tête de boeuf* 14193, Antwerp 1464–66; *Tête de boeuf* 14237, Namur 1474) with parchment reinforcing strips in the centers of the quires; ff. 104; 210 × 145 (ca. 160 × 105) mm. $1\text{–}3^{12}$(through f. 36) 4^{10} $5\text{–}8^{12}$ 9^{10}. No catchwords. On the first 3 quires the leaves are signed a–f and the indication of quire may follow in either roman or arabic numerals (a, b, c, . . . ; aii, bii . . . ; a3, b3 . . .). On quires 6–8, the leaves are shown by arabic numerals and the quires by the arabic numerals 3–5 (counting from the quire beginning at f. 37) with the designation "quaternus" (1 3 quaternus, 2 3 quaternus . . . ; 1 4 quaternus, 2 4 quaternus . . .). 29–33 long lines, frame ruled in dry point. Written in a secretary script of academic type; a second person added material on ff. 34v–36 (art. 4) and 103v (art. 25). Space reserved for opening initials, 3- and 2-line. 1-line initials and initials within the text filled in yellow.

Bound, s. XV, in doeskin, now white but once dyed pink, over bevelled wooden boards; evidence of a clasp closing to a pin on the center back cover. Pastedowns cut from an English antiphonal, s. XIII, with portions of the office for sext through vespers of Palm Sunday (front pastedown) and prime through none of Passion Sunday (back pastedown); width of text, 185 mm., written in a liturgical gothic hand; square notation on 4-line staves.

Written in England. On the upper margin of f. 1, "Smith Lo./ ⟨?⟩ I22 ⟨?⟩" corrected to "I12" (?). In the collection of the Tollemache family of Helmingham Hall, Suffolk, who began collecting at the turn of the seventeenth century. N. 16 in the old Helmingham catalogue; small paper label on the front pastedown "L.J.VI.21" corrected to "L.J.IV." For a brief history of the Tollemache collection, see the Sotheby catalogue, 14 June 1965, iii–viii. Tollemache sale, Sotheby's, 6 June 1961, lot 16 to the Huntington Library.

Secundo folio: Asplena vel splendilio
Bibliography: Chronica, 4.

HM 26054 — England, s. XV^2
ARMA CHRISTI, roll — *fig. 125*

The vernacul y honowr hym & the/ that the made thrugh his preute . . . and lest schall without hend/ Ihesu crist vs þethere send Amen. [dorse blank]

IMEV 2577. R. Morris, ed., *Legends of the Holy Rood; Symbols of the Passion and Cross-Poems.* EETS os 46 (London 1871) 171–93, here with text similar to London, Brit. Lib., Add. 22029, but with the picture and verses on the hammer (vv. 101–104) placed after the verses on the ladder (v. 124), and missing vv. 71–72 while vv. 77–78 were copied erroneously in their place, probably due to confusion at the break between the 2 membranes. See R. H. Robbins, "The 'Arma Christi' Rolls," *Modern Language Review* 34 (1939) 415–21.

Parchment, roll of 2 membranes, 1,638 × 103 (1,530 × 63) mm. 148 lines of verse, very faintly ruled in ink. Written in a mixed hand with anglicana and early secretary forms.

Twenty-four illustrations colored in pink, green and gold, in an unskilled style, and generally similar to those shown by Morris for Add. 22029: 1, the Vernicle with the face of Christ in the center of a large cloth, geometrically divided; 2, knife for the Circumcision; 3, pelican in its piety; 4, thirty pieces of silver; 5, lantern; 6, sword and stave; 7, rod; 8, a hand with strands of Christ's hair and the hand that slapped him; 9, cloth to blindfold Christ; 10, dice and the unseamed coat; 11, two scourges; 12, crown of thorns; 13, pillar placed sideways across the roll, and entwined with ropes; 14, standing Christ holding the cross; 15, three nails; 16, vessel; 17, rod with sponge; 18, spear; 19, ladder; 20, hammer; 21, tongs; 22, the face of Christ in the center with a Jew spitting at him from either side; 23, cross with three nails, placed sideways across the roll; 24, sepulchre with Christ's body lying in it.

Kept in a green silk bag with a drawstring; s. XIX.

Written in England in the second half of the fifteenth century. Acquired by the Huntington Library at Sotheby's, 11 April 1961, lot 139.

Bibliography: Chronica, 5.

HM 26061 — England, s. XIII^{med}
BIBLE and MISSAL — *fig. 55*

Bible with a missal copied straight on after Psalms, thus placing it in the center of the book; books of the bible generally in the usual order (see Ker, *MMBL* 1:96–97), but with the prayer of Manasses after 2 Paralipomenon, the prayer of Solomon after Ecclesiasticus, Baruch (its "epistola" before the text) on an inserted bifolium, and Acts after the Gospels; there are 38 prologues (24 in the New Testament) and a summary of Genesis.

1. ff. 1–9v: [added, s. XV^1, lacking first leaf] //*Numerus habet 36 capitula versus 6,* (populum) diminuat *1,* (tentoria) figunt *2,* (numeratur) levi *3,* (tabernaculum) portant *4,* (quo modo fiat) aqua zeli *5*/ . . . [for Apocalypse:] (reges terre) flebunt *18,* (beati qui ad cenam nupciarum agni vocati sunt) ad cenam *19,* (mortui) surgunt *20,* (ornatam viro suo) sponsam *21,* (dicit sponsus) venio iam *22.*

Mnemonic verses, beginning defectively, on the contents of the chapters of the books of the Bible, each chapter represented by a numbered word or words, further explained by suprascript words (here in parentheses) that do not fit the meter; for example, in Numbers there are 36 chapters, thus 36 words or phrases, given in 6 verses; the first verse, representing the first 5 chapters of Numbers, is "Diminuat figunt levi portant aqua zeli." A version of Stegmüller 1182; see also Walther, *Initia* 17610; by Alexander de Villa Dei.

2. 10–21v: [added by the same hand] Epistle and Gospel readings *"secundum usum sarum"* for the temporale (from the first Sunday in Advent through the Saturday after the 25th Sunday after Trinity), for the dedication and the reconciliation of a church, for the sanctorale (from Andrew through Linus, including the feasts of Wulstan, 19 January; Richard of Chichester, 3 April; Translation of Richard of Chichester, 16 June; Translation of Thomas of Canterbury, 7 July, followed by "Festum reliquiarum," which was established for Salisbury cathedral in 1319 as the first Sunday after the feast of Thomas; Anne, 26 July; Cuthburga,

31 August; Edith, 16 September; "Wolstani" (for Wulfram), 15 October; Hugh of Lincoln, 17 November), for the common of saints, for votive masses of the Trinity, Holy Spirit, Holy Cross, Mary (throughout the liturgical year), one's guardian angel, for peace, *pro serenitate aeris, pro pluvia, tempore belli, pro ipso presbitero, pro fratribus et sororibus, pro sponsalibus, pro iter agentibus, pro defunctis, pro peste animalium, pro infirmandum, pro peccatis.*

3. ff. 22–176v: Old Testament, through Psalms:
f. 22, *Incipit epistola eusebii iheronimi ad desiderium de omnibus divine historie libris,* Frater ambrosius tua michi munuscula perferens detulit . . . , *Incipit prefacio,* Desiderii mei desideratas accepi epistolas . . . [Stegmüller 284, 285]; f. 23v, De die primo in quo lux facta est . . . tollent secum ossa eius in terram suam [Stegmüller 9653, here an abbreviation of the contents of Genesis only]; f. 24, Genesis; f. 35, Exodus; f. 45, Leviticus; f. 52, Numbers; f. 61v, Deuteronomy; f. 71, *Incipit prefatio sancti Ieronimi presbiteri in librum ihesu nave et iudicum,* Tandem finito pentatheuco moysi velut grandi fenore . . . [Stegmüller 311]; f. 71v, Joshua; f. 78, Judges; f. 85, Ruth; f. 86, *Incipit prefatio beati Ieronimi presbiteri in libro regum,* Viginti duas esse litteras apud hebreos . . . [Stegmüller 323]; f. 123v, *Incipit prologus in paralipomenon,* Si septuaginta interpretum pura et ut ab eis . . . [Stegmüller 328], 2 Paralipomenon followed by the prayer of Manasses, *Oracio,* Domine omnipotens deus patrum nostrorum abraham ysaac et iacob et seminis eorum iusti . . . [Stegmüller 93, 2]; f. 142, Ezra; f. 144v, Nehemiah; f. 148v, Tobit; f. 151v, Judith; f. 155, Hester; f. 158v, *Incipit prologus in beatum Iob,* Cogor per singulos scripture divine libros . . . [Stegmüller 344]; f. 166, Psalms, with one verse per line, omitting the words that do not fit on the line; painted initials at the usual 8-part division, and parted initials at Pss. 51, 101, 119; the psalms numbered in lead in the margins to 157 (including the sections of Ps. 118, itself counted as 116).

ff. 177–191v: Missal:
4. f. 177, a small leaf, 172 × 115 mm., cut from another book, blank on the recto except for an added list, s. XV, of the incipits of 10 canticles with book and chapter number; f. 177v, in a contemporary hand, "Communicantes" for Christmas, Epiphany, Easter, Ascension, vigil of Pentecost and Pentecost; "Hanc igitur" for Easter.

5. f. 178: Prefaces for 10 feasts.

6. ff. 178v–180: Crucifixion miniature and the Canon of the Mass, from the daily preface through 3 prayers for communion.

7. ff. 180–183v: Collect, secret and postcommunion for various masses for the dead: *in anniversario* in 2 forms; *in annuali; pro familiaribus, pro patre et matre, pro benefactoribus, pro fratribus congregationis* (. . . beata maria semper virgine et beato michaele archangelo intercedente . . .), *pro quiescentibus in cimiterio, pro feminis, pro quolibet speciali, pro omnibus fidelibus defunctis; pro vivis et defunctis* in 3 forms and with readings, *de sancto spiritu, de sancta maria, de apostolis, de sancto oswaldo* (king), *de beato augustino* (of Hippo), *de beato laurencio, de beata maria magdalena, de beata katerina* (of Alexandria), *de omnibus sanctis, pro specialibus amicis, pro pace, pro iter agentibus, pro quacumque tribulatione, pro serenitate aeris, pro amico vivente, pro pluribus amicis, pro temptacione carnis, pro sacerdote, pro se ipso* in 2 forms, *oracio communis.*

8. ff. 183v–191v: Full services for the masses *de angelis, de sancto spiritu, de sancta cruce, de sancta maria* (throughout the year), *de incarnatione domini, de sancto stephano, de sancto iohanne* (the Evangelist), *de innocentibus* (this and the following with collect, secret and postcommunion only), *de sancto thoma* (of Canterbury), *in die epiphanie, in die purificationis, in die pasce, in die ascensionis, in die pentecostes, de trinitate;* collect, incipit of Epistle and Gospel reading, secret and postcommunion for the 25 Sundays after Pentecost (*sic,* not Trinity), for the Sundays in Advent, the Sundays after Epiphany, Septuagesima and the 2 following Sundays, 5 Sundays in Lent, Passion Sunday, Palm Sunday, Easter and the following 5 Sundays, the Sunday after Ascension; collect, secret and postcommunion for the vigil of the Ascension; full offices for John the Baptist, Peter, Paul, Assumption, Nativity of the Virgin, All Saints.

9. ff. 192–282v: Old Testament, Proverbs through Maccabees:
f. 192, *Liber salomonis id est parabole eius secundum ebraicam veritatem translate ad* [*sic*] *eusebio ieronimo presbitero petente chromatio et eliodoro episcopis, Ieronimus,* Iungat epistola quos iungit sacerdotium . . . [Stegmüller 457]; f. 197, Ecclesiastes; f. 199, Song of Songs; f. 200, Wisdom; f. 203v, *Incipit prologus in libro ihesu filii sirach,* Multorum nobis et magnorum per legem . . . [biblical introduction treated as prologue]; f. 213v, Et inclinavit salomon genua sua . . . [de Bruyne, *Sommaires,* 562]; f. 214, *Incipit prefatio sancti Ieronimi in ysaiam prophetam,* Nemo cum prophetas versibus viderit . . . [Stegmüller 482], one leaf missing after f. 214 with loss of Is. 5, 2–10, 4; f. 224v, *Incipit prologus sancti Ieronimi presbiteri in Iheremiam prophetam,* Hieremias propheta cui hic prologus scribitur . . . [Stegmüller 487]; f. 238v, Lamentations; f. 240, *Incipit epistola quam misit Ieremias ad abductos captivos . . . ,* Propter peccata que peccastis ante deum . . . [Bar. 6, 1–72, copied out of its normal position]; f. 240v, *Incipit prologus in libro baruch,* Liber iste qui baruc nomine prenotatur . . . [Stegmüller 491], Baruch ending at 5, 9, the last chapter having been copied above, all of Baruch by a second hand on added leaves; f. 242, *Incipit prologus ezechielis prophete,* Hezechiel propheta cum ioachim rege iuda . . . [Stegmüller 492]; f. 254v, *Incipit prologus danielis prophete,* Danielem prophetam iuxta septuaginta interpretes . . . [Stegmüller 494]; f. 260, *Incipit prologus duodecim prophetarum,* Non idem ordo est xii prophetarum . . . [Stegmüller 500]; f. 260, Hosea; f. 261v, Joel; f. 262, Amos; f. 263v, Obadiah; f. 263v, Jonah; f. 264, Micah; f. 265, Nahum; f. 265v, Habakkuk; f. 266, Zephaniah; f. 266v, Haggai; f. 266v, Zechariah; f. 268, Malachi; f. 269, *Incipit prologus sancti Ieronimi,* Machabeorum libri duo prenotant prelia . . . [Stegmüller 551].

10. ff. 282v–348v: New Testament:
f. 282v, *Incipit ieronimi presbiteri prologus iiii evangelistarum ad damasum papam,* Beatissimo papa damaso ieronimus. Novum opus me facere cogis ex veteri . . . , *Eusebius cypriano fratri in domino salutem,* Ammonius quidam alexandrinus magno studio . . . , Ieronimus damaso papa. Sciendum etiam ne quis ignarum . . . , *Incipit prefatio sancti Ieronimi,* Plures fuisse qui evangelia scripserunt . . . quam ecclesiasticis vivis canendas, *Incipit argumentum evangelii sancti mathei,* Matheus ex iudea qui et levi sicut in ordine primus ponitur . . . [Stegmüller 595, 581 and 601 run on, 596 lacking last lines, 590]; f. 292, *Incipit argumentum evangelii secundum Marcum,* Marcus evangelista dei electus et petri in baptismate filius . . . [Stegmüller 607]; f. 296v, *Incipit prologus super lucam,* Lucas syrus natione antiochensis arte medicus . . . [Stegmüller

620]; f. 305v, *Incipit prefatio Sancti Ieronimi in evangelio Iohannis,* Hic est Iohannes evangelista unus ex discipulis dei . . . [Stegmüller 624]; f. 312v, *Incipit prologus in actus apostolorum,* Lucas natione sirus cuius laus in evangelio . . . [Stegmüller 640]; f. 321v, *Incipit prologus in epistola ad romanos,* Romani qui in urbe roma . . . [Stegmüller 675]; f. 325, *Incipit prologus in epistola ad chorinthios,* Chorintii sunt achaii [*sic*] et hii similiter . . . [Stegmüller 685]; f. 328, *Incipit prologus in epistola ad chorinthios,* Post actam ab eisdem chorinthiis penitentiam . . . [Stegmüller 699]; f. 330v, *Incipit prologus ad Galathas,* Galathe sunt greci. Hii verbum veritatis . . . [Stegmüller 707]; f. 331v, *Incipit prologus in epistola ad epheseos,* Ephesii sunt asiani. Hii accepto verbo . . . [Stegmüller 715]; f. 333, *Incipit prologus,* Philippenses sunt macedones. Hii accepto verbo veritatis . . . [Stegmüller 728]; f. 334, *Incipit prologus in epistola ad colocenses,* Colosenses et sicut laodicenses sunt asiani . . . [Stegmüller 736]; f. 334v, *Incipit prologus,* Thessalonicenses sunt macedones qui in christo ihesu . . . [Stegmüller 747]; f. 335v, *Incipit prologus,* Ad thessalonicenses secundam scribit epistolam apostolus . . . [Stegmüller 752]; f. 336, *Incipit prologus,* Thimotheum instruit et docet . . . [Stegmüller 765]; f. 337, *Incipit prologus,* Item thimotheo scribit de exhortatione martyrii . . . [Stegmüller 772]; f. 337v, *Incipit prologus,* Tytum commonefacit et instruit . . . [Stegmüller 780]; f. 338, *Incipit prologus,* Philemoni familiares litteras facit . . . [Stegmüller 783]; f. 338, *Incipit prologus in epistola ad hebreos,* In primis dicendum est cur apostolus paulus . . . [Stegmüller 793]; f. 340, *Incipit prologus super epistolas canonicales,* Non ita est ordo apud grecos . . . [Stegmüller 809]; f. 340v, James; f. 341v, 1 Peter; f. 342v, 2 Peter; f. 343, 1 John; f. 344, 2 John; f. 344, 3 John; f. 344v, Jude; f. 344v, Apocalypse.

11. 349: [added in the upper margin in a contemporary hand, the names of the letters of the Hebrew alphabet in red ink with the Latin meaning of each name in brown ink above it] *Aleph,* doctrina; *Beth,* consilio; *Gimel,* Retributio . . .

12. ff. 349–379v: *Hic incipiunt interpretationes hebraicorum nominum secundum ordinem literarum alphabeti incipiencium de a et primo,* Aaz interpretatur apprehendens vel apprehnsio . . . Zusim consiliantes eos vel consiliatores eorum. *Ista sufficiant de interpretationibus nominum hebraicorum.* [Stegmüller 7709]

13. f. 379v: 6 short poems added in a contemporary hand: *De ordine* [*li*]*brorum* [*bib*]*lie,* Quinque libri moysi, Iosue, iudicumque sequuntur . . . [5 verses]; *De opere sex dierum,* Prima facta die duo celum terra leguntur . . . [6 verses; Walther, *Initia* 14619]; Quinque libri moysi iosue iudicum samuelem . . . [9 verses; Walther, *Initia* 16027 ?]; *De x plagas,* Prima rubens unda rane tabesque secunda . . . [5 verses; Walther, *Initia* 14595]; *De x precepta,* Disce deum colere nomenque dei retinere . . . [5 verses; Walther, *Initia* 4527]; Quatuor est primus primis tribus alter opimus . . . [5 verses; Walther, *Initia* 15297].

14. f. 379v: added in a second contemporary hand in the lower margin: Ys. Ie. bar. eze. dan. . . . [2 verses on the prophets]; Roma. corinth. gal. Ephe. phili. Colo. thessalo. thimo. . . . [2 verses on the Pauline epistles]; In omni processione uniformi multiplicetur aggregatum ex extremis [?] per medietatem processionum et habebitur summa tocius; ff. 380–381 blank, except for 4 erased inscriptions, s. XV^2, on f. 381, of which only the third remains somewhat legible:

Qui non vult dum quidem [?] dum vellet forte nequibit [Walther, *Proverbia* 24417].

15. f. 381v: note, s. XIV^{med}, on neither adding to nor subtracting from the word of God, referring to Deut. 4, 2, Prov. 30, 6 and Apoc. 22, 19; in the same hand, "Non auditur verbum in quo michi male" and a list of the books of the Bible, not in the order of this manuscript: Genesim, Exodum, Leviticum, Numeri, Deuteronomi, Primus Iosue, Secundus Iudicum, Tercius Samuel, Quartus regum, Quintus Ysaias, Ieremias, Ezechiel, Octavus 12 prophete.

Parchment, ff. ii (modern paper) + ii (modern parchment) + 381 + ii (modern parchment) + ii (modern paper); 220 × 154 (156 × 103) mm. 1^{10}(–1; contemporary foliation, ii–x) 2^{8} 3^{4}(through f. 21) 4–11^{12} 12^{16} 13^{22}(–22; no loss of text) 14^{14}(through f. 168) 15^{16}(+ 6, f. 174; + 9, f. 177) 16^{6}(through f. 191) 17^{12} 18^{12}(–12, after f. 214, with loss of text) 19–20^{12} 21^{12}(+ 2 and 3, a bifolium, ff. 240–241) 22^{16} 23–27^{12} 28^{20}(through f. 348) 29^{10}(+ 11) 30^{14} 31^{6}(through f. 379) 32^{4}(–2, 3; stubs remain). Catchwords in the inside lower margin, usually cropped. Signatures, a i–a iiii, in quire 2 only. 2 columns: of 35–36 lines for the Epistle and Gospel readings (quire 2); of 58 lines for the bible; of 47 lines for the prefaces, Canon, some of the masses (ff. 178–185, second half of quire 15); of 51 lines for the remainder of the missal (quire 16); of 51 lines for the *Interpretationes* (quires 29–31). Ruled in lead usually with the 2 top, middle and bottom lines full across, triple rules between the columns and an additional narrow double rule in the upper and outer margin; on ff. 32–69v, 192–309, the 3 top, middle and bottom lines full across, and a single rule in the outer margin. Slash pricking in the 3 outer margins. Written in a gothic book hand by four scribes: i, ff. 22–69v, 192–239v, 242–308v; ii, ff. 70–176v; iii, ff. 309–348v; iv, ff. 349–379v; the missal, ff. 179–191v, by a different hand, as well as the added materials: ff. 1–21v (arts. 1, 2) by one hand, s. XV^{1}; f. 177, a different hand; ff. 240–241, another hand, which also recopied the first 10 lines of f. 242 over an erasure (Lam. 5, 14–22, Bar. 6, 1–72, prologue to Baruch, Bar. 1, 1–5, 9) to supply the otherwise missing text to Baruch.

Full page Crucifixion miniature with Mary and John, f. 178v, facing the Canon of the Mass, with Jesus's face rubbed, in good style, of the type found in the so-called Robert of Lindesey group and similar to the Crucifixion in the Peterborough psalter (Cambridge, Fitzwilliam Museum, MS. 12).[1] Seven historiated initials, 13- to 9-line: f. 22 (prologue), Jerome writing, against a gold background; f. 24 (Gen.), the length of the text, the Creation in 6 polylobe medallions and, at the bottom, a larger compartment with the Crucifixion with Mary and John, against gold background; f. 166 (Psalms), David playing his harp; f. 284 (Mt.), the Evangelist, as a young man, checking the point of his quill; f. 292 (Mk.), Mark writing, as his lion (without wings or mane) turns to look at him; f. 297 (Lk.), Luke sharpening his quill, as his ox (blue, without wings) looks on; f. 306 (John), the initial I in colored segments the length of the text, surmounted and bitten by John's eagle, which clutches in its claws a bearded head (John the Baptist?). Painted initials begin books of the Bible, 12- to 7-line, in white-patterned blue or maroon, enclosing stylized vegetation or animal forms in blue, maroon, beige, green and orange. Initials for prologues, 10- to 4-line, in parted red and blue with flourishing in both colors; 2-line initials alternating red with blue flourishing and blue with red; unornamented 1-line initials alternating red and blue within the text, in the Psalms and in the *Interpretationes.* Running headlines and chapter numbers, placed in the margins, alternating red and blue letters. Considerable contemporary and later marginalia for liturgical and study purposes, including: on f. 159, upper margin, "Rubee figure distingunt libros moralium" referring to arabic numerals in red ink, 1–35, added in the margins of Job, ff. 159–165v, to tie to the books in the *Moralia* of Gregory the Great; in Proverbs, ff. 192–197, Grosseteste indexing symbols in brown ink in the margins, somewhat cropped; see R. W. Hunt, "Manuscripts containing the Indexing Symbols of Robert Grosseteste," *Bodleian Library Record* 4 (1952–53) 241–54 and R. H. Rouse, "New Light on the Circulation of the A-Text of Seneca's Tragedies,"

HM 26061

JWCI 40 (1977) p. 285 n. 12 citing this manuscript; in the Gospels, concordance notes (?) in red ink; in the Gospels, Acts and Epistles, notes in brown ink on readings for the Mass throughout the year. Later medieval foliation, s. XIV or XV, in lead in arabic numerals, on ff. 22–176 as [1]–155 and on ff. 192–348 as 156–314, thus excluding the added material (arts. 1, 2) and the missal. Some leaves with contemporary repairs in the outer and lower margins.

Bound in beige calf, November 1968; front cover of medieval binding, whittawed skin over wooden boards, sewn on 4 bands, with evidence of 2 fore edge clasps; shelved separately.

Written in England in the middle of the thirteenth century, with the missal as an integral part of its original structure, as in Boston, Public Library, MS 202 and Paris, B.N. lat. 10431. The votive mass on f. 182v, "pro fratribus congregationis," with its invocation of the Virgin and Michael Archangel, may point to an origin in a house of canons regular dedicated to them. The presence of the indexing symbols suggests that the bible belonged at an early date to a Franciscan or to a cleric who had been to Oxford, since these symbols were employed primarily at Grey Friars, Oxford. The heading for the added fifteenth century Epistle and Gospel readings identifies that portion as Sarum use; readings for the feast of the relics of Salisbury cathedral are given on f. 17v. Given to the Huntington Library in 1953 by Mrs. Sidney H. Burchell in memory of her husband.

Secundo folio: [f. 23] audit clamorem
Bibliography: Aspects of Medieval England, n. 34 open at ff. 178v–179. *Chronica,* 5. N. Morgan, *Early Gothic Manuscripts* [*I*] *1190–1250* (Oxford 1982) 125–26 with plates of ff. 166, 178v.

---

[1] We thank Prof. Harvey Stahl for this information.

HM 26068 — Edinburgh, 1591
ESTHER INGLIS, DISCOURS DE LA FOY — *fig. 36*

ff. 1–51: *Discours de la Foy. Escrit a Lislebourg par Esther Langlois, Francoise M D XCI* [f. 2, Dedicatory epistle to Queen Elizabeth:] A treshaute et puissante Princesse Elizabeth Roine d'Angleterre et cetera, Madame, combien que ie soye peu exercée . . . De votre Majestie La treshumble, tresobeissante et tresaffectionnée servante a Jamais, Esther Langlois, Fille Françoise. [f. 9, Poem to Queen Elizabeth by Esther Inglis:] Princesse de valeur dont les nobles A yeux . . . ; [f. 10, Poem to Queen Elizabeth by Nicholas Inglis, father of Esther:] Foelix ante alias regio foelicior ipsa . . . ; [f. 11, Title:] *Sommaire Discours de la Foy Contenant Quarante Stances,* [f. 12, Text:] Cependant ô Chrestiens, que Satan travaille/ Et que son lieutenant nous dresse une bataille . . . Ne nous pourront jamais distraire d'avec toy. Fin. [f. 50:] *Hexasticha hoc in libello varie descripta,* Multiplici rogitas cur iam vestimur amictu . . . Texuit has calamo Galla puella suo. N[icolaus] A[nglus] D[ictae] P[uellae] P[ater]. [f. 50v:] *Advertissement,* Madame, apres avoir tirè le pourtraict de la Religion Chrestienne . . . de pouvoir a Jamais vous faire treshumble service. [f. 51:] *Huius ipsius Libelli Prosopopoeia,* Filia me scripsit mandante vtroque Parente/ Exilii calamo taedia discutiens.

Discours de la Foy in 40 6-line stanzas, dedicated to Queen Elizabeth; possibly not complete as the *advertissement* (f. 50v) mentions "certain nombre de vers, les uns en Anglois, les autres en françois," and there are now none in English. Copied (but possibly not written?) by the calligrapher Esther Inglis in Edinburgh, 1591. See D. Laing, "Notes Relating to Mrs. Esther (Langlois or) Inglis, the celebrated Calligraphist," *Proceedings of the Society of Antiquaries of Scotland* 6 (1868) 284–309, and D. J. Jackson, *Esther Inglis: Calligrapher, 1571–1624* (New York: privately printed at The Spiral Press, 1937), listing 41 manuscripts. HM 26068 unrecorded; only one other known manuscript, London, Brit. Lib., Sloane MS 987, bears an earlier date (1586).

Paper (Grapes, Heawood 2153, Antwerp 1598, and a Crown atop an unidentifiable device, hidden in the gutter on f. i only), ff. ii (contemporary paper) + 52 (f. 52 pasted to f. 51) + i (contemporary paper); 100 × 151 (70 × 119) mm. Collation beginning with f. ii: 1^2 2^4 3^4(replacement leaf attached to stub of original 3rd leaf) 4^2 5–12^4 13^6 14^2(+ a leaf pasted to 2nd leaf). Catchwords in the inside lower margin on the verso of each leaf in the dedicatory epistle; versos blank and no catchwords thereafter. 10 long lines in dedicatory epistle; 13–14 lines of verse in the poems of Queen Elizabeth; usually 6 lines of verse throughout the text. Frame ruled in black ink, double bounding lines, with additional double rule above top of frame to enclose space for running titles on recto of each leaf. Each of the 40 stanzas written in a different script or different sized script by Esther Inglis. 2-line initials in black, most with flourishing, begin stanzas.

Bound in contemporary parchment with gilt decorations; holes in both covers for 2 fore edge ties; gilt edges.

Written in 1591 in Edinburgh by Esther Inglis for Queen Elizabeth. Belonged to Sir Richard Ellys (1688?–1742), whose library was described in the transactions of the Gentlemen's Society at Spalding, 24 June 1742 (unpublished). Given by his niece, Mrs. Lloyd of Wympole Street, to Sir Richard's chaplain, Andrew Gifford, who noted the circumstances on f. ii verso; his armorial bookplate on the front pastedown with a pressmark added in ink, "B.d.1." Bequeathed by Gifford with the remainder of his library to the Bristol Baptist College in 1784; their later bookplate and 2 pressmarks, "Z.e.39" and "Z.h.10," on the front pastedown. See Ker, *MMBL* 2:186–201 for the manuscripts retained by the Baptist College; this one sold, Sotheby's, 11 December 1961, lot 176 with plate of f. 2 to the Huntington Library.

HM 26298 — Italy (?), s. XIV^{in}; England s. XV^1
GUILLELMUS DURANTIS, RATIONALE DIVINORUM OFFICIORUM — *fig. 66*

1. ff. 1–8: [Chapter list and subject index, alphabetical through the first two letters, with references given to the book, treatise and lettered section of the text] *Hic incipiunt rubrice libris Rationalis divinorum officiorum qui s. liber dividitur in 8 partes* . . . Zona sive cingulum quid sunt nomina, 3 parte tractato 3. laus sit deo. [f. 8v, ruled, but blank]

2. ff. 9–253v: [Prologue] *Racionale divinorum officiorum incipit Rubrica.* Quecumque in ecclesiasticis officiis rebus ac ornamentis consistunt . . . [f. 10, Text:] Prius est ut de ecclesia et eius partibus videamus . . . ut apud misericordissimum

iudicem pro peccatis meis devotas orationes effundant. *Explicit rationale divinorum officiorum.*
Schulte, 2:155.

Parchment, ff. iii (modern paper) + i (contemporary parchment) + 253 + ii (modern paper); 315 × 215 mm. Art. 1, the quire containing the index on ff. 1–8, was added in England, s. XV¹: written space, 235 × 145 mm., 2 columns of 46 lines, English book hand, 2-line blue initials with red penwork. Art. 2, the main text: written space, 235 × 137 mm. 2 columns of 50 lines, ruled in lead with a narrow space allotted in the inner and outer margin for notes; pricking visible in upper and lower margin. Collation beginning with the index: $1\text{–}30^8$ 31^{12} + one leaf added at the end. Catchwords in unadorned frames in lower right corner. Signatures occasionally present as letters and roman numerals (on the index), or as a series of slashes, or as both progressive letters and roman numerals (ai, bii, ciii, diiii on ff. 217–220). Main text written in a gothic book hand with southern features, using olive-brown ink. On ff. 127v and 168, lightly written pecia marks to the left of the text in ink frames, as follows: f. 127v, "Finis xxx pet." on Book 5, treatise 4, across from the section of text reading: ". . . ita exultant hodie christiani deiectis perversis imperatoribus qui ecclesiam persequebantur in odium nominis christiani. In VI feria fit commemoratio passionis domini . . ."; on f. 168, "Finis xl pet." on Book 6, treatise 29, across from the section of text reading: ". . . nisi forte mortis periculo iminente, omnis igitur ecclesie protes quoniam per anni circulum . . ."

Historiated initial, f. 9, 10-line, grey on blue ground with author in bishop's dress holding his book; dusky pink background patterned in white; stylized acanthus leaf and ball extensions along the length of the text, with some touches of burnished gold. The 8 non-historiated initials beginning each book are similar in style (ff. 10, 29v, 38v, 50v, 113, 134v, 223, 245). Secondary initials, 3-line, alternate red and blue with swirled flourishing of the opposite color, and occasionally with both colors in the flourishes. The 2 colors alternate in the paragraph marks and running headlines across the opening. Rubrics in red throughout. A careful round gothic hand has corrected the text and has filled in the marginal notes in the allotted space. An English cursive hand, s. XV, has added some marginal notes, has extended the running headlines to include the treatise number and subject, and has divided the text of each treatise into the lettered sections which are used in the index. The letters progress according to the length of each treatise, e.g. Book 3, treatise 31 covers a–z, aa–zz, aaa–ddd. On f. iii verso, an English hand, s. XV, has noted: "Wilelmus Durhant [corrected to "Durandus" by a seventeenth century hand] erat nomen compilatoris huius libri ut dictum est."

Bound, s. XIX, in English black morocco over bevelled wooden boards; large brass fore edge clasp closing to the top; gilt edges; marbled endpapers.

The pecia marks and the initials would suggest this manuscript was written in Bologna; the script, however, is not Bolognese letter and resembles more that of southern France, s. XIV^in^. By the beginning of the fifteenth century, the manuscript was in England, as shown by the index on ff. 1–8, the marginalia and 2 erased possession marks on f. iv recto (3 or 4 lines) and verso (1 line), both in an English hand; f. iv as read with the use of a reagent by H. C. Schulz and J. F. Preston in 1962: "Iste liber ⟨?⟩ x^i^ pat' 'pn̄o/ dn̄o Thome [inserted] Arch⟨?⟩ quinque libri pr⟨?⟩/ trad pry ⟨?⟩ forth anno ⟨?⟩ xci"; f. iv verso: "Iste liber [erased]." Belonged to Charles John Wilson, 3rd Baron Nunburnholme (1904–74); his sale, Sotheby's, 11 December 1961, lot 161. Acquired by the Huntington Library at that time.

Secundo folio: [f. 10, Text] quarum institutio
Bibliography: Chronica, 5.

HM 26341 England, s. XVI[med]
HISTORICAL MISCELLANY

1. f. 1: *Laudes Brytanniae, De Brytanniae Laudibus quidam sic scripsit,* Illa quidem longe caelebri splendore beata/ Glebis lacte favis supereminet insula cunctis . . . [Walther, *Initia* 8687].

2. ff. 1–72v: [Henry of Huntingdon] Habet a miridie [*sic*] Galliam Belgicam cuius proximum littus transmeantibus aperit civitas quae dicitur Rutupi portus . . . unde comparet quantae rex Stephanus audatiae et animi pericula non reformantis fuerit.

T. Arnold, ed., *Henrici Archidiaconi Huntendunensis Historia Anglorum.* RS 74 (London 1879) 6–279, to the year 1147, here considerably abridged and lacking the chapters "De Summitatibus" and "De miraculis" normally found in the post 1145-editions; in these 2 features (text up to 1147; omission of Books 8 and 9) similar to Glasgow, University Library, Hunterian U.6.6. (288).

3. ff. 73–87: *Decreta Willelmi Bastardi et emmendationes quas posuit in Anglia,* Hic intimatur quid Willelmus rex Anglorum cum principibus suis constituit post conquisitionem Angliae. In primis quidam unum deum super omnia volumus per totum regnum nostrum venerari unam fidem christi semper inviolatam custodiri . . . Et hoc praeceptum non sit violatum super forisfacturam meam planam. [f. 74:] *Leges Eadwardi quas Willelmus postea confirmavit,* Post acquisitionem Angliae Willelmus Rex iiii° anno regni sui consilio baronum suorum fecit summoneri . . . tamen in foro regio empto mercato suo cum testibus et cognitione vendentium.

F. Liebermann, *Die Gesetze der Angelsachsen* (Halle 1903) 1:489–91, 627–70.

4. ff. 87v–88v: Primus dux Normanniae Rollo qui et Robertus in baptismo dictus regnavit annis 30 . . . Huic successit Stephanus nepos eius annis 18.

Genealogy of the Norman dukes from Rollo through Stephen, often following the texts of art. 3; see London, Brit. Lib., Roy. 13.A.XVIII.

5. ff. 89–90v: *Chronica monasterii Sancti Albani,* Habent chronica Sancti Albani quendam fuisse Merciorum regem Warmundum nominatum qui Warwicum civitatem condidit. Huic filium fuisse Offam primum qui usque ad annum fere trigessimum cum mutus permansisset . . . ac si res esset fatalis quaesitu non invenitur.

W. Wats, ed., *Matthaei Paris Monachi Albanensis Angli Historia Major . . . duorum Offarum Merciorum Regum* (London 1640; this section with separate title page dated 1639) 1–32, the lives of the 2 Offas, here considerably abridged.

6. ff. 91–104: *Willegodus primus abbas Sancti Albani,* Offa rex cum ecclesiam conditam monachis multis variis e regionibus ob sanctitatem electis replesset . . . Iohannes de Marins successit Romam profectus cum 4 monachi ubi confirmatus cum non parvam pecuniam consumpsisset reversus est anno 1302°, rexit feliciter sex annos et 3/4 bonus et prudens cum fuisset antea prior 14 annos. Mortuus est anno 1308°. [f. 104v, blank]

H. T. Riley, ed., *Gesta Abbatum Monasterii Sancti Albani a Thoma Walsingham . . . compilata.* RS 28 (London 1867) vol. 5, p. 4–vol. 6 p. 109, to the year 1308, here considerably abridged.

HM 26341

Paper (Fleur-de-lis, Heawood 1445, Schieland 1526–65; on ff. 73–88, *Pot,* somewhat similar to Briquet 12517, Puys-Notre-Dame 1589), ff. ii (modern paper) + i (contemporary paper) + 104 (+ f. 36 bis, blank, thus omitted in contemporary foliation) + ii (contemporary paper) + ii (modern paper); 208 × 160 (166 × 105) mm. Collation beginning with contemporary flyleaf: $1–9^4$ 10^6 $11–18^4$(through f. 72) $19–22^4$(through f. 88) $23–26^4$ 27^2(contemporary flyleaves). 25–35 long lines, vertical boundaries marked by folding. Written in a rapid cursive which deteriorates in the course of writing. Frequent finding notes in the margins. Red paragraph marks; initials with the text overwritten in red. Foliated in arabic numerals by the writer. Lower margins badly damaged by damp and mold; repaired, 1982.

Bound, s. XVII, in limp parchment now reinforced with paper boards; evidence of 2 fore edge ties; barely legible on the front cover, "H. Huntingdon Leges conquestoris et Cronicarum Sancti Albani. 1565. Thomas Lambard 1634" (transcribed before binding repair); on the spine, "Manuscr. H. Huntingdon Leges Conquestoris Et Cronicarum Sancti Albani."

Written in England presumably by 1565 (date on the cover) by the antiquary Laurence Nowell, and left by him with his friend, the antiquary William Lambarde (1536–1601), when Nowell left England for the Continent in 1567; see R. M. Warnicke, "Note on a Court of Requests Case of 1571," *English Language Notes* 11 (1973–74) 250–56. N. 3 in the list of Nowell-Lambarde manuscripts printed by J. Nichols, *Bibliotheca Topographica Britannica* (London 1780–95) 1:510–12, at the time in the possession of Multon Lambard; n. 10 in the same list is a transcript done from this manuscript by Lambarde in 1565 of the abridged Henry of Huntingdon (art. 2). For a discussion of Nowell-Lambarde books and manuscripts, see R. Flower, "Laurence Nowell and the Discovery of England in Tudor Times," *Proceedings of the British Academy* 21 (1935) 47–73 (where, however, the antiquary Laurence Nowell is conflated with his cousin by the same name, who was Dean of Lichfield); to which add Los Angeles, University of California, University Research Library, MS 170/529, a commonplace book in both Nowell's and Lambarde's hands. Francis Edwards Cat. (November 1909) n. 184. Not in Hodgson sale catalogue of Lambarde books and manuscripts, 18 June 1924. Acquired by the Huntington Library from Maggs in July 1962.

HM 26560 — England, s. XIV^med^
MARIALE

ff. 2–312: [f. 2r–v, Chapter list, breaking defectively at Bk. 5, ch. 27:] *Explicit prologus. Capitula i libri et cetera,* Quod nullus inveniatur dignus in laude virginis. Quod debeant eam omnes laudare quamvis digna laus non suppetat. Quod omnis creatura ea debeat laudare quia ad statum debitum per eam reformatur. Quod per ipsam petenda est gratia ubi digne laudetur . . . De septem donis. De vita contemplativa beate virginis// [f. 3r–v, Prologue, beginning defectively:] //que floribus in varios succos mirabili artificio . . . de beato iob sumo loquendi principium. [f. 4, Text:] *Quod nullus in laude beatissime virginis inveniatur dignus, liber primus,* Iob, Nunquid levabis in nebula vocem tuam. Nebula est caro virginis in qua divinitas latuit unde regum liber iii . . . Merito itaque laudatur in sabbato ex qua et in qua et per quam sabbatum vere quietis illuxit. *Esdre iii. Conclusio operis,* Factum est ut populus terre impediret manus populi iude et turbaret eos in edificando . . . ignoscat omnipotens deus et donet omnibus qui circa hoc opus laboraverunt graciam in presenti et gloriam in futuro per sue gloriose matris merita. Amen. [f. 312v, blank]

HM 26560

Anonymous collection of texts regarding the Virgin Mary, as yet unpublished. It appears to have been compiled in England in the thirteenth century, and is known in 3 other manuscripts: Cambridge, Pembroke College 22 (s. XIV; Bury St. Edmunds), beginning imperfectly in the chapter list; London, Lambeth Palace 52 (s. XIV), preceded by an alphabetical index attributed to Jacobus de Voragine; Salisbury Cathedral 62 (s. XIII), which lacks substantial portions of the text. The text is attributed in the prologue (lacking here) to "quodam fratre ordinis predicatorum"; the latest writers mentioned in the prologue and in the list of authors cited (ff. 311v–312) are Richard Fishacre (d. 1248) and Robert Grosseteste (d. 1253).

Parchment, ff. iii (early modern paper) + 313 (1 and 313, contemporary pastedowns) + iii (early modern paper); 388 × 250 (307 × 170) mm. $1^{12}(-2)$ $2\text{–}16^{12}$ 17^{10} 18^{14} $19\text{–}24^{12}$ 25^{10} 26^{14}. Catchwords present; quire and leaf signatures in lead in letters (a–z, tironian 7, diagonal slash, horizontal bars) and roman numerals; evidence also of leaf signatures in ink in arabic numerals. 2 columns of 38 lines. Ruled up to f. 111v (with some variation) in lead with top and bottom 2 lines full across, narrow double bounding lines to the left of each column and with an additional narrow double rule in the 4 margins; from f. 112 on, ruled in ink, usually with only the single top and bottom line full across and with the vertical double rules now placed to the far left and right of the written space. Written by at least 4 people in large school book hands: i, ff. 2–81; ii, ff. 81v–108v (end of a quire); iii, ff. 109v–110v; iv, ff. 110v–312. Corrector's marks in the lower outer corner of many leaves and frequently at the end of the quire.

Opening initials of the books (3 letter I's running the length of the text, with their extensions; others, 5-line and 2-line) in white-patterned blue or pink decorated with both colors and with some gold and silver, including some animal forms and trilobe leaves at the ends of the extensions. 2-line parted red and blue initials infilled with void designs and with red and blue cascade borders the length of the text; 1-line initials in the chapter list, f. 2r–v, and in the authorities list, ff. 311v–312, alternating blue with minimal red flourishing or red with purple. Yellow tinted initials within the text; alternating red and blue scribbled lines as line fillers in the chapter list. Finding notes in the margins; running headlines alternating red and blue letters. In the section written by the first scribe, occasional well executed flourishing in brown ink, sometimes touched in yellow (e.g., ff. 2, 25, 36v). A few sketches by another person, usually in relation to the adjacent text: f. 8, a set of eyes (in the text, "oculos"); f. 252, 2 hands holding apples (in the text, "pomum in manu sua"); f. 257, a cross (in the text, "iuxta crucem"). Face brackets on, e.g., ff. 126, 144, 278v; nota bene hands on, e.g., ff. 118, 122, 217v. Elaborate L-shaped scroll nota bene marks, s. XVI?, on, e.g., ff. 76, 82, 107v.

Bound, s. XVIII, in stained calf; evidence from a previous binding of 2 fore edge clasps and chain marks on f. 1 top and bottom center.

Written in England in the middle of the fourteenth century. Late medieval notes of ownership including valuation or price erased from ff. 1v and 3, lower margin. On f. 1v, "Mariale magistri Thomae la Warre," probably the Thomas la Warre (ca. 1342–1427) who converted the rectory of Manchester into a collegiate church (Emden, *BRUO,* 1111). Listed by Ker, *MLGB,* 129 as having belonged to the collegiate church of the Blessed Virgin Mary in Manchester. On f. 2, "Laurentius Vause grammatice magister me possidet"; the Roman Catholic Laurence Vaux (1519–85) was warden of the Manchester church when the college was dissolved in 1559. Listed by Bernard among the books of another warden of Manchester College, Richard Wroe (1641–1717), n. 7160: "Mariale Bernardini de Bustis, Fol. Fuit hic Liber Tho. le Ware Coll. Mancuniensis Fundatoris." Bookplate of Le Gendre Pierce Starkie (b. 1796); sold from the estate of Guy Piers Le Gendre Starkie of Huntroyde, Lancs., by Sotheby's, 12 December 1962, lot 136 to the Huntington Library.

HM 26560

Secundo folio: [f. 5, Text] tuo assensu
Bibliography: Chronica, 5.

HM 26959 London, 1430
VINCENT OF BEAUVAIS, SPECULUM DOCTRINALE, alphabetical compendium *fig. 10*

ff. 1–97: *Incipit quartum speculum Vincentii doctrinalis compositum per alphabetum et ad materias distinctum et primo de A. Actor. Abstinencia* est virtus qua gule voluptates in nobis restringimus aut resecamus. Valerius libro 2. Fuit antiquorum illa simplicitas in potu ciboque . . . *De accidia* . . . *De accepcione et contemptu munerum* . . . [f. 96v, *De zelo et correpcione. Actor.* Zelus est fervor animi . . .] nam contra homines severissime adversum peccantes ingemimus et ipsi eadem committimus. Deo gracias. Amen. *Explicit speculum fratris vincencii belvacensis ordinis predicatorum per distinctiones ad materias distinctum Sub anno domini 1430 in london.*

Abbreviation of materials mainly in Bks. 4 and 5 of the *Speculum doctrinale* of Vincent of Beauvais, arranged alphabetically by topic. One other manuscript is known, Basle, Universitätsbibliothek, B.XI.3, ff. 238–308 (s. XIV; belonged to the Dominicans of Basle). The work was studied from the Basle manuscript by Ph. Delhaye, "Un dictionnaire d'éthique attribué à Vincent de Beauvais," *Mélanges de science religieuse* 1 (1951) 65–84.

Parchment, ff. i (modern paper) + 97 + i (modern paper); 178 × 120 (115 × 67) mm. $1–11^8$ 12^8(+ 9). Catchwords in lower right margin, most enclosed by scrolls; quire 1 with no visible signatures; quires 2–12, marked +, a–k and the leaves in roman numerals. 26 long lines, ruled in ink with the top and bottom 2 lines full across. Written by 2 scribes: i, ff. 1–8v in an anglicana formata hand probably by an Englishman; ii, ff. 9–97 in an anglicana formata hand possibly by a foreigner working in London. Opening initial, 6-line, in a German or Dutch style in light blue with red flourishing and infilled with void leaf designs; secondary initials, 3- or 2-line, bulbous and plain in the same light blue, with guide letters visible; alternating red and light blue paragraph marks. In quire 1, 1-line initials tinted yellow. Sources cited underscored in red; rubrics throughout. On f. 97v, 6 brief extracts from the text in the same mid-fifteenth century secretary hand that occasionally annotates the text: "De providencia et partibus eius . . ." On f. 97, the text is followed by a 3-line note added in a sixteenth century hand, "Idcirco intermittitur Lex, et non procedit in aeternum, quia improbus circumsidet iustum. Idcirco prodit ius Lubricatum," and two Hebrew inscriptions in a single hand, the first "alleluia," the second a transliteration of the name "Robert Varchoff."[1]

Bound, s. XVIII, in quarter calf; marbled paper boards; morocco label on the spine: "Quartum Speculum Vincentii MS 1438."

Written in London in 1430, as signed on f. 97. Belonged to Sir Thomas Phillipps, who had acquired it from Thomas Thorp shortly before 1840; Phillipps MS 9622; Phillipps sale, Sotheby's, 21 March 1895, lot 1134. H. W. Edwards Catalogue 106 [1963] n. 61; acquired from Edwards by the Huntington Library in July 1963.

Secundo folio: meus in seipsam
Bibliography: Chronica, 5.

[1] We thank Rabbi Norbert Weinberg for this information.

HM 26960
FLORILEGIUM

England, s. XIII[in]

ff. 1–147: An owner-produced collection of theological materials, mainly in prose in the form of full sermons, which are sometimes reduced to *sententiae;* the preaching material towards the end is arranged schematically into distinctions. Among the authors cited are Stephen Langton as archbishop (e.g. f. 57), John of Cornwall (e.g. f. 23v) and Bernard (e.g. f. 92). There are a few sections in verse, and considerable later marginalia with didactic verses or proverbs, the majority of which are unattributed, although some are ascribed to Bernard or to the Church Fathers. The collection, made up of numerous parts, was apparently put together over a period of time by one or more writers; the divisions between the texts are not always clearly distinguishable. The texts have contemporary cross-referencing, consisting of quire numbers, leaves within the quire, sometimes the page, the position on the page, a mention of the rubric and a tie mark, for example: f. 91v, "Ad idem in anteriori parte ultimi folii iiii[ti] quaterni versus finem. Et in anteriori parte secundi folii v quaterni circa medium de herbis" (with no corresponding marks on ff. 24, 26 to which this note refers); f. 104, "Ad idem in dextera parte penultimo folio xvi quaterni" (with a tie mark) and its reverse reference on f. 131v, "Ad idem in sinistra parte vii [*sic*] folio xiiii quaterni" (with the matching tie mark). Other marginalia consist of finding notes, often touched with color, and nota marks; running headlines have been added on ff. 110–123.

1. ff. 1–2v: [Begins incomplete, quire 1 lacking; verses:]// Triplex stulticie genus est qua probra paravitur/ Si nimias geris ore minas de nemo timebit . . . Recta fides, spes firma, duplex dilectio semper/ Ferveat assiduis precibus iustus tamen ora.

2. ff. 3–5v: *Incipit collectum Sancti ysidori,* O Dilecte fili dilige lacrimas noli differre eas. Tantum promtus esto ad lamentare quantum fuisti pronus ad culpam. Qualis tibi fuit ad peccandum intentio . . . illic remuneratio amittitur. Iustis in celo non in terra mores promittitur. Vide quisquis hoc legis ne quod legendo respicis vivendo condempnas. *Explicit collectum sancti ysidori.*

3. ff. 6–10: [Marginal note: ysidorus adhuc] *Incipit liber eiusdem de conflictu viciorum atque virtutum,* Apostolica vox clamat per orbem atque in procinctu fidei positus ne securitate torpeant . . . Deo contra de illo qui per increpationem dicitur. Argue sapientem et amabit te.

In the form of a dialogue; the speakers, in pairs, are: Superbia, Humilitas, Inanis gloria, Timor domini, Symylatio vere religionis, Religio vera, Inobedientia, Beata subiectio, Invidia, Congratulatio fratrum, Odium, Vera caritas, Detractio, Libertas iuste correptionis, Ira, Paciencia, Pretervia, Mansuetudo.

4. ff. 10–31: [Sermons or sermon material, usually without rubrics] Qui in domo dei per conditionem manet diabolus est cum eo . . . ; Incongruum est latere corpore et lingua per totum orbem vagari . . . ; Iuvenilem etatem senili auctoritate compesce . . . ; Cave ne hominum rumusculo aucuperis . . . ; Filius mittitur ad redeptionem [*sic*] nostram . . . ; *Salomone,* Tria sunt insaturabilia et quartum quod numquam dicit sufficit. Infernus et os vulve . . . ; *Salomone,* Timor domini disciplina sapientie et gloriam precedit humilitas . . . ; *Idem,* Meror in corde viri humiliabit eum . . . ; *Idem,* Spes que differtur affligit animam

. . . ; Via stulti recta in occulis eius qui autem sapiens est audit consilia . . . ; Est quasi dives cum nichil habeat . . . ; Benefacit anime sue ubi misericors . . . ; *De tristicia,* Non contristabit iustum quicquid ei acciderit . . . ; *De Invidia et quomodo noxia est,* Vita carnium sanitas cordia putredo ossuum . . . ; *De superbia et eius contradictoria humilitate,* Ubi fuerit superbia ibi et contumelia. Ubi autem humilitas . . . ; *De odio et eius contradictoria videlicet caritate,* Odium suscitat rixas et universa delicta aperit karitas . . . ; *Salomone,* Circulus aureus in naribus suis mulier pulcra et fatua . . . ; Fili mi si spoponderis pro amico delixisti aput extraneum manum tuam . . . ; *de dominica,* Amica christi est ecclesialis anima sancta . . . ; *Salomone in cantica,* Totus desiderabilis est dilectus meus et ipse est amicus meus merito dignus . . . ; *Sponsa de sponso In canticis,* Venter illius eburneus distinctus saphiris. Venter christi dilectissimi sunt fragiles in ecclesia qui eburnei dicuntur . . . ; Iusticiam commitatur religio que est mundicia vite . . . ; *De decem plagis egypti,* Nota quod sicut egyptii x^{cem} plagis percutiuntur. Ita filii israel preceptis liberantur . . . ; *Lucas In illo ewangelio. Erat Iesus eiciens demonium et illud erat mutum,* Cum inmundus spiritus exierit ab homine ambulat per loca arida querens requiem . . . Inmundus autem spiritus exivit ab homine quando diabolus exivit a iudeis cum legem acceperunt . . . ; Hec enim duo mala odit omnipotens deus in omnibus hominibus scilicet revertendi neggligentiam et salutis desperationem . . . ; Scimus quia ad maiorem mentem commovent dolorem dampna maiora . . . ; Fuerunt michi lacrime mee panes dies ac nocte et cetera. Panis lugentium habundantia est lacrimarum . . . ; Aliquis mittitur in vineam hora prima et alius hora undecima . . . ; Omne peccatum est vicium . . . ; *Ieronimus Damaso pape,* Quales clerici de decimis et rebus ecclesie vivere debeant . . . ; Qui in uno offendit reus est omnium . . . ; Et vocabitur nomen eius admirabilis et cetera. Admirabilis est in nativitate consiliarius in predicatione . . . ; Ave maria gratia plena. Bene credo et angelis et hominibus grata, hominibus per fecunditatem, angelis per virginitatem . . . ; Emant aromata sua tres mulieres, mens, lingua, manus . . . ; Infirmitati mortalium omnipotens pater benigne providens in ecclesia tria constituit medicos, loca, remedia . . . ; Apprehendent vii mulieres virum unum id est vii gratie virum unum id est christum . . . ; [a series of short *sententiae*]; Ego sum via, veritas et vita dicit dominus. Poluta sunt michi labia ut iustis loquar . . . ; [rubric added in the margin: In ascensione domini] Ascendit christus in altum captivam duxit captivitatem dedit dona hominibus . . . ; In vita sancti basilii legitur quod eo agente divina misteria ebreus quidam se christianus commiscuit . . . ; [rubric added in the margin: Moyses ad populum] Exeamus de egypto in viam trium dierum et cetera. Exeamus fratres dilectissimi de egypto huius mundi in viam trium dierum scilicet corpore, mente et opere . . . ; Septem panes quibus reficimus isti sunt. Primus panis verbum dei in quo vita hominis est . . .

5. ff. 31v–33: [Dialogue] *Cecilia virgo ad tiburcium,* Si ista sola esset vita et non alia, iuste illam perdere timeremus . . . illa eterna vita succedit quam dei filius nobis donare dignetur qui vivit et regnat per omnia secula seculorum. Amen.

6. f. 33r–v: *Versus Sibille de secundo Adventu Iudicis,* Iudicii signum tellus sudore madescet/ E celo rex adveniet per secula futurus . . . Et coram hoc domino reges sistentur ad unum/ Recidet e celo ignisque et sulphuris Amnis.
Walther, *Initia* 9907.

7. ff. 33v–35: [Sermon material] Construe super eum peccatorem, spalmista [*sic*] davit. Diabolus construitur super aliquem quatuor modis scilicet ad aufferenda temporalia . . . ; short exerpts from Bernard, Jerome, the Bible, Augustine, St. Peter, Anselm *in Apologetico.*

8. ff. 35–36v: [Monastic material] *Quomodo diabolus placitat contra hominem,* Verum sciendum est quia placitat diabolus contra hominem quomodo improbum placitor contra alium aliquem . . . ; *Similitudo inter monachatum et potionem et inedicum et Abbatem,* Attendant novicii quia sic agit qui monachatus arripit difficultates . . . ; *Similitudo inter angelos et sanctos,* Est preterea quedam vera societas inter angelos et sanctos quam debent habere nutriti in claustro monachi inter se et conversos . . . ; *De vestibus monachi,* Quod viles nigrasque fert vestes monachus ut se vilem reputet peccatoremque commonet . . . ; *De corona et tonsura monachi,* Corona denique capillorumque tonsura enim esse debere sacerdotem et regem demonstrat . . . ; *De spirituali sacrificio Monachi,* Officium sacerdotis erat in lege generis diversi peccora mactare; hoc igitur similiter officium debet esse leonem ne et crudelitatis lupum rapacitatis . . .

9. ff. 36v–38: [*Sententiae*] *De tribus hominum ordinibus,* Tres quippe sunt hominum ordines videlicet orantes, agricultores, defensores . . . ; *De vii donis spiritus sancti,* Septem quippe sunt dona spiritus sancti, videlicet timor, pietas, scientia, fortitudo, consilium, intellectus, sapientia; horum donorum ut dictum est timor est primum . . . ; *De tribus generibus verecundie,* Tria etenim sunt verecundie genera que et ipsa exterius operantur diversa. Alia namque est coram deo timor . . . ; *De tribus generibus que notantur in iuvene,* In iuvene quoque tria notantur quibus ad probitatem venturus prenoscitur, hec autem sunt taciturnitas, corporis continencia, verecundia . . .

10. ff. 38–39v: [Sermon material] *De diversis alimentis,* Sicut enim alimentis diversis ad perfectam corporis etatem . . . ; *Exemplum,* Qui caret culto merito esurit si alieno incidere nolit . . . ; *De detractione,* Comedit namque alter alterum et quasi morsum in eo facit quocienscumque aliquis aliquem male loquendo viliorem efficere . . . ; *De caritate,* Qui enim non diligit manet in morte, plus namque peccat qui amorem proximi a corde alterius minuit . . . ; *De scientia, voluntate et usu,* Cum in omnibus actionibus nostris sine opere querendum sit quibus pocius utendum si ut boni efficiamur . . . ; *Similitudo inter desides et peccantes,* Ad quid istud tantillum tenebo, Non ex re tam parva sapiens ero . . . ; *De Quadrato lapide,* Quadratus lapis sex equalia habet latera, in quod horum inciderit . . .

11. ff. 39v–40v: [*Exempla*] *Similitudo de molendino,* Cor hominum simile est molendino semper molenti quod dominus quidam cuidam servo suo custodiendum dedit . . . ; *De quadam matrona,* Matrona quedam filias suas cum ancillis suis magistre comendavit ut eas opera mulieribus congrua doceat . . .

12. ff. 40v–43: [Sermon material] *De voluntate propria,* Multa mala existunt in proprie voluntatis familia et ex sese quondam exercitium faciunt . . . ; *Commendatio superne ierusalem,* Commendatio superne ierusalem. Ibi namque iura legum in inquinabilia optime ibi consuetudines . . . ; *De beatitudinibus anime,* Hec sunt quatuordecim beatitudines anime, scilicet pulcritudo, agilitas, fortitudo, libertas, sanitas, voluntas . . . ; [short excerpts from Gregory, Ezechiel, Proverbs, *De Samsone,* Isidore].

13. ff. 43–47v: [Sermons] *In Ysaia legitur,* Rorate celi de super et cetera. Ysaias his verbis in quibus tres continentur petitiones . . . ; *Sermo,* Astitit regina a destris tuis in vestitu deaurato circumdata varietate. Regina ista beata est virgo maria . . . ; Rorate celi de super et cetera. Per celos dei sedes, per nubes prophete et apostoli . . . ; Sint lumbi vestri precincti et lucerne ardentes in manibus vestris ut custodientes vigilias noctis . . . ; *Sermo,* In exodo legitur, Dixit dominus ad moysen, Ascende ad me in montem et esto ibi. In veteri testamento tria festa celebrabantur . . .

14. ff. 48–50v: [Cut out with only stubs or small pieces remaining; f. 50v:] // . . . *hec dicta sunt de symone sacerdote magno In Libro Iesu filii syrac,* Ioseph filius tuus vivit et ipse principatum tenet totius terre egypti . . .//

15. ff. 51–57v: [Sermons or sermon material] Videtur michi uniuscuiusque sermo divine scripture simul esse alicui seminum . . . ; Qui res terrenas adquiri desiderat, requiem mentis deserit quam querebat . . . ; Nesciat sinistra tua quid faciat dextera tua id est non admisceate laudis appetitus . . . ; Adam peccavit ex pietate ne molestaret uxorem suam sed illa eva ex malitia . . . ; [rubric added in the margin: Gregorius] Depredari desiderat qui thesaurum suum in puplico pertat . . . ; *Lucas evangelista,* Quis habebit amicum et ibit ad illum media nocte dicens amicus meus venit ad me de via et non habeo quod ponam ante eum. Comoda michi tres panes. Nichil plus voluit ille quam tres . . . ; *Libro regum tertio,* Dixit salomon semet edifica tibi domum in ierusalem et habita ibi et non egredieris inde huc atque illuc quacumque ante die egressus fueris . . . ; *In canticis canticorum libro primo,* Vulnerasti cor meum soror mea sponsa wlnerasti cor meum. Soror christi est primitus credens synagoga . . . ; *In Iob, Gregorius,* Astra non sunt munda in conspectu eius . . . ; *Evvangelista lucas,* Omne regnum in seipsum divisum desolabitur et domus supra domum cadet. Homo est regnum ihesu christi . . . ; *Propheta david,* Iustum deduxit dominus per vias rectas . . . , Hic nota quinque, quod deduxit dominus iustum per rectas scilicet per decem mandata decalogi . . . ; *Matheus evangelista,* Ductus est ihesus in deserto a spiritu ut temptaretur a diabolo. Queritur a quo spiritu . . . ; Ieiunavit christus in monte. Ieiunavit quoque moyses nam et helyas in deserto. Christus ut nos redimeret . . . ; *Matheus Ewangelista,* Egressus ihesus secessit in partes tyri et sydonis . . . Nota tria in cananea mulieres fidem, pacientiam et humilitatem . . . ; *helias propheta in monte oreb,* Zelo zelatus sum pro domino deo excertituum quia derelinquerunt pactum domini filii israel. Helias propheta latitans in spelunca in monte oreb . . . ; *Gregorius in moralibus,* Quatuor sunt quippe qualitates quibus viri iusti anima in compunctione vehementer afficitur . . . ; *Stephanus Cantuariensis archiepiscopus* [added in the margin: Paulus ad ephesios] Que sit longitudo latitudo sublimitas et profundum crucis . . . ; Cum feceris prandium divites invitare noli, sed pauperes ante omnia . . . ; *Spalmista,* Vovete et reddite. Vos karissimi novistis tria videlicet castitatem, obedientiam et proprie voluntatis carentiam . . .

16. ff. 58–74v: *De septem diebus,* Primo facta die duo celum terra leguntur/ Fit firmamentum spera sequente die . . . [line 7] Ecclesiam sanctam designat terra fidelem . . . Vel lacrimas agra denotet hec ut siquis ad Aram/ Accedat culpas flectibus ante lavet.

The text presents New Testament events alongside their Old Testament counterparts; the first 6 lines correspond to the beginning of the *Aurora* of Peter Riga, ed. P. E. Beichner (Notre Dame 1965).

17. ff. 75–78v: [Sermons] *Matheus,* Ascendit ihesus in naviculam transfretavit et venit in civitatem suam. Christus suscepit crimen humanum . . . ; *Sermo de beata virgine,* Ave maris stella dei mater alma, vertens sum aperire os meum hodie karissimi inter tantos bonos ac peritos in utroque testamento doctores . . . ; *Lucas ewangelista,* Nuptie facte sunt in cana galilee et erat ibi mater ihesu. Dilectissimi sollempnitas presentis diei ab omnibus christi fidelibus debet celebrari . . . ; *Iezechiel,* Quatuor facies uni et quatuor penne uni . . . Per faciem quisque cognoscitur . . . ; *Contra claustralium superbiam,* Mei erunt manasses et effraim id est seculares fructificantes et contemplativi claustrales Ruben et simeon . . . ; [leaf missing between ff. 78–79]

18. f. 79: [Distinctions] *Puer,* Puer innocens est, purus, simplex, verax, munificus . . . [with entries on Piscis, Predicator attributed to Bernard, Piscator].

19. ff. 79–89: [Sermons] Gaudent in celis anime sanctorum qui christi vestigia sunt secuti. Maius erit gaudium sanctorum qui in hiis miseriis fuerunt in celo quam angelorum . . . ; Balaam dixit filio suo, fili ne sit formica sapientior te . . . ; *Malachias iii,* Inferte omnem decimationem. Sciatis vos perdisse habundantiam quia defraudasti me parte mea . . . ; *Apocalipsis,* Quod vides scribe in libro et mitte septem ecclesiis. Primo videndum est quis et cui . . . ; *Bernardus,* Securum habes o homo accessum ad dominum . . . ; *Christus in passione,* Tristis est anima mea usque ad mortem. Primo prope mortis anxietatem . . . ; *Genesis,* Penitet me fecissem hominem. Nota quia penitentia vel dolor cordis cadit in dominum . . . ; Quesivi virum qui interponeret maceriam et staret contra me . . . ; Quis est iste qui venit de edom et cetera. Vox est angelorum admirantium christi ascensionem . . . ; *Stephanus Cantuariensis Archiepiscopus,* Qui veri ihesu expetit amicitias multorum patitur inimicitias . . . ; Superbia est extollentia proprie persone cuius species sunt quatuor . . . ; *Davit,* In circuitu impii ambulant. Dilectissimi est circuitus malus et est circuitus bonus . . . ; *Consolatio quedam,* Quatuor sunt genera ovium, infirme, fete, valide, erronee . . . ; *De sancto petro sermo ad vincula,* Nunc scio vere quia misit dominus angelum suum et cetera. Dilectissimi fodiamus litere parietem et inveniemus thesaurum intelligentie desiderabilem . . . ; *Iacobus Apostolus,* Si quis in verbo non offenderit, hic perfectus vir est . . . Similiter et magne naves modico ubi impetus dirigentis voluerit . . . ; *Super ewangelium Mathei de spiritibus,* Cum immundus spiritus exierit ab homine et cetera. Videamus primo qui sunt septem spiritus boni . . . ; *Ieremias,* De excelso misit dominus ignem in ossibus meis Karissimi de igne spiritus sancti quo hodie apostolorum corda sunt ignita . . . ; *Super illud evangelium Mathei Gregorius,* Cum natus esset ihesus et cetera. In omnibus signis que vel nascente vel moriente domino sunt monstrata . . . ; *Canonica petri prima,* Christus passus est pro nobis vobis relinquens exemplum ut sequamini vestigia eius . . . ; *Augustinus in libro confessionum,* Ve laudabili vite hominum si remota misericordia discutiens eam . . . ; *bernardus,* Optime prorsus circumcidit nos et superflua resetat universa paupertas hec voluntaria . . . ; *Iob,* Si abscondi quasi homo peccatum meum et celam in sinu meo iniquitatem meam. Audi mirabile quid. Iob libenter in terra confitetur homini . . . ; Legimus christum ihesum tres mortuos resuscitasse filiam videlicet archisinagogi adhuc in domo mortuam iacentem . . . ; Deus enim non nostra sed nos querit. Cum melior sit anima . . .

20. f. 89v: *Questio est,* utrum persona assumpsit personam vel persona naturam vel natura personam vel natura naturam. Si respondes persona assumpsit perso-

nam, hec est falsa quia christus non est persona . . . ; [genealogy:] *Testimonium istud sumptum est in epistula sancti Ieronimi contra Helwidum,* Sancta maria mater domini et maria mater iacobi alphei et ioseph . . . ;

21. f. 90: *Thema ascensione,* Ascendo ad patrem meum et patrem vestrum dominum meum et dominum vestrum. In Iohanne. [followed by several other single-line excerpts, some with bracketed variant readings, e.g. Estote imitatores mei sicut filii karissimi: 1. a peccatis abstinendo; 2. paupertatem diligendo; 3. salutem animarum zelando . . .]

22. ff. 90v–91v: [Short sermon material] Ingresso zacaria templum domini et cetera. Octo sunt in hiis que diximus colligenda . . . ; Christus apparuit nobis et cetera. Karissimi ut ait doctor gentium brevis est sermo . . . ; Inveni quem desideraverat anima mea et cetera. Invenit eum primo beata virgo in utero . . . ; Deus quibusdam est manna propter dulcedinem. Aliis lignum vite . . . ; Et veniet quasi ymber nobis temporaneus et serotinus terre. Item linearis. Iudeus qui non recipit temporaneum . . . ; Super illum locum osee vi. Venite et revertamur ad dominum quia ipse cepit . . . Ibi nota. Hebrei somptuant sibi salutem post circulum mille annorum . . . [followed by bracketed material].

23. ff. 92–97v: [Sermons] *In quodam sermone beati maximi episcopi,* Quam mirifico misterio dominus noster ihesus christus vel tactu corporis sui vel transitu glorie sue . . . ; [distinctions on:] Verbum caro factum est . . . ; *Iob ultimo capitulo,* Non sunt invente tam speciose mulieres sicut filie Iob in universa terra. Iob interpretatur dolens . . . ; *Ieremias,* Filie Iob tres filie christi pulcrerrime [*sic*] et sibi spirituali dilectione karissime tres quarum prima est veritas confessionis . . . ; *Augustinus super illum locum. Implete ydrias aqua,* Miraculum domini nostri ihesu christi quod de aqua vinum fecit non est mirum eis qui novunt quia deus fecit . . . ; *Quare religiosi sunt cum principibus,* Ne veritatem falsitas obumbret, ne eternitati iniquitas prevaleat . . . ; *Sermo Sancti sebastiani ad martires,* O fortissimi milites christi o instructissimi bellatores divini prelii per nimiam animi victoriam fortiter pervenistis ad palmam . . . ; *Questio de caritate,* Quidam enim asserunt quod caritas semel habita non amittitur, alii contra dicentes quod habita sepe amittitur . . . ; *Psalmista davit,* Ascendit deus in iubilo. Duo sunt hic notanda. Quis ascendit quod notatur ibi deus, qualiter ascendit . . . ; *Gregorius In moralibus,* Sepe enim dum castitatis mundicia aliquis extollitur . . . ; *In moralibus,* Mortui enim estis et cetera. Gregorius. Si enim uno in loco sint mortuus et vivus . . . ; *Leo papa,* Timeat qui cum iustis in seculo non dolet ne cum peccatoribus supplicio perenni laceretur . . . ; *Paulus Ita epistula sua,* Et sicut non probaverunt domini habere in noticia . . . [the biblical passage]; *In decretis xl Distinctione Ibidem,* Tria sunt genera elemosinarum una corporalis scilicet egenti dare quicquid poteris . . . ; *Eodem libro,* Due sunt elemosine una cordis. Alia pecunie . . . ; *Gregorius super illum locum,* Abhominationes egyptiorum altissimo imolant israelite domino. Super quo loco Gregorius in moralibus. Quid namque stultius videmur mundo . . . ; *In decretis,* Quid enim prodest ulli suo errore non potui qui consensum preparat . . . ; *Ieronimus ibidem,* Ut lexiva per cinerem humidum fluens lavat et non lavatur . . . ; *In Distinctione,* Qui donant ystrionibus graviter delinqunt. Non enim attendunt . . . ; *Ambrosius,* Non satis est bene velle, sed etiam velle facere bene . . . ; *Ieronimus xxxvi causa distinctione ultima,* Non mediocriter errat qui magno bono prefert mediocre bonum . . . ; *Pius papa Ibidem,* Nichil

prodest homini ieiunare . . . ; *Ieronimus Ibidem,* Nichil enim sic iocundum est sicut cibus bene digestus . . . ; *Matheus,* Vigilate quia nescitis qua hora dominus vester venturus sit, prima vigilia contemptus mundi . . .

24. f. 98: [On the Creed] *De Symbolo,* Simbolum grece latine sonat iudicium id est collatio . . . ; *Quomodo xii apostoli fecerunt simbolum,* Damasus papa constituit ut symbolum cantetur ad missam . . . ; *De symbolo misse,* Constantinopolitanum quoque symbolum xii clausulas dinoscitur continere prima Credo in unum deum . . .

25. f. 98v: Seven "themes" from the Bible.

26. ff. 99–100: [Continuous text and gloss, with the lemmata underlined] Qui timet. *Dimidiavit dies suos* et dicit per re timore. *Vadam ad portas inferni,* Unde non despetans . . .

27. ff. 100–104: [Sermon material] *Ysidorus xxxii causa Questio Septima,* Non solum et cetera. In cuius decreti fine dicitur. Intra cetera septem vicia fornicatio maximi est sceleris . . . ; *Matheus,* Confiteor tibi pater celi et terre et cetera. *Augustinus,* Hec vox confiteor non semper est peccatoris . . . ; *Gregorius,* Sepe in exteriori opere ante occulos hominum inordinati Apparere metuimus . . . ; Perit omne quod agitur si non sollicite in humilitate custoditur . . . ; *xiii causa questio prima,* Precepit dominus discipulis suis ut commederent et biberent eaque aput auditores suos erant . . . ; Sparsis foris mentibus ad semetipsum redire cuique difficile est. Quia prava itinera . . . ; [bracketed material:] hee sunt septem claves sapientie: 1. interrogare humilite, 2. audire diligente . . . ; *Moyses ad pharaonem,* Deus hebreorum vocavit nos ut eamus iter trium dierum in solitudinem et sacrificemus domino deo . . . ; *Dominus ad moysen,* Moyses quid clamas ad me. Respondet. Voces aput aures domini faciunt verba nostra . . . ; Multis auctoritatibus probatur quod nullus potest facere elemosinam de rebus male adquisitis . . . ; Movet me quid ait. Extendisti manuum tuam et devorant eos terra. Quasi ut devorarentur a terra . . . ; Si quis bonum fecit causa vane glorie . . . ; Zacheus cupiebat videre ihesum sed non poterat propter multitudinem circumstantium . . . ; Gregorius super illum locum illius evangelii mathei. Cum natus esset Ihesus ubi ait de magis. Per aliam viam reversi sunt in regionem suam. Magnum vero vobis aliquid magi . . . ; Cantemus domino gloriose enim magnificatus est et cetera. Multa legimus cantica in scripturis sed hoc primum omnium est quod egyptiis et pharaone submersis post victoriam canitur . . . ; Grande malum est propria voluntas qua fit ut bona tua tibi bona non sunt . . . ; Sobrie et iuste et pie vivamus in hoc seculo expectantes beatam spem . . . ; Ecce confidis super baculum arundineum id est super regem egypti . . . ; *Ieremias secundo,* Virgam vigilantem ego video. Et dominus bene vidisti quia vigilabo ego et cetera. Super quo ieronimus. Pro virga vigilantem septuaginta baculum nuceum transtulerunt . . . ; *Augustinus in libro de verbis domini,* Utantur divites consuetudine infirmitatis sue sed doleant se aliter non posse . . . ; Duplicem contra christi milites mundi producit aciem . . . ; *De Ieiunio,* Ieiunium fratres scimus esse dei artem, christi castra . . . ; *De saturitate,* Fames ieiunii est amica virginitatis, inimica luxurie . . . ; *Que sunt ale ieiunii,* Misericordia et pietas sunt ale ieiunii per quas tollitur et portatur in celum . . . ; *Ysayas,* Querite dominum dum inveniri potest. Super quo beatus bernardus. Attende tres esse causas que interim occurrunt . . .

28. ff. 104v–109v: [One sermon] Audierunt hostes iude et beniamyn quid filii captivitatis edificarent templum domino deo israel in ierusalem, irati sunt valde. In Iuda exprimitur virtus confessionis . . .

29. ff. 110–123v: [This section set apart from the others in terms of layout and script; see below] *Bernardus de passione domini,* Respice in faciem christi tui et videbis eum dorso flagellato . . . ; *De caritate,* Si per viam vere caritatis volumus currere . . . ; *Augustinus de fide,* Fides est res audax et improba perveniens quo non pertingit intelligencia . . . ; *Augustinus de spe,* Spes est certa expectacio future beatitudinis . . . ; *De Quatuor Cardinalibus virtutibus Et Primo De Prudentia, Tullius,* Prudentia est rerum bonarum et malarum, utrumque discretio in fuga mali et electione boni. Seneca. Quia prudens est respicit ad omne tempus . . . ; *De Iusticia Philosophus,* Iusticia est constans et perpetua voluntas ius suum unicuique tribuens . . . ; *De Temperantia Philosophus,* Temperantia est virtus vel potentia refrenandi illecebris . . . ; *De Fortitudine Philosophus,* Fortitudo est virtus que nec adversitatis incursu frangitur . . . ; *De perseverantia Ieronimus,* Cepisse multorum est ad culmen vero pervenisse paucorum . . . ; *De Recidivatione Ysidorus,* Irrisor est et non penitens qui adhuc agit quod penitet . . . ; *De Adulatione Gregorius,* Curari vulnus neggligitur quod dignum laudis premio videtur . . . ; *De Predicatione Ieronimus,* Illa vox audientium corda penetrat quam proferentis vita commendat . . . ; *De Paupertate Bernardus,* Magna est abusio ut velit frater dives vermiculus vilis . . . ; *De Prelatis Gregorius,* Contra subditos in esse debet rectoribus et iuste consulens misericordia et pie semens disciplina . . . ; *Ad Claustrales Bernardus,* Ubi necessitas cogit dispensatio excusabilis est . . . ; *De Meditacionibus Beati Bernardi,* O Anima insignita dei ymagine decorata similitudine, desponsata fide . . . ; *Idem De Penis Inferni,* Nichil aliud in inferno audietur nisi flectus et planctus gemitus et ululatus . . . ; *De Gaudio celi Bernardus,* O civitas celestis mansio secura patria totum continens quod delectat . . . ; *Consolatio Contra Infirmitatem Gregorius,* In omelia dominice resurrectionis scribit beatus gregorius de sancto petro apostolorum principe dicens. Considerandum est nobis Cur omnipotens deus eumquem cuncte ecclesie preferre disposuerat . . . ; *De Corpore Christi Augustinus xxxvi capitulo Distinctione v*[a], Nos in specie panis et vini quam videmus res invisibiles . . . ; *De Penitencia Innocentius ii*[us] *xxxiii capitulo Distinctione v*[a] *et Distinctione vi*[a] *Et deinceps,* Tempus inquit penitentie est usque in ultimum articulum vite . . . ; [running headlines added, s. XV: Nota hic bene qualiter christus est querendus] Ihesum querentis nazarenum crucifixum surrexit, non est hic. Angelus ad mulieres. Tria possint hic notari, Quis queritur . . . ; *Exemplum de caritate,* Super ewangelium illud Luce. Duo de discipulis ihesu ibant in emaus secunda feria pasce. Gregorius. Quidam paterfamilias cum tota domo sua magno hospitalitatis studio serviebat . . . ; *Paulus,* Si quis spiritum christi non habet, hic non est eius. Ibi Gregorius. Quasi quidam titulus divine possessionis est iste spiritus amoris . . . ; *De Potestate Divina,* Sapientia edificavit sibi domum. Ibi Leo papa id est corpus hominis assumpsit . . . ; *In Iohanne,* Pacem meam do vobis pacem relinquo vobis. *Augustinus,* Pax est serenitas mentis, tranquillitas animi . . .

30. ff. 124–135: [Distinctions, arranged alphabetically, with brackets; ff. 132–133, only stubs remain] Amicus; Ancilla; Amor dei . . . [ends at "Crux tollitur"]

31. ff. 135v–139: [Sermon material] Crux est vinculum obedientie et penitentie cui astrincti sunt omnes contemplativi . . . ; In corde est duplex lepra, propria

voluntas et proprium consilium . . . ; Lepra proprii consilii eo perniciosior est . . . ; Mentior si ne videre potui quosdam quorum paupertas talis erat . . . ; Sunt quidam qui sciunt et possunt et volunt preesse . . . ; Inobedientia assumit sibi quoniam nomen obedientie ut solo nomine glorietur . . . ; Inter abusiones huius seculi sola maior est senis obstinatio qui morti proximus mortis adventum non abhorret . . . ; Ordo claustri et ordo curie secularis diversus est. Ibi. Sedes in consiliis cum divitibus . . . ; *De peccato obstinationis,* Omne peccatum in spiritu sancto est obstinacio vel gratie impugnacio . . . ; Ieiunent membra que peccaverunt. Bernardus. Ieiunet occulus a curiosis aspectibus . . . ; Sanctus quippe symeon didicerat a prophetis quod veniret filius dei . . . ; Multis modis fiunt excusaciones in peccatis . . . ; Videant in quanto periculo sint pro quibus etiam ecclesia palam orare non audet . . . ; Habet diabolus refectorium in quo pascitur quod est invidia . . . ; *Gregorius,* Qui vult mereri bonum quod expetit . . .

32. ff. 139v–142: [Sermons] Ioel primo. Residuum eruce comedit locusta et residuum locuste comedet brucus et residuum bruci comedet rubigo. Eruca vermis est qui in oleribus maxime invenitur . . . ; Cum descenderet et tos, pariter descendebat et manna. In tore figuratur verbum domini eo quod refrigerat . . . ; Renes vestros accingetis calciamenta habentes in pedibus baculos tenentes in manibus et commedetis festinanter. De lya legitur quod succinctis lumbis venit iesrael [*sic*] . . . ; *Ioel primo,* Expergiscimini ebru et flete et ululate omnes qui bibitis vinum in dulcedine quoniam periit ab ore vestro, Expergisci. Qui in ymo viciorum iacetis . . .

33. ff. 142v–145v: [Distinctions, arranged as lists] De superbia; Invidia; Ira; Accidia; Cupiditas; Castrimargia; Ebrietas; Libido; Fornicatio; Cecitas; Peccatum in Lingua; Peccata in deum; Peccata claustri quo ad prelatos; Peccata claustri quantum ad officiales; Peccata claustri quo ad claustrales; Adhuc quo ad claustrales.

34. f. 146: [Five short passages] Sapientia edificavit sibi domum . . . ; Multi autem straverunt vestimenta sua in via . . . ; Osanna id est salvifica subaudi quia tu es . . . ; Mulier sterilis et cetera. Mulier ista significat synagogam . . . ; Quod continet omnia et spiritus sanctus qui continet omnia et regit . . .

35. ff. 146v–147: [Sermons] Poterat enim unguentum hoc venundari trecencis denariis. Notetur glosa Ieronimi qui dicit iudam sub pretextu avaricie . . . ; *Augustinus de verbis domini secundum Iohannem,* Augustinus de verbis domini in ewangelio secundum iohannem. Super illum locum. Non turbet cor vestrum. Credimus in dei filium qui sepultus est . . .

36. f. 147v: Paschal tables added.

Parchment, thick and velvety, ff. i (modern parchment) + 147 + i (modern parchment); 150 × 110 (110 × 75) mm. 1–3^{8} 4^{8}(+ 2) 5^{8}(to f. 41) 6^{6}(ff. 42–47) 7^{10} 8^{12} 9^{6}(ff. 70–74; 5 is a stub) 10^{8}(5 is cut away between ff. 78–79, apparently with text missing) 11^{8} 12^{10}(–6, 9) 13–14^{12} 15^{10} 16^{8}(1 and 2 are stubs, but with text) 17^{8}. Signed in roman numerals on the last folio verso of each quire in the upper margin, II–[XIII]; the first quire is now missing. 20–29 long lines, ruled in lead often with double bounding lines; written on the top line. Written by several hands in a small spiky littera textualis. Rubrics, when present, are usually in red; on ff. 110–123, they are in the ink of the text touched in green, as are the authorities carefully listed in the margins. Initials are seldom more than 2 lines in height, and usually plain red; occasionally they may be in green, yellow or a bright turquoise blue. The first letters of the distinctions on ff. 124–135 are touched in red, green, yellow or bright blue with only one color used on a given opening; on ff. 140–147 the initials have simple flourishes of another color. Sketches of animals in the lower margins of ff. 10, 14v, 30v and 59; on f. 36 a large sketch colored in green showing a monk and an angel conversing. On f. 39, a strip of outer margin has been sliced and twisted into a slit as a tab.

Bound, s. XX, in white pigskin over pasteboards.

Written in England in the first third of the thirteenth century. In sale catalogue 106 of H. W. Edwards, 1963, n. 22. Acquired by the Huntington Library at that time.

Bibliography: Chronica, 5; *Aspects of Medieval England,* n. 32 open at f. 36.

HM 27186 — England, s. XIII^{ex}, XIV^{med}
STATUTES, roll

1. membrane 1: Anna tribus Ioachim Salome Cleophas Marias/ Tres parit has dicunt [*sic*] Ioseph Alpheus Zebedeus . . . [in 4 verses on the genealogies of the 3 Marys; cf. Walther, *Initia* 1056–1069].

2. membranes 1–6: Statute of Westminster II, 13 Edward I, ending ". . . Et si dimissio facta fuerit antecessori iaceat visus sicut prius fieri consuevit"; *SR* 1:71–95.

3. membrane 1 dorse: Statute of Winchester, 13 Edward I; *SR* 1:96–98.

4. membranes 1 dorse – 3 dorse: Notes on points of law in French, similar to material printed in W. H. Dunham, ed., *Casus placitorum.* Selden Society 69 (London 1952).

5. membranes 3 dorse – 5 dorse: Statute I, 14 Edward III; *SR* 1:281–89.

Parchment, roll, 365 × 25.2 cm. Formed of 6 membranes, measuring ca. 76, 68, 71, 65, 66 and 25 cm. respectively. Catchwords in center of lower margin of each membrane (none on dorse). 424 lines on the front, 450 lines on the dorse, frame ruled in dry point. Written by 2 scribes in anglicana scripts: i, arts. 1–4; ii, art. 5. Contemporary note on the dorse, "Statuta regis Edwardi."

Written in England in the late thirteenth century; art. 5 added in the middle of the fourteenth century. Apparently belonged to the Cistercian house of Coggeshall (listed with a query by Ker, *MLGB,* p. 53): a seventeenth century note on the dorse, "Found in the Abbey of Coxall in Essex at the tyme of the dissolution." On the dorse in a modern hand, "134." Acquired by the Huntington Library from Sotheby's, 10 June 1963, lot 160.

Bibliography: Aspects of Medieval England, n. 4. *Chronica,* 5.

HM 27187 — England, s. XIV^{med}, XV^{in}
ROBERT HOLCOT; WILLIAM WOODFORD; FRANCISCUS DE MAYRONIS — *fig. 157*

Composite volume

I.

1. ff. 2–113v: //esse contingentem et 1^{am} teneor credere esse necessariam si

dicatur quod non teneor assentire omnibus equaliter . . . Ad 11^{m} quando queritur quid appeciit, superius dictum fuit et cetera. Explicit lectura.

Robert Holcot, *Quaestiones super quattuor libros sententiarum Petri Lombardi* (Lyons: Jean Trechsel, 1497); Hain 8763. Kaeppeli, *SOPMA* 3499. Stegmüller, *Rep. Sent.* 737. Here with the first leaf torn away, the second *questio* of Bk. 1, "Utrum sit ipsum complexum vel res significata per complexum," not copied, and with Bk. 4 copied before Bk. 3 (but each with its proper numerical designation); Bk. 3 contains 4 *questiones:* "Utrum filius dei potuit incarnari"; "Utrum finale premium boni viatoris sit beatitudo" (in printed text as Bk. 4, quest. 8); "Utrum angelo confirmato conveniat deputari ad custodiendum hominem viatorem" (in printed text as Bk. 2, quest. 4); "Utrum demones libere peccaverunt" (in printed text as Bk. 2, quest. 3).

2. f. 113v: Incipiunt tituli questionum in hoc libro contentarum super primum sentenciarum. Utrum quilibet viator existens in gratia in assentiendo articulis fidei mereatur, 1 . . . Utrum demones libere peccaverunt, 18. Expliciunt tituli questionum in hoc volumine contentarum.

Chapter list in the order of this manuscript, with Bk. 4 preceding Bk. 3; the heading for the *questio,* "Utrum finale premium . . . ," added in the lower margin by the same hand that added folio references.

3. ff. 114–117: [added in another hand] Chapter list of each *questio* and its *articuli* in the order of this manuscript; alphabetical subject index with reference to the *questiones* (not the folios): Abraham . . . absolvere . . . acceptor personarum . . . accidencia . . . visio christi . . . virtus . . . voluntas . . . Xps . . . Explicit tabula super hoc opus. Deo gracias.

4. ff. 117v–118: [added by the same hand as art. 3] [U]trum beata virgo fuerit concepta cum peccato originali. Et arguo quod non, primo ex accidente . . . omnis pene ab eo quem reconciliavit. [f. 118rb–118v, blank]

5. f. 119r–v: [added by the same hand as arts. 3, 4] potest igitur sine assensione dividi tria, primum quod voluntas creata non tenetur semper se conformare voluntate beneplaciti ipsius dei . . . quia nisi deus coageret in persecutionibus ipsi nichil agerent et sancti nichil paterentur.

II.

6. ff. 120–164v: Venerabili in christo patri ac illustri domino thome cantuariensi archiepiscopo tocius anglie primati et sedis apostolice legato humilis suus servitor frater Willelmus Wydford devotissimum humilitatis et subiectionis famulatum. Reverendissime pater, mandatis vestris obtemperando causas condempnacionis articulorum per vos nuper dampnatorum . . . si in hiis dictis alicubi recessi a via veritatis et parcere michi velet vestra dominacio quamvis hoc opus non habeat in singulis articulis discussionem plenam quia pro completa discussione tot articulorum tempus quadragesimale per vestram reverenciam taxatum fuit nimis breve. Scripta in castro de framlynham in vigilia pasche per auctoritatem vestram venerabilem atque dominacionem ad catholice fidei defensionem conservet Ihesus christus feliciter per tempora longiora. Amen. Witford minor.

William Woodford, *De causis condempnacionis articulorum xviii dampnatorum Jo. Wyclif,* pr. in E. Brown, ed., *Fasciculus Rerum Expetendarum et Fugiendarum prout ab Orthuino Gratio . . . editus* (London 1690) 1:190–265; on f.

163v, lines 19–22, Thomas Arundel given as archbishop of Canterbury (1396–1414), Robert Braybroke as bishop of London (1382–1404), Richard II as king (1377–99; printed text and secondary sources give Henry IV, 1399–1413), John of Gaunt as duke of Lancaster (1340–99). See Emden, *BRUO,* 2081–82. See J. I. Catto, "William Woodford, O.F.M. (c. 1330–c. 1397)," unpublished D.Phil. dissertation, Oxford 1969, listing 20 manuscripts of this work, including the present manuscript on pp. 306–08.

7. ff. 164v–165: *Augustinus de ieiunio sabbati ad casulanum,* Si nullo modo liceret sabbato ieiunare 40 continuos dies . . . sine ullo scrupulo vel disceptacione facite. Explicit augustinus de ieiunio sabbati ad Casulanum. Amen. [f. 165v, blank]

Excerpts from the letter from Augustine to Casulanus; *PL* 33:136–151.

8. ff. 166–174: *Memoriam fecit mirabilium suorum et cetera,* Tria sunt preconia quibus mundani principes solent principaliter commendari . . . in corpore organico et christi corpus in hoc sacramento. Explicit sermo de corpore christi quem composuit frater franciscus de maronis doctor sacre theologie. Ihesus amen. [f. 168v:] *Quodcumque ligaveris super terram et cetera,* Mt. 16, Duos fines ultimos futuros esse in fine seculi describit augustinus 13 libro de civitate dei quorum unus est dampnatorum pena eterna . . . qui solem suum facit oriri super bonos et malos et pluit super iustos et iniustos cui est honor et gloria in secula seculorum amen. Explicit sermo fratris francisci de maronis de potestate clavium.

Franciscus de Mayronis, 2 sermons; Schneyer, 80 (?) and 131.

9. ff. 174v–180: *Utrum per scripturam veteris testamenti poterit probari* quod christus in lege promissus iam venit. Arguitur primo quod non quia cum iudei acceptent . . . Tenendum est igitur firma fide christum in carnem venisse propter dicta patriarcharum. Non plus hic de adventu messie. Ihesus amen. [ff. 180v–181v, blank; f. 182, a 12-line note in a contemporary running hand; f. 182v, blank]

Parchment, ff. iii (contemporary parchment; i, former pastedown) + 182 (the first leaf torn away; + 89 bis; 182, former pastedown).

I. s. XIV^{med}, ff. 2–119; 260 × 184 (220 × 130) mm. $1^{12}(-1)$ $2\text{–}10^{12}$. Catchwords in lightly sketched frames in the shape of fish, mice or grotesques. 2 columns of 47 lines ruled in lead with an additional double rule in all 4 margins. Written in a deteriorating littera textualis. The remaining lower inner corner of f. 1 shows decoration on the opening page to have consisted of a bar border of colored segments and trefoil leaves. Alternating red and blue 3-line initials with flourishing of the other color; letters of the running headlines and paragraph marks alternating red and blue. Side notes in the hand of the scribe enclosed in the same pen sketches as the catchwords. Contemporary foliation in arabic numerals, [1]–119.

II. s. XV^{in}, ff. 120–182; 254 × 181 (198 × 125) mm. $1\text{–}5^{8}$ 6^{6}(through f. 165) 7^{8} $8^{8}(-7, 8)$ 9 (composed of 3 singletons?). Catchwords in the script of the text in the right lower margin. Leaf signatures usually i–iiii, but as ai–aiiii on ff. 166–169. 43–47 long lines, frame ruled in crayon; pricking in the outer margins of the conjunct leaves, ff. 120 and 127, but not used. Written in a poorly formed current anglicana script. Opening initial, f. 120, 5-line, in gold on a particolored blue and pink ground with trailing floral spray of blue, orange and tan spoon leaves and green tendrils, across the inner and upper margins. 3-line blue initials with red flourishing; red paragraph marks. Contemporary pagination, 1–92 on ff. 120–165v (arts. 6, 7).

Bound, s. XV, in doeskin over wooden boards; sewn on 5 bands; remains of 2 fore edge clasps closing to pins on back. Notes, possibly added at the time of the binding (apparently not in the scribes' hands): f. 1, remaining lower corner, "Sunt//"; f. 119, "hic sunt 10 quaterni"; f. 120, lower margin and f. 180, upper margin, "Sunt 9 quaterni istius opusculi." Badly wormed boards and endleaves.

Written in England, the first part in the fourteenth century, the second at the beginning of the fifteenth. The 2 parts were together when owned by Robert Rede, O.P., bishop of Chichester (1396–1415): on f. i verso, "Liber magistri Roberti Reede Episcopi Cicestrensis in quo continentur lectura holcote super iiii^{or} libri sententiarum in parte cum tabula eiusdem cum tractatu valde bono magistri W. Whydeford edito contra hereticas opiniones et erroneas positas per magistrum I. Wyclyff." Rede bequeathed his books to the Dominican convent of Kings Langley in Hertford; see Emden, *BRUO,* 2209 and Ker, *MLGB,* 105. At some time in the fifteenth century the manuscript may have passed to St. Albans: "De studio abbatis" appears 5 times on ff. ii and iii verso; 10 other St. Albans books bear this note; see R. W. Hunt, "The Library of the Abbey of St. Albans," in *Medieval Scribes, Manuscripts and Libraries: Essays presented to N. R. Ker,* ed. M. B. Parkes and A. G. Watson (London 1978) 251–77, and Ker, *MLGB,* 164–68, listing HM 27187 with a query. Belonged to James Fairhurst, as part of his collection of mainly sixteenth and early seventeenth century ecclesiastical materials, which he had gathered in an effort to locate lost portions of Matthew Hale's library; on the Fairhurst collection, see the introduction to *Will of Aethelgifu: a Tenth-Century Anglo-Saxon Manuscript,* trans. and examined by D. Whitelock, with a note by N. R. Ker and analyses by Lord Rennell (for the Roxburghe Club 1968) 1–4. "XII" in modern pencil on f. i. Sold through Messrs. Morgan Grenfell and Co. Ltd., Sotheby's, 10 June 1963, lot 162 to the Huntington Library.

Secundo folio: [Pt. **I:**] esse contingentem; [Pt. **II,** f. 121:] (quali-)tates carnis
Bibliography: Aspects of Medieval England, n. 20 open at f. 120. *Chronica,* 5.

HM 27486 — England, s. XV^{med}
BEDE, HISTORIA ECCLESIASTICA; etc.

1. ff. 1–46v [Prologue:] De prima christianitate missa in Anglia ab eleutherio papa . . . de sancto Petro abbate eiusdem monasterii primo. [Text:] *Incipit liber quem composuit sanctus et venerabilis Beda presbiter de gestis Anglorum,* Anno ab incarnatione domini centesimo quinquagesimo sexto . . . ut apud omnes fructum pie intercessionis inveniam. Amen. *Explicit liber quem composuit Beda de Gestis Anglorum.*

An epitome of the *Historia ecclesiastica;* for the full text, see B. Colgrave and R. A. B. Mynors, eds., *Bede's Ecclesiastical History of the English People* (Oxford 1969); this manuscript discussed on p. lv. See also M. L. W. Laistner, *A Hand-list of Bede Manuscripts* (Ithaca 1943) 70 and 103.

2. ff. 46v–47v [*Epistola Cuthberti de obitu Bedae:*] *Quedam epistola de transitu Venerabilis Bede presbiteri,* Dilectissimo in christo lectori Cutwino Cuthbertus condiscipulus in deo salutem eternam. Munusculum quod misisti . . . sed brevitatem sermonis ineruditio lingue facit. *Explicit.*

CPL 1383. *BHL* 1068. *PL* 90:63–66.

3. ff. 47v–54v: *Incipit vita sancte Marie egipciace,* Secretum Regis celare bonum est . . . et adorando spiritu et nunc et semper et in secula seculorum. Amen. *Explicit.* [f. 55r–v blank]

PL 73:671–690, attributed to Sophronius.

4. ff. 56–90: *Incipit epistola Bede ad Notelinum de templo Salomonis,* Hortatur nos vas electionis et magister gencium . . . [f. 57, Text:] Domus dei quam edificavit Rex Salomonis . . . ac diligentes quos dominus benedicit pusillos cum maioribus. *Explicit expositio venerabilis Bede presbiteri de templo Salomonis.*
CPL 1348. *PL* 91:735–808. Laistner, 78.

5. ff. 91–93v [Bede, *Epistola ad Pleguinam:*] *Incipit epistola venerabilis Bede presbiteri de sex etatibus seculi,* Fratri dilectissimo et in christi visceribus honorando plegwino Beda in domino salutem. Venit ad me . . . deus omnipotens fraternitatem tuam sospitem conservare dignetur. *Explicit epistola venerabilis bede presbiteri ad fflegwinum de sex etatibus seculi.*
C. W. Jones, ed., *Bedae Opera de temporibus* (Cambridge 1943) 304–15, and *Bedae Venerabilis Opera.* CC 123c (Turnholt 1980) 615–26, mentioning this manuscript. Laistner, 120, listing 4 other manuscripts.

6. ff. 93v–99 [Bede, *In Cantica canticorum libri VII:*] *Incipit liber Bede contra iulianum divine gratie repugnatorem,* Scripturus dei iuvante gratia in cantica canticorum primo ammonens putavi lectorem . . . dico in india iudea et egipto geruntur non nisi per eorum qui hiis interfuere scripta nosce [*sic*] valemus. *Explicit.* [ff. 99v–100v, blank]
CPL 1353. *PL* 91:1065–1077, part of Book I only. Laistner, 70.

Parchment (poor quality), ff. i (contemporary parchment) + 100 + iii (contemporary parchment); 237 × 168 (154 × 114) mm. 1–10^{8} 11–12^{10}. Catchwords present; quires and leaves signed in letters and arabic numerals. 33–34 long lines frame ruled with brown crayon. Written in a school secretary hand. 2-line blue initials with red flourishing; 1-line initials alternating red and blue. Running headlines; chapters numbered in the margin.
Bound, s. XVII, in English brown calf sewn on 5 original (?) bands, now drawn into pasteboards; old pastedowns re-used, the one on the back with a note, s. XV, "prec. ii marc."; evidence of 2 fore edge clasps; edges speckled in red.

Written in England in the middle of the fifteenth century, possibly in Yorkshire. C. Plummer, *Venerabilis Baedae Historia Ecclesiastica* (Oxford 1896) 2:118 observed of this manuscript that its "scribe probably had local knowledge," since the name of the village near Catterick where James the Deacon lived, otherwise unnamed, is here specified as "seynt iemestret" (end of Book 2, on f. 14); this detail was also noted by a seventeenth century reader, who has collated the text. On f. 99 a contemporary hand notes a financial transaction: "Solut. Willelmo ⟨cropped⟩ iii s. i d. Al⟨cropped⟩ Waltero xxx ⟨cropped⟩ et iii d. pro⟨cropped⟩." In an eighteenth century hand, Greek letters on pastedown, and "ΑΧΩ" on f. 1. Sold in 1836 by Thomas Thorpe to Sir Thomas Phillipps; Phillipps 9428 and the Phillipps shelfmark in pencil on the front pastedown; the number also in ink on f. i verso. Belonged to George Dunn (1865–1912) of Woolley Hall; his sale, Sotheby's, 11 February 1913, lot 400 to Bertram Dobell (1842–1914). Untraced according to Laistner in 1943. Sale, Sotheby's, 6 July 1964, lot 236 to the Huntington Library.

Secundo folio: esse prodiderat
Bibliography: Schenkl 1814. Römer, i, 338 (erroneously). *Chronica,* 5.

HM 27523 France, s. XV[1]
BARTHOLOMAEUS ANGLICUS, LIVRE DES PROPRIETES DES CHOSES, trans. Jean Corbichon *fig. 97*

1. ff. I–IX: [Chapter list] *Cy sont les rebriches de tous les chapitres qui sont contenus en tous les livres des proprietes des choses. Et parle premierement des rebriches du premier livre,* Cy commence la table des Rubriches du premier livre des proprietes des choses translate de latin en francoys par le commandement de charles le quint par la grace de dieu Roy de france et le translata maistre Iehan de corbeichon de l'ordre Saint augustin l'an de grace mil ccc lxxii . . . Le xxxvi chapitre parle des noms des aucteurs qui sont alleguez en ce present livre. *Explicit. Il y a en ce livre xi*[c] *iiii*[xx] *et xix chapitres.* [f. IXv, blank]

2. ff. 1–277v: [Prologue] *Cy commence le livre des proprietes des choses translate de latin en francois l'an mil trois cens sexante et douze par le commandement du roy charles le quint de son nom regnant en france noblement et puissaument en ce temps. Le prologue,* A treshault et puissant prince Charles le quint de son nom par la digne prouveance de dieu Roy de france paissible seignourie soit donnee de celuy par qui les Roys Regnent et de par le translateur de ce livre qui pour cause de sa petitesce nommez ne se doibt soit offerte et presentee honeur et reverence . . . [f. 2, Prologue:] *Le prologue de l'acteur,* Comme ainsi soit que les proprietes de choses ensuient leur substance pour ce selon l'ordre de la distinction de substances sera l'ordre et la distinction des proprietes des choses desquelles a l'ayde de dieu ay ceste oeuvre compilee . . . [f. 2v, Text:] *Ci fault le prologue de l'acteur. Et commence le premier livre qui est de dieu et des noms divins qui sont dis de dieu,* En commensant a declairer aucunes choses des proprietes et des natures des choses tant espirituelles comme corporelles . . . Theophile, Varro, Virgile. *Ce livre des proprietes des choses fut translate de latin en francoys l'an de grace mil CCC lxxiii par le commandement de tres puissant Charles le quint de son nom regnant en ce temps en france puissaument. Et le translata son petit et humble chapelain frere iehan Corbechon de l'ordre saint Augustin maistre en theologie de la grace et promocion dudit prince et seigneur tresexcellent. Deo gratias.*

Bartholomaeus Anglicus, *De proprietatibus rerum* in the French translation of Jean Corbichon, of which there are several incunable editions; in HM 27523 art. 1 lists 20 books, the last of 36 chapters; however, in the text the "20th" book begins, f. 273, with the rubric, *Ci commence le traite de la difference des nombres et des mesures . . .* ; this and the remaining chapters numbered as Book 19, chapters 114–149. For lists of manuscripts, not including HM 27523, see Stegmüller 1564–1567, Zumkeller, n. 468 and M. C. Seymour, "Some Medieval French Readers of *De Proprietatibus Rerum,*" *Scriptorium* 28 (1974) 100–03.

Parchment, ff. iii (modern paper) + IX (art. 1, parchment) + 277 + iii (modern paper); 380 × 290 (255 × 210) mm. 1^{10}(–1; art. 1) 2–35^{8} 36^{6}(–6). Catchwords in the hand of the text in the lower right margin; quire signatures in black ink in the lower left corner of the first recto: c–z and aa–oo (a and b presumably cropped); traces of quire and leaf signatures following the same sequence, in red ink in the lower right corners of leaves: f. 12, b.iiii; f. 84, l.iiii; f. 177, y.i. 2 columns of 47 lines, ruled in ink; pricking visible in upper and lower margins. Written in a bâtarde script.

HM 27523

Nineteen miniatures introducing each book, framed by simple burnished gold bands, with backgrounds often as feathery gold or silver rinceaux against black or dark pink grounds; opening miniature, f. 1, the width of both columns, ca. 200 × 160 mm., divided into 4 compartments: upper left, God, as a young man, creates heaven and light, and holds a roundel around which is inscribed: J'ay fait le ciel et la lumiere pour estre a homme chambriere; upper right, God creates fire, air and water, holding a roundel inscribed: J'ay fait le feu l'air et la mer pour que homme bien me doit amer; lower left: God creates the earth, holding a roundel inscribed: J'ay fait la terre bien garnie pour donner a homme sa vie; lower right, Charles V hands the Latin text to Jean Corbichon, saying on a scroll: De tout cecy les proprietes en cler francois nous translatez; the roundel placed at the center of the 4 compartments contains a coat of arms (see below); full border of black ink sprays, gold motifs and regularly placed, but sparse, colored acanthus leaves. Remaining miniatures, the width of one column, 19- to 13-line height: f. 7v, God and 3 rows of angels above a gaping hell mouth, which is receiving the fallen angels; f. 17v, creation of Adam in the Garden; f. 28v, a doctor lectures to his students on the humors of the body, while on a shelf behind are urine bottles and apothecary jars; f. 36v, a doctor stands before 2 cripples; f. 66v, an old man, hunchbacked, addresses 3 men of different social situations; f. 78, a teacher lectures to his students; f. 101v, a man, holding an astrolabe, stands talking to 2 others against a brilliantly striped sky; f. 117v, a seated man with an astrolabe talks to a cleric against a sky similar to the preceding one; f. 125v, a teacher lectures to his students; f. 128v, a man, standing against an orange scroll background, points to a roundel of a starry sky, pink castle, trees, grass and water; f. 134, in 4 compartments, an eagle, a swan, a stork, a rooster; f. 145, a man talking with 2 others, in a landscape of rivers, hills, trees and a graded blue starry sky; f. 152v, a landscape of converging rivers, a tree at either end and a mountain in the center; f. 160v, a landscape with rivers, trees, hills, castles and churches; f. 181, converging rivers, hills, castles; f. 192v, 3 tall fruit-bearing trees framing 2 smaller ones, against a low horizon and a graded starry sky; f. 228, 9 compartments containing a hedgehog, a lion, a bear, a monkey, a wolf (?), a boar, a dog, a stag and a horse; f. 260, a teacher lectures to his students. Initials for books, 7- to 3-line, in white-patterned blue or pink, infilled with colored trilobe leaves on a gold base; chapter initials, 4- to 1-line, alternating blue with red penwork or red with blue; alternating red and blue paragraph marks; rubrics throughout.

Bound, s. XVIII, in French polished calf; red edges.

Written in France, possibly Brittany, in the first half of the fifteenth century. The first owner was a member of the Laval family, whose coat of arms is in the roundel on f. 1: or, on a cross gules 5 escallops argent, semé of alerions azure (Rietstap, vol. 4, pl. 33). On f. I, shelf mark or notarial mark composed of a large flourish or paraph and the number "cinq," found on manuscripts of the library of the Château d'Anet, sold in Paris in 1724; this manuscript [n. 98] in that sale. The mark is on a number of manuscripts and printed books now in Vienna, for which see O. Pächt and D. Thoss, *Die illuminierten Handschriften und Inkunabeln der Österreichischen Nationalbibliothek: Französische Schule* (Vienna 1974) vol. 1, pls. 141, 155, 156 and vol. 2, pls. 410, 412.[1] Acquired by J. B. Denis Guyon de Sardière with a portion of the Château d'Anet collection; his sale, Paris 1759, lot 227. Sold by Mme H. Lestourgie to the French book dealer Brieux. Acquired by the Huntington Library in 1964 through H. Levinson, Beverly Hills.

Secundo folio: [f. II, Chapter list] mention. Et sera; [f. 2, Text] diligence esquelx livres
Bibliography: Chronica, 5–6; *Aspects of Medieval England,* n. 43 open at f. 101v. D. Byrne, "The Boucicaut Master and the Iconographic Tradition of the 'Livre des Propriétés des Choses'," *Gazette des Beaux-Arts* 92 (1978) 149–64, citing this manuscript on p. 163, n. 22.

---

[1] We are indebted to M. François Avril for the identification of this mark.

HM 28174 England, s. XIV[ex]
JACOBUS DE VORAGINE, LENTEN SERMONS *fig. 76*

1. ff. 1–132: [Jacobus de Voragine, Lenten Sermons] //derari, primo quantum ad naturam prout scilicet sunt homines ad ymaginem dei facti . . . ad secundam resurrectionem in gloriam. Ad quam meritis et precibus gloriose virginis matris sue et omnium electorum suorum ipse filius dei nos perducat, qui cum patre et spiritu sancto vivit et regnat per infinita secula regna. Amen. *Expliciunt sermones quadragesimales compilati a fratre Iacobo de voragine archiepiscopo Ianuense cuius anime propicietur deus. Qui scripsit carmen sit benedictus amen.*
Jacobus de Voragine, Lenten sermons; Schneyer end of 201, 202–292. Kaeppeli, *SOPMA* 2157.

2. ff. 132v–143v: [Unidentified sermons] Cor contritum et humiliatum deus non despicies. in psalmo. Tale cor deo est acceptum quia huius petit deus proverb. 22. Fili probe michi cor tuum quia sic est de deo . . . ; [f. 134v:] Nemini quicquam debeatis nisi ut invicem diligatis. Rom. 13. Nota quatuor esse debita quatuor indebita spiritualia significanda . . . ; [f. 135:] Prudencia sua percussit superbum. Io. 18. Legitur in speculo historiali quod philippus pater alexandri magni invenit mirabilem equum . . . ; [f. 135v:] Si possides amicum in temptacione posside illum et ne defacili ei credas teipsum eccl. 6. Multi amiciciam divitum querunt . . . ; [f. 136:] Pugnetis adversus naciones que convenerunt dispendere vos. Mach. 3. Tres sunt naciones que nos convenerunt dispendere scilicet mundus, caro et diabolus . . . ; [f. 136v:] Qui vicerit non leditur a morte secunda. Apoc. Refert alexander nequam de naturis rerum quod virgilius in civitate romana palacium construxit . . . ; [f. 137:] Hortamur vos ne in vacuum graciam dei recipiatis. Cor. 6. Ille invanum graciam recipit qui graciam sibi infusam ad effectum producere . . . ; [f. 139:] Scito et vide quid feceris quia amarum et malum est reliquisse te dominum deum tuum. Ier. 2. Cum homo mortaliter peccat deum a se expellit . . . ; [f. 140:] Revelabitur ira dei de celo super omnem pietatem. Ro. Qui se difficile reddit ad opus pietatis exercendum pietatem exceptare non oportet . . . ; [f. 140v, 3 lines only of the sermon here, and in the margin, the note "cave hic"; the complete sermon on f. 151:] Quare moriens dominus israel morietis dicit dominus. Revertimini ad me. Ys. 18. . . . ; [f. 140v:] Quid est hoc. Exod. xiiii°. et prothemate hodierno. Reverendi domini triplici de causa solent homines querere questiones . . .

3. ff. 143v–144: [14 short Latin verse compositions]: C ter erant mille decies sex unus et ille . . . [3 lines, with the note "Isti versus inveniunt quod anno domini M° ccc° lxi° in festo sancti mauri abbatis fuit ille magnus ventus secundum computacionem ecclesie anglie"; also in HM 37539, f. 154]; Mille ter C xl pestis fuit anno [with note "Nota bene pestilencia"]; Christi millenis C ter decies quater annis . . . [4 lines on English victory over the French, also in HM 37539, f. 154]; M C ter X penta miserosa ferox violenta . . . [2 lines on the plague, with note "Maxima mortalitas"]; Mors communis in M ter C pentaptata decem [with note "Magna pestis"]; Ecce flat hoc anno maurus in orbe tonat [with note "Magnus ventus"]; Quatuor ista timor odium dilectio census . . . [2 lines, with note "Quatuor pervertunt iudicium"; Walther, *Initia* 15330]; Munus fit iudex fraus est mercator in urbe . . . [4 lines, Walther, *Initia* 11487]; Cur me sic fecit, cur me promittit ut errem . . . [4 lines, with note "Isti sunt 8 modi

excusandi falsi et mali ubi patet per raciones oppositas contentas in versibus hic sequentibus]; Cur vis posse gradi, cur spernis terevocantem [4 lines]; Illa reviviscunt que mortificata fuerunt . . . [2 lines, with note "facta in mortali peccato non valent ad incrementum glorie]; Pressus mortali bene fac ut gracia detur . . . [2 lines with note "facta in mortali valent ad tria ut patet hic in versibus"]; Cur homo troquetur, ut ei meritum cumuletur, ut Iob . . . [5 lines, Walther, *Initia* 3927]; Spes in mundanis quam fallax quam sit inanis . . . [4 lines].

4. ff. 144v–151: [Ghost story of Guido de Corvo] Augustinus in libro de fide ad petrum dicit, Miraculum est quicquid arduum vel insolitum . . . Anno sue incarnacionis m° ccc^{mo} xxiiii° xvi die decembris in provincia provincie et in civitate glesti [*sic,* but later "alesti"] que per xxiiii^{or} leucas distat a vicennia, obiit quidam civis nomine gwido de corvo . . . Prior autem dicte domus nomine frater Iohannes Goby . . . Et extunc nichil de spiritu ulterius auditum fuit in illo loco. Unde opinabatur quod residuum penitencie sue complevit in purgatorio communi. *Explicit spiritus gwidonis.*

B. Hauréau, *Notices et extraits* (Paris 1890) 2:328–44, portions of the text printed; this manuscript does not correspond to any of the others mentioned as far as dates, places, names. See also G. Schleich, "The Gast of Gy," *Palaestra* 1 (1898) i–lxviii and 1–230, especially pp. lv–lxi, a prose Latin version differing from HM 28174, which contains much doctrinal matter omitted in Schleich's edition. Kaeppeli, *SOPMA* 2370.

5. ff. 151–184: [Unidentified sermons] [f. 151, the sermon begun on f. 140v:] Quasi moriens dominus israel morietis dicit dominus revertimini ad me. Ys. 18. Nota si homo sit dampnatus imputandum est sibi et non deo . . . ; [f. 153:] Convertimini ad me in toto corde vestro. ioel. Nota quod quatuor requiruntur ad hoc quod peccator convertatur, primum est gracie dei infusio . . . ; [f. 154v:] Diligite iusticiam qui iudicatis terram. Sap. 1. Iusticia est tribuere unicuique quod suum est . . . ; [f. 155:] Lignum vite est hiis qui apprehenderint eam. Prov. 3. Bene dicitur crux ligni. Nam per primam invenitur deus qui ait. Io. Ego sum via . . . ; [f. 155v:] Oculi mei semper ad dominum qui ipse evellet de laqueo pedes meos. In psal. Nota quod dyabolus laqueum peccatorum parat . . . ; [f. 156:] Donec deficiam non recedam ab innocencia mea et quod cepi tenere non deseram. Iob 27. Nota ubi perseverancia non sequitur frustra . . . ; [f. 156v:] Caro concupiscit adversus spiritum et spiritus adversus carnem. Ad gal. 5. Augustinus. caro dicitur concupiscere quia hoc secundum ipsam agit animam . . . ; [f. 156v:] De propiciatu peccatorum noli esse sine metu neque adicias peccatum super peccatum et ne dixeris miseracio domini est magna, multitudinis peccatorum meorum miserebitur. Eccl. 5. Nemo propter misericordiam dei peccandi audaciam prestet . . . ; [f. 157:] Rectorem te posuerunt, noli extolli esto in illis quasi unus ex ipsis. eccl. 23. Nota quod ille qui regit tineri debeat et amari . . . ; [f. 157:] Posce sapienciam que melior est auro. Sepe contingit quod homo spiritualiter ad mortem tendit ut patet eccl. 8. multos perdit aurum sed sapiencia ab illa infirmitate liberat et ad vitam eternam reducit . . . ; [f. 161v:] Egredietur dominus de loco sancto suo ut visitet iniquitatem habitatorum terre. Ys. 28. Audiant hic falsi advocati. Numquid istum decipient . . . ; [f. 163v:] Nolite detrahere alterutrum fratres mei, qui detrahit fratri aut qui iudicat fratrem suum detrahit legi et iudicat legem. Iacob. 4. Est de detractore sicut de sanguissuga que insidiatur omnibus venientibus . . . ; [f. 165:]

Loquere que ad sanam decent doctrinam. Ad thi. 1. Timere debent et precipue religiosi ne loquuntur nisi de necessariis et utilibus. Ro. 15. Non enim audeo loqui aliquid eorum . . . ; [f. 165v:] Omnes qui credebant erant pariter et habebant omnia communia. Act. 2. Ubi legitur quod conversis ad fidem quod erant in vinculo caritatis . . . ; [f. 166v:] Nescis quia miser es et miserabilis. Ap. 3. Si nescis homo miseriam tuam vide principium tuum, medium et finem et invenies quia plenus es miseriis. Iob. Homo natus de muliere . . . ; [f. 167v:] Prepara animam tuam ad temptacionem. Ecc. 2. Tres sunt spirituales hostes qui nos temptant quorum sunt temptaciones diverse et ideo diversitudo . . . ; [f. 169:] Non simus inanis glorie cupidi. Galath. 6. Advertite karissimi quod viciosus est ventus vane glorie quia sua malicia fructum bonorum operum avellit . . . ; [f. 169v:] Recordare domine quid acciderit nobis intuere et respice obprobrium nostrum hereditas nostra versa est ad alienos. Tren. ult. Hec vox generis humani per diabolum a regno celesti fuit exhereditater . . . ; [f. 170:] Dedisti metuentibus te significacionem ut fugiant a facie archus. Ps. Hic signans tribulaciones temporales quibus figuratur homini ut fugiat a facie archus . . . ; [f. 171v:] Panis quem ego dabo caro mea est pro mundi vita. Io. 28. Sciendum est quod panis triticeus fit de grano frumenti et ut de grano isto loquor qualiter ex eo fit panis de quo conficitur corpus christi . . . ; [f. 174v:] Veniet finis universe terre id est tota affeccio quam habent homines ad prima temporalia finem capienti. Est enim duplex dilectio scilicet dei et mundi que simul stare in homine non potest. Io. 2. Si quis diliget mundum . . . ; [f. 179:] Qui sine uxore est solicitus est quomodo placeat deo. Cor. 7. Nemo ita bene ad negocium spirituale peragendis disponitur nec ad verum iudicium exequendum . . . ; [f. 179v:] Turris fortissima nomen domini ad ipsam currit iustus et exaltabitur. Prov. 18. Solent homines ad tuta loca currere propter duo scilicet propter municionem loci ut est in castris . . . ; [f. 180v:] Speciose et delicate assimilavi filiam syon. Ie. 6. Fertur quendam fuisse imperatorem et habuisse filiam tenerime nutritam. Que sui iuris effecta, eo contempto secuta est raptorem . . . ; [f. 182:] Particula bone diei [*sic*] non te pertranseat [*sic*]. Ecc. 14. Nota quod dies quo mortuus est salvator noster pro peccatis nostris ex quadam prerogativa bona dies vocatur . . .

Parchment, ff. i (former pastedown) + 184 + i (former pastedown); 280 × 195 (197 × 120) mm. 1–14[8] 15[8](+ a half leaf added between 7 and 8, f. 120) 16–22[8] 23[8](8 was the pastedown). Catchwords written horizontally across the inner bounding line, often in a red-touched frame; quire and leaf signatures consist of letters and roman numerals. The first quire, lettered "a," is missing. Quires 5–8 use a double system, the quire being shown by both a letter and a progressive arabic numeral, the leaves by the usual roman numeral (f1 i, f1 ii . . . , g2 . . . , h3 . . . , i4 . . .). 37 long lines ruled in lead, with the 2 top and bottom horizontal lines extended the width of the bifolium; pricking visible in the 3 outer margins. Written in an anglicana formata script. Initials, 2-line in blue with red penwork; alternating red and blue paragraph marks; red used for slashed initials within the text, underlining, and framing marginalia. Descenders of the bottom line usually extended with flourishes. Marginalia, as text-finders, in the hand of the scribe; manicules sometimes decorated in red (e.g. ff. 132v, 138). Marked "corrected" in the center lower margin, not only quire by quire, but often on successive folios (e.g. 96–100 with quire ending at 96v).

Bound, s. XV, in whittawed leather over bevelled wooden boards, sewn on double bands, which are attached differently to the front and back covers: on the front cover, the 2 top and 2 middle bands brought together and pegged in a single hole per pair, and the 5th band pulled straight; on the back cover, the double bands are separated, pulled away from the book at an angle and pegged into the same hole as the adjacent half-band, forming a continuous zig-zag pattern. Two red leather fore edge straps closing to small brass eyes on the edge of the back cover; part of one strap and one eye survive. Spine crudely strengthened with a piece of brown leather (the same repair on the binding of HM 36337, also a Tollemache book).

Written in England at the end of the fourteenth century; possibly of monastic origin. On f. 184v, notes in an early sixteenth century hand: "Sciant presentes et futury quod ego Iohannes Wodedale" and "Willelmus Sponar possessor huius libri est. Si quis furetur cito per collum pendetur." On the back flyleaf: "feria 4ta xii d; feria 5ta vi d; feria sexta xvi d." A price, s. XVI, "1^{l} 8^{s}," on f. i verso identified in the Sotheby catalogue (see below) as in the same hand as a similar note in lot 1, that book being a collection of sermons from a monastic house in eastern England, s. XII^{med}. Belonged to the Tollemache family of Helmingham Hall, Suffolk, who began collecting around the turn of the seventeenth century. For a brief history of the Tollemache collection, see Sotheby catalogue, 14 June 1965, iii–viii. N. 56 in the old Helmingham catalogue; small paper label on the inner front cover reads "L.J.III. (corrected to "V") 2.," presumably the shelf mark in the Tollemache library. Tollemache sale, Sotheby's, 14 June 1965, lot 17 to Maggs for the Huntington Library.

Bibliography: Chronica, 6. *Aspects of Medieval England,* n. 31, open at f. 144v.

HM 28175 — Northern France, s. XV^{in}
BOOK OF HOURS, Sarum use

1. ff. 1–3v: misbound leaves, now: f. 1, suffrage of Christopher [. . . michi famulo tuo . . .]; ff. 1v–2, blank except for illegible erased notes; f. 2v, full page miniature of Christopher; f. 3, blank; f. 3v, full page miniature of the Annunciation.

2. ff. 4–6v: Calendar, beginning defectively at July, with the usual English feasts, some added later, in red and black ink; Latin month verses [Walther, *Initia* 14563]; the qualifier "pape" has been crossed out (14 October, 26 November, 31 December), as well as the entry for Thomas of Canterbury (29 December).

3. ff. 7–8v: misbound leaves, now: f. 7, blank; f. 7v, full page miniature of Veronica; f. 8, suffrage of John the Baptist; f. 8v, blank.

4. ff. 9–27v: Hours of the Virgin, apparently Sarum use, although, due to missing leaves between ff. 25–26, all of none, vespers, and part of compline are gone; hours of the Cross worked in; suffrages after lauds of the Holy Spirit, the Trinity, the Cross, Michael, John the Baptist, John the Evangelist, Peter and Paul, Andrew, Stephen, Lawrence, Thomas of Canterbury, Nicholas, Mary Magdalene, Catherine of Alexandria, Margaret, All Saints, for peace; following compline is the Salve Regina, with the versicles, Virgo mater ecclesie . . . and the prayer, Omnipotens sempiterne deus qui gloriose virginis et matris marie . . . [*HE,* 62–63]; added in a later cursive hand: f. 12r–v, *Oracio inter elevaciones corporis et sanguinis dei,* O decus christi recrea me, O anima christi sanctifica me . . . ; f. 12v [in another hand], O lorde have marssye one my soull . . . [Hanna, "Addenda," n. 37]; f. 22v, O that my toung could but expres the misserys that my hart doth daly torment [Hanna, "Addenda," n. 38]; f. 27r–v, Gaude virgo mater christi que per aurem concepisti . . . [*RH* 7013]; Omnipotens sempiterne

deus qui divina salutacione gabrielis . . . ; Stella celi extrippavit [*sic*] que lactavit dominum mortis pestem quam plantavit . . . ; A fame pestilencia morte subitanea et dampnacione . . . ; Gaude flore virginali honoreque speciali . . . [the 7 Joys, *RH* 6809].

5. ff. 28–35v: Prayers to the Virgin, as follow: *Has videas laudes que sacra virgine gaudes* . . . , Salve virgo virginum stella matutina . . . [a farcing of the Salve Regina attributed to Bonaventure, *Opera,* Vatican, 1668, 6:466–67], with the prayer, Deus qui de beate marie virginis utero . . . [Bruylants, *Oraisons* 2, n. 230]; *Oracio de domina nostra,* O intemerata . . . orbis terrarum. Inclina mater . . . [masculine forms; Wilmart, 488–90]; *Oracio de domina nostra,* Obsecro te . . . [divided into 2 parts at "Veni et festina in auxilium"; masculine forms; Leroquais, *LH* 2:346]; *Oracio,* Ave mundi spes maria . . . [Walther, *Initia* 1945] with Adiuvet nos quesumus domine deus . . . ; *Quicumque hec septem gaudia in honore beate marie virginis . . . a papa clemente qui hec septem gaudia proprio stilo composuit,* Virgo templum trinitatis . . . [Philippus de Grevia; Wilmart, 329, n.]; added in a later hand: f. 33v, Ave digna ave flos ave virgo ave nubes . . . ; f. 35v, Take heed of him that ⟨page cropped⟩ Doth.

6. ff. 36–40: Prayers to Christ, as follow: *Ad ymaginem domini,* Omnibus consideratis paradisus voluptatis . . . [attributed to Johannes Lemovicensis; divided into 10 parts, the last 2 to the Virgin and to St. John; Wilmart, 584, note to p. 527] with the prayer, Omnipotens sempiterne deus qui unigenitum filium tuum . . . ; *Incipit oracio venerabilis bede presbiteri* . . . , Domine ihesu christe qui septem verba . . . [Leroquais, *LH* 2:342]; *Oracio,* Precor te piissime domine propter illam caritatem . . . [Wilmart, 378, n.]; *Oracio,* Deus qui voluisti pro redemptione mundi a iudeis reprobari . . . ; *Oracio,* Ave ihesu christe verbum patris filius virginis . . . [Wilmart, 377, n.]; *Oracio,* Ave principium nostre creationis . . . mihi famulo tuo N . . . [Wilmart, 23, n.]; *Oracio,* Ave verum corpus domini nostri ihesu christi . . . [Wilmart, 373–76]; *Oracio,* Ave caro christi cara inviolata crucis ara . . . [Wilmart, 366, passim]; *Quilibet dicenti hanc oracionem . . . papa bonifacius sextus concessit . . . ad supplicacionem philippi regis francie,* Domine ihesu christe qui hanc sacratissimam carnem . . . [Wilmart, 378, n.]; f. 40v, ruled but blank except for the added note, O cupid I graunt thy might is much for sure thou loveth thy dart to shent at such [Hanna, "Addenda," n. 36].

7. ff. 41–49: Penitential psalms (leaf missing after f. 43, with loss of text from the fifth psalm, Ps. 101, 23, to the end), gradual psalms (cues only for the first 12), and litany, including Edward, Alan, Christopher, Lambert among the martyrs; Remigius, Bavo, Vedast, Audoenus, Aegidius, Amand and Robert among the confessors; Bridget, Christina, Sexburga, Milburga, Osyth and Radegundis among the virgins; f. 49v, ruled, but blank except for an ownership note (see below).

8. ff. 50–61v [f. 50, blank]: Office of the Dead, Sarum use.

9. ff. 62–69v [f. 62, blank]: Commendation of souls (Pss. 118, divided, and 138) and the prayers, Tibi domine commendamus animam . . . , and Misericordiam tuam domine sancte pater omnipotens deus . . . ; added on f. 69v, "blessed is he that keppethe godes commandemente and so is he that" (ending here), and an invocation to Christopher.

10. ff. 70–72v: *Incipit psalterium de sancta cruce* (Pss. 21–30, 6 with cues only for Pss. 22–24, 26 and 29).

11. ff. 73–80v [f. 73, blank]: Psalter of St. Jerome, Verba mea auribus percipe . . . , and the prayer, Liberator animarum mundi redemptor ihesu christe . . . ; f. 80v, added in a cursive hand, *pro pestilencia bona oracio,* Sancte deus sancte fortis sancte et immortalis agnus dei . . .

Parchment, ff. ii (modern paper) + 80 + ii (modern paper); 192 × 135 (122 × 80) mm. The book now consists entirely of singletons sewn together in groups of 4 and bearing on the first recto in pencil in a modern hand the signatures a-u; no catchwords. 24 long lines, ruled in pale red ink. Written in a gothic book hand.

Seven full page miniatures, usually in narrow gold and colored frames with sparse black ink spray foliage, with blue and pink flowers and pale green and silver leaves; all are blank on the recto. The miniatures are: f. 2v, misbound, Christopher with the Christ Child on his shoulders; no hermit; f. 3v, misbound, Annunciation, the angel holding a long scroll; f. 7v, misbound, Veronica holding the Vernicle cloth; f. 13v (Lauds), Betrayal of Jesus, by a different artist, in a narrow arched compartment surrounded by a full, broad, red band border of tarnished silver acanthus leaves twisted about a green rod; f. 50v (Office of the Dead), funeral service with monks and mourners; f. 62v (Commendation of souls), 3 souls carried in a sheet held by 2 angels to God the Father in nebuly, against a gold scroll background, with a gold line traced around the edges of the various figures; f. 73v (Psalter of St. Jerome), Jerome writing at his desk, with the same gold line traced around the figures and gold scroll background; no lion. On the leaves facing these miniatures and the now-missing miniatures, 8- or 7-line initials in white-patterned orange or blue with colored trilobe leaf and vine infilling against a cusped gold ground; narrow bar border of color and gold in a U-shape or as 2 bars the length of the text, terminating in trilobe leaves; the remaining margins with black ink sprays and small colored flowers. 5-line initials in gold on particolored blue and dusky rose grounds/infilling; 2-line initials in gold on extravagantly cusped blue or pink grounds with infilling of the other color; 1-line initials in gold with black flourishing or in blue with red. Rubrics throughout. A small rectangle cut out of the margin of f. 54 with no loss of text. Very simple sketches of human figures on ff. 10, 49v, 66v, 67v, 70 (more capable, representing Jesus), 73v and 74.

Bound, s. XIX, by J. Leighton, Brewer St. in brown pebble morocco, with gold-starred blue endpapers; gilt edges.

Written possibly in northern France for export to England. Ownership notes of the sixteenth century on f. 5v: George brakye ba⟨?⟩, John bra⟨?⟩, Tomas conyers, Robert cony⟨?⟩; on f. 12v: . . . george Conyers; on f. 49v: George Conyers ave this bouke and so ffourthe, Finis. Sale by G. A. Leavitt, New York, 6 February 1888, n. 164. Acquired by Samuel Bowne Duryea, with his bookplate on the front pastedown; bequeathed with other material to the Long Island Historical Society in 1895; listed by C. A. Nelson, *The Manuscripts and Early Printed Books Bequeathed to the Long Island Historical Society by S. B. Duryea* (Brooklyn 1895) p. 15. Sold by the Society at Sotheby's, 5 July 1965, n. 234, with a plate of ff. 7v and 73v; acquired by the Huntington Library at that time.

Bibliography: Chronica, 6.

HM 28177 — England (?), s. XIII^in
PETER THE CHANTER, VERBUM ABBREVIATUM

1. ff. 1–11v: //Item Gregorius. Sicut viciosi lectoris est manifeste dicta exponere . . . scilicet opus superbie, que est fons et origo//; [4 leaves missing; ff. 12–

27v:] //Quid ergo. Eadem faciemus que ceteri . . . Prima unicitas est fidei sacra [catchword:] mentorum//; [6 leaves missing; ff. 28–37v:] //sibi invicem subministrantium . . . Que ad litteram in hiis observanda sunt et que non, auctoritate scripturarum proferemus. Scriptum [catchword:] est enim lex domini//

Peter the Chanter, *Verbum abbreviatum, PL* 205:26–59, 72–118, 136–163. See J. W. Baldwin, *Masters, Princes and Merchants: The Social Views of Peter the Chanter and His Circle* (Princeton 1970) 2:246–65, who does not mention this manuscript; this is the short version without marginalia.

2. f. i r–v [back flyleaf]: //dabitur ei statim vel postea, nisi aliud iterim faciat unde mereatur id amittere . . . et elemosina pro quibus tecum vivimus et regnamus qui cum patre et spiritu sancto. *In die ascensionis,* Elevatus est sol in celum et luna stetit inter ordine suo. Hodie fratres karissimi est ascensionis domini iocunda festivitas, hodie destructa est humani generis captivitas . . . similes et pares fieri volebant//

A leaf from a homilary.

Parchment, ff. 37 + i (contemporary parchment); 263 × 175 (174 × 103) mm. 1^8(-1) 2^8(-5 through 8) $3\text{–}4^8$ 5^8(-1 through 6) 6^8. Quires signed in roman numerals on the last leaf verso; catchwords in the script of the text in the corner of the inner margin. 39 long lines. Ruled in brown crayon, with double vertical bounding lines, and the first, middle and last 3 horizontal lines full across; pricking visible in the inner and outer margins. Written above the top line in an upright littera textualis. Initials, usually 2-line, alternating in red and blue with plain tendrils and filigree, except on ff. 8–19 (what remains of quires 2 and 3), which are in plain red only, with no tendrils. Rubrics in a rather orange-tinged red. In the margins: notes to the rubricator, contemporary corrections to the text, and "exemplum" or "nota" marks in red, in black ink, or in crayon; 3 unidentified proverbs in the lower margin of f. 8: Cum bene pugnabis cum cuncta subacta putabis [Walther, *Initia* 57?]; Que primo infestat vincenda superbia restat; Hec nisi vincatur promissa corona negatur.

Folio i (back flyleaf): 249 × 178 (209 × 142) mm. 2 columns of 33 lines, ruled with a fine brown lead point. Written in a spiky minuscule bookhand above the top line. One initial, 2-line, in green.

Bound, s. XIX², in brown leather with an embossed overall pattern of oriental figures; remains of fore edge ties.

Written in England (?) in the first third of the thirteenth century. Acquired from H. W. Edwards, Newbury, Berks. in 1965.

Secundo folio: [now f. 1] Item Gregorius. Sicut
Bibliography: Chronica, 6.

HM 28561 — England, s. XV^med-ex^
HIGDEN, POLYCHRONICON, trans. John Trevisa; etc. — *fig. 127*

1. ff. 1–5v: *Dialogus inter militem et clericum, Clericus* y wonder sir noble kny3t þat in fewe daies tymes beþ chaungid ri3t is yburied lawes biþ ouertorned . . . Also in þe tyme of gospel hit is writen þe holy day is made for man and nou3t man for þe holy day. *Explicit dialogus inter clericum et militem.*

Ps. William Ockham, *Dialogus inter militem et clericum,* trans. J. Trevisa.

HM 28561

A. J. Perry, ed., *Dialogus inter Militem et Clericum, Richard FitzRalph's Sermon: 'Defensio Curatorum,' and Methodius: 'þe Bygynnyng of þe World and þe Ende of Worldes' by John Trevisa.* EETS os 167 (London 1925) 1–37; this manuscript described, xxv–xxvii, but not used in the edition because it had been mislaid.

2. ff. 5v–20v: *Incipit sermo domini archiepiscopi Armacani,* Demeþ nought by þe face but riȝtful dome ye deme. John 8° c°. Holy fadir in þe bigynnyng of my sermoun I make a protestacioun . . . þerfore I conclude & pray mekelich & deuoutlich as I prayed in þe first þat I touchid: demeþ nouȝt bi þe face et cetera. *Explicit.*

Richard FitzRalph, *Defensio curatorum,* trans. J. Trevisa, pr. by Perry, 39–93.

3. ff. 21–23v: In þe name of crist here bigynneþ þe boke of methodii þe bisshop of þe chirche of paterenis and martir of martir of [*sic*] crist . . . And wicked men wiþout ende shul suffre peyne. Wherefore þe lord vouche he saaf to delyuer vs. qui cum patre et cetera. *Explicit liber metodii episcopi.*

Ps. Methodius, *The Beginning of the World and the End of Worlds,* trans. perhaps by J. Trevisa, pr. by Perry, 94–112.

4. ff. 24–32: [Alphabetical subject index in Latin, with reference to books and chapters] Abraham lib. 2 cap. 10, Abdon dux Israel lib. 2 cap. 10, Abessa dux Israel lib. 2 cap. 24, De Abendon monasterio lib. 5 cap. 7 . . . De christi etate et operibus lib. 4 cap. 5, De christi passione lib. 4 cap. 6, De zenone imperatore lib. 5 cap. 3, De zorababel et cetera lib. 3 cap. 10.

5. ff. 32–40v: [Alphabetical subject index in English, with reference to books and chapters] [A]ppolyn delphicus temple lib. 1 cap. 22, Athene is ybuld lib. 1 cap. 22 . . . Wenche sleep hir silf lib. 3 cap. 33, Wondres of Iulius deþ & dedes lib. 3 cap. 42 [perhaps finishing incomplete: "wondres," written in a noting hand in the lower margin, intended as a catchword? f. 40 bis r–v, an added singleton, the width of one column only and ruled with the extra spaces for book and chapter numbers; blank]

6. ff. 41–42: Siþþe þat babel was ybuld men spekiþ diuerse tonges . . . þan alle þat ben ywrite in þe boke of lyf shal wynde wiþ him into þe blisse of heuen and be þere in body and soule and se & knowe his godhed and manhed in Ioy wiþout eny ende. *Explicit dialogus.*

A text with modernized spelling by A. W. Pollard, "Dialogue between a Lord and a Clerk upon Translation, From Trevisa's Translation of Higden's *Polychronicon,*" *Fifteenth Century Prose and Verse* (Westminster 1903) 203–08.

7. f. 42r–v: Welþe and worshipe to my worthy and worshipful lord sir Thomas lord of Berkley. I Iohan Treuysa youre prest and youre bedman . . . to se god on his blisful face in ioy wiþout eny ende. Amen. *Explicit epistola.*

A text with modernized spelling by A. W. Pollard, "The Epistle of Sir John Trevisa, Chaplain unto Lord Thomas of Barkley upon the translation of *Polychronicon* into our English tongue," *Fifteenth Century Prose and Verse* (Westminster 1903) 209–10.

8. ff. 43–319v: *Incipit prefacio prima,* Aftir solempne and wise writers of art and of science þat had swetnesse & likyng al her liftyme . . . ; [f. 44v:] *Prefacio secunda ad historiam,* And for þis cronicle conteyneþ beringes and dedes of

meny tymes . . . ; [f. 44v:] *Prefacio tercia ad historiam,* To hem þat wole haue ful knowelech of stories it nedeþ eiȝte þinges to knowe . . . ; [f. 46, Text:] *De orbis dimensione priscianus in Cosmagraphia* [*sic*], Iulius Cesar by Counsaile of þe senatours and elder men of Rome loked and serched stories . . . [f. 192v:] and regned in bretaigne as it were xxx[ti] yere anone to þe convertynge of Constancius [catchword:] Philippus wiþ his sone philip// . . . [f. 193] //and died at þe laste by treson of his wif in þis maner . . . þis translacion is endide in a þursday þe xviii day of Aueril þe yere of oure lorde a þousande þre hundred foure score and seuen þe tenþe yere of king Richard þe second aftir þe conqueste of englande þe yere of my lordis age sir Thomas lorde of Berkeley þat made me make þis translacion fiue and þritty. *Explicit.*

C. Babington and J. Lumby, eds., *Polychronicon Ranulphi Higden monachi cestrensis.* RS 41 in 9 volumes (London 1865–86) through 8:345 and with Trevisa's continuation, 347–52. Verse sections written in long lines: *IMEV* 2736.2, 2831.4, 1426.6, 746.5, 4189.5, 2361.5, 3218.3, 399.5, 1637.6, 1811, and Hanna, "Addenda," n. 28. This manuscript lacks 3 quires between ff. 191–192 with loss of text, in the RS edition, 5:73 line 8 to 5:371 line 9.

9. ff. 320–325: *Hic metrice tractatur de regulis ab aluredo primo fundatore universitatis Oxoniensis circiter Annum domini D CCC lxiii usque ad henricum sextum,* Aluredus rex anglorum primusque monarcha/ Belliger invictus in scripturis bene doctus . . . Hoc tunc in fine verborum queso meorum/ Prospera quod statuat regna futura deus. Amen.

Walther, *Initia,* 883. 115 verses on the kings of England from Alfred to Henry VI, followed, ff. 320v–325, by several documents concerning Richard II (his renunciation of the throne), Henry IV, Henry V, Henry VI and Edward IV (his claim to the throne of France with 2 genealogical tables, ff. 323v and 324v); f. 325v, ruled, but blank.

10. ff. 326–337v: *Turpine the Archebisshop of þe Bataille of Rouncivale. Here begynneth þe prologe of Turpines Story,* Tvrpyne by the grace of god Archebiship of Reynes a bisye ffoluere and of grete Emperoure Charlis a ffelow with leoprande Dene of Akim gretinge and helthe euerlastinge in god . . . ; [Chapter list:] *B*[rubricator's error for H]*ere beginneth the Titulus of þe Chapitres of the Storye of the Bataille of Rouncivale of grete Charles the Emperoure, Capitulum 1*[m], [H]ow seynt Iame aperid to Charlis; *Capitulum ii,* [H]ow þe wallis of pampilione fylle down by hem selffe . . . ; [f. 326v, Text:] *How seint Iame apered to king Charles, Capitulum 1*[m], [A]fter oure lord ihesu criste had sufferid deþe and paid þe Rawnsome for synfulle man . . . þen Roulonde lete him goo, and he callid to god to helpe him. And anone//

Ps. Turpin, *Historia Karoli Magni,* ending defectively in the 26th of 36 chapters, as announced in the chapter list. No Middle English prose version mentioned in Wells, *Manual;* see H. M. Smyser, ed., *The Pseudo-Turpin* (Cambridge, Mass., 1937), in Latin.

Parchment (poor quality), ff. i (contemporary parchment) + 337; 380 × 277 (264 × 176) mm. 1–4[8] 5[8](+ 9, f. 40 bis) 6–24[8] 3 quires missing here 25–39[8] 40[8](–8, after f. 320) 41[8](–7, 8 after f. 325) 42[8] 43[8](–5 through 8). Catchwords in the lower right margin; beginning with quire 18, additional catchwords occur variously within the quires. Quire and leaf signatures through quire 32 as letters and roman numerals, the quires marked +, a–x (the "x" on quire 23; presumably "y" on quire 24; "z," tironian 7 and "cum" symbol possibly on the 3 missing quires?), aa–hh on quires 25–32. On quires 33 to the end, only the leaves are signed, using roman numerals. 2 columns of 40 lines ruled in lead, with top and bottom 2 lines full across; on some leaves ruling appears to be in dry point alone or in mixed dry point and lead, as if the point of the lead were bad (e.g., ff. 162, 166, 171, 174, 178, 184, 260, 261); pricking visible in all 4 margins with double holes at the second line from the bottom of the inside and outside margins. Written by four scribes:

i. late anglicana formata script with secretary forms: ff. 1–78 col. A l. 5; f. 78v col. A l. 11–end of column; ff. 81–82 col. B l. 4; f. 87 col. B l. 31–87v col. A l. 23; f. 100v col. A l. 1–29; ff. 101v col. A l. 1–102 col. A l. 11; f. 104 col. B l. 20–end of f. 104; f. 105 col. A l. 1–105v entire col. A; ff. 109–111v; f. 123, entirely.

ii. secretary script: f. 78 col. A l. 5–78v col. A l. 10; ff. 78v col. B l. 1–80v; ff. 82 col. B l. 4–87 col. B l. 31; ff. 87v col. A l. 23–100; ff. 100v col. A l. 29–101; ff. 102 col. A l. 11–104 col. B l. 20; f. 104v; ff. 105v col. B–108v; ff. 112 col. A–122v; ff. 123v–319v.

iii. late anglicana formata script with secretary forms: ff. 320–325 (art. 9).

iv. secretary script: ff. 326–337v (art 10).

Decoration was left at varying stages of completion up to f. 138; thereafter it was abandoned entirely (excepting art. 10). Full borders composed of narrow gold and color strips with acanthus leaves and ink sprays ending in green leaves, flowers and gold motifs occur on ff. 1 (art. 1) and 88 (Book 2), with 5- or 4-line particolored pink and green initials, infilled with acanthus leaves and set on cusped gold grounds; both borders with coats of arms (see below). Similar initial on f. 43 (First preface) with a full border of the narrow strips on 2 sides and wide bands on the other 2 sides, composed of regularly twisted pink and blue acanthus leaves; on f. 46 (Text) the same combination of narrow strips and wide bands, but with secondary initials. Full border on f. 21 (art. 3) of the narrow strips alone, with secondary initials. Other borders composed of narrow gold and color strips the length of the text, with acanthus leaves and ink sprays extending into the upper and lower margins occur with major initials (as above): 5-line particolored pink and green (f. 5v, art. 2) or green and orange (f. 24, art. 4) with leaf or flower infilling on cusped gold grounds; these borders also occur with the 2 styles of secondary initials, used more or less alternately: either 4- or 3-line white-highlighted blue or pink on cusped gold grounds (e.g., f. 41, art. 6) or 4- or 3-line gold on white-highlighted particolored pink, blue or orange grounds (e.g., f. 42, art. 7). Other initials, 2-line in gold on white-patterned particolored pink and blue grounds with small ink sprays terminating in green leaves and gold motifs. In red are paragraph marks and underlining of sources cited, headings and chapter numbers. Stages of the unfinished decoration are apparent on ff. 26v, 27v and 28v with the outline of the border decoration and of the initials, to which gesso has been applied; on ff. 25, 26, 27 and 28 the gold has been added; on ff. 83, 85, 87 (for example) the first base of color is present; on ff. 81 and 82 the ink sprays and the outlining of the bar border were completed, but colors still lack final modelling and highlighting. In quires 10 (ff. 73–80), 16 (ff. 121–128) and 18–41 (ff. 137–325) spaces were reserved for the initials indicated by guide letters. On f. 326 (art. 10), plain blue 4- or 3-line initials; the remaining initials in art. 10 by guide letter only; rubrics throughout this section. Pen trials throughout; on f. i, practice alphabets, s. XVI. Illuminated initials cut out on ff. 54v, 64v, 65.

Bound, s. XV, in 3 layers of leather over bevelled wooden boards; earlier 2 layers, once dyed pink, now faded; evidence of 2 fore edge straps closing to pins on the back cover; of the original 10 brass bosses, 3 are missing; sewn on 7 thongs.

Written in England towards the middle and the end of the fifteenth century. Arms of the first owner in the borders of ff. 1 and 88; on f. 1: ermine, a mill-iron sable; on f. 88: quarterly 1 and 4 the same arms as above, 2 and 3 per pale azure a lion (or a fox?) rampant argent and gules 2 lions (or foxes?) rampant argent. Miscellaneous pen trials include the following names: s. XV: f. 255, in lead, "Welby Willm"; back pastedown,

"Johnn Hornywold the son off Richard Hornywold." Notes, s. XVI: f. i, "George Hornby" and, on f. i verso, notes on his father Robert's marriage and the births of the latter's children (1503–14); f. 150, "Thys Is ye layste wyll of me Wyllyam barray mayde y xxx[th] yer of ye reyng of youre sofereyng kyng"; f. 164, "Ihon harry"; back pastedown, "Robard smythe was marryed the xix daye of octobar ano 1500/30/7," and "þis boke longyth to Rycharde Welby gentyllman." Brief marginal notes (ff. 287, 299v, 319) in the hand of William Cecil, Baron Burghley (1520–98). On f. i, a note in an eighteenth century hand concerning the authorship and translation of the text. On the front turn-ins "W.1.10," s. XVIII–XIX; on spine, printed label, "Tf 14." Listed among the books belonging to the Marquess of Exeter at Burghley House, Stamford in the HMC, *6th Report, Appendix* (1877) p. 234; their sale, Christie's, 15 July 1959, lot 132 with plate of f. 70v. Sold by F. Hammond Booksellers, with a sale pamphlet including plates of ff. 43 and 46 (noticed in *Scriptorium* 27, 1973, Bull. Cod. 87) to J. Howell Books in San Francisco in 1965. Acquired by the Huntington Library from Howell's at that time.

Secundo folio: keys of þe kyngdom
Bibliography: Chronica, 6. *Aspects of Medieval England,* n. 18 open at f. 43.

HM 28562 — Flanders, s. XV[ex]
JEHAN DE WAVRIN, CHRONIQUES D'ENGLETERRE — *fig. 139*

ff. 1–332v: [Jehan de Wavrin, *Chroniques d'Engleterre*] Ad fin que vous sachies la cause pour quoi ne a quel tiltre les guerres de france et d'engleterre encomnencerent premierement . . . descouvert a bbrestmoustier ou il fut enterre de lez madame phelipe de henault sa femme. Et atant prent fin le Second voulumne de ces croniques d'engleterre Et commencera le Tiers au couronnement du Ieune Roy Richard Iadis filz au noble prince de galles. Cy fine le second voulume des croniques d'engleterre.

Volume 2 of 6 volumes, covering the years 1337–77. Portions edited by William Hardy and Edward Hardy (pts. 4, 5), *Recueil des Croniques et Anchiennes Istories de la Grant Bretaigne, a present nomme Engleterre, par Jehan de Waurin.* RS 39 (London 1864–91); the edition covers only the years to 688 and 1399–1471.

Paper (Briquet, *Armoiries, trois fleurs de lis* 1741, Troyes 1470; and *Ancre* 393, Paris 1479), ff. i (early modern) + 332 + i (early modern); 385 × 285 (258 × 193) mm. $1\text{–}17^8$ 18^8(–8, after f. 143) $19\text{–}41^8$ 42^8(–5, 6, 7). Catchwords written horizontally in inner right corner, often cropped; quires and leaves signed with letters of the alphabet (a–z, tironian 7, "cum" abbreviation, then again from a on) and roman numerals. 2 columns of 44 lines, ruled in lead with single bounding lines; slash-form pricking visible in the 3 outer margins. Written in a bâtarde script.

Miniatures in water color grisaille with pink, red, gold or green for accent. The underlying sketches of the 2 large miniatures, ff. 1 and 62, are still visible; that on f. 1 includes *pentimenti* of 2 small grinning dogs in the foreground (caricature?). Opening miniature, f. 1, 31 lines in height, and width of both columns, depicting the coronation of Edward III; full border in floral pattern of black, gold and red. On f. 62, 24-line miniature of the celebration for the institution of the Order of the Garter. Four smaller miniatures, the width of one column: f. 112, 20-line, the seige of Calais; f. 163v, 21-line, soldiers; f. 204, 20-line, a battle scene; f. 265, 17-line, the death of Queen Philippa. Initials, some with cadel designs (ff. 7v, 69, 82v, 145v, 155 and 157), rubrics, and paragraph marks in red ink. Incorrect early modern foliation at lower right corner of text.

Bound in green velvet, quite worn and rebacked, over wooden boards, with the arms of Stuart encircled by the collar of the Order of the Bath (?) impressed in blind on both covers, now barely visible.

Written in Flanders toward the end of the fifteenth century. Unidentified coat of arms in the lower margin of f. 1: tierced in pale, 1, per fess, in chief, chequy or and azure a bordure gules (Counts of Dreux; Rietstap, vol. 1, pl. 226), and in base, or 2 pallets azure a chief gules; 2, azure 2 crosses flory or in chief and in base; 3, per fess, in chief, or 2 pallets azure a chief gules, and in base, chequy or and azure a bordure gules; en surtout an escutcheon gules 3 hands sinister or. Belonged to Jean Baptiste Denis Guyon de Sardière, son of Mme de la Mothe-Guyon, with his signature on ff. 1 and 332v; catalogued for his sale, Paris 1759, lot 2188; the collection, however, was bought *en bloc* by the Duc de la Vallière (1708–80) before the sale; not identified in La Vallière's catalogue. Later acquired by Sir Charles Stuart, Baron Stuart de Rothesay (1779–1845), British Ambassador to Paris, 1815–30; Stuart sale, Sotheby's, 31 May 1855, lot 896 to Sir Thomas Phillipps. Phillipps' small paper label on spine, 17700. Acquired by the Huntington Library at the Phillipps sale, Sotheby's, 30 November 1965, lot 33 with plates of ff. 1 and 62.

Secundo folio: L'amendoit on son
Bibliography: Chronica, 6.

HM 30313 — England, s. XVI²
RIPLEY (?), ALCHEMICAL SCROLL

1. [Richard Carpenter?] Of the Sunne take the light/ The red Gum that is so bright/ And the Moone doe allsoe/ The white gum there keepe to . . . But in the Matrix wher the bee put/ Looke never the vessell bee unshut/ Till they haue ingendred a Stone/ In all the woorld is not such a one.

IMEV 2656. E. Ashmole, ed., *Theatrum Chemicum Britannicum* (London 1652) 275–77, and R. H. Robbins, ed., *Secular Lyrics of the XIVth and XVth Centuries* (Oxford 1956) 82–84, here in 42 verses, of which only 15 correspond to the text printed by Robbins (his vv. 1–12, 34–36). See also Schuler, n. 105, citing this manuscript.

2. [George Ripley? First block of text, 36 verses:] On the ground there is a hill/ Allso a Serpent in a well . . . Of the white Stone and the red/ Here truly is the very deede. [Second block, 40 verses:] [Take thy] father that phebus soe bright/ [That] sit so highe in Maiestie . . . Sum behinde & some before/ As philosephers there him gaue. [Third block, 12 verses:] In the sea withouten lees/ Stoude the Byrd of Hermes . . . Vnderstand now well A Right/ & thancke God of this Sight. [Fourth block, 38 verses:] I Shall Now tell without Leesinge/ hou & what is My Generation . . . And make them All thre but one/ Loe here is the philosephers Stone.

IMEV 1364.5. Ashmole, here reversing the order of his blocks of text, to be read 378–79, 377–78, 376–77, 375–76. See R. H. Robbins, "Alchemical Texts in Middle English Verse: Corrigenda and Addenda," *Ambix* 13 (1966) 62–73, citing this manuscript as *olim* Dyson Perrins on pp. 70 and 73 (in a list of known manuscripts). Schuler, n. 464.

3. In the name of the Trinitie/ Harke here and ye shall see . . . All maner Good men in his Degree/ Amen amen for Charitie. [dorse blank]

Hanna, "Addenda," n. 20 printing this text in full. See also Oxford, Bod. Lib., Ashmole 1480 article 15 (s. XVI) and Ashmole 972 article 16 (Ashmole's notes in an interleaved copy of his *Theatrum Chemicum Britannicum*).

Parchment, roll of 6 membranes; 3,247 × 392 mm. 196 lines of verse. Written in an italic script, badly rubbed in some areas. Four large illustrations in ink and watercolor, ca. 760 mm. in height. In the first (process for the White Stone), Aristotle (?) holding a large retort within which are 8 circles containing monks looking at human figures in glass bottles, each bottle being linked by a chain to a circle containing 2 men holding a book. In the second picture (process for the Red Stone), a fountain supported by a column held by one of 3 naked figures standing in a pool; 7 philosophers stand on pinnacles around the fountain, in which a naked man and woman are eating grapes from a vine; on the base of the fountain is a green dragon with a frog jumping from its mouth; below it, "The Red Lyon" and "The Grene Lyon" warm their paws at a fire. In the third picture (process for the Elixir of Life), the white bird of Hermes standing on a globe, eating its wing. In the fourth, a sun above a crescent moon which is held in the mouth of a dragon standing on a winged globe; inside the sun are 3 linked circles identified as "the white stone," "the red stone" and "the Elixir vitae." Below the winged globe, the final verses written on a scroll held by a king and a pilgrim (representing George Ripley?). For plates of New Haven, Yale University, Beinecke Library, Mellon MS 41, a Ripley alchemical scroll very similar to HM 30313, see *Alchemy and the Occult: A Catalogue of Books and Manuscripts from the Collection of Paul and Mary Mellon given to Yale University Library,* compiled by Laurence C. Witten II and Richard Pachella (New Haven 1977) 3:271–88.

Written in England in the second half of the sixteenth century. A number of other rolls with variations of this text and with similar illustrations were produced about the same period; London, Brit. Lib., Add. 5025 is dated 1588. Belonged to C. W. Dyson Perrins (1864–1958). Acquired by the Huntington Library from Sotheby's, 9 December 1958, lot 42 with a plate of the upper part of the second picture, showing the fountain.

Bibliography: Chronica, 6.

HM 30319 — England, s. XV[1]
MATTHEW PARIS, FLORES HISTORIARUM — *figs. 91, 92, 158*

1. ff. i–iii verso: [commentary] //postea facit mencionem de poeta famoso et facundo et ponit responsionem quam dedit vir historiographus qui vocatur Livius . . . [f. i verso, text:] *De Cacuvio* [*sic*] *et eius arbore capitulo 16,* Cacuvius flens arrio vicino ait . . . [f. i verso, commentary on this text:] Valerius ad sui propositi probacionem et consilii Ruffino dati confirmacionem adducit . . . [f. iii, end of text:] quo ego timeo. Sed ne orestem scripsisse videtur. Vale. [f. iii verso, end of commentary:] quod adulator dicitur blandus amicus, veritas autem amara est rugose frontis et tristis offendit correctos. *Explicit Epistola Valerii ad Ruffinum de uxore non ducenda cum Exposicione eiusdem.* [added in the margin, after the erasure of "quod Aleyn":] quod frater R. Aleyn.

Commentary of John Ridevall[1] on the *Dissuasio Valerii ad Ruffinum philosophum ne uxorem ducat* by Walter Map, lacking approx. the first ⅔. The text in M. R. James, ed. and trans., rev. by C. N. L. Brooke and R. A. B. Mynors, Walter Map, *De nugis curialium, Courtiers' Trifles.* Oxford Medieval Texts (Oxford 1983) 288–313. On the commentary see R. J. Dean, "Unnoticed commentaries on the *Dissuasio Valerii* of Walter Map," *Mediaeval and Renaissance Studies* 2 (1950) 128–50; also found, for example, in Cambridge, University Library, Ff. 6.12, and in Oxford, Bod. Lib., Digby 147 and Douce 147.

2. f. iii verso: [D]ux henricus lancastrie disponsavit filiam dompni de Beaumond de qua genuit dominam Blaunch. Iohannes de Gaunte . . . de qua idem david genuit alium David secundum Comitem de Asselles, qui quidem David secundus genuit duas filias quarum una filia mater fuit hugonis Halsham Militis. [f. iv recto–verso, blank]

Genealogical notice concerning Sir Hugh Halsham of Coombes, Sussex (d. 1442), through David, Earl of Atholl (1309–35).

3. ff. v–vi verso: Nomina sanctorum quorum reliquie hic in Bello continentur hec sunt. In primis de ligno crucis domini qui est sanctus sanctorum, illo excepto philacterio quod de auro et gemma fulgida confectum est . . . [D]e sancta Lucia virgine, [D]e sancto Ignacio episcopo et martyre. [added below the text:] ths. Bryd.

List of over 150 relics at Battle Abbey; no other list recorded for the Abbey.

4. ff. 1–94: *Incipiunt Cronica de adquisicione regni Anglie per Willelmum ducem Normannie et de pactis inter Willelmum ducem et haroldum,* Anno gracie M°lxvi° Willelmus dux normannorum applicuit in angliam Cuius adventus causa fuit hec. Cum dux haroldus filius Comitis Godwini generis regis Edwardi in predio iuris sui scilicet apud Boseham perhendinaret . . . [f. 24v:] Hugo quoque de Mohaut factus// [ff. 25–26v:] //nocte illa quiescens post laborem dormivit . . . tria castella super regem francorum // [ff. 27–28v:] //Iohannis desidiam fallacem . . . licet inviti et cum murmure assen// [ff. 29–31v:] //paulum londoniis. Eodem anno in vigilia purificationis . . . Interim rex Iohannes accensus furore// [f. 32r–v:] //ander de Savenesby in Cestrensem rome . . . qui de rege baronias tenebant in capi// [ff. 33–34:] //lanus ad restaurandum pape thesaurum . . . quod rapidus erat in verbo// [ff. 35–74v:] //iuvare eundem Iohannem . . . apud Neuyn in Snowdonia in cho// [ff. 76–77v:] //delibus et apud Berewicum . . . apud veterem crucem lapideam Westmonasterii consederunt// [ff. 75r–v, 78–94:] //dirent. Post hec elegerunt . . . Et ordinatum est per concilium regis istum cardinalem non plus debere habere quam acceperat olim Octobonus cardinalis et legatus in anglia, scilicet dimidium postulati. [f. 94v, blank]

By Matthew Paris. H. R. Luard, ed., *Flores Historiarum.* RS 95 in 3 volumes (London 1890), listing 20 manuscripts, HM 30319 unrecorded, although it appears to belong to a group of 5 other manuscripts descended from a manuscript of Merton Priory, now Eton Coll., 123. HM 30319 covers the period 1066–1306, but with considerable loss of text due to 28 (?) missing leaves; in Luard, 1:579–2:99, 2:110–2:118, 2:128–2:135, 2:148–2:161, 2:182–2:185, 2:195–2:202, 2:210–3:62, 3:83–3:87, 3:281–3:327. The text has been carefully collated with another manuscript, mistakes erased and corrected throughout.

5. ff. 95–105: In Civitate antiochia Rex fuit Antiochus nomine a quo et ipsa civitas nomen accepit . . . Casus suos ipse descripsit et duo volumina fecit. Unum in templo diane ephesiorum, aliud bibliotece sue exposuit. [scribe's note in the lower margin:] *Prave feci finem penitet me quod fixi pennam.*

G. A. A. Kortekaas, ed., *Historia Apollonii Regis Tyri* (Groningen 1984); listed p. 20.

6. ff. 105v–106v: Lucius imperator romanus regi Arthuro inimico suo salutem quam meruit. Miramur plurimum quod tu ausus es aperire oculos tuos contra nos . . . Arthurus rex britannie et francie imperatori respondet per suas litteras et raciones. Dato quod ego sum rex britannie et francie . . . usque ad reditum suum regendam et voluit quod regnaret ut rex quia heredem non habuit de corpore suo procreatum.

Exchange of letters between the Roman emperor Lucius and King Arthur, leading to a war in which Lucius is killed, followed by an account of Mordred's rebellion and Arthur's death.

7. ff. 106v–107: Anno domini millesimo ducentesimo nonagesimo nono Margareta soror Regis francie philippi applicuit apud dovore in festo Nativitatis beate marie . . . sed corpus eius [of Edward I] fuit dilatum in angliam et sepultum apud Westmonasterium anno proximo sequenti citra festum sancti andree apostoli xviii die mensis octobris et cetera. [ff. 107v–108v, blank]

Notes on various events, 1299–1307.

Parchment, ff. ii (modern parchment) + vi (contemporary parchment, with text) + 108 (last was pastedown) + ii (modern parchment); 246 × 182 mm. Manuscript written over a period of time, each article (except 6 and 7) by a different scribe. Arts. 1–3 on a quire of 6 leaves. Art. 1, ff. i–iii verso, written space 193 × 124 mm., 54 long lines, frame ruled in crayon, written by Richard Aleyn, cellarer of Battle Abbey, 1459–63, in a littera textualis for the text and in a littera cursiva for the commentary; 2-line initials, slashed initials within the text, paragraph marks and rubrics, all in red. Art. 2, f. iii verso, on lines ruled in ink for this text, written in a littera textualis formata; space reserved for a 2-line initial, initials within the text washed in yellow or brownish-pink. Art. 3, ff. v–vi verso, written space 180 × 122 mm., 2 columns of 26 lines ruled in ink with pricking in the inner margin, written in a littera textualis formata by Thomas Bryd, cellarer of Battle Abbey, 1436–38; 2-line blue initial and 1-line initials of the saints' names washed in color, usually in brownish-pink, but some in green or yellow on f. vi verso. Arts. 4–7, written space 160 × 125 mm. through f. 86, thereafter 175 × 125 mm. $1–3^8$ 4^2(ff. 25–26, center bifolium) 5^4(ff. 27–30, the 2 outer bifolia) 6^2(ff. 31–32, center bifolium) 7^2(ff. 33–34, center bifolium) $8–12^8$ 13^2(ff. 76–77, center bifolium, now misbound; should precede f. 75) 14^{10} 15^8(through f. 94) 16^8 17^6. Quires signed in crayon with roman numerals in the lower margin of the first leaf recto, [1]–17; the first quire with leaf signatures in the same position. Catchword, f. 50v, in inner right corner in a noting hand. Written in 3 scripts: i, ff. 1–94 (art. 4); ii, ff. 95–105 (art. 5); iii, ff. 105v–107 (arts. 6, 7).

Opening initial, f. 1, 4-line gold with light green infilling and floral spray, frame in lower and outer margin of colored segments and sparse leaves, around which a snake is entwined, reaching upwards for a parrot, in an unskilled style; similar initials on ff. 72v, 73, 95. 5- to 3-line initials, blue only up to f. 11 included, then in alternating red and blue, then red only, then red, green or blue, all with red and green flourishing in a rough idiosyncratic style; some of the flourishing incorporates figures, such as a king's head (f. 11v), birds (f. 37v), animal heads (ff. 57v, 59v, 65v), a face (f. 91). Some sketches in crayon for flourishing on, e.g., ff. 16, 23v, 29v, 65. Red and green paragraph marks, initials in the text touched in red, nota marks in the margins often filled in colors. Rubrics frequently entered in the margins and enclosed by rope frames.

Bound, s. XIX^{in}, by Charles Smith in green morocco, gilt; gilt dentelle on the turn-ins; gilt edges.

Written in England in the early fifteenth century; art. 1 copied by Richard Aleyn, cellarer of Battle Abbey, 1459–63, and art. 3 by Thomas Bryd, cellarer, 1436–38. Evidently bound together at least by the time it was given to Battle Abbey by John Newton, cellarer, 1457–59, and abbot, 1463–90. Inscriptions, s. XV^{med}, on ff. v and 108, "Liber monasterii sancti martini de bello ex dono [f. 108: domini] Iohannis Nuton Abbatis cum signo IN" followed by a leaf flourish. Newton also owned a *Brut Chronicle,* now University of Chicago, Joseph Regenstein Library, MS 254, which bears the same "IN" initials and leaf flourish on f. 1; inscriptions in both manuscripts in black/brown ink. Belonged to Edward Willoughby, who used 3 bifolia of this manuscript as book covers: of the bifolium ff. 25–26, on f. 26v, upside down, his signature and the date 13 September 1725; of the bifolium ff. 33–34, on f. 34v, upside down, his signature and the date 17 March 1725; of the bifolium ff. 76–77, on f. 77v, upside down, the inscription "Domus Edward Willoughby," his signature and the date 1723/4; this last bifolium foliated (by Willoughby?) 4–5, right side up. In the upper margin of f. 1, s. XVIII (?), "Cronica Johannis Londoniensis monachi Cantuariensis ecclesie." Acquired in 1836 from Thomas Thorpe by Sir Thomas Phillipps; Phillipps number on the small paper label on the spine, 8517. Phillipps sale, Sotheby's, 28 November 1967, lot 109 with a plate of f. 1 to the Huntington Library.

Secundo folio: [f. 2, art. 4] sed castellum
Bibliography: Ker, *MLGB,* 8. *Chronica,* 7. For a description of the Battle Abbey papers at the Huntington Library, acquired in 1923, see *Guide to British Historical Manuscripts* 1–20.

---

[1] We thank Prof. Ralph Hanna for this identification and for the reference to other manuscripts.

HM 30957 — Spain, s. XVII^{in}
LUIS DE LA CRUZ, DERROTERO

ff. v–184: [Dedicatory poem:] Al Capitan Luis de la Cruz Piloto Mayor . . . ; [f. vi recto, Title page, containing a dedication to Don Francisco de Guzman, Marqués de Ayamonte:] *Ynstruccion y avisos excelentes de las derotas y carrera de las yndias* . . . ; [f. vii recto, Word to the reader:] beso los Pies . . . ; [f. 1, Text:] *Capitulo primero de la derrota de la barra De sant lucar a las yslas De canaria,* Partiendo de la barra de san lucar . . . nombre de Jesus. [ff. 184v–199v, blank]

Sailing instruction for the route from San Lucar, Spain, to the West Indies and Florida, with a description of duties and payment of ship's personnel (ff. 150v–177v) and table of latitudes (ff. 178–184). Dedicatory poem indicates that Luis de la Cruz is the author.

Paper (*Croix Latine* not dissimilar from Briquet 5688 and 5704, both Perpignan, respectively 1596 and 1595, but here with the initials R and MS [?]), ff. vii + 199; 195 × 142 (160 × 90) mm. Collation beginning with f. iv: 1–7^{20} 8–10^{16}(through f. 184) 11^{16}(–16, now the pastedown and torn loose from the quire). 20–26 long lines with vertical bounding lines defined by folds in the paper. Written in a cursive script in 3 hands: i, f. v; ii, ff. vi–vii verso, 1–26v; iii, ff. 26v–184. Chapter headings in a slightly larger version of the same script. Contemporary foliation, 1–183.

Bound, s. XVII, in limp parchment with remains of 2 fore edge ties; title on the spine in a round gothic script "derrotero de la Carrera de las India[s]."

Written probably about 1600, since Luis de la Cruz is first listed as master of a ship in 1585 and his name last appears in the records of the Archivo de Indias in Seville in a law suit of 1615. Internal evidence shows the volume was written after 1565 since the town of St. Augustine, Florida, founded in that year, is mentioned. Notes on front cover

"SN 118," and on front pastedown, "$SEE" (?). A letter, dated 22 July 1968, on file in the Huntington Library from Dra. Lourdes Díaz-Trechuelo of the Escuela de Estudios Hispano-Americanos de Sevilla suggests that this manuscript may have been in the private library of the Marqués de Ayamonte, to whom the book is dedicated. After his death it probably passed into the library of his relative, the Conde-Duque de Olivares, a library consulted by A. León Pinelo for his bibliography published in 1629. Purchased by the Huntington Library from the Spanish bookseller José Porrúa Turanzas, 24 March 1967.

Bibliography: A. León Pinelo, *Epitome de la biblioteca oriental i occidental, nautica i geografica* (Madrid 1629) 149. A. González de Barcia Carballido y Zúñiga, ed., *Epitome de la Bibliotheca oriental, y occidental, nautica, y geografica de don Antonio de Leon Pinelo* (Madrid 1737) 1:1148. N. Antonio, *Bibliotheca hispana nova* (Madrid 1788) 2:32. M. Fernández de Navarrete, *Biblioteca marítima española* (Madrid 1851) 2:355.

HM 30986 — England, s. XIV[2]
SARUM MANUAL — *fig.* 77

1. ff. 1–4v: *Omnibus dominicis diebus per annum* . . . , Exorciso te creatura salis . . . qui custodiat foveat protegat visitet et defendat omnes habitan//

Benedictio salis et aque, ending defectively due to damage on f. 4; A. J. Collins, ed., *Manuale ad usum percelebris Ecclesie Sarisburiensis.* HBS 91 (Chichester 1960) 1–4.

2. ff. 4v–8v: //*In primis inquirat sacerdos ab obstetrice utrum sit infans masculus an femina* . . . ut habeas vitam eternam et vivas in secula seculorum. Amen.

Ordo ad cathecuminum faciendum, beginning defectively due to damage on f. 4; *Manuale,* 25–31.

3. ff. 8v–11v: *Quando fons fuerit mundandus et de pura aqua renovanda quod sepe debet fieri propter aque* [catchword:] *corruptionem//* [f. 9:] //fontis utero in novam renata creaturam . . . *et sanctificatis fontibus olei et crismatis infusione baptizetur. Post hec//*

Benedictio fontis, with 3 leaves missing between ff. 8–9, and ending defectively; *Manuale,* 31 and 34–35.

4. ff. 12–19v: //*impedimentum aliquod proponere voluerit et ad hoc probandum caucionem prestiterit. . . . sed anima non potest esse sponsa alterius quam christi quia cum demone fornicatur nec est matrimo-*[catchword:]*nium spirituale//*

Ordo ad faciendum sponsalia, beginning defectively due to loss of 2 leaves between ff. 11–12, and ending defectively due to loss of a quire between ff. 19–20. Vows of both spouses in English on ff. 12v–13; *Manuale,* 45–58.

5. ff. 20–21v: //serpentis suavem a patribus nostris gustatum . . . Ipse det tibi vitam et victoriam et benedictionem in seculum seculi. Amen. *Sequatur,* Benedicat te deus pater//

Benedictiones pomorum, elemosine, panis, scuti et baculi, beginning and ending defectively, with loss of one quire before f. 20 and 1 leaf after f. 21; *Manuale,* 66–69.

6. ff. 22–27: //non approximabunt. Tu es refugium meum a tribulacione . . . et omnium peccatorum tuorum pius indultor. Qui vivit et regnat cum deo patre.

Ordo ad visitandum infirmum, beginning defectively; exhortation, explanation of the Articles of the Creed, absolution and blessing are replaced in this manuscript (as in others; see *Manuale,* 100, n. 11) by a single rubric; *Manuale,* 98, Ps. 31, 6–100 and 106, line 29–107.

7. ff. 27–34: *Priusquam inungatur infirmus incipiat sacerdos antiphonam,* Salvator mundi . . . in trinitate sanctificet quem omnes gentes venturum expectant ad iudicium. Qui cum deo patre et eodem spiritu sancto vivit et regnat deus per omnia secula seculorum. Amen.

De extrema unctione; *Manuale,* 107–112.

8. ff. 34–37: *Cum vero anima in exitu seu dissolutione corporis visa fuerit laborare* . . . de gehenne incendiis et ab omnibus angustiis. Amen.

Commendatio anime in articulo mortis; *Manuale,* 114–118, with litany as printed.

9. ff. 37–45v: *Sequatur commendacio animarum et dicatur in camera vel in aula . . . et sic deinceps in superiore gradu. Singula vero responsoria a duobus ad caput corporis//*

Commendatio animarum (after death), ending defectively due to loss of 1 leaf between ff. 45–46; *Manuale,* 118–132.

10. ff. 46–64v, 68–71v, 75–77v: //tus est. *Antiphona,* Dominus. Amen. *Psalmus,* Levavi oculos meos . . . Vide humilitatem meam et labo// [f. 55:] //videre bona domini in terra vivencium . . . Attenuati sunt oculi mei [catchword:] suspicientes// [f. 68:] //[added in the upper margin, s. XVI: et omnis qui vivit et] credit in me non morietur in eternum . . . Bonitatem fecisti cum servo tuo Domine secundum verbum tuum// [f. 75:] //Mirabilia testimonia tua domine ideo scrutata est . . . tu venia misericordissime pietatis absterge. Per christum dominum nostrum. Amen. Requiescant in pace. Amen.

Vigilie mortuorum and Commendatio animarum (to be sung over the corpse in the church or in the graveyard), beginning defectively and with 3 internal breaks, respectively of 1, 2 and 2 folios: *Manuale,* 133, line 10–137, line 26 (ff. 46–54v); 137, line 32–140 (ff. 55–64v); 141, line 9–143, line 15, Ps. 118, 65 (ff. 68–71v); 143, line 15, Ps. 118, 129–144 (ff. 75–77v); the Missa pro Defunctis was not copied in the manuscript.

11. ff. 65–67v, 72–74v: //iudicas populos in equitate et gentes in terra dirigis . . . qui credit in me eciam si mortuus fuerit [catchword and continuation on the text line, s. XVI:] vivet// [f. 72:] //mater mea et soror mea vermibus Ubi est ergo nunc prestolacio mea . . . Auditui meo dabis gaudium et leticiam et exulta//

The 3 outer bifolia of a quire (lacking central bifolium) from another manuscript, folded backwards so that leaves 1–3 (ff. 72–74) now follow leaves 6–8 (ff. 65–67); they have been placed here so that the text on ff. 65–67v may remedy the deficiency between ff. 64 and 68 of the main manuscript; the text on ff. 72–74v is superfluous (repeating what is on ff. 59–62v) and was evidently only retained for a more secure binding of the conjunct leaves. The text is: *Manuale,* 140, line 32, Ps. 66, 5–141, line 8 (ff. 65–67v) and *Manuale,* 138, last line, Job 17, 14–140, line 22, Ps. 50, 10 (ff. 72–74v).

12. ff. 77v–89v: *Post missam accedant duo clerici de ii[a] forma ad caput defuncti* . . . et anime omnium fidelium defunctorum per dei misericordiam in pace requiescant. Amen. *Secundum Hankok.*

Inhumatio defuncti; *Manuale,* 152–162.

13. ff. 90–95: *In nocte nativitatis domini dum canitur ix responsoria . . .* laus creatori resonet congrua amen dicant omnia.
Evangelium in nocte nativitatis Domini; *Manuale,* 5–6.

14. ff. 95–98: *In nocte epiphanie dum canitur ix responsoria cum suo versu . . . Finito evangelio sacerdos in capa serica incipiat,* Te deum laudamus.
Evangelium in nocte epyphanie; *Manuale,* 6–7.

15. ff. 98–101v: *In purificatione beate marie cantata hora sexta fiat benedictio luminis . . . Postea accendantur candele et distribuantur cantore incipiente antiphona,* Lumen ad revelationem *ut in processionali continetur.*
Benedictio cereorum in Purificatione; *Manuale,* 7–9.

16. ff. 101v–104v: *Feria iiii*[a] *in capite ieiunii post vi*[a] *in primis fiat sermo ad populum si placuerit . . . Tunc eat processio ut in processionalibus continetur.*
Feria quarta in capite ieiunii; *Manuale,* 9–12.

17. ff. 104v–105v: *Dominica in ramis palmarum post aspersionem aque benedicte . . .* omnis incursio demonum eradicare et explantare ab hac crea-[catchword:]tura florum//
Benedictio frondium in Dominica palmarum, ending defectively; *Manuale,* 12–13.

Parchment, ff. iii (modern paper) + 105 + iii (modern paper); 290 × 190 (195 × 122) mm. 1^8 2^8(–1, 2, 3, 7, 8) 3^8 one quire missing here 4^8(–3, after f. 21) 5–6^8 7^8(–4, after f. 45) 8^8(–6, after f. 54) 9^8 10^8(–1, 2, 7, 8; ff. 65–67 and 72–74, 3 bifolia from another manuscript, wrapped around the remaining leaves of the original quire) 11^8 12^8(–8, after f. 89, possibly blank) 13–14^8. Catchwords in brown or red ink according to the text of the next quire, and enclosed in ink frames of the same color. Quire and leaf signatures in letters and short horizontal strokes, [a] through "p"; the "h" signing ff. 44, 45 of quire 7 is in red, due to red ink of extensive liturgical directions on these leaves. 2 columns of 24 lines, ruled in lead (in ink on ff. 20–45v) with single bounding lines; slash pricking in the 3 outer margins. Written in a textura script by "Hankok" who signed his name on f. 89v. A "Frater J. Hancok" copied Dublin, Trinity College, D.4.4 (424), treatises on grammar and rhetoric; although that manuscript is mainly in an anglicana script, the textura of its headings appears to be in the same hand as HM 30986, perhaps in more haste. Music in black on red 4-line staves.

Opening initial, f. 1, 5-line, in particolored dull rose and blue, infilled with leaves and vine on a gold ground, the whole on a particolored ground, reversing the colors of the initial; C-shaped bar and foliage border, with leafy tendrils extending into the outer margin. On f. 90 (beginning the service), a similar 3-line initial, colored and infilled with leaves on a gold ground; C-shaped border. Initials on ff. 41, 50, 90 (beginning of the gospel) in gold on white-patterned particolored dull rose and blue grounds; those on ff. 41 and 50 with short sprays of daisy buds. 3- and 2-line blue initials with red flourishing and infilling of void leaves and balls; 1-line initials alternating red and blue; 1-line initials within the text tinted yellow; paragraph marks in blue; liturgical directions in red throughout. Within the music, cadel initials with washes of light purple, green or yellow and occasional faces in profile. Corrector's marks in lead at the end of each quire, near the catchword.

Inserted leaves, ff. 65–67 and 72–74, 264 × 180 (184 × 120) mm., constituted the 3 outer bifolia of a quire, now folded in the reverse of their original position: quire and leaf signatures on ff. 73, 74 composed of a letter (cropped) and roman numerals, ii and iii. Catchword on f. 67v in a frame touched in red. 21 long lines ruled in lead. Written in a textura script. Music in black on red 4-line staves, with cadel initials, less well done than those of the main manuscript, often enlivened with profile faces washed in pale green, yellow or with some red. Text initials very similar to those of the main manuscript: 2-line blue initials infilled with void leaves and balls and flourished in red; 1-line initials alternating red and blue; 1-line initials within the text washed in yellow; blue paragraph marks.

Bound, s. XIX, in purple morocco by Maltby, Oxford; gilt edges.

Written in England ca. 1350–80. Belonged to the Rev. Edward S. Dewick (1844–1917); his sale, Sotheby's, 17 October 1918, lot 89. Acquired by John Meade Falkner (1858–1932); a letter dated 1 January 1919 discussing text and re-binding from E. Gordon Duff affixed to f. ii, with his collation of the manuscript and a note in the hand of E. V. Stocks, Durham University Librarian, 1903–34; Meade Falkner sale, Sotheby's, 12 December 1932, lot 263 with pl. of ff. 89v–90 to Quaritch (another 12 manuscripts which once belonged to Meade Falkner are now Claremont, California, Claremont Colleges, Honnold Library, Crispin MSS 5, 8, 10, 11, 13, 14, 16, 17, 19, 22, 23, 37). Acquired by James P. R. Lyell (1871–1949) from Quaritch, 7 April 1943, according to Lyell's notes on the front pastedown; of his collection of some 250 medieval manuscripts, 100 were bequeathed to the Bodleian Library and the remainder sold by his executors to Bernard Quaritch in 1951; see introduction by de la Mare, *Lyell Catalogue,* for further information and bibliography. Quaritch Cat. 699 (1952) n. 102 to James R. Page (1884–1962); his number JRP 351. Bequeathed to the Huntington Library with his collection on the Book of Common Prayer.

Secundo folio: (te-)cum vivit

Bibliography: The Book of Common Prayer, The James R. Page Collection. Loan Exhibition held at the Henry E. Huntington Library . . . commemorating the Coronation of Queen Elizabeth II, June 2 1953, n. 1 with plate of f. 82v. *A Descriptive Catalogue of the Book of Common Prayer and related materials in the Collection of James R. Page,* compiled by D. Bowen (Los Angeles 1955) 1–2 with plate of f. 82v. *Manuale,* ix n. 13. Bond and Faye, 18. de la Mare, *Lyell Cat.,* xxviii.

HM 31052 — Bohemia (?), s. XIV/XV
GRADUAL, fragment

Ad te levavi animam meam . . . et semitas tuas edoce me. *Sequitur inmediate Gloria patri et filio.* Gloria patri//

Opening leaf of a gradual with the introit of the first Sunday of Advent.

Parchment, 1 leaf; 568 × 405 (395 × 270) mm. 5 lines of text and music, ruled in lead with double vertical bounding lines and with single horizontal rules limiting space for top and bottom of minims; pricking for the text lines in the outer margin, and for the staves at the edges of the written space. Written in a liturgical book hand; music in square notation on red 4-line staves. Opening initial, ca. 165 × 140 mm. (the height of 2 lines of text and music), in stippled gold enclosing in its upper compartment a sainted Benedictine abbot (or bishop?), seated, holding an apple (?) in one hand, his crozier in the other, and the Gnadenstuhl between his knees; in the lower compartment, under a gothic canopy and against a tessellated background, a kneeling king holding his soul, as a small naked figure, between his praying hands (probably David). Elaborate full border of elongated red, blue and gold acanthus leaves, with, in the lower border, a knight in prayer before Catherine of Alexandria. The knight's arms are on his chest and twice in the outer margin, where they alternate with the knight's crest; for arms and crest, see below. Grotesques in the margin include ladies pelting wildmen with rocks from a turret;

an old man (?) spinning; a woman bending over; a seated woman touching her bare foot; an old man coming out of a small church (?); a hunting scene with dogs, rabbit, owl and hunter; 2 kneeling women holding flat, narrow objects in their mouths, facing one another, with the same white cloth wrapped around both their necks; a ram and a lion fighting; a seated donkey playing a psaltery; an obscene ape; a dog and a cat fighting; a snail grotesque and a dragon fighting; a cock with a long tongue (?); a grinning man-lobster-feline grotesque holding a spear, with a pot on his head; another dragon. On the verso, 2 large initials (the height of one line of text and music), in heavy black penwork with some void design. Leaf considerably worn and rubbed, especially on the recto.

Written at the turn of the fourteenth century in eastern Europe, perhaps Bohemia. Arms of the first owner, gules a fess argent between 3 sea-gulls (?) argent, 2 and 1, supported by a pair of seated lions; crest of the first owner, a bearded old man's head in profile, couped at the bust, proper, with a long cap curled forward, gules, supported by a pair of angels. Belonged to Alice Parsons Millard (1873–1938); following her death, friends acquired George (d. 1918) and Alice Millard's collection of materials on the evolution of the book, and donated it to the Huntington Library.

Bibliography: De Ricci, 24. [S. B. Dakin and R. O. Schad] *The Alice and George Millard Collection Illustrating the Evolution of the Book* (Ward Ritchie Press [1939]) p. 12. *Chronica,* 7.

HM 31151 — England, s. XII$^{2/4}$
AUGUSTINE, AGAINST HERESY — *figs. 42, 159*

1. ff. 5–52v: *Aurelii augustini liber primus incipit contra epistolas iuliani et aliorum de heresi pelagiorum,* Noveram te quidem fama celeberrima predicante . . . et ut petant providenter instruit et petentes clementer exaudit. *Explicit liber aurelii augustini contra epistolas iuliani et aliorum de heresi paelagianorum.*
PL 44:549–638.

2. ff. 53–55v: *Incipit sermo arrianorum,* Dominus noster ihesus christus deus unigenitus primogenitus totius creationis . . . per unigenitum eius filium deum et salvatorem nostrum in spiritu sancto nunc et per omnia secula seculorum amen. *Explicit sermo arrianorum.*
PL 42:677–684.

3. ff. 55v–70: *Aurelii Augustini doctoris contra istam arrianorum perfidiam liber incipit,* Eorum precedenti disputationi hac disputatione respondeo . . . ne nimis longum faceremus hoc opus nostrum. Quod tandem isto fine concludimus. *Explicit liber Augustini doctoris respondentis contra Arrianorum perfidiam.*
PL 42:683–708.

4. ff. 70–108: *Incipit eiusdem contra adversarium legis et prophetarum liber unus,* Librum quem misistis fratres dilectissimi nescio cuius hęretici inventum . . . Quę si dominus voluerit quantotius explicare curabo.
PL 42:603–666.

5. ff. 108–136: *Incipit beati augustini de genesi contra manicheos liber primus,* Si eligerent manichei quos deciperent eligeremus et nos . . . et sine aliquo

prȩiudicio diligentioris tractationis quȩ michi videbantur exposui. [ff. 136v–138v, ruled, but blank]
PL 34:173–220.

6. ff. 139–162: *Aurelii Augustini Doctoris Contra Pelagianos et Celestianos Hereticos Hypponosticon Liber Incipit,* Adversarii catholicȩ fidei dum contra regulam veritatis . . . nisi gratia per ihesum christum dominum nostrum subvenerit salutaris. [f. 157v:] *Augustinus contra pelagianos de prȩdestinatione divina,* Addere etiam hoc quam maxime huic operi oportet . . . gratiam predestinationis indebitam prorogare. Amen.
Ps. Augustine. *CPL* 381. *PL* 45:1611–1648 (Bks. 1–4), 1657–1664 (Bk. 6).

7. ff. 162–172v: *Contra Felicianum arrianum,* Extorsisti michi dilectissime fili optate ut de unitate trinitatis . . . Tunc separatus est a zizaniis segetem cum iustis cȩperit adhibere mercedem.
Virgilius Thapsensis. *CPL* 808. *PL* 42:1157–1172.

Parchment, ff. 174 (of which 1 is the pastedown, 2–4 front flyleaves, 173 back flyleaf, 174 pastedown); 318 × 200 (229 × 137) mm. i^4 $1–16^8$ 17^6(through f. 138) $18–19^8$ 20^6 21^8 22^4 ii^2. Catchwords occasionally in lower right margin, cropped. 2 columns of 36 lines, ruled in lead, single vertical bounding lines, central rule between the columns; exterior prickings visible. Written by 4 scribes in good book hands: i, ff. 5–52v; ii, ff. 53–136; iii, ff. 139–157v; iv, ff. 157v–172v. See E. Parker McLachlan, "The Scriptorium of Bury St. Edmunds in the Third and Fourth Decades of the Twelfth Century: Books in Three Related Hands and Their Decoration," *Mediaeval Studies* 40 (1978) 328–48 and plates, esp. p. 334 listing HM 31151 among the manuscripts of Group B, whose scribes share related elements with one of the two distinctive Bury hands.

Major initials, 8- to 3-lines, of varying quality, in red, purple, green or blue occasionally with small leafy tendrils in the same color or with touches of another color; those after f. 139, with scribes iii and iv, of finer execution; up to f. 56, 1-line initials within the text in colors; ff. 56–97, 2- and 1-line initials in red only; thereafter in the ink of the text. Ink drawings in the lower margins of ff. 57, 58v (reproduced in the 1968 Sotheby catalogue, see below) and 106v respectively of a lion, a dragon and a pointing hand; smaller sketches or trials in lead on ff. 107v, a shrine, and 108, a dragon and a lion. On ff. 3v–4, effaced drawings of an archer (f. 3v, mainly in lead, the head only in ink) and a king (f. 4, in ink, approx. 16 cm. high), probably a sketch of the martyrdom of St. Edmund, but apparently extraneous to this manuscript; see E. Parker McLachlan, pp. 339 n. 52 and 343–44. Contemporary running headlines; rubrics in red; corrections over large erased passages, e.g. on ff. 93, 94; *nota bene* hands e.g. on ff. 22, 61, 78; face brackets on ff. 59, 80v; frequent marginal notes in lead. Foliated in early form arabic numerals in crayon in the upper margin recto of arts. 3–7, beginning afresh with "1" at each article. On ff. 1v–2, pen trials, s. XV, "In my beginninge god," "Jhesus of nazareth kynge of the Jews."

Bound, s. XII/XIII, at Bury St. Edmunds in parchment over oak boards, square edges flush with the book block, semi-circular tabs at head and foot of spine. Fore edge clasp on later medieval pink leather strap fastening to pin on center back. Brass chain staple and one iron link at the center lower edge of the front cover. Remains of a whittawed leather chemise under rear pastedown. Plate of the binding in the 1968 Sotheby catalogue (see below). Regarding Bury bindings, see G. Pollard, "The Construction of English Twelfth Century Bindings," *The Library.* Transactions of the Bibliographical Society, ser. 5, 17 (1962) 1–22, pls. I–II. In a red box made by J. S. Wilson and Sons, Cambridge.

Written at Bury St. Edmunds in the second quarter of the twelfth century. Regarding the Bury scriptorium, see E. Parker [McLachlan], "The Scriptorium of Bury St. Edmunds in the Twelfth Century," unpublished Ph.D. dissertation, University of London 1965. Identifiable with no. xlii in the twelfth century catalogue of the abbey, ed. M. R. James, *On the Abbey of S. Edmund at Bury.* Cambridge Antiquarian Society Octavo Publ. 28 (Cambridge 1895) 23–32. Regarding the library see Ker, *MLGB,* 16–22 and R. Thomson, "The Library of Bury St. Edmunds in the Eleventh and Twelfth Centuries," *Speculum* 47 (1972) 617–45. The table of contents on the pastedown, the Bury pressmark "A.10" on the pastedown and on f. 5, and the note on the pastedown "In custodia .s. laugham [?]" are in the hand of the fourteenth century Bury *armarius* Henry of Kirkestede; see R. H. Rouse, "Bostonus Buriensis and the Author of the *Catalogus scriptorum ecclesiae,*" *Speculum* 41 (1966) 471–99. The contents of the manuscript are itemized in the thirteenth century Franciscan *Registrum Anglie de libris doctorum et auctorum veterum,* and in Kirkestede's "Catalogus scriptorum ecclesiae," items I.3, 22, 165, 186, 226, 366, 373. Upon the Dissolution the manuscript appears to have been acquired from the Bury library by Sir Nicholas Bacon, Lord Keeper, who owned lands at Redgrave, Suffolk, that had belonged to the abbey. The property was acquired towards the end of the seventeenth century by Sir John Holt (1642–1709), whose niece married, ca. 1750, Thomas Wilson, ancestor of George Holt Wilson of Redgrave Hall, Suffolk. This manuscript and 2 others from Bury (another volume of Augustine, the companion to HM 31151, now Cambridge, Mass., Harvard University, Houghton Library, Richardson MS 26, and one of Jerome, now London, Brit. Lib., Egerton MS 3776) were in the G. H. Wilson sale, Sotheby's, 21 July 1910, lot 159 (both Augustines) to Quaritch. Quaritch Catalogue 321 (1912) n. 249 (both Augustines) with a plate of the Harvard volume, and Quaritch Catalogue 357 (1920) n. 380 (both Augustines) to A. Chester Beatty (1875–1968). See E. G. Millar, *The Library of A. Chester Beatty* (Oxford 1927–30) 1:94–95 with plate 73 of Western MS 25 (the Harvard volume) and 1:96–97 with plate 74 of Western MS 26 (HM 31151), f. 139. The 2 Augustines were divided at the Chester Beatty sale, Sotheby's, 7 June 1932, when the volume now at Harvard was sold as lot 6, with a plate; the present Augustine, HM 31151, was acquired by the Huntington Library in the Chester Beatty sale, Sotheby's, 3 December 1968, lot 6 with plates of f. 139, the binding, and the drawing of the dragon on f. 58v.

Secundo folio: que in paradiso
Bibliography: Römer, i, 330. *Chronica,* 7.

HM 31189 — England, s. XIV^{ex}
PETER RIGA, AURORA

ff. 1–282: [20 line prologue by a Premonstratensian canon:] [*De*] *utilitate legendi hunc librum,* Nil homini melius quam si divina legendo . . . Intima declinat noxia vana fugat. [Teacher's preface:] Omnis scriptura divinitus inspirata . . . interfectionem dyaboli a christo. [f. 2, Peter Riga's prose preface:] *Incipit prefacio,* Frequens sodalium meorum peticio cum quibus conversando florem infancie exegi . . . et veritatis fulgor patenter illuxit. [f. 3, Text:] *Incipit Aurora de operibus vi dierum. Incipit Genesis,* Primo facta die duo celum terra leguntur . . . [f. 276v:] Efficit et validum nullisque minis ruiturum// [f. 277:] //Est laban sathanas cuius nomen sonat album . . . Signat eos quibus est danda beata quies//

The third edition of the *Aurora* of Peter Riga, with occasional interpolations of Aegidius of Paris, in the following order: f. 3, Genesis; f. 31, Exodus; f. 54v, Leviticus with prologue and with the verses *de avibus* (Beichner, p. 171) placed at the end; f. 69v, Numbers; f. 80, Deuteronomy with prologue; f. 85, Joshua; f. 89v, Judges; f. 95, Ruth; f. 96v, 1–4 Kings with prologue; f. 124v, Tobit ending with an additional 14 lines: Helizabeth genitrix . . . fertilis absque uno; f. 132v, Daniel; f. 146v, Esther ending with 4 lines by Aegidius: Inde quod evasit . . . nomen imposuere phurim; f. 151, Judith; f. 154v, 1–2 Maccabees with prologue; f. 163, Gospels with prologue; f. 217v, Acts with Aegidius' prologue: Dixi me finisse . . . faveto michi; f. 236v, Job with prologue; f. 250v, Song of Songs with prologue, ending defectively on f. 276v; f. 277, *Recapitulationes* beginning defectively in the section *Sine D* and ending defectively in the section *Sine R*. P. E. Beichner, ed., *Aurora Petri Rigae Biblia Versificata.* Publications in Mediaeval Studies 19 in 2 vols. (Notre Dame 1965). Stegmüller 6823–6825.

Parchment (thick and fuzzy), ff. i (modern parchment) + i (contemporary parchment) + 282 + i (modern parchment); 226 × 146 (170 × 63) mm. $1–23^{12}$ 24^{12}(–1 through 3 and 10 through 12). Quires signed in red roman numerals on the last leaf verso. 29 lines of verse. Ruled in lead with the top and bottom 2 horizontal rules full across; 3 vertical rules to the left of the text serve to separate the first letter of each verse from the rest of the line; in the lower and outer margins additional sets of narrow rules; slash pricking in outer margins. Written in a clear anglicana formata. 2-line initials alternating in red and blue. Rubrics and arguments in long lines extending to narrow rules in the outer margin. Running headlines with book and chapter number on each page, added s. XIV/XV. Fore edges damp rotted.

Bound in 1971 in white quarter leather over wooden boards; 2 fore edge clasps; covers from the previous binding of eighteenth century English speckled calf with the Dysart arms (stamp A; see below) mounted as doublures; edges speckled in red.

Written in England at the end of the fourteenth century. On f. i, "Liber magistri Willelmi Waverton Rectoris ecclesie de Tankerslay"; Waverton, a Queen's College "poor boy" in 1399, was rector of Tankersley in the West Riding of Yorkshire from 1420 until his death in 1440 (Emden, *BRUO,* 2000). 2 small parchment strips, 38 × 227 mm., from a deed relating to Yorkshire, s. XVI (?), signed "J. Chenche" removed from previous binding and shelved separately. Possibly among the manuscripts collected by Sir Lionel Tollemache ca. 1600; rebound in the mid-eighteenth century by Sir Lionel Tollemache, 4th Earl of Dysart (1708–70); the collection was dispersed in private sales 1953–56 and by auction in 7 Sotheby sales, 1955–71; for a brief history of the collection, see Sotheby's, 14 June 1965, pp. iii–viii with plates of the Dysart arms and crests used on the bindings, and E. Wilson, "The Book-stamps of the Tollemache Family of Helmingham and Ham," *The Book Collector* 16 (1967) 178–85. This manuscript sold by Sotheby's, 14 June 1965, lot 14. Acquired by the Huntington Library in July 1969 from Dawson's, Pall Mall, Cat. 200 (1969) n. 6.

Secundo folio: litterarum veritatem
Bibliography: Schenkl 4704. *Chronica,* 7.

HM 31543 GRADUAL

Northern Italy, s. XV

ff. 1–58: Gradual, as follows: ff. 1–10, feasts of the Virgin, beginning defectively; ff. 10v–17, Secundus, including a prose; ff. 17–22, Holy Spirit; ff. 22–25, Sebastian; ff. 25v–28v, Raphael; ff. 29–32v, Kyrie, Agnus dei, Gloria in excelsis deo; ff.

33–42, Mass for the Dead; f. 42r–v, added, s. XVII, Stella celi extirpavit . . . [*RH* 19438]; ff. 43–58v, sung portions of the Office of the Dead.

Parchment, ff. 58; 325 × 230 (250 × 180) mm. 1^8(-1, 2, 3) 2^8 3^8(-4, cancelled by the scribe?) 4^8 5^4(ff. 29–32) 6^8 7^2(ff. 41–42) 8–9^8. Quires signed, s. XVII, in both square capitals and cursive script with letter of the alphabet in the center of the first leaf recto ("B" through "I"). 5 lines of text and music; the minims of the text between faint ink ruling; double vertical bounding lines the length of the leaf. Written in a round gothic book hand; music, in square notes, on red 4-line staves.

Major initial for office of Secundus, f. 10v, the height of text and music, 60 mm., in punched gold, decorated with small red flowers, and set on a square ground of brown ink leaf designs and beading. Other major initials, also the height of text and music, in parted blue and gold, or in red and blue against penwork grounds of red alone, or of red and blue; secondary initials, slightly more than the text in height, 25 mm., alternating red and blue, with penwork of the other color up to f. 11, thereafter, red initials with brown penwork; after f. 14, the penwork usually not completed; rubrics in red. Contemporary foliation in red roman numerals, at the top of each recto through f. 13, ff. iiii–xvi.

Bound in old limp parchment.

Written in Italy, probably for use in Asti, to judge from the prominence accorded to St. Secundus and its later history. The manuscript remained in that area until the nineteenth century, when it belonged to members of the Morando family, who, among much other miscellaneous marginalia, signed on ff. 19v, 42v: "Morando Giovanni Maria, 1850, Nativo di Revigliasco" and "Morando Giuseppe figlio di Giovanni, 1847, Nativo di Rivigliasco." Other marginalia by a different hand, perhaps earlier, include the name of "Jeronimus Zavorinus" on f. 58. Part of the front pastedown, apparently with ownership inscription, torn away. Given to the Huntington Library by James D. Hague in 1971.

HM 31544 — Germany, s. XV
CHOIR BOOK, fragment

//et ecce sedes posita erat in eo et in medio sedis et in circuitu eius quatuor animalia . . . et aspectus hominis erat in eis aeuia aeuia alleluia, *vers.*, De medio autem eius quasi// . . . //corpus suum et alterum similiter velabatur Sub quo Gloria patri . . . *resp.*, Audiebam sonum alarum quasi sonum aquarum multarum quasi sonum subli//

Common of Evangelists, beginning in vespers (?) and continuing into a section of matins; text not continuous.

Parchment, 1 bifolium, with string still running down the gutter; 500 × 340 (390 × 254) mm. 12 lines of text and music; sets of double prick marks along both inner margins correspond to the heights of the minims of the text, suggesting ruling not presently visible; above and below the text, ruling in red ink with the upper and lower bounding lines full across; double vertical bounding lines the length of the leaf; music on red 4-line staves. Initials, the height of the text and music (except for a letter "I" along the outer margin of the first leaf verso, 240 mm.) in blue with red void penwork infilling often in leaf designs, or with the colors reversed, or as strapwork with red pen designs; rubrics in red.

Written in Germany in the fifteenth century. Given to the Huntington Library by James D. Hague in 1971.

HM 31911

HM 31911 England, s. XIV^{in}
BRACTON, DE LEGIBUS ET CONSUETUDINIBUS ANGLIAE

1. f. ii: [tipped in] Memorandum on the meaning of the name Bengough, dated 10 July 1847 from the Bristol City Library; ff. iii verso–iv verso: Bengough family tree dated 1847 and continued by a later hand through 1887.

2. ff. 1–4v: [added in a different hand] Chapter list to Bracton with divisions into 4 books and with references in roman numerals to quires and in arabic numerals to paragraphs, beginning afresh with each quire.

3. f. 4v: [Prayer:] Deus cui omne cor patet et omnis voluntas loquitur et quem nullum latet secretum . . . ; [note on herbs:] Decoquantur . . . et ex istis herbis lavetur membrum paciens [*sic*] unde versus, Salvia castoreum lavendula primula veris/ Nasturtium ruta curant paralitica membra; [verses:] Per subitum saltum Tedaldus fertur in altum/ Ex odio fratrum fit pater ille patrum; De gregorio x^{o} qui ante vocabatur Tedaldus hec dicta sunt; Nescio quid sit amor nec amo nec amor nec amavi/ Set scio si quis amat uritur igne gravi . . . [10 verses; Walther, *Initia* 11740]; In die paraceven anno domini M^{o} ccc^{o} dominus Iohannes de Arderne capellanus domini Rogeri de Brabazon in visione vidit hos versus sequentes ultra sedem Regis Edwardi tercii in magna aula Westm. scriptos littera crocei coloris, Fellea famina ructuat emphia curia regis/ Aurea lamina conteret omnia pondera regis . . . [political prophecy in 6 verses; Roger le Brabazon was justice of the King's Bench in 1296]; Lucius est piscis lupus et tirannis aquarum/ A quo discordat lucius iste parum . . . [6 verses; Walther, *Initia* 10431], Hii supradicti versus fuerunt de quodam lucio papa.

4. ff. 5–263: *Que sunt Regi necessaria. Incipit liber domini Henrici de Bracton,* In rege qui recte regit necessaria sunt duo hec, arma videlicet et leges . . . [f. 74, rubric added in the margin in a different hand:] *Incipit liber secundus,* Cum sint quedam crimina capitalia . . . , [f. 101, rubric added in the margin in a different hand:] *Incipit liber 3us,* Dictum est supra qualiter possessio . . . , [f. 195, rubric in the written space in the hand of the scribe:] *Incipit liber quartus de iure et proprietate et de tractatu super breve de Recto, de essoinis et dilationibus* . . . , Expedito tractatu de assisis et recognitionibus . . . qui sunt ad fidem domini Regis sive inde preceptum habuerint sive non. *Explicit liber Henrici de Bractoun de legibus et consuetudinibus Anglicanis.*

G. E. Woodbine, ed., *Bracton on the Laws and Customs of England,* trans. with revisions and notes by S. E. Thorne (Harvard University Press and the Selden Society 1968–77); this manuscript not recorded.

5. f. 263: Statute for religious men, 7 Edward I; *SR* 1:51.

6. f. 263r–v: Extenta manerii; *SR* 1:242–43.

7. ff. 263v–264: *De plumbo,* Ceo fet asaver ke fother de plum est de xxx fotmal . . . Ras de ayl est de xv gleynes e chescon gleyne est de xxv testes. La Centeyne de pesson est de viii^{xx}.

Assize of weights and measures, here without introductory material and in French; *SR* 1:205.

8. f. 264: Sachez ke quant le quart de furment est vendu per xii deners dunkz peisera le payn a ferxing de Wastel vi livres xvi souz . . . et ben pount il ceo

fere. Ceste assise est generale pur tut Engleterre. Ceste assise fust delivere per les mayns W. benet clerc anno regni regis henrici filii Regis Iohannis xlv°.

Assize of bread and ale, here in French; *SR* 1:199–200.

9. ff. 264–265: Quam prona sunt etatis studia et quanto vivamus diucius tanto proniora et hec quare plurimi sunt contractus utpote conductiones emptiones venditiones obligationes . . . [f. 264v:] Cartas igitur obligationes seu conventiones facere proponentes curam subscriptis adhibeant . . . Ego A. de B. et heredes mei vel assignati totam terram predictam cum pertinentiis sicut prius dictum est prefacto C. de B. et cetera. *Explicit ordinacio Cartarum.*

10. f. 265: Le dener peisera xx greyns eliz de furment . . . et le bussel peisera e tendera viii galuns.

11. f. 265r–v: View of frankpledge, in Latin; *SR* 1:246–47.

12. ff. 265v–267: Magna Carta, 9 Henry III; *SR* 1, charters, 22–25.

13. f. 267: Metra iuvant animos comprendunt [*sic*] plurima paucis/ Pristina commemorant hec sunt tria gratia legenti [Walther, *Initia* 10972]; a copy of a writ of entry brought by William of Sparesholte against Gerald de Insula dated at Winchester, 21 September in the year of "our" reign 13; Diva potens nemorum terror silvestribus apris/ Cui licet amfractus ire per ethereos . . . , Brute sub occasu solis trans gallica regna/ Insula in occeano est undique clausa mari . . . [the *Versus Bruti ad Dianam* and the *Responsio Diane* in 14 verses; Walther, *Initia* 4598].

14. f. 267v: Carta de foresta, 9 Henry III, ending defectively . . . Nul chasteleyn ou autre tyegne plee de la foreste ou de vert ou//; *SR* 1, charters, 26–27.

Parchment, ff. i (modern parchment) + iii (modern paper) + 267 + i (modern parchment); 298 × 205 (225–228 × 158–163; ca. 246 × 185 in chapter list) mm. 1^{4} $2\text{–}22^{12}$ 23^{12}(–12 with loss of text). Catchwords in inner lower margin. Quire signatures in roman numerals beginning with the text (present quire 2), in ink in the center lower margin, written on the recto of each leaf of the quire in quires 2–14, but on the recto of only the first leaf of the quire in quires 15–23; the quire numbers are repeated in lead in the upper margin of each leaf of all quires. Leaf signatures, where visible, different in each quire, using horizontal or vertical slashes, letters or roman numerals written in lead, red ink or turquoise, and placed at various positions in the lower margin. 2 columns of 46 lines (3 columns of 51 lines in the chapter list), ruled in lead, 3 lines between the columns; round prick marks in the 4 corners of the written space; in quire 2, the 3 lines between columns pricked with slash marks on either side of a round prick mark. Written in an anglicana script; the chapter list (art. 2) and the texts on f. 267r–v (arts. 12, 13) by a second hand, and the short texts on f. 4v (art. 3) by a third scribe. 3- and 2-line blue initials with red flourishing; paragraph marks alternating red and blue; rubrics in red, not completed on ff. 228–234, 254v–263. Considerable marginalia in several contemporary and later hands. Narrow strips of parchment in the outer margins of ff. 74, 101, 190, 195 slashed free on 3 sides to be twisted into fore edge tabs, now torn away except on f. 190.

Bound in 1973 in calf with 2 fore edge clasps; previous binding in eighteenth century parchment, spine gilt, green morocco title label.

Written in England in the early fourteenth century. On f. 267v, ownership note, s. XV, "P. bonar‹?›." According to the Sotheby catalogue description, the name "W. Mildmay" (perhaps Sir Walter Mildmay, Chancellor of the Exchequer, d. 1589) was written on a detached flyleaf, no longer with the volume. Owned by George Bengough of Bristol in 1847; his notes on ff. ii–iv. Acquired by the Huntington Library from Sotheby's, 8 July 1970, lot 100.

Secundo folio: [f. 6, Text] intelligatur habitus
Bibliography: Chronica, 7.

HM 34807 — England, s. XIII²
PETER COMESTOR, HISTORIA SCHOLASTICA — *fig. 54*

1. f. i: Old Testament genealogies schematically displayed in an English hand of the end of the thirteenth or early fourteenth century; f. i verso, blank, except for ownership mark (see below).

2. ff. 1–246: [Prologue] Reverendo patri et domino Willelmo dei gratia senonensi archiepiscopo . . . Causa suscepti laboris fuit instans petitio sociorum . . . [f. 1, Text:] Imperatorie maiestatis est in palatio ["tres" added in the margin, s. XIV] habere mansiones . . . qui prius albula dicebatur, undecimus silvius Agrippa. [f. 137r–v, blank; text follows directly from f. 136v to f. 138, beginning 4 Reg.:] Porro Ochosias filius Achab regnare cepit in samaria . . . de Iohanne filio symonis prosequentes. [f. 197v, in the margin, note of missing text, s. XV, being the inset "additiones"; f. 198, blank; f. 198v, beginning the New Testament:] Mortuo symone qui ultimus v filiorum Mathathie asamonei dux . . . et nota differentiam, translatus enoch subvectus est helyas, ascendit ihesus propria sui virtute. *Explicit hystoria evangelium.*
Peter Comestor, *Historia scholastica; PL* 198:1053–1524C, 1525B–1644.

3. ff. 246–278v: *Incipiunt capitula hystorie actuum apostolorum,* Anno nonodecimo imperii tyberii cesaris adhuc procuratore iudee pilato . . . et in loco honorabili scilicet in cathacumbis. *Explicit hystoria Actum apostolorum Radulph*[*i*?].
Peter of Poitiers, *Historia actuum apostolorum;* Stegmüller 6565 and 6785; *PL* 198:1645–1722. Stegmüller 7091–7092 notes a similar case of the name Radulphus, whether possessor or author, added to the end of a Biblical commentary in a manuscript once at St. Paul's, London.

The whole volume was compared with another manuscript in the fourteenth century and the missing portions (the "additiones") were noted, for example: f. 64, "deficit ca. 22 et 23"; f. 70, "deficit 17, 18 & 19"; f. 77v, "deficit 3^m^ ca^m^."; f. 78, "deficit usque 12"; f. 81v, "deficit 29 & 30"; f. 85, "deficit hic." The same hand attempts to supply the biblical chapter numbers. Occasional longer notes in the margins in the same hand as f. i (for example, ff. 12, 13, 27, 54v), or in another hand of the fourteenth century (for example, ff. 77, 136v), or in a hand of the sixteenth century (for example, ff. 179, 184v–188v). On f. 136v, a list of the 6 ages of the world added in a late fifteenth century hand with a 7th added in another hand.

Parchment, ff. i (modern paper) + 278 + i (modern paper); 174 × 126 (134 × 95) mm. $1–11^{12}$ 12^{8}(–5, 6, 7; through f. 137) $13–17^{12}$(through f. 197) 18^{6} $19–24^{12}$ 25^{4}(–4). Quires 10–15 apparently signed on each (?) leaf in blue with the letters G–M. Catchword on f. 137v, in the inner corner, cropped. 2 columns of 40 lines, some columns divided into 2 narrower columns (e.g. on ff. 98v, 100); ruled in lead; double bounding lines. Written in an English book hand. Opening initial, 6-line, parted red and blue with filigree infilling around 4 blue rosettes, with red and blue cascade and flourishing to frame the inner and upper margins. Blue initials, 2-line, with red and blue cascade or red flourishing; initials within the text touched in red; paragraph marks alternating in red and blue. Running headlines in red and blue.

Bound, s. XIX, in faded green calf.

Written in England in the second half of the thirteenth century. On f. i verso, written in pale red ink in a mid-sixteenth or seventeenth century legal anglicana script, probably in explanation of the name "Radulphus" on f. 278v: "This booke appears to have been examined by Radulph de Baldock, Deane of Saint Paule 1297." Ralph de Baldock, bishop of London, 1306–13, and chancellor of England, 1307, owned a number of books: Emden, *BRUO*, 2147–49 prints the list of the 37 books found in Baldock's study (June 1313) and of the 126 "libri scolastici" which Baldock bequeathed to St. Paul's in London; included at item 12 is "Historie scolastice cum aliis scriptis"; however, this book does not appear in St. Paul's 1458 catalogue, printed by W. Dugdale, *History of St. Paul's Cathedral in London* (London 1716) 60–70. The manuscript belonged to Ebenezer Jacob, whose bookplate is on the front pastedown; later owned by John Broadley, with his bookplate on f. i; his sales, Evans, 12 July 1832 and 19 June 1833 (these catalogues not available to us). Acquired by the Huntington Library in 1971 from Lathrop C. Harper, Catalogue 200 (Spring 1970), n. 9 with a plate of f. 92.

Secundo folio: dicunt eum
Bibliography: Chronica, 7.

HM 35300 — England, s. XV^{med} and XIII^{ex}
BEDE, HISTORIA ECCLESIASTICA; etc. — *fig. 113*

Composite volume

I.

1. f. i verso: Biographical note on Bede in the hand of Robert Elyot.

2. ff. 1–109v: *Incipit prefacio venerabilis Bede presbiteri in ecclesiasticam historiam gentis anglorum ad regem Colwulfum,* Gloriosissimo Regi Colwlfo Beda famulus christi et presbiter. Historiam gentis anglorum ecclesiasticam . . . litteris mandare studuimus; [on f. 2r–v, chapter list of Book 1; f. 2v, Text:] Britannia occeani insula quondam albion nomen fuit . . . et parere semper ante faciem tuam. [followed directly by the last paragraph of the preface:] Preterea omnes . . . apud omnes fructum pie intercessionis inveniam. Amen. Deo gratias. Finito libro sit laus et gloria christo.

B. Colgrave and R. A. B. Mynors, eds., *Bede's Ecclesiastical History of the English People* (Oxford 1969); on p. lvii this manuscript is described among those containing "the common text of southern England in the later Middle Ages." See also M. L. W. Laistner, *A Hand-list of Bede Manuscripts* (Ithaca 1943) 95. Caedmon's hymn in Old English in the outer margin of f. 82 in the hand of the scribe.

3. f. 109v: Verses on Bede as follow: Suscipe nostrorum rex historiam populorum/ Quam lege scribe proba cunctos hanc nosse labora/ Scribens in sceda sedet hic sua dogmata Beda/ Ex anglis natus doctissimus atque probatus/ Nam

Scripturarum tractando profunda sacrarum/ Mundum doctrinis ceu sol perlustrat opimis [these 6 verses, in a different order, also occur in Oxford, Magdalen College, MS lat. 105]; *Scriptor,* Nunc pater o Beda tibi supplico tu michi te da/ Hostis ne preda sim per mea crimina feda; [last 2 verses in another hand:] Sancte pater Beda temptantis deprime feda/ Ne sibi sim preda protectoris michi te da.

4. f. 110: Extitit hic Beda doctor venerabilis idem . . . [7 couplets using the name "Beda" in the different grammatical cases, labelled in the margin "in nominativo casu" (twice), "in genitivo," etc.; also in the margin, "Isti versus extracti erant de quadam parva rotula doctoris gaskun," apparently in reference to Thomas Gascoigne (d. 1458); all this in the hand of Robert Elyot]; Iaru non Iarum sancto Bede dedit ortum [in the hand of Robert Elyot]. [f. 110v, blank]

II.

5. ff. 111–130: *Incipit prefacio Bede presbiteri in Actus Apostolorum missa Acce episcopo,* Domino in christo desiderantissimo et vere beatissimo acce episcopo beda perpetuam in domino salutem. Accepi creberimas beatitudinis tue litteras . . . , [f. 11v, Text:] *Incipit expositio in Actus Apostolorum, Primum quidem sermonem* . . . , De omnibus se dicit christi factis et dictis se scripsisse . . . cursum consumavi fidem servavi. Amen.

M. L. W. Laistner, ed., *Bedae Venerabilis Expositio Actuum Apostolorum et Retractatio.* Mediaeval Academy of America Publ. 35 (Cambridge, Mass. 1939) 3–90; this manuscript listed on p. xxxvi, n. 15. See also Laistner, *Hand-list,* 21.

6. ff. 130–131v: *Descriptio situs terre a Beato Beda provinciarum civitatum insularum huic libro congruendum* [*sic*], Acheldemach est ager sangwinis qui usque monstratur in bely . . . quod in eo populus stans desuper atque spectans ludos scenicos contemplaretur. *Explicit expositio bede presbiteri in Actus Apostolorum.*

Laistner, "Nomina regionum atque locorum de Actibus Apostolorum" in *Expositio* . . . , 149–58.

7. ff. 131v–170: *Incipit in epistola Iacobi Apostoli Exposicio venerabilis Bede presbiteri, Iacobus dei et domini nostri ihesu christi servus duodecim tribubus que sunt in dispersione salutem,* Dixit de hoc Iacobo apostolus paulus . . . Et hoc non ab inicio temporis alicuius sed ante omne seculum et nunc et in omnia secula seculorum. Amen. Amen. Amen. *Explicit exposicio venerabilis bede in epistola iude apostoli.*

Bede, Commentary on the Catholic Epistles, *PL* 93:9–130. Laistner, *Hand-list,* 31.

8. f. 170: [*quaestio* added in a cursive script:] Queritur utrum virgo maria in concepcione filii sui spiritu sancto in aliquo cooperata fueret . . . ipsa sola a deo sicud mulier viro commixta unde tota substancia christi filii de matre sua. [added in the same hand, with the author attribution in the margin:] *Hugo de Sancto victore,* Inter amorem huius mundi et amorem dei hoc distare . . . bibatur suavissimum poculum caritatis. [f. 170v, blank, except for erased pen trials, including: Edwardus dei gratia Rex Anglie dux ybernie; domine labia mea; Pater noster.]

HM 35300

Parchment, ff. i (contemporary parchment) + 170; 261 × 187 mm. A composite volume in 2 parts.

I. s. XV^med, ff. 1–110, ruled space: 182 × 125 mm. 1–13⁸ 14⁸(–7, 8). Catchwords in the innermost corner, sometimes enclosed by a scroll (ff. 32v, 40v); quires and leaves signed in letters and roman numerals. 2 columns of 32–40 lines, ruled in ink, usually frame only; pricking occasionally visible in the upper and outer margins. Written in an anglicana formata by 2 (?) scribes, the second somewhat inconsistent: i, ff. 1–8, 47va line 23–109v (except for the last 2 lines); ii, ff. 9–47va line 23. 5- to 3-line parted red and blue initials; full red and blue cascade border and red flourishing on f. 1; bracket borders in the same style for beginnings of other books (omitted for Book 4). 2-line blue initials with red flourishing; 1-line initials alternating red and blue in the chapter lists. Running headlines and chapter numbers added by a contemporary hand.

II. s. XIII^ex, ff. 111–170, ruled space: 186 × 138 mm. 1^{20} 2^{20} 3^{20}; note, however, that all the leaves appear to be singletons, stitched together and reinforced by a parchment strip wrapped around each gathering. Quires 1 and 2 signed in arabic numerals on the last leaf verso. 2 columns of 40–45 lines written above the top line; ruled in brown crayon and in lead; pricking often visible in the lower and outer margin. Written in an early anglicana script. 5- to 2-line blue initials with red flourishing, different from those in pt. **I.** The rubrics and some underscoring in the same red as the flourishing. Instructions to the rubricator in crayon. In the upper margin of f. 111 in the hand of the scribe, "Sancti spiritus assit nobis gratia."

Bound, s. XV, in whittawed leather over bevelled wooden boards; 2 fore edge brass clasps catching on the back cover, the straps restored; remains of 2 paper labels on the spine, the upper one illegible, the lower "K." On the back cover, a label under horn: "V. Beda de gestis Anglorum. Idem super actus apostolorum et epistolas canonicas. *2° fo.* et prassini" as is common on books from Syon Abbey. Some modern restoration.

Written in England, pt. **I** in the middle of the fifteenth century and pt. **II** at the end of the thirteenth. Belonged to Robert Elyot, fellow of All Souls College and vice-provost of Eton until his death in 1499. His characteristic profile face brackets and pointing hands occur mainly in pt. **II**, e.g., on ff. 121v, 124v, 125 (the hands) and on ff. 150, 155v, 164v (the face); these are in the same orange-tinged red ink as some of the underscoring and marginal notes; the faces, hands, underscoring and notes, including arts. 1 and 4, also occur in black ink (e.g. ff. 134v–135); N. R. Ker, "Robert Elyot's Books and Annotations," *The Library* ser. 5 vol. 30 (1975) 233–37 with plates. Given by him to the Bridgettine abbey of Syon at Isleworth, Middlesex, as attested by the note on f. i verso: "Liber domus Sancti Salvatoris de Syon ex dono magistri Roberti Elyot Anno domini 1490. Orate pro Anima eius." Identified as K.59 in the early sixteenth century catalogue of that abbey printed by M. Bateson, *Catalogue of the Library of Syon Monastery, Isleworth* (Cambridge 1898) 87; see Ker, *MLGB,* 185, and Emden, *BRUO,* 638. Belonged to Augustine Styward, who wrote his name on f. 1; given by him to the library of the church of St. James in Bury St. Edmunds in the year of its foundation, 1595: on f. i verso, "Augustinus Stywarde dono dedit Bibliothecae in Ecclesia D. Jacobi infra villam de Buria S. Edmundi Anno Domini 1595 Augusti 29 et Aetatis sue tricesimo sexto." Styward also owned Oxford, Bod. Lib., Bodley 130 (SC 27609), a herbarium from Bury. Regarding the Styward family, see W. Rye, *Genealogist* n.s. 1 (1884) 150–57 and 2 (1885) 34–42. On f. 1, s. XIX, "St. James' Library in Bury St. Eds."; on the front pastedown a small round label, "Church Congress Exhibition, 111."; the same label on New Haven, Yale University, Beinecke Library, MSS 287 and 417. Sold by St. James, Sotheby's, 12 July 1971, lot 36 with facsimile of the Syon inscription on f. i verso and with a plate of the back cover.

Secundo folio: [f. 3] et prassini; [f. 112] transito necessarium
Bibliography: Schenkl 4959. *Chronica,* 7.

HM 36336 England, s. XVI^{in}
ADAM OF EYNSHAM, MAGNA VITA SANCTI HUGONIS, abbrev.
fig. 147

1. ff. 1–95v: [Prologue of the abbreviator:] *Incipit prologus abbreviationis vite beati Hugonis Lincolniensis episcopi et confessoris,* Inspecta serie descriptionis vite beati Hugonis quam composuit [followed by a blank space] de quo in salutacione . . . hic ad capitula alia transferuntur. Ad maiorem autem tocius operis evidentiam premittuntur. Hic ante libellum primum capitula per ordinem singulorum librorum. [Prologue of Adam of Eynsham:] Dominis et amicis in christo carissimis Reverendo priori et qui cum eo sunt sanctis Withamensibus monachis servorum suorum minimus frater A. vite qui nunc est et future gaudia. Silencium michi . . . [f. 2v, Chapter list of Book 1:] *Incipiunt capitula primi libri,* Qualiter Hugo genitricis solacio destructus et . . . [f. 3, Text:] *Capitulum primum,* Hugo genitricis solacio tum necdum etatis metas excessisset orbatus est . . . propter accessum confluentis populi magis congruere ab oriali [*sic*] ipsius edis regione ad gloriam dei qui vivit et gloriatur super omnia, deus benedictus in secula. Amen.

The Long Abbreviation by an anonymous Carthusian of Adam of Eynsham's *Magna Vita Sancti Hugonis;* the complete version by Adam of Eynsham printed in D. L. Douie and H. Farmer, eds., *The Life of St. Hugh of Lincoln* 2 vols. (London 1961); this manuscript, at the time untraced, discussed on pp. l–li. The Long Abbreviation printed in *PL* 153:943–1114, with variants from the Prologue and Book 1, chapters 1–7 from this manuscript printed by J. F. Dimock, ed., *Giraldi Cambrensis Opera.* RS 21 (London 1877) 7:237–42. The other known manuscripts of the Long Abbreviation are Toulouse, Bibl. Mun. MS 483 (s. XIV; belonged to the Carthusians of Toulouse) and Edinburgh, National Library of Scotland, MS 9999, acquired by them in 1972 from the London Charterhouse (s. XIV^{in}); see description in Ker, *MMBL* 1:9–12.

2. ff. 95–96v: *Bulla specialis domini pape honorii tertii de canonizacione beatissimi et gloriosissimi Hugonis Lincolniensis episcopi,* Honorius episcopus servorum dei venerabili fratri episcopo . . . , Non repulit Dominus plebem suam . . . Datum viterbii xiii kal. martii Pontificatus nostri anno quarto; *Bulla generalis domini pape honorii de canonizacione et translacione beati hugonis Lincolniensis Episcopi,* Honorius episcopus et cetera Universis christi fidelibus . . . , Divine dignacio pietatis . . . Datum viterbii xiii kal. marcii Pontificatus nostri Anno quarto; *Item alia bulla de translacione eiusdem,* Honorius et cetera venerabili fratri episcopo Lincolniensi . . . , Cum venerabile corpus beati Hugonis . . . Datum viterbii Pontificatus nostri Anno 4to.

Three bulls of Honorius III relating to the canonization of Hugh of Lincoln; A. Potthast, *Regesta pontificum romanorum* . . . (Berlin 1874–75) n. 6195; printed by Dimock, 243–46.

3. f. 97: O quam grata dei pietas pia gratia . . . ; Deus qui beatum hugonem confessorem tuum . . . ; [4 lines ending incompletely, added by a contemporary hand:] Postea mirabar tunc non sine litibus esset/ Prima dies caussam [*sic*] percipe famis ait . . . [f. 97v, ruled, but blank]

The two prayers printed by Dimock, 246–47.

Parchment (monastic: thick and fuzzy on both sides), ff. ii (contemporary parchment) + 97 + ii (contemporary parchment); 274 × 204 (182 × 128) mm. $1\text{–}2^8$ 3^6 $4\text{–}5^8$ 6^8(–7, with no loss of text) 7–12^{8} 13^{4}. Catchwords in the lower margin; quires and leaves signed in letters and roman numerals; the leaves also signed a–d in the first half of the quire. 32–33 long lines, ruled in rose-colored ink, the final quire in crayon; single vertical bounding lines, with the top and bottom 2 lines full across; pricking visible in the lower and outer margins. Written in a well formed bastard secretary hand with chapter headings in a smaller script; occasional large looped bottom-line descenders. Opening initials on f. 1 for the rubric and prologue with black strapwork, tinted in red; one top-line ascender, f. 58v, in similar style; 2-line red initials; initials within the text slashed in red.

Bound after 1510, when the Dutch binder John Reynes immigrated to London, and apparently before 1519, when he discontinued use of his unsigned roll tool of a dog, a bird and a bee; see J. B. Oldham, *English Blind-Stamped Bindings* (Cambridge 1952) An.*b*(3) 556 used here in conjunction with his pineapple stamp, Oldham 437, and by the same author, *Shrewsbury School Library Bindings* (Oxford 1943) plate 9 of B:111.29, similar to the binding of HM 36336. Bound in brown calf over wooden boards with evidence of 2 fore edge straps dyed pink, closing to hooks (1 remains) on edge of back cover.

Written in the early years of the sixteenth century, possibly at the London Charterhouse. The preparation of the parchment and the careful attention paid to quire structure, script, chapter headings and punctuation are concomitant with Carthusian origin. Its Reynes binding would point to the London house (although there is no sign of their ex-libris), or to Henry V's Carthusian foundation at Sheen. Provenance unknown until it appears in the late nineteenth century at Belton House, Grantham, in the library of Sir Adelbert Wellington Brownlow (1844–1921), whose bookplate is on the front pastedown: Rietstap, vol. 1, pl. 332 but differenced by, on the first quarter, argent, a sinister hand couped at the wrist gules and, on the escutcheon, sable, a cross engrailed argent between 4 fleur-de-lis of the same; the motto "Opera illius mea sunt." Exhibition label (of the Victoria and Albert Museum?) affixed to the front pastedown, Case 88, exhibited by Earl Brownlow. Brownlow sales, Sotheby's, 15 April 1929, lot 785 and Sotheby's, 6 December 1971, lot 15 with a plate of the binding. Acquired by the Huntington Library at that time.

Secundo folio: Nosse quippe
Bibliography: Chronica, 7.

HM 36337 — England, s. XIII^{in}
FLORILEGIUM — *fig. 51*

1. ff. 1–3v [contemporary flyleaves, included in the foliation; ff. 1–2 are a bifolium from a missal, England, s. XII^{2}, here bound reversed]: [f. 1r–v, canon of the mass:] //fides cognita est . . . offerimus preclare maiestati tuę de tuis donis ac datis//; [f. 2r–v, prefaces, noted with neumes on 4-line staves with C or F clef indicated:] //cęlestis exercitus, ymnum glorię tuę canimus . . . Celi cęlorumque virtutes ac beata seraphim socia exultacione//; [f. 3, title:] Liber scintillarum, meditaciones beati Bernardi Et de trinitate cum multis aliis; [added later:] excepciones biblie; [f. 3v, contents of the Liber Scintillarum, s. XIII/XIV:] De caritate, De Paciencia . . . De personarum acceptis, De itinere; [f. 3v, contents of the volume, s. XV:] Libri contenti in hoc volumine videlicet Liber scintillarum vii cum versibus, Excepciones biblie, tractatus de verbis defectivis, De trasgressione [*sic*] ade, Beda de trinitate, Tractatus de sequentia sancti Michelis, De miseria humane condicionis, Pater noster expositus, Sermones qui sicut incipiunt Vide iacob scalam, Meditaciones bernardi.

2. ff. 4–54v: [Defensor of Ligugé] *Liber scintillarum primus. De caritate incipit,* Dominus dicit in evangelio Maiorem caritatem nemo habet . . . et multi sunt qui intrant per eam. *Liber scintillarum explicit.* [followed by an erasure of 2 lines; f. 55r–v, well washed material of undetermined date, illegible under ultraviolet light]

H. M. Rochais, ed., *Defensoris Liber Scintillarum. CC* 117 (1957) 1–308. Here in 7 books of 58 chapters in all. Additional extracts from the Fathers added in the outer margins in the fourteenth century by 2 hands; those on f. 6 added over an erased note; book numbers and occasionally topics added as running headlines. A list of 285 surviving manuscripts given by H. M. Rochais, "Les Manuscrits du 'Liber Scintillarum'," *Scriptorium* 4 (1950) 294–309; this manuscript not included.

3. f. 56: Infans vagit, ovis balat, rugire leones . . . est hominumque loqui quod dico prevalet omni. [12 verses on the voices of animals]; Excaturizat aves, pisces eventerat ille/ Ustulat hic porcos, excoriatque boves; Fons scaturit, vinum [?] scatet, pullos scaturizat/hustullat porcos excoriatque boves [the last 2 verses added in an anglicana script, s. XIII/XIV].

4. ff. 56v–60: [Poem on old age] Magne [*sic*] fuit quondam capitis reverentia cani . . . Et fugiunt freno non remorante dies/ Cernis ut ignavum corrumpunt ocia corpus. [ff. 60v–61, previous text washed; f. 61v, blank]

Anonymous poem in ca. 200 lines of elegiac couplets.

5. ff. 62–81: *Incipiunt exceptiones de libro Genesis. Quid sit annalis historia,* Annalis historia est rei facte per annum complete commemoratio. Kalendaria historia est alicuius insignis rei . . . [chapter 2:] *Quid sit febris effimera,* . . . [chapter 3:] *Quid sit allegoria,* . . . [chapter 4:] *Unde dicuntur elementa,* . . . [chapter 5:] *Sentencia platonis aristotilis Epicuri Moysi,* . . . [last chapter: *Quod petrus et paulus uno eodem die sint passi,* . . . :] Petrus vero crucifixus est in vaticano vico scilicet qui est extra civitatem ubi fiebant dolia. *Explicit actus apostolorum.*

Definitions, descriptions and exegesis on the Old and New Testaments, with emphasis on the latter; occasional citations from the Fathers and Zacharias.

6. f. 81: *Ex dictis egregii pape gregorii,* Tribus moris culpa perpetratur, Suggestione, Delectatione, Consensu . . . , *Item Gregorius,* Quattuor moris peccatum perpetratur in corde . . .

7. ff. 81v–83v: *Incipit de verbis defectivis,* Plurima deficiunt vario cum tempore verba/ Deficiunt alia plurima per genera . . . Que bene verba tenet versificalis apex. [6 verses; Walther, *Initia* 14194]; *Versus de verbis defectivis,* Cedo, sodes, faxo, cepi, sis, infit et inquit/ Nolo, facello, volo, queso, capello, fero . . . Designata tunc dulciter ista placunt. [6 verses]; *Tractatus de verbis defectivis,* Sunt verba defectiva ut donacius ait, Alia per modos ut cedo . . . Super piget redet inflectuntur. *Explicit.*

8. ff. 84–87: [Hildebert of Le Mans] *De transgressione ade triformi,* Vicit adam veterem gula, gloria vana, cupido . . . Nox aurora dies umbra figura deus. *Explicit.*

Hildebert of Le Mans, 69 short verse pieces generally in the order listed by P. Von Moos, *Hildebert von Lavardin, 1056–1133.* Pariser Historische Studien 3 (Stuttgart 1965) 373–74: reversed are his nn. 3–4, 22–23, 35–36; n. 65 is omitted; the last 2, not on his list, are Walther, *Initia* 15912 and 11581.

9. ff. 87v–90: *Beda de trinitate,* Omnipotens deus pater et filius et spiritus sanctus, unus atque trinus. Unus videlicet in natura . . . Vigilare dei est in defensionem electorum suorum et ultionem inimicorum se manifestum demonstrare. *Explicit.*

Eucher of Lyons, extract from *De formulis spiritualis intelligentiae,* printed in *PL* 42:1199–1206 as Ps. Augustine, *De essentia divinitatis,* pt. I.

10. ff. 90–95: *Tractatus de sequencia Sancti Michaelis,* Nota hoc nomen canticum nec stricte nec large accepi . . . Idem est ergo alleluia quod laudate universalem id est dominum. *Explicit.*

11. ff. 95–97v: [Brief exegetical texts with rubrics as follow:] *De septem hostibus,* Septem sunt hostes de quibus in deuteronomio dicit, per unam viam venient . . . ; *De triplici modo compassione,* Triplex est compassionis modus . . . ; *De Sunamite et helyseo,* Dixit sunamitis viro suo de heliseo . . . ; *Ubi antichristus nascetur,* Nascetur antichristus in babilone de tribu Danielis iuxta quod Iacobus ait . . . ; *De tribus missis in natali domini,* Tres misse que in natale domini celebrantur . . . ; *De pascha,* In diebus hiis est pascha dei id est transitus quando transivit de hoc mundo ad patrem . . . [f. 97, blank; f. 97v:] *De mendacio,* Perdes omnes qui loquuntur mendacium . . . ; *De perfectione vite,* Tria sunt que ducunt hominem ad vite perfectionem, Cordis contritio . . .

12. ff. 97v–109v: *Incipit liber de miseria humane conditionis editus a lothario diacono cardinali sanctorum Sergii et Bachi qui postea Innocentius iii*^{us} *appellatus est,* [Prologue:] Domino patri Karissimo petro portuensi episcopo Lotharius . . . Modicum ocii quod inter multas angustias . . . , [Text:] Quare de vulva . . . terrores, fames, sitis, frigus, cauma, sulphur et ignis ardens in secula seculorum. *Explicit liber Domini pape Innocentii iii de Contemptu Mundi.*

M. Maccarone, ed., *Lotharii Cardinalis (Innocentii III) De Miseria Humane Conditionis.* Thesaurus Mundi (Lugano 1955); see also R. E. Lewis, ed., *Lotario dei Segni (Pope Innocent III) De Miseria Condicionis Humane.* The Chaucer Library (Athens, Georgia 1978), with list of manuscripts, HM 36337 not included.

13. ff. 110–112: *Pater noster,* hec est oratio dominica ceteris oracionibus omnibus et instituentis auctoritate sublimior et utilitate petitionum fecundior . . . ad illas delicias dilectores suos nos assumat summe bonus ihesus christus qui est benedictus in secula Amen.

14. ff. 112–165v: Septem scale quibus ascenduntur regna celorum prima castitas . . . [f. 163:] Preceptum obediencia obedienciam signa comitantur. *Explicit;* [f. 163v, in the upper margin, *Additiones ut supra:*] *Beda in omelis illa,* Si diligitis me mandata mea servate et cetera, Quinquagesima die post occisionem agni data est lex . . . [followed by 11 other sermons; f. 165:] Sepe in evangelio causa designatur nomine sui effectus . . . Omnia michi ex patre nota in quibus electorum salus consistit per me scietis. [f. 166, blank]

Exegetical passages on texts from the gospels; frequent use of texts of the Fathers and occasional distinctions in the margins in schematic form.

15. f. 166v: [Charm to staunch blood] *Pur seink estanger,* Iesu crist notre seignur el flum Iordan entra/ Cent cinquaunte veines de euue i truva/ Cent cinquaunte veines chescun home a/ estaunche saunc par tutes les vertuz ke damnedeus a. [f. 167, blank]

16. f. 167v: Table of roman numerals and their Latin names, one to one million. [ff. 168–169v, previous text washed; notes in lead point on f. 169v]

Parchment, ff. 169 (of which 1–3 are medieval flyleaves; previous text washed from ff. 55r–v, 60v–61, 168–169); 163 × 120 (117 × 78, 107 × 89, etc.) mm. 1^{2}(+ 3, added as a flyleaf) $2–7^{8}$ 8^{4}(through f. 55) 9^{10}(–7, 8) $10–13^{8}$ 14^{2}(ff. 96–97) $15–23^{8}$. Quires 17–22 signed b–g in lower inner corner of the first recto. Art. 2 in 25 long lines; the other texts in 2 columns of 34–35 lines; both written on the top line; ruled in crayon and lead point; pricking visible. Written by 2 people: i, art. 2, in a spiky littera textualis; ii, ff. 62–165v, in a small spiky littera textualis. Art. 2, 3- to 2-line initials up to f. 25v (thereafter uncompleted) and rubrics in orange-tinged red; in the other texts, 3- to 2-line initials, placed outside the written space, in red, dark green or light blue. Running headlines added to art. 2, s. XIV^{in}. Invocations to the Trinity and the Holy Spirit in upper margins, ff. 84, 98, 122, 130.

Bound in contemporary (?) calf (varnished later) over oak boards; evidence of a fore edge strap closing to pin on back cover; tabs to mark texts on lower edge of ff. 81, 97, 112; pastedowns removed; spine crudely strengthened with a piece of brown leather (the same repair on the binding of HM 28174, also a Tollemache book).

Written in England in the first third of the thirteenth century. Cloth label on spine: "MS 8." Belonged to the Tollemache Library, Helmingham Hall: n. 24 in the old Helmingham catalogue; label on inside of front cover: "L.J.II.6" altered to "L.H.II.28" and "24" in pencil. For a brief history of this library, see the Sotheby catalogue, 14 June 1965, iii–viii. Acquired by the Huntington Library from Alan G. Thomas, Catalogue 28 (1972) n. 4.

Secundo folio: [f. 5] Qui diligit me
Bibliography: Schenkl 4705. *Chronica,* 7–8.

HM 36701 DEVOTIONS

Flanders (?), s. XVI^{1}
fig. 31

1. ff. 1–3: Hec sunt precepta et ceremonie atque iudicia que mandavit Dominus Deus vester . . . et fecerimus omnia precepta eius coram domino deo nostro sicut mandavit nobis.

Deut. 6, 1–25.

2. ff. 3v–4v [rubric on f. 3]: *Sequitur Ad Deum in cruce pendentem Oratio devota,* O Dulcis ihesu vulnera cor meum amore tuo, ut penitentie et amoris lachryme sint michi panes die ac nocte . . . ; *Alia ad Deum Oratio,* Per signum sancte crucis de inimicis nostris libera nos deus noster, with versicle, response and prayer, Deus qui sanctam crucem ascendisti . . . ; *Alia Oratio,* Domine ihesu christe fili dei vivi pone passionem . . . ; *Alia Oratio,* Obsecro te domine ihesu christe ut passio tua sit virtus mea . . .

3. ff. 5–15: Gospel pericope from John (1, 1–14) and the prayer, Protector in te sperantium . . . [Perdrizet, 25]; Passion according to John (18, 1–19, 42); gospel pericopes from Luke (1, 26–38), Matthew (2, 1–12) and Mark (16, 14–20); *Oratio,* Concede quesumus omnipotens deus ut qui unigenitum tuum redemptorem nostrum ad celos ascendisse credimus . . . [Bruylants, *Oraisons,* 2, n. 136].

4. ff. 15v–27v: Prayers as follow: *Oratio Dominica,* Pater noster qui es in celis . . . ; *Salutatio Angeli,* Ave maria gratia plena . . . ; *Oratio devotissima,* Maria mater gratie mater misericordie . . . ; *Symbolum fidei,* Credo in deum patrem omnipotentem . . . ; *Benedictiones mane et sero dicende pro gratia,* Benedicat me imperialis maiestas protegat me regalis divinitas . . . [*HE,* 88]; *Alia recommendatio ad Deum,* Benedictio dei patris omnipotentis et filii et spiritus sancti venerande trinitatis et individue unitatis . . . ; *Oratio sancti Augustini pro peccatis Devotissima,* Deus propicius esto michi peccatori . . . [*HE,* 125]; *Oratio ante ymaginem pietatis d*[*evota*?], Precor te amantissime domine ihesu christe propter illam eximiam charitatem tuam . . . [Wilmart, 378, n.]; *Post elevacionem et sacramenti perceptionem oratio,* Anima christi sanctifica me . . . [Leroquais, *LH* 2:340]; *Ad Deum salvatorem nostrum Oratio,* Ave rex noster fili david redemptor mundi quem prophete predixerunt . . . with versicle and prayer, Omnipotens sempiterne deus qui unigenitum tuum salvatorem nostrum carnem sumere, crucem, coronam spineam . . . ; *Ad gloriosam virginem mariam Oratio,* Ave sanctissima maria mater dei regina celi porta paradisi . . . ; *Beati Bernardi Ad Virginem Mariam oratio,* Per te accessum habeamus ad filium tuum o benedicta inventrix gratie . . . ; *De sancto Michaele archangelo oratio,* Sancte Michael archangele domini nostri ihesu christi qui venisti in adiutorium populo dei . . . ; *Ad proprium Angelum oratio,* Obsecro te angelice spiritus cui ego indignus peccator ad custodiendum commissus sum . . . , followed by an antiphon, Angele bone qui michi datus es custos . . . , a versicle, response and prayer, Deus cuius providentia humano generi supernorum spirituum presidium subministrat . . . ; *De sancto Iohanne baptista oratio,* Sancte Iohannes baptista electe dei . . . , with versicle, response and prayer, Sancti Iohannis baptiste nos quesumus domine preclara comitetur oratio . . . ; *Ad omnes sanctos patriarchas et prophetas,* Sancti patriarche et prophete per quos omnipotens deus multa miracula seculis dignatus est ostendere . . . ; *Ad omnes sanctos Dei Antiphona,* Sancti dei omnes intercedere dignemini . . . , with versicle, response and prayer, Omnipotens sempiterne deus qui nos omnium sanctorum tuorum merita . . . ; *De dulcissimo nomine ihesu Oratio,* Sponse matris ecclesie ihesu rex summe glorie . . . ; *Canticum sanctorum Ambrosii et Augustini incipit,* Te Deum laudamus . . . ; *Ante sacram Communionem oratio,* Domine non sum dignus ut intres sub tectum meum sed tu domine qui dixisti . . . ; *Oratio,* O Salutaris hostia que celi pandis ostium bella premunt hostilia . . . ; *Post sacramenti Communionem Oratio,* Anima christi sanctifica me . . . [Leroquais, *LH* 2:340; same prayer on f. 19r–v]; *Alia devota Oratio,* Hec sunt convivia que tibi placent que nobis orphanis reliquisti. O patris sapentia natus de virgine . . . ; *Item alia oratio,* Vera perceptio corporis et sanguinis tui . . .

Parchment, ff. i (paper) + ii (parchment) + 27 + ii (parchment) + i (paper); 107 × 75 (83 × 50) mm. 1^4 2–3^8 $4^8(-8)$. 19 long lines, frame ruled in brown ink. Written in an italic script with rubrics usually in a humanistic script.

Illumination, f. 3v, 12-line, depicting the Crucifixion with Mary and John on one side, and a man kneeling in prayer at Jesus' left; 2 smaller illuminations, 8-line, on f. 19v (Ave rex noster fili david), showing Jesus in glory holding a globe and blessing, and on f. 20v (Ave sanctissima maria mater dei), the Virgin and Child in glory standing on a crescent. A 3-line initial on f. 5 and 2-line initials as gold branches on shaded square grounds of blue, green or red, or as white branches on a shaded gold ground; 1-line initials in painted gold on square colored grounds. Rubrics in pale red ink. Marginalia, in a contemporary hand, on the back flyleaf, f. ii verso: pie Iesu Domine Miserere nostri.

HM 36701

Bound, s. XVI (?) in parchment over pasteboard, with the title "pia scripta <?> et cetera" written on the spine and on the front cover; parchment flyleaves from a French printed book (calendar?), s. XV or XVI, text barely visible horizontally along the outer and inner margins.

Written, according to a note in a cursive hand on f. i, in Brussels in 1539; also on f. i, the name "P. noels," and on the back flyleaf, f. iii verso, "F.N." On the front pastedown an armorial bookplate with the legend "Reverendus Admodum Dominus Johannes Franciscus Bosselaer Sancte Romane Ecclesie Protonotarius." An attached English book dealer's slip states that the manuscript was in the Renier Chalon collection. Given to the Huntington Library in 1972 by Mr. and Mrs. James Graham.

Bibliography: Chronica, 8.

HM 37539 England, s. XV[1]
ROSARIUM

1. ff. 1–151v: [*Rosarium,* first leaf missing] //unde augustinus super Iohannem omelia finali Petrus apostolus . . . , *Abstinencia* duplex est scilicet corporalis et spiritualis. Abstinencia corporalis est ordinata gubernacio corporum in victu et vestitu . . . , *Abusiones* 12 sunt per augustinum, prima sapiens sine operibus bonis . . . , *Acceptio* personarum est iniusticia qua prefertur persona per se propter causam indebitam . . . *Accidia* . . . *Accusacio* . . . *Addicio* . . . *Ymago* triplex est scilicet equalitatis imitacionis et representacionis . . . *Ypocrisis* est exterior similacio sanctitatis . . . *Zelus* duplex est scilicet bonus et malus. Bonus zelus aliquando sumitur pro sponsali dilectione . . . et Iacobus 3° ubi enim est zelus et contencio ibi inconstancia et omne opus pravum et cetera. [rubric erased]

Stegmüller 10080. The anonymous late fourteenth century Lollard collection of extracts known as the *Rosarium,* here containing 303 entries but missing 2 (?) at the beginning and at least 1 on the leaf torn out after f. 63 (between the entries for *Labor* and *Lex*); this manuscript belongs to the third and shortest version. See A. Hudson, "A Lollard Compilation and the Dissemination of Wycliffite Thought," *Journal of Theological Studies* 23 (1972) 65–81, listing 14 manuscripts of this version, and, by the same author, "A Lollard Compilation in England and Bohemia," *ibid.* 25 (1974) 129–40 with 2 more manuscripts of this version; HM 37539 not recorded. See also C. von Nolcken, ed., *The Middle English Translation of the Rosarium theologie, a selection.* Middle English Texts 10 (Heidelberg 1979).

2. ff. 152–154 [added in a contemporary hand, possibly that of the scribe of the main text] Gloriam propriam querit . . . [brief gloss on John 7, 18]; a series of biblical passages supporting the articles of the Creed; Sex sunt note in quibus totus cantus disponitur, scilicet ut re mi fa sol la. *Ut* prima petri 2°, *Ut* abstineatis vos a carnali et spirituali desiderio illicito; *Re* Iacobi 4°, *Re*sistite diabolo et fugiet a vobis . . . Et si quis has notas transgreditur deo discordat; Genesis ex le nu deu Iosue iudicumque . . . [Walther, *Initia* 7140; mnemonic verses in syllables for the order of the books of the Bible, the numbers of the chapters written above the name of each book]; a short outline of biblical passages to be read throughout the periods of the liturgical year with a note on their relation-

ship to the year; Confortat stimulat arcet . . . [12 verbs, each with a biblical reference suprascript, e.g., on the 3 above: Luc. 22, Reg. 19, Tob. 8]; [G]allus habet 7 proprietates. Prima est antequam cantat verberat se alis suis . . . [paragraph with moralization on the "gallus" to mankind]; Marchus romanis sed iohannis asianis/ Lucas achaiis matheus scribit ebreis [Walther, *Initia* 10679, in a second hand]; Sectus ysaias lapidatus et ieremias . . . [Walther, *Initia* 17447, in the second hand]; Bernardus, multiplica prebendas, labora ad archidiaconatum aspr<damaged> ad episcopatum gradatim ascendes sed in puncto ad inferna descend<damaged> [in the first hand]; Cur homo torquetur: ut ei meritum cummuletur . . . ne fastus ei dominetur . . . [Walther, *Initia* 3927, in a third hand, written in *distinctio* form, each line followed by the revelant biblical source]; Iob probat inclinat paulum sese manifestat/ In ceco purgat maria punit herodem [Walther, *Initia* 9864, in the third hand]; under the heading *De hereditate sacerdocium,* a list of biblical sources in a fourth hand.

3. f. 154: [Historical verses in the fourth hand:] Mens caro conardus cui lex improperabit/ princeps edwardus caroli sedem vacavit; Christi millenis ter c decies quater annis/ ffrancorum venus rubet equorum luce Iohannis/ De quo gaudere potest anglia Francia flere [also in HM 28174, f. 143v]; Ter c M decies sex unus et ille/ luce tua maure vehemens fuit impetus aure [also in HM 28174, f. 143v, referring to a great wind on 15 February 1361]; *Schrevesbery,* Anno domini millesimo cccc^{mo} tercio fuit bellum apud Schrevesbery [note on the battle of Shrewsbury, 1403, in the second (?) hand].

Parchment, ff. ii (paper) + ii (modern parchment) + 154 + ii (paper); 186 × 123 (139 × 90) mm. $1^8(-1)$ 2^8 $3–6^{10}$ 7^8 8^8(-1 torn out after f. 63 with loss of text) $9–13^8$ $14–16^{10}$ 17^8 18^6. Catchwords enclosed in ink frames; quires signed in arabic numerals on the last leaf verso; quires and leaves signed in letters and roman numerals in the normal position. 36 long lines ruled in lead; pricking in the outer margin, with 2 holes for the last line. Main text written by one person in an English book hand influenced by anglicana; additions (arts. 2 and 3) in several other hands. First initial of each alphabetical section, 4-line, in parted red and blue with red flourishing; secondary initials, 3-line, in blue with red flourishing, sometimes including a face or grotesque (e.g. ff. 19v, 23v, 56v, 65v); alternating red and blue paragraph marks. Occasional marginalia with additional texts, often trimmed by the binder; verses on f. 10v, added to the section *Antichristus,* Cum fuerint anni complete [*sic*] mille ducenti . . . [Walther, *Initia* 3617]; on f. 22v, added to the section *Columbe,* Grana legit volitat sociata cadavera vitat . . . [Walther, *Initia* 7291].

Bound, s. XVIII, in Dutch (?) calf with gilt tooled panels on the spine and the title "Concordanti [*sic*] Bibliorum"; covers blind tooled with border and corner fleurons; red morocco label pasted on the spine, "333."

Written in England in the first half of the fifteenth century. Among the erased pen trials on f. 154, s. XV, "Ric[ardus ?] pruton." Belonged to the Lincolnshire antiquary Maurice Johnson (1688–1755) of Ascough Hall. According to a long note in his hand, f. ii r–v, it was given to him by "M[r] Ferrour de Sancto Botulpho" in 1728, and it was n. XCIX in the catalogue of Ascough Hall Library. The note also explains that the small painted medallion of Moses on f. iii was copied by Johnson's son from a drawing by Dr. William Stukeley (1687–1765) of a medal in the latter's collection. On the front pastedown, Johnson's armorial bookplate, engraved by George Vertue, and a pencilled shelfmark "Crassus.E.16." Acquired by the Huntington Library from Alan Thomas (London) 1973.

Secundo folio: [now f. 1] unde augustinus
Bibliography: Chronica, 8.

HM 37542 Spain, 1611 (?)
SALCEDO, RELACION DEL COMERCIO DE LAS INDIAS

ff. 1–10: *Relacion sacada de los papeles del comercio y trato de las yndias Con los Reynos de espania y de unas probincias de ellas a otras—Relator El doctor salçedo,* Ano de 602 se despacho cedula de su magestad . . . lo demas adbirtiendo muy particularmente de lo que en ella se contiene. [f. 10v, blank]

Excerpts of documents written from 1602 to 1611 regarding shipping between Spain and the New World.

Paper (watermark generally as *Croix Latine,* Briquet 5704, Perpignan 1595, but here with the initials B.F.), ff. 10; 290 × 205 (275 × 155) mm. 5 bifolia of which the first and the last appear to function as folded sheets while the middle 3 bifolia are placed inside one another to make a gathering of 6 leaves. 38–39 long lines, unruled, and set to the far right of the page, leaving no margin on that side. Written in a cursive script. 2 sets of contemporary or slightly later foliation on ff. 3–10 as 742–749 (cancelled) and 279–286; the contemporary foliation on ff. 1–2 has been cropped, and may read 740–741, 277–278 or (if these leaves belong at the end) 750–751, 279–280 (?).

Formerly bound with HM 177, vol. 2; separated in 1975.

Written in Spain after 1611, the last date mentioned in the text. On f. 1, upper left corner, "39" in ink, possibly indicating its number in a series of Spanish documents; in center of upper margin, "33," in pencil. See description of HM 177 for provenance.

HM 39465 England, s. XV^med^
ASTRONOMICAL MISCELLANY *fig. 110*

1. f. i verso: *Elementa; Qualitates; Tempus; Humores; Etates* [with 4 items listed for each, followed by a discussion of the humors]; A nona noctis donec sit tercia luna . . . [Walther, *Initia* 56].

2. ff. 1–18v: Tractatus de spera in 4^or^ capitula dividimus dicentes primo quid sit spera . . . [f. 2, Text:] Universalis mundi machina in duo dividitur scilicet ethereum et elementarem regionem . . . aut deus nature patitur aut mundana machina dissolvetur. *Explicit tractatus de* [small space filled by a contemporary hand: *machina mundi*] *R. Elys.*

Extracts from Johannes de Sacrobosco, *De Sphaera;* Thorndike and Kibre, 1602. For the full text, see L. Thorndike, *The Sphere of Sacrobosco and its Commentators* (Chicago 1949) 76–117. Marginalia on ff. 1–3v in italic hands, s. XV^ex^ and XVI^med^.

3. ff. 18v–19v: Diagrams and notes regarding eclipses of the sun and the signs of the zodiac.

4. ff. 20–30: *Hic incipit practica Astrolabii,* Nomina instrumentorum sunt hec: primum est armilla suspensoria ad capiendum altitudinem . . . et qualis fuerit comparacio punctorum ad 12, talis est comparacio stature tue ad planitiem et cetera. *Explicit practica Astrolabii R.E.*

Messahala, *De operatione vel utilitate astrolabii;* printed by R. T. Gunther, *Early Science in Oxford* (Oxford 1929) 5:217–31.

5. ff. 30v–37: [rubric added by a contemporary hand:] *Hic incipit Compotus manualis secundum usum Oxoniensem,* Filius esto dei celum bonus accipe grates/ Fructus alit canos et gallica bellica danos . . . [Prose:] Est autem primus versus discurrens per 28 loca designans ciclum solarem . . . Solsticium estus sic dat baptista iohannes. *Explicit compotus manualis et cetera.*

John of Garland; Thorndike and Kibre, 561 and Walther, *Initia* 6525; verses interspersed with prose sections.

6. ff. 37v–44v: [rubric added by a contemporary hand:] *Hic incipit Algorismus secundum usum Oxoniensem,* Hec Algorismus Ars presens dicitur in qua/ Talibus indorum fruimur bis 5 figuris . . . Tali quesita radix patet arte reperta. *Explicit et cetera.* [followed by multiplication tables; f. 45, text washed and now illegible]

Alexander de Villa Dei; R. Steele, ed., *The Earliest Arithmetics in English.* EETS es 118 (Oxford 1922) 72–79, vv. 1–258, with Latin prose sections after vv. 142, 147, 151, 158, 166, 174.

7. ff. 45v–62v: *De impressionibus,* Ad noticiam impressionum habendam secundum doctrinam aristotilis in primo metheororum . . . ad 2^{m} dicendum quod fulmine et huiusmodi et non tonitruum sicut creditur a wlgis et cetera. [f. 63, blank]

Thorndike and Kibre, 55 (?); also in Cambridge, Gonville and Caius College, MS 402 (411), ff. 204–214.

8. ff. 63v–64: [Notes in prose and verse on weights and measures] Nota quod ista figura 1 dicitur scrupulus et denotat id quod pondus 20^{ti} granorum ferri vel ordei . . . ; Collige triticeis medicine pondera granis/ Grana quater v scrupuli pro pondere sume . . . [Thorndike and Kibre, 234; Walther, *Initia* 3027]; Scrupulus est pondus 1 d. . . . omnium aliorum ponderat duas marcas et cetera. [f. 64v, blank except for pen trials, see below]

Parchment (poor quality), ff. iii (early modern paper) + i (contemporary parchment) + 64 + iii (early modern paper); 157 × 117 (110 × 80) mm. 1^{10} $2–5^{12}$ $6^{8}(-7, 8)$. Catchwords in right lower margin, underlined in red; leaf signatures in arabic numerals in the last 2 quires. 21–30 long lines, frame ruled in brown crayon. Written in a poor secretary script. Plain 3- and 2-line red initials; on f. 29, initial in the shape of a dragon. Verse brackets, paragraph marks and underlining of rubrics in red; nota bene signs filled in red in the margins. Running headlines on ff. 45v–59v. Diagrams on ff. 17, 18r–v, 19, 28, 44v. Contemporary foliation in arabic numerals, 1–34.

Bound, s. XVIII, in English panelled calf with red morocco label on the spine, "Sphaera &C., MS."

Written in England in the middle of the fifteenth century by R. Elys, who gives his name on f. 18v, his initials on f. 30, and his monogram on f. 44v. On f. iv, an erased ex libris (?), an erased prayer, "O mater christi . . . ," and a faded recipe "for a salet," s. XV^{ex}. On f. 64, s. XVI^{med}, both names in the same hand: "Robert Lawes of Sarsingam in norffolke" and "John hutchenson scholemaister of Castleacre in the afforesayd countie." On f. 1, s. XVI^{ex}, "Liber Guil[elmi] Martialis Tractatus de mundi machina per R. Elys vide in fine huius." Of the seventeenth century: f. 64v, "Liber iste est meus hyndus [?]

nomine dicor," "Thomas Cary" and, f. iv by the same hand, "Capt."; also on f. iv, "Precium x . . ." written over by the signature of Robert Davies (ca. 1658–1710) of Llannerch and Gwysaney. N. 22 in the 1740 catalogue of the Davies library (that number in ink on the front pastedown) and n. 73 in the 1778 catalogue; for the history of the collection, see H. D. Emanuel, "The Gwysaney Manuscripts," *The National Library of Wales Journal* 7 (1952) 326–43. Not in the listing of the Gwysaney manuscripts in the HMC, *6th Report,* pt. I (1887–88) 418–21, not placed on deposit in the National Library of Wales, 1947–59, nor in the Davies-Cooke sale of the collection, Sotheby's, 15 June 1959. Book dealer's label, s. XX, on the front pastedown: William Wesley & Son, 28 Essex Street, Strand, London. Belonged to the Royal Meteorological Society, though not in Ker, *MMBL* 1:230–31; their sale, Sotheby's, 9 July 1973, lot 51 to the Huntington Library.

Secundo folio: universalis mundi
Bibliography: Chronica, 8.

HM 39467 — France, s. XV^ex^
PRAYER ROLL

1. Penitential psalms and litany, including Gervasius and Protasius among the martyrs; Hilary, Julianus, Saturninus, Hippolytus, Denis, Maurice and Eustachius among the confessors; Gemma, Neomadia, Radegundis and Sapientia among the virgins.

2. Short hours of the Dead; hymn, Veni creator spiritus, mentes tuorum visita . . . [*RH* 21204].

3. Short hours of the Conception, Eya mea labia nunc annunciate . . . [*RH* 5307].

4. Prayers as follow: *De beatissima atque sanctissima trinitate,* Te invocamus, te adoramus, te laudamus . . . with versicle, response and prayer, Omnipotens sempiterne deus qui dedisti famulis tuis in confessione . . . ; [to the Trinity] Domine sancte pater omnipotens eterne deus qui coequalem . . . , Domine ihesu christe fili dei vivi qui es verus . . . , Domine spiritu sancte deus qui coequalis . . . [*HE,* 124–25]; *Ad dominum nostrum ihesum christum,* O Beatissime domine ihesu christe respice digneris super me miserum peccatorem . . .

5. *Quiconques dira ceste oraison cy apres escripte en passant par ung cymitiere* . . . , Avete omnes anime fideles . . . with the prayer, Domine ihesu christe salus et liberacio . . . [Leroquais, *LH* 2:341].

6. Mon benoist dieu Ie croy de cuer et confesse de bouche . . . [Sonet 1150].

Parchment, 1 roll composed of 7 membranes of varying length (from 150 to 690 mm.); 360 × 18 centimeters (width of text: 10 centimeters). Ruled in pale red ink; pricking still present. Written in 2 sizes of a bâtarde script according to liturgical function.

Three miniatures, the width of the text, framed by a simple painted gold band: (Penitential psalms), 75 mm. high, David kneeling before a half-figure of God the Father who appears in the sky; quite badly rubbed; (Hours of the Dead), 90 mm., the Three Living and the Three Dead; (Hours of the Conception), 75 mm., the meeting of Joachim and Anne at the Golden Gate. Two historiated initials, approximately 4-line, one (Avete omnes anime fideles) with a skull, the other (Mon benoist dieu) with Jesus the Redeemer. 4- and 3-line initials in blue with white shading against a pale flesh-tone ground with gold filigree; 2- and 1-line initials in painted gold against square grounds of blue, brown or flesh-tone; ribbon line fillers in the same colors. Rubrics in pale pink.

Written in France. Belonged to F. S. Ferguson. Acquired by the Huntington Library in April 1973 from the book dealer J. F. T. Rodgers, *Catalogue* 3 (London 1973) n. 37.

Bibliography: Chronica, 8.

HM 39872 England, s. XV$^{3/4}$
JACOBUS MAGNUS, BOOKE OF GOOD CONDICIONS, trans.

ff. 1–122v: Here begynneth the tabill of þe Rubriches of the booke of good condicions. Otherwyse called the Sophiloge of wysdom. The whiche seid booke is deuided in v partes. The first parte spekith of the vii dedely synnes and of Remedies ageyns theym . . . *The first part,* Here begynneth the Rubriches of the first parte. First how pride displesith god . . . [f. 3v, Text:] *Here begynneth the first part of this booke called good condicions, the which spekith of þe remedies þat is ageyns the vii dedly synnes. And first how pride displeseth god. The first chapitre,* Pride wolde compare to God in as muche as thei glorifi in þey self and in the goodes that they haue of the whiche thinges the gloire is principally due to god . . . wherby it apperith þat the hoope of theym availleth litil that seith that this worlde shall endure right longe. *Here endeth the booke called the Sophiloge of wysdome otherwyse called the booke of good condicions. Deo gracias.*

An English translation of the *Livre de Bonnes Meurs,* itself a paraphrased translation of Jacques Legrand, *Sophilogium.* HM 39872 is of the same English version as Glasgow, University Library, Hunterian T.3.16 (78), but different from the Caxton translation printed by Caxton himself in 1487, by Pynson in 1494 and by Wynkyn de Worde in 1507. See B. Lindström, "The English Versions of Jacques Legrand's *Livre de Bonnes Meurs,*" *The Library* ser. 6 vol. 1 (1979) 241–54 and "Book of Good Manners," *ibid.* ser. 6 vol. 2 (1980) 224, discussing this manuscript. HM 39872 lacks one bifolium between ff. 27–28, containing part of Book 1, chapter 10 and the beginning of chapter 11.

Parchment, ff. i (modern parchment) + 122 + i (modern parchment); 224 × 156 (135 × 88) mm. 1–3^{8} 4^{8}(–4 and 5 after f. 27 with loss of text) 5–15^{8} 16^{4}. Catchwords in the center or right-center of the lower margin; quires and leaves signed in letters and roman numerals. 23–24 long lines, ruled in pale red ink, with the top and bottom 2 lines full across; slash pricking in the 3 outer margins. Written in a bastard secretary script.

Spaces of 16 and 10 lines reserved on ff. 59v (Part 3) and 102 (Part 5), presumably for miniatures; the spaces of 16, 17 and 9 lines on ff. 3, 49v and 77v may also have been intended for miniatures, although Parts 1, 2 and 4 begin on the following pages (3v, 50, 78). 5- to 3-line initials in blue and pink with white designs on gold grounds, ink spray border including acanthus and strawberries (?) imitative of French or Flemish decoration, in C-shape (f. 1), the length of text and across the top margin (f. 78) or the length of the text (ff. 3v, 50, 59v). 3-line initials in gold on blue/pink grounds; those on ff. 6v and 95v with foreign-influenced sprays; initials within the text and some top-line ascenders daubed with yellow. Paragraph marks alternating blue and pink; rubrics in the same deep rose-colored pink; some pink and blue jigsaw line fillers. Running headlines, s. XVI^ex, reading "the firste part" through f. 27v; from f. 23 on, the numbers of the parts given as "f" (for "first"?) on part 1, and thereafter in roman numerals.

Bound, 1974, in quarter leather and wooden boards, 2 fore edge clasps; previous binding, s. XIX, in tan calf, blind tooled.

Written in England in the third quarter of the fifteenth century. On the front pastedown, bookplate of the Rev. Henry Campbell, chaplain to the 18th Earl of Shrewsbury; bequeathed by him in 1874 to Beaumont College, Old Windsor, Berkshire; see M. F. Bond, "Some Early Books at Beaumont College," *Berkshire Archaeological Journal* 54 (1954–55) 53–55. Sale of the Beaumont manuscripts, Christie's, 28 June 1973, lot 49 with plate of f. 1. Acquired by the Huntington Library from Harry A. Levinson (Beverly Hills) in 1973.

Secundo folio: [f. 2, Chapter list] gouerne and teche; [f. 4, Text] eete of the fruit
Bibliography: Chronica, 8.

HM 41537 — Northern France, s. XIII^in
PETER THE CHANTER, VERBUM ABBREVIATUM — *figs. 52, 160*

ff. 1–98v: Verbum abbreviatum fecit dominus super terram. Si enim verbum de sinu patris nobis missum, immo si filius dei incircumscriptibilis . . . [chapter 2:] Gregorius autem brevitatem lectionis commendans . . . [chapter 3:] *De brevitate et commoditate questionum,* Post hec de brevitate questionum vel disputationis agendum est . . . [chapter 153, *De proprietate monachorum,* . . . :] quia non nisi coacti per obedientiam ad eas claustrales accedebant. Modo autem sunt vendicie et empticie. [f. 98:] *Incipiunt tytuli capitulorum,* [first entry added in a cursive hand:] de brevitate lectionis; De brevitate et commoditate, *ii;* De temeritate questionum et temerariis disputationibus, *iii* . . . [with incorrect chapter numbers up to 46] . . . De pena eterna semper habenda in memoria, *cli;* De gaudio et premiis beatitudinis eterne, *clii;* Contra proprietatem monachorum, *cliii.*

Peter the Chanter, *Verbum abbreviatum; PL* 205:23–370, the short version with marginalia. See J. W. Baldwin, *Masters, Princes and Merchants: The Social Views of Peter the Chanter & His Circle* (Princeton 1970) 2:246–65 for a discussion of the versions of the text and of the surviving manuscripts. HM 41537 is the manuscript from Cambron (termed C) used by the editor of the *Verbum abbreviatum,* the Belgian Benedictine Georges Galopin, for his edition published at Mons in 1639[1] and reprinted by Migne. Chapter numbers in the outer margin, but not entered in the text by the rubricator. The text has been corrected throughout. Carefully made marginal finding notes in the hand of the scribe: references to the psalms, names of authors cited, virtues and vices treated and major topic headings. Frequent additions in the margins in the hand of the scribe. Occasional *distinctiones* in schematic form; on f. 1, lower margin, a *distinctio* of 14 parts in schematic form, headed *"Insolubilia cantoris.* De reconciliando cum fratre quem offendisti . . . De omissione mandatorum dei generaliter." On f. 98v, lower margin, in a contemporary hand, "Summa magistri petri cantoris parisiensis de questionibus matutina lib. 5° incipit: Tota celestis philosophia in bonis moribus et fide consistit, distincta per c. <erasure> 1113 capitula, primum quid sit penitencia et quid penitere. Ultimum vero utrum ligna et lapides ecclesie consecrate possint adsumi ad officinas fratrum," referring to the *Summa* of Robert of Courson[2]; see Baldwin 1:23–25 and 2:14.

Parchment, ff. iii (modern parchment) + 98 + iii (modern parchment); 259 × 190 (178 × 115) mm. 1–11[8] 12[10]. 2 columns of 42 lines, ruled with lead point; double bounding lines, the top, middle and bottom three horizontal lines full across; pricking in outer margins. Written in a well-formed early gothic book hand, with the top line in chancery style. Opening initial, 6-line, parted red and blue with red and brown floral filigree; chapter initials alternating in red and blue, occasionally with conservative pen scroll work; initials in green ink, ff. 41v, 43v, 45v (*Salum* corrected to *Malum*), 46v. Notes to the rubricator occasionally found in the margins.

Bound in brown morocco with blind stamps of the Evangelists and of "Salvator" by Zaehnsdorf; gilt edges; in a cloth case.

Written in the opening decades of the thirteenth century (with letter unions, but still written above the top line), possibly at the Cistercian abbey of St. Mary at Cambron. The volume belonged to St. Mary's and bears the thirteenth century ex libris of the abbey: "Liber beate Marie de Camberone" on f. 1; "de Camberone" is entered in the lower recto margin every few leaves throughout the volume; on f. 98v, s. XV, "de camberone beate marie, Ihesus Maria" in red. This manuscript is possibly to be identified with item 61 in the 1782 catalogue of the Cambron library, "Liber magnus Petri Cantoris qui dicitur Verbum abbreviatum, item Casus penitentiales editi a fratre Remondo," ed. R. Plancke, *Les catalogues des manuscrits de l'ancienne abbaye de Cambron,* Société des Bibliophiles Belges, Mons, 40 (1938) 41, 44. It has been suggested that Chicago, Art Institute MS 20.214, a Raymond manuscript, was the second part mentioned in the 1782 catalogue; however, Plancke does not accept it as a Cambron manuscript, and its size as given by De Ricci, 18 × 13 cm., and its binding, "original wooden boards," would imply that it was not part of HM 41537. The Huntington manuscript itself shows no evidence of ever having been joined to another text. In ink, on the front pastedown, "M 73." Sold at Sotheby's, 16 July 1928, lot 213, "Property of a Nobleman." N. 44 in the library of C. H. St. John Hornby (1867–1946), whose bookplate (Shelley House, Chelsea) is on the front pastedown. Acquired from him by Major J. R. Abbey, whose initials, "J.A.," manuscript number "3215," and date of acquisition "15-9-1946" are carefully entered in ink on a back flyleaf; his sale, Sotheby's, 25 March 1975, lot 2952 to the Huntington Library.

Secundo folio: (pam-)pinosa sed
Bibliography: Chronica, 8.

---

[1] We thank Prof. John Benton for this identification, which was kindly confirmed by Prof. John Baldwin.
[2] We are indebted to Prof. John Baldwin for this identification.

HM 41761 — Netherlands, 1443
HUGH OF ST. VICTOR, HOMILIES ON ECCLESIASTES — *fig. 15*

ff. 1–119: [ff. 1–14:] *Incipit prologus in omelias Magistri hugonis super ecclesiasten,* Que de libro salomonis qui ecclesiastes dicitur nuper vobis coram disserui . . . sed a vobis intellectu gaudeatis. *Explicit prologus. Incipit omelia prima. Verba ecclesiastes filii david regis iherusalem,* Titulus est libri iste in quo breviter et qualitas exprimitur . . . in rebus volubilibus et tempore transeuntibus [*PL* 175:113–130]; [ff. 14–16v:] *Omelia secunda,* Generatio preterit et generatio advenit . . . minus fortassis proficit ad edificationem [*PL* 175:130–133]; [ff. 16v–22:] *Omelia tertia,* Verba ecclesiastes que cuncta sub sole vana esse testantur . . . in universitate subsequenter ostendit [*PL* 175:133–139]; [ff. 22–30v:] *Sequitur. Cuncte res difficiles* . . . , Cum res quelibet in superstite sua cernitur . . . vanitas vanitatum et omnia vanitas [*PL* 175:139–149]; [ff. 30v–33v:] *Omelia quinta,* Ego ecclesiastes fui rex israel in iherusalem . . . , Sermones sapientum etiam et enigmata eorum . . . verba narrationis eius revertamur [*PL* 175:149–153]; [ff. 33v–49v:] *Omelia sexta. Ego ecclesiastes* . . . , Primum michi hoc nequaquam pretereundum videtur . . . sed faciem videas veritatis [*PL* 175:153–172]; [ff. 49v–64:] *Omelia septima,* Cumque me convertissem . . . , Audivimus supra . . . et disponit omnia suaviter [*PL* 175:172–190]; [ff. 64–76:] *Omelia octava,* Diutius fortassis quam tractatus brevitas postularet . . . quod nostram veraciter vanitatem agnoscimus [*PL* 175:190–204]; [ff. 76–84v:] *Omelia nona,* Multi sunt sermones hominis . . . et animos habeamus alacriores [*PL* 175:204–215]; [ff. 84v–102v:] *Omelia decima,* Omnia tempus habent . . . , Quesierat supra ecclesiastes . . . ad non esse pocius moveatur [*PL* 175:215–236]; [ff. 102v–119:] *Omelia undecima,* Modo de temporibus exivimus . . . et utrum hec ipsam aliis post se profutura sint ignorant. [*PL* 175:236–256]. *Expliciunt omelie Magistri hugonis super ecclesiasten fideles utique et omni acceptione dignissime. In profesto beati Andree apostoli anno domini M° cccc° xliii°.* [ff. 119v–120v, ruled, but blank]

Hugh of St. Victor, *Homilies on Ecclesiastes, PL* 175:113–256; the division of the manuscript into 11 homilies does not correspond to the 19 part division of the printed text. See Goy 2.2.4.9 (pp. 329–40); this manuscript not recorded.

Parchment, ff. ii (contemporary parchment) + 120; 225 × 159 (149 × 110) mm. $1\text{–}15^8$. Catchwords in inner corner in a noting hand; quires and leaves signed with letters and roman numerals. 2 columns of 29 lines, ruled in lead; prickings visible in outer margins. Written in a well-formed hybrida. Opening initial, 7-line, in blue with void design and red flourishing. 3- or 2-line initials in red or blue; initials within the text slashed in red; red paragraph marks and running headlines across the opening.

Bound, s. XV^2, in brown calf over wooden boards with diagonal rules in diamond patterns; marks of 4 corner bosses on front and back; evidence of 2 fore edge clasps and of a label on the upper front cover; 2 nail holes on the lower edge of each cover; rebacked. Pastedowns removed in 1975 and catalogued separately as HM 41785 from a late ninth century sacramentary from St. Amand.

Written in the Netherlands in 1443. Belonged to the Augustinian house of Bethlehem near Louvain: f. ii verso, erased, "Hoc volumen pertinet Bethle[hem] ⟨?⟩ regularium prope lovanium." Notes in French in pencil on f. i, including "vente Vergauwen ⟨?⟩ n. 425." On f. i verso, "Purchased of George Perkins Humphrey about 1890, Rochester, New York"; in a different hand on f. ii, "Craig Carlton Miller 1933." Given to the Huntington Library in 1971 by Mrs. Creighton Sibley Miller in memory of her husband.

Secundo folio: dicitur et
Bibliography: Chronica, 8.

HM 41785 — Northern France, ca. 860–880
SACRAMENTARY, fragment — *fig. 39*

f. 1r–v: //⟨erasure⟩catione placatus ⟨damaged⟩sti seu emandes sordibus delictorum et dites fructu operum bonorum . . . Quos caelesti recreas munere perpetuo domine co⟨damaged⟩// f. 2r–v: //supplicum tuorum vota per caritatis officia . . . matura quaeque desiderans exercere libera caritate. Per dominum nostrum ihesum christum filium tuum//

J. Deshusses, "Encore les Sacramentaires de Saint-Amand," *Revue Bénédictine* 89 (1979) 310–12.

Parchment, 2 leaves; approx. 225 × 170 (190 × 130) mm. 25 long lines ruled in hard point. Written in an even caroline minuscule with rustic capitals in red and green.

Written at the Benedictine abbey of St. Amand ca. 860–880, as identified by Bernhard Bischoff. Former pastedowns in HM 41761 which had belonged to the Augustinian canons of Bethlehem near Louvain; removed and catalogued separately in 1975.

Bibliography: Chronica, 8.

HM 45146 — England, s. XIII/XIV
CARTULARY, fragment

1. f. 1: William I, De subjectione Eboracensis archiepiscopi. 1072, with crosses. H. W. C. Davis, *Regesta Regum Anglo-Normanorum* 1 (Oxford 1912) n. 64.

2. f. 1r–v: Stephen, De libertatibus ecclesie Anglie. 1136, *SR* 1:3.

3. f. 1v: John, Ut libere sint electiones totius anglie. 1214, *SR* 1:5.

4. ff. 1v–3: John, Magna Carta. 1215, *SR* 1:9–13. f. 3v, blank.

Parchment, ff. 3; 391 × 283 (310 × 205) mm. Although consecutive, ff. 1–2 are not conjunct. 46–49 long lines ruled in lead. Written by one person in a formal littera textualis with occasional anglicana features. 2-line alternating red and blue initials with filigree and tendrils. Running headlines in the hand of the text. Two early foliations: in roman numerals in the headlines by the hand of the text: xiii, xiiii, xiv; in roman numerals in the upper right corner in a fifteenth century hand: $\overset{\text{xx}}{\text{c}}$iiii, $\overset{\text{xx}}{\text{c}}$iiii i, $\overset{\text{xx}}{\text{c}}$iiii ii. Occasional erasures and corrections by the scribe, one early modern correction, several late nineteenth century pencil corrections. Running headlines, *De libertate Ecclesiastica.*

Written in England at the end of the thirteenth or in the early fourteenth century. Formerly ff. 180–182 of large cartulary, presumably ecclesiastical. Belonged to Sir Thomas Phillipps (name and number 16502 on lower margin of f. 1v). Pencil numbers 28, 835. Acquired by Homer D. Crotty (1899–1972), a trustee of the Huntington Library, shortly after 1945. Given to the Huntington Library by Mrs. Homer Crotty in 1972.

Bibliography: Chronica, 8.

HM 45147 — England, s. XV^2
REGISTER OF WRITS

ff. 1–104v: Register of writs, beginning defectively in the section on trespass and ending defectively in the section on writs of attaint; at least 7 quires missing with loss of text at the beginning (2 quires), after f. 56 (3 quires), f. 64 (1 quire), f. 72 (1 quire) and an unknown amount at the end; sporadic running headlines and 4- to 2-line initials, or spaces for initials, to signal chapter divisions.

Parchment, ff. 104; 271–292 × 179–190 (164–195 × 108–119) mm. Collation: (2 quires missing here) $1–7^8$ (3 quires missing here) 8^8 (1 quire missing here) 9^8 (1 quire missing here) $10–13^8$ (unknown number of quires missing here). Catchwords in the center of the lower margin through quire 7, and in the right lower margin in quires 8–13; quire signatures in red roman numerals in the lower right corner of the first leaf of each quire, from iii on quire 1 to xxi on quire 13; apparent additional quire signatures in brown ink occur on the first leaf of the first 7 quires: 4, 10, i, ii, 3, 7, 4. 33–45 long lines, ruled in lead; top and bottom 2 lines full across in quires 8–9; 2 vertical rules in the outer margin form a column approximately 25 mm. wide for notes; slash prick marks in the 3 outer margins, remaining most visible in quires 8–9, 12–13. Written in legal anglicana scripts by 3 scribes: i, ff. 1–40v, 73–88v (quires 1–5, 10–11); ii, ff. 41–56v (quires 6–7); iii, ff. 57–72v, 89–104v (quires 8–9, 12–13). Plain red 3- and 2-line initials; blank spaces reserved for initials on the leaves copied by the third scribe; paragraph marks in red, omitted on some leaves. Contemporary foliation in roman numerals in the upper right corner of the recto of the leaves, xvii–cxx on ff. 1–69. Marginal notes in the hand of the scribe, usually set off by a red paragraph mark; occasional running headlines. Some marginalia and pen trials in other hands, s. XVI. Damage from damp in the last quire; on the last few leaves, rust marks in a vertical line approximately 40 mm. from the outer edge.

Bound, s. XVII, in limp parchment sewn ledger style, i.e. tied through the spine; "1671" written on the front cover.

Written in England during the second half of the fifteenth century. On the inside front cover, a pledge note, "Remanet in plegium [manuscript: "pplm̄"] iiii s. iiii d." A slip from an American (?) book dealer's catalogue tipped into the volume; the price code "srsts" in pencil in the upper margin of f. 1. Belonged to Homer D. Crotty (1899–1972), a trustee of the Huntington Library; given to the Library by his estate.

Bibliography: Chronica, 9.

HM 45717 — England, s. XII^ex
SUETONIUS, DE VITA CAESARUM — *fig. 46*

ff. 1–117v: Annum agens cesar sextumdecimum patrem amisit . . . abstinentia et moderatione insequentium principum. [f. 118r–v, blank]

Greek words entered by scribes; corrected throughout by the second scribe; the section 10, 1 – 12, 2 was omitted from its place on f. 96 and then inserted on ff. 97v–98 between parts of 20, 1. M. Ihm, ed., *C. Suetoni Tranquilli Opera* (Leipzig 1907).

Parchment (thick), ff. i (modern paper) + i (medieval parchment) + 118 + i (modern paper); 217 × 150 (148 × 112) mm. $1–14^8$ 15^8(–7, 8 excised). Catchwords in lower right corner, many of them cropped. 2 columns of 30 lines, ruled in brown lead, with top and bottom 2 or 3 lines often full across; single bounding lines; pricking visible in the 3 outer margins. Written above the top line by 2 hands in an English minuscule script: i, ff. 1–16v; ii, ff. 17–117v. Opening initial on f. 1, somewhat damaged, 9-line, in red infilled with blue and green arabesque tendrils; the other 11 initials, 10- to 4-line, in similar style in green, blue or metallic red, either plain or with arabesque infilling in other colors (e.g. ff. 17, 40v, 56, 69); 1-line initials in ink of text placed outside of ruled space. Rubrics added for the beginnings of books in an uneven hand of the end of the thirteenth century; occasional marginalia of the same date. On f. ii verso (which may be one of the 2 missing leaves of quire 15, transferred to the front of the book, as it shows no sign of the damage of f. 1, nor of the chainmarks), and on f. 118v faint notes in lead, s. XIII^{ex}/XIV^{in}, mentioning "sancti Bernardi monachorum precepta."

Bound, s. XVIII, in English speckled calf; chain marks on the inner lower margin of f. 1 and successive leaves.

Written at Bury St. Edmunds at the end of the twelfth century; thus not manuscript no. xxvii in the mid-twelfth century catalogue of the abbey: "Epistole senece et sidonius, suetonius [erased]," ed. M. R. James, *On the Abbey of St. Edmund at Bury.* Cambridge Antiquarian Society Octavo Pub. 28 (Cambridge 1895) 24. Probably to be identified with the entry for Suetonius in the "Catalogus scriptorum ecclesiae" of Henry of Kirkestede. See Ker, *MLGB,* 21, and R. M. Thomson, "The Library of Bury St. Edmunds Abbey in the Eleventh and Twelfth Centuries," *Speculum* 47 (1972) 617–45, this manuscript discussed p. 639, n. 141. Bury pressmark, s. XIV², crossed out, in the upper right margin of f. 1: "S. 18." Received in the library of Sion College after the Great Fire of 1666 and before the publication in 1697 of Bernard, *Catalogi* where it is cited, 2:107, no. 4087. Sion College stamped ex libris on ff. 1, 40v, 117v, and its shelf mark, Arc. L.40.2/L. 9, on the front pastedown and on the round label on the spine; "anc. 2=3" in red ink on the front pastedown and on f. i. Sion College sale, Sotheby's, 13 June 1977, lot 71 with plate of f. 94; acquired by the Huntington Library, in part with funds given in memory of William D. Truesdell.

Secundo folio: verit. Questori
Bibliography: Schenkl 4485. Ker, *MMBL* 1:270.

HM 46015 — England, s. XIII²
GREGORY IX, DECRETALS, fragment

1. f. 1r–v: [Text] //procurator proposuit ex adverso quod cum olim ad petitionem patronorum ecclesie amoriensis . . . apud apostolicam sedem quam apud ecclesiam revenatem [*sic*] unde//; [Gloss:] //pervenit ff. pro emptore quod vulgo ff. pro legato ⟨cropped⟩ quia episcopus non potest deponere ius unius ecclesie et dare alteri . . . et [*sic*] notum ut iudici prout dicit dominus azo et alii dicunt sicut p. quod etiam de facto et inducunt ad hoc ff. de pet. here. 1. f. sed primum verius est quod de tali facto//

Gregory IX, *Decretals,* 1.4.8–1.5.3 with gloss of Bernardus Parmensis.

2. f. 2r–v: [Text] //Tue fraternitati et infra, utrum clericos qui ad partes ierosolimitanas . . . vel predecessores ipsius de pacifica sic obtenta consuetudine iurisdicionem aliquam in ipso monasterio vel in huiusmodi abbatiis//; [Gloss:]// tue commendaciis [*sic*] vel etiam dimissoriis lxxi di. c. penultim. et f. et xix q. ii due sunt . . . et correctio ex consuetudine potius habetur ut s. de electione dudum dic super hoc ut dixi s. e. cum satis//

Gregory IX, *Decretals,* 1.22.3–1.23.10 with gloss of Bernardus Parmensis.

Parchment, 2 leaves from the same book; 365 × 255 (245 × 107) mm. Text in 2 columns of 47 lines, ruled in lead; pricking visible in the inner margin. Text written in a littera textualis; the gloss in a rounder noting script. 3- to 2-line initials alternating in red and blue with flourishing of the other color. *Nota bene* hand, f. 1v. Marginalia, s. XV.

HM 46015

Written in England in the second half of the thirteenth century. Leaf 2 bears the names "Richard," "Chrisostimos" and the motto "Gloria vos titillat ambos" in one or more seventeenth century English hands. The leaves were apparently once used as pastedowns in a binding to judge from the stains; however their size suggests that they were not originally part of HM 19916 from which they were removed. HM 19916 was acquired by the Huntington Library from Sotheby's, 15 June 1959, lot 205.

HM 46554 England, s. XIII[in]

PETER OF POITIERS, DISTINCTIONES SUPER PSALTERIUM

fig. 50

1. ff. 1–65v: *Incipiunt distinctiones super psalterium,* Facies michi tentorium in introitu thabernaculi quatuor pretiosis coloribus contextum. Thabernaculum quo in nobis deus habitat . . . *Cum omnes prophetas et cetera. David dicitur prophetarum eximius:* propter regiam dignitatem ut, Inveni David servum meum, oleo sancto meo unxi eum; propter multam humilitatem, ut Inveni virum secundum cor meum . . . velut in Beatitudine recipiamur; unde, Petite a me et accipietis, pul. [catchword:] et apud vobis//

Stegmüller 6783; see also P. S. Moore, *The Works of Peter of Poitiers* (Notre Dame 1936) 78–96. Here arranged in schematic form, i.e., the scriptural word that is being interpreted is placed to the left of the text, with lines radiating to the different senses; ends defectively.

2. ff. 66–89v: [Anonymous distinctions] *Angeli,* potestas superna. In psalmo, Qui facis angelos suos [*sic*] spiritus . . . *Anni* . . . *Aurum* . . . *Argentum* . . . *Aquilo* . . . *Auster* . . . [*A*]*rea* . . . [*A*]*rbor* . . . [*A*]*rundo* . . . [*A*]*rcus* . . . [*A*]*rma* . . . [*A*]*sinus* . . . [*A*]*ries* . . . [*A*]*gnus* . . . [*A*]*per* . . . [*A*]*ves* . . . [*A*]*le* . . . [*A*]*quila* . . . [*A*]*ccipiter* . . . [*A*]*que* . . . [*A*]*byssus* . . . [*A*]*tria* . . . [*A*]*ltare* . . . [*A*]*rcha* . . . [*A*]*uris* . . . [*A*]*er* . . . [*A*]*ger* . . . [*A*]*cervus* . . . [*A*]*urora* . . . [*B*]*abilonia* . . . [*V*]*ir* . . . [*V*]*irgo* . . . [*V*]*ultus* . . . [*V*]*ertex* . . . *Unguis* . . . [*U*]*bera* . . . [*U*]*terus* . . . Secretum consilii, unde, De cuius utero egressa est glacies.

Distinctiones in simple form, primarily of figurative meanings, in alphabetical order with space left for additional *distinctiones* at the end of each alphabetical section. Regarding distinction collections see A. Wilmart, "Un répertoire d'exégèse composé en Angleterre vers le debut du XIIIe siècle," *Mémorial Lagrange* (Paris 1940) 307–46, and R. H. and M. A. Rouse, "Biblical Distinctions in the Thirteenth Century," *Archives d'histoire doctrinale et littéraire du Moyen Age* (1974) 27–37.

Parchment, ff. ii (parchment) + 89 + i (paper); 220 × 157 (art. 1: 183 × 140; art. 2: 190 × 120) mm. $1^8(+9)$ $2–11^8$, signed on last leaf verso at 2 different times in roman numerals, I-VIII; occasional catchwords. 44–45 (art. 1) and 38–39 (art. 2) long lines. Ruled in lead point and brown crayon; double bounding lines; art. 1 in 2 columns of ca. 28 mm. width for the lemmata and ca. 110 mm. for the text. Prickings visible in outer margins; in art. 2 also visible in the inner margin. Written by 4 persons: i, ff. 1–9v; ii, ff. 10–65v; iii, ff. 66–73; iv, ff. 74–89v; the first writer corrects the second, e.g. ff. 10v, 11; in brownish ink. Plain initials in red, occasionally in blue or with blue penwork. Art. 1: distinctions noted in red in schematized form in the left margin, except for ff. 18v–20, 49v–65v, where they are left unfinished. Art. 2: f. 66, 3-line initials alternating in grey-blue, ochre and green. On ff. 74, 82–84, 2- and 1-line initials alternating in red and green; on ff.

74v–75, mainly in green, the alternating red not filled in. On ff. 1–9v, careful penwork, heads of birds (e.g. eagle, ff. 1v, 3) and animals. On f. 1 (top margin cropped): "Sancti Spiritus." Pen trials on ff. i and ii verso.

Bound, s. XVII, in limp vellum; on the spine: *Distinctiones super Psalterium;* on front cover: Ms. N° 216.

Written in England in the opening years of the thirteenth century. Inside the front cover, "P:B:" and "Ms. N° 216." Belonged to Thomas Mostyn, with his armorial bookplate and signature, the date 1744, and the number 75 on f. ii; many of the Mostyn manuscripts were collected by Sir Thomas Mostyn (1535–1617). Mostyn shelfmark in pencil on inside front cover, "$\frac{H}{4}$ C." Mostyn sale, Sotheby's, 13 July 1902, lot 31. Sotheby's, 11 July 1978, lot 39 to the Huntington Library.

Secundo folio: plantant secus

Bibliography: HMC, *4th Report* (1874), Appendix, 358, n. 216. Schenkl 4790. *HLQ* 42 (1978–79) 73 with a plate of f. 7v.

HM 47405 England, s. XV^med^
WALTER BURLEY, DE VITA ET MORIBUS PHILOSOPHORUM
fig. 104

1. ff. 1–103v: *De vita philosophorum et moribus veterum tractaturus multaque ab antiquis auctoribus in diversis libris de ipsorum gestis sparsim scripta reperi in unum colligere laboravi plurimaque eorum responsa notabilia et dicta elegancia huic libello inserui que ad legencium consolacionem et morum informacionem conferre valebunt. De Talete philosopho,* Tales philosophus asianus ut ait laertius in libello de vita philosophorum . . . scripsit eciam librum de naturalibus questionibus ad cosdre regem persarum. *Explicit liber de vita philosophorum.*

H. Knust, ed., *Walter Burley, De vita et moribus philosophorum.* Bibliothek des litterarischen Vereins in Stuttgart 177 (Tübingen 1886); this manuscript lacks his chapter 128, "Justinus" and reverses the order of "Ovid" and "Marcus Verrius Flaccus"; it incorporates the Ps. Seneca, *De remediis fortuitorum malorum* (ff. 89v–94). See J. O. Stigall, "The Manuscript Tradition of the *De vita et moribus philosophorum* of Walter Burley," *Medievalia et Humanistica* 11 (1957) 44–57 for a list of 105 manuscripts, HM 47405 not included; the Diogenes chapter, edited by Stigall by way of example, is here reduced to one sentence: "*De diogene poeta,* Diogenes babilonicus stoicus philosophus catonis tempore claruit" (f. 81v), as in the 1472 Cologne edition printed by Arnold ter Hoernen. (*GW* 5783).

2. f. 103v: [added verses, the first 5 lines by one contemporary hand, the last possibly by another] Nunc lege nunc ora nunc cum femore labora/ Sic erit hora brevis et labor ipse levis [Walther, *Proverbia* 19350]; Inspice mentem discute mores acta resolve/ Semper ab hiis et in hiis potis cognoscere quid scis [Walther, *Proverbia* 12523]; Dum regunt vulve dicet gens tota simul ve<cancelled>; Est homo res fragilis durans nunc tempore// [ends incomplete; Walther, *Proverbia* 7486]. [f. 104r–v, ruled but blank]

Parchment, ff. iii (modern paper) + 104 + iii (modern paper); 198 × 140 (123 × 82) mm. 1–13⁸. Catchwords in lower right corner. 27 long lines ruled in red ink with the top 2 lines and the bottom line full across; single vertical bounding lines; pricking occasionally visible in the 3 outer margins. Written in a bâtarde hand.

Opening historiated initial, 9-line, in white-highlighted pink on a gold ground with thin blue, rust and green acanthus leaves and spiky sprays in Continental style along the inner margin; in the center of the initial, a philosopher lecturing to his students, by the Master of Sir John Fastolf. 2-line blue initials with red flourishing; alternating blue and rose-colored paragraph marks; rubrics in the same rose-colored ink.

Bound, s. XVIII, in English russia; marbled endpapers; rebacked.

Written in England, or perhaps in France where it may have received its historiated initial and marginal spray, but in England from an early date, as shown by the distinctly English decoration of the 2-line blue initials, and by the finding notes in the margins in an English hand. The only other copies of English provenance noted by Stigall are Cambridge, Trinity College O.2.50 (1154), Philadelphia (Pennsylvania), Temple University, Ms. 567 and Vatican, Reg. lat. 7147. On f. ii, "Hic liber est meus/ Testis est Deus," and the signature "Robt. Hill"; on f. iii, "R. Hill 1792." All three are heavily crossed out in ink. Acquired by the Huntington Library from Alan G. Thomas (London) in 1979 with the support of the Lois and Keith Spalding Endowment Fund.

Secundo folio: olmas emere

HM 47543 — France, 1702
ANTIPHONAL

1. pp. iii–37: *Officium Sanctae Sindonis In Primis Vesperis, fait en L'annee mil sept cens deux et cetera* . . . , Ioseph vir bonus et justus accessit ad Pilatum . . . [*Resp. Beatae Mariae De Mercede in tertio nocturno*] *Vers.*, Tua sancta intercessione adiuva nos virgo inmaculata. Cuius. Gloria Patri et Filio et Spiritui sancto. Cuius.

Antiphonal with responses for the feasts of the Holy Shroud, St. Mary in Mount Carmel, the Holy Innocents, Joachim, Joseph and Our Lady of Mercy [this last possibly by a different hand].

2. p. 38: [added in a careful cursive hand] Variation of the Office for the Holy Shroud outside of Easter time.

Paper, pp. i–iv + 38, with contemporary pagination; 435 × 280 (385 × 220) mm. One gathering of 20 leaves + one leaf at the end. Eight lines of text and music, with pricking for both along inner and outer margins; music in square notation on red 4-line staves; height of the minims controlled by lead ruling. Written in a humanistic script, using a dark black acidic ink. The title, p. iii, in large square roman capitals, enclosed by a heavy black ink frame and red ruling; rubrics often in combined italic and humanistic display scripts in both red and black ink. Opening initial, p. 1, the height of the text and music, in red with red-touched pen and ink drawing of two flowers; other initials, same size, in plain red. Corrections to the text and music on strips of paper glued over the offending section (see pp. 6, 7, 8, 19).

Bound in a single large sheet of limp parchment, the reverse of which is completely covered by long lines of a sixteenth century bâtarde script in French, probably a document.

Written in France in 1702, perhaps for a Carmelite house. On pp. i and 38, the flourished signature of Urbain Roges, and on p. 38 the number "184." Acquired in Paris between

1910–1926 by the artist Elmer E. Pattee, and given to the Huntington Library in August 1980 by his son-in-law, Robert G. Steele.

HM 47544 — Italy (?), s. XV^2
BOOK OF HOURS, fragment

1. f. 1r–v: //vero in medio umbre mortis non timebo mala . . . Dirige me in veritate tua et//

From matins of the Office of the Dead.

2. f. 2r–v: //*Ad primam,* Deus in adiutorium meum intende . . . Quoniam alieni insurrexerunt adversum me et//

From the Hours of the Virgin, at prime; possibly use of Rome: the hymn is Memento salutis auctor . . . ; the antiphon, Assumpta . . . ; the psalm, Deus in nomine tuo salvum me fac . . .

3. f. 3r–v: //De cruce deponitur hora vespertina . . . perducat nos ad gaudia paradisi. Amen.//

Short hours of the Cross from the hymn for vespers to the end.

Parchment, ff. lxxx (modern parchment, stained on the edges to give an older appearance) + 3 single leaves + lxvi (modern parchment, as above); 98 × 70 (54 × 35) mm. After a first gathering of 10 leaves, all the remaining 22 quires are of 6 leaves; the 12th contains the 3 medieval leaves tipped in. 15 long lines on ff. 1 and 3, 14 long lines on f. 2, ruled in pale red ink. Written in a rounded gothic script. Decorated in the style of northern French manuscripts: 5-line initial in white-decorated blue on a cusped gold ground, infilled with colored trilobe leaves; a U-shaped narrow band border of gold and color around the text; outer border of black ivy vine, gold motifs, 2 swirls of narrow acanthus leaf in red, orange, blue and green, and flowers. 2-line initials in burnished gold with pink infilling on a blue ground, or vice versa; 1-line initials alternating gold with black penwork, or blue with red penwork; initials within the text slashed in red. Red rubrics.

Inserted in an early metal binding with gilt decoration, over wooden boards; remains of a fore edge clasp; much repaired; on the back pastedown, a fragment of a sixteenth century printed leaf with a poem in octaves, in Italian.

Written possibly in Italy in the second half of the fifteenth century. A label on the front pastedown, "D 113." On f. 1, modern pencil foliation, "152"; on f. 3, with the same numbering, "18." Faint pencil marks on the lower margin of f. 3 resemble the price code of Dawson's Book Shop, Los Angeles. Given to the Huntington Library in 1975 by Mrs. Edward J. Loftus.

HM 47619 — England, s. XV^{med}
OLD TENURES; NATURA BREVIUM

1. ff. ii verso–iii: Notes, s. XV, on the number of vills, etc. in England; mnemonic verses on the return days in Michaelmas, Hilary, Easter and Trinity terms; a couplet in a more formal hand, "Dat crux lucia mereres [?] karismata dies/ Ne sis in angaria quarta sequens feria"; ownership notes (see below); notes in prose on the beginnings and endings of the terms; a note defining measurements

of land, "In libro de domsday sub titulo terre Regis in comitatu Surr. inter al. continetur sic, xxiiii acres terre faciunt unam virgatam . . ." (printed in English by HMC; see below); ff. iii verso–v verso, blank.

2. ff. 1–6v: Calendar in red and black, including the feasts of David (1 March), Chad (2 March), "Resurrectio domini" (27 March, in red), Richard of Chichester (3 April, in red), Dunstan (19 May, in red), Translation of Richard of Chichester (16 June, in red), Anne (26 July, in red).

3. ff. 7–13v: //ou tenementz sount donez a un homme a un certeyn terme . . . astringitur ratione debeti vel contractus absolucio perpetua et cetera.

Old Tenures, beginning defectively in the section on mortgages, with 18 sections, continuing beyond the 1521 Pynson edition with *Service de frank ferme* and *Auncienne demesne;* at the end, a number of short definitions, *Sute service* through *Obligatio* (f. 13r–v).

4. ff. 14–69v: Dicitur q'il ad breve de droit patent et brief de droit clos . . . et s'il ne demande deinz l'an donques le proscheyn//

Natura brevium, ending defectively in the writ *Quale ius.*

5. ff. 70–117v: Subject index to statutes, *Accusacions* to *Wurstede,* with no later additions in the spaces reserved for that purpose.

6. back flyleaf iii: Ownership note (see below); a proverb, "Multa volumus, pauca scimus et minora possumus"; a biblical passage (Luke 14, 26); a citation attributed to Augustine on living a good life to avoid a bad death.

Parchment, ff. i (modern paper) + iv (contemporary parchment) + 117 + iii (contemporary parchment) + i (modern paper); 214 × 160 (156 × 112 in the calendar; 156 × 95 for text in arts. 3 and 4, but 112 wide with ruling for nota bene marks; 160 × 125 in art. 5) mm. 1^6 2^8(–1; through f. 13) 3–15^8. 34 long lines, ruled in lead with top and bottom 2 lines full across; additional set of narrow double rules in the outer margin of arts. 3 and 4 for nota bene marks; additional vertical rule 2/3 across page for column of statutes cited in art. 5. Calendar ruled in ink; slash prick marks visible in this section. Calendar written in a textura script; the rest of the manuscript in a legal anglicana script by the same scribe who copied a statute book in Auckland Public Library, Med. MS S1571[1] (plate of f. 131v of that manuscript in D. M. Taylor, *The Oldest Manuscripts in New Zealand,* Wellington, 1955, pl. 28). For related scribes in other legal manuscripts, see K. L. Scott, "A late fifteenth-century group of *Nova Statuta* manuscripts," in *Manuscripts at Oxford: an exhibition in memory of Richard William Hunt (1908–1979)*, ed. A. C. de la Mare and B. C. Barker-Benfield (Oxford 1980) 102–05, and K. L. Scott, *The Mirroure of the Worlde, MS Bodley 283 (England, c. 1470–1480): The Physical Composition, Decoration and Illustration* (Oxford, Roxburghe Club, 1980) 45–50, 66–68, to which add EL 9 H 10, ff. 1–49.

Opening initials, ff. 1, 14 and 70 in 3- and 2-line gold on white-patterned blue and maroon grounds with black ink sprays terminating in green and gold leaves or in pink and blue leaves; 3-line blue initials with red flourishing; in the calendar, 2-line initials alternating in blue with red flourishing and in gold with blue; alternating red and blue paragraph marks. Calligraphic initial with 2 sketched faces, signed "w.w.," on the Byrley ownership note, f. ii verso (see below). On the back flyleaves, rough sketches in crayon of a stag (?), a dog's head, an interlace design and a bird's head.

Bound, s. XX, in vellum from a document as recovering over earlier pasteboards; earlier spine label laid down; previous binding in red-brown calf, English, ca. 1780.

Written in England during the middle years of the fifteenth century; the latest date in the text is 23 Henry VI, i.e. 1444–45 (on, e.g., ff. 74v, 84v, 86); the calendar does not include Osmund, canonized in 1456. The manuscript may have been copied in London by or for a stationer associated with the Inns of Court, as suggested by the existence of other legal manuscripts in related hands; the presence of Dunstan in the calendar may point to a connection with Clifford's Inn. On f. ii verso, twice, the name of Thomas Byrley; on the third back flyleaf, "Ihesu mercy/ of Byrley constat/ Lady helpe/ ‹?›" and "Ihesu haue mercy on me so al men." A Thomas Byrley was admitted to Lincoln's Inn in 1501; see *Records of the Honorable Society of Lincoln's Inn, Admissions* (1896) 1:29 and *The Black Books* (1897) 1:122. The same man apparently owned a statute book now in Lincoln's Inn, Hale 176 (Misc. 12) with the inscription, "Thome Byrley constat liber." Note, s. XVI, on f. ii verso, "Thomas Hever [or Henery?] Arthur Towers Francis Arm [?] J. Anthony Francis Anderson ‹?›." Belonged to Philip Carteret Webb (1700–70); his sale, 25 February 1771, lot 2814 to John Lowes of Ridley Hall, Northumberland; Lowes' book plate on the front pastedown and, on f. ii, his acquisition note and collation of the text of the Old Tenures against the 1521 Pynson edition. By 1877 owned by Sir Henry Ingilby, Bart., of Ripley Castle, Yorkshire; in the sale of Lt. Col. Sir William Henry Ingilby (1874–1950), Sotheby's, 21 October 1920, lot 171. Sold by Leighton, Cat. II, 2 (1921) n. 671 to Coella Lindsay Ricketts of Chicago (d. during or before 1941). Acquired by the Huntington Library from Sotheby's, 24 June 1980, lot 60 with a plate of ff. 69v–70.

Secundo folio: [f. 7] ou tenementz
Bibliography: HMC, *6th Report, Appendix* (1877) 357. De Ricci, 649. J. H. Baker, "Migrations of Manuscripts," *Journal of Legal History* 1 (1980) 305.

[1] We thank Mr. Jeremy Griffiths for this information.

HM 47641 — Italy, s. XV^{med}
PORTABLE CALENDAR — *fig. 17*

ff. 1–8: Full calendar, missing the leaves for February, October, November and December, with some grading, written in a round gothic script in black, blue and red; included are the feasts of "Georgii martyris ferrariensis patroni" (24 April, in red, maius duplex), "Maurelii episcopi ferrariensis martyris" (7 May, in blue, maius duplex), Bernardinus (20 May), "Festum nivis" (5 August). Each leaf is blank on the verso, except for the month name, which, when the calendar is folded, appears at the top on the outside of the leaf.

Parchment, ff. 8; open: 110 × 83 mm.; folded: 55 × 30 mm. The 2 outer thirds of each leaf fold vertically inwards over the middle third; the entire leaf is then folded horizontally downward in half. Tabs extending from the bottom of the middle third of each leaf, together with protective morocco flaps front and back are held by a brass clip with a loop at its other end, 50 × 32 mm., so as to hang the calendar from a belt. The clip is engraved with the sacred monogram "IHS" on one side, and with the Man of Sorrows on the other. This unit slides into a rectangular brass case which narrows towards a hole at the top, just large enough for the brass clip to slip through, so that the case rests on the shoulder of the parchment leaves. The case, 88 × 33 × 15 mm., is engraved: Felice chi pesa ogni suo paso/che del'opera raguarda el fine (J. Sanguinacci; in L. Frati, *Rime del codice isoldiano*, Bologna 1913, 1:264). On case front and back are images of the Crucifixion, and of John of Tossignano in bishop's dress, holding the sacred monogram; below his feet, the inscription: Beatus Iohannes de Tossiniano Iesuatus Ieronimi Episcopus Ferrariensis. For other examples of this type of folding portable book, see M. C. Garand, "Livres de poche médiévaux à Dijon et à Rome,"

Scriptorium 25 (1971) 18–24, and H. Bober, "The Zodiacal Miniatures of the *Très Riches Heures* of the Duke of Berry," *JWCI* 11 (1948) n. 6 pp. 26–27; to which add Ballarat Fine Arts Gallery, Victoria, MS Crouch 4; Cambridge, Mass., Harvard University, Houghton Library, Typ. 278H; New York, Pierpont Morgan Library, M.941; Oxford, Bod. Lib., Douce 71; Sotheby's, 22 June 1982, lot 73; Venice, Museo Civico Correr, Spalato Breviary.

Written probably in Ferrara, between 1450 (canonization of Bernardinus) and 1455 or 1458 (canonization of Vincent Ferrer and institution of the Feast of the Transfiguration, neither of which appear in the calendar). John of Tossignano was bishop of Ferrara, 1432–1446. Sold by Gilhofer and Ranschburg, Lucerne, 14 June 1932, lot 598 with plate of the case. The numbers 2718 (crossed out) and 2882 on a rectangular, red-edged paper label affixed to the fitted pasteboard box containing the calendar. Belonged to Alice Parsons Millard (1873–1938); following her death, friends acquired George (d. 1918) and Alice Millard's collection of materials on the evolution of the book, and donated it to the Huntington Library.

Bibliography: [S. B. Dakin and R. O. Schad] *The Alice and George Millard Collection Illustrating the Evolution of the Book* ([Los Angeles] Ward Ritchie Press [1939]) p. 9.

HM 47753 — Italy, s. XV^{ex}
MESUE, LIBER DE SIMPLICIBUS MEDICINIS

1. ff. 1–5: Medical recipes added by 2 contemporary hands; ff. 5v–6v, ruled, but blank.

2. ff. 7–109v: *Incipit liber hebemesue de simplicibus medicinis,* [Prologue] In nomine dei misericordis cuius nutu sermo recipit gratiam et doctrina perfectionem Principium verborum filii hamet filii helii filii abdebla regis damasceni verbus cecidit . . . [f. 7v, Chapter list:] *Distinctio capitulorum libri primi,* Quatuor intentionum agregabimus sermonem in libro nostro primo. Prima intencio ponit condiciones in electione et posse medicinarum solutionem faciencium . . . [f. 8, Text:] *Continet ergo liber iste primus xxxvi capitula. Capitulum primum sermo utilis de electione medicinarum* . . . , Dicimus quod medicina lexativa [*sic*] non est a re complexionali . . . [f. 108, De elleboro . . . :] *Dosis,* Eius est a karatis vi usque ad 3.ii vel usque ad 3.i.

Johannes Mesue the Younger, *Liber de simplicibus medicinis,* printed in his *Opera medicinalia,* Venice 1479; Hain 11108.

3. ff. 109v–113: *Incipit liber graduum hebemesue,* Absinthium calidum est in primo gradu siccum in secundo. Agaricus duobus modis est masculus et femina, lauda femina qui uterque calidi sunt in primo gradu . . . [f. 113, Zizannia . . . :] Plante leonis duo sunt genera maius et minus frigida et sicca in ii^{o} super carbunculos apposita prodeest. *Explicit liber hebemesue de simplicibus medicinis. Deo gratias.*

Thorndike and Kibre, 11.

4. f. 113r–v: [Alphabetical glossary] Alhosorum id est species zuri duri, Alhase id est thimum, Alharmel id est cuta . . . Taraxaton dicitur endivia vel silvestris scariola, Zirugen id est hermodattilus.

5. ff. 113v–191v: *Incipit liber iohannis damasceni filii mesuhe calbdei quod est agregatio vel antidotarium electorum confectionum et incipit liber tercius,*

[Prologue:] Sicut in libris urinarum [*sic*] ex hiis que experti sumus quedam rememoracione digna ex quarum agregatione sumam conteximus quam gerbadin [*sic*] nostrum vocamus . . . [Text:] *Incipit prima distinctio de electuaris delectabilibus,* Prima distinctio que est electurariorum subdivisionem habet quedam enim ex eis delectabilia sunt . . . [f. 191v, Oleum philosophorum . . . :] Et est in eo virtus calefactiva resolutiva penetrativa consumptiva superfluitatum Et confert//

Johannes Mesue the Younger, *Grabadin medicinarum,* printed in his *Opera Medicinalia,* Venice 1479; here breaking defectively near the end.

Paper (*Arbalète* surmounted by a flower, not in Briquet), ff. iv (modern paper) + 191 + iv (modern paper); 212 × 136 (125 × 80) mm. 1^{6} $2–4^{10}$ 5^{10}(–6, after f. 41 with loss of text) 6^{10} 7^{10}(–a leaf in the second half of the quire; excised?) $8–19^{10}$ 20^{10}(–8, 9, 10). Catchwords written vertically along inner bounding line. 2 columns of 26 lines faintly ruled in lead. Written in a running hand with humanistic forms; the first line of each chapter in an oversize gothic display script. Opening initial, f. 7, 6-line, in gold on a parted dark pink and blue ground with a floral band border of vines and flowers the length of the text; opening initial of chapter list, f. 7v, 4-line, in gold with red flourishing and infilling; 3- and 2-line initials alternating red and light blue; initials within the text filled in yellow; rubrics; alternating red and blue paragraph marks. On ff. 8, 17, 49, in the upper margin, s. XVI, "Iesus"; on f. 36 upside down in the lower margin, in a later (?) hand, "Al Molto Magnifico Signor."

Bound, s. XX, with sixteenth century covers, blind tooled in a twisted rope pattern, laid down; evidence of 2 fore edge clasps.

Written in Italy at the end of the fifteenth century. The ex libris of a sixteenth century owner has been cancelled on f. 7, but it appears to be the same name as on f. 6: "Ioannes Maglionus semper tenere cupit." Inscription on f. 3, in the same hand as the note on f. 36: "All Magnifico Signor Claudio et Claudina Maria." On the front pastedown, the armorial bookplate of Noel F. Barwell, with his motto "Non minus sed solus quam eum solus" and the date, 1902. Acquired by the Huntington Library in 1952 from Mrs. A. P. Haigh of Long Beach, California with the help of the Lois and Keith Spalding Endowment Fund.

Secundo folio: [f. 8, Chapter list] lavacionum; [f. 9, Text] super quibus non

HM 47937 — France, s. XIII^in^
ARNULF OF ORLEANS, fragment

//⟨damaged⟩ quasi diceret *Nisi dimisso milite* id est pacifico et inermi. *Potui* si vellem. *Motu surgente* in principio belli moti. *Foro* . . . , *Medio* . . . , *Dum* . . . , *Bella relegem* . . . , *Extremum orbem* . . . , *Transcendam* . . . , *Ardentes* . . . , *Eripiam* . . . [ending on the verso:] *Ad phicia,* ad festa apollinis a phitone dicta sicut in festo palmarum ubique gencium//

Expanded version of the commentary by Arnulf of Orleans on Lucan's *Pharsalia,* Bk. 6.321–409[1]; see B. M. Marti, ed., *Arnulfi Aurelianensis Glosule super Lucanum* (American Academy in Rome 1958) 327–32.

Parchment, 1 leaf; 210 × 157 (180 × 140) mm., 2 columns of 48 lines, ruled in lead (?), pricking in the outer margin. Written in a minuscule script with the lemmata underscored in ink. On the recto, a circle labelled "tessalya" in the center, with the cardinal directions along the perimeter; outside the circle, 5 irregularly shaped projections with the names of the mountains surrounding Thessaly.

Written in France in the early thirteenth century. Loose in HM 1345 when that book was acquired by Henry E. Huntington in 1926 from A. S. W. Rosenbach.

---

[1] We are grateful to Prof. B. Marti for this identification.

HM 48048 ANTIPHONAL — Italy, s. XVII

1. f. 1v: Title page, *Antiphonarium de tempore et sanctis,* followed by a rayed circle inscribed "Ave Maria," probably s. XX.

2. ff. 2–74: Temporale from the first Sunday after Easter until Advent.

3. ff. 74v–177v: Sanctorale from Anthony of Padua (13 June) to Clement (23 November), including the feasts of Clare, Francis and Didacus.

4. ff. 177v–178: Table of contents, s. XVIII, with reference to foliation, added at the same time, ending: *Finis huius operis quem P. Regulus a vurno huius Almę Provincię Tuscię ex obediença sui superioris restaurabat anno domini 1719. Si tibi hoc opus placet deo gratias age et si tibi non placet deo gratias age, vade et ora pro scriptore;* followed by a rayed circle containing the YHS monogram, probably s. XX.

Parchment; according to the eighteenth century foliation used in this description, ff. 178, but missing ff. 23, 65, 89, 94, 112, 130, 136–158, 162–163 and 167, so that the actual number of leaves present is 146; 530 × 388 (430 × 292) mm. 1^{8}(+ 1, 10, 11) 2^{12}(–12) 3–4^{12} 5^{12}(+ a leaf in the first half) 6^{14}(–6) 7^{14} 8^{12}(–2, 7) 9^{12} 10^{12}(–1) 11^{12}(–7) two quires (?) missing here 12 (3 bifolia remain; the center bifolium, ff. 162–163, is missing) 13^{10}; many "bifolia" are actually attached singletons. The only leaf written entirely in prose, f. 112v, has 15 long lines ruled in ink with added lines to define space for the minims. Usually in 5 lines of text and music, the text in a round gothic book hand, the music on red 4-line staves.

Twenty-seven historiated initials or border designs added in the late nineteenth or early twentieth century, of which eleven are partially or completely based on compositions of Girolamo da Cremona and Liberale da Verona in Sienese choir books; see M. G. Ciardi Dupré, *I Corali del Duomo di Siena* (Siena 1972); most are signed "David [?] Gray Apl. 7/23"; the subject is frequently inappropriate to the feast and the letter has occasionally been rendered incorrectly. The initials are: f. 1v, "Ave Maria" in a rayed circle; f. 6v, 2 putti placing a collar on a stag (Ciardi Dupré, pl. 176); f. 9v, Christ triumphant (Ciardi Dupré, pl.214); f. 18v, Michael Archangel, with Renaissance ornament in the lower margin (Ciardi Dupré, pl. 87); f. 24v, the 3 Kings, one with a halo, who kisses the Baby Jesus' foot (Ciardi Dupré, pl. 185); f. 27, a young Renaissance gentleman with halo, sword and palm leaf, and ornament in the lower margin; f. 28, an elegant young saint riding on a white horse and holding the standard of Christ; in the lower margin, a haloed figure with a palm leaf; f. 32v, Virgin and Child; f. 40v, David in penitence in a landscape (Ciardi Dupré, pl. 239); f. 41, Jesus walking in a landscape (Ciardi Dupré, pl. 262); f. 47, 2 angels in prayer; f. 52v, Christ triumphant (Ciardi Dupré, pl. 220); f. 66, 3 shields, based on Sienese models, in the lower margin: gules, a griffin rampant argent; red flourishes on a shield per fess argent and sable; azure, bentwise "Libertas" or; f. 67v, Crucifixion with Mary and Mary Magdalene, and Renaissance ornament in the outer margin; f. 74v, busts of a young angel and of Jesus (?); f. 75, a young gentleman with halo and standard; f. 75, Jesus, his finger touching the mute man's mouth (Ciardi Dupré, pl. 266); f. 79v, a bishop and a young angel; f. 80, a praying angel; f. 84v, George in armor with Renaissance ornament in the border; f. 92v, angels playing musical instruments and Peter, with Renaissance ornament in the outer margin; f. 104v, the Good Shepherd and a bishop; f. 113, a monstrance (Ciardi Dupré, pl. 105), and the Veronica; f. 119v, a young armored saint on a prancing white horse, holding the standard; on the initial, the same 3 coats of arms as on f. 66; f. 120, bust of an angel; f. 124, Silvester baptizing Constantine (Ciardi Dupré, pl. 105); f. 127v, an allegorical representation of a Wind (Ciardi Dupré, pls. 242, 243). Initials contemporary to the text, usually red, but towards the end of the book alternating red and blue; both colors on ff. 8v, 12v, 134v. Initials within the text as cadels, sometimes with sketched faces or washed in yellow. Rubrics throughout.

Bound, s. XVIII, in wooden boards with large bosses and studs on all sides and along spine; rebacked; cracks in the wood repaired with small brass plates on the inside. Thumb holes cut along the lower edge of each leaf; book marks of yellow silk and red braid hang from a wire attached to the top of the spine. Leaves from another antiphonal used as flyleaves (foliated as ff. 1 and 178, now scraped and written over) and as pastedowns (the front pastedown, once present as shown by offset on front cover, now missing; the back pastedown now lifted) from a book very similar to the present one. Two stoles and a strip of silk formerly loose in the volume; on a large, carved, pseudo-gothic lectern.

Written for use in a Franciscan house, after the canonization of Didacus in 1588. In 1719 P. Regulus added the table of contents and identified himself as being from "Vurno," probably the town of Vorno in the province of Lucca, which would have fallen under the jurisdiction of the Franciscan province of Tuscany. Date and source of acquisition by the Huntington Library unknown.

HM 48570 — England, s. $XV^{3/4}$
CHRONICLE OF ENGLAND

1. f. 1: [notes on chronology added, s. XV] Notandum est quod secundum Cestrensem in libro polecronice libro 1° capitulo 4° octo fuerunt modi calculandi annos . . . Novissime vero christiani Anno ab incarnatione domini supputarunt [C. Babington, ed., *Polychronicon Ranulphi Higden Monachi Cestrensis.* RS 41 (London 1865) 1:34–36]; Nota quod sex sunt etates seculi prima ab Adam usque ad noe . . . a christo usque ad finem mundi [Higden, 1:32–34]; Et nota quod in presente volumine . . . versus finem mundi [much rubbed but apparently on the 4 dating systems used in this chronicle; ff. 1v–2v, blank]

2. ff. 3–87: Britannia que et Anglia dicitur a Bruto nomen est sortita que ante ipsius adventum albion dicebatur. Est autem insula illa beatissima omnium insularum. Cuius insule Brutus post expulsos gigantes habitator . . . In cuius rei evidenciam quidam legatus apostolicus in scocia tunc existens dictam camisiam postmodum domino pape ut dicitur deferebat. [ff. 87v–88v, blank]

A chronicle of England from Brutus to the murder of James I of Scotland in February 1437. Dates entered in the margins; some fifteenth century side notes in the hand of the scribe; extensive notes by various hands of the seventeenth century in Latin and in English in the margins and on f. 88v (with references to folio numbers in another book).

HM 48570

Parchment, ff. iv (early modern paper) + 88 (1 and 2 as flyleaves) + v (early modern paper); 184 × 136 (125 × 81) mm. 1–11[8]. Catchwords in the script of the text; quire and leaf signatures as letters and roman numerals. 24–29 long lines, frame ruled in ink. Written in a secretary script. Opening initial, f. 3, 5-line, in gold on a cusped ground with ink sprays of simple green and gold foliage; colors of infilling and ground (red?) now washed away. 3-line blue initials with red flourishing. Early modern foliation up to f. 23 in arabic numerals. Pen trials, upside down, on ff. 28v–29, including "Be it knowne vnto all men by these presents." Some damage from damp.

Bound, s. XVIII, in English mottled calf over pasteboards; rebacked by Bernard Middleton, s. XX.

Written in England in the third quarter of the fifteenth century. Belonged to Edward Sanders of Floore, Northants., his signature and the date 1607 on f. 2v; marginalia possibly in his hand. Also on f. 2v, a seventeenth century note referring to 2 other manuscripts of this chronicle: one in St. Benedict's College, Cambridge (Corpus Christi College, MS 311) and another in Sir Robert Cotton's Library, probably Cotton Vitellius D.xii (T. Smith, *Catalogus . . . Bibliothecae Cottonianae,* 1696, p. 93), destroyed in the fire of 1731. Belonged to Arthur Annesley, 1st Earl of Anglesey (1614–86), historian and Lord Privy Seal to Charles II, his signature and date, August 2, 1681, on f. 1; his sale by Thomas Philipps, London, 25 October 1686, lot 18, p. 77. Acquired by James Sotheby (d. 1720), principal collector of the Sotheby Library at Ecton Hall, Northants.; his signature in the upper margin of f. 3. Descriptive notes signed J.S., February 27, 1722, mounted on f. i. On the front pastedown, book plate of C. W. H. Sotheby, and short note signed F.E.S., 24 December 1890. Sold by the executors of N. W. A. Sotheby, Sotheby's, 8 December 1981, lot 93 to Alan G. Thomas (London). Acquired from him by the Huntington Library in March 1982.

Secundo folio: viro utique

HM 49124 DEVOTIONS

Germany, s. XV²

1. f. 1r–v: [misbound] Suffrages of Augustine and Catherine of Siena.

2. ff. 2–15v: Penitential psalms beginning defectively in Ps. 31, 2, and litany including Matthias (in red ink) among the apostles; Augustine, Dominic (twice) and Louis (of Toulouse?; all in red ink) among the confessors; Catherine (of Alexandria?), Ursula, Apollonia, Odilia and Catherine of Siena (all in red ink) among the virgins; leaf missing after f. 9 with beginning of litany.

3. ff. 16–19: Prayers. [f. 19v, ruled, but blank]

4. ff. 20–49: Office of the Dead, Dominican use. [f. 49v, ruled, but blank]

5. ff. 50–58: Prayers, beginning and ending defectively, and including on ff. 55v–57v a prayer headed *Oratio ad patronos ordinis nostri dedicata* (to Dominic, Peter martyr, Thomas Aquinas, Vincent Ferrer, Catherine of Siena) and on f. 57v, a prayer to Matthias. [ff. 58v–59v, ruled, but blank]

6. ff. 60–67: Prayers. [ff. 67v–68v, ruled, but blank]

7. ff. 69–71: [added by a contemporary hand] Ave mitis Imperatrix/ Ave vite Restauratrix . . . [*RH* 1965; 18 stanzas of 4 verses each, each verse per stanza beginning with the same letter].

8. ff. 71v–76: [added in a later hand] Prayers. [ff. 76v–78v, ruled, but blank]

9. ff. 79–87v: Seven prayers attributed to Thomas Aquinas. [f. 88r–v, ruled, but blank]

10. ff. 89–97v: Long hours of Mary Magdalene.

11. ff. 97v–106v: Prayers in hierarchical order (Angels, Apostles, Martyrs, Confessors, Virgins, All Saints).

12. ff. 107–117: Long hours of Eternal Wisdom.

13. ff. 117–122: Prayers. [ff. 122v–123v, ruled, but blank except for later ownership note; see below]

14. ff. 124–125: Suffrages, including one of Odilia. [f. 125v, ruled, but blank]

15. ff. 126–136v: Long hours "de beato Dominico confessore patre nostro," followed by prayers to Dominic and Catherine of Siena.

16. ff. 136v–144: Prayers and gospel readings for various canonical hours, including 2 prayers attributed to Thomas Aquinas; f. 144v [added by a contemporary hand] *Sanctus Gregorius papa hic scripsit karolo magno,* Balsamus et cera munda cum crismatis unda . . . [*RH* 24055?]

17. ff. 145–150: Short hours of Catherine of Alexandria, followed by prayers to Catherine of Alexandria and to Vincent Ferrer.

18. ff. 150–153: Prayers. [f. 153v, ruled, but blank]

19. ff. 154–166v: Long hours against sin, followed by prayers to Louis confessor (of Toulouse?), Apollonia, the Holy Spirit.

20. ff. 166v–172v: Prayers for the dead, preceded by indulgences of Pius II and John IV; litany for the dead. [f. 173r–v, ruled, but blank]

21. ff. 174–185: Fifteen O's of St. Bridget, followed by a prayer to Jesus, Domine ihesu criste fili dei vivi ad honorem et gloriam tremende passionis . . . me indignum famulum tuum ludowicum [the name in red ink] dignare absolvere . . .

22. ff. 185v–191v: Metrical hours of the Passion, beginning Gloria tibi domine Qui tuo sacras lumine/ Tempora noctis medie Natus de maria virgine . . . [*RH* 27364].

23. ff. 192–194v: Suffrages of Peter martyr, Ursula and Jerome [f. 195r–v, ruled, but blank]

24. ff. 196–207: Prayers to say before communion. [f. 207v, ruled, but blank]

25. ff. 208–216: Prayers to say after communion. [ff. 216v–217v, ruled, but blank]

26. ff. 218–226v: *Incipit Sertum seu Crinale gloriose virginis Marie ex quinquaginta flosculis figurarum atque enigmatum compositum per venerabilem magistrum Iohannem parisiensem sacre Theologie professorem eximium Amen,* Ave salve gaude vale o maria non vernale, sed hiis rosis spiritale . . . [*RH* 2098, here attributed to Jean Gerson, 1363–1429; 5 stanzas of 10 verses each, each verse per stanza beginning with the same letter], followed by prayers to the Virgin. [f. 227r–v, ruled, but blank]

27. ff. 228–238v: Devotions on the life of Mary and of Jesus for the rosary, followed by prayers to the Virgin.

28. ff. 239–241: Devotions for the canonical hours on the sorrows of the Virgin. [f. 241v, ruled, but blank]

29. ff. 242–243v: Prayers to Thomas Aquinas and to Barbara; ff. 243v–244v, added in a contemporary hand, prayer to Jesus; f. 245r–v, ruled, but blank except for later ownership note and pen trials (see below); on back flyleaf, s. XVI, the couplet, Walther, *Initia* 14318 (?), Post hominis mortem querunt tria avide sortem/ Vult vermis carnem, animam Sathan, proximus rem.

Paper (watermark, *Armoiries, Fleur de lis* similar to Briquet 1744, Paris 1482, Cologne 1481–94 and various other places in northeastern Europe), ff. i (modern paper) + ii (contemporary paper) + 245 + i (contemporary paper) + i (modern paper); 89 × 67 (70 × 42) mm. 1^{10}(–1, 10; 1 replaced by another leaf) $2–5^{10}$ 6^{12}(–1, 10 after ff. 49 and 57) 7^{10}(–9 after f. 67, probably blank) 8^{10}(through f. 78) 9^{10}(through f. 88) 10^{10}(through f. 98) 11^{10}(–9, 10 after f. 106) 12^{10} 13^{10}(–a leaf in the second half) 14^{10}(–10 after f. 134, no loss of text) 15^{10}(through f. 144) 16^{10}(–1, no apparent loss of text; through f. 153) $17–18^{10}$(through f. 173) $19–20^{10}$ 21^{2}(through f. 195) 22^{12}(through f. 207) 23^{10}(through f. 217) 24^{10}(through f. 227) 25^{10} 26^{8}. Quire structure and arrangement of texts show production in booklets. Quires marked in blue ink with letters of the alphabet and in pencil with numbers, both systems modern and incorrect. Usually 18 long lines, frame ruled in ink. Written by one person in a German littera cursiva with additions by 3 other people: i, ff. 69–71 and 144v, in a contemporary hand; ii, ff. 71v–76, in a sixteenth century hand; iii, ff. 243v–244v, in a contemporary hand. 6- to 1-line red initials, occasionally washed in yellow; rubrics and underlining in red. Damage to ff. 98v and 227v suggests that engravings, once pasted to these pages, have since been removed. Contemporary foliation: 49–50 (on present ff. 2–3), 68–70 (on present ff. 20–22), 99–106 (on present ff. 50–57), 108–117 (on present ff. 58–67), 119 (on present f. 68) 120–127 (on present ff. 79–86). Contemporary foliation shows 48 leaves missing at the beginning of the volume (one of which probably now mounted as f. 1), 1 leaf missing between the present ff. 3 and 20 (actually after f. 9), 1 leaf missing between the present ff. 22 and 50 (actually after f. 49), 1 leaf missing between the present ff. 57 and 58, 1 leaf missing between the present ff. 67 and 68; the discrepancy between the 2 sets of foliation at the present f. 68 (in contemporary foliation, f. 119) and the present f. 79 (in contemporary foliation, f. 120) is due to the foliator having omitted numbering the quire of then blank leaves, now ff. 69–78 (with same watermark and ruling as rest of volume).

Bound, s. XV, in red leather over pasteboards, stamped with diagonal rules and an enclosed rosette; remains of a fore edge clasp, closing back to front; remains of red leather fore edge tabs; rebacked.

Written in northwestern Germany (as suggested by the veneration shown to Odilia and Matthias, patrons respectively of Strasbourg and Trier), after 1461 (the date of canonization of Catherine of Siena), for and probably by a Dominican (see arts. 2, 4, 5, 9, 15, 17) whose name seems to have been Louis: on f. 184v is a prayer for ". . . me indignum famulum tuum ludowicum . . . ." On f. 245, ownership note of "Frater Balthasarus Schuop anno domini 1572." Sixteenth century ex libris of a convent, probably Dominican, in Frankfurt on f. ii, "Iste libellus pertinet ad Conventum Franckfordiciensem Anno domini [15]78." Eighteenth century pressmark, presumably of the same convent, on f. iii verso, "No. 4910 C[onventus] fr[atrum] O[rdinis] P[raedicatorum]." Given after the secularization by a Professor Schütz, teacher of Latin, to his student on 16 January 1813 according to the note on f. 123, "Dieses Manuscript habe ich von meinem lateinischen Lehere herr Professor Schütz zum Geschenk bekommen ⟨?⟩stag den 16ten Januar 1813"; the lower edge of this leaf cut away, possibly to remove the student's signature. On f. i verso, "This volume was picked up on the field of Gravelotte, shortly after the battle [of the Franco-Prussian war, west of Metz, 18 August 1870] by James Audus Hirst Esq. of Adel near Leeds who gave it to his daughter Ethel Adela (Mrs. W. A. Harding)." Mrs. Harding, an author, and her husband, Walter Ambrose Harding of Madingley Hall, Cambridgeshire, died in 1942. Acquired by James Thorpe in Cambridge, England, ca. 1950; given by him to the Huntington Library in July 1983.

HU 1051 England, s. XV^{in}–XVI^{ex}
ALCHEMICAL, MEDICAL and TECHNICAL COMPILATION

1. ff. 1–2v: Et inter ceteras res illa est quam te non oportet ignorare . . . Et cum tibi dant diversa signa et adversa declina semper ad meliorem et probabiliorem partem. Completus est tractus de signis et moribus naturalibus hominum Ad regem magnificum Alexandrum qui dominatus fuit totius orbis dictusque monarcha in septembrione.

Aristotle, *De physiognomia;* see W. J. Wilson, "Catalogue of Latin and Vernacular Alchemical Manuscripts in the United States and Canada," *Osiris* 6 (1939) 419–61, especially p. 421.

2. ff. 3–4v: Naturam primam dare cuique suam voluit deus atque/ Iuxta naturam scit dare cuique suam locum . . . Per quem securum non diruit ulla ruina/ Si quem non teneat non tenet ille locum.

Thorndike and Kibre, 904; Walther, *Initia* 11614; here in 134 verses.

3. ff. 4v–6v: Ver estas Autumpnus yemps sunt iiii^{or} Anni/ Tempora diversis dissociata modis . . . Quando igitur laicus ratione regente mederi/ Egrotis qui non noverit ista potest.

Thorndike and Kibre, 1685; Walther, *Initia* 20124a; here in 139 verses; these verses also follow those of art. 2 in Oxford, Corpus Christi College, MS 95.

4. ff. 7–8v: Here begynnyth a tretys of meystyr pawlyn for to knowe ye febultes yat grouyn to seknes in mane and in woman for to see yar waturs And to gyf yame medycyns for to conuert theme & cetera. Fyrst ther ben 4 elymentes in ye word and of them man ys made . . . for yt ys parell to take cold and surfets for ye dropsy.

Treatise on diet according to the 4 seasons, the 4 elements and the 4 humors.

5. f. 8v: Beten ys An erbe of many vertuys. What maner of man yat berys beyten vp on hyme yer shall no maner venumys best do hyme no herme . . . and yf he have Any thyng to do he shall be sped well in hys ["Iurney" deleted and corrected to:] doyng.

Passage on the properties of the herb betony; see R. H. Robbins, "Medical Manuscripts in Middle English," *Speculum* 45 (1970) 401, n. 22.

6. ff. 9–18v: Six alchemical recipes in English and in Latin; Wilson, p. 422.

7. ff. 18v–19: Maius opus dicitur quando fit aurum . . . ; *Opus Imperatorii,* Mercurii crudi partes sex optime lune . . . ; *Ferrum,* scilicet in ferro parum . . .
Three notes on alchemical matters.

8. f. 19v: Memorandum quod capellanus gilde corporis christi et beati georgii de Blida recepit per manum Thome Chamburlayn de stipendio ii li. vi s. viii d. . . .

Note of sums received by the chaplain of the Guild of Corpus Christi and of St. George of Blyth, Notts., including the names of Hugh Peke, John Watson, Thomas Hemyng, Sir Robert Clyfton, Stephen Pumry (?), John Wolfe and Richard Dowson; see HMC, *Report on the manuscripts of the late Reginald Rawdon Hastings, Esq.* (1928) 1:417–30, especially p. 418.

9. f. 20: Que sunt sacramenta necessaria et que voluntaria . . . ex sanctificacione aliquam invisibilem quam conferas. [f. 21v, blank, except for pen trials]

10. f. 21r–v: Spiritus principales sunt 4^{or} scilicet sulfur, auripigmentum, argentum vivum, sal armoniaci qui spiritus quoque vocantur angeli sive anguli . . . Et cuprum convertit in argentum. Et hoc vocatur alixer in omnibus libris.

11. ff. 22–23: Seven alchemical recipes in Latin; f. 23v, blank.

12. ff. 24–29v: *Metaforum paradisus,* Quatuor sunt species tantum necessarie ad elixir componendum videlicet Argentum vivum, Sulphur citrinum fugiens . . . et nominibus ‹faded› spirituum sublimatorum et ‹faded› matutina [catchword:] et ve‹?›t//

Hortulanus, condensed by Johannes Dumbeler de Anglia (?); Wilson, p. 423.

13. f. 30r–v: *Saturnus fundendo in acetum mundificatus,* Nota, Dicunt philosophi quod lapis fit ex una re et cum uno et unum est . . . et est resolutiva et congelativa et rigativa multas faciens operaciones. *Explicit hec aqua.*

14. f. 31r–v: //similiter et pone in distillatorio cum suo recipiente . . . qui dicitur mensis vulgaris quod est magnum secretum huius artis.

Ps. Pliny; Wilson, p. 424; here beginning defectively with a tie mark and the note "verte 32 folia" to a now-lost f. 68 according to the contemporary foliation, which numbers this leaf as f. 36.

15. f. 32r–v: Septima operacio et pars huius operis est practica virtutis elixirii . . . Elixir vero corporum tingit minus quam spiritum quia tingit nisi centum.

Johannes de Rupescissa; Wilson, p. 424.

16. f. 32v: Est in mercurio quicquid querunt sapientes/ Corpus ab hoc anima spiritus tinctura trahuntur . . . Hec petra divina prius alba deinde citrina/ Cum fuerit aurina vestra deducta carina//

Wilson, p. 424; Walther, *Initia* 21054, here ending defectively.

17. f. 33r–v: //sub diafragmate ad cor suffocandum . . . Nichil efficacius spasmum cedat quam nobilissima quinta essencia vel in eius absencia aqua ardens.

Johannes de Rupescissa; Wilson, pp. 424–25.

18. f. 33v: Audite secreta que loquar dilectique verba oris mei. Spiritus ubi vult spirat . . . gutta una et se per mensem teneat in quiete//

Roger Bacon (?); Wilson, p. 425, ending defectively.

19. f. 34: *Aqua corosiva sic debet fieri,* Accipe de urina puerorum . . . que utimur ad opus nostrum benedictum et cetera.

Ps. Pliny; Wilson, p. 425.

20. ff. 34–35v: *Incipit tractatus optimus in quo plinius philosophus quid sit lapis qua materia debet fieri et quomodo* . . . et cum aceto vini filtrati modificando vaporando et per 4 horas sublimando et per todidiem//

Ps. Pliny; Wilson, p. 425, ending defectively.

21. ff. 36–38v: Four alchemical recipes in English and in Latin; Wilson, pp. 425–26.

22. ff. 38v–39v: Inmundum corpus est plumbum quod Alio nomine Ascop interpretatur . . . id est fumus albus, leo viridis et aqua seu terra fetida.
Morienus; Wilson, p. 426; written in spaces left blank by previous scribes.

23. f. 39v: Assob arabice, Alumen interpretatur latine . . . in Aurum purissimum convertetur quo melius reperire non potest.

24. ff. 39–43v: [Table of values:] *Here begynyth the Rate off ynglysshe money first for mytis,* 20 mytis makyse a grayne . . . [f. 41, Table of values of 51 foreign coins:] The glydren of gaunte with a lyon is worth iii s. iiii d. . . . [f. 43, Table for setting the price of silver by weight:] *The Rate of bying of all maner off siluer after xviii d. the Coynage of a li. wher of the kyng hath xii d. . . .* [f. 43v, Table for setting the price of gold by weight:] *The Rate of bying of fyne gold after iiii s. the Coynage of a li. wher of hath to þe kynges mynte ii s. vi d. . . .*
Hastings Report, pp. 418–21, in part printed directly, in part in resumé; Wilson, p. 426.

25. ff. 44–45: *Hec sunt dicta sanctorum de virtute sacramenti Altaris de fructu misse prout sequitur,* Paulus apostolus dicit Missa precellit et est dignior ceteris oracionibus . . . iuste petimus aut hic aut in futuro.
Also citing Bernard, Jerome, Ambrose, Chrysostomus, Luke, Matthew, John the Evangelist, Augustine; the quotations on f. 44v crossed out.

26. ff. 45–46v: Five alchemical recipes, the first and the last, *Opus ad solem* and *To make sylver,* printed in *Hastings Report,* pp. 429–30; Wilson, p. 427.

27. f. 47r–v: List of 47 chapels, churches, monasteries, priories, convents, etc. in London, Southwark and Westminster.

28. f. 48: [Cost of making colored letters] Small lettris blew & rede the C at i d. a M^{l} vi d. Small lettris blew & rede florisshid precium C ii d. a M^{l} x d. Small lettris gold & blew florisshid þe C iiii d. a M^{l} x d.
Hastings Report, p. 421; Wilson, p. 427.

29. f. 48: Table of the value of farthings, pence, etc.; notes on the number of days in a year; the rhyme, xxx^{ti} days hath Nouembre, Iune Aprill & Septembre/ Of xxviii there is but one & all þe remenunt xxxi.

30. f. 48v: Table entitled *Compotus frumenti,* according to the day and the year; table of currency exchange, Numerus marcarum conversus in libras . . .

31. f. 48v: Two medical recipes, *For blered Eyn* and *For Runnyng Eyn,* written in spaces left blank by the previous scribe; printed in *Hastings Report,* p. 427.

32. f. 49: Conclusion of a medical recipe in English; printed in Wilson, p. 427.

33. f. 49r–v: Inmundum corpus est plumbum quod Alio nomine Ascop . . . aqua seu terra fetida. Anatron id est sal nitri.
Morienus; Wilson, p. 428, and above, art. 22.

34. f. 49v: Phebus fonde first the crafte of medecine/ By touche of poues & vryne Inspections . . . Among all other ther is no thyng mor mete/ To the help of man then temperat diete. [Followed by a list of the number of days in each month.]

IMEV 2751. Schuler, n. 425. Printed in *Hastings Report,* p. 421 and in R. H. Robbins, ed., *Secular Lyrics of the XIVth and XVth Centuries* (Oxford 1955) 76.

35. f. 50r–v: Numbers, 1–1,000,000 written out in Latin with the corresponding arabic numeral in digits.

36. f. 50v: Two recipes, *To make Mercury* and *To wryte with gold of florysshe,* printed in *Hastings Report,* p. 429.

37. f. 51r–v: Five alchemical notes; Wilson, p. 428.

38. f. 52r–v: Vitrum lapis est arte confectus vi ignis avecenna dicit . . . Et ultimo avicennus dicit quod pulvis inde potatus in vino expellit petram renum et vesice et cetera. [Followed by a table of equivalent terms:] Argentum vivum, Spiritus fugiens, anglice quik siluyr . . .

39. f. 53r–v: *Opus perfectissimum sine mendacio vocatur liber divinalis,* Super vas istud reponatur vitrum factum ut urinale ponitum versum . . . Et omnia predicta dicit flos Regis in suis capitulis si intelligis et cetera. *Explicit.*

40. f. 54: Sciendum quod nichil sine experiencia sufficienter sciri potest. In uno solo consistit veritas quarum lapis veritas vocatur . . . res est hec tum [?] una.

41. f. 54: Mors argenti vivi est principium artis nostre . . . luna vera et fixa ut dicit hermes.

42. ff. 54v–56: Four alchemical recipes in English and in Latin; Wilson, p. 429; f. 56v, blank.

43. f. 57: *Thinges noted out an Olde book yat was Peter de Moyes,* Borax ita fit, combure tartarum donec fiat album . . . et pone omnia iterum ad sublimandum ut supra et sic reiterando. [ff. 57v–62, blank]

44. f. 62v: A horse hath xviii propertees: iii of an Ox, iii of an asse, iii of a fox, iii of an hare & vi of a woman. Thre of an ox: brod yed, brod fronted & syde garnesyde . . . Esy att sterop & soft beryng et cetera.

Printed in *Hastings Report,* p. 421.

45. f. 62v: Recipe, *For to make a water to gylde ony maner metall.*

46. ff. 63–66v: //sanctum Thomam. Anno domini Millesimo C lxx° passio sancti Thome martiris Cantuariensis . . . Anno domini M° ccc xxii° ingressus est Robertus Bruys in comitatu karliolensi cum toto excercitu stetit totam patriam// [f. 66:] //et opida intrini [= of Antrim?] captivante. Eodem Anno [1417] constancie electus fuit papa martinus . . . Eodem anno moritur Robertus halam Episcopus Sarisburiensis. [New paragraph:] [A]nno domini 1421 Occisus fuit dux clarencie . . . Eodem anno [1430] post nativitatem domini in Anglia est Reversus et cetera.

Fragments of a chronicle of England and Scotland covering 1170–1322 and 1417–1430, missing one leaf with loss of text after f. 65.

47. ff. 66v–71v: Fifteen medical and alchemical recipes in Latin and in English; Wilson, pp. 429–30.

48. f. 72: Means of determining infertility, *For to know wheder ye fautt be in ye mone or ye woman,* printed in *Hastings Report,* p. 422; followed by "Contra palisim lingue semen sinapis masticatum et sub lingua retentum valet," and a medical recipe, *For to Clensse ye hed,* crossed out.

49. f. 72v: Two alchemical recipes; Wilson, p. 430.

50. ff. 73–74v: //Alius philosophus unquam exposuit seu declaravit ita ut in me increpare non possis . . . sine quorum sciencia nullus veniet ad operacionis incrementum et cetera.
Ps. Pliny; Wilson, pp. 430–31, and below, art. 52.

51. ff. 75–77: Eight technical recipes in English, printed in *Hastings Report,* pp. 427–29, *For to floresshe with gold on colors or on parchement, To ley golde on cuppes of horne, glasse or ston, To make Curyus warke on glasse wyndosse after ye be aneled, To do syluer on yrun, To make Turnesoll, To make a museke, For to make boe glew, To make byse.*

52. ff. 77v–82v: *Hic incipit tractatus optimus in quo exponit et aperte declarare plinius philosophus quid sit lapis philosoficus et ex qua materia debet fieri et quomodo* . . . a die solis que vulgariter dies dominica nuncupatur solis et cetera, luna a die lune, Mars a die Martis, et cetera.
Ps. Pliny; Wilson, pp. 431–32, and above, arts. 14, 19, 20, 50.

53. ff. 83–84: *Incipit liber xxx verborum,* Iam scis tu fili qui hanc scientiam et doctrinam queris . . . Et hoc modo facias donec compleatur numerus et hoc est verbum 30 quod tu scire debes si deus voluerit. *Explicit liber 28* [*sic*] *verborum.*
Geber (?); Wilson, pp. 432–33.

54. f. 84v: Note on pharmaceutical weights and four alchemical recipes in Latin; Wilson, p. 433.

55. f. 85: Iuce of lekes with gotes galle/ For euyl heryng help it shall . . . It is gud for dronkyn men/ A raw lek to ete & comfortyth ye brayn.
IMEV 1810. Printed in *Hastings Report,* p. 422 and in Robbins, *Secular Lyrics,* p. 77.

56. f. 85: Four culinary recipes in English, the first three printed in *Hastings Report,* pp. 426–27 out of order, *Leche Lumbard, A chawdryun for a swanne, Lesche, Muda* (?).

57. ff. 85v–86v: Twelve medical recipes of which the nine in English are printed in *Hastings Report,* pp. 422–24; the titles of two of the Latin recipes are in cipher: *For swellyng of legges, For a marmole, Pr4pt2r 1m4r2m m5l32r3s* [= Propter amorem mulieris, by inscribing her name on the Eucharist and, after various procedures, giving it to her to eat or drink unawares; Wilson, p. 434]; *Ad 1p1r32nd*[*um*] *c2r1s* [= Ad apariendum (*sic,* for "aperiendum") ceras, by writing magical words with bat's blood on new parchment, putting it in one's mouth and blowing on the seal; Wilson, p. 434]; *For ye goute, For the goute, For akyng & swellyng in ye ballokke, Anoyer, For to staunch blud when ye mast veyn is kervyn, Yf a man be in gret perel of bledyng, For scallyd hedes,* a charm in Latin against dog bite (Wilson, p. 434).

58. ff. 87–88: Eighteen technical recipes in English, the first beginning acephalously, the others printed in *Hastings Report,* pp. 424–25: *To mak brasyl water*

substancial in a crudde, To dry brasil water when it is cruddid to be substancial for alumpnars or steynars, Vermyloun, To mak dorre, To mak swerte colour, For mak purpure, To mak yelow for horse treese and hayr, For colours, To mak anoyer dorre, To mak a tanned water, To temper mader, To mak syse for gold or syluer, To mak blewe, To mak blac water, To mak sable, To mak a cloth for to shyne when it is wroght, To mak rosett.

59. ff. 88v–90: Six recipes in Latin, of which five alchemical and one technical, *Ad faciendum scripturam auream, argenteam, eneam vel cupream;* Wilson, pp. 435–36.

60. f. 90v: Two technical recipes, *To mak fyne green* and *For to gylt,* printed in *Hastings Report,* pp. 425–26; a list of five herbal waters and their properties, and a medical recipe, printed in *Hastings Report,* p. 427; two medical recipes in Latin.

61. ff. 91–103: Ninety-four alchemical recipes in Latin, numbered by the same person who foliated the manuscript, in several series usually beginning afresh with 1 on the recto of each new folio; Wilson, pp. 436–42; f. 103v, blank.

62. f. 104r–v: Six related alchemical recipes in Latin, usually ending "et serva ad opus," the last entitled *Opus lunare,* to make silver; seven short notes on alchemical matters, the whole numbered by the foliator; Wilson, pp. 442–43.

63. f. 105: Three alchemical recipes in Latin, numbered by the foliator; Wilson, p. 443.

64. f. 105v: *Incipit prologus in speculum de secretis philosophorum,* Cum studii solertis indagine universarum rerum artificia philosophia comperit secundum utilitatem tamen fili karissime exquisicionis alkamie magisterium adinvenit . . . et impensam amisisse merito deplorabit.

Aristotle, variant fragment of *De perfecto magisterio;* Wilson, p. 443.

65. ff. 106–107v: *Incipit liber de secretis philosophorum,* In nomine domini nostri ihesu christi ad instructionem multorum circa hanc doctrinam studere volencium quibus deest copia librorum, hic libellus edatur titulusque speculum stultorum intitulatur . . . et tocius huius rei completum sub maximo compendio propter penuriam librorum. Lauda deum et ei gracias age cui semper sit laus honor et gloria Amen. *Explicit Speculum Alkymie secundum Rogerum Bacon.*

Roger Bacon; Wilson, p. 443.

66. ff. 107v–109: *Incipit liber de 12 Aquis,* Prima aqua est de aqua rubea, Secunda de penitrativa . . . continue rubebit et colorem aureum retinebit. *Explicit tractatus de 12 aquis.*

Aristotle (?), numbered in 12 sections by the foliator; Wilson, p. 444.

67. ff. 109–110v: Aqua ad dissoluendum omnia metalla . . . quia timeo ne eam habentes in superbia extollantur. *Explicit.*

Petrus Hispanus, waters numbered 2–21 by the foliator; Wilson, pp. 444–45.

68. ff. 110v–123v: 144 alchemical recipes in Latin, many by title only and cross-referenced to the "other book," i.e. art. 61; numbered in the margin by the foliator in several series beginning afresh with 1 on the recto of each new folio; Wilson, pp. 446–55.

69. ff. 124–125: Seven alchemical recipes in Latin, the second and the third, *Plumbum simile argento facere* and *Ex ere argentum vel elidrium vel aurum facere,* being nn. 79 and 209 of the *Mappae clavicula* (R. P. Johnson, "Some Continental Manuscripts of the *Mappae Clavicula,*" *Speculum* 12, 1937, pp. 84–85, citing this manuscript); quotations from "Dancim [?] philosophus," "Morienus philosophus," and "quidem philosophus Maria"; Wilson, pp. 455–56.

70. f. 125v: One recipe, *For to make lyme for byrdes,* printed in *Hastings Report,* p. 429.

71. ff. 126–127: Archilaus dicit, Accipe de Mercurio quantum vis et tere cum aceto acerimo . . . et pone super omnia corpora et fiant luna bona. [f. 127v, blank]

72. ff. 128–129: //duavit hominem ad interitum. Nam si aliquis illorum panniculorum quantum unius acris est acumen rumpatur . . . Nunc dicendum est de Tractatibus ad omnes Plagas sanandas in corpore humano. De Tractatibus faciendis. De unguentis faciendis. De unguentis Calidis//

Six paragraphs of a medical treatise on tumors, plasters, salves, wounds, etc., beginning defectively and ending unfinished; Wilson, p. 456.

73. f. 129v: Mercure is flos florum for by hyr myght she calcyns euery mettall to powder . . . for by hyr power she calcyns metall colde more yen fyre may do by heyte.

Liber patris sapientie (?); Wilson, p. 456.

74. ff. 130–140v: Approximately twenty-two alchemical recipes and notes in English and in Latin, with one added at the end in another hand; Wilson, pp. 456–58.

75. f. 141: Five recipes for glue in Latin, the last added in a different hand; Wilson, p. 458.

76. ff. 141v–142: Six technical recipes, the five in English printed in *Hastings Report,* p. 426: *To mak Syment for ston, For to mak a fenestrall, To mak red wax, To mak vynegar, To make Blak leddyr, Ad faciendum encaustum;* Wilson, pp. 458–59.

77. ff. 141v–142: Three recipes in Latin, added in spaces left blank by the previous scribe, *Multiplicacio cere, To kytt a glasse with a feder* (printed in *Hastings Report,* p. 426); *Multiplicacio Croci;* Wilson, p. 459.

78. ff. 142v–144: *De pictura cuiuscumque ligni,* Cum preterea tabulam, ymaginem vel aliquid ligneum depingere volueris, provideas tibi bonum glutum factum de corde cervi et pergameno quod inferius exprimitur . . . [f. 143v:] Deinde si volueris totum coloribus depictum preter aurum vel argentum poteris vernizare ut melius luceat. Hoc modo facies cum omni ligno. [New paragraph:] Colam sive glutum superius memoratam hoc modo facies, Accipe ollam et impone cornua cervorum cesa in parvis partibus . . . cum aliquo instrumento deponatur tunc quid clarius elucescit.

79. ff. 144–145: Four recipes in Latin, *Pillule gloriosissime Rogeri regis quibus utebatur singulis diebus eis etiam utebatur papa Alexander, Ad faciendam scripturam in Calibe, Ad sculpendum litteras in Calibe, Ad colorandum litteras sculptas in metallo quando vis colorare;* Wilson, p. 459.

80. ff. 145–147: Alkamia est scientia docens transformare genera metallorum in aurum verum et argentum verum. Hec quidem confici possunt ex quatuor spiritibus et 7 metallis. Spiritus autem dant colorem . . . Ecce instrumenta quibus operamur in scientia.
Ebrardus; Wilson, pp. 459–60.

81. ff. 147–148: Seven alchemical recipes and notes in Latin; Wilson, pp. 460–61.

82. f. 148v: *Incipit liber de aquis et primo de aqua preciosa herbarum,* Actus mirabilis quas composuit Petrus hispanus cum naturali industria quarum prima est aqua preciosa herbarum et est mirabilis in virtute ad visum conservandum necnon clarificandum et contra omnem maculam in oculo que sic fit. Recipe Rute feniculi . . . *De aqua Seminibus,* Recipe semen petrocilii apii anisii maracei carui ver-[catchword:]-vene ava//
Thorndike and Kibre, 1328 (?), here ending defectively.

Paper, in quarto, consisting of parts of several manuscripts of separate origin but by now impossible to distinguish precisely one from the other, brought together in the late fifteenth century. Watermarks: 3 types of *Tête de boeuf* similar to Briquet 14183, Belfort 1458, to Briquet 14193, Antwerp 1464–66 and to Briquet 15068 or 15089, Bordeaux 1462 or Soleure 1488; 5 types of Hand, similar to Heawood 2472, 1511–12, to Heawood 2475 but with a circle in the palm, 1519–25, to Heawood 2473 but with an identified ornament in the palm, 1512–19, to Briquet 11355, Sassenberg 1533 and to Briquet 11154 but with a five-pointed star, Rouen 1561; *Fleur* similar to Briquet 6654, Rome 1452–53; *Char* similar to Briquet 3537, Palermo 1465. ff. ii (modern paper) + 148 + ii (modern paper); 222 × 147–165 (135–178 × 80–132) mm. Collation cannot be determined, as all leaves are mounted on stubs. Catchwords on f. 29v (different from following text, even though contemporary foliation is consecutive) and on f. 148v. Scattered signatures: on f. 22, "4" in the lower right corner; on ff. 83–90, in the center of the lower margin, "ay," "aȝ," "ah," "ak" (leaves with contemporary foliation, 50–53), "q," "re," "at," "av" (leaves with contemporary foliation, 69–72); on ff. 141–148, in the center of the lower margin, "am" to "at" (leaves with contemporary foliation, 73–80). 20–38 long lines; 2 columns on ff. 40, 48v, 50. Possibly frame ruled in lead, but difficult to see; ff. 63–67 and 128–140, fully ruled in lead; apparent slash prick marks visible in the upper and lower margins of these leaves. Written by 13 people, usually in current anglicana scripts with some secretary forms (unless otherwise stated); the second copyist was also responsible for the contemporary foliation and for the numbering of some of the recipes; the divisions are: i, ff. 1–8v, s. XV^{med}; ii, ff. 9–19, 21r–v, 36–38v, parts of 39–56 (with copyist vii), 62v, 66v–71v, 72v–82v, 125v–127, 129v–140v, in a large and clumsy mixed hand, s. $XV^{med/ex}$; iii, ff. 19v–20v, s. XV^{med}; iv, ff. 22–29v, anglicana, s. XV^{in}; v, ff. 30–31v, 34–35v, s. XV^{ex}; vi, ff. 32–33v (marginalia by copyist ii), s. XV^{med}; vii, parts of ff. 39–56 (with copyist ii), 62v; viii, ff. 57, 140v bottom, (an italic note on f. 148?), secretary script, s. XVI^{ex}; ix, ff. 63–66v, secretary script, s. XV^{med}; x, f. 72; xi, ff. 83–90, 90v bottom – 125, 141–148; xii, f. 90 top (possibly the same as xi); xiii, ff. 128–129, secretary script with textura for the rubrics, s. XV^{med}. Generally unornamented; the most formal section, ff. 128–129 (art. 72), with 2-line calligraphic initials in blue and with rubrics in alternating red or blue. On ff. 1–6v, plain red 2-line initials and 1-line initials within the text touched in red; on f. 83, a plain red 1-line initial; on ff. 141, 144v–145, 148v, 2- and 1-line plain red initials, 1-line initials within the text touched in red and red paragraph marks. Sketch of distilling equipment in red ink in the lower margin of f. 148v. Corrector's mark in the outside lower corner of the recto and the verso, ff. 91–123. Contemporary foliation by the second copyist (with the modern foliation used in this description given in parentheses): 1–21 (1–21), 27–37 (22–32), 44–46 (33–35), 48–60 (36–48), 43–44 (49–50), 27–

37 (51–61), 39 (62), 96–98 (63–65), 109–111 (66–68), 127 on the verso (69), 146 (70), 167 on the verso (71), 147 (72), 172–173 (73–74), 177–184 (75–82), 50–53 (83–86), 69–72 (87–90), 184–218 (91–125), 218–219 (126–127), 114–126 (128–140), 73–80 (141–148).

Bound in 1971, with each leaf mounted on a stub and many leaves covered with crepeline.

Written in England during the fifteenth and sixteenth centuries. The second copyist appears to have been responsible for gathering together parts of several manuscripts, annotating them, foliating them and numbering the recipes in various sections. Among the pen trials on f. 125v what may be a copyist's or an owner's name, "[w]ell beloved rotgers." On f. 1, ca. 1600, "Jo. Bisshop," the same person who signed another alchemical and medical compilation formed of several manuscripts and formerly in the Hastings collection (*Hastings Report,* p. 430; alienated before 1926?). Belonged to the Hastings family, earls of Huntingdon. Purchased with the Hastings papers in January 1927 from Maggs, who had acquired the material from Edith Maud Abney-Hastings, Countess of Loudoun; for a description of the collection, see *Guide to British Historical Manuscripts,* 78–144.

Bibliography: De Ricci, 122.

RB 17862 GEOMETRICAL PROPOSITIONS

Wittenberg, 1553

Bound after John Peckham, *Perspectiva communis* [Milan: Petrus de Corneno, ca. 1482]; Hain 9425.

ff. 1–11v: [Brief paragraphs under the following rubrics:] *De supputatione motus solis, De conversione temporis oblati in tempus astronomicum, De reductione, De medio solis motu inveniendo, De auge invenienda, De argumento solis, De aequatione investiganda, De hypothesibus solis facientibus ad intelligendum calculum tabularum brutenicarum, Definitiones* [of various kinds of circles], *Explicatio diagrammatis.* [ff. 9v–10, 12r–v, blank]

Paper (watermark similar to Piccard, *Ochsenkopf* XVI, 123, Ansbach, Nürnberg, etc., 1480–82), ff. 12; 302 × 210 (230 × 130) mm. 1^{12}. Catchwords at the lower right corner of the text on each page. Number of lines varies; unruled. Written in one vigorous cursive hand. Headings in red rustic capitals or in red cursive. Rough compass diagrams, ff. 6r–v, 8, 11r–v.

Bound, s. XIX, in German half calf over marbled pasteboards; printed red leather label on the front cover.

Written by Philip Melancthon at Wittenberg in 1553; place and date in the upper right corner of f. 1 in the same hand as the text. See S. Leigh Sotheby, *Observations upon the Handwriting of Philip Melanchthon Illustrated with Fac-Similes* (London 1839) pl. XIV, II of parts of f. 1. Belonged to Dr. Georg F. B. Kloss of Frankfurt; his sale, Sotheby's, 7 May 1835, lot 4635 to Thorpe; Thorpe Cat. (1836) n. 838 to Sir Thomas Phillipps; his n. 9028 on the first leaf of the printed book and on the small paper label on the spine; Phillipps sale, Sotheby's, 5 June 1899, lot 868. Belonged to the collector of Lincolniana, Oliver R. Barrett (1873–1950); sale of a "notable American collector" by the American Art Association, New York, 20 December 1920, n. 580 to J. Adams for Henry E. Huntington.

Bibliography: De Ricci, 120. Mead, n. 3502.

RB 68069

RB 68069 Germany, s. XV[ex]
EXEMPLA; HOMILIES; LIFE OF CATHERINE OF SIENA

Bound after *Sermones Amici ex corrupto reintegrati* (Basle: Nicholaus Kessler, 1501).

1. ff. i verso—1: [preceding the printed book] Table of contents, from the *Sermones* of the printed book through the Life of St. Catherine, excluding Walburga (art. 34).

2. ff. 1–5v: *Dominica 2ª post octavam pasche,* Obsecro vos tamquam advenas et peregrinos abstinere vos a carnalibus desideriis, i Petrus 2. Plinius in libro de immortalitate anime dicit Qui corpus suum nutrit inimicum suum nutrit, est enim inimicus pessimus caro nostra . . . Non enim facile capitur a dyabolo qui bono vacat exercicio quod ⟨?⟩.

3. ff. 5v–9v: *In festo penthecoste,* Ille docebit vos omnia, Iohannis xiiii. Beatus Augustinus sic dicit Sicud omnis perfectio corporalis a spiritu corporeo est Sic omnis perfectio spiritualis est a spiritu sancto est [*sic*]. Et quia omne defectum appetit suam perfectionem quia natura secundum se est imperfecta . . . quia facit eos sanctos et spirituales facit in quibus operatur. Proprietates enim sunt hec: Purgat, per primum intelligitur donum timoris; Liquefacit, per 2ᵐ donum pietatis . . . Inflammat, per 7ᵐ donum sapiencie. Ista omnia apposita ut sis.

4. ff. 9v–10v: *Coronacio imperatoris,* Primo duo episcopi Monasteriensis et Myndensis infra sacrarum ornat se et induit admodum subdyaconi Leodiensis et Traiectensis admodum dyaconi et cetera ante regale solium producunt coronandum . . . acclamerunt ipsi salutem laudem et gloriam sigillatim ad regale solium prestiterunt eidem debite fideliter homagium.

5. f. 10v: Item nota quod cor Augustini Oculi dyonisii Thome digiti quibus christum voluit tangere Os christi et manus origenis. Ista adhuc habent suum esse, Cor Augustini vivit et servatur in padua integrum et cum cantatur gloria tibi domini se movet . . . Cor sebastiani plenum passione, cor petri martyris plenum zelo, finis.

6. ff. 10v–11: *Enigmata,* Item nota quod quatuor fuerint enigmata que proposuit regina saba regi Salomoni ut habetur 3 Responsiones. Primum fuit de duobus pueris similibus quorum unus fuit masculus et aliter femella . . . et cuius non est comedere non comedat paganus comedit et non iudeus.

7. f. 11r–v: *De 4ᵒʳ viduis,* Narrat Ieronimus in libro 2º contra Iovionianum [*sic*] de quatuor viduis que renubere noluerunt . . . et idcirco virum alium non intendo accipere, finis.

8. ff. 11v–12: *Quid est homo,* Nota quidam rex cuidam philosopho quinque questiones proposuit. Prima questio fuit quid est homo . . . cum david, ecce ego in iniquitatibus conceptus sum et in peccatis meis concepit me mater mea.

9. f. 12r–v: *De tribus generibus hominis,* Rex quidam habuit tres filios qui cum mori debuit Primogenito dedit hereditatem, Secundo dedit thesaurum, Tercio dedit annulum preciosum . . . quia per fidem tamquam per annulum christus christianos sibi desponsavit.

10. f. 12v: *De perseverancia,* Fuit quidam heremita deo devotus desiderans christum videre in humanitate, christus sibi apparuit in quadam via in sua humanitate eo nesciente . . . et ego recipiam te in regnum mei patris eterni ubi vives mecum in eternum, finis.

11. ff. 13–15: Convertimini ad dominum deum, Iohelis 2. Beatus Benedictus in sermone de capite Ieiunii qui incipit Convertimini ad me in toto corde vestro, Volens nobis dare formam vere penitencie et conversionis devote ad deum sic inquit, Attende . . . et ergo tu deus propicius esto michi peccatori, Luce 18, quam propiciacionem nobis.

12. ff. 15–19: *Miracula quedam de katherina senensi,* Item anno domini M ccc lxx in civitate senensi fuit quidam vocatus Andreas . . . et ibi construeret monasterium feminarum quod et ipse fecit de licencia speciali et auctoritate felicis redordationis [*sic*] domini gregorii xi, finis.

13. ff. 19–20: *De pietate et valore dominice oracionis sive pater noster,* Erat quedam paupercula habens nisi ortum olerum quem porci sepe propter sepis vetustatem infrigentes vastaverunt . . . dabimus hec omnia propter deum et intremus aliquam religionem et serviemus domino usque in finem vite quod et fecerunt, finis.

14. f. 20r–v: *De valore pater noster,* Quadam vice dum beatus odalricus pergeret ad dominum apostolicum conduxit quamdam pauperculam que usque ad eius reversionem pro eo singulis diebus unum diceret pater noster . . . quo relato sanctus presul sibi indulsit et bene contentus fuit.

15. ff. 20v–21: *Exemplum de sancto bartholomeo apostolo,* Vir quidam devotus nomine combertus existens in heremo tantam infestacionem sustinuit a demonibus qui ipsum nitebantur in desperacionem . . . Iterum sanctus bartholomeus accessit imperans demonibus ut ipsum restituant celle sue quod et factum est.

16. ff. 21–22v: *Exemplum de sacramento et nigromancia,* Tres erant clerici, unus de austria, alius saxo et tercius bavarus qui valde cupiebant in nigromancia informari. Venerunt ergo ad quendam magistrum in madenborch nomine albertus . . . qui et sic unus illorum fuit et dicebatur rodingerus, finis.

17. ff. 22v–28: *In festo marie magdalene,* Dimissa sunt ei peccata multa quoniam dilexit multum, Luc. vii. Dicit beatus Ambrosius Quod peccatum est transgressio legis divine et celestium inobediencia mandatorum . . . Satisfecit ungendo corpus domini, finis.

18. f. 28v: *De sancto Iacobo introductio quedam,* Laudent illum celum et terra. Videmus autem secundum consuetudinem quod quinque genera hominum solent laudari primo homines pollentes virtute . . . et ipse fortis valde fuit quia de morte triumphavit, finis.

19. ff. 29–30: *De sancta Anna,* Fuit in regno ungarie quidam militaris et dives et potens qui habuit unicum filium procopium nomine . . . et claret multis miraculis ut patet intuenti ipsius vitam, amen.

20. ff. 30v–32v: *De Anna sancta mater virginis marie,* Erat enim vir quidam valde dives et potens in ungaria habens unicum filium dilectum xv annorum, patre mortuo, filius nonnullam substantiam inutiliter consumpsit . . . Et inventum est et gavisi sunt valde et cetera.

21. ff. 32v–34: *De sancta katherina martyre exemplum,* Antistes quidam mediolanensis nomine Sabinus vir vite venerabilis beate virgini marie et beate katherine a iuventute devotus . . . In huius rei testimonium annulus et cartula episcopo tradita usque hodie reservantur apud mediolanum. Hec petrus ravenensis, finis.

22. f. 34r–v: *Exemplum de iudeo et crucifixo,* Iudeus quidam salvatoris ymaginem ab ecclesia furtive subtraxit . . . et ea inventa iudeum comprehendentes lapidaverunt, finis.

23. ff. 34v–36: *De institucione ordinis carthusiencium,* Fuit quidam magnus clericus acta regens parisius magister in theologia canonicus beate marie . . . adiuvante domino qui novit eos qui sunt eius qui est auctor et fautor omnium ordinum cui laus et honor.

24. f. 36: *De gaudiis beate marie virginis,* Erat quidam monachus qui cottidie consuevit beate virgini eam laudando recitare eius gaudia . . . Septimum quod omnino secura sum quod gloria mea numquam deficiet vel excrescet, finis huius Amen.

25. f. 36v: *Honorare quinque vulnera christi bonum est,* Miles quidam a frederico imperatore captus et suspensus . . . Vocetur ergo sacerdos qui me expediat et communicet ac inungat, quo peracto, iam dormivit in domino, amen.

26. ff. 36v–38: *Feria v*[ta] *post invocavit,* Ecce sanus factus es noli peccare, Iohannes v. Circa litteram notandum est quod in ierusalem sicut habetur ex scriptura tres erant piscine, prima erat extra civitatem in loco eminentiori . . . et per hec poteris in penitenciam piscine descendere sed homo habet impedimenta.

27. f. 38v: *De sancto Augustino exemplum,* Erat quidam episcopus nomine sigilbertus hic multum dilexit beatum Augustinum et die nocteque diversis orationibus venerabatur . . . In cuius latere vulnus quas sagitte infixum videtur satis mirabile, finis.

28. f. 39r–v: *Quare deus permittit demones intrare homines,* Dicendum est quod propter quinque rationes. Primo permittit ratione superiore et enormitatis cuiuscumque peccati . . . ut ipsi sancti invocentur et liberacionem impetrent a deo.

29. ff. 39v–41: *Quare dominus dedit homini precepta,* Respondetur propter tres raciones. Primo propter expergefactionem seu experienciam nostre proprie condicionis . . . ad penam sicut achor preterivit mandatum domini et penitus est.

30. ff. 41–42: *Dyaboli modus temptandi in extremis hominem,* Ordo temptacionis quod sustinet agonizans iuxta gradus mortis qui est triplex. Primus gradus est cum vene incipiunt desiccari . . . qui pro te intercesserunt ad percipiendum premium remuneracionis omnium bonorum cuius particeps sis.

31. f. 42r–v: *Quare dyabolus non potest se in effigie crucifixi presentare,* Respondetur propter tria, primo quia est summe superbus . . . interpellantis redimentis et sic videbitur in iudicio.

32. ff. 42v–43: *De beato dominico,* Hic magnus vocabitur in regno celorum, Mt. 26. Aristoteles iiii ethicorum dicit quod pulcritudo consistit in magno corpore

. . . qui se intromittit de gloria de iudicio et vindicta. [ff. 43v–48v, ruled, but blank]

33. ff. 49–102v: *Incipit vita beatissime katherine virginis de senis,* Fuit vir unus de civitate senensi regionis tuscie nomine Iacobus. Et erat vir ille simplex et absque dolo et fraude ac timens deum . . . ad osculum pacis hilariter est recepta ac inter eas collocata. Finis huius vite sancte katherine. [f. 102v:] Notandum est autem quod ista extracta sunt et abreviata ex legenda sancte virginis katherine de senis quam composuit Venerabilis frater Raymundus de capua doctor sacre theologie et magister generalis ordinis predicatorum, huius sacratissime virginis confessor. Et licet infinita quasi ut ita dicta gesta eius et miracula tam in vita eius quam post transitum glorie ostensa, his sunt pretermissa tamen cursus vite eius qui quasi totus miraculosus et super naturam extitit luculenter hinc potest considerari.

Raimundus de Vineis Capuanus, *Legenda S. Catharinae senensis,* here in abbreviated form with respect to the version printed in the *Acta Sanctorum* (Antwerp 1675) 30 April, 859–947; see Kaeppeli, *SOPMA* 3419.

34. ff. 102v–106v: *De sancta Walburga virgine,* Postquam nacio anglorum per beatum gregorium a gentilitatis errore ad fidem est conversa multi illorum ob celestis spei remuneracionem in franciam devenerunt . . . sic quod eciam nimium verecundaretur. Tandem accessit quadam//

Paper (*Ochsenkopf* of Piccard's type X, 401–489), ff. i (parchment; before the printed book) + 106; 210 × 160 (165 × 110) mm. $1\text{–}8^{12}$ 9^{12}(–11, 12). Evidence of catchwords in the lower right corner. 30–35 long lines, frame ruled in lead. Written by one person over a period of time in a running hybrida script. 3-line red initials; 1-line initials in the text slashed in red.

Bound, s. XVI^{in}, in German pigskin over boards, with diagonal rules and stamps (quite worn) of flowering plants in circles (same stamp on RB 54171-72 and RB 102369), fleurs-de-lis in lozenges, an eagle with a halo in lozenges and free rosettes; remains of a brass fore edge clasp, closing from back to front; mark from a chain hasp on top of rear board.

Written in Germany at the end of the fifteenth century. "678" in an early modern hand on a label on the spine. Belonged to Leander van Ess (1772–1847); his number "404" in pale red ink on the first leaf of the printed book. Sold by him to Sir Thomas Phillipps. On a printed paper label on the upper spine, "130" corrected by hand to "630," the number of this book in the *Catalogus Incunabulorum* of former van Ess books in the Phillipps collection. In ink on the inside front cover and on a square printed label on the lower spine, the number "409." N. 660 in the bound Rosenbach typescript in Rare Book Department files. The Phillipps incunabula acquired by Henry E. Huntington through A. S. W. Rosenbach in 1923.

Secundo folio: inobedienciam indignus

RB 73098 — Germany, s. $XV^{3/4}$
MARTIN OF TROPPAU, MARGARITA DECRETI

Bound after *Vocabularius utriusque juris* (Nürnberg: Anton Koberger, 1481); Copinger 6361.

ff. 1–205v: [f. 1, Prologue:] Inter alia que ad fidelium christi doctrinam scripta sunt ius canonicum ad ipsorum doctrinam et consolacionem conscriptum reperitur . . . Hoc opusculum inchoans ab a prima littera usque ad extremam litteram alphabeti deduxi. Ipso iuvante qui est principium et finis regnans in secula seculorum benedictus. [Following the end of the prologue without break:] Insuper dignetur perscrutare huiusmodi lector solicite me inter minores minimum Sextum decretalium et clementinas modo et forma quo ut supra presenti tabule circa cuiuslibet decretalis finem ordinarie inservisse. Circa annos domini M° ccc° xcvi anno postremo lecturatus missiensis ad laudem omnipotentis dei eius matris benedicte ac sancti francisci confessoris. [Text:] Aaron sacerdotium approbatur d. xxii *sacrosancta* . . . [Zizania] tunc angeli colligent zizaniam in fasciculos ad colligendum frumentum xxiii q. i paragrapho i in fine xxxiii q. iii *Quantus.*

Schulte, 2:137–38; a brief collation against the 1489 Strasbourg edition (Hain 10845) shows considerable differences in the order of the quoted words and topics and in the quoted phrases. Kaeppeli, *SOPMA* 2973.

Paper (*Coeur* similar to Briquet 4293, Hirschberg 1474), ff. i (contemporary paper) + 205; 305 × 215 (236 × 137) mm. Collation including f. i: $1\text{–}16^{12}$ $17^{12}(-12)$ $18^{6}(-3$ through 6). 2 columns of 48 lines ruled in dry point. Written in a littera currens. Alternating red and blue initials in 2 sizes: 5-line for each new letter of the alphabet, 3-line for the topics under each letter; 1-line initials within the text slashed in red.

Bound, s. XV, in German white pigskin, blind tooled with a circular stamp of the Virgin and Child in glory, a roll tool of animals chasing or fighting one another, and a fleur-de-lis; 2 fore edge clasps closing back to front; strips from an eleventh or early twelfth century manuscript used as reinforcement; titles written on bottom edge and on front cover: Vocabularius juris; Tabula martiniana; on the spine, the titles in a later hand and a square printed paper pressmark label: G 426.

Written in Germany in the third quarter of the fifteenth century. Belonged to the Carthusian house at Buxheim; ex libris in the upper margin of f. 1 of the printed book, "Cartusiae in Buxheim," and in the lower margin, their book stamp. Not in the mid-fifteenth century catalogue of Buxheim, P. Ruf, ed., *Mittelalterliche Bibliothekskataloge Deutschlands und der Schweiz* (Munich 1932) 3:1. Acquired from Otto Vollbehr in March 1925 by Henry E. Huntington.

Secundo folio: causa committitur
Bibliography: Mead, n. 1188. Bond and Faye, 23.

RB 86299 — France, before 1428
OSWALD, OPUS PACIS — *fig. 7*

Bound after Johannes Chrysostomus, *Homiliae XXI* (Brussels: for the Brethren of the Common Life, 1479); Hain-Copinger 5038.

ff. 1–42v: [Prologue] *Incipit prologus in opus pacis,* Quoniam difficillimum est ad correctionem librorum iuxta statutorum nostrorum tenorem per totum ordinem faciendam haberi posse exemplaria domus cartusie originalia . . . [f. 1v, Text:] *Secuntur cautele in correctione librorum observande generales,* Ad corrigendum igitur libros subsequentia sunt diligenter previdenda per que ritus et uniformitas ordinis non immutatur . . . satis claret ex eorum usu quando u diptongetur vel non. [f. 42, Conclusion:] Sic igitur hoc opus conclusurus precor legentem ut cum aliquid sibi insolitum invenerit in uno loco querit in alio . . .

in nobis sibi habitaculum faciat. Cui cum patre et spiritu sancto par est potestas et gloria nunc et in secula. Amen. Explicit opus pacis in cartusia editum [author's name added above the line: a fratre oswaldo ibidem monacho] pro libris corrigendis deserviens quibuslibet aliis domibus eiusdem cartusiensis ordinis. [added:] Hunc librum ad nimiam instantiam et importunitatem domini Iohannis bernsau ego frater osvaldus dimisi ei quamvis michi necessarius foret 〈following passage of almost 2 lines painted over in red to cancel〉 communicetque omnibus pie desiderantibus. Scriptum manu propria, sicut etiam ipsum librum manu propria scripsi. Feria sexta post reminiscere anno 1428; ita ordinavi 〈1 line painted over in red to cancel〉. [ff. 43–44v, ruled, but blank]

Edited in part by P. Lehmann, "Bücherliebe und Bücherpflege bei den Karthäusern," in *Erforschung des Mittelalters* 3 (Stuttgart 1960) 129–42. Frequent notes in the margin possibly in the hand of the scribe.

Paper (*Cercle* similar to Briquet 2952, Valréas 1404? and Geneva 1424/27; *Main* similar to Briquet 10635, Alsace 1420), ff. 44; 200 × 140 (152 × 90) mm. 1^{12} $2\text{–}3^{10}$ 4^{12}. Catchwords in the gutter, ff. 12v, 32v. 28–32 long lines, frame ruled in ink. Written in a hybrida script. Lumpy initials of German type: 4-line red initial with simple void design on f. 1; 4-line space reserved, f. 23v; plain red 3- and 2-line initials; 1-line initials within the text filled in red; also in red, the chapter numbers, rubrics and a nota bene hand pointing to the conclusion on f. 42.

Bound, s. XV, in brown calf over wooden boards with blind stamps (one of which is an eagle displayed?) in a grid pattern; remains of 2 brass fore edge catches on the front cover and straps on the back cover; rebacked; original spine laid down; alternating leather and parchment fore edge tabs marking homilies and the beginning of the *Opus pacis.* Parchment label on spine, "Omelie Iohannis Crisostomi"; in ink on the front cover, top center, "C 16." Front flyleaf, Germany, s. XII^{med}, parchment, 38 long lines (but bottom cut off); recto: //〈?〉 romana civitas michi teste 〈?〉tuit. Nec ea intentione hoc illis scriptas . . . scribimus generaliter omnibus tenere 〈?〉damus. Pascha//; verso: //lentium perveniret scripsimus fratri et coepiscopo nostro petro ut si ita esset . . . vos augustino episcopo anglorum genti ordinato et illuc directo scripsisse de his quos olim ad fidem//.

Written by the author Oswald according to the colophon, "Scriptum manu propria, sicut etiam ipsum librum manu propria scripsi," probably at the Grande Chartreuse, where Oswald was prior, to judge from the paper. Completed on Friday, 5 March 1428. Both the printed book and the manuscript belonged to Weidenbach, the house of the Brethren of the Common Life in Cologne. The printed book bears the following notes: f. i, "C 24 16 [second number cancelled] C 24 Liber domus presbiterorum et clericorum in Wydenbach [last 2 words cancelled]"; f. iii, "Omelie beati Iohannis crisostomi sexterni xx [last 2 words cancelled] I 7. Liber domus presbiterorum et Clericorum in Wydenbach Colonie iuxta sanctum panthaleonem." On f. 1 of the manuscript, "Liber domus presbiterorum zo Wydenbach apud sanctum panthaleonem in colonia et habent eum pro alio libro [qui?] ex isto scriptus fuerit," indicating that it was given in return for the manuscript copied from it. Acquired by Henry E. Huntington in March 1925 from Otto Vollbehr.

Secundo folio: deinde considerent
Bibliography: Mead, n. 5027. Bond and Faye, 23.

RB 86438 — Italy, s. XV^{ex}
PALLADIUS

Bound after Columella, *De cultura hortorum* (Padua: D[ominicus?] S[iliprandus?], ca. 1480); *GW* 7181.

RB 86438

ff. 1–5v: *Palladii Rutilli Tauri Emiliani de Institucione* [*sic*] *Liber ad Pasiphilum virum doctissimum feliciter incipit,* Habes aliud indultae fidei testimonium pro usura temporis hoc opus de arte institucionis [*sic*] . . . [Text:] Pasiphile ornatus fidei cui iure fatemur/ Si quid in archano pectoris unbra regit [*sic*] . . . Aspera sed miti rusticitat [*sic*] leges. [ff. 6–7v, blank]

R. H. Rodgers, ed., *Palladii Opus Agriculturae, De Veterinaria Medicina, De Insitione* (Leipzig 1975) 293–301; see also Rodgers, *An Introduction to Palladius,* University of London, Institute of Classical Studies, Bulletin Supplement n. 35 (London 1975) for the tradition of the *Carmen de insitione,* pp. 59–65, and for a list of the manuscripts, this one not recorded.

Paper (*Etoile* of the general type of Briquet 6077, Palermo 1479 with sim. var. also Venice 1460–71), ff. 7; 210 × 143 (145 × 113) mm. $1^{6}(+6)$. 24 lines of verse written in a hasty cursive humanistic hand, heading on f. 1 in an epigraphic display script. Opening initial, 4-line, in plain red; 2-line plain red initials, versals touched in red, headings lined through in red.

Bound in modern paste paper boards.

Written in Italy at the end of the fifteenth century; the person who copied the Palladius text may also be the one who annotated the Columella; the red underscoring and the red touching of initials appear in both to be by the same person. Acquired by Henry E. Huntington from Otto Vollbehr on 23 March 1925.

Secundo folio: Conexumque nemus
Bibliography: Mead, n. 3901.

RB 87637 — Italy, s. XV^ex
CICERO; JULIUS CAPITOLINUS; PETRARCH

Bound after Gregory the Great, *Explanatio in septem psalmos poenitentiales* (Mainz: Jacob Meydenbach, 1495); Hain 7941.

1. f. i verso: In isto volumine sunt opera sequentia. i, Marci Tullii Ciceronis de Somno Scipionis; x, Vita divi Antonini pii imperatoris Augusti; xxvi, Magni Basilii libellus in ebrios per Bartholomeum mirabella Siculum e greco in latinum conversus; xxxii, Guarini veronensis ypothesia ad Hieronimum filium suum; liii, Epistole Cratis per Anastasium Constantinopolitanum Abbatem e greco in Latinum converse; ⟨?⟩xx, Epistola beati Bernardi super regimine domus; ⟨?⟩xxvii, Epistole magni Turci per Lauduvium equitem Hierosolimitanum traducte; ⟨?⟩vii, Epistola Pii summi pontificis ad Ducem Burgundie; ⟨?⟩xvi, Epistole ad illustrissimum dominum Regem Alfonsum Aragonum per Ianuenses misse; ⟨?⟩xv, Pogii florentini Oratoris eloquentissimi faceciarum Liber; [added in a similar hand:] ⟨?⟩x, De potenciis anime Tractatus beati Thome de aquino.

Only the first 2 items listed actually appear in the manuscript; art. 4 (see below) not in index; outer margin cropped with loss of beginning of the folio references.

2. ff. 1–9v: *Marci Tullii Ciceronis De Somno Scipionis Liber incipit Feliciter,* Cum in Africam venissem A. manlio Consule ad quartam legionem . . . Ille discessit. Ego somno solutus sum. *M. T. C. de somno Scipionis finit. Deo gratias.*

K. Büchner, ed., "Somnium Scipionis: Quellen, Gestalt, Sinn," *Hermes, Zeitschrift für klassische Philologie, Einzelschrift* 36 (1976) 2–16.

3. ff. 10–21v: *Vita Divi Anthonini Pii Imperatoris Augusti Incipit Foeliciter,* Anthoninus pius Cesar imperator augustus pater patrie a C. Iulio xvi° Adriano in principatu successit. Cepit autem anno ab urbe condita . . . [f. 11v:] ut Adrianus honori et quieti viri talis consuleret. *Auguria Eius Imperii,* Cum autem Ytaliam regeret tale imperii augurium ei factum est . . . [f. 21:] cuius felicitatem pietatem seccuritatem [*sic*] et cerimonias semper obtavit. Fecit autem columnam in urbe que adhuc suo nomine nuncupatur quam modo carbones et Malbrante Duce maxime progenies tenent . . . faustine corpus perungi maxime partem illam corporis ubi libido concupiscentie vehementius inflammatur quo facto mox cessavit tentatio. *Divi Anthonini Pii Imperatoris Vita finit. Deo Gratias.*

D. Magie, ed., *Scriptores Historiae Augustae* (London 1922) 1:100–30, with significant differences between this manuscript and the printed text.

4. ff. 22–24v: *Patrarcha* [*sic*] *ut illis temporibus Orator vel maximus hanc fabellam ad quendam fratrem religionis beati francisci ex familia aut gente Columnea Rome podagricum e Greco sermone in latinum summa in illum dilectione ab eo traductam dedit,* Anilem tibi fabellam sed ex re ut ait Flaccus Garrio . . . proinde si pellere vis podagram pelle delicias si malum omne pelle divicias [*sic*]. Vale diu felix. [f. 25r–v, blank]

V. Rossi, ed., *Le Familiari di Francesco Petrarca* (Florence 1933) 1:131–33, letter III, 13.

Paper (*Main,* similar to Briquet 11154, Palermo 1482 or 11165, Perpignan 1505), ff. i (contemporary paper) + 25 (but "17" skipped in foliation); 198 × 142 (126 × 80) mm. $1–3^8$ with vertical catchwords between pen flourishes, reading from top to bottom. 20–21 long lines frame ruled in dry point with double vertical bounding lines. Written in 2 humanistic scripts: i, ff. 1–21v (arts. 2, 3); ii, ff. i verso (art. 1) and 22–24v (art. 4). On f. 1, 4-line parted dark blue and red initial; 4-line red initials on ff. 10, 11v, 21; 1-line initials placed outside text space within the vertical rules; first line of text in arts. 2 and 3 and the first word in art. 4 in a Byzantinizing display script.

Bound, s. XVI, in Italian limp parchment, remains of 2 leather fore edge ties; on the spine, s. XVII(?), "1495 et MS" and, s. XVI, "Gregorii pape in septem psalmos penitentiales explanatio"; on the top edge, "Gregorii in 7 Psalmos."

Written in Italy. Acquired by Henry E. Huntington from Otto Vollbehr in March 1925.

Secundo folio: timorem Scipio
Bibliography: Mead, n. 52. Bond and Faye, 23. B. L. Ullman, "Petrarch Manuscripts in the United States," *IMU* 5 (1962) n. 84. D. Dutschke, *Census of Petrarch Manuscripts in the United States* (Padua 1986) n. 114.

RB 89797–98 DIRECTIONS FOR PRIESTS

Germany, s. XV[ex]

Bound after Antoninus Florentinus, *Confessionale* (Strasbourg: Martin Flach, 1488); *GW* 2128; and after Johannes Moesch, *Tractatus de horis canonicis dicendis* (Augsburg: Anton Sorg, 1489); Hain 11534.

RB 89797–98

1. ff. 2–7 [f. 1r–v, ruled, but blank]: [S]i contingit quod sacerdos ante consecracionem vel post consecracionem moritur aut sensibus alienatur . . . Respondet S[anctus?] T[homas?] Quod si hoc ante consecracionem contingat tunc non oportet quod oficium [*sic*] misse per alium compleatur . . . Inter omnia enim opera meritoria missa est primatum, hec gregorius et tantum de hiis dubiis. [5 verses:] *Per deum dicat cum patrem prespiter orat . . . Si spiritus alius eiusdem dicere debes.* [f. 7v, ruled, but blank]

Ten doubts on the celebration of the Mass under difficult circumstances, usually answered by "S.T.," and occasionally by "Sanctus Thomas," Landolfus, Augustine or Gregory; followed by verses on how prayers end, Walther, *Initia* 13935.

2. ff. 8–12: [S]ciendum est quod penitenciarum alia publica alia solempnis alia privata. Publica est cum alicui iniungitur peregrinacio cum baculo cubitali . . . hec est abusio ut ibi litiges ubi peccatum te ipsum accusaberis. [f. 12v, blank]

List of sins for which absolution must be obtained from a bishop or from the pope.

3. ff. 13–20: [M]ateria baptismi debet esse pura de aqua de flumine fonte sew putio vel de mari . . . Si alias vere penitet sacerdos potest eam absolvere. [ff. 20v–22v, ruled, but blank]

Instructions for a priest on the form and matter of baptism, communion and confession, and procedures if something should go wrong in the administration of these sacraments.

4. ff. 23–24: *De novo sacerdote sermo,* [V]as electionis est michi iste ut predicet [*sic*] nomen meum coram regibus et principibus, *Act. ix.* Licet hec verba dicta sunt ad ananiam possunt tunc dici . . . qui sic incipit, Ite ostendite vos sacerdotibus.

5. f. 24v: Honorabilis domine Thoma hiis literis certiorem vos reddo qualis in causa in qua consultum me habuiste tale do vobis responsum quando cum queritur utrum filii duorum compatrum per quorum neutrum deventum est ad compaternitatem possunt contrahere matrimonium prout est in casu vestro. Respondetur quod sic . . . quod non possunt contrahere ut supra dixi et cetera. Ex yarst⟨?⟩ xvii die mensis Iulii 1489. Erasmus hagawer [?] decretoris doctor.

Letter concerning matrimony between persons related by compaternity.

Paper (*Ochsenkopf* similar to Piccard XI, 303, Bolzano and Rattenberg, 1487, 1488), ff. 24; 197 × 132 (ca. 175 × 95) mm. 1–2^{12}. 30–39 long lines, frame ruled in lead. Written in a running hybrida script. Space reserved for 3- and 2-line initials; 1-line initials in the text slashed in red; underscoring in red.

Bound, s. XV/XVI, in German quarter leather over wooden boards; remains of a fore edge clasp closing bottom to top; pastedowns removed; reinforcement strips around the spine from a twelfth century missal, with neumes. On the spine, a paper label, "⟨?⟩ 175"; label removed from the front cover.

Written in Germany at the end of the fifteenth century as a complement to the printed texts with which it was bound. Acquired by Henry E. Huntington from A. S. W. Rosenbach in February 1925.

Secundo folio: aut ab integris
Bibliography: Mead, nn. 420 and 1049.

RB 100304 — Italy, s. XVI^1
GIORGIO VALLA, excerpt

Bound after *Astrolabii canones* (Venice: Paganinus de Paganinis, ca. 1497–98); *GW* 2759.

ff. 1–5v: *Ex Giorgio Valla, De signis et partibus et scrupulis primis ac secundis ipsorum,* Memorandum iam nobis est quo pacto recensi a nobis supputandi numeri referuntur ad signa ad signorum partes quas iuniores gradus vocant . . . *De compositione* . . . *De subtractione* . . . *De multiplicatione* . . . *De divisione* . . . Nullus siquidem hic numerus ablatus est sed sola pars sola atqui pars numerus neutiquam est monadis siquidem habet rationem.

Giorgio Valla, *De expetendis et fugiendis rebus opus* (Venice: Aldus Manutius, 1501) volume 1, "De arithmetica," Bk. 4, chapters 6–10.

Paper (*Sirène,* somewhat similar to Briquet 13891, Rome 1531–35), ff. 5; 210 × 152 (139 × 100) mm. $1^6(-1)$. 33–34 long lines. Written in an Italian gothic littera currens. Rubrics and arithmetical tables carefully entered. Modern pencil foliation in the printed book, 1–30, and in the manuscript, in the same hand, 85–89.

Bound, s. XIX/XX, in German half vellum over pasteboards.

Written in Italy towards the beginning of the sixteenth century by the same person who occasionally annotates the printed text. In the lower margin of the first leaf of the printed text, s. XVI, the signature of Franciscus Mariotti Asculanus. Acquired by Henry E. Huntington from Otto Vollbehr in March 1925.

Bibliography: Mead, n. 3012.

RB 101445 — Italy, s. XVI^1
GRAMMATICAL TREATISE

Bound after Hubertinus Clericus Crescentinatis, *Commentum super Heroides Ovidii* (Casale Monferrato: Antonius de Corsiono and Guilelmus de Canepa, 1481); Reichling 12208.

1. ff. 1–12v: [Q]uoniam de partitivis tractare decrevimus de hiis quam brevi dici posset Dicendum est et id solum scribendum nobis utile visum fuerit . . . [f. 8:] [P]articipium quo loco verbi fongimur est illud quod significat per modum fluxus . . . Dum perdit tempus dum comparat asscociamus [*sic*] Istis compositum dum simplex sit tibi verbum deo finis. Expliciunt participia sequntur ⟨word cancelled⟩ cumparativa amen.

Grammatical treatise in 2 parts, translating certain examples into an Italian dialect, which sometimes includes place names: f. 5v, "sono stato a l'uno e a l'atro de pavia e de milano"; f. 6, "veni papia ianua et vercelis"; f. 6, "mi sun andato a l'un e a l'atro de casale", f. 6v, "montis calvi et vignalis"; f. 8, "inter mediolanum et papiam."

2. ff. 13–18v: [C]omparativum Nomen est illud quod cum intellectu positivi vel cum aliquo participe sensu positivi magis ad verbum significat ut albior id

est magis albus . . . Ideo utimur genitivo singulari pro plurali ut optimi cuiusque animus pro bonorum omnium animus Amen.

Grammatical treatise, using examples from Latin literature.

Paper (ff. 1–12, *Serpent* of the same type as Briquet 13804, San Secundo 1486 and Briquet 13835, Luzerna 1553, both towns in Piedmont; ff. 13–18, *Raisin* similar to Briquet 12995, Brunswick 1438–45, this type of grape cluster of Piedmontese origin), ff. 18; 190 × 135 (ca. 112 × 70) mm. 1^{12} 2^{6}. Art. 1, 19 long lines ruled in ink; art. 2, 21–27 long lines, not ruled. Written by one person in two scripts: art. 1, in a littera textualis; art. 2, in a littera textualis currens. Spaces reserved for 2-line initials; beginning word of each section in a display script.

Bound, s. XIX^{in}, in Spanish mottled parchment with original calf spine.

Written during the first half of the sixteenth century in northwestern Italy to judge from the place names used in art. 1 and from the watermarks of the paper; the printed book with which it is bound originates in the same area: Casale Monferrato (given in its old form in the colophon, Casal di San Vaso) is in the province of Alessandria. Acquired by Wilhelm Richter of Berlin in Munich, May 1906; the date appears on the back flyleaf of the book and in the typewritten inventory of Richter's collection, compiled in 1919, in which this book is n. 162. Sold through A. S. W. Rosenbach in October 1924 to Henry E. Huntington.

Bibliography: Mead, n. 4190.

RB 102160 PENITENTIARIUS

Germany, s. XV^{med}

Bound before Albertus Magnus, *Sermones de tempore et de sanctis* (Speier: Peter Drach, not after 1475); *GW* 772.

ff. 1–38v: *Vadam ad montem mirre* [Prologue:] *Hec proposicio pro themate assumpta* Scribitur originaliter in canticis canticorum capitulo iiii et sunt verba sponse que in amore verfecenti [*sic*] prorumpit ad sponsum . . . [f. 3, Text:] Iste libellus cuius subiectum est penitencia seu modus penitendi dividitur prima sua divisione in duas partes . . . debent considerari Sed constructio istius litere ad dominum festinandi potest ex quarto dubio presentis litere et cetera. *Hec est finis huius penitentiarii.*

Bloomfield, *Virtues and Vices* 6304.

Paper (*Raisin,* Briquet 12995, Braunschweig 1438–45, and *Ochsenkopf,* similar to Piccard, VII, 539, Würtemburg 1447), ff. 38; 288 × 208 (180 × 124) mm. $1\text{–}2^{12}$ 3^{14}. 2 columns of 28–39 lines frame ruled in ink. Written in a hybrida currens with lemmata in a littera formata. Opening initial, 10-line, in red with leaf infilling, framed by written text on 4 sides; lemmata lined through in red; initials within the text touched in red; headings for the text divisions in the margin in red frames.

Bound, s. XVI^{in}, in German calf over wooden boards, with diagonal fillets on both covers; remains of 2 fore edge clasps, closing back to front; 2 nail holes on front cover. Front and back pastedowns from an antiphonal, with portions of a service for Pentecost; Germany, s. XIII^{ex}, ca. 283 × 222 (221 × 172) mm., 2 columns of 16 lines of text and music; neumes on 4-line staves with indication of C and F clefs.

Written in Germany towards the middle of the fifteenth century; in the lower margin of f. 24v, "anno quadragesimo quarto." On f. 1, upper margin, s. XVI^{in}, "Liber Ecclesiae sancti Nicolai salaeye [?] Latsarinae in Enge<cropped>"; on the front pastedown, the eighteenth century bookplate of the Premonstratensian abbey of Sayn, near Koblenz. Acquired by Henry E. Huntington from Otto Vollbehr (n. 11309) in 1925.

Secundo folio: dei dicitur
Bibliography: Mead, n. 1412.

RB 102312 Germany, s. XV^{ex}
MISCELLANY with ST. PATRICK'S PURGATORY

Bound after Thomas Aquinas, *Quaestiones de duodecim quodlibet* (Cologne: Johannes Koelhoff the Elder, 1485); Hain 1405.

1. ff. 1–6: Omnis utriusque sexus. Ista decretale editus est per Innocencium tercium ad reformandum humanum genus a labe actualium peccatorum . . . quanto magis in spirituali considerantur tanto magis ad concupiscenciam provocaret. Et sic est finis.
   Commentary on Decretals, V, tit. 38, cap. 12 regarding confession.

2. f. 6: Alligor affligor spernor sternorque flagellor/ Ut te dampnatum reddam patri bene gratum/ Solum cor michi da pro quo fero verbera tanta/ Ut sit in exemplum credentibus et in templum.

3. ff. 6–10: [E]xcellentissimo principi ac domino domino karolo Regi romanorum semper augusto Suus servitor minimus frater Conradus ordinis predicatorum provincie Scotonie [*sic*] professor sacre theolo[g]ie cum omnimoda reverencia tanto principi debitur . . . Noverit vestra imperialis maiestas . . . 3^{a} figura ponitur Ezechielis xxxviii ubi dicitur prophetante ezechiel reviviscant ossa et cetera. Expliciunt figure operum christi cum declaracionibus eorundem.
   Conrad of Halberstadt, *Figure operum Christi;* see Kaeppeli, *SOPMA* 761, listing 3 manuscripts of German origin; present manuscript not known to Kaeppeli.

4. ff. 10v–21: *Testimonia omnium prophetarum,* [H]ic inducuntur testimonia omnium prophetarum per magistrum Gotfridum viterbiensem episcopum inducta qui sunt domino nostro ihesu christo ad defensionem fidei christiane et Iudeorum confusionem. [f. 11, Text:] [C]um omnes veteris testamenti historias secundum moysen et Iosephum et secundum alios auctores . . . quia in novissimis conversi erunt iudei mortuo prius antichristo et cetera. Explicit tractatus super omnes prophetias que de christo sunt et cetera.
   Godfrey of Viterbo, *Pantheon de universo Veteri et Novo Testamento.* Stegmüller 2610; this section printed in *Pantheon* (Basle 1559), "Testimonia omnium prophetarum," cols. 322–70.

5. ff. 21–29: *Iheremias primo,* A a a domine deus nescio loqui quia puer ego sum; *Ro. 13,* Abiciamus opera tenebrarum et induamur arma lucis . . . *Deu. 31,* Utinam saperent et intelligerent ac novissima providerent.
   Selected biblical verses in alphabetical order with citation of book and chapter; a few additions in a contemporary hand.

6. f. 29: *Augustinus,* [N]ullius enim missam audias quem indubitanter sis habere concubinam alias peccati illius particeps efficiaris. Sanctus Iheronimus in libro

obitus sui dicit eu domine mi quid dicam. Quid hodie sacerdos te commedunt in altari . . . fit in eiusdem peccatis conscivis per se et pene particeps. Bene considera et attende istam gravem supradictam sentenciam iheronimi.

7. ff. 29–32: [Geert Grote] Sequuntur quedam dicta magistri gherhardi groten ex sermone suo predicato coram universo clero traiectensi in sinodo generali. Primum dictum meum est hoc quod notorius fornicator per evidenciam facti . . . et tenebre flagellum frigus et ignis diaconis aspectus flagellum frigus.

8. ff. 32–33: Sequitur epistola magistri Eggardi dicti magni ad quondam sacerdotem. Amice in christo solus ille qui tibi christo amicus est vere tibi amicus est . . . et ignita tela dyaboli mundi et carnis spiritualibus fidei doctrinis carismatibus et noscere repellere. Amen. Hanc epistolam composuit venerabilis magister Gotfridus dictus Grote quam mittebat cuidam sacerdoti.

W. Mulder, ed., *Gerardi Magni Epistolae* (Antwerp 1933) 94–99.

9. ff. 33–41v: *Incipit liber de purgatorio in hibernia,* Patri suo in christo preoccupato [*sic*] domino N. [*sic*] abbati frater h. monachorum de psaltereia minimus cum continua salute patri filius obedientie munus. Iusisstis [*sic*] pater venerande ut scriptum . . . [f. 33v, Text:] Vir [*sic*] magnus sanctus patricius qui a primo est secundus . . . transferat in prefatam beatorum requiem ihesus christus dux et dominus noster cuius nomen gloriosum permanet et benedicat in secula seculorum amen.

St. Patrick's Purgatory, attributed to Henry of Saltrey, here with prologue, the story of the Irishman, the 2 homilies, the tales of the 2 Hermits and epilogue; see Ward, *Cat. of Romances* 2:435–52.

10. ff. 41v–42: *Oratio,* [O] regum rex legum lex in cunctos da scienciam Tu michi domine in lux redde pacienciam . . . Die ire tue dire me venire iube ire in celi residenciam Amen. [ff. 42v–45v, blank]

Paper (similar to Piccard *Ochsenkopf* XI, 242, Oberschwaben, Braunschweig 1470–1480, and to *Ochsenkopf* XV, 360–361, various localities in Germany, 1474–1482), ff. 45; 289 × 209 (215 × 140) mm. 1–3[12] 4[12](–7 through 9). 2 columns of 47–55 lines, frame ruled in lead. Written in a littera currens. 3- and 2-line initials in red, frequently not supplied; 1-line initials touched in red and some underlining on ff. 1, 12v–13, 20v–21; some rubrics in red.

Bound, s. XV[ex], in stamped calf with round "ihesus" and "maria" stamps alternating with small rosettes in the outer border; in the central panel, diagonal fillets enclose lozenges of a floral spray in an urn (?); remains of chain fastening in top rear cover; 2 fore edge clasps, back to front; pastedowns of a fifteenth or sixteenth century document (?), face down.

Written in Germany towards the end of the fifteenth century. On f. i of the printed book, "Orate pro domino Tilemanno Wikenberch quondam plebano in arberge prope C[?]zerstede et pro domino Bodone [?] Lochendorp testamentario eius." "N.271" in an early modern hand on the front pastedown. Belonged to Leander van Ess (1772–1847); his initials in pale red ink on the second leaf of the printed book. Sold by him to Sir Thomas Phillipps. On a printed paper label once on the upper spine, but now loose in the book, "32" corrected by hand to "332," the number of this book in the *Catalogus Incunabulorum* of former van Ess books in the Phillipps collection. In ink on the inside front cover and on a square printed label on the lower spine, the number "705." N. 78 in the bound Rosenbach typescript in Rare Book Department files. The Phillipps incunabula acquired by Henry E. Huntington through A. S. W. Rosenbach in 1923.

Secundo folio: (mu-)lieris ex
Bibliography: Mead, n. 648. Bond and Faye, 23.

RB 102369 Germany, s. XV¹ and XVᵉˣ
THOMAS CLAXTON; ROBERT COWTON; etc.

Bound with Thomas Aquinas, *Summa Theologie* (Venice: Antonius de Strata, 1482); Hain 1443.

Composite volume

I.

1. ff. i–xix [preceding the printed text]: Tables to the *Summa Theologie,* divided into 7 parts: f. i, [D]e actione corporalis creature q. 117 et habet 6 articulos . . . [beginning only, *Actio* to *Bonitas*]; f. i verso–iii verso, *Tabula questionum prime partis Doctoris sancti secundum ordinem alphabeti,* Actio corporalis creature q. 117 et habet sex articulos . . . Ypostasis subsistencia et essencia sit idem quod persona in divinis q. 29 art. 2°. *Finis prime tabule huius summe scilicet prime partis sancti Thome laus sit deo;* f. iii verso, De actione angelorum in homines q. iii . . . ; f. iv, blank; f. iv verso–xv verso, *Incipit Tabula articulorum prime partis Doctoris sancti secundum ordinem Alphabeti,* Actio angelorum que est invicem se illuminare q. 106, Articulos require infra in littera A in ly. Angelus . . . ; ff. xv verso–xvi verso, *Tabula materiarum prima 2^{e}* [*sic*] *Sancti Thome secundum ordinem alphabeti,* De actibus imperatis a voluntate q. 17 . . . ; f. xvi verso–xviii verso, *Tabula materiarum prime 2^{e}* [*sic*] *Sancti Thome secundum ordinem Alphabeti,* Abstinencia q. 46, Acceptio personarum q. 63, Accidia q. 37 . . . ; f. xviii verso–xix, *Tabula materiarum 3^{cie} partis Sancti thome secundum ordinem Alphabeti,* De assumpcionis modo quantum ad ordiendum q. 6 . . . ; ff. xx–xxi verso, blank.

II.

2. ff. 1–8v: *Questio magistri Thome claxton correspondens primo libro sententiarum,* Utrum essencia divina est personis in divinis communicandum. Quod non arguitur sic. Essencia divina non est a se communicanda . . . notificat a quacumque alia a se persona divina. Et sic est finis huius questionis. *Explicit questio reverendi doctoris magistri thome claxton ordinis fratrum predicatorum provincie anglie correspondens primo libro sententiarum.*

3. ff. 9–11v: Utrum sacra scriptura ad hoc quod plenarie intelligatur requirat quod quadrupliciter exponatur. Quod questio sit falsa probatur multipliciter et primo sic. Nulla est sacra scriptura . . . eorum habitudo secundum statum illum similiter sub anagogia continetur scripture sacre sicut et status beatificus beatorum. Quem statum nobis concedat ihesus christus amen. *Explicit questio fratris thome Claxton ordinis predicatorum sacre theologie doctoris de mistica theologia scripta in oxoniis.*

Stegmüller, *Rep. Sent.* 902. Emden, *BRUO,* 426, for this and the preceding article. A note in the margin of HM 503, f. 51v refers to Claxton as "a precher & doctor of dyvynyte in þe chayere at oxenforde."

4. ff. 11v–12v: Supponitur primo quod multipliciter sumitur materia primo pro privacione essencia [?] infinite que tenet se per modum materie in omni re creata . . . et ratione cuius tollitur compositio generis ex materia quasi et forma sibi proportionaliter et cetera. *Explicit pulchra posicio de origine differenciarum substancialium de predicto subiecto et cetera.* [ff. 13–14v, blank]

5. ff. 15–53: Utrum habitus theologie sit forma simplex per abnegationem compositionis ex principiis sui generis essencialiter distinctis. Quod non videtur. Idem secundum idem non est causa . . . [f. 40v, end of Bk. 1:] *Explicit scriptum fratris Roberti cowton inceptoris sacre theologie ordinis fratrum minorum super primum sententiarum reportatum oxonie per me fratrem Iohannem Geuenstey ordinis predicatorum.* . . . libra eligit illud quod est minus bonum non sub ratione qua minus et cetera. *Explicit scriptum fratris Roberti Couton inceptoris sacre theologie ordinis fratrum minorum super 2^m^ sententiarum scriptum in oxoniis et cetera.*

Abbreviation by Richard Snetisham of Robert Cowton's *Questiones* on the Sentences. Stegmüller, *Rep. Sent.* 735. See also A. G. Little, *The Grey Friars in Oxford.* Oxford Historical Society 20 (Oxford 1892) 222–23, and Emden, *BRUO,* 507 for Cowton and 1725 for Snetisham.

6. f. 53r–v: Utrum filius dei incarnatus fuisset si homo non peccasset. Quod sic arguitur quia naturalem dignitatem a quodam debet homo consequi . . . sed secundum formam deitatis debet tamen caput ecclesie secundum formam servi quia sic est similis suis membris et cetera. [ff. 54–56v, blank]

III.

7. ff. 57–65: *Questio de unitate formarum,* Quia questionem de formarum gradibus per me ad multorum instanciam disputatam . . . [Text:] Quantum ergo ad primum potest argui sic. Ordini pluralium in partito debet . . . resolucio usque ad materiam primam quia si ita esset organisacio. [ff. 65v–68v, blank]

8. ff. 69–75v: Utrum intellectus sit unus numero in omnibus hominibus. Et arguitur primo quod non quia illa sunt unum . . . magis reddunt hanc posicionem improbabilem quam sustinent eandem [?]. Et ideo non plus de ista questione ad presens. [ff. 76–80v, blank]

IV.

9. ff. 81–110: Abstractio est duplex scilicet forme a materia et universalis a particularibus q. 40 art. 3°. Abstractum . . Abstrahere . . . Christus simul fuit viator et comprehensor ideo mereri potuit q. 62 art. 9° ad 3^m^.

Alphabetical subject index to the *Summa theologie,* with which this manuscript is bound.

V.

10. f. 111: Utrum divina essencia est personis in divinis communicandum, 1. Ista questio est magistri thome claxton ordinis predicatorum provincie anglie corrispondens primo libro sentenciarum. Utrum sacra scriptura ad hoc quod plenarie intelligatur Requirat quod quadrupliciter exponatur, fo. 9 . . . Utrum in divinis sit equalitas personarum cum circumincessione earundem, 32. [f. 111v, blank]

Chapter list, unfinished, of f. 1 through the present f. 33, copied in slightly over one column.

I. ff. i–xxi, Germany, s. XV$^{med/ex}$, paper (*Ochsenkopf* similar to Piccard's type X, 111–379), 285 × 205 (205 × 150) mm. 1^{10}(–7) 2^{8} 3^{8}(–3 through 6). 2 columns of 40–42 lines, frame ruled in dry point or by folding. Written in a small littera currens. 2- and 1-line initials in red; initials within the text slashed in red; red rubrics and underscoring. Bound before the printed text.
II. ff. 1–56v, Germany, s. XV^{1}, parchment (outer and inner leaves of each quire) and paper (*Monts* similar to Briquet 11686, Udine 1406–07; *Armoiries* similar to Briquet 1742, Cologne 1489; *Croissant* similar to Briquet 5276, Breslau 1372; *Flacon* similar to Briquet 6256, Montpellier 1404), 285 × 205 (224 × 161) mm. 1–4^{14}. Catchwords in the inner margin. 2 columns of 54–75 lines, frame ruled in lead. Written in a small littera currens. 8- and 7-line initials in red or blue with infilling of the other color, containing leaves in void technique (by the same person who decorated the printed text); on f. 41, 7-line parted red and blue initial; 3-line initials and paragraph marks alternating red and blue; initials within the text slashed in red; rubrics in red. In the outer margin of f. 1, a small painted profile head of a man. Bound after the printed text.
III. ff. 57–80, Germany, s. XV$^{med/ex}$, paper (*Ochsenkopf* similar to Piccard's type X, 111–379 as above in pt. **I**, and another similar to Piccard XIII, 706, Augsburg, Innsbruck 1472–74), 285 × 205 (225 × 153) mm. 1–2^{12}. 2 columns of 42–52 lines, frame ruled in dry point. Written in a littera currens. 3-line red initials; initials within the text slashed in red; underscoring and paragraph marks in red. Bound after the printed text.
IV. ff. 81–110, Germany, s. XV$^{med/ex}$, paper (*Buchstabe P* similar to Piccard's type VIII), 285 × 205 (201 × 156) mm. 1^{8} 2^{10} 3^{12}. 31–32 long lines, frame ruled in lead. Written in a littera currens. 3- and 2-line red initials; initials within the text slashed in red; rubrics and underscoring in red. Bound after the printed text.
V. f. 111, Germany, s. XV$^{med/ex}$, paper (no watermark), 218 × 198 (250 × 175) mm. 2 columns of ca. 57 lines; vertical rules in ink. Written in a littera currens. Formerly loose in the volume.

Bound, s. XV^{ex}, in German stamped calf over wooden boards, sewn on 4 bands; on front and back cover, perpendicular fillets form an outer border of large rosettes alternating with small rosettes on either side of an upright leaf, or alternating with a thistle; in the central panel, repeated vine-like tooling whose resulting ogives enclose a thistle; remains of 2 fore edge clasps, back to front; 4 corner pieces; 4 bosses on the back, now missing; unidentified pattern of holes on the front cover; holes from the nails of a chain hasp on the upper edge of the back cover. The same binding on RB 104537, and on RB 54171–72 and RB 104671 (both mentioned in entry for RB 104537).

Written in Germany, pt. **II** during the first half of the fifteenth century; the rest of the manuscript between the middle and the end of the century. The name of Iohannes Geuenstey on f. 40v may represent the person who originally took the notes rather than the scribe. Belonged to Leander van Ess (1772–1847); his signature and n. 417 in pale red ink on f. 1 of the manuscript. Sold by him to Sir Thomas Phillipps. On a printed paper label on the upper spine, "88" corrected by hand to "288," the number of this book in the *Catalogus Incunabulorum* of former van Ess books in the Phillipps collection. In ink on the inside front cover and on a square printed label on the lower spine, the number "278." N. 77 in the bound Rosenbach typescript in the Rare Book Department files. The Phillipps incunabula acquired by Henry E. Huntington through A.S.W. Rosenbach in 1923.

Secundo folio: [pt. **I**] de dei patri; [pt. **II**] sed dte. representare; [pt. **III**] per quam agit; [pt. **IV**] angeli corpora.
Bibliography: Mead, n. 2631.

RB 103317 — Germany, s. XV²

PETRUS AUREOLI, COMPENDIUM SACRE SCRIPTURE

Bound after Werner Rolewinck, *Fasciculus temporum* [Strasbourg: Johann Prüss, not before 1490]; Hain 6916.

ff. 1–93: [Prologue:] [V]enite ascendamus ad montem domini et ad domum dei Iacob et docebit nos vias suas. Isaie ii° capitulo et Michee iiii°. Scriptura divina potest dividi in viii partes principales secundum viii modos docendi quos assumit . . . [f. 4, Text:] [P]rima itaque pars sacre doctrine que politica et legislativa est . . . Incipit igitur Genesim parte politica et tractat de domino legem iniungente . . et suavitatis odorem ut accedat quod scriptum est. Canticorum tercio ascendit sicut virgula fumi ex aromatibus mirree et thuris et universi pulveris pigmentarii. [f. 93v, blank]

Stegmüller 6422; several early editions.

Paper (letter Y surmounted by a cross; not in Briquet), ff. 93; 285 × 205 (230 × 156) mm. $1–7^{12}$ $8^{10}(–10)$. 2 columns of 43–46 lines, frame ruled in ink. Written in a littera currens. 2-line spaces reserved for initials. Corrections added in the margins in the hand of the scribe. In upper margin of f. 1, s. XVI, biographical note on Petrus Aureoli.

Bound, s. XV/XVI, in German brown calf over wooden boards, the front cover ruled with a double fillet forming an outer border, an inner border (filled with lush acanthus) and a central panel, itself divided into lozenges. Stamps in the central panel: "Ihesus," "Maria" and "Iohannes" within circles; a rosette within a circle; a stylized fleur-de-lis within a square; a lion rampant within a lozenge; the 4 Evangelists' symbols within circles (Kyriss, Tafel 33, stamps 6–9; Cologne, Carthusians, 1481–1519); a shield of the same shape as Kyriss, Tafel 35, stamp 3, although the charge on the shield cannot be determined. Back cover, a simpler arrangement using some of the same stamps. Remains of 2 fore edge clasps, closing back to front. Back pastedown, a legal text, Italy, s. XV, 286 × 195 (250 × 156) mm. 60 long lines, 2-line alternating red initials with purple harping or blue with red; offset on front cover of what was probably a pastedown from the same manuscript. Title, *Fasciculus,* on the fore edge.

Written in Germany in the second half of the fifteenth century. Belonged to the Carthusian house in Dülmen, Westphalia (founded 1476); on f. i, "Liber Carthusiensium prope dulmaniam" and a pressmark, "i 67," which also occurs on the spine. Also on f. i, a contemporary note, "Pro d. tynan. gre⟨?⟩hoff sig." and the signature, s. XVIII–XIX, "Arthur Douglas Wagner." Belonged to Sir Charles Thomas-Stanford (1858–1932); his bookplate tipped in before the flyleaf. Acquired from him by Henry E. Huntington through A. S. W. Rosenbach in September 1924.

Secundo folio: felicitatem vel
Bibliography: Mead, n. 336. Bond and Faye, 23–24.

RB 103500–01 — Germany, ca. 1478–80

PASTORAL MISCELLANY

Bound before and between Johannes Herolt, *Sermones discipuli super epistolas dominicales* (Cologne: Conrad Winters, ca. 1477–78), Copinger 2936, and Guillelmus Parisiensis, *Postilla super epistolas et evangelia* (Reutlingen: Michael Greyff, 1478), *BMC* 2:575.

1. ff. 1r–v, 3–8: Alphabetical subject index to the 2 printed books, referring to folio number. The present f. 1, a fragment, bound in reverse.

2. ff. 8–9v, 2r–v [misbound]: Calendar including the following entries, Reinold (7 January), "Valerii archiepiscopi trevirensis" (29 January), "Lutgeri episcopi monasteriensis" (26 March), "Arbogasti episcopi argentinensis" (29 March), Translation of Liborius (28 April), "Adventus sancti liborii episcopi" (28 May), "Maximini archiepiscopi Trevirensis" (29 May), Cantianus, Cantius and Cantianilla (31 May), "Medechardi archiepiscopi trevirensis [*sic* for tornacensis]" (8 June), Ulric (4 July), Kilian (8 July, in red), Liborius (30 July), Meinulf (5 October, in red), "Severi archiepiscopi trevirensis" (22 October), "Severi archiepiscopi coloniensis" (23 October), Cunibert (12 November), Fridolin (14 November), "Illatio sancte marie" (26 November), "Nicetii archiepiscopi trevirensis" (5 December), David (30 December).

3. ff. 8–9v, 2r–v: [brief texts in the margins below the calendar] *Hugo in persona* Christi dicit serva salutem tuam . . . , *In scripturis* sanctis sunt profunda misteria . . . , *De vana laude,* Amator vane laudis de uno ribaldo . . . , *Contra Accidiam,* Proverbiorum 12, Nolite declinare . . . , *Contra gulam et ebrietatem,* Albricanus brixensis vitare debemus commesstiones.

4. f. 10r–v: [brief texts on the duties of a preacher] Predicator tria in se habere debet. Primus debet cogitare qualiter vel quid aut unde loquatur . . . , Predicator debet esse verax. Baltasar rex libenter audivisset levia et sibi placabilia a daniele . . . , Predicator debet tria peccatoribus proponere . . . , Predicator bonus debet peccatorem ad viam reducere veritatis tribus modis. . . .

5. ff. 111–113: *De Sacramentis,* Sacramenta ecclesie septem sunt. Primus est baptismus in aqua et spiritu sancto . . . item splendor solis non polluitur si sordidam fenestram pertranseat.

6. ff. 113–117: [brief texts concerning the powers of the priesthood] *Sequitur de sacerdotibus,* Sacerdos a quibus possit absolvere a quibus non licet dominus, sacerdotibus claves contulerit ligandi et solvendi . . . , *Sacerdos absoluit vere* sicut enim potest ligare auctoritate clavium . . . , *Sacerdotis officium* non usurpent sibi layci, hoc dico propter quosdam modernos hereticos qui dicunt se missas posse celebrare . . . , *Sacerdotibus* obedit creatura insensibilis Ideo vult dominus ut eis distincte loco sui obediatur in omnibus . . . , *Sacerdotum magna est dignitas . . . , Dupliciter deus honorat sacerdotes . . . , Sacerdotibus est obediendum . . . , De Auctoritate et potestate sacerdotum. Sacerdotibus magna auctoritas* seu potestas est collenda . . . , *Sacerdotium christi tripliciter honoravit . . . , Excommunicare potest* sacerdos aliquem pro triplici contemptu . . . , *Decimas bene solvere* est valde utile. . . .

7. 117–118v: [brief texts on the following:] *De parentibus. Parentes sunt honorandi* duplici honore . . . , *Parentes honorantes plurima bona consequentur . . . , Parentes non honorantes . . . , Ieiunias potius in quadragesima . . . , Ieiunium cur sit xl^{a} diebus . . . , Ieiunare excusantur* infirmi . . . , *Ieiunare tenentur . . . , Ieiunium duplex est* malorum et bonorum . . . , *Ieiunii veri* multiplex est effectus. . . .

8. f. 118v: *De Amore,* Amor intensus socium non patitur. . . .

9. f. 118v: *Propheta,* Non est propheta sine honore in patria sua . . . [6 short extracts from the New Testament].

10. ff. 119–121v: *Temptacio,* Circa temptationem quattuor sunt nominanda . . . promisit deus diligentibus se. Tu autem domine miserere nobis deo gratias. Amen.

11. ff. 121v–122: *Exposicio dominice oracionis, Pater noster et cetera,* Sciendum quod ista oracio dicitur oratio dominica . . . et in tua gloria admirabili cum sanctis tuis perpetue gloriari. Amen.

12. f. 122: *Duodecim articuli fidei per apostolos. Petrus,* Credo in deum patrem omnipotentem creatorem celi et terre. . . .

13. f. 122v: *De die dominico, Qui non* servatis dies dominicos et alias festivitates . . . iocunditas civium iustorum et piorum humilium et castorum.

14. f. 123r–v: Distinctions and short verses on mercy, mercy of God, virtues and vices, and other subjects.

15. f. 216v [Last leaf of incunabulum]: Upper ⅔ lacking; remainder contains additional notes in Pilter's hand (see below).

Paper (quire 1, *Main* similar to Briquet 11422, Dieuze 1486; quire 2, *Lettre P* similar to Briquet 8532, in many localities 1483–84), ff. 10 + 10; 268 × 208 (207 × 150) mm. Two quires, one of 10 leaves (of which one is missing in the first half) bound before Herolt's sermons, the other of 10 leaves bound between the 2 incunabula; ff. 10, 111–112 are part of the first incunabulum, ff. 123, 216 are part of the second. In long lines and 2 columns of 44–47 lines; frame ruled in hard point; calendar fully ruled in lead. Written by Johann Pilter in a running hybrida script. Initials, including those by Pilter in the printed book, are outlined in green and brown, infilled in orange with void white patterns and penscrolls in orange and green. Manuscript and printed book contain Pilter's notes in lower margin for the subject index; occasional rubrics; foliation in the upper recto in arabic numerals, and in the lower recto in arabic numerals through the first printed book; ff. 113–118, arabic foliation crossed out (ff. 103–105) and refoliated aia, aiia, aiiia, aiiiia . . . axa; occasional longer notes by Pilter, e.g., f. 166v (contemporary foliation, f. 269v), f. 78 (contemporary foliation, f. 181). Each printed volume separately foliated, s. XIX/XX. Opening leaves misbound and damaged with loss of text.

Bound, s. XIX^{in}, in mottled grey paper boards, remains of pink leather fore edge tabs.

Written in western Germany, ca. 1478–80, by Johann Pilter, who also decorated and annotated the printed book and left his name at various places in the volume: f. 111 (at end of Herolt's *Sermones*), "Ego Iohannes pylter pro nunc possessor huius libri eundem illuminavi anno 1480 In Ieiunio quadragesimali deo gratias"; f. 174v (contemporary foliation, f. 277v), "Anno domini M° ccccIxxviii° Hos sermones et postillas Ego Iohannes pylter mecum duxi de Treveri circa festum sancte Margarete cum ibi presens eram cum clusenario meo de Wehene scilicet hinrico tuleman deo gratias. Amen"; f. 215v (contemporary foliation, f. 318v, at the end of the printed book), "Istum librum ego Iohannes pylter plebanus in Sydinchuss concessi ad bonam custodiam devoto patri domino conrado lovelinaus [?] terciario in hovegeismare usque ad revocationem, in presentia domini Iohannis Conradi et Iohannis de Ad‹?› ipso die beate Anne in Buren, anno 1487." Johann Pilter wrote and gave a number of manuscripts to Eberhardsklausen (Windesheim Congregation) near Trier between 1459 and 1486 (see Bénédictins du Bouveret, *Colophons de Manuscrits* . . . , Fribourg 1965–82, nn. 10976–10982). He came from Warburg in the diocese of Paderborn, held a benefice in Buren, and served as rural priest in Zidinchuss near Buren; he is probably not the same person as Johannes de Buren, d. 1503 (*Colophons,* nn. 9085–9095). Regarding the house and its members, see P. Dohms, *Die Geschichte des Klosters und Wallfahrtsortes Eberhardsklausen an der Mosel.* Rheinisches Archiv 64 (Bonn 1968). This book was not among the books which Pilter left to Eberhardsklausen and which passed to the Staatsbibliothek in Trier in 1802, since he gave it to a Franciscan of Hofgeismar (cf. note f. 215v), where it apparently remained until the secularization. Belonged to Leander van Ess (1772–1847); his initials in pale red ink on f. 3 of the manuscript. Sold by him to Sir Thomas Phillipps. On a printed paper label on the upper spine, "183," the number of this book in the *Catalogus Incunabulorum* of former van Ess books in the Phillipps collection. In ink on the front pastedown and on a square printed label on the lower spine, the number "119." "81" in modern pencil on f. 3. Nn. 407–408 in the bound Rosenbach typescript in Rare Books Department files. The Phillipps incunabula acquired by Henry E. Huntington through A. S. W. Rosenbach in 1923.

Bibliography: Mead, nn. 730 and 1591.

RB 103533 — Germany, s. XV^2
COMMENTARIES ON PETER LOMBARD

Bound before Werner Rolewinck, *Fasciculus temporum* [Cologne: Ludwig von Renchen, ca. 1483]; Hain 6914.

1. ff. 1–86v: Cupientes aliquid et cetera. Hic queruntur quinque. Primo utrum aliquis veritati insistere debeat que excedit facultatem sui intellectus . . . [f. 57:] voluit bonam christi passionem. Qui est super omnia deus benedictus in secula seculorum. Amen. Deo gracias. *Explicit prim*⟨erasure⟩ *sententiarum sancti thome scriptum. Tercii sententiarum distinctio i,* Dividitur liber iste in duas partes, in prima determinat de incarnacione, in secundo prosequitur condicionem filii dei incarnati . . . [f. 83v:] Ad iii de eterno dicendum quod eternum in quantum eternum caret fine persona quamvis sit eterna et sic careat fine secundum se// [rest of column and following page blank; note in the lower margin, "hic deficiunt 4^or^ articuli de resurrectione"; f. 84v:] [C]um supra habitum sit et cetera. [added, "distinctio xxii," *sic,* for 23:] Circa partem istam queruntur 4^or^. Primo an diffinitio fide quam tradit apostolus sit recte assignata . . . [f. 86v:] fides est una licet diversa enunciabilia formentur sed diversum modum accipiendi ut accipiatur presens preterita vel futura. [ff. 87–89v, blank]

Hannibaldus de Hannibaldis, *Super libros I–IV Sent.* Stegmüller, *Rep. Sent.* 309 and Kaeppeli, *SOPMA* 1684; several early editions, often as Thomas Acquinas, *Scripta ad Hannibaldum.* Here in an abbreviated version, Bks. 1 and 3 only (the latter lacking dist. 22, as noted by the scribe), with loss of text due to missing leaves before f. 1 (? 1 leaf) and after ff. 12 (2 leaves), 22 (2 leaves), 33 (1 leaf), 43 (2 leaves), 53 (1 leaf).

2. ff. 90–100v: [C]um igitur venit plenitudo temporis ut ait apostolus misit deus filium suum natum de virgine et cetera. Determinato in libro precedenti de rerum exitu a principio. In hoc tertio incipit magister determinare de reditu divinarum rerum in finem scilicet deum . . . [f. 93, second distinction:] [E]t quia in homine tota humana natura vicio corrupta erat totam assumpsit et cetera. Postquam magister determinavit de incarnatione ex parte assumentis . . . [f. 96, third distinction:] [Q]ueritur eciam de carne verbi an priusquam conciperetur obligata esset peccato et cetera. Ostenso quid filius dei in natura humana et quo ordine assumpserit hic ostendit quale sit quod assumptum est . . . In oppositionem prime partis conclusionis arguitur Omnes virtutes anime vegetalis scilicet active secundum commentationem qui in 2° de anima ponit hanc distinctionem.

RB 103533

Unidentified commentary on the third book of the Sentences of Peter Lombard, similar to Stegmüller, *Rep. Sent.* 1063 or 1361 (both anonymous); here probably ending incomplete.

Paper (art. 1, *Lettre P* similar to Briquet 8685, Düsseldorf 1464 and to Briquet 8690, Nivelles 1461; art. 2, *Lettre P* similar to Briquet 8598, Colmar 1465), ff. 100; 209 × 205 (210 × 150) mm. First part of art. 1 apparently copied on quires constructed with the outer bifolium in parchment, of which only 1 leaf survives, f. 33, the rest having been cut away: 1^{14}(–1, 14) 2^{12}(–1, 12) 3^{12}(–1; the twelfth leaf is f. 33) 4^{12}(–1, 12) 5^{12}(–1, 12) $6–8^{12}$ 9^{12}(–12, art. 2). Remaining catchwords on f. 33 (does not match following leaf) and for quires 6 and 7. No signatures on quire 1; quire and leaf signatures on quires 2–5 begin respectively b2, b3, b4, b5; stubs remain between these quires and the adjacent leaves often are partially cut through. Art. 1 in 2 columns of 46 lines ruled in lead; written in a littera textualis. Art. 2 in 2 columns of 48 lines, ruled in hard point; written in a small littera cursiva. Opening initial, f. 1, 10-line, crudely done in red with leaf infilling; 3- and 2-line red initials, a few with simple decoration such as a jester's profile on f. 7 and a monk's profile on f. 8v; in the lower margin of f. 6, a sketch in red ink of a hound chasing a hare. Rubrics, headlines at the change of distinctions, and paragraph marks in red up to f. 68; thereafter omitted and space for initials left blank.

Covers removed; only the front pastedown and part of the back remain, the latter from a Hebrew manuscript (*Babylonian Talmud, Sotah* 46b).[1]

Written in northern Germany in the second half of the fifteenth century. Belonged to Leander van Ess (1772–1847); his name and number "416" in pale red ink on f. 1 of the manuscript. Sold by him to Sir Thomas Phillipps. Possibly n. 258 (? but printed in Basle: Henricus Wirzburg de Vach, 1481) or n. 890 (? but printed in Strasbourg: Johannes Grüninger, 1480) in the *Catalogus Incunabulorum* of former van Ess books in the Phillipps collection; the covers of the book are missing and the *Catalogus* number, normally on a label on the spine, is no longer present, if indeed it ever were. In ink on the former front pastedown and on a square printed label on the lower spine, the number "537." N. 618 in the bound Rosenbach typescript in Rare Book Department files. The Phillipps incunabula acquired by Henry E. Huntington through A. S. W. Rosenbach in 1923.

Secundo folio: iustos viros
Bibliography: Mead, n. 804. Bond and Faye, 24.

[1] We thank Rabbi Norbert Weinberg for this information.

RB 104537 — Paderborn, etc., 1470(?)–92
DURANDELLUS — *fig. 26*

Bound after Petrus de Aquila, *Quaestiones in IV libros Sententiarum Petri Lombardi* (Speier: Peter Drach, 1480); Hain 1325.

ff. 1–98v *Evidencie Durandi super primum Sententiarum,* Supra prologum primi sententiarum sunt duo articuli. *Primus est contra illud quod dicit Thomas in questionibus disputatis q. ix ar. 9 videlicet rubrica* de eodem non potest esse scilicet fides et scientia . . . [f. 18v:] *Et sic explicit recensio ad ea que continentur super primum sententiarum per me fratrem hinricum dazeborch ordinis predicatorum conventus wartbergensis anno domini m° cccc lxx°* [space] *in octava vigilie marie visitacionis pro tunc me lubeck exeunte* . . . [f. 46:] Expliciunt hec super secundum sententiarum per manus fratris hinrici dazeborch lectoris per anno domini m° cccc° 90 . . . [f. 62v:] Expliciunt hec super 3m librum Sententiarum per me fratrem Hinricum dazeborch ordinis predicatorum Conventus Wartbergensis Terminarius pro tunc Paderbornensis. In vigilia Beati Mathie apostoli que tunc occurrebat 4ta feria post invocavit de ieiunio Anno Domini m cccc 91. Deus sit benedictus in sempiterna secula. Amen. . . . [f. 96:] Sic ergo apparet quod solo deo qui est ultimus finis omni tamquam immediato obiecto fruendum est Cui est gloria in secula seculorum. Amen. Benedictus deus. *Expliciunt reprobationes Durandi super 4m Anno domini M° cccc° lxxxxii. In die Corone domini. In Paderborn per me fratrem hinricum dazeborch conventus Wartbergensis Ordinis predicatorum pro tunc terminarius exeuns Paderbornen. anno meo in ibi undecimo Cuius laus et honor sit deo trinitati. Amen.* [ff. 96–97v, Subject index:] *Anima . . . Angelus . . . Ydee,* Plures sunt in deo primo [libro] distinctione 36 articulo 2°. [f. 98r–v, a discarded folio from this text, written but not rubricated, or foliated, bound at the end of the text.]

Evidenciae contra Durandum I–IV, Stegmüller, *Rep. Sent.* 191. Kaeppeli, *SOPMA* 923, citing this manuscript. Each *distinctio* and article divided into 4 sections denoted by the letters A-D for purposes of reference; the letters are not used in the subject index, which refers rather to the *distinctio* and article. Carefully corrected throughout; full marginal gloss in the hand of the writer on f. 1 only; thereafter sporadically.

Paper (several crowns of the type of Briquet, *Couronne* 4758, Namur 1463 and sim. var. Luxembourg, Metz and 2 incunabula printed in Lubeck; and of Piccard, *Kronen* I, 278, Erbach 1460–66), ff. 98; 398 × 280 (290 × 178) mm. 1–12^8 13^8(-2 through 8, + 1 at the end). 2 columns of 62–67 lines, frame ruled in lead. Written in a poorly formed littera currens; the beginning words of each section in a somewhat more formal book hand. Opening initial, 16-line, parted red and blue with short tendrils; remaining book and secondary initials, 6-line, either parted red and blue, or red only. Running headlines; foliated in early form arabic numerals circled in red.

Bound, s. XVex, in German stamped calf over heavy bevelled wooden boards, sewn on 7 bands; on front and back cover, perpendicular fillets form an outer border of small rosettes on either side of an upright leaf, alternating with large rosettes; in the central panel, repeated vine-like tooling whose resulting ogives enclose a thistle plant; remains of 2 fore edge clasps, back to front; 8 corner pieces; 4 bosses on the back, now missing; pattern of holes on front cover not clear; holes from the nails of a chain hasp on the upper edge of the back cover; spine missing and in poor condition overall. The same binding on RB 54171–72 (see below in this description), RB 102369 (separate description), and RB 104671 (see below in this description).

Written at least in part at Paderborn between 1470 (?) and 1492 by Henricus Dazeborch of the Dominican house in Wartburg. Henricus also copied 7 leaves bound before Peter Lombard, *Sententiarum Libri IV* (Basle: Nicolaus Kesler, 1489), Hain 10196 and Thomas Aquinas, *Scripta ad Hannibaldum* (Basle: Nicolaus Kesler, 1492), Copinger 579, bound together as Huntington Library RB 54171–72. Henricus' material contains mnemonic and study devices on the Sentences: 1. Res tres mens genuit essencia velle potestas/ Esse coevus amor uterque prius genitus dant . . . [also in Frankfurt, Stadts- und Universitätsbibliothek, MS Barth. 99, f. 364], signed "Et finit quartus liber sententiarum metrice per me hinricum dazeborch ordinis predicatorum Anno domini M° cccc 91° in Paderborn pro tunc terminarius ibidem"; 2. Aut fruimur rebus cunctis aut utimur ipsis/ B<?> lege domini trinum necnon probat unum . . . [Walther, *Initia* 1878], signed "Finit hec Sententiarum metrice <?> 5a feria hora vesperarum per me fratrem hinricum dazeborch ordinis predicatorum Terminarius in Paderborn Anno domini M° cccc° 91"; 3. Cum difficultas verbalis multum impediat animum a speculatione veritatis . . . [Franciscus de Mayronis, *De usu terminorum;* Stegmüller, *Rep. Sent.* 1342, 1 and G. E. Mohan, "Initia Operum Franciscalium," *Franciscan Studies* ser. 2, vol. 35 (1975) 75], signed "Explicit tractatus Brevis et utilis de terminis theoycalibus anno et cetera 90 Sabbato post festum beati dominici patris nostri per me fratrem hinricum dazeborch." Possibly also in the hand of Henricus Dazeborch, although unsigned, are 3 manuscript leaves containing a *questio* of Henry of Gorichem (Stegmüller, *Rep. Sent.* 322) on the Sentences bound before Henry of Gorichem, *Quaestiones in S. Thomam* [Esslingen: Conrad Fyner, not after 1475], Hain 7806, Huntington Library RB 104671. Another printed book with manuscript material by Henricus Dazeborch is known through the bound Rosenbach typescript of Phillipps incunabula (in Rare Book Department files). In 1923 A. S. W. Rosenbach offered to Henry Huntington a copy of Johannes Herolt, *Sermones discipuli super Epistolas dominicales* [Cologne: Conrad Winters, de Homborch, ca. 1478], Copinger 2936, which contains a manuscript table copied by Henricus Dazeborch and dated 1481. The volume was returned or disposed of as duplicate (of RB 103500) at an unknown date; present location unknown. A Henricus de Dosburch is listed on the flyleaf of Berlin, Deutsche Staatsbibliothek, MS lat. 544 (th. fol. 145); that manuscript dated Leipzig, 1464; no medieval provenance given.

In RB 104537, on the second leaf of the printed book, the initials of Leander van Ess (1772–1847) in pale red ink. Sold by him to Sir Thomas Phillipps. Identified as n. 210 in the *Catalogus Incunabulorum* of former van Ess books in the Phillipps collection, although the upper part of the spine (the normal location for this number) is missing. In ink on f. i and on a square printed label on the lower spine, the number "29." N. 62 in the bound Rosenbach typescript in Rare Book Department files; this number in pencil on f. i. The Phillipps incunabula acquired by Henry E. Huntington through A. S. W. Rosenbach in 1923.

Secundo folio: (defen-)sive et
Bibliography: Mead, n. 1402. Bond and Faye, 24.

RB 104566 — Eastern Europe, s. XV²
SERMONS; JORDANUS OF QUEDLINBURG

Bound after Franciscus de Platea, *Opus restitutionum* (Cracow: Printer of Turrecremata, 1475); Copinger 4763.

1. ff. 1–91v: *Cum ieiunatis scribitur Math. vi,* Introductio a tempore quo cognoscimus inter bonum et malum heu semper plus peccamus quam bonum facimus . . . [Holy Friday] Egressus ihesus trans torrentem Cedron et cetera. Queritur ex quo per unam guttulam nos redimere potuit . . . ipsum satisfaceremus nisi passione christi iuvaremur et cetera.

Thirty-seven sermons for Lent, the same in Kórnik, Biblioteka Kórnicka Polskiej Akademii Nauk, sygn. 55, ff. 304–362.

2. ff. 91v–97v: *Tibi dabo claves regni celorum, Mt. 16,* Hic videnda sunt plura, primo quare dicte sunt claves penitencie, 2° quis tenetur recipere claves penitencie . . . quia pocius debet homo omnia mala sustinere quam mortaliter peccare. Facit c. Sacris quod metus causa et cetera. [f. 95:] *Tibi dabo claves regni celorum et cetera, Scribitur Mt. 6* [*sic*] De istis clavibus dicit Richardus super quartum sententiarum Quod sunt quedam potestas date Ecclesie in prelatis suis ad aperiendum et claudendum regnum celorum quod clauditur homini per peccatum

vel per obligacionem ad penam pro peccato . . . sibi celum aperitur et clauditur. Et tantum de clavibus Ecclesie et cetera.

3. ff. 97v–98v: Est zelus improbus qui solet seducere multos. Unde notandum quod sunt nonnulli qui noxias saciunt . . . Audiens hoc vicinus dives recessit ab eo valde in vita sua emendatus et cetera.

4. ff. 99–100: Subject index to the material on ff. 1–98v with reference to a numbering system in the upper margins of those leaves.

5. ff. 100v–130v: *Passio Iordani per articulos, Inspice et fac secundum exemplar Quod tibi in monte monstratum est. Exo. 25,* Et si christus ubique in scriptura dicatur mons ratione summitatis sue excellentissime perfectionis . . . [f. 102:] *Primus articulus, Primus articulus dominice passionis est pavoris et tristicie assumptio, nam ut dicit augustinus cena domini facta et pedis locione celebrata . . . vel alias sicut deus oranti vel meditanti devotionem ministrabit. Amen. Amen Sit laus deo patri.*

Jordanus of Quedlinburg, *Meditationes de passione Christi;* here with arts. 1–55, 58, 63–65 (although labelled in the manuscript 1–56, 60, 64–65), abbreviated with respect to the 1492 Basle edition; Zumkeller, n. 646; Stegmüller 5141.

Paper (3 types of *Balance* similar to Briquet 2528, Zwickau 1470; 2406, Wörth 1466; 2454, Wiener-Neustadt 1476; 4 types of *Ochsenkopf* similar to Piccard XII, 857, in many locations 1457–70; XIII, 213, Augsburg 1470; XII, 651, Nürnberg 1462–63; XII, 902, Lienz 1470–73), ff. 130; 290 × 210 (209–224 × 140–146) mm. $1–8^{12}$ 9^{16} 10^{12} 11^{12}(-7 through 12). Arts. 1–4 in 2 columns of 36–46 lines, frame ruled in ink; art. 5 in 2 columns of 49 lines, fully ruled in lead. Written by 5 scribes in running littera textualis scripts: i, ff. 1–24va; ii, ff. 24va–36v; iii, ff. 37–98v; iv, ff. 99–100 (art. 4) and marginal notes throughout; v, ff. 100v–130v (art. 5). Opening initial, f. 1, 5-line, in red decorated with knotwork and infilled with leaves; in arts. 1–3, 3- and 2-line red initials, 1-line initials within the text slashed in red, authorities underscored in red. In art. 5, 4- to 1-line red initials, 1-line initials within the text slashed in red, authorities underscored in red, marginal finding notes in red. Numbering system referring to the opening, not to the leaf, in the upper margins of arts. 1–3 as the sequence of the alphabet followed by a roman numeral, ai, bi, ci . . . aii, bii, cii . . . sv, tv.

Bound, s. XV, in whittawed leather ruled with diagonal fillets, over bevelled wooden boards, sewn on 5 bands; remains of 2 fore edge clasps closing back to front; chain marks on top and bottom of rear board; handwritten label on spine, s. XIX.

Written in eastern Europe in the second half of the fifteenth century. The writer of the index (art. 4) may have overseen the production of this manuscript. He numbered the openings of arts. 1–3 (written by 2 other copyists) for the index which he compiled on ff. 99–100. The last 2 leaves of arts. 2–3 and the index occupy the beginning of a large quire of different paper; to this a third copyist, who ruled both the frame and lines of ff. 100v–130v, added art. 5, the *Passio* of Jordanus of Quedlinburg. Round ink stamp on the inside of the front cover, s. XX^{in}, "Bundesdenkmalamt, Wien." Acquired by Henry E. Huntington from A. S. W. Rosenbach in June 1925.

Secundo folio: (concu-)piscen[tia?] iuget
Bibliography: Mead, n. 5066.

HM 51848

The following manuscripts received too late for inclusion of descriptions in regular sequence.

HM 51848 — Germany, s. XV^2
IOHANNES HEROLT; PEREGRINUS DE OPPELN

1. ff. 1–49v: Iohannes Herolt, *Postilla Discipuli super epistolas dominicales et de sanctis secundum sensum litteralem* [Kaeppeli, *SOPMA* 2394].

2. f. 49v: Short passages identifying the recipients of the Pauline epistles, based on the biblical prologues.

3. ff. 50–121v: Iohannes Herolt, *Sermones Discipuli super evangelia dominicalia et de sanctis secundum sensum litteralem* [Kaeppeli, *SOPMA* 2393, here breaking defectively after the first leaf of the sanctorale and lacking the entire common of saints].

4. ff. 122–227v: Peregrinus de Oppeln, *Sermones de tempore et de sanctis* [Kaeppeli, *SOPMA* 3194, here breaking defectively in the entry for Clement].

5. f. 228r-v: Prayers to say in various occasions, added in an early modern hand, beginning defectively.

6. ff. 229–243v: Four collations on John the Baptist.

7. f. 243v: Prayer added in the same hand as art. 5.

Paper (*Tête de boeuf* similar to Briquet 14871 or 14873), ff. ii + 243 + i; 285 × 205 (210 × 150) mm. Gatherings mainly of 12 leaves; catchwords in center of lower margin in script of text. 2 columns of 45–52 lines, ruled in dry point. Written in a careful cursive script. Major initials, 4- to 11-line, in red or green with infilling, often of both colors, in void design, some with sketched profile faces; minor initials, 4-line, alternating plain red and green; 1-line initials within text slashed in red; paragraph marks and rubrics in red. Marginal finding notes in the hand of the scribe. Contemporary (?) foliation in arabic numerals through f. 227.

Bound, 1986, at the Huntington Library in white pigskin. Previous binding (retained in case with book), s. XVI, in pigskin over boards, with roll of renaissance ornament and 4 small compartments, 220 × 17 mm.: "Salvator" (half figure of Christ, blessing and holding cross-and-orb, facing left), "S. Iohannes Tau" (presumably John the Baptist, as he is normal to this sequence in sixteenth century German binding rolls; half figure, holding a book, facing left), "S. Paulus .O." (half figure of Paul, holding sword and book, facing left), "Rex .O. Davit" (half figure of David holding harp, facing right); for this roll, see K. Haebler, "Rollen- und Plattenstempel des XVI. Jahrhunderts," in *Sammlung Bibliothekswissenschaftlicher Arbeiten* 42 (Leipzig 1929) 227, Munich-41; the "Tau" after "S. Iohannes" could be the binder's initial "T" (also normal practice), for an example of which see Haebler, "Rollen-," *ibid.* 41 (Leipzig 1928) 440, F. T.-1, a very similar roll signed "F. T." On the previous binding of HM 51848, remains of 2 fore edge clasps closing from bottom to top.

HM 52435

Written in Germany in the second half of the fifteenth century; it may have belonged to a Dominican house, as the two identified authors are of that order. On f. 1, early modern ownership note of the Benedictine monastery of St. Peter and St. Paul in Bregenz, Austria. Also on f. 1, signature of Alexander Valpy. Given to the Huntington Library by Mrs. Julian Binstock in 1985.

HM 52435 England, s. $XII^{2/4}$
AMBROSIASTER, COMMENTARY ON THE PAULINE EPISTLES

frontispiece

ff. 1–129v: *Incipit tractatus Ambrosii episcopi in epistola Ad Romanos,* Principia rerum requirenda sunt ut noticia earum possit haberi . . . [f. 1v] *Incipit Tractatus Sancti Ambrosii In Epistola Ad Romanos,* Paulus servus ihesu christi. Apud veteres <nostros ratione> nomina componebantur ut ysaac propter risum . . . ut securos illos faciat et erigat ne timeant que irrogari possunt a perfidis sed in persecutione alacres//

Commentary by Ambrosiaster on the Pauline Epistles. *CPL* 184. *PL* 17:45–332D, 411B–420, 441–462, 421A, 423C–426A, 488D–494C. This manuscript missing 4 quires after f. 112 (end of commentary on 2 Corinthians, all of Galatians, all of Ephesians, beginning of Philippians); missing one leaf after f. 126 (part of Colossians); missing undetermined amount after f. 127 (end of Colossians, all of 1 Timothy, beginning of 2 Timothy); missing undetermined amount after f. 129 (end of 2 Timothy, all of Titus, all of Philemon); 1 and 2 Thessalonians are copied before Colossians. Each epistle commentary remaining with incipit (Romans, 1 and 2 Corinthians, 1 and 2 Thessalonians, Colossians) is prefaced by a chapter list; the chapter lists in this copy of Ambrosiaster retain forms of the Vetus Latina recension. The prologue to 2 Corinthians is that printed in the *PL* (not the one beginning "Sciens sanctus apostolus profecisse epistolam . . ." printed by A. Souter, "The Genuine Prologue to Ambrosiaster on Second Corinthians," *Journal of Theological Studies* 4, 1903, 89–92), although the text of the commentary itself on 2 Corinthians begins differently here (but not in any large manner for any of the other commentaries) from that of the *PL:* "Paulus apostolus Ihesu Christi. Queritur cur in omnibus epistolis contra usum epistolarum primo suum nomen ponat . . ." A. Souter, *A Study of Ambrosiaster* (Cambridge 1905) 15, n. 12; same author, *The Earliest Latin Commentaries on the Epistles of St. Paul* (Oxford 1927) 57; H. J. Vogels, "Die Überlieferung des Ambrosiasterkommentars zu den Paulinischen Briefen," *Nachrichten der Akademie der Wissenschaften in Göttingen, Philologisch-Historische Klasse* (1959) 115, n. 5, all citing the present manuscript as "Bramshill House, IV." Vogels lists 72 manuscripts of this text.

Parchment, ff. 129; 340 × 260 (270 × 157) mm. $1–15^8$ 16^8(– 6 after f. 126) + 2 leaves of a later quire. Quires counted in roman numerals in the center of the last leaf verso, [I]-XIIII on quires 1–14, and XIX-XX on quires 15–16; these 2 quires also signed C-D in the center of the first leaf recto. Ruled in dry point with top first and third (or occasionally second and fourth) lines and bottom last and third from last lines full across; double vertical rules on both sides of both columns (thus 4 central rules). 2 columns of 39–41 lines, with text copied above top line. Written by 2 scribes in minuscule scripts: i, ff. 1–112v; ii, ff. 113–129v (the quires with additional signatures, C-D); both use a smaller size script for the chapter lists, and a form of rustic capitals for the rubrics. The first scribe uses as "catchword" the latter part of a word that he was forced to divide and carry from one column to the next due to limitations of space. Four opening initials with scrollwork in the text section copied by the first scribe: f. 1 (prologue; somewhat damaged by damp), 24-line, in green, blue and red, inhabited by monks; f. 1v (Romans), approx. 26-line, but extending into the lower margin and cropped at the bottom, in pen outline without color, biting lions and foliage; f. 54 (1 Corinthians), 31-line, in green, blue and red, with men, animals and grotesques all grasping on to or holding one another; f. 90 (2 Corinthians), 20-line, in dark green, blue and red, with biting dragons. Three opening initials in simpler style in the text section copied by the second scribe: f. 118v (1 Thessalonians), 14-line, parted blue and green; f. 124 (2 Thessalonians), 14-line, purple; f. 126v (Colossians), 7-line, red with purple flourishing. Secondary initials, 5- or 4-line, and minor initials, slightly over 1-line, in green, light purple or red; those from f. 113 on, where the second scribe worked, occasionally with some void design or parted. Rubrics frequently in colored ink, e.g. f. 1 in blue and purple; ff. 1v and 54, green and red; f. 90, green, blue and red; f. 118, purple. Running headlines across the openings; biblical quotations signalled in the margins.

Bound, s. XV, in calf over wooden boards, tooled and stamped in somewhat different patterns for the front and back covers by the "Fishtail" binder in Oxford; see Oldham, p. 22, stamps 160 and 162; remains of 2 clasps, closing from bottom to top, and evidence of a label formerly on the back cover.

Written in England at Winchcombe Abbey ca. 1130–1140, by two scribes, the first of whom is the same scribe who copied the Bede now Oxford, Bod. Lib., Douce 368 (see N. R. Ker, *English Manuscripts in the Century after the Norman Conquest*, Oxford 1960, pl. 24). The two manuscripts were also decorated by the same artist; see A. Heimann, "A Twelfth-Century Manuscript from Winchcombe and its illustrations: Dublin, Trinity College, MS 53," *JWCI* 28 (1965) 86–109, citing this manuscript on pp. 107–108, and with a reproduction of the initial, f. 1v; Sotheby's catalogue, 11 December 1979, lot 46, also links the illumination of the present manuscript with that in two other Winchcombe books (Cambridge, University Library, Mm.3.31; London, Brit. Lib., Cotton Tiberius E.iv). See Ker, *MLGB*, pp. 198–199 for a list of surviving books from Winchcombe Abbey, including HM 52435 (as Camarillo, Doheny Lib., 50). This book was still at Winchcombe under the energetic direction of Richard Kidderminster (abbot, 1488–1525), when it received its present binding, as did another Winchcombe book in similar binding, an Augustine, now Oxford, Jesus College, MS 102. Said in the literature (Dawson's typescript description [1950]; Doheny catalogue 1955; Bond and Faye 1962; Christie's sale catalogue 1987; see below) to have belonged to Sir John Prise (1502/03?–1555), a commissioner for the visitation of the monasteries in 1535 and 1539. This ownership seems posited on the fact that Jesus College 102 belonged to Prise and that the two manuscripts (the present one and Jesus College 102) are in very similar bindings. However, the binding of both was certainly done while the books were still at Winchcombe. Moreover, Prise's will directs that his books go to Hereford Cathedral (where one is presently so identified) and to Jesus College (where 2 are so identified); neither of the other Winchcombe books that passed by inheritance through the Cope family shows any evidence of ownership by Prise (Cope sale, lot 9, later Sotheby's, 11 December 1979, lot 46, now Oxford, Bod. Lib., Lat. th. d. 46[1]; Cope sale, lot 171, untraced). See N. R. Ker, "Sir John Prise," *The Library*, ser. 5, vol. 10 (1955) 1–24, esp. p. 15, listing an Ambrosiaster that did belong to Prise (London, Brit. Lib., Burney 42; whence some of the present confusion?), p. 14, emphasizing the Cirencester (Gloucestershire) and St. Guthlac (Hereford) origin of most of Prise's books, and pp. 19–20, discussing the Winchcombe origin of the present manuscript in the context of Prise's ownership of Jesus College 102. May have belonged to Sir Walter Cope; see A. G. Watson, "The Manuscript Collection of Sir Walter Cope (d. 1614)," *Bodleian Library Record* 12 (1987) 262–297, discussing this manuscript on pp. 274, 291–292. The book was in the library of the descendants of Sir Anthony Cope, a brother of Sir Walter; it was recorded in the Cope inventory compiled ca. 1772 as n. 6. Sale of Sir Anthony Cope of Bramshill Park, Winchfield, Hampshire, Sotheby's, 4 March 1913, lot 4 to Barnard. On the front pastedown the bookplate of E. F. Bosanquet; his sale, Sotheby's, 24 June 1944, lot 64 to Maggs. Also on the front pastedown, in pencil, the note, "George A. Goyder, Maltby, Oxford, 1944"; sold by him to Maggs in 1950. On the back pastedown, the name of Dawson's Book Shop in Los Angeles and the date June 1950 (but not their price code); a typescript description from Dawson's is with the book. Acquired at that time from Dawson's by Carrie Estelle Doheny, on whose collecting see E. Shaffer, "Reminiscences of a California Collector: Mrs. Edward Laurence Doheny 1875–1958," *The Book Collector* 14 (1965) 49–59. Doheny accession number 6385 on f. 129v. Mrs. Doheny left her extensive collection of manuscripts, books, William Morris materials, paperweights, Western Americana, paintings and tapestries to the library she built at St. John's Seminary in Camarillo, California, in the archdiocese of Los Angeles, as a memorial to her husband. Sold by the archdiocese through Christie's, 2 December 1987, lot 141 with reproduction of initials on ff. 1, 1v, 54, 90 to Maggs for the Huntington Library as a gift of the Dan Murphy Foundation in memory of Bernardine Murphy Donohue.

Secundo folio: enim filius hominis
Bibliography: HMC, *3rd Report, Appendix* (1872) 242, n. IV. Schenkl 4747. [Carey S. Bliss and Amelia B. Bliss], *Catalogue of Books and Manuscripts in the Estelle Doheny Collection, Part Three* (Los Angeles 1955) p. 3 and pl. VI of f. 54. Bond and Faye, p. 13 n. 50.

[1] I thank Andrew Watson for supplying, in a great rush, the present location of this manuscript and the following bibliography on Sir Walter Cope.

INDEX 1
DATED MANUSCRIPTS

INDEX 2
OTHER MANUSCRIPTS CITED

Index 2: MSS Cited

INDEX 3
PERSONS AND INSTITUTIONS (MAINLY OWNERS)

Index 3: Owners

INDEX 4
SCRIBES

See also "Autograph manuscript" in General Index

Index 4: Scribes

INDEX 5
ARTISTS

Index 5: Artists

INDEX 6
ICONOGRAPHY

Miniatures of HM 268, Lydgate, *Fall of Princes* (pp. 231–232) and of HM 936, Boccaccio, *Des cas des nobles hommes et femmes* (pp. 282–283) are not indexed. For iconography of individual saints, see Saints Index.

Index 6: Iconography

Index 6: Iconography

INDEX 7
SAINTS

Saints' names are standardized, for the most part, according to F. G. Holweck, *A Biographical Dictionary of the Saints* (St. Louis and London 1924; repr. 1969). Saints as authors of texts are entered in the General Index. Iconographic scenes with saints (such as Annunciation, Baptism of Christ, Last Supper, etc.) are to be found in the Iconography Index. Entries for saints in this index are specified as follows:

{i} = illustration
{k} = calendar
{l} = litany
{m} = mass
{n} = narrative (*Legenda aurea*, pp. 590–94, not indexed)
{o} = office
{p} = prayer

Index 7: Saints

INDEX 8
INDEX OF MIDDLE ENGLISH VERSE NUMBERS

INDEX 9
GENERAL INDEX

General Index

CHART OF THE BOOKS OF HOURS

Arrangement is alphabetical according to use, then chronological; the arabic numerals refer to numbered articles in descriptions.

	AMIENS		BESANÇON		CHÂ-LONS-SUR-MARNE	CHAR-TRES	LAN-GRES
Call number	HM 1126	HM 1167	HM 1137	HM 1141	HM 1265	HM 1150	HM 1169
Country of origin	France	France	France	France	France	France	France
Date	XV^{2}	XV/XVI	XV^{1}	XV^{med}	XVI^{in}	XV^{ex}	XV^{ex}
Calendar	1	1	2	1	2	1	1
Pericopes of the Gospels	2	4	3	2	3	3	
Passion accord. to John		3				12	
Obsecro te/O Intemerata	2	10	9	8	4, 8	10	7
Votive mass of the BVM							
Hours of the BVM	3	7	6 (undet. use)	3	5	4	4
Changed office of the BVM							4
Penitential psalms; litany	4	8	7	6	6	7	5
Gradual psalms							
Hours of the Cross	5	5	4	4		5	4
Hours of the Holy Spirit	6	6	5	5		6	4
Hours of the Eternal Wisdom							
Other hours							
Office of the Dead	7	9 (3 lessons)	8	7	7	8	6
Commendation of souls							6
Suffrages of saints		10	3			9, 11, 13, 14	7
Psalms of Passion/Psalter of St. Jerome/other psalms							
Prayers	8	10		9	1, 6, 8	2, 9–11, 14	2–3, 6, 7
Didactic materials		2					
Language other than Latin	French	French	French	French	French	French	French

Charts

	PARIS							
Call number	HM 1142	HM 1151	HM 1156	HM 1160	HM 1138	HM 1099	HM 1100	HM 1129
Country of origin	France	France	France	France	France	France	France	France
Date	XV^{in}	XV^{in}	XV^{in}	XV^{in}	XV^{1}	XV^{med}	XV^{med}	XV^{med}
Calendar	1	1	1	1	1	1	1	1
Pericopes of the Gospels	2	2	2	3	2	2	2	2
Passion accord. to John			6	2				8
Obsecro te/O Intemerata	2	8	2	3	4	8	2	8
Votive mass of the BVM								
Hours of the BVM	3	3	3 (?)	4	3 (?)	3	3	3
Changed office of the BVM								
Penitential psalms; litany	4	4	7	7	5	5	4	6
Gradual psalms								
Hours of the Cross	6	5	4	5		6	5	4
Hours of the Holy Spirit	missing	6	5	6	6	7	6	5
Hours of the Eternal Wisdom								
Other hours								
Office of the Dead	7	7	8	8	8 (3 lessons)	9 (undet. use)	7	7
Commendation of souls								
Suffrages of saints	8	8	9		9	4	9	
Psalms of Passion/Psalter of St. Jerome/other psalms								
Prayers	5	8	2, 6, 9	8	3, 4, 7, 9	4	8	7, 8
Didactic materials								
Language other than Latin	French	French	French	French	French	French	French	entirely in French

PARIS

Call number	HM 1130	EL 34 A 1	HM 1128	HM 1154	HM 1163	HM 1133	HM 1147	HM 1168
Country of origin	France	France	France	France	France	France	France	France
Date	XV^{med}	XV^2	XV^2	XV^2	XV^2	XVI^{in}	XVI^{in}	XVI^1
Calendar	1	1	1	1	1	1	1	1
Pericopes of the Gospels	2	2	2	2	2	2	2	2
Passion accord. to John					2			
Obsecro te/O Intemerata	2	2	2	2	3	2	9	2
Votive mass of the BVM								
Hours of the BVM	3	3	3	3	4, 8	3	4	3
Changed office of the BVM								
Penitential psalms; litany	4	4	4	4	5	4	7	6
Gradual psalms								
Hours of the Cross	5		5	5	4	5	5	4
Hours of the Holy Spirit	6		6	6	4	6	6	5
Hours of the Eternal Wisdom								
Other hours								
Office of the Dead	7 (?)	5	7	7	6	7 (undet. use)	8	7
Commendation of souls								
Suffrages of saints		6		8	8	8	9	8
Psalms of Passion/ Psalter of St. Jerome/other psalms								
Prayers	8	6	8	8	3, 7	9	3, 9	
Didactic materials								
Language other than Latin	French	French	French	French	French	French	French	

Charts

	ROME							
Call number	HM 1104	HM 1123	HM 1134	HM 1136	HM 1143	HM 25779	HM 1132	HM 1148
Country of origin	France	France	Flanders	Flanders	France	Italy	Italy	Flanders
Date	XV^{in}	XV^{med}	XV^{med}	XV^2	XV^2	XV^2	XV^{ex}	XV^{ex}
Calendar	1	1	1	1	1	1	1	1
Pericopes of the Gospels	2	2	3 (John only)	5	2			6
Passion accord. to John			10		2			
Obsecro te/O Intemerata	15	2	3	9	3			2
Votive mass of the BVM				4				
Hours of the BVM	3	3	5	6	4	2	2	7
Changed office of the BVM								7
Penitential psalms; litany	4	4	7	7	7	3	6	8
Gradual psalms								
Hours of the Cross	11	5	6	2	5	4	4; 5 (long)	4
Hours of the Holy Spirit	8	6	2 (long)	3	6			5
Hours of the Eternal Wisdom								
Other hours	6, 7, 9, 10, 12, 13		4					
Office of the Dead	5	7 (?)	8	8 (3 lessons)	8	5	3	9
Commendation of souls								
Suffrages of saints	15 (XV^{ex})		9, 11	9	9			3
Psalms of Passion/ Psalter of St. Jerome/other psalms					11, 12, 13			
Prayers	14; 15 (XV^{ex})	8, 9	3, 9, 10, 11		3, 10			2, 8
Didactic materials	16 (XV^{ex})							
Language other than Latin	Provençal	French	French		French			

ROME

Call number	HM 1157	HM 1174	HM 25773	HM 1170	HM 1181	HM 48	HM 1101	HM 1124
Country of origin	Flanders	Flanders	Flanders	France	France	France	France	France
Date	XV^{ex}	XV^{ex}	XV^{ex}	XV^{ex}	XV/XVI	XVI^{in}	XVI^{in}	XVI^{in}
Calendar	1	1	1	1	1	1	1	1
Pericopes of the Gospels	6	5		2	2	2	2	3
Passion accord. to John						2	2	3
Obsecro te/O Intemerata	8	9	7	3	3	9	2	2
Votive mass of the BVM	5	4	3					2
Hours of the BVM	7	6	4	4	4	3	3	4
Changed office of the BVM	7	6	5	4	4	3	3	4
Penitential psalms; litany	9	7	6	5	8	6	4	9
Gradual psalms								
Hours of the Cross	3	2		6	6	4	5	6
Hours of the Holy Spirit	4	3		7	7	5	6	8
Hours of the Eternal Wisdom								
Other hours						8		5
Office of the Dead	10	8		8	9	7	7	10
Commendation of souls								
Suffrages of saints	8	9		9	10	9	8	2, 11
Psalms of Passion/ Psalter of St. Jerome/other psalms								
Prayers	2, 7, 8, 11	9	2		5, 11	9	3	3, 7, 11
Didactic materials								
Language other than Latin				French	French			

Charts

ROME

Call number	HM 1139	HM 1161	HM 1165	HM 1171	HM 1149	HM 1164	HM 1135	HM 1166
Country of origin	France	France	France	France	Flanders	Flanders	Italy	Spain
Date	XVI^{in}	XVI^{in}	XVI^{in}	XVI^{in}	XVI^{in}	XVI^{in}	XVI^{in}	XVI^{1}
Calendar	1	1	1	1	1	1	1	2
Pericopes of the Gospels	6 (John only)	2	2	3				3,12 (both John only)
Passion accord. to John				3				
Obsecro te/O Intemerata	7	3	2	7	7			
Votive mass of the BVM							4	8
Hours of the BVM	3	4	4	4	4	4	3	7
Changed office of the BVM	3	4	4	4		4	3	7
Penitential psalms; litany	4	5	5	5	5	5	6	9
Gradual psalms								11
Hours of the Cross	3	6	4	4	2	2	10	4
Hours of the Holy Spirit	3	7	4	4	3	3	11	5
Hours of the Eternal Wisdom								
Other hours				4				6
Office of the Dead	5	8	6	6	6	6	8	10 (missing)
Commendation of souls								
Suffrages of saints	3, 7	9	7	8	8	8	5	13
Psalms of Passion/ Psalter of St. Jerome/other psalms	2							
Prayers	7	9	3, 7	7, 9	7, 9	7	2, 5, 7, 9	3, 12
Didactic materials	7			2				
Language other than Latin	French	French	French	French	French		Italian	

	ROME		ROUEN			ST. QUENTIN
Call number	HM 1088	HM 1102	HM 1145	HM 1166	HM 2590	HM 1172
Country of origin	France	Rome	France	France	France	France
Date	1513	1549	XV²	XV²	XV²	XV²
Calendar	2	2	1	1	1	1
Pericopes of the Gospels	3; 6 (John only)	3	2	2	3	
Passion accord. to John		3				
Obsecro te/O Intemerata			8	2		10
Votive mass of the BVM						
Hours of the BVM	5, 7	4	3	3	2	2
Changed office of the BVM	8					
Penitential psalms; litany		5	4	4	4	5
Gradual psalms						
Hours of the Cross	5	7	5	5		3
Hours of the Holy Spirit	5	8	6	6		4
Hours of the Eternal Wisdom						
Other hours						
Office of the Dead		6 (3 lessons)	7 (as in Sarum)	7 (as in Sarum)	5	6 (3 lessons)
Commendation of souls						
Suffrages of saints	4	9	3	3	2, 6	4, 7
Psalms of Passion/Psalter of St. Jerome/ other psalms						
Prayers	4, 6, 9, 16		3, 8	8		7–9, 11
Didactic materials	1, 10–15, 17–18	2				
Language other than Latin	French	French	French	French	French	French

Charts

SARUM

Call number	HM 1346	HM 19913	HM 28175	HM 1125	HM 1086	HM 1087	HM 1144	HM 1344
Country of origin	England	England	N. France	N. France/ Flanders	Flanders	Flanders	Flanders	Flanders
Date	XIV^1	XV^{in}	XV^{in}	XV^{med}	XV^{med}	XV^{med}	XV^{med}	XVI^{in}
Calendar	1	1	2	1	1	1	1	1
Pericopes of the Gospels				14				2
Passion accord. to John								3
Obsecro te/O Intemerata			5	7	6	5	5	5
Votive mass of the BVM								
Hours of the BVM	2	2	4	6	5	4	4	4
Changed office of the BVM								
Penitential psalms; litany	3	3	7	9	7	9	7	6
Gradual psalms	3	3	7	9	7	9	7	6
Hours of the Cross		2	4	6	5	4	4	4
Hours of the Holy Spirit				2				
Hours of the Eternal Wisdom								
Other hours								
Office of the Dead	4	4	8	10	8	10	8	7
Commendation of souls		5	9	11	9	11	9	8
Suffrages of saints	2	2	1, 3, 4	4, 6	4, 5	3, 4	3, 4	4, 5
Psalms of Passion/ Psalter of St. Jerome/other psalms		6	10–11	12–13	10	12–13	10–11	9–10
Prayers	5	7	4–6	3, 5, 7–8, 14	2–3, 5–6	2–3, 5–8	2–3, 5–6	3, 5, 6, 11
Didactic materials	6–8				11			
Language other than Latin	French		English	French	English		English	English

	SENS	TROYES	WINDESHEIM		
Call number	HM 1153	HM 1146	HM 1155	HM 1127	HM 1131
Country of origin	France	France	Netherlands	Netherlands	Flanders
Date	XV^2	XV^{ex}	XV^{med}	XV^2	XV/XVI
Calendar	1	1	2	1	2
Pericopes of the Gospels	2 (John only)	2			
Passion accord. to John					
Obsecro te/O Intemerata	8	5			7
Votive mass of the BVM					7
Hours of the BVM	3 (?)	5	3	2	4
Changed office of the BVM					
Penitential psalms; litany	6	6	6	8	5
Gradual psalms					
Hours of the Cross	4	3	4 (long)	6 (long)	3
Hours of the Holy Spirit	5	4			
Hours of the Eternal Wisdom			5	4	
Other hours					
Office of the Dead	7 (3 lessons)	7	11	13	6 (3 lessons)
Commendation of souls					
Suffrages of saints	8		7		8
Psalms of Passion/Psalter of St. Jerome/other psalms					
Prayers			8, 9	3, 5, 7, 9–12, 14	3, 6–7, 9
Didactic materials			1, 10	1	
Language other than Latin	French	French	G. Grote Dutch	G. Grote Dutch	

UNDETERMINED USE;
fragments; some prayerbooks

Call number	HM 1159	HM 1179	HM 1200	HM 1173	HM 47544	HM 1248	HM 1180	HM 1250
Country of origin	England?	France	Flanders	France	Italy?	Flanders	France	France
Date	XV^{in}	XV^{in}	XV^{med}	XV^{2}	XV^{2}	1478	$XV^{4/4}$	XV^{ex}
Calendar			1	1		2		1
Pericopes of the Gospels			2	2				2
Passion accord. to John							2	
Obsecro te/O Intemerata			2, 10	7		9		2
Votive mass of the BVM			9	3				
Hours of the BVM	missing	missing	5 (undet. use)	5 (undet. use)	2 (use of Rome?)	not present	not present	3 (undet. use)
Changed office of the BVM								
Penitential psalms; litany			7	6		3		4
Gradual psalms						3		
Hours of the Cross		2 (long)	3	4	3		1 (long)	3
Hours of the Holy Spirit		3 (long)	4				5 (long)	3
Hours of the Eternal Wisdom								
Other hours		4					3, 7	
Office of the Dead	missing	not present	8 (3 lessons)	8 (use of Rome)	1 (defective)	4 (Sarum use?)	not present	5 (undet. use)
Commendation of souls	1					5		
Suffrages of saints	2	5, 9	11			7, 8	1	
Psalms of Passion/ Psalter of St. Jerome/other psalms						6, 10	11	
Prayers		6–9	6, 10	9–10		7–9	4, 6, 8–10	
Didactic materials								
Language other than Latin			French	French				

UNDETERMINED USE; fragments; some prayerbooks

Call number	HM 39467	HM 1140	HM 1158
Country of origin	France	Nether-lands	Italy
Date	XV^{ex}	XV^{ex}	XVII^{in}
Calendar		1	
Pericopes of the Gospels			
Passion accord. to John			
Obsecro te/O Intemerata			
Votive mass of the BVM			
Hours of the BVM	not present	not present	not present
Changed office of the BVM			
Penitential psalms; litany	1	8	3
Gradual psalms			
Hours of the Cross		2	1
Hours of the Holy Spirit			2
Hours of the Eternal Wisdom			
Other hours	3		
Office of the Dead	2 (short)	not present	not present
Commendation of souls			
Suffrages of saints		7, 9	
Psalms of Passion/ Psalter of St. Jerome/other psalms			
Prayers	4–6	3–6, 9–12	
Didactic materials			
Language other than Latin	French	G. Grote Dutch	

CHART OF THE PORTOLAN ATLASES

Geographical Areas on Maps and Portolan Atlases

T-O maps not included; see General Index under "Map" for references. Geographical descriptions in derroteros not included; see descriptions of HM 1788 (p. 587) and HM 30957 (p. 692).

	HM 10	HM 25	HM 26	HM 27	HM 28	HM 29	HM 30	HM 31	HM 32	HM 33	HM 34	HM 35	HM 37	HM 38	HM 39	HM 40	HM 41	HM 42	HM 43	HM 44	HM 45	HM 46	HM 47	HM 132,f.4v	HM 160,f.141	HM 427	HM 1092	HM 1548	HM 1549	HM 2098	HM 2515	HM 217 [forg-	HM 218 eries]
Adriatic Sea						x	x						x														x						
Aegean Sea	x	x	x	x	x	x	x	x	x	x	x	x	x	x				x															
Africa					x																											x	
Africa, Eastern	x	x	x	x	x				x	x							x			x													
Africa, Northern						x			x		x	x		x			x										x						
Africa, Northwestern	x	x	x	x	x	x			x	x		x		x	x		x			x							x				x		
Africa, Southern						x			x	x					x		x			x													
Africa, Western						x			x	x		x								x										x			
Arabia					x	x			x	x					x		x			x							x					x	
Asia																											x					x	
Asia, Eastern	x	x	x	x	x	x			x	x					x		x																
Asia, Southern	x	x	x	x	x										x					x							x						
Atlantic Ocean, North	x	x	x	x	x				x	x		x			x				x	x										x			
Atlantic Ocean, South						x									x					x													
Australia (Terra Java)						x			x													x											
Black Sea	x	x	x	x	x				x	x		x			x		x			x							x						
British Isles	x	x	x	x					x							x						x			x		x	x	x	x			
Caribbean Sea						x			x	x					x		x			x													
Central America						x			x	x					x		x			x													
Ceylon																											x						
Corsica														x													x						
East Indies	x	x	x	x	x	x			x						x		x			x													
Europe	x	x	x	x	x	x			x	x		x			x	x	x			x		x					x	x	x			x	
Europe, West coast	x	x	x	x											x															x	x		
France																						x					x				x		
Germany																						x					x						
Greece																											x						

	HM 10	HM 25	HM 26	HM 27	HM 28	HM 29	HM 30	HM 31	HM 32	HM 33	HM 34	HM 35	HM 37	HM 38	HM 39	HM 40	HM 41	HM 42	HM 43	HM 44	HM 45	HM 46	HM 47	HM 132, f. 4v	HM 160, f. 141	HM 427	HM 1092	HM 1548	HM 1549	HM 2098	HM 2515	HM 217 [forg-	HM 218 eries]
Iceland	x														x					x													
India					x				x						x		x			x							x						
Indian Ocean	x	x	x	x	x	x			x	x					x		x			x													
Italy	x	x	x	x	x						x			x													x						
Japan										x							x			x													
Madagascar									x	x					x		x			x													
Mediterranean Sea	x	x	x	x	x	x	x		x	x	x	x	x	x	x	x	x	x		x								x	x		x	x	
Mexico						x			x	x					x		x			x													
Near East					x					x					x												x	x					
Newfoundland						x			x	x					x		x			x													
North America																																x	
North America, East coast	x	x	x	x	x	x			x	x		x			x		x		x	x													
North America, West coast	x	x	x	x	x					x					x		x			x													
Pacific Ocean	x	x	x	x	x					x																							
Palestine	x																																
Persian Gulf						x				x					x												x						
Red Sea						x			x	x					x												x						
Russia	x									x																	x						
Sardinia											x			x													x						
Scandinavia	x				x							x				x	x			x								x	x				
Sicily											x			x													x						
South America					x																											x	
South America, Eastern						x									x		x			x													
South America, Northeast	x	x	x	x		x			x	x					x				x	x													
South America, Northwest										x					x					x													
South America, Southern						x			x	x					x		x			x													
South America, West coast	x	x	x	x	x												x																
Spain & Portugal	x	x	x	x	x				x			x		x						x		x					x				x		
Spitsbergen																							x										
Turkey																											x						
World	x	x	x	x	x																x	x		x		x	x						x
Armillary sphere	x		x	x	x																												
Table of declinations	x	x	x	x	x	x											x			x		x											

LIST OF FIGURES

Figures 1–37 are of dated/datable manuscripts

List of Figures

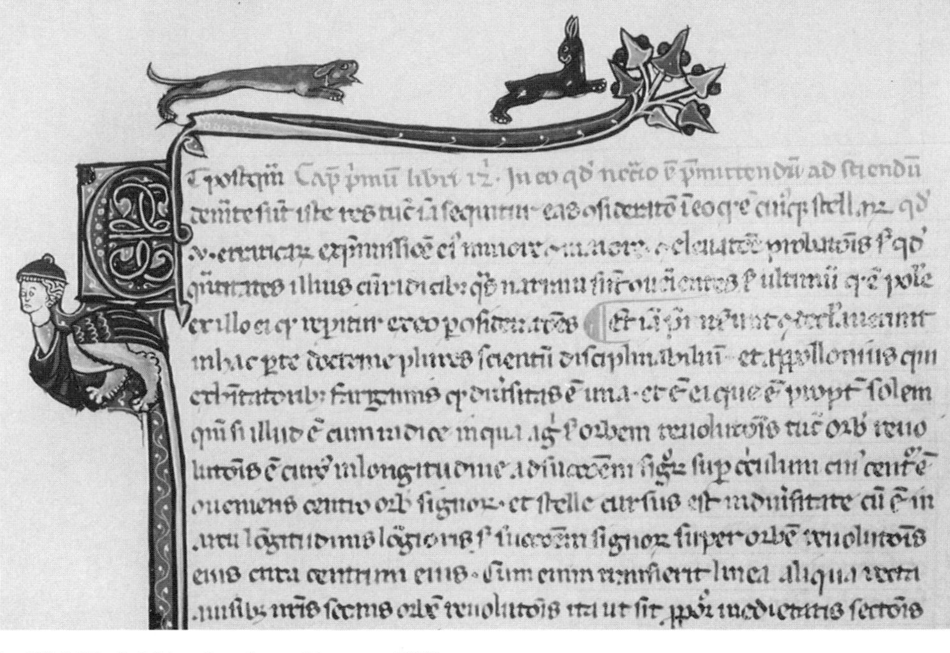

1. HM 65, f. 184v; Southern France, 1279

2. HM 65, f. 241; Southern France, 1279

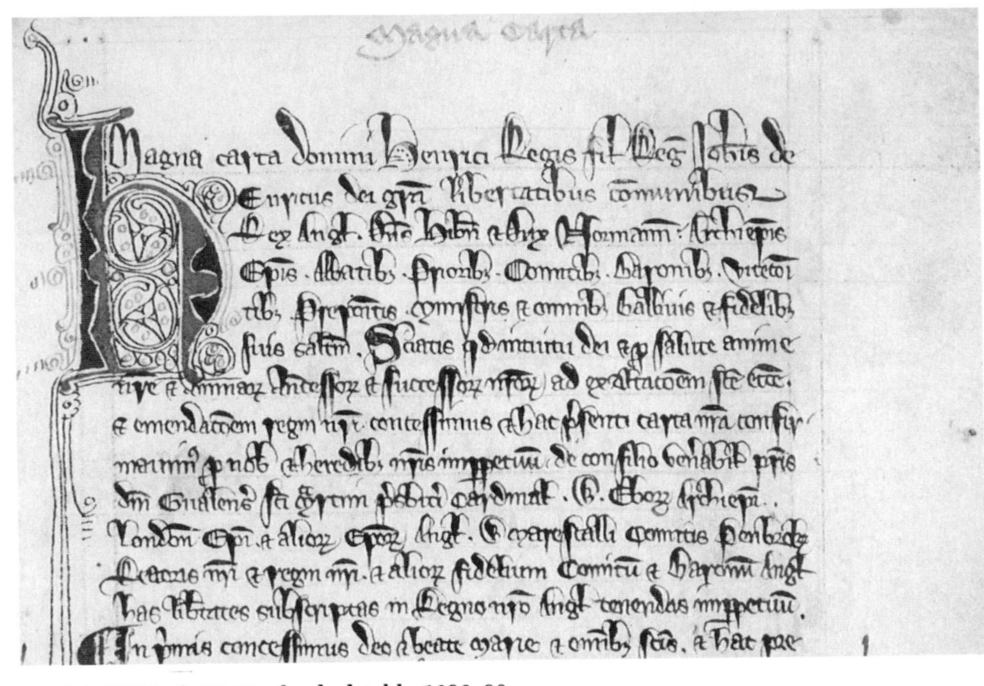

3. HM 25782, f. 17; England, datable 1286–90

4. HM 19918, f. 17; England, datable ca. 1320

5. EL 7 H 8, f. 180; England, 1368

6. BA 30, f. 21v; England, 1408–10

7. RB 86299, f. 1; France, before 1428

8. EL 26 A 3, f. 181; France, 1410

9. EL 26 A 3, f. 213; France, 1415

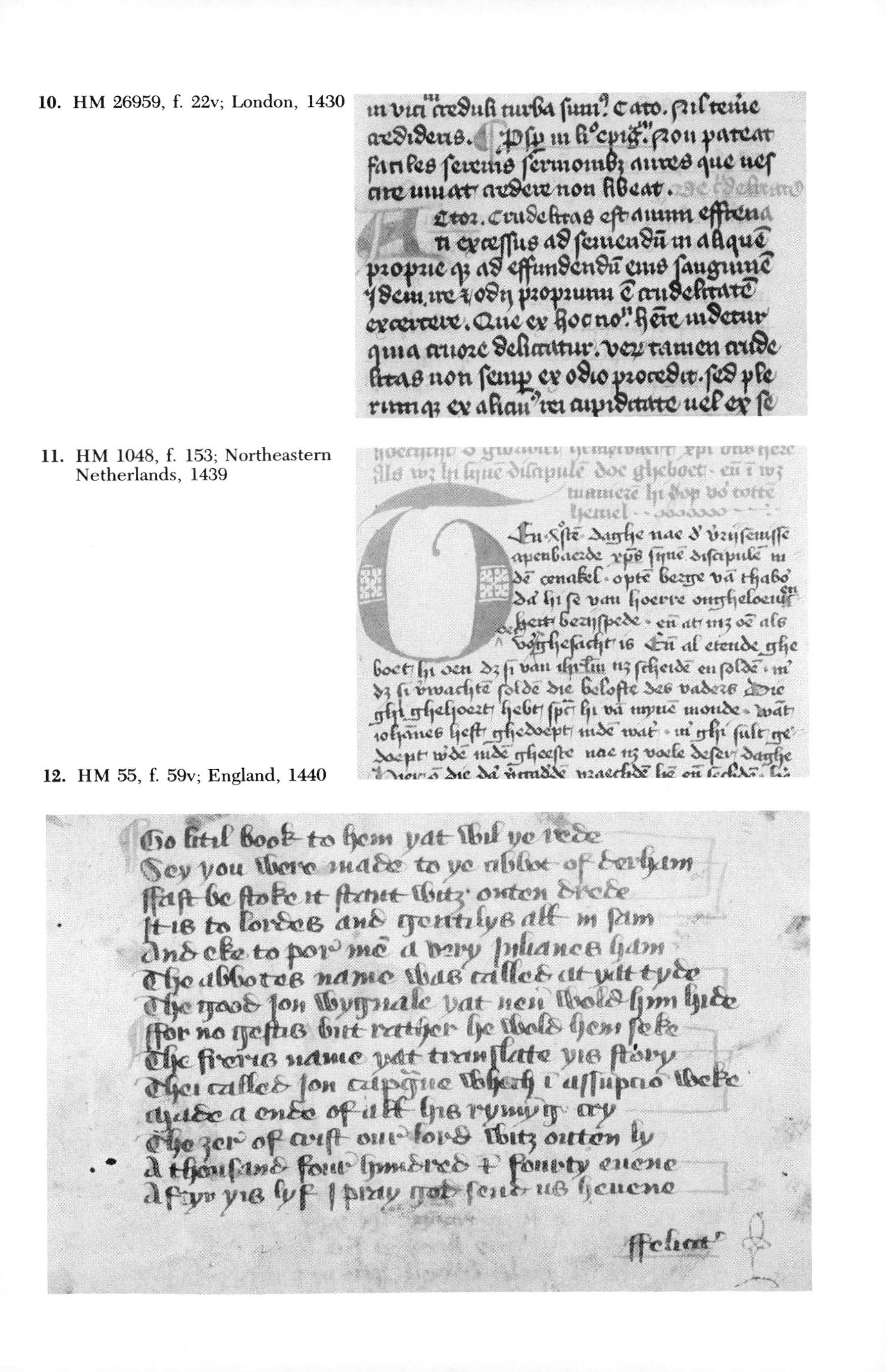

10. HM 26959, f. 22v; London, 1430

11. HM 1048, f. 153; Northeastern Netherlands, 1439

12. HM 55, f. 59v; England, 1440

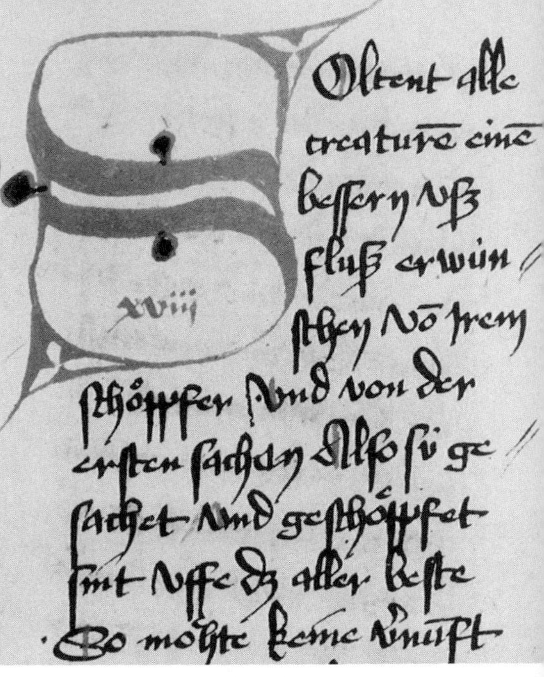

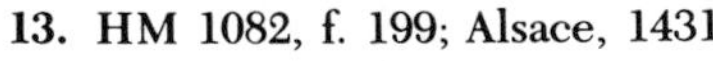

13. HM 1082, f. 199; Alsace, 1431

14. HM 1082, f. 286v; Alsace, 1431

15. HM 41761, f. 1; Netherlands, 1443

16. HM 932, f. 10v; England, 1447

Incipit prologus i omeli
as. magistri hugonis super
ecclesiaste.
Que de li
bro salo
monis q
ecclesiastes
dicitur
nup vob
cora disserui: breuiter nuc
pstringens q̄a queda ibi
digna memoria videbant
stilo signaui. Omnis scriptu
ra secūdu primam interpreta
tione exposita, et clarius

negant ubi est: vel appo
nenda supstitiose conten
dut ubi nō est. Et propter
in hoc ope nō multu ego
laborandū estimo tropolo
gys siue misticis allego
riaru sensib; p tota dūtax
at enarrationis eius serie
pquirendis. Precipue cu ipe
auctor hic nō tā morib; in
struendis vel misteriis e
narrandis intendat: q̄ ut
cor hūanu ad reru munda
naru conteptu manifesta
rationu veritate atq; ex

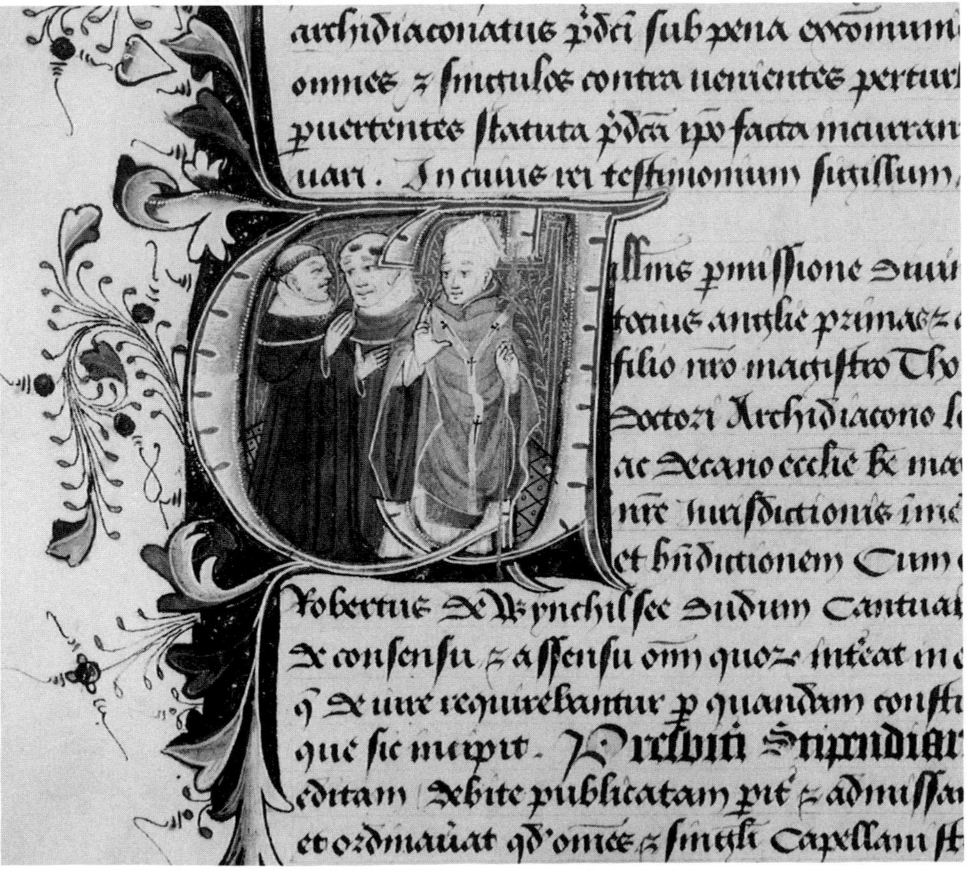
archidiaconatus p̄dci sub pena excommuni
omnes & singulos contra venientes pertur
puertentes statuta p̄dca ipo facto incurran
uari. In cuius rei testimonium sigillum

illmus pmissione diui
torius anglie primas & a
filio nro magistro Tho
doctori Archidiacono
ac decano ecclie be ma
nre iurisdictionis ime
et bndictionem Cum
Robertus de Wynchilsee dudum Cantuar
de consensu & assensu om quor interat in
q de iure requirebantur p quandam consti
que sic incipit. Presbiteri stipendiari
editam debite publicatam pit & admissam
et ordinauit qd omes & singuli Capellani

17. HM 47641, May; Italy, datable 1450–55

18. HM 1080, f. 137v; Florence, 1452–53

19. HM 744, back flyleaf recto; England, 1463

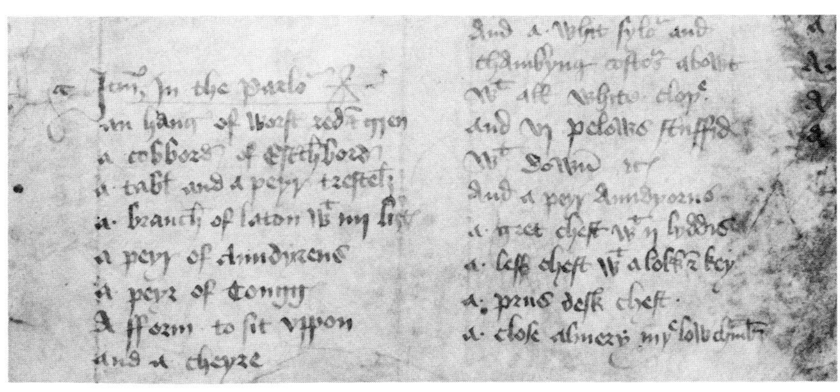

20. HM 1040, f. 1; Rome, 1456

CECILI CIPRIANI EPI CARTAGIN EPLA · LI · IN

Bene ammones Donate karme. Nã
et promisisse me memini et reddẽ
di tempestiuũ prorsus hoc temp⁹
est: quo indulgente uindemia
solutus animus inquietem so
lemnes ac statutas animi fatigã
tis inducias sortiatur. Locus
etiam cum die conuenit: et mulcendis sensibus:
ac fouendis adlenes auras blandientis autumni
ortoꝝ facies amena consentit. Hic iocundũ ser
monibus diem ducere: et studentibus fabulis in
diuina precepta conscientiaꝫ pectoris erudire. Ac
ne eloquiuꝫ nostru arbiter prophan⁹ impediat: aut
clamor intemperans familie strepentis obtundat.
Petamus hanc sedem: dant secessum uicina secre
ta: ubi dum erratici palmituꝫ lapsus nexibus
pendulis per arundines baiulas repūt: uitea por
ticũ frondea tecta fecerunt. Bene hic studia in au
res damus: et dum in arbores: et in uites quas

21. HM 937, f. 1; Flanders, 1461–62 (75% reduction)

22. HM 937, f. 33; Flanders, 1461–62

vne montaigne du pays de eubee · En
la crupe de celle montaigne · Le roy
amplius pere de palamedes · fist alumer
grans brandons et falos par nuit · Af
fin que les gens retournans de la bataille
de troies cuidassent que illec feust vng
port bon et seeurs · Et les nefs des grec
qui illec arriuerent furent peries et aussi
les hommes qui dedens estoient par les
rochiers cornus qui sont en la mer prez
du mont capharrus · Et fist naui
plus cela nuit pour vengier la mort

filius Regnavit
[illegible] filius eius
[illegible] frater eius
[illegible]

Danius filius eius

Morindus crudelior

[illegible]
[illegible] Morindus
[illegible] quinque filios
[illegible] progenitos
[illegible] gesta [illegible]
[illegible]
progenitus
[illegible]
[illegible]
[illegible]
[illegible]

Elidurus — Argallo — Gorbodianus progenitus — Vigenius — Peredurus

Gerontius filius Eli[duri] — Morganus filius progenitus Argalli — Enniaunus 2 filius — Redallo — Rimo

[illegible] repleverunt insulam

militantes corrupte [illegible]
Deno tumultu commovit
sublata est potestas. Et
Ediles facti sunt consulibus [illegible]

Anno ab urbe con[dita]
a [illegible]
Gaius Julius Cesar factus est
ta est ei Gallia et Illiria
qui per novem annos tam Ge[rmanos]
[illegible] bella gessit [illegible]
[illegible] subiugandum Galli[os]
Suevos perdomuit
subiugavit et Brit[annos]
tributarios fecit
[illegible] pugnavit
Beda [illegible]
[illegible] venit Jul[ius]
[illegible] Britannia
Beda libro primo ca[pitulo]

Julius consul [illegible]
et Gallos qui [illegible]
[illegible] bellum [illegible]

24. HM 142, f. 54v; England, 1467

25. HM 142, f. 60v; England, 1467

23. HM 264, "f. 10"; England, datable 1461–64

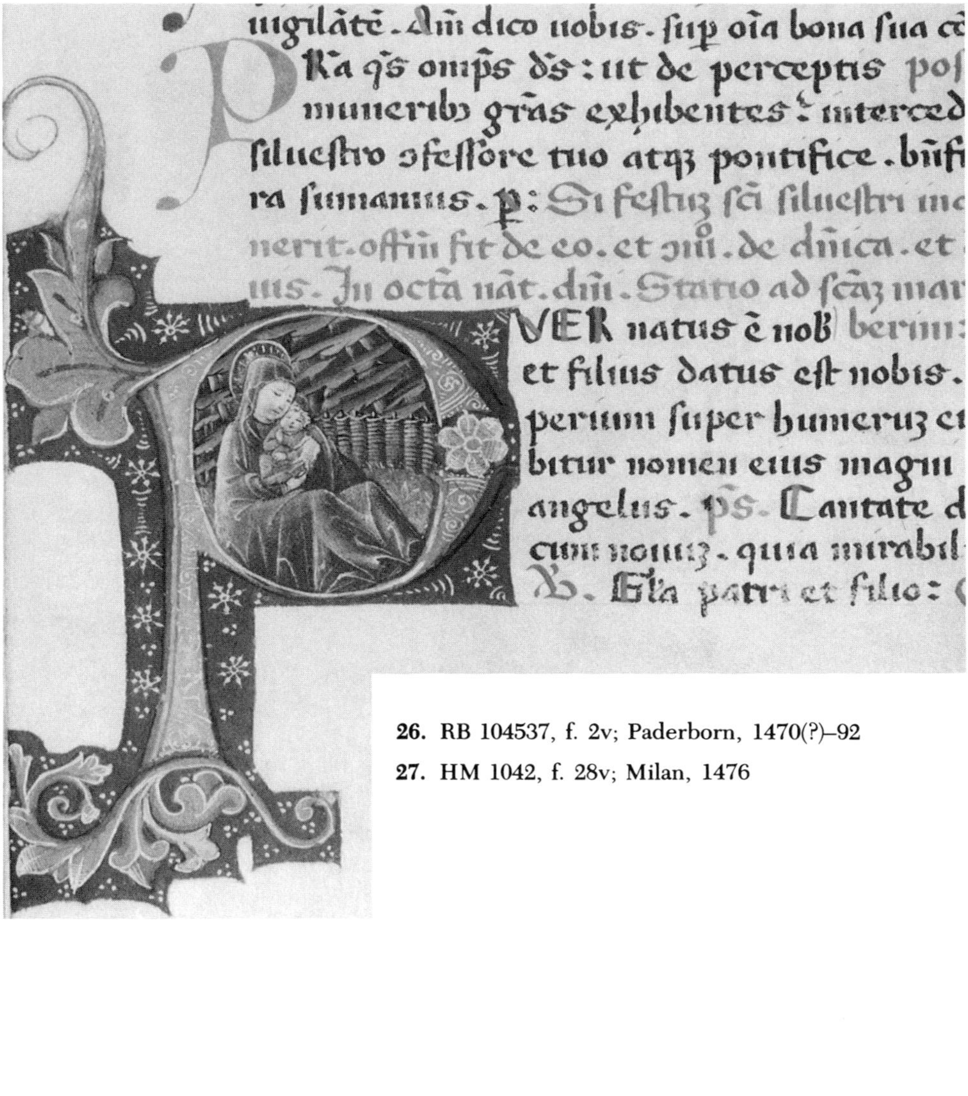

26. RB 104537, f. 2v; Paderborn, 1470(?)–92

27. HM 1042, f. 28v; Milan, 1476

28. HM 1248, f. 155; Flanders, 1478

29. HM 83, f. 16v; Lübeck(?), 1486–88

30. HM 1088, f. 54; France, 1513

31. HM 36701, f. 19v; Flanders(?), 1539(?)

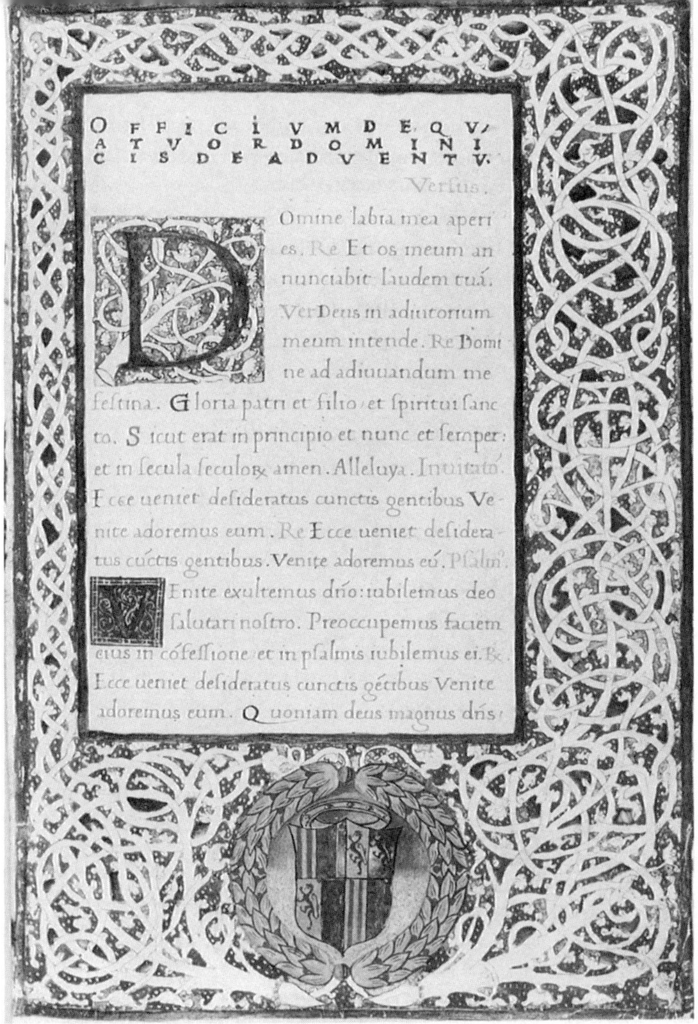
OFFICIVM DE QVATVOR DOMINICIS DE ADVENTV.
Versus.
DOmine labia mea aperies. Re Et os meum annunciabit laudem tuá.
Ver Deus in adiutorium meum intende. Re Domine ad adiuuandum me festina. Gloria patri et filio et spiritui sancto. Sicut erat in principio et nunc et semper: et in secula seculorum amen. Alleluya. Inuitato.
Ecce ueniet desideratus cunctis gentibus Venite adoremus eum. Re Ecce ueniet desideratus cúctis gentibus. Venite adoremus eú. Psalm.
VEnite exultemus dño: iubilemus deo salutari nostro. Preoccupemus faciem eius in cófessione et in psalmis iubilemus ei. Re
Ecce ueniet desideratus cunctis gétibus Venite adoremus eum. Quoniam deus magnus dñs

32. HM 1046, f. 18; Southern Italy, 1519 (50% reduction)

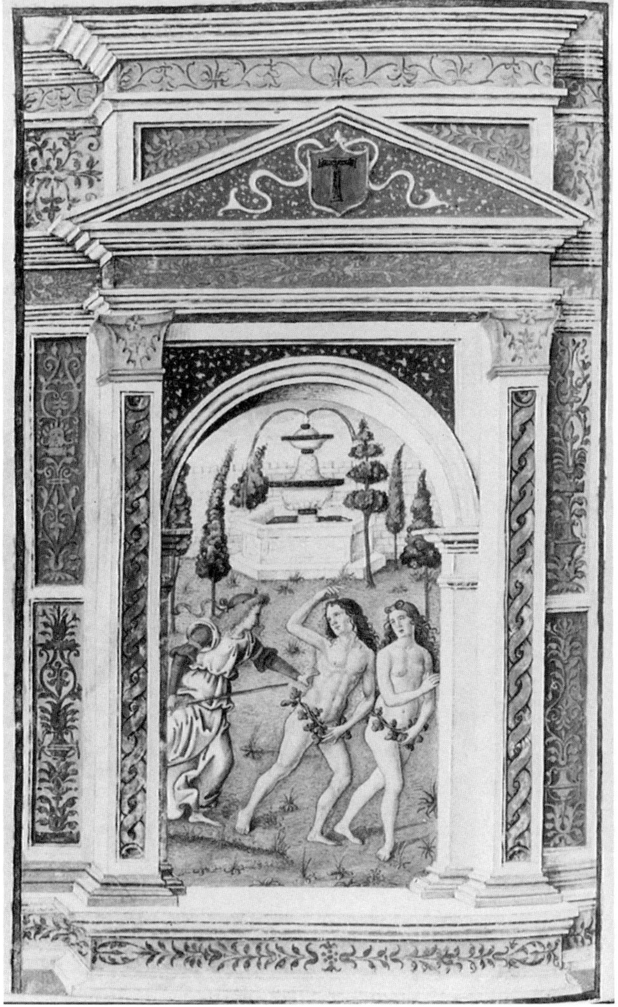

33. HM 1046, f. 87v; Southern Italy, 1519 (50% reduction)

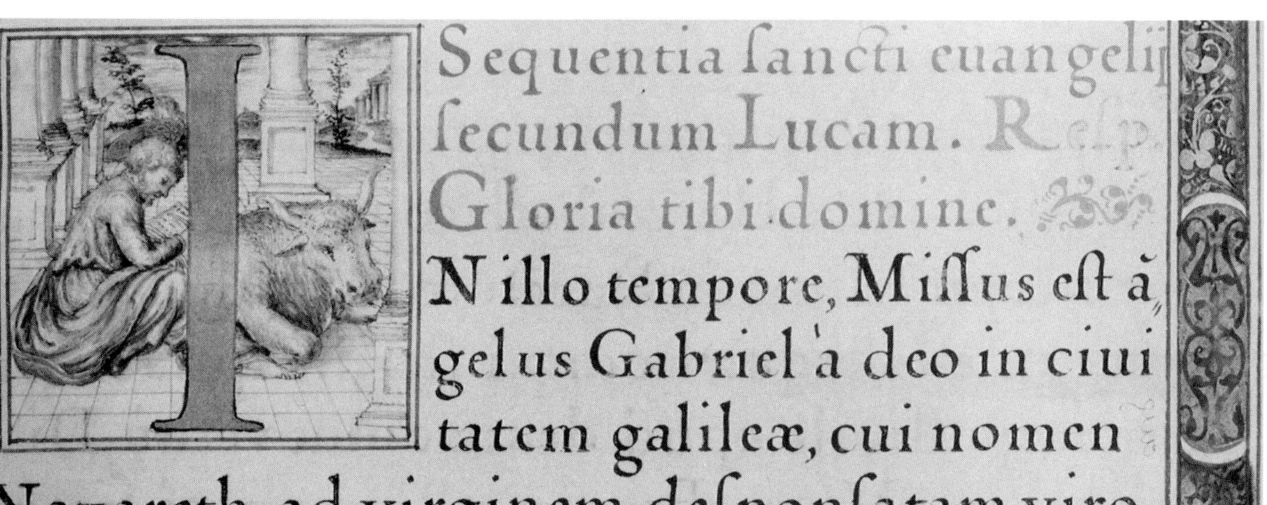

Sequentia ſancti euangelij ſecundum Lucam. Reſp. Gloria tibi domine.

IN illo tempore, Miſſus eſt angelus Gabriel a deo in ciuitatem galileæ, cui nomen Nazareth, ad virginem deſponſatam viro, cui nomen erat Ioſeph, de domo Dauid, & nomen virginis Maria. Et ingreſſus angel⁹ ad eam, dixit. Aue gratia plena, dominus tecum, benedicta tu in mulieribus. Quæ cũ audiſſet, turbata eſt in ſermone eius, et cogitabat qualis eſſet iſta ſalutatio. Et ait angel⁹

34. HM 1102, f. 22; Rome, 1549

35. HM 160, f. 103; England, 1567 (80% reduction)

36. HM 26068, f. 23; Edinburgh, 1591

DISCOVRS DE LA F. CHRE.

XII.

Son peché, non la loy, est cause de sa perte:
Le sens est donc tout clair & la raison aperte,
Que l'homme par la loy ne peut prendre renfort:
Donc tout consideré, nous concluons qu'au monde
Par la loy du Seigneur, sans qu'ailleurs on se fonde,
Est cognu le peché, du peché vient la mort.

O misericordiosissimo
señor Iesu xpo a
Vos sea alabança gloria y hon-
ra perpetua que a la tarda &
Vra sagrada passion a las
diez horas fuestes preso y a-
tado y miserablemente [illegible]
do y de Vios disciplulos los
quales huyan de miedo aban-
donado yo os Ruego muy be-
nito señor libra me de los
Vinculos de mys pecados

37. HM 1053, ff. 13v–14; Spain, 1591

38. HM 1158, ff. 74v–75; Italy, s. XVII^{in}

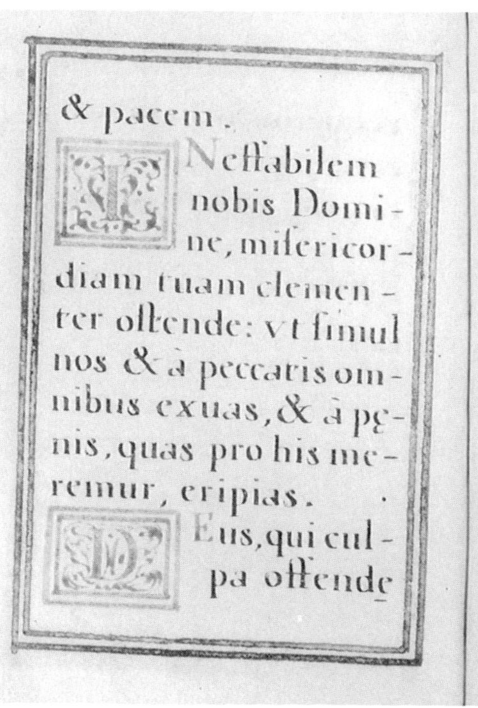

& pacem.
Ineffabilem nobis Domine, miſericordiam tuam clementer oſtende: vt ſimul nos & à peccatis omnibus exuas, & à pęnis, quas pro his meremur, eripias.
Deus, qui culpa offendę

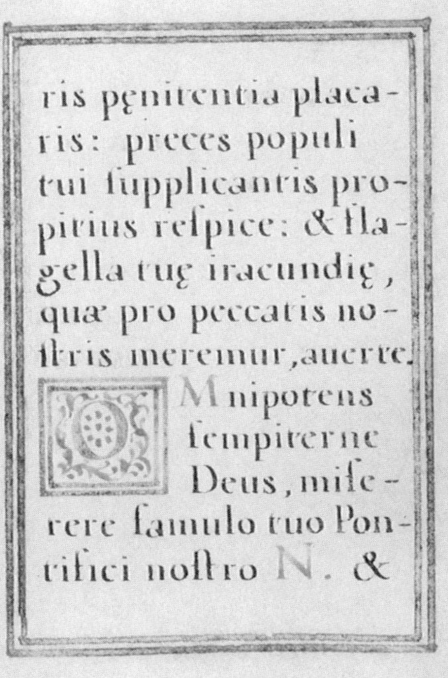

ris pęnitentia placaris: preces populi tui ſupplicantis propitius reſpice: & flagella tuę iracundię, quæ pro peccatis noſtris meremur, auerte.
Omnipotens ſempiterne Deus, miſerere famulo tuo Pontifici noſtro N. &

39. HM 41785, f. 2; Northern France, ca. 860–80

40. HM 62, vol. 1, f. 161; England, s. XI^2

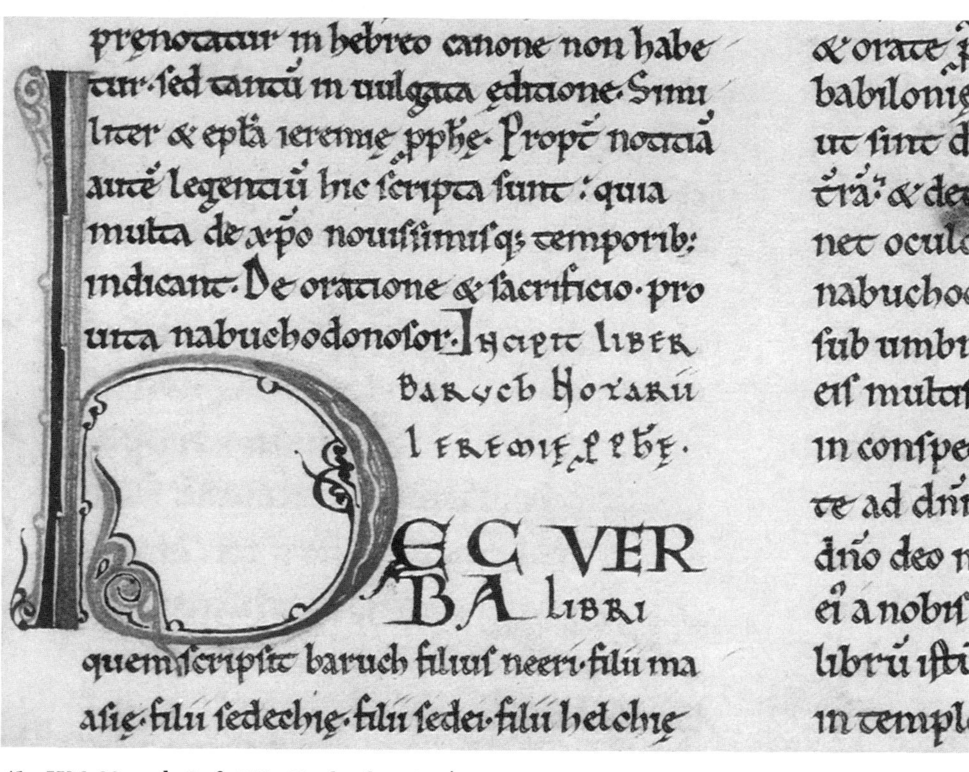

41. HM 62, vol. 2, f. 259; England, s. XII^{in}

42. HM 31151, f. 139v; England, s. XII$^{2/4}$

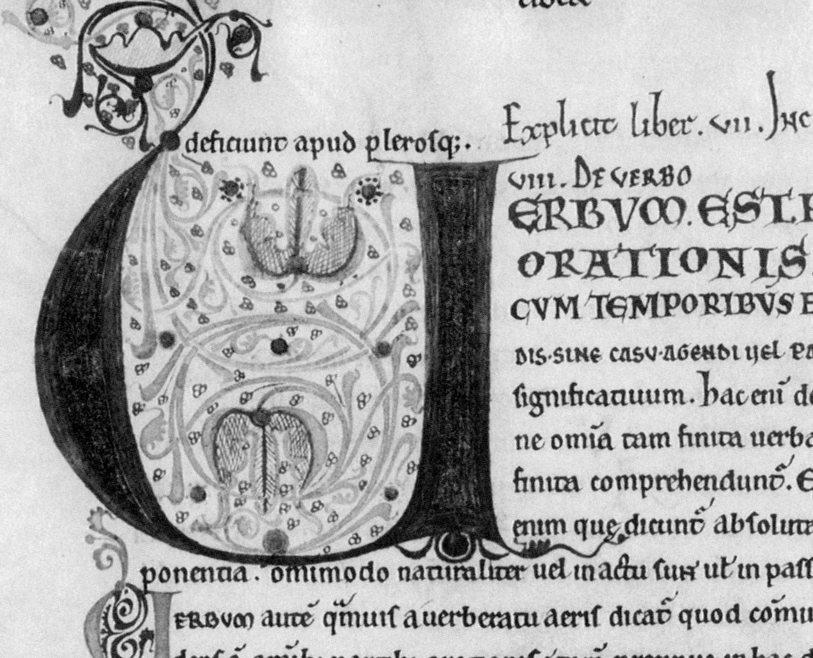

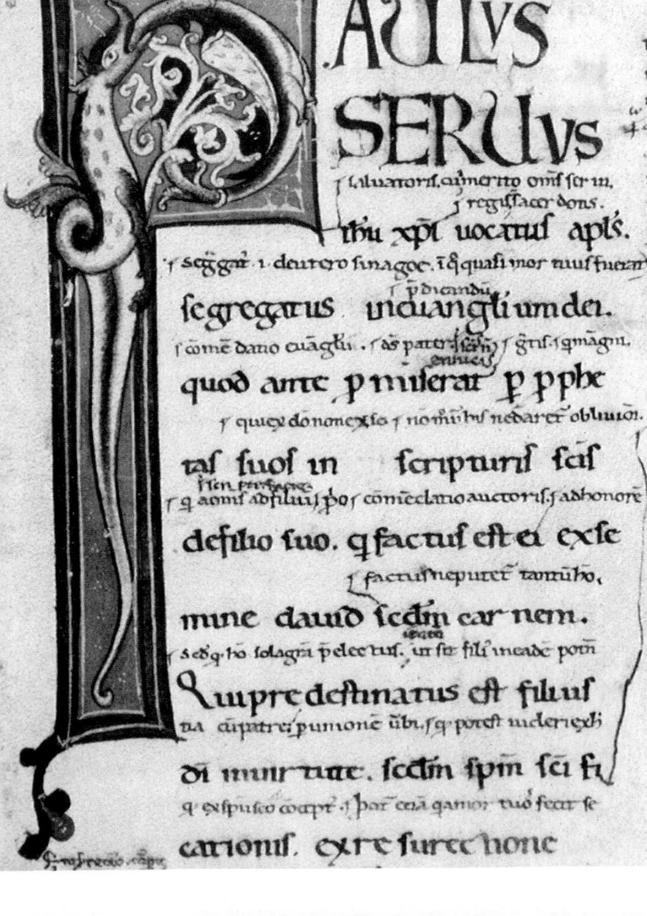

43. EL 9 H 11, f. 99v; England, s. XII$^{2/4}$ (95% reduction)

44. HM 56, f. 1; Italy, s. XII^{med}

45. HM 26052, f. 235; England, s. XII^{2} (80% reduction)

46. HM 45717, f. 98v; England, s. XII^{ex} (90% reduction)

ee peccato. an ignoratis inqt: q'm quicumq; bap
tizati sumus in xpo ihu. in morte ipsi' baptizati
Si g hinc osten d puulos pctis. xxxi. sumus
dim mortui ee peccato. quia in morte ipsi'
xpi baptizati sum'. pfecto & paruuli q baptizant
in x. peccato moriunt: quia in morte ipsi' + ipsi
baptizant. Nullo eni excepto dictu e. qcumq;
baptizati sum' in x ihu: in morte ipsi' baptizati

47. HM 19915, f. 29v; England, s. XII/XIII

48. HM 19915, f. 42; England, s. XII/XIII

49. HM 1081, vol. 2, f. 5v; s. XIII (60% reduction)

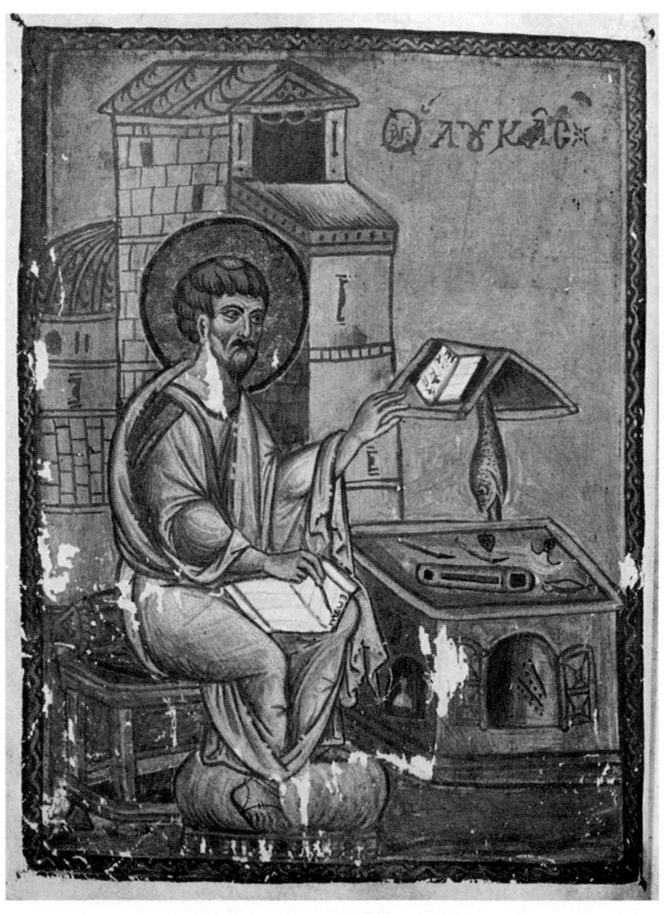

50. HM 46554, f. 5; England, s. XIII^{in}

51. HM 36337, f. 98; England, s. XIII^{in}

52. HM 41537, f. 9v; Northern France, s. XIII^{in}

53. HM 1069, f. 3v; Italy, s. XIII^{med}

54. HM 34807, f. 132; England, s. XIII^{2}

55. HM 26061, f. 178v; England, s. XIII^{med}

56. EL 9 H 4, f. 2; England, s. XIII^2 (72% reduction)

58. HM 1073, f. 219; France, s. XIII²

57. HM 1072, f. 222v; France, s. XIII²

59. HM 1035, f. 1; Southern Italy, s. XIII²

60. HM 1079, f. 53v; Bohemia, s. XIII^2

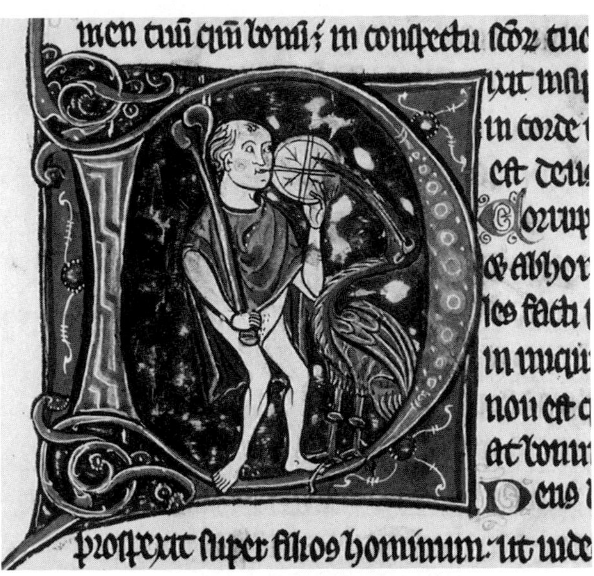

61. HM 1054, f. 41; Northern France, s. XIII^{ex}

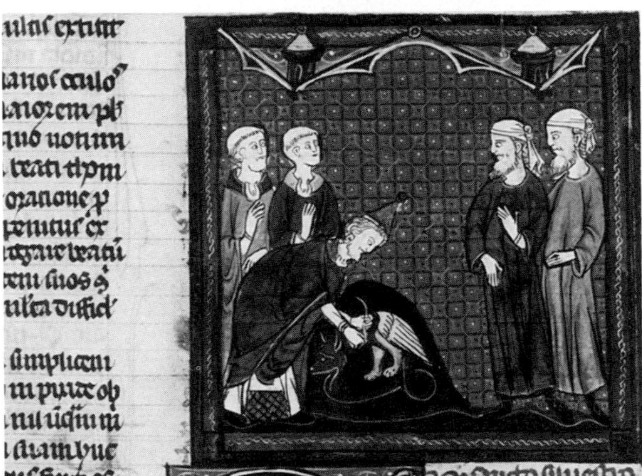

62. HM 3027, f. 13v; France, s. XIII^{ex} (80% reduction)

63. HM 1050, f. 60v; Flanders, s. XIV^{in}

65. HM 19999, f. 121v; England, s. XIV[1]

64. HM 19999, f. 191; France, s. XIII[ex]

66. HM 26298, f. 9; Italy(?), s. XIV[in]

67. HM 1084, f. 204v; Italy, s. XIV[1]

68. HM 1346, f. 85; England, s. XIV[1] (57% reduction)

69. EL 9 H 17, f. 85v; England, s. XIV[1] (72% reduction)

70. EL 9 H 17, f. 15v; England, s. XIV[1]

71. HM 1034, f. 78v; Spain, s. XIV[med]

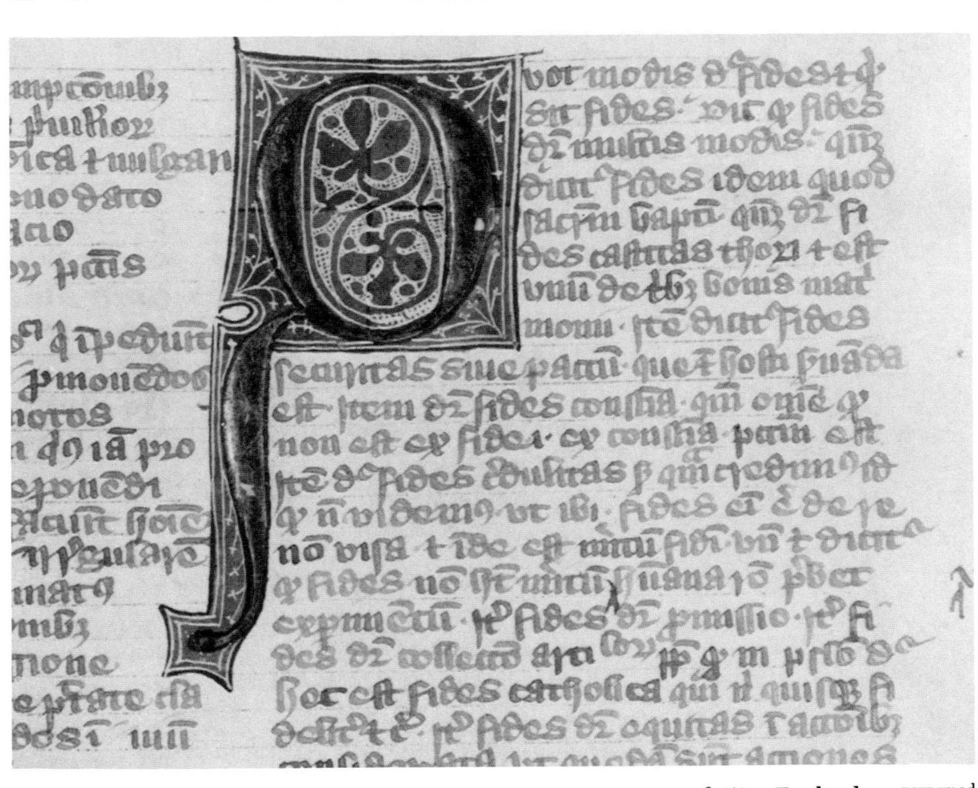

72. HM 132, f. 51v; England, s. XIV^{med}

73. EL 9 H 3, f. 3; England, s. XIV^{med}

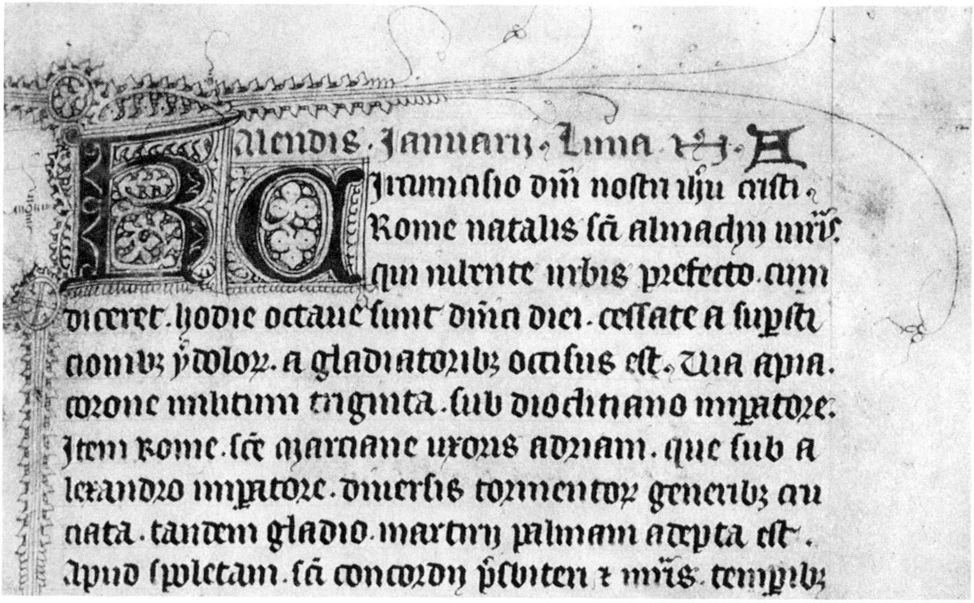

74. EL 9 H 15, f. 9; England, s. XIV^2 (79% reduction)

75. EL 9 H 9, f. 137v; England, s. XIV^2

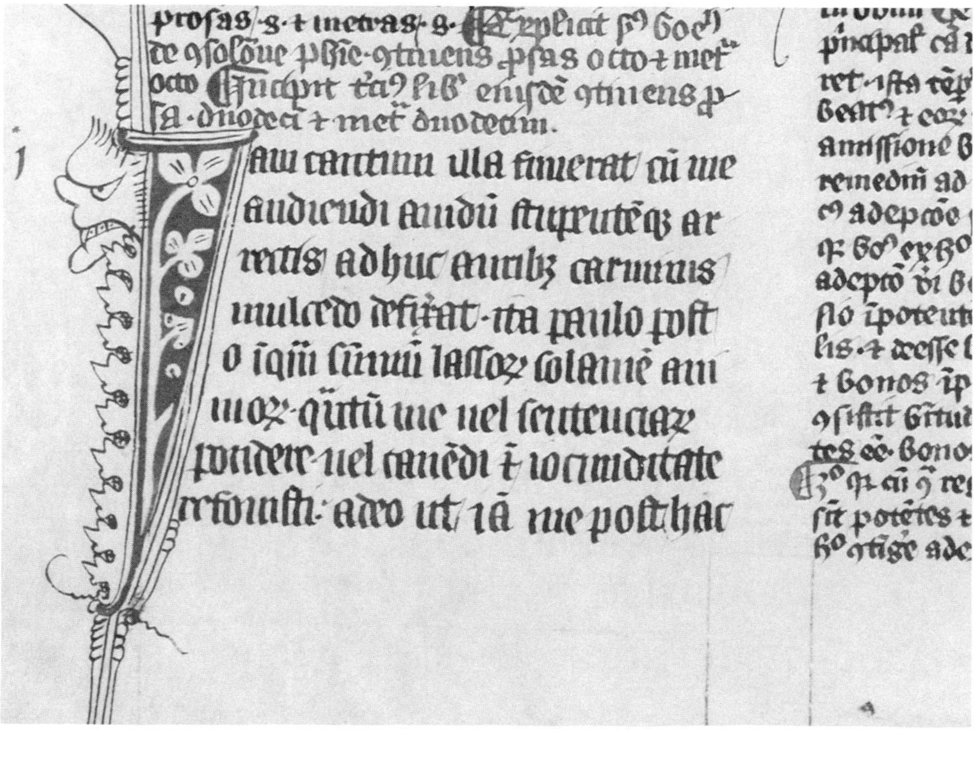

76. HM 28174, f. 132v; England, s. XIV[ex]

77. HM 30986, f. 37v; England, s. XIV[2]

78. HM 137, f. 19v; England, s. XIV/XV

79. HM 129, f. 213v; Ireland, s. XV^{in}

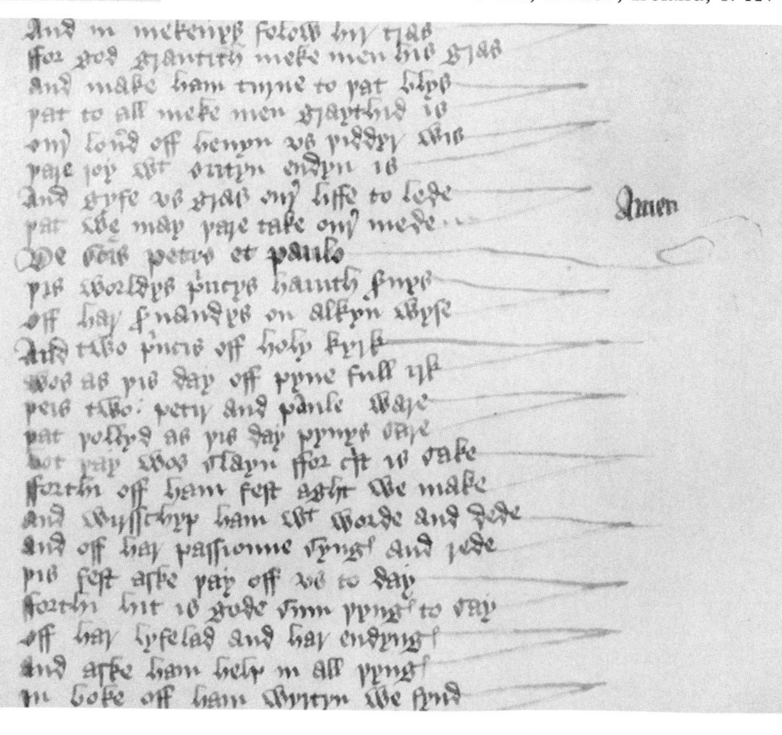

80. HM 19913, f. 122; England, s. XV^{in}
(90% reduction)

81. EL 26 C 9, f. 153v; England, s. XV^{in}

Magna Carta

Henricus dei
gratia Rex An
glie et Domi
nus Hibernie
Archiepiscopis E
piscopis Ab
batibus Prio
ribus Comitibus Baronibus Justiciariis
Vicecomitibus Prepositis Ministris
et omnibus Balliuis et fidelibus suis pre
sentem cartam inspecturis salutem. Sci
atis quod nos intuitu dei et pro salute
anime nostre et animarum antecessorum et suc

centum marcas. Heres vel he
litis de feodo militari int
solidos ad plus. Et qui m
exit minus det secundum
consuetudinem feodorum
Si aliquis heres talium
fuit dominus eius non
diam eius nec terre sue
maginum eius cepit et po
heres ad etatem peruenit
annum et fuerit in custod
ditatem suam sine rel
fine. Ita tamen quod si

Ce feust myse en le liure de monsr Johan lors
nomez ore Regent de ffrance et Duc de Bedford

Un to the rial estaat excellente
I humble clerc with al hertes humblesse
This book presente & of your reverence
Byseeche I pardon and forgevenesse
That of myn ignorance & lewednesse
That have I write it in so goodly wyse
As that me oughte [?] ben to youre worthynesse
Myn pen hath custumed bysynesse
So dulled that I may no bet souffyse

I drede lest that my maister Massy
That is of fructuous intelligence

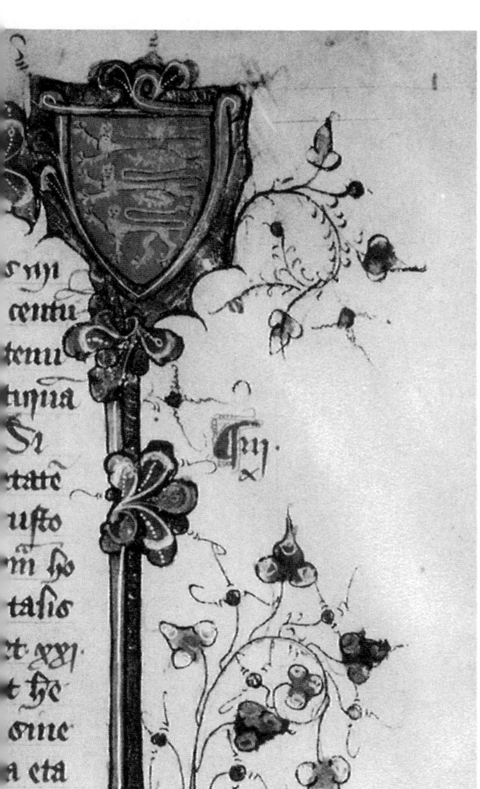

82. HM 19920, f. 1; England, s. $XV^{1/4}$

83. HM 111, f. 37v; England, s. $XV^{1/4}$

84. HM 1156, f. 75v; France, s. XV^{in}

85. HM 1142, f. 61v; France, s. XV^{in}

88. HM 1036, f. 2; Italy, s. XV^{1} (90% reduction)

87. HM 1179, f. 115; France, s. XV^{in} (95% reduction)

89. HM 1033, f. 102; Italy, s. XV^{in}

90. HM 26012, f. 1; England, s. XV^{1} (65% reduction)

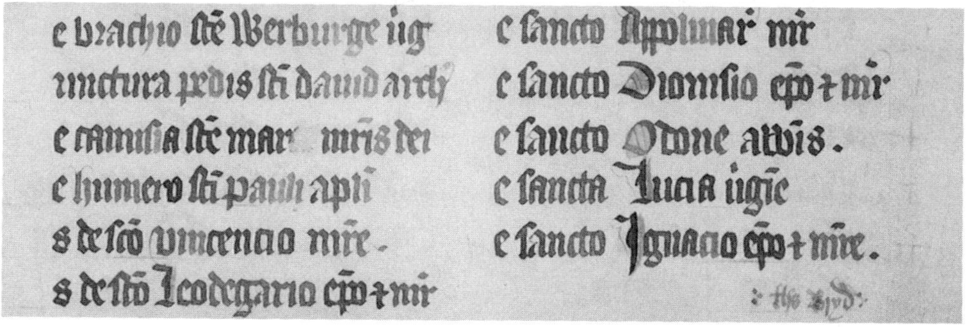

91. HM 30319, f. iii; England, s. XV[1]

92. HM 30319, f. vi verso; England, s. XV[1]

93. HM 115, f. 2v; England, s. XV[2/4]

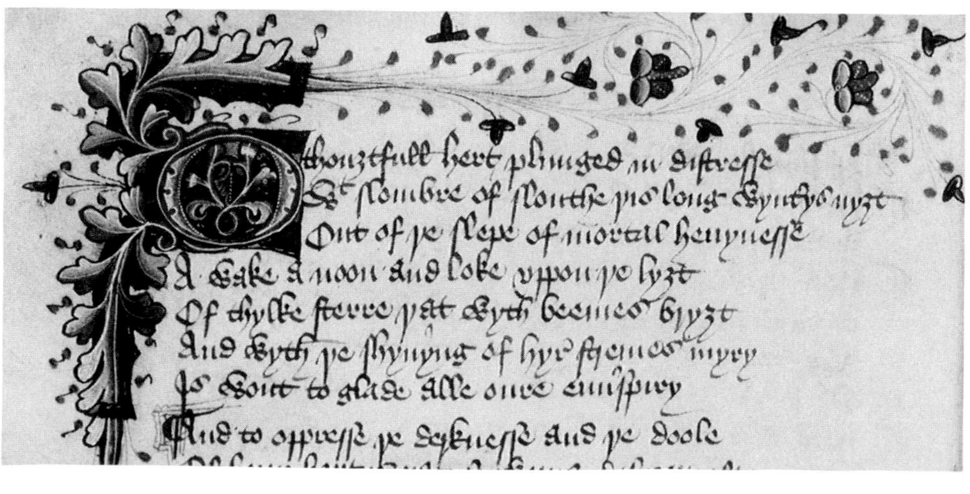

95. HM 150, f. 13v; England, s. XV^{1} (75% reduction)

94. HM 1067, f. 148v; England, s. XV^{1} (65% reduction)

Deus in adiutorium
meum intende.
Domine ad ad

96. HM 1137, f. 50; France, s. XV[1] (74% reduction)

97. HM 27523, f. 28v; France, s. XV[1]

98. HM 1087, f. 135; Flanders, s. XV^{med}

99. HM 1125, f. 62; Flanders or northern France, s. XV^{med}

100. HM 1100, f. 52; France, s. XV^{med}

101. HM 1141, f. 60; France, s. XV^{med}

103. HM 1123, f. 124; France, s. XV^{med}

102. HM 1099, f. 85; France, s. XV^{med} (95% reduction)

104. HM 47405, f. 1; England, s. XV^{med}

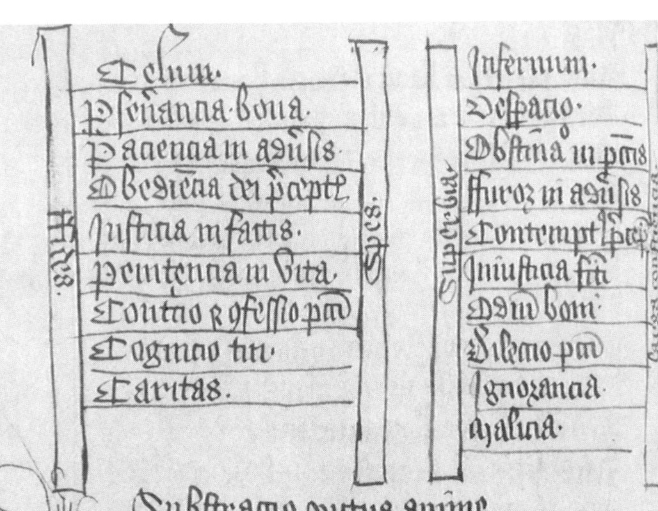

105. HM 124, f. 45v; England, s. XV^{med}

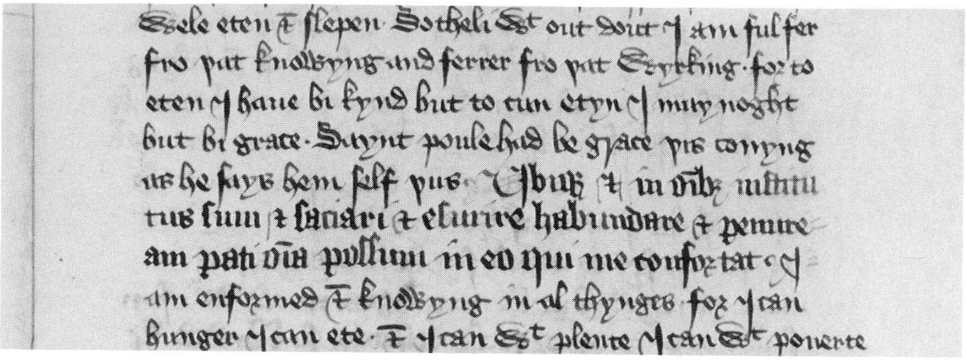

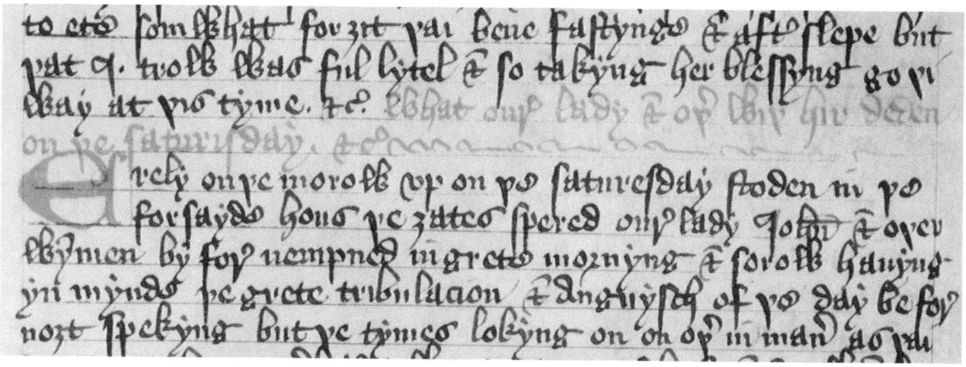

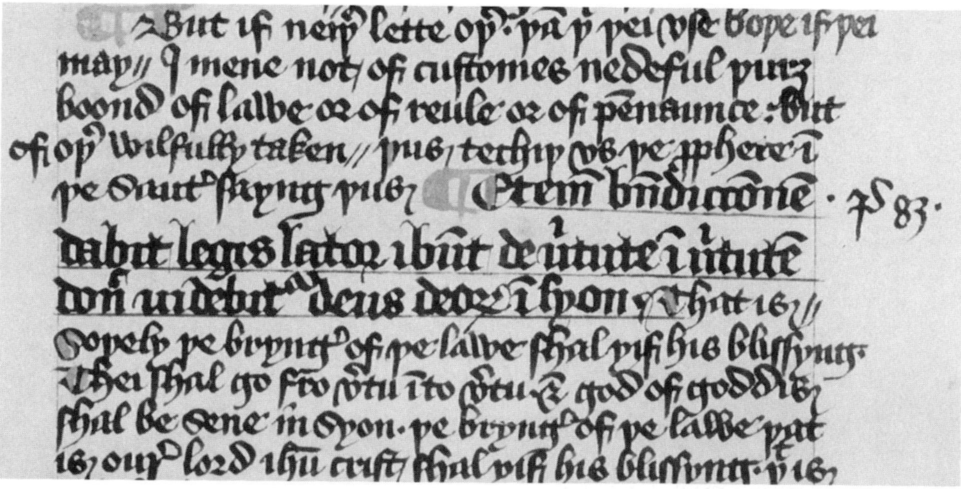

106. HM 112, f. 63; England, s. XV^{med}

107. HM 149, f. 91v; England, s. XV^{med}

108. HM 266, f. 49; England, s. XV^{med}

109. HM 1336, f. 36; England, s. XV^{med}

110. HM 39465, f. 18v; England, s. XV^{med}

111. EL 26 A 13, f. iii; England, s. XV^{med}

Grettest envie wher is grettest pees
Grettest a wayt wher is most riches
And grettest ease wher is rest & pes
Wher most discorde most is hevynesse
And of al sorowe sorowfullest ertresse
Is thilke sorowe that doth a man constreyne
After prosperite adversite sodeyne

Noble princes to avoyde al disentres
Amonge youre sylf discordes doth represse
Beth nat envious nor prous causles
Werketh nothyng of hasty wilfulnesse
Lat discression be youre governesse
For ther mot folowe yf ye part on tweyne
After prosperite adversite sodeyne

Ext mordre to Bothas did ap
pere After the mysthif of Eu
menydes The grete quene wt
a ful pitous chere
Moder of alisaundre Olympiades
Borne of the lyne of Eacydes
Amonge the quenes hir story bereth witnesse
Excelled al other of bewte & richesse

She was doughter to neptolonyus
The myghti kyng of Epirothes
And had suspecte hem neptanabus
Be enchauntement put hym sylf in pres
Of wilfly trouthe to make hir reckles
But Bothas here for to save hir name
Sett but a litel of hir disclaundrous diffame

This saide quene right faire of hir visage
Was first brought forth in thilke region
Wher al the worthy of blood & of lynage
Held ther sceptres & ther riche crown
Throughout al grece wt ful possession
So that this quene that tyme myghti & feire
Was of bewte called the lodesterre

But amonge al hir gret prosperite
hir youthe flouryng & most sodeyn noblesse
hir joye was medled with grete adversite
Whan phelip macedo to hir gret hevynesse
Was mortally wounded in distresse
In Scithia by a certeyn nacion
Called triabolys as made is mencion

For in that contre upon a certeyn day
Wher as he faught & did his besy peyne
To gete a cite & at the sege lay
And for thassaut did his stuffe ordeyne
He lost unwarly on of his eyen tweyne
That when the quene beheld his sodeyn wounde
She fyl for sorowe even plat to grounde

Another thyng bookys specifie
Troubled hir fame be gret hevynesse
The suspecte sclaundre of advoutrie
Wrought be neptanabus enchauntyng hir fame
The light eclipsyng of hir high noblesse
Be swifte report for to hyndre hir name
What fleeth moor swyfte than doth wykked fame

112. HM 268, f. 95v; England, s. XV^{med} (54% reduction)

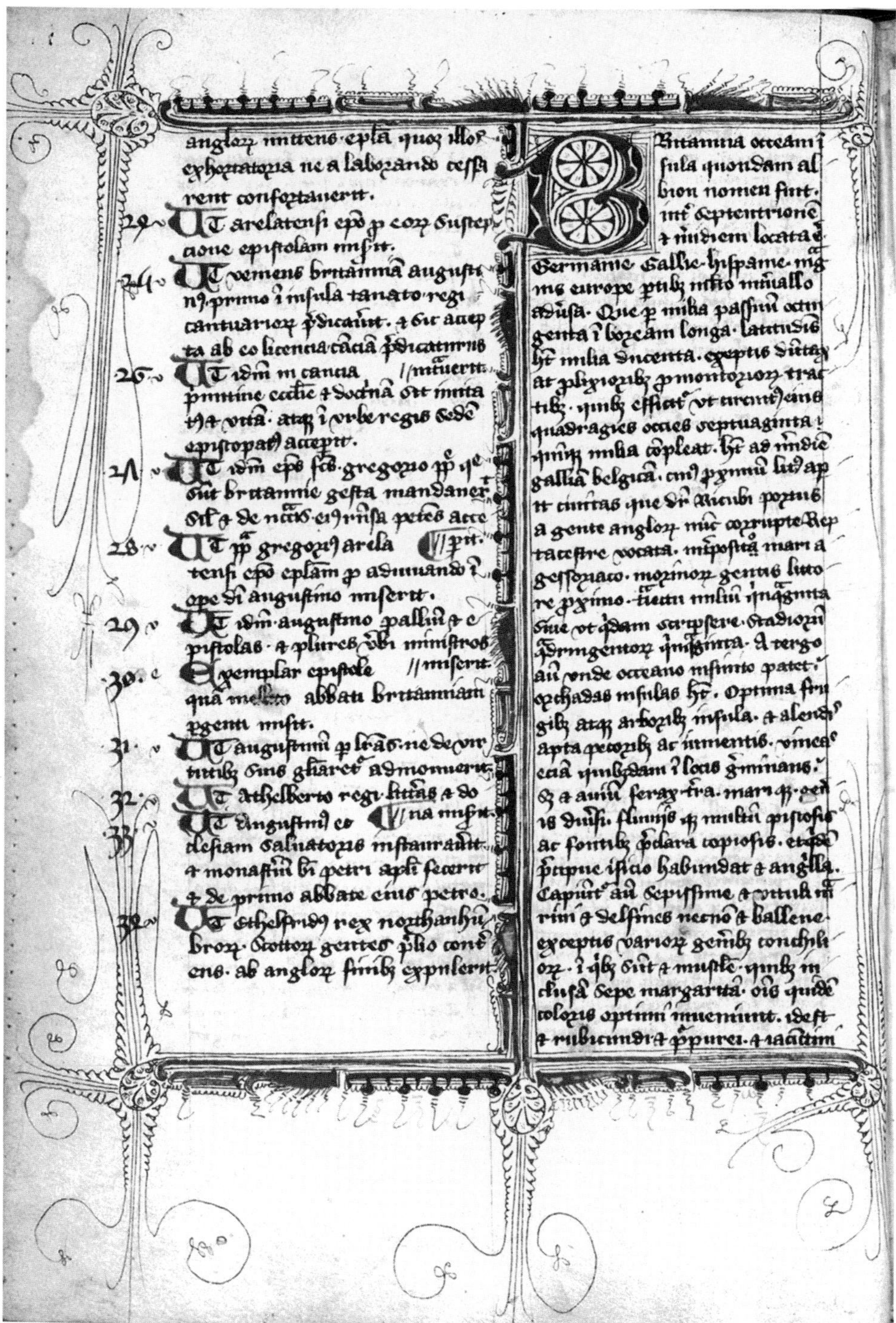

113. HM 35300, f. 2v; England, s. XV^med (80% reduction)

114. HM 19960, f. 13v; England, s. XV[med]

115. HM 195, ff. 101v–102; Germany, s. XV[med]

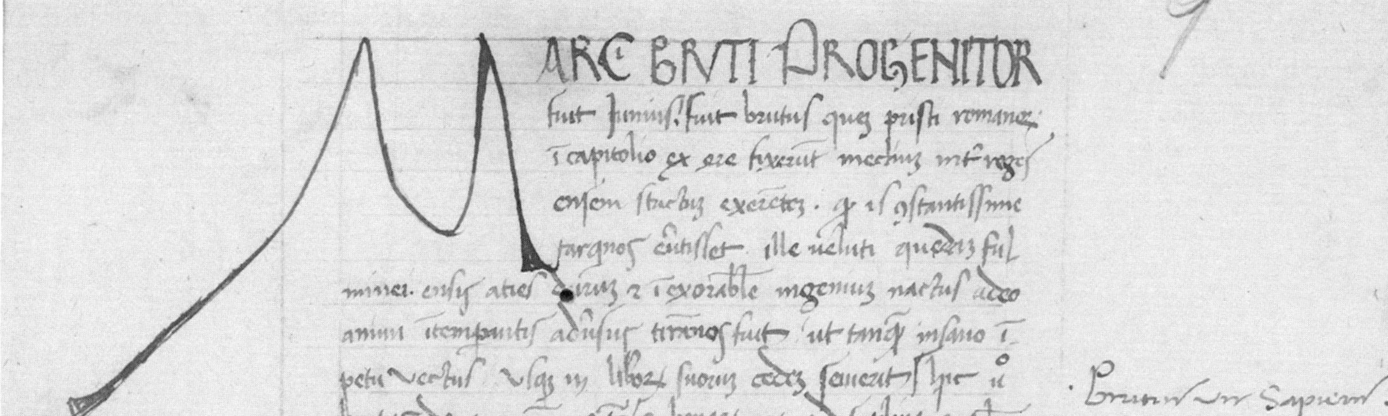

116. HM 1029, f. 1; Italy, s. XV^{med}

117. EL 34 B 6, f. 55v; Italy, s. XV^{med}

118. HM 1077, f. 159; France, s. XV^2 (90% reduction)

119. HM 1126, f. 155; France, s. XV^2 (90% reduction)

120. HM 1128, f. 186v; France, s. XV[2] (90% reduction)

121. HM 1143, f. 142v; France, s. XV[2] (90% reduction)

122. HM 1163, f. 129v; France, s. XV^2 (90% reduction)

123. HM 1136, f. 22v; Flanders, s. XV^2 (90% reduction)

124. HM 1173, f. 84; France, s. XV^2

This knyfe betokneth the circumcision
that dystruyd owre synnes all' & som
off owre fore fadyr adame
when ymost we tak the kynd of ma~
ffrom temptation of lechery
Lorde kepe me tyll' I dye

The pellycan his blode doth bled
ther with his byrdys for to fed
hit betokneth up on the rode
owre lorde fed us with his blode
when he us boȝt owt of hell
In ioy and blis with hym to dwell
and be owr fadyr and owr fod
and we his chyldren meke and gode

The pens all' so that Judas tolde

125. HM 26054 (roll); England, s. XV^2 (75% reduction)

126. EL 9 H 10, f. 48v; England, s. XV^2

127. HM 28561, f. 43; England, s. XV^{med-ex} (56% reduction)

128. HM 936, f. 49v; France, s. $XV^{3/4}$ (90% reduction)

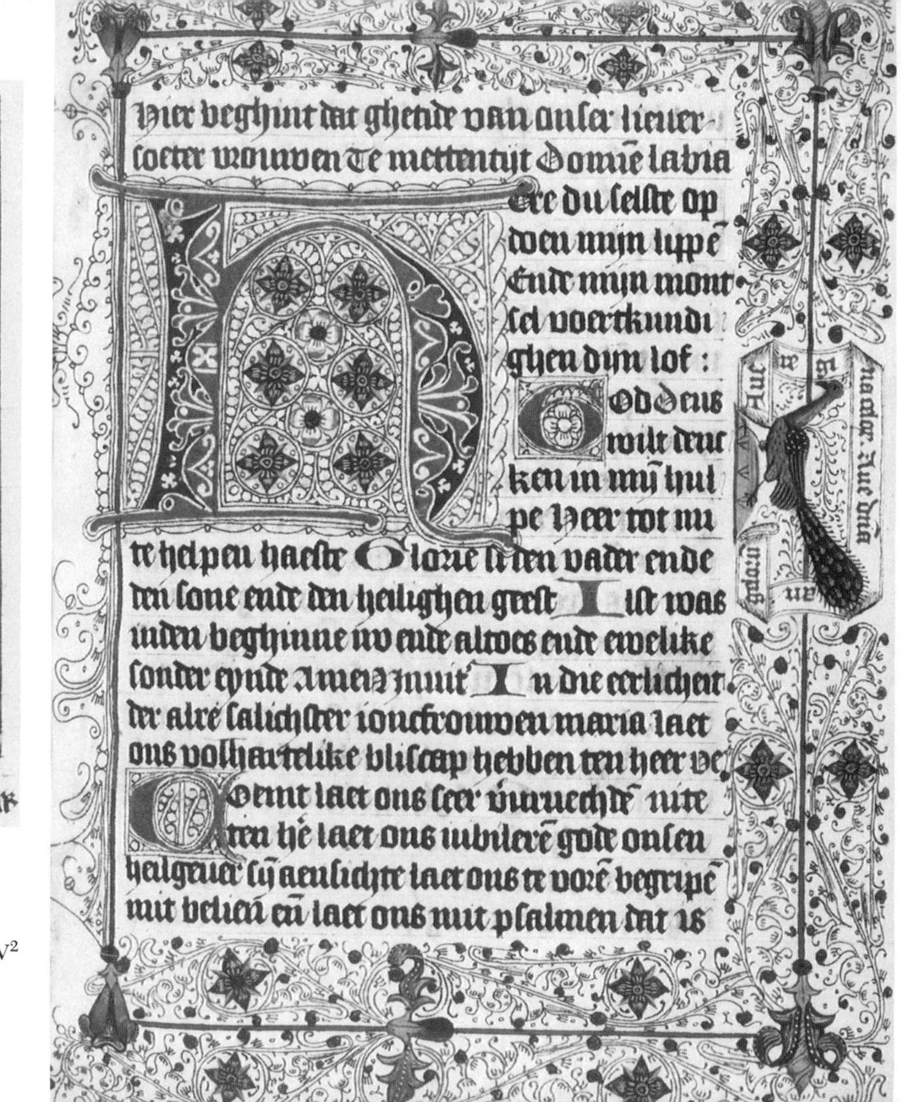
Hier beghint dat ghetide van onser lieuer-
vrouwen te mettentijt Domine labia
Here du selste op
doen mijn lippe
Ende mijn mont
sel voertkundi
ghen dijn lof :
God deus
wilt deuc
ken in mij thul
pe Heer tot mi
te helpen haeste Glorie si den vader ende
den sone ende den heilighen geest Als hi was
inden beghinne nv ende altoes ende ewelike
sonder eynde Amen Inuit In die eerlicheit
der alre salichster ioncfrouwen maria laet
ons volhertelike bliscap hebben ten heer ve
Coemt laet ons seer vrolike ... uite
... laet ons iubileren gode onsen
heilgemaker ... laet ons te voren begripe
mit belien ... laet ons mit psalmen dat is

129. HM 1127, f. 11; Netherlands, s. XV^2

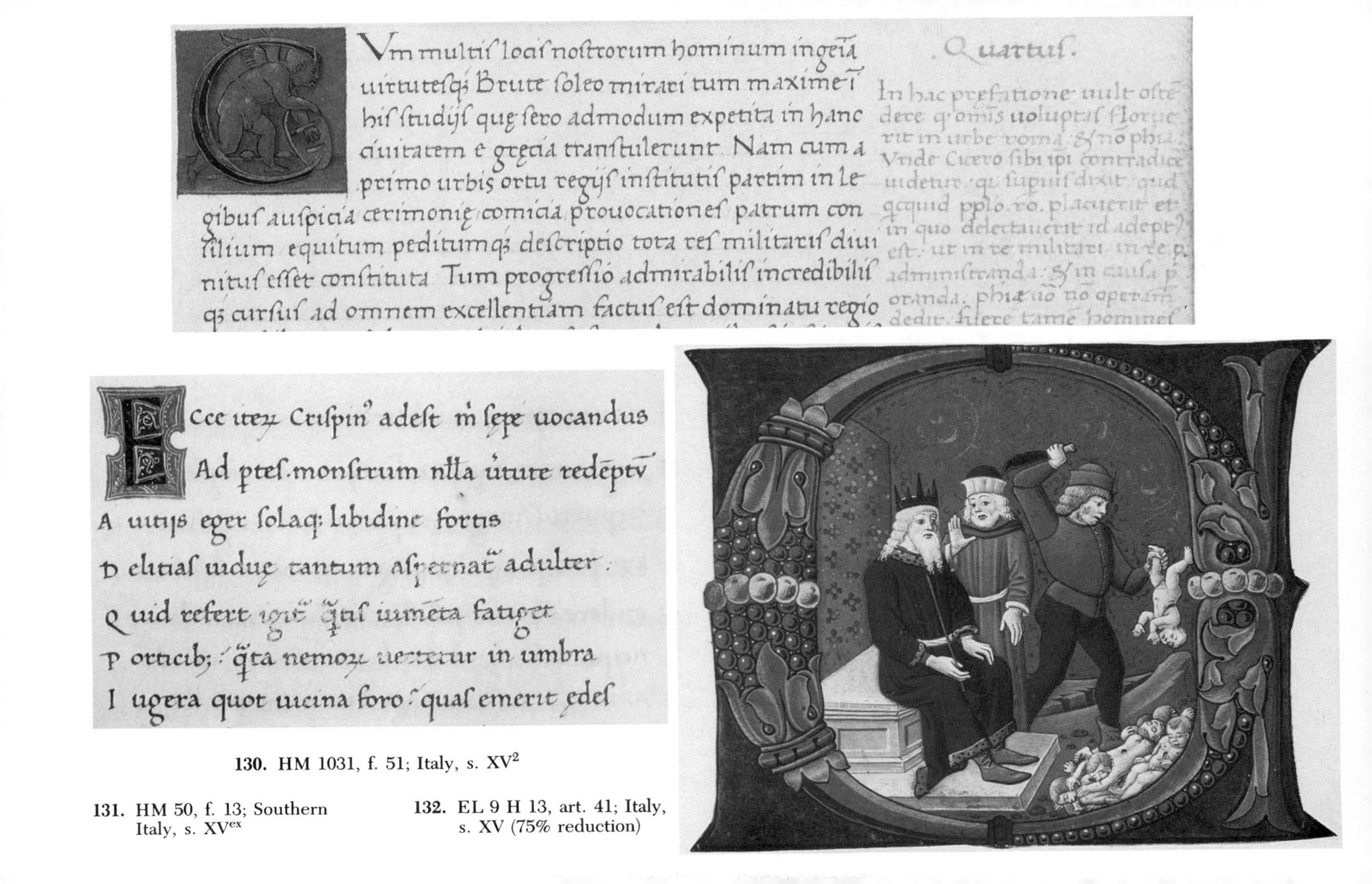

130. HM 1031, f. 51; Italy, s. XV^2

131. HM 50, f. 13; Southern Italy, s. XV^{ex}

132. EL 9 H 13, art. 41; Italy, s. XV (75% reduction)

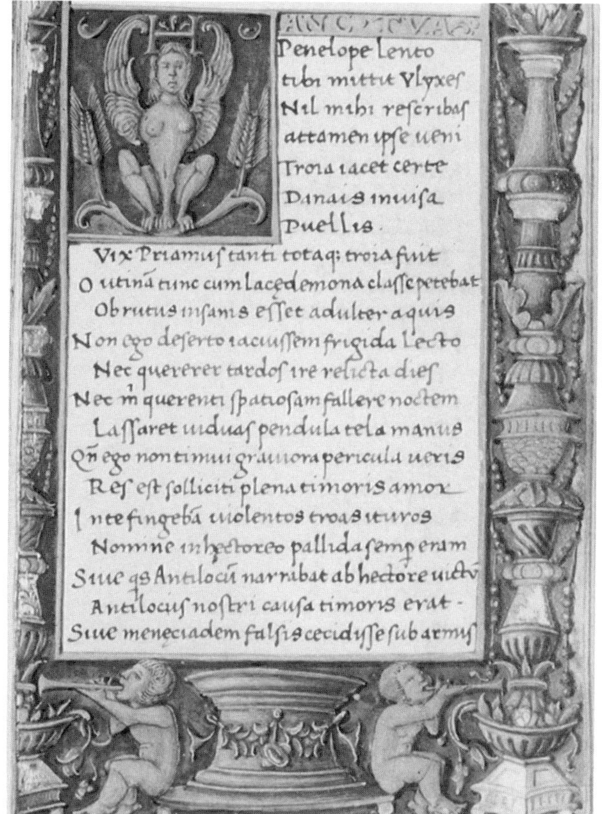

133. HM 1038, f. 61; Italy, s. XV^{ex}

134. HM 1028, f. 1; Southern Italy, s. XV^{ex} (65% reduction)

135. HM 1041, f. 125; Southern Italy, s. XV^{ex} (65% reduction)

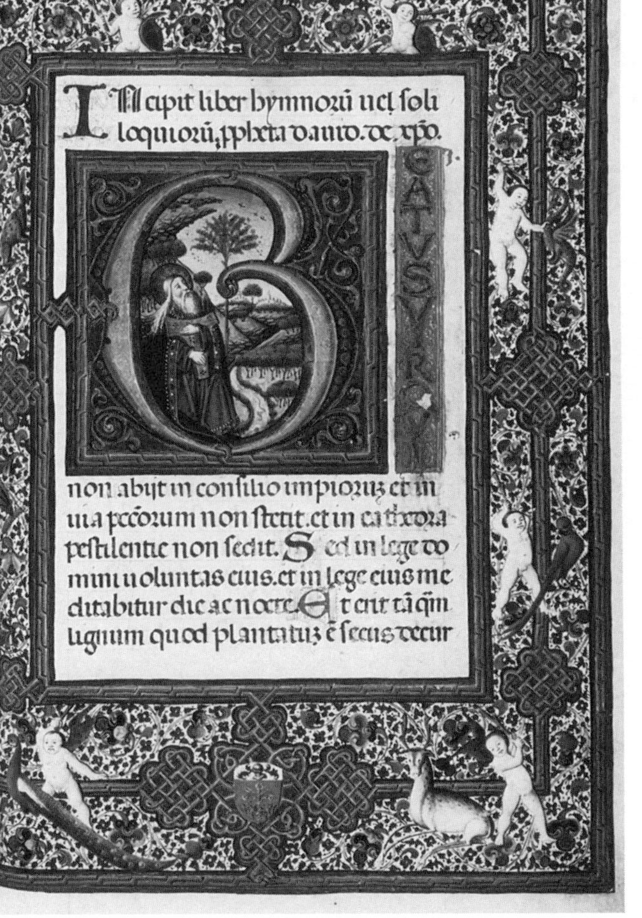

136. HM 1064, f. 17; Southern Italy, s. XV^{ex} (65% reduction)

137. HM 1150, f. 36v; France, s. XV^{ex}

138. HM 1180, f. 35v; France, s. XV$^{4/4}$ (90% reduction)

139. HM 28562, f. 265; Flanders, s. XV^{ex}

140. HM 1140, f. 32v; Northwestern Netherlands, s. XV^{ex}

141. HM 1157, f. 96v; Flanders, s. XV^{ex}

cuius gloriam predicamus
in terris eius precibus adiu
uemur in celis. Per christum
dominum nostrum. Amen.
De sancto nycholao anthiphona
Beatus ny-
cholaus
adhuc pu
erulus mul
to ieiunio
macerabat
corpus. V. Ora pro nobis be
ate nycholae. Ut digni effi
ciamur promissionibus christi.
Oremus. Collecta
Deus qui beatum ny-

142. HM 1148, f. 23v; Flanders, s. XV^{ex}

144. HM 1131, f. 93; Flanders, s. XV/XVI

143. HM 1174, f. 14v; Flanders, s. XV^{ex} (85% reduction)

145. HM 1162, f. 98v; Spain and Flanders, s. XVI[1]

146. HM 60, f. 75v; France, s. XV/XVI (78% reduction)

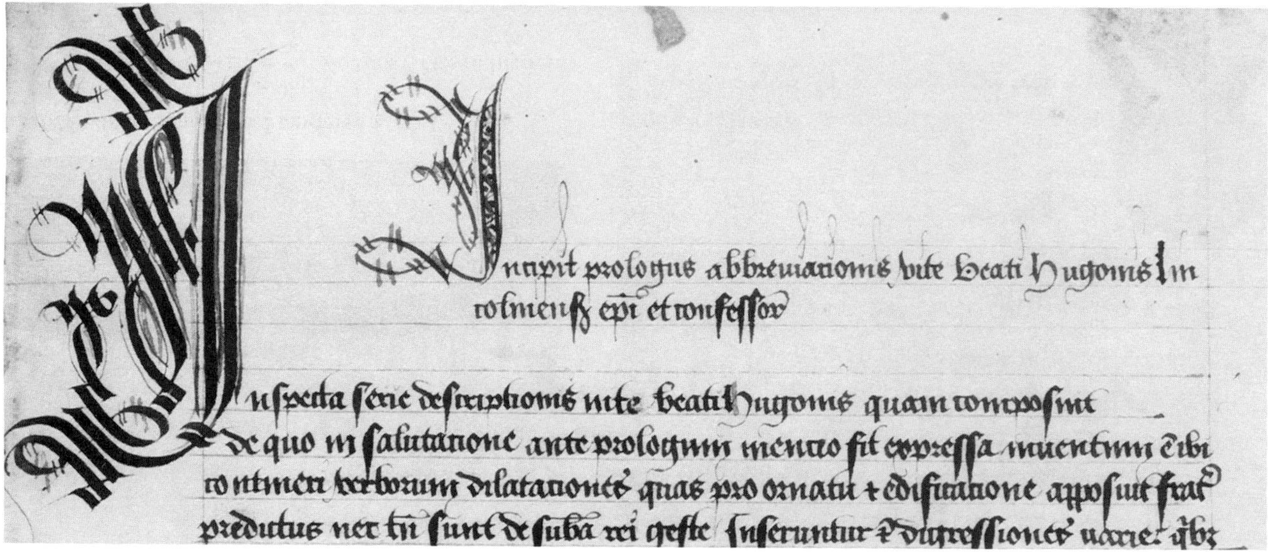

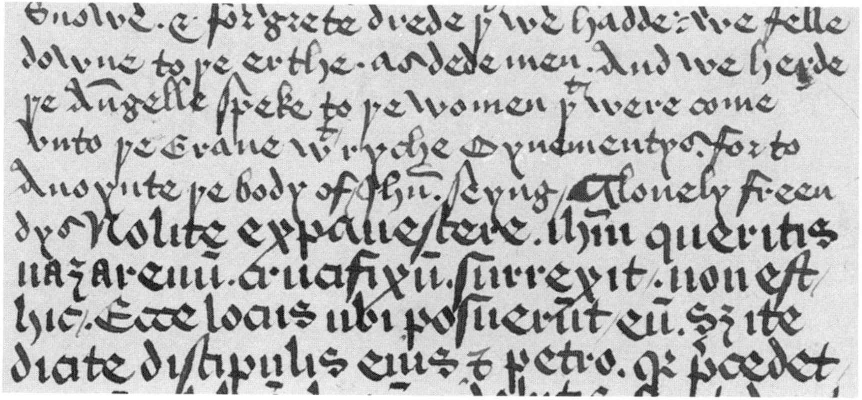

147. HM 36336, f. 1; England, s. XVI^{in}

148. HM 144, f. 47v; England, s. XV/XVI

149. HM 1165, f. 89; France, s. XVI^{in}

150. HM 1124, f. 123; France, s. XVI^{in} (65% reduction)

MEmento ſalutis auctor q noſtri
quondam corporis ex illibata
virgine naſcendo formam ſumpſeris.
Maria mater gratie mater miſericordie
tu nos ab hoſte protege & hora mortis
ſuſcipe. Gloria tibi domine qui natus
es de virgine cum patre & ſancto ſpiri

151. HM 48, f. 37v; France, s. XVI^{in} (90% reduction)

152. HM 1727, f. 1; Flanders, s. $XVI^{2/4}$

153. HM 49, f. 1v; France, s. XVI^{1} (90% reduction)

154. HM 903, f. 1

155. HM 19915, f. i verso

156. HM 25775, f. 128v

157. HM 27187, f. iii verso

158. HM 30319, f. 108

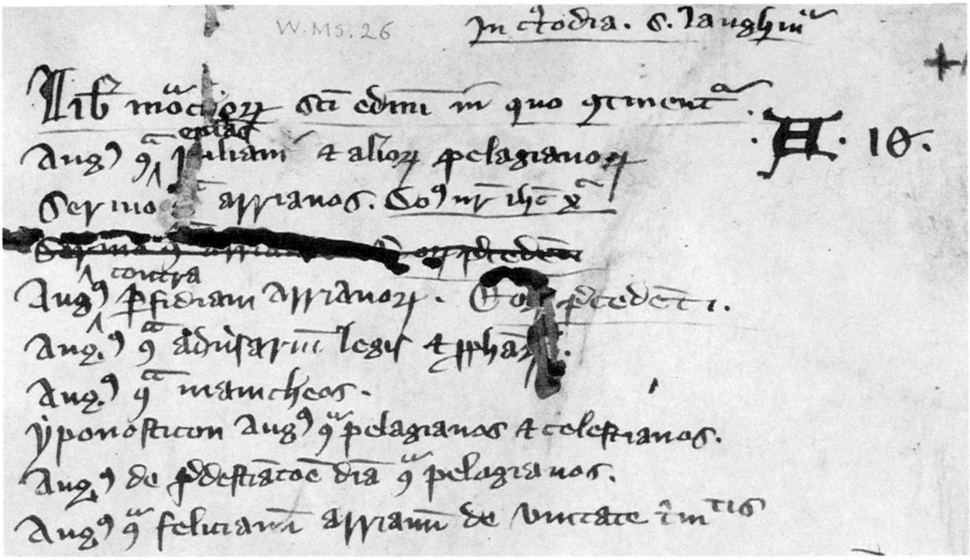

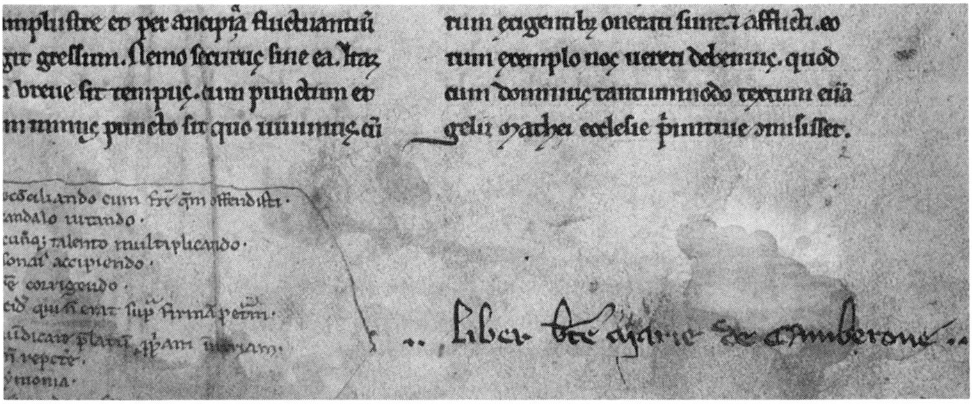

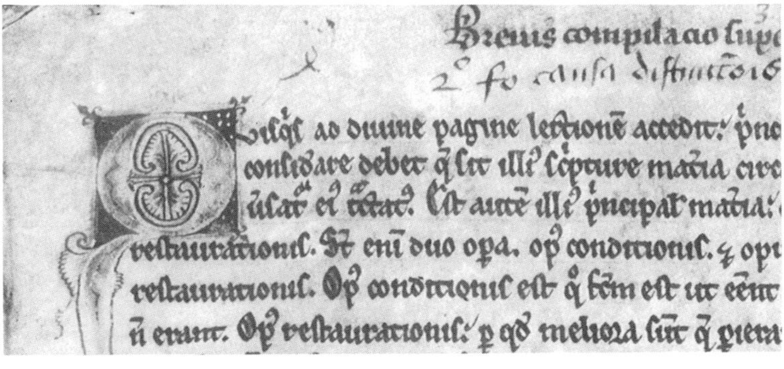

159. HM 31151, front pastedown

160. HM 41537, f. 1

161. HM 19914, f. 3